D1289808

PENGUIN BOOKS

A HISTORY OF THE MIDDLE EAST

Peter Mansfield was born in 1928 in Ranchi, India, and was educated at Winchester and Cambridge. In 1955 he joined the British Foreign Office and went to Lebanon to study Arabic at the Middle East Centre for Arabic Studies. In November 1956 he resigned from the foreign service over the Suez affair, but remained in Beirut working as a political and economic journalist. He edited the *Middle East Forum* and corresponded regularly for the *Financial Times*, the *Economist*, the *Guardian*, the *Indian Express* and other newspapers. From 1961 to 1967 he was the Middle East correspondent of the *Sunday Times*, based mainly in Cairo. After 1967 he lived in London, but made regular visits to the Middle East and North Africa, and in the winter of 1971–2 he was visiting lecturer on Middle East politics at Willamette University, Oregon. As editor his books include *The Middle East: A Political and Economic Survey* and *Who's Who in the Arab World*. He has also written *Nasser's Egypt*, *Nasser: A Biography*, *The British in Egypt*, *The Ottoman Empire and Its Successors*, *Kuwait: Vanguard of the Gulf* and *The Arabs*, a comprehensive study generally believed to be his magnum opus, which is also published by Penguin. Peter Mansfield died in 1996, and in its obituary notice *The Times* praised him as 'Eloquent, scholarly, free from convention . . . [He] earned himself a distinguished place by forty years of thoughtful work and the passion of his convictions.'

Nicolas Pelham studied Arabic in Damascus, before joining a London law firm specializing in Islamic law. In 1992 he moved to Cairo as editor of the *Middle East Times*, and then joined the BBC Arabic Service producing documentary programmes from across the Arab world. In 1998 he moved to Morocco as correspondent for the *Economist*, the BBC and the *Observer*. In 2005 he moved to Jerusalem as a senior analyst for International Crisis Group, reporting on Israeli and Palestinian affairs.

A History of the Middle East

Fourth Edition
revised and updated by Nicolas Pelham

PETER MANSFIELD

PENGUIN BOOKS

PENGUIN BOOKS
Published by the Penguin Group
Penguin Group (USA), 375 Hudson Street,
New York, New York 10014, USA

USA | Canada | UK | Ireland | Australia | New Zealand | India | South Africa | China
Penguin Books Ltd, Registered Offices: 80 Strand, London WC2R 0RL, England
For more information about the Penguin Group visit penguin.com

First published in Great Britain by Penguin Books Ltd 1991
First published in the United States of America by Viking Penguin,
a division of Penguin Books USA Inc., 1991
Published in Penguin Books (UK and USA) 1992
Second edition published in Penguin Books (UK) 2003
Published in Penguin Books (USA) 2004
Third edition published in Penguin Books (UK) 2010
This fourth edition published in Penguin Books (UK and USA) 2013

LIBRARY OF CONGRESS CATALOGING-IN-PUBLICATION DATA
Mansfield, Peter, 1928–
A history of the Middle East / Peter Mansfield.—Fourth edition / revised
and updated by Nicolas Pelham.
pages cm
ISBN 978-0-14-312190-9
1. Middle East—History—19th century.   2. Middle East—History—
20th century.   I. Pelham, Nicolas.   II. Title.
DS62.4.M36 2013
956—dc23   2013019936

Printed in the United States of America
1   3   5   7   9   10   8   6   4   2

Set in Bembo Book MT Std

To Luis Cañizares

Contents

Maps

THE MIDDLE EAST TODAY

International Boundary

0   1000 Km
0   600 Miles

CASPIAN SEA

• Tabriz

• Tehran

IRAN

Baghdad   Isfahan •

Abadan
Basra •
          • Shiraz
• Kuwait
       • Bushire

KUWAIT

PERSIAN GULF

Jubail •
Damman •
Dhahran •
            Sharja
QATAR   Dubai •
      Abu Dhabi •
BAHRAIN

GULF OF OMAN

• Muscat

• Riyadh

UNITED ARAB EMIRATES

ARABIA

OMAN

ARABIAN SEA

REPUBLIC OF YEMEN

• Salala

• Mukalla

Socotra Island

INDIAN OCEAN

• Aden

GULF OF ADEN   SOMALIA

Foreword to the Third Edition

In his concluding chapter, 'Prospects for the Twenty-first Century', written two decades ago, Peter Mansfield proved remarkably prescient. He predicted the resurgence of an armed Islamic movement across the Middle East. He foresaw that Arab regimes, however slim their power-bases, would survive. But there was one prediction where he went badly awry. In the concluding paragraph of the *History*, Peter ventured that as the Cold War faded away, the United States would lose its *raison d'être* as a military presence in the Arab world, and 'would hardly maintain its superpower status in the region'.

Perhaps had Western policy-makers harkened, much of the subsequent bloodshed might have been averted. Certainly it is hard to argue that the Middle East is any better for the military intervention that followed. When he completed the first edition almost two decades ago, the United States was at the peak of its power. It was celebrating victory after chasing Iraq out of Kuwait; the mujahideen it backed in Afghanistan had won their *jihad* against the Soviet Union, and Arab states were for the first time preparing to sit down publicly with Israel to negotiate an end to their conflict.

In hindsight it looks a more innocent age. US policies in a region ten thousand miles away have boomeranged, at a cost of thousands of American lives both at home and in the Arab world. After returning to war with Iraq, the US is beating a retreat with the country's promised political and economic reconstruction still unrealized. In Afghanistan as well as many places elsewhere, the US is fighting its former allies. And after two decades of on-off negotiations, the promised end of conflict between Israel and the Arab world remains as elusive as ever. And under America's watch hundreds of thousands of Middle Easterners have perished in continuing conflicts in Iraq,

Algeria, Sudan and Israel/Palestine. US credibility in the region is in tatters.

This update of the *History* attempts to analyse what went wrong. In two new chapters, it looks at unfolding US policy towards Iraq, the Arab–Israeli conflict, and the evolving *jihadi* movements. It suggests that rather than seek to opt for regime change from without, US interests would be better served by working with the existing political movements on the ground. Peter understood that to resolve conflicts, societies have to be at peace not just with their enemies but also with themselves. 'What the Arab world urgently needs is more democracy, wider political participation and much greater respect for human rights,' he wrote two decades ago.

Almost universally, the deficit is greater today than it was then. Since Peter wrote his book, the Middle East has shrunk in on itself and become a more embittered, suspicious and intolerant place. Cosmopolitan cultures have atomized into their communal parts. For the vast majority of Arabs, the promise of independence has failed to materialize. For Palestinians, their homeland has been cut into an obstacle course of walls and checkpoints, rendering movement for an entire population the most restricted anywhere on earth. From where I write, I like millions of others can travel barely five minutes without being asked for my papers.

Whether the United States can yet be a force for good in the region is much debated. The outpouring of support President Obama received following his May 2009 Cairo address is testimony to the belief of many that it can. Clearly too a superpower cannot withdraw from a region that fuels the world. But as the past decade has shown, America's armadas, bombings and military bases spark more problems than they solve. And after President Obama invested his political capital in Israel and Iran with no immediate dividend, scepticism abounds that persuasion and soft power can do any better.

Recent books on the Middle East commonly end with a prophecy of better days ahead. Invariably those written in recent years have had their dreams dashed. But if there is now a silver lining, it is that as the US prepares to withdraw from Iraq, the peoples of the

Middle East are again honing their own methods of conflict resolution and self-determination. As Peter notes, 'over the centuries, the Middle East has confounded the dreams of conquerors and peacemakers alike'. Come the next edition, perhaps the region will again be able to look forward to more Pax and less Americana.

I am grateful to Luis Cañizares, to whom Peter dedicated his *History*, for trusting me to don Peter's mantle and update the text; to my agent Michael Sissons for seeking me out; and to Simon Winder of Penguin for his patience. My contribution has benefited greatly from the editors I have been fortunate to work with during my years in the region: Barbara Smith and Xan Smiley, Middle East editors at *The Economist*; Roula Khalaf at the *Financial Times*, and Rob Malley at International Crisis Group. Throughout my travels I have benefited from the insight and encouragement of countless friends and colleagues, including several in conflict zones who risked their well-being to ensure mine. Above all thanks go to my wife, Lipika, who dreamt as a child in lush Bengal that she would be cast out to a desert, and for almost two decades has supported me in making it come true.

Nicolas Pelham
Jerusalem, February 2010

A History of the
Middle East

1. Introduction: from Ancient to Modern

'The Middle East' is a modern English term for the most ancient region of human civilization. Before and during the First World War, 'the Near East', which comprised Turkey and the Balkans, the Levant and Egypt, was the term in more common use. 'The Middle East', if employed at all, referred to Arabia, the Gulf, Persia (Iran)/Mesopotamia (Iraq) and Afghanistan. After the First World War Allies had destroyed the Ottoman Turkish Empire and established their hegemony over its former Arab provinces, 'the Middle East' gradually came to encompass both areas. This trend was reinforced during the Second World War, when the entire region was seen as a strategic unit in the struggle against the Axis powers. Egypt was the site of the Allies' Middle East Supply Centre. At the end of the war, Cairo also became the headquarters of the Arab League, which linked Egypt with the independent Asian Arab states. The Turkish Republic, which had joined NATO and saw its destiny as part of Europe, scarcely belonged to the Middle East any more.

The term 'the Middle East' is Eurocentric. The people of the Indian subcontinent understandably find it irritating. For them after all, the region is 'the Middle West'. 'Why not "West Asia"?' they might ask. But this has the disadvantage of excluding Egypt. Similarly, 'the Arab world', now in common usage, excludes Israel and Iran which, to say the least, are both at the centre of the region's concerns, although 'the Arab world' does have the advantage of including the North African Maghreb states, which are increasingly partners in the affairs of the region in spite of the practical failure to achieve political union of the two halves of the Arab world. 'The Middle East' seems likely to continue in use for some time. It is not even confined to European languages: in Arabic – *Asharq al-Awsat* – it is the title of the Saudi Arabian newspaper with the largest international circulation of all Arab newspapers.

Common usage, however, should not allow us to lose sight of the drawbacks of the term, of which the most important is that it assumes a Western domination of the world. That distinguished scholar the late General John Bagot Glubb enjoyed reminding his readers that, in terms of civilization and culture, the Middle East region was in advance of western Europe for all but the last five hundred of the five thousand or so years for which human history can be traced back. Archaeologists will continue to dispute whether the Nile Valley and Delta, narrow but richly fertile, or Mesopotamia, the land of the twin rivers, the Tigris and the Euphrates, can claim precedence as the cradle of human civilization, but it is their joint role in the development of mankind which matters.

Hammurabi, King of Babylon in the eighteenth century BC, formulated the first comprehensive code of law which has survived. Akhenaten, Pharaoh of Egypt in the fourteenth century BC, had the first conception of a single all-powerful deity. Some fifty years later Rameses II – 'the Great' – created an empire which covered most of the Middle East region.

In the huge arc of territory which stretches from the Euphrates around the northern edge of the Syrian Desert along the eastern Mediterranean to the Nile Valley, much of human history was made. It was the Fertile Crescent, because either river irrigation or winter rainfall nurtured productive farmland and settled populations. The central portion of this arc is the isthmus of land which connects Egypt with Anatolia (central Turkey). Bounded on the west by the Mediterranean and on the east by the Syrian Desert, it is some 500 miles long and 75 miles wide. Later called the Levant, it today comprises Lebanon, Israel and the western parts of Syria and Jordan. All the great powers of the ancient world fought over and occupied this stretch of land; it contains the oldest continuously inhabited towns on the earth, such as Jericho and Byblos (Jubail). It was the birthplace of Judaism and Christianity. The name of its most famous city, Jerusalem, still arouses more passionate responses than any other.

The glorious if violent history of this territory was shaped by its geography. Its features run north and south. First the narrow coastal plain, then the upland chain from the Alawite or Nusairiyah mountains of Syria to the north, through Mount Lebanon, Galilee, Samaria and Judaea to Beersheba. To the east of this a deep rift is formed by the valley of the Orontes, the Bekaa Plain, the Jordan Valley leading to the Dead Sea, the Gulf of Aqaba and the Red Sea, and then another mountain chain – the Anti-Lebanon, Mount Hermon, Kerak and the mountains of Moab. Because the winter rains are blown in from the west, the land is most fertile on the coast and the western slopes of the mountains. Eastwards the farmlands become pasture, until they merge into the limestone steppe of the Syrian Desert stretching to Mesopotamia. The city of Damascus stands like a port on the western edge of this wilderness, which was always a more formidable barrier than the Mediterranean Sea.

This short causeway along the eastern Mediterranean between Egypt and present-day Turkey was the scene of an astonishing and productive mixture of peoples and cultures. They came from all directions. The non-Semitic and highly civilized Sumerians from Mesopotamia dominated Syria for about a thousand years, from 3500 BC. They were defeated by the Semitic Amorites, nomads from central Arabia, but the Sumerians taught their conquerors how to write and how to farm the land. Babylonians in the middle of the third millennium were followed by Egyptians, who first conquered the coastal plain of Syria at about the same time. The Egyptians were frequently driven out by the new invaders such as the warlike Hittites from Asia Minor, who took all of Syria in 1450 BC, but just as often they returned and recovered control.

The settled inhabitants of Syria and Palestine were known as Canaanites from about 1600 BC. Almost certainly they did not constitute a single race but were formed through a mingling of peoples, some of whom came from the sea and some from the desert. They never created a powerful imperial state of their own; they submitted to the successive waves of conquerors, paid them tribute and traded with them. They were skilful workers in metal.

One people who came to settle on the Levant coast in about 1400 BC was the extraordinary seafaring Phoenicians, who established trading colonies on most of the Mediterranean shore and even on the Atlantic coasts of Europe and Africa. Carthage, Tyre and Sidon are the most famous of these. The name 'Phoenician' derives from the Greek word for purple – the Tyrian purple dye was renowned throughout the ancient world. Many Lebanese of today like to think of the Phoenicians as their ancestors.

Another wave of invaders came from central Arabia – the Aramaeans. By about 1200 BC they had gained control over Damascus. They took their culture from the more civilized, settled inhabitants of Syria, but it was their Semitic language – Aramaic – which became the *lingua franca* of the region and was spoken by Jesus Christ a thousand years later.

About a century after the Phoenicians the Hebrews, having escaped from Egypt, invaded the land of Canaan from the east, seized Jericho and gradually subdued its settled population in the hills. But they had to contend with a new wave of invaders from across the Mediterranean – the Philistines – who settled on the coastal plain, giving their name to the region: Palestine (*falastin* in Arabic). The struggle ebbed and flowed until David, King of Israel, united the Hebrew tribes, captured the Jebusite town of Jerusalem and made it his capital. There his son Solomon built the first Jewish temple. The Kingdom of Israel lasted some two centuries before it split into two – the Kingdoms of Israel and Judah. In about 720 BC the newest great power from northern Iraq – the Assyrians – overran the two little Jewish states and caused them to disappear. From then on there was never an independent Jewish state until the twentieth century, although the Jews had a degree of autonomy in the Maccabean kingdom (166–163 BC) and its successor, the House of Herod. When the Jews rebelled against the Roman Empire in AD 70, the Emperor Titus destroyed Jerusalem. Their final revolt was put down by Hadrian in AD 135 and the Jews were scattered; only a few thousand remained in Galilee.

The Jews stood apart from the other peoples who invaded and

settled in Syria and Palestine in two important respects. One was
that in general they did not intermarry and assimilate with the other
peoples of the region. The other was their religious genius, which
produced the first of three great monotheistic faiths. The Ten
Commandments and the Judaic legal code which derives from them
were by far the highest system of morality to be developed by
mankind before the coming of Christ. But because the Jews regarded
themselves as a distinctive people, specially chosen by God, Judaism
was never a proselytizing religion. There was no question of huge
masses of humanity converting to the Jewish faith, as was the case
with its two successors – Christianity and Islam.

From about the end of the ninth century BC, the character of the
invasions of Syria/Palestine began to change. It was now less a matter
of migrating peoples seeking a better place in which to settle – 'a
land of milk and honey' – than of great powers aiming to conquer
and impose their rule over the existing inhabitants. The Assyrians,
who had their capital at Nineveh near Mosul in modern Iraq, first
appeared in Syria in about 1100 BC, but it was their King Shalama-
neser III (859–824 BC) who founded the Assyrian Empire, which
lasted for more than two centuries and finally conquered Egypt.
The former great empire of the Pharaohs had been in sad decline
since the time of Rameses III of the Twentieth Dynasty (twelfth
century BC), who was the last to display military genius in the field
of battle. Irrigation works fell into disuse and trade decayed. Egypt
was governed by local despots in the cities of the Nile Delta, which
were constantly attacked and finally defeated by the Assyrians.

The Assyrians were in turn defeated and overthrown by the Chaldean dynasty of Babylon. In 597 BC their King Nebuchadnezzar
took Jerusalem. But the Chaldean Empire was short-lived. Further
east, in present-day Iran, a new and dynamic state was formed by
the uniting of Medes and Persians. Their King Cyrus II – 'the Great'
– reigned from 559 to 530 BC and founded an empire which covered
the whole of western Asia in the modern Middle East and more,
from the Indus River to the Aegean Sea and the borders of Egypt.
In 525 BC the successors of Cyrus conquered Egypt with little

difficulty, and it could be said that for the Egyptians two thousand years of foreign rule had begun.

The Persians were then masters of the whole civilized world of the time, apart from China. In the western province of Syria and Palestine, Aramaic was the official language. Administration was efficient, roads were built and taxes were collected regularly. The region enjoyed two hundred years of peace and prosperity.

As we have seen, the local indigenous population was a melting-pot of races, both non-Semites who had come mainly from the west and north and Semites who had come mainly from the east – the Arabian peninsula. The word 'Semite' derives from Shem, the eldest son of Noah, from whom all the Semitic peoples are supposed to be descended. However, it is not a racial but a linguistic term, invented in the late eighteenth century by the German historian Schlözer to denote the languages which were spoken in Mesopotamia, Syria and the Arabian peninsula and which from the first millennium BC spread into North Africa. All the Semitic languages have striking similarities in their syntax and basic vocabularies, just as there are affinities between the social institutions, religious beliefs and even the psychological traits of the peoples who speak them. Almost certainly there was once a single 'proto-Semitic' language spoken by the people of Arabia which had dialectical variants.

The northwards migration of Semitic peoples from the Arabian peninsula was continuous, tending to reach a peak about every thousand years. The Arabs are first mentioned in Assyrian inscriptions of about 850 BC as a nomadic people of the north Arabian desert who paid their tribute to their Assyrian overlords in the form of camels – which had first been domesticated in the Arabian peninsula some five hundred years earlier.

The racial origins of the Arabs are highly obscure. The Arabs of today have inherited a tradition that they come from two stocks – the Qahtanis and Adnanis. The former originated in the rain-fed highlands of south-western Arabia and are descended from the patriarch Qahtan. The latter came from the north and centre of the peninsula and are descended from the patriarch Adnan. Almost every Arab tribe claimed descent from one or the other. Of the two, it is the southerners or Yemenis who now form half the population of Arabia and are called the 'true Arabs', the sons of Adnan being called *Mustarib* or arabized peoples. Although today there is no obvious racial difference between those who call themselves Qahtanis and those who call themselves Adnanis, there are two recognizable racial types among the general population of Arabia. The tall people with clean-cut, hawk-like features come mainly from the north; while those in the south tend to be shorter with softer and more rounded features – in origin they are probably related to the Ethiopians. It is therefore ironic that it is the southerners who are considered the 'true Arabs', for it is the northerners who provide the popular image of the Arab and it was in central and northern Arabia that the classical Arabic tongue – the vehicle of Arab/Islamic civilization – developed.

It was many centuries before the whole Middle Eastern and North African region (apart from Persia and Turkey) became arabized. In 336 BC Philip, King of Macedon, united the warring Greek city-states, and it was his son Alexander who launched the astonishing series of conquests which overthrew the magnificent but decadent Persian Empire. Greek thought and culture had already started to penetrate Syria/Palestine and Egypt before Alexander the Great's arrival. A thousand years of Graeco-Roman civilization on the eastern and southern shores of the Mediterranean had begun.

The Persian/Arabian Gulf was included in Alexander's empire. When he reached the limits of his eastern conquests, in India in 326 BC, he set out to return to Persia by land. But he had in mind a great sea-traffic between Babylon, the capital of his eastern empire, and India. So he ordered his admiral, Nearchos, to return to the Euphrates via the Gulf at the head of his huge fleet. Nearchos reported on the existence of two strategic islands at the head of the Gulf. The larger had wild goats and antelope, which were sacred to the Goddess Artemis, and Alexander ordered that it should be named Ikaros after the island in the Aegean Sea which it resembled. A fortress outpost was established which lasted about two hundred years. Today Ikaros is called Failaka and is part of Kuwait.

Alexander's dream of a vast united Hellenistic empire did not survive his early death, as his conquests were disputed between his generals. But Hellenistic civilization remained dominant in the successor empires which stretched from Persia to Egypt, and the cities which Alexander founded continued to flourish. Egypt prospered under the wise rule of the early Ptolemys. Alexandria, with its library and museum, became a splendid city and the intellectual centre of the world. Palestine for a time came once again under Egyptian rule. The rest of Syria and Asia Minor (Turkey of the present day) fell into the hands of Seleucus, the Persian ruler of Alexander's former eastern empire. He founded Antioch, which he named after his father, and this became the capital of Syria for the next nine centuries.

Hellenism first began to retreat in Persia, but even here it was a slow process. Two hundred years after Alexander's death, the Seleucids in Persia were overthrown by the Parthians, a predatory nomadic tribe from the region of the Caspian Sea. The Parthians assimilated Greek government practice and continued to make use of the Greek language in addition to their own. Some Greek cities of Seleucid foundation continued to flourish. Hellenistic influence began to weaken only in the first century AD.

In Syria/Palestine Hellenism was more lasting, but its degree of influence varied greatly. As might be expected, it was greatest to the north and west on the Mediterranean coast, where Laodicea (modern Latakia) and Berytus (Beirut) were typical Greek cities. East of Mount Lebanon, towards the Syrian Desert, Hellenistic influence declined. In fact the whole region was a blend of Hellenism and Semitic Aramaic culture in varying proportions. In both the Ptolemaic and Seleucid Empires the senior civil servants, and the leading businessmen, scholars and intellectuals were Greek. Both empires encouraged immigration from Greece, but the Greeks remained a minority. In their armies the Greeks formed the core or phalanx bearing pikes, but the archers and slingers were Arabs, Kurds and Persians.

Little more than a century after Alexander's death saw the beginning of the rise to power of the Roman Republic. After the final defeat of Carthage in 211 BC, Rome gained mastery over the western Mediterranean. It then turned its attention to the east and invaded Greece. There followed more than 150 years of chaos and war in the eastern Mediterranean region. The rival Seleucid and Ptolemaic Empires fought each other beneath the looming shadow of Rome, and went into a long decline. As always, local powers in Syria took the opportunity to assert themselves.

In Palestine, the small Jewish community enjoyed some freedom to manage its own affairs in the Judaean hills around Jerusalem. The Jewish people were divided between a Hellenized educated upper class which broadly accepted Seleucid rule and a peasantry which clung to their Judaic faith. When, in 168 BC, the Seleucid King Antiochus Epiphanes ordered the altar of Zeus, 'the abomination of desolation', to be set up in the Holy Temple in Jerusalem, Judas Maccabaeus, the son of a priest, led the fervent Jews in a revolt. Although Judas was killed, his family founded a dynasty of priest-princes – the Hasmonaeans – who gradually extended their rule to cover most of Palestine as the Seleucid Empire disintegrated. They were succeeded under the Romans by the related House of Herod.

Further to the east another independent state was established by the Nabataeans, with their headquarters in Petra (south Jordan) and Madain Saleh (Saudi Arabia). In the second century BC their powerful commercial kingdom stretched deep into the Arabian peninsula and flourished by controlling the caravan trade which brought Chinese and Indian spices, perfumes and other luxuries from southern Arabia to Syria and Egypt. The Nabataeans spoke Arabic, but their writing was Aramaic. Their culture was superficially Hellenic. The people of present-day Jordan regard them as their ancestors.

The consolidation of Roman power in the eastern Mediterranean was delayed by the civil war and anarchy in Rome. However, in the 60s BC the triumvirate of generals Pompey, Caesar and Crassus took power, and Pompey set about establishing Roman power in Asia Minor and the eastern Mediterranean. He invaded Syria and took Jerusalem. But Roman rule was not yet firmly established. The Parthians inflicted a savage defeat on the Roman legions and for a time occupied Syria. It was not until after both Pompey and Caesar had been assassinated that Caesar's successor Octavian – the Emperor Augustus, who reigned from 29 BC to AD 14 – incorporated the entire Middle East region from Egypt to Asia Minor into the Roman Empire. Only Persia and present-day Iraq remained under Parthian control. Augustus ignored the demands of some of his generals that the defeat of the Roman legions be avenged, preferring to have peace in order to organize Rome's new eastern provinces.

The eastern Mediterranean region – Asia Minor, Syria and Egypt – settled down to several centuries of the Pax Romana, which in general meant efficiency, good order and justice in accordance with Roman law. The road and tax systems were greatly improved. Egypt became an important supplier of food to the imperial capital and a military base for the Roman armies. The Romans cleared the Red Sea of pirates and revived the trade through it to India. Egypt was a Roman colony in the fullest sense, living under iron military government and paying exorbitant taxes. The Greek ruling class co-operated with the colonial power and retained its privileged position.

Egypt, with its population densely concentrated in the Nile Valley and Delta, lends itself to authoritarian centralized government. Roman rule in Syria was rather more relaxed. In the eastern or 'Semitic' half of the region, the Romans allowed the local rulers to retain their autonomy – provided they did not become over-ambitious and threaten the settled populations to the west. It was indirect rule of the kind employed by the British in their empire in Asia and Africa some eighteen centuries later. Thus the Nabataeans continued to control east Jordan and Damascus until in AD 106 the Emperor Trajan, exasperated by their spirit of independence, brought them under the subjection of Rome. A century later, Palmyra in the central Syrian Desert emulated the Nabataeans in achieving power and prosperity through control of the caravan trade-routes to the east until its queen, Zenobia, defied Roman authority, only to be defeated and to have the region's autonomy repressed.

The western or Mediterranean region of Syria, with its great and flourishing Greek cities founded under the Seleucids, was more directly incorporated into the Roman Empire. The educated urban population, a fruitful synthesis of Mediterranean and Semitic races, was part of the empire's professional and intellectual élite. These people mixed easily with the Roman officials, and many acquired Roman citizenship. Many Syrian lawyers, doctors, historians and administrators – not to mention poets and actors – achieved distinction and fame. Hellenized Egyptians played a similar role. Antioch and Alexandria were, after Rome, the two largest and most magnificent cities of the empire. While Latin was the official language of government, Greek was the *lingua franca*. Several of the later Roman emperors were either wholly or partly Syrian, although it has to be said that two of these – Caracalla and Elagabalus, from Homs – were among the least admirable. However, Caracalla can claim credit for the decision to grant Roman citizenship to the whole empire in AD 212. Philip 'the Arab', an able ruler, did something to redeem Syria's reputation during his brief reign.

Despite the easy racial mixture of the cities, a gulf – and especially a linguistic gulf – remained between the cities and the peasants and tribesmen of the countryside. In Syria these spoke Aramaic; the nomads and semi-nomads on the fringes of Arabia spoke Arabic. In Egypt the majority of the population spoke the ancient Egyptian language. But it was in Palestine that the clash of cultures was most violent, and yet perhaps most productive.

In 40 BC the Romans appointed Herod from Idumaea (Edom) in southern Palestine as King of Judaea, with Jerusalem as his capital. In his long reign he extended his effective rule over most of Palestine, earning the title of 'Herod the Great'. An Arab by race, he was a Jew by practice and he saw himself as the protector of the Jews. He rebuilt the Temple of Jerusalem, but as a Hellenizer and a Roman protégé he was detested by the pious Jews. His reign ended in bitterness and violent dispute over his succession in which he ordered the notorious massacre of the innocent infants of Bethlehem. Thus he also became the ogre of Christian tradition, as it was in the little

Herodian kingdom that the Jewish founder of the Christian religion was born, lived and was executed – the founder of the religion which in time triumphantly converted the entire Graeco-Roman world.

Jesus and his Apostles were Jews, and Christianity was originally a movement within Judaism. But the Christian message made little headway among the Jewish people and so it was soon directed towards the gentile world instead. It was the task of the early Christian apologists to define the Christian gospel as both the correction and the fulfilment of Greek and Roman philosophy, and their intellectual achievements in the first three centuries after Christ were considerable. However, the simple message of the Sermon on the Mount made its first appeal to the poor and underprivileged masses of the Graeco-Roman world. Despite official persecution, it thrived and spread – the martyrdom of Jesus providing a model for suffering and endurance. Christianity is thought to have arrived in Egypt with St Mark, before the end of the first century AD, and it spread rapidly among the mass of the Egyptian people, although the Greeks and the Hellenized upper class generally remained pagan.

The persecution of Christianity in the empire occurred in waves which were interspersed by periods of toleration, but for three centuries Christianity gained converts. Although still a minority – the majority clinging to the old state religions, of which the cult of the emperor was the most popular – Christians formed a substantial proportion among all classes, including members of the imperial family and the Roman aristocracy, by the time the last wave of persecution was instituted by Diocletian, at the beginning of the fourth century AD. They were dynamic and well-organized, and within a few years of Diocletian's abdication his successor, Constantine the Great, declared Christianity to be the official religion of the Roman Empire. Whether Constantine's conversion was genuine or whether he had recognized Christianity as the conquering faith is immaterial.

The rise of Christianity was favoured by the decline of the empire. Throughout the third century AD the empire had been beset by internal divisions – indeed, for periods it was ruled by rival emperors – and assaulted from outside its borders by Goths and Persians. At times the empire had seemed on the verge of collapse, until it was rescued once more by an able emperor or army commander. In the east, the Parthian Empire was replaced in AD 224 by that of the Sassanids from west Persia, who claimed descent from the great dynasty of Cyrus and Darius. The Sassanian Empire lasted for four centuries, in which it was almost constantly at war with the rival great power in the west. Shapar I, the second Sassanid ruler, took the title of 'King of Kings of Iran and non-Iran', thus emphasizing his claim to dominion of the world.

In AD 330, on the ancient site of Byzantium on the Bosporus where Europe meets Asia, Constantine founded the city that bore his name. Constantinople became the capital of the eastern half of the Roman Empire – still formally united – and, as the centre of power and wealth shifted eastwards, Constantinople overtook Rome in magnificence. Half a century later, on the death of the Emperor Theodosius, the empire was divided between his two sons. The Christian, Hellenic–oriental Byzantine Empire was born. While the western half of the empire collapsed under the weight of barbarian invasions, Byzantium continued to rule the Balkans, Asia Minor, Syria, Palestine and Egypt.

The eastern Roman Empire was able to maintain control over the Middle East region for three centuries. The greatest threat it faced was not from Goths and Germans in Europe but from the aggressive and expansionist Sassanian Persians to the east. However, for at least two hundred years the Byzantines were able to secure peace with the Persians through diplomacy. It was only when Justinian the Great (527–65) decided to devote his energies to the reconquest of the western Roman provinces and the reuniting of the empire – efforts which were partially and temporarily successful – that the Persian danger increased. Between 534 and 628 the Persians repeatedly invaded and occupied Syria and had to be thrown back. In 616 they conquered both Egypt and Asia Minor and laid siege to Constantinople. By the time the Emperor Heraclius defeated the Persians and restored the empire's frontiers, Byzantium and

Persia, although still the two superpowers of the ancient world, were overstretched and weakened. Meanwhile, in AD 570 or 571, in obscure and impoverished Arabia an extraordinary man had been born who would plant the seeds of a new and much greater power that would come to overwhelm them. The Prophet Muhammad, who was born in Mecca, one of the largest settled and trading communities in western Arabia, was a man of genius and inspiration who helped to transform the history of mankind – a fact which is acknowledged not only by the one-fifth of the human race who subscribe to the faith that he founded.

There are two aspects of the Islamic religion which are of special importance to the subsequent history of the Middle East. The first of these is that while Muslims do not believe Muhammad to be divine – for Islam is the most fiercely monotheistic of faiths, adhering to the belief that 'there is no God but God' – they do regard him as the last of God's messengers, or the seal of the prophets, who include Moses and Jesus. They therefore hold that Islam is the ultimate faith, which completes and perfects the two other heavenly religions – Judaism and Christianity. If mankind as a whole has not yet accepted the truth, it is due to the failings of the community of Muslim believers.

The other important fact is that, while Muslims believe in paradise and the soul's immortality, their faith is far from other-worldly. The Prophet, unlike Jesus, was a political leader and organizer of genius, and in Islam there is no separation between religion and politics and no concept of a secular state. The Holy Koran, which for Muslims is the literal word of God, is the continuing inspiration for all Muslim thought and actions, but it is not a comprehensive code of law. Muslims have therefore looked also to the example of the Prophet and his companions. Their words and deeds, known as their *sunnah* or habitual modes of thought and action, were collected in the *hadith*, or traditions of the Prophet, which were handed down through a line or reliable witnesses. Together the Koran and the *sunnah* form the sources of the Islamic *sharia*. This is normally translated as 'Islamic law', but it is much more than this. It is neither canonical law (Islam has no priesthood) nor secular law, because no such concept exists in Islam: it is rather a whole system of social morality, prescribing the ways in which man should live if he is to act according to God's will. If he contravenes the *sharia*, his offence is against God and not the state.

This is the ideal. Since the earliest times, Arab and Muslim rulers have assumed secular powers to some degree – and none more so than those of today – but the ideal continues to have a powerful influence on the hearts and minds of all Muslims. It accounts for the potent force of utopianism among Arabs – the belief that if they were to return to the ways of the Prophet and his companions the triumph of Islam in this world would be assured. In the West this is usually described as fundamentalism, but in a real sense all Muslim believers are fundamentalist, because they know that the Holy Koran was God's final message to mankind. The triumph of the West in the last two or three centuries is seen by Muslims as an aberration of history.

It is not surprising that the Arabs of today are still inspired to the point of obsession by the story of the first achievements of Islam. When, at the age of forty, Muhammad underwent the religious experience which turned him into a prophet and leader, the Arabian peninsula was a conglomeration of petty autonomous states grouped around tribal confederations. The largely nomadic people were mainly animists by religion, worshipping a variety of spirits who were often based in a particular rock or shrine. They had no written codes of laws; crimes were restrained by the lasting fears of vengeance. No such restraints applied to communal acts of violence, however, and the frequent inter-tribal disputes could be settled only by reference to an arbiter, a wise authority on tribal customs. This was not a high culture which could remotely be compared with that of Byzantium or Persia, but it had a matchless asset in the Arabic language, with its limitless power and flexibility and the supreme artistic achievement of its poetry.

Although proud and independent, the people of Arabia were not immune to outside influences. Through their contacts with the

Christian Byzantines and Abyssinians, and Zoroastrian Persians, they had begun to acquire some monotheistic ideas when Muhammad began his mission. By the time he died, in his early sixties, the new faith had been accepted throughout most of Arabia. In one generation he had succeeded in welding the scattered and idolatrous tribes of the peninsula into one nation worshipping a single, all-powerful god.

If the achievements of the Islamic faith in the lifetime of Muhammad were remarkable, those during the brief rule of his three successors, or caliphs – the Rashidoun or Rightly Guided Ones – were even more astonishing. The small forces of the faithful went on to challenge the two great empires of Byzantium and Persia. Within ten years they had defeated the Sassanid Persians, captured their capital Ctesiphon on the Tigris and driven them out of Mesopotamia. They then turned their attention to the Byzantine provinces of Syria and Egypt. The Arab army swept on through North Africa, and within another fifty years, in AD 711, had crossed into Spain.

After the conquest of Syria and Egypt, the Arabs spent another ten years destroying what remained of the Sassanid Empire. The Byzantine Empire, however, was to last another eight hundred years. Although the Arabs took Cyprus, Rhodes and Cos and twice besieged Constantinople, they never conquered and held Anatolia, which continued for several more centuries to be shared between the Byzantines and the Christian kingdom of Armenia.

Within thirty years of the Prophet's death, decisive events were to shape the future of Islam and of the Prophet's Arabian homeland. In AD 656 the Caliph Omar's successor, Othman, was assassinated. His natural successor seemed to be Ali, first cousin of the Prophet and husband of his daughter Fatima. But Ali was opposed by the ambitious and able Arab general Muawiya, whom Omar had appointed governor of Syria and who, like Othman, belonged to the powerful Umayyad family of Mecca. The defeat of Ali and his son Hussein by the Umayyads led to the first and only great division in Islam: between the Sunnis, or 'people of the *sunnah*', who are the great majority, and the Shia or 'partisans' of Ali, who continue to regard Muawiya and his Umayyad successors as secular usurpers.

Today about 10 per cent of the world's Muslim population are Shiite, and most of these are in Iran and the Indian subcontinent. There are scarcely any Shiites in Africa. In the Levant they are important in Lebanon, where they form 40 per cent of the population and probably outnumber the Sunnis.

In the Arabian peninsula the great majority of the people have remained Sunni, although there are important Shiite minorities on the eastern fringes. The Zaydis, who inhabit the mountains of Yemen, also belong to a branch of Shiism. But Sunnism and Shiism continued in dispute over Persia (Iran) until, in the sixteenth century, Shiism was adopted as the ruling faith. In Mesopotamia (Iraq), the majority of the population have remained Shiite, and the Shia holy cities of Najaf and Karbala are on Iraqi territory, but Sunnis are still politically dominant. This has a significant bearing on the modern history of the region.

The triumph of the Umayyads not only caused a split in Islam: it made Damascus the capital of the new Arab/Islamic Empire. After a century, in AD 750, the defeat of the Umayyads by the Abbasids, a rival revolutionary movement based in east Persia, shifted the centre of power to Baghdad, inaugurating the Golden Age of Islam – one of the highest peaks of human civilization.

In the vast territories in which Islam was triumphant, two processes – allied but not identical – began to operate: 'arabization' and 'islamization'. In Iraq, Greater Syria, Egypt and the North African countries of the Maghreb, the Arabic languages began gradually to overwhelm the existing tongues. (Kurdish in northern Iraq and the Berber tongue, Tamazight, in Algeria and Morocco have survived.) In Syria/Palestine and Egypt, Greek continued to be used in administration for a time until Arabic was made the official tongue. In the Fertile Crescent, the Arabic which was already spoken in the east and in the Arabian peninsula steadily replaced Aramaic, which now barely survives in one or two villages north of Damascus and in northern Iraq. Similarly, the Coptic language of the ancient Egyptians was progressively extinguished as the Arab occupation changed into full-scale colonization and assimilation, although it survived at least until the seventeenth century.

Islamization was less complete than arabization because substantial communities of Christians and Jews, respected and tolerated by Islam as 'People of the Book', clung to their faith and survived. But the spread of Islam was more extensive than that of the Arabic language. It moved swiftly to Samarkand and the borders of India, and in subsequent centuries huge populations in the Indian subcontinent, in China and in south-east Asia converted. But here Arabic was confined to religious observance. The language and culture of the Persians survived both their conquest by the Arabs and their acceptance of the Islamic faith, although the Persian Farsi language adopted the Arabic script and an extensive Arabic vocabulary. Today only about one-fifth of the Muslims in the world are Arabic-speaking.

The Turks were not conquered by the Arabs, but they were largely converted to Islam in the tenth century, and their language was invaded by a stream of Arabic words from the vocabulary of religion, science and culture. Turkish was also written in the Arabic script. The twelfth century, when Persian became the literary language of western Asia, saw a second linguistic invasion. Turkish writers adopted Persian and Arabic grammatical constructions as well as words, to create the synthesis of Ottoman Turkish.

Three languages – Arabic, Persian and Turkish – therefore came to be spoken or written by the vast majority of the inhabitants of the Middle East region. According to modern nationalist terminology, the people who spoke these languages were Arabs, Persians and Turks.

Only three important minorities resisted assimilation and retained their national identity – Armenians, Kurds and Berbers. The Armenians had a continuing national existence from the sixth century BC, in what is now eastern Turkey and part of Soviet Transcaucasia, and they can claim to be the oldest Christian nation, with their own Armenian Apostolic Church. They had an independent kingdom for several centuries before their conquest and absorption into an Islamic Empire in the fourteenth century, and, although later dispersed throughout the Middle East and beyond, they remain loyal to their language, religion and culture.

The Kurds are a mountain people whose ancient history has often overlapped with that of the Armenians. They speak an Indo-European group of dialects, related to Persian. Unlike the Armenians, they have never had their own independent state, but they have been less dispersed and today they inhabit an arc of territory from north-western Iran through north-eastern Iraq and Syria to eastern Turkey.

The Arabs were aided in their conquest by the debilitating struggles between the Byzantine and Persian Empires, and also by the unpopularity of the imperial rulers among their subject peoples. To create their own lasting empire the Arabs had to succeed better in the art of government than their predecessors. The achievement of these former barbarian nomads was astonishing, and undoubtedly the nature of the Islamic faith – austere, simple, comprehensible and just – provides the reason. There is no cause for surprise that Arabs of today should believe that a return to the principles and practice of those days should restore their greatness.

Initially the tribal warriors of pure Arab descent formed a military aristocracy who numbered no more than a few hundred thousand. Non-Arabs who embraced Islam – Persians, Egyptians, Levantines of mixed race or North African Berbers – were called *mawalis* or clients. But this aristocracy of the Arabs did not last.

Although Islam's relationship with Arabia and the Arabic language is indestructible, racial distinction among the faithful is contrary to both the letter and the spirit of the Holy Koran. As marriage with *mawali* women was frequent, assimilation proceeded swiftly, and in the process the term 'Arab' began its gradual change from the name for a beduin nomad of the Arabian peninsula to its present meaning of anyone whose culture and language are Arabic.

Under the Abbasid caliphate, a great movement of ethnic as well as cultural assimilation took place within the Islamic Empire. While Arabic came to be accepted first as the dominant language and then as the *lingua franca*, the 'pure' Arabs also gradually abandoned their claims to aristocracy. The principle of ethnic equality came to be accepted. Thus the language and religion of the Arabs acted as the cement which held this great edifice together. Its strength and prosperity lay in the fact that the splendid Persian and Hellenic civilizations which had been overwhelmed were not destroyed: for a time the new Arab rulers left the existing systems of government and administration largely intact, until they had assimilated them and developed their own synthesis.

The transfer of the empire's capital from Damascus to Baghdad shifted its centre of gravity eastwards. Interest in the Mediterranean declined, and oriental influences, such as the Persian taste for absolute monarchy, increased. The removal of frontier barriers made Baghdad the centre of a vast and increasingly prosperous free-trade area in which most sections of the population had the opportunity to engage in vigorous commercial activity. Arab ships sailed to China, Sumatra, India and southwards along the east coast of Africa as far as Madagascar. Learning and culture also flourished in this Islamic Golden Age. At first it was mainly a question of translation into Arabic of the great scientific and philosophical works of the ancient civilizations, but soon the Islamic Empire brought forth its own towering achievements in science, literature and the arts.

As in all other human empires, the seeds of decline were already sprouting when this empire was apparently at its zenith. Despite the remarkable system of communications radiating from Baghdad, effective power could not be exerted over the more distant provinces for long. In Egypt and in eastern Persia, authority was delegated to local commanders who made themselves autonomous. The Arabs who had earlier supplied the vanguard of the imperial forces felt alienated from their new arabized rulers and no longer enlisted, so the caliph took to importing Turkish slave-boys known as Mamlukes from what is now Soviet Turkestan to be trained as soldiers who would maintain the security of the empire. Although speaking Turkish, the Mamlukes were not all ethnic Turks but included Kurds, Mongols and other central Asian peoples. These mercenaries made effective soldiers, but they soon realized their ability to seize control for themselves. In 861 they assassinated the caliph in Baghdad and set up a military dictatorship. In 867 a Turk named Ibn Tulun seized power in Egypt. He easily occupied Syria and once again brought it into an association with Egypt. This was to last, with intermissions, until the whole region came under the domination of the Ottoman Turkish Empire in the sixteenth century.

The great Arab/Islamic Empire which had lasted more than two centuries and covered the whole of the contemporary known world except for northern Europe and China was breaking up. In the early part of the eighth century the Arabs had held Spain and half of France. They soon withdrew from France, but later occupied Sicily and much of southern Italy. However, the move of the capital from Damascus to Baghdad weakened the empire's control in the Mediterranean and now, at the end of the ninth century, this was broken entirely. The Arabs retained their cultural dominance for at least another two centuries, and Baghdad continued to be a great centre of culture and learning, but effective power was exercised by the uncultivated Turkish military caste.

This Turkish hegemony was broken for a time, however. In AD 969, Egypt, after a century of unstable rule by Turkish military dynasties, was invaded from the west by a new Arab power. This was the Fatimid dynasty, which took its name from the Prophet's daughter Fatima, the wife of the caliph Ali. Before moving to North Africa the Fatimids had originated in Syria as leaders of the Shiite Ismaili movement, which was dedicated to the overthrow of the Abbasid caliphate. They were regarded as heretical enemies by Baghdad.

Just north of the old Arab/Muslim capital of Fustat, the Fatimids founded Cairo as their new capital and established a rival caliphate to that of Baghdad, with its own empire of great splendour. For a time this stretched westwards across the Maghreb to the Atlantic and into Sicily. Although Fatimid power did not extend eastwards, the instability in Baghdad meant that much of the oriental trade which was the source of Abbasid wealth was diverted from the

Persian/Arabian Gulf to the Red Sea. Cairo prospered at Baghdad's expense.

Syria/Palestine resumed its historical role as the battlefield for the struggle between the rival rulers of the Tigris–Euphrates and Nile Valleys. But a new element added to Syria's misery: the Byzantines, who had suffered three centuries of Arab/Muslim invasions, took their opportunity for revenge. Between 962 and 1000, Syria was invaded thirty-eight times by successive Byzantine emperors.

In 1018 the Fatimid caliph Hakim became insane and declared himself to be God. After his death, a new religion emerged with the belief that Hakim had not died but had only disappeared, and would return in triumph to inaugurate a golden age. Taking their name from one of their leaders who fled to Mount Lebanon, Ismail al-Darazi, the Druze are important because, although never numerous (some 600,000 now live in the Middle East), they are one of the few of the many sub-Shiite sects which appeared at that time to have survived to the present day and have played a crucial role in the history of the region. (Another sub-Shiite sect is the Alawite or Nusairi, that first flourished around Aleppo in the tenth century. This sect has also survived and today forms about 10 per cent of the population of Syria. The fact that President Assad and other key members of his regime belong to this sect has had a significant bearing on the modern history of Syria.)

In spite of their repeated invasions of Syria/Palestine, the Byzantines were not able to hold this region. In fact the Byzantine, Abbasid and Fatimid Empires were all in a state of decline in the first half of the eleventh century, when a new force burst on the scene. Oghuz Turkish nomads from central Asia, who became known as Seljuks, after one of their chiefs, invaded Persia and in 1050 captured Baghdad, reducing the Abbasid caliph to the status of a vassal. In 1071, they took Syria and Palestine and drove the Fatimids back to Egypt. By the end of the century the Seljuk Empire included Persia, Mesopotamia, Syria and Palestine. But the Turkoman warriors of the Seljuk army were looking to the rich lands of the Byzantine Empire to the west. In 1071 the Seljuk sultan Arp Arslan routed a huge

Byzantine army and captured the Byzantine emperor. The Muslim Turks were then able to settle in Asia Minor.

For four centuries, Byzantium had protected western Christendom from Islamic invasion and expansion from the east. With the Byzantine Empire now in danger of collapse, the Emperor Alexius Comnenus (1081–1118) appealed to Pope Urban II for men to help fight the infidel invaders. On 27 November 1095 the Pope called for recruits to march to the relief of their fellow-Christians in the east and to restore the security of the western pilgrim-routes to the Holy Land.

The consequent invasion of the Middle East by the Christians of western Europe – the First Crusade – was initially successful. Jerusalem was captured in 1099 and its Muslim and Jewish populations were massacred. A Latin kingdom of Jerusalem and three other crusader principalities were established. The Abbasid caliphs of Baghdad and the Seljuk sultans were largely indifferent to Syria and Palestine, which lay on the periphery of their interests. After one abortive attempt, the Fatimids of Egypt abandoned any effort to recover Jerusalem for Islam. In Syria itself the local Turkish regimes, normally in a state of mutual hostility, frequently allied themselves with the crusaders against each other.

The petty Christian states, which were manifestly inferior in culture and civilization (the Muslims were astonished by the crusaders' primitive medical knowledge, for example), were not regarded as a serious threat to the world of Islam. But the crusader states were not content with mere tolerated survival. They became embroiled with their neighbours, and eventually caused the divided Muslim states to unite in a *jihad* or holy war against them. In 1187 the Kurdish leader Saladin recovered Jerusalem (and, in contrast to the crusaders eighty-eight years previously, spared the lives of those who surrendered). Further crusades were launched in the following century which enabled the diminished Christian states on the coast of Syria and Palestine to survive for a time, but after little more than two centuries they had disappeared.

Apart from a few magnificent castles and some of their blood through intermarriage, the crusaders left little which endured. Their greatest achievement was drastically to weaken the superior civilization they encountered and to undermine its moral standards. However, in one vitally important respect the crusaders showed that they had an advantage over their Muslim enemies: this was their ability to create sound and workable political institutions. These were feudal rather than democratic, but they enshrined the notion of the rights and obligations of the different sections of society – princes, knights, merchants and peasants. The power of the ruler was not unlimited, and the succession was usually achieved by consent rather than force. In the Muslim lands, on the other hand, although both the principles and procedures of law governing human relationships were more sophisticated and rational, the practice of government was normally arbitrary and unlimited. The tribal democracy of the early caliphs, whose power was limited by a *Majlis al-Shura* or consultative council, had generally given way to despotism.

It has been wisely observed that the most disastrous effect of the crusades on the Islamic heartland was Islam's retreat into isolation:

Although the epoch of the Crusades ignited a genuine economic and cultural revolution in Western Europe, in the Orient these holy wars led to long centuries of decadence and obscurantism. Assaulted from all quarters, the Muslim world turned in on itself. It became over-sensitive, defensive, intolerant, sterile – attitudes that grew steadily worse as worldwide evolution, a process from which the Muslim world felt excluded, continued.

This was the long-term consequence. At the time, the triumphant elimination of the Christian invaders was seen as proof of the superiority of the Islamic faith, which, as always has to be remembered, Muslims believe to be designated by God to succeed and perfect the other monotheisms. A few contemporary Muslim chroniclers were prepared to acknowledge the virtues of the system of government in the crusader states, but such comparisons were considered irrelevant once these states had been eliminated.

With the final defeat and expulsion of the crusaders, Islam was triumphant throughout the Middle East region. In Egypt, the splendid but short-lived Ayyubid dynasty founded by Saladin was replaced by the Mamlukes, who at the end of the thirteenth century extended their empire to Syria. The Seljuks gradually pushed forward their domains in Anatolia at the expense of Byzantium, whose decline had been accelerated by the crusaders who in their Fourth Crusade, at the beginning of the thirteenth century, caused a struggle in Constantinople between western Latin and eastern Greek Christians. The Seljuk dynasty in Asia Minor was known as 'the Sultanate of Rum' (Arabic for Rome), a Muslim inheritor of the eastern flank of the Roman Empire.

In the beginning of the thirteenth century, the Muslim world had to face a new and terrifying threat: the Mongols. Like the nomadic Turkish tribes before them, the Mongols burst out of central Asia into the rich lands of the Fertile Crescent. In 1220 Genghis Khan seized Persia; in 1243 his successors routed the entire Seljuk army and went on to occupy the Sultanate of Rum. In 1258 Genghis Khan's grandson Hulagu captured Baghdad and eliminated the last ghostly relic of the Abbasid caliphate, as his armies completed the destruction of the great irrigation works of Mesopotamia.

It seemed as if nothing could prevent the Mongols from overruning Syria and Egypt. But the Egyptian Mamlukes rallied to inflict a crushing defeat on the Mongols at Ain Jalout in Palestine in 1260. In that it saved the heartlands of the Muslim world from being overwhelmed, this was one of the decisive battles in the history of the world. The Mongol threat was far greater than that of the Christian crusaders, but it was also short-lived. Eastern and western Christians both nursed hopes that the Mongols could be converted to Christianity. Instead, in 1295, the Mongol khan announced that he had become a Muslim. The struggle for the Middle East continued to be within the world of Islam.

The three centuries of Mamluke rule in Egypt and Syria showed many of the aspects of an advanced civilization. With the demise of Baghdad and the reduction of Muslim Spain, the great centres of Islamic learning and literary and artistic achievement were now Cairo, Damascus and Aleppo. Exquisite architecture and artefacts have survived from the period. These cities were wealthy and prosperous, as trade poured through both to and from the East. But these centuries were disastrous in the way that power was exercised and in the development of political institutions. If Muslim society was relatively stable, its rulers were not. The Mamlukes' code prevented the founding of a hereditary dynasty, and in matters of government they fell back on their ferocious and unyielding military tradition. Mamluke sultans of Egypt rarely lasted more than a few years before they were ousted by a stronger rival. Similarly, Mamluke generals fought each other for the governorship of Syria. As the Mongol Empire declined, there was no longer an external threat to enforce the unity that had been achieved at Ain Jalout.

The Mamlukes were not aware that their fate was being sealed by events that were taking place in Asia Minor. At the end of the thirteenth century this was the territory of some dozen Turkish warrior-princes, or ghazis, who had overwhelmed most of the provinces of the Byzantine Empire. Nominally tributaries of the Mongol khans, they had become increasingly independent. One of these, named Osman, was the founder of a dynasty and empire which grew to control most of the world of Islam for four centuries.

The first Osmanlis – or Ottomans, as they became known in the west – were distinguished among their fellow-ghazis by their wisdom and statecraft. In many ways they resembled the first caliphs of Islam – the Rashidoun or Rightly Guided Ones – in that they combined a passionate and simple faith with a chivalrous and tolerant attitude towards the mainly Christian inhabitants of the lands they conquered. Some of these Christians converted to Islam, but even those who did not frequently welcomed the firm justice of Ottoman rule in contrast to the anarchic misgovernment of the decadent Byzantine Empire.

In the second half of the fourteenth century, Osman's grandson Murad I, the first great Ottoman sultan, crossed the Hellespont to extend the young empire into the Christian Balkan states. He applied the principle of toleration to allow non-Muslims to become full citizens and rise to the highest offices of state, so at this very early stage establishing the character of the vast multilingual and multi-ethnic Ottoman Empire, which had much in common with the Roman Empire.

Murad conquered the Balkans; his son Bayezid I devoted himself to the acquisition of the whole of Asia and the final reduction of Constantinople. He failed at the final hour because of a sudden new threat from the east – the Tartars, who appeared like a reincarnation of their Mongol cousins two centuries earlier. Tamerlane, the terrifying Tartar leader, came close to destroying the Ottoman Empire in its infancy and restoring the ghazi principalities to Byzantium, but he died on his way to new conquests in China. The Ottomans recovered and a generation later produced another outstanding leader in Mohammed II – 'the Conqueror' – who in 1453 finally captured Constantinople and overwhelmed the last relics of the Byzantine Empire.

Western schoolchildren have been taught that, by scattering the legacy of Greece and Rome, the Muslim conquest of Constantinople launched western Christendom into the Renaissance. In fact, although this momentous event had a profound and lasting effect on the imagination of mankind, it marked only the final stage of the withdrawal of non-Muslim power from the Middle East: for many generations the Byzantine Empire had been no more than a shadow of its former dominating presence.

Europe was already well aware of the Ottoman threat. The Venetians, Hungarians and others had tried to stem the tide by forming temporary alliances with the Ottomans' rivals in Asia Minor. After the fall of Constantinople, the infidel Turk was for two centuries a towering menace which threatened to burst out from the Balkans and overrun central Europe. Twice – in 1529 and 1683 – the Ottoman forces were on the point of occupying Vienna and overwhelming the Habsburg Empire. In weapons and military strategy – especially the early use of firearms – they were superior, and they had rapidly turned themselves into a formidable naval power which could match anything the Europeans could put to sea. Edward Gibbon's famous speculation about the consequences for Europe if the Arab/Muslim armies had continued their advance northwards into France in the eighth century (students of Oxford and Cambridge studying the Holy Koran instead of the Bible) could equally have been applied to the Turkish invasions eight centuries later. The Arabs were turned back as much by the unappealing climate of northern Europe as by the army of Charles Martel, leader of the Christian Franks; the Turks from Asia Minor were more accustomed to the frost and snow. The Renaissance monarchs of Europe constantly attempted to combine their forces for new crusades against the world of Islam but, in contrast to their predecessors in the earlier crusades, they were acting not on behalf of Christian pilgrims to the Holy Land or Christian minorities in the Middle East but to protect themselves.

In its first two centuries, the greater part of the Ottoman Empire's remarkable energies was directed towards Christian Europe. However, after Mohammed the Conqueror had consolidated the Ottoman hold on Asia Minor, his grandson Selim I, known as 'the Grim', turned his attention towards Asia. In Persia the Safavid dynasty had been established when Ismail, known as 'the Great Sufi', proclaimed himself shah in 1501. Shortly afterwards he declared Shiite Islam, which was already the faith of most of his subjects, to be the official religion of the empire. In 1508 he occupied Iraq. Selim the Grim – also known as 'the Just' for his severe Sunni orthodoxy – defeated Ismail in a great battle in the Valley of Chalderan, near Tabriz. In 1514 he went on to annex the high plateau of eastern Anatolia, which provided the Ottoman Empire with a vital strategic defence against invasion from the west.

More than two centuries of struggle and intermittent warfare between the Sunni and Shiite Empires ensued. Militarily the Ottomans usually had the upper hand, but Persian cultural influence remained a powerful force in the Turkish Empire, and even when the Ottomans established their definitive control over Mesopotamia in the seventeenth century the majority of its Arabic-speaking people remained Shiite. Shah Ismail may be regarded as the founder of modern Persia (Iran). Unlike the Ottomans, the Safavids had no ambitions to invade and conquer Christian lands. Apart from disputed Mesopotamia, the territories of the Persian Empire remained roughly the same until modern times. But within these borders a great national and religious revival took place. Shah Abbas I, who reigned from 1587 to 1629, was an outstanding military leader, administrator and patron of the arts. Although a zealous Shiite Muslim, he was tolerant towards Christians, allowing the Carmelites and other orders to set up missions and build churches at Isfahan and elsewhere. The Safavid dynasty declined under his less able successors, but Persia remained established as a dominant power in the region. Although encroached upon by its neighbours, it never suffered the dismemberment which was the fate of the Ottoman Empire.

After his defeat of Persia, Selim turned upon the Mamlukes. Although courageous fighters, in their weakened and semi-anarchic condition these were no match for the superior training and discipline of the Ottoman army. After a battle near Aleppo in 1516, in which the aged Mamluke sultan Qansuh al-Ghawri died of a stroke and his army was annihilated, Selim easily occupied Syria and Palestine. The following year he invaded Egypt and inflicted a final defeat on the Mamlukes outside the walls of Cairo. While he was in Egypt, Selim received a delegation from the Arab sharif, or ruler, of Mecca, who offered him the keys of the Holy City of Islam and the title of 'Protector of the Holy Places'. The standard and cloak of the Prophet were transferred to Istanbul.

The North African or Barbary states as far as Morocco soon accepted Ottoman suzerainty. Yemen in south-western Arabia became an Ottoman pashalik, or governorate, in 1537. Of the Arabic-speaking world, only Morocco in the far west, Oman in south-eastern Arabia and the central Arabian peninsula, sparsely inhabited by beduin, remained outside Ottoman control. Although it was not until the eighteenth century that the Ottoman sultans officially adopted for themselves the title of 'Caliph of Islam', their claim to leadership of Sunni Islam was henceforth disputed only by rebels with local followings in outlying provinces.

It is hardly surprising that the Arabs of today tend to see their four Ottoman centuries in the darkest terms. Their ancestors had allowed first military leadership and then political leadership in the Islamic world to pass into Turkish hands. Except in the outer extremities of the Arab world, where the Arabs retained some political independence, the Turks were indisputably the governing race. In contrast, the Persians in their own vast homeland were rivals rather than subjects of the Ottoman Turks. Just as wounding to Arab pride was the fact that the Arabic language, the glory of Arab civilization, had yielded its cultural leadership in Islam. Arabic remained the language of religion, as it was bound to be, but Turkish and Persian, after absorbing profound Arabic influence, developed more vital independent cultural worlds of their own.

Nevertheless, the Ottoman Empire was a splendid Islamic civilization. It reached its zenith under the son of Selim the Grim – Sulaiman the Magnificent, or Lawgiver, who reigned from 1520 to 1566 and was therefore an exact contemporary of the great Renaissance monarchs of Europe – the Habsburg Emperor Charles V, Francis I of France and the Tudor Henry VIII of England. Sulaiman added Hungary, Rhodes and North Africa to his empire, although he failed to take Vienna. But he was much more than a great military campaigner: he was a fine administrator and a stern but humane dispenser of justice. A considerable poet in his own right, he encouraged all the arts at his court. Like all great civilizations, the Ottoman absorbed and transformed various external cultural influences. The first sultans took from the Byzantines. Selim and Sulaiman brought in craftsmen from Tabriz in western Persia to beautify Istanbul. Under Sulaiman, with the help of Sinan – the son of a Christian from Anatolia and one of the finest architects of all time – the work that had begun with Mohammed the Conqueror was completed, and Istanbul became a city of true magnificence at the point of confluence of eastern and western civilization.

All great multiracial empires decline and dissolve. The Ottoman

Empire was far more extensive and enduring than the powerful states that had been established by other warrior nomads from central Asia – the Seljuks, Mongols and Tartars – but decline began rather less than halfway through the five centuries of the empire's life, and from then on the decadence was virtually unremitting. Attempts to reform and revive the empire actually contributed to its break-up and decline.

It is not possible to ascribe the decline to any single cause; it is certain only that the seeds of the empire's decadence had been sown when it was apparently at its zenith under Sulaiman the Magnificent. For some further hundred and fifty years it remained a great power that was still capable of instilling in successive Popes and the Christian states of western Europe a lively dread that they would be overwhelmed by the Turkish infidel. It was the second Ottoman defeat at the gates of Vienna – in 1683, at the hands of the forces of the King of Poland – which finally removed the Turkish threat. The balance of power had turned unremittingly against Istanbul. But in 1683 no one in Europe could be confident of turning back the Muslim advance. It took time for fears to recede.

While no simple diagnosis can be made of the cause of the transformation of the empire into the 'Sick Man of Europe', there are certain characteristics which suggest themselves. Often they were originally reasons for the empire's strength and success, but they became weaknesses as they were unadaptable to changing circumstances. In the first place the empire was a huge military organization in which military values and ideals were supreme. It was also highly centralized, in the sense that virtually all land within the empire belonged to the Ottoman state. It was feudal in so far as much of the best land was allocated as fiefs to the Ottoman military aristocracy; but only in rare cases could this land be inherited, and thus the empire never developed a European kind of feudal nobility to balance the power of the monarch. If this European type of feudalism is an essential stage towards the ultimate development of capitalism, this suggests a reason why the empire gradually fell behind the European states in terms of material and industrial power.

On the other hand, the lack of a landed aristocracy meant that the early empire was socially egalitarian to an exceptional degree. Not only Muslims but also Christians and Jews – ex-slaves and men of the humblest birth – could rise to the highest offices of state, provided they converted to Islam. Sulaiman the Magnificent's outstanding grand vizier Ibrahim was born a Christian Greek. Beyond doubt the empire benefited from the use of these unusual sources of talent and ability.

Converted Christians were the source of one of the strangest and most distinctive institutions of the Ottoman empire – the Janissaries (that is *yeni-cheris*, or new troops). In the fourteenth century, Murad I began the practice of recruiting Christian boys, handpicked for their good physique and ready intelligence, to form a highly disciplined and superbly trained militia which became the core of the Ottoman army. Forbidden to marry, they lived monastic lives which were devoted to the sultan. As the empire expanded, they were used to put down ruthlessly any signs of disorder or insurrection among its huge population.

The empire did not have a hereditary aristocracy, but it did have a ruling class. This consisted of the army officers, the senior civil servants and the men of religion – the muftis and leading *ulama* (Muslim scholars). They represented the sultan's authority which it was their function to preserve. Beneath them were the *rayas (rai'yah* in Arabic – the 'flock' or 'shepherded people'), who consisted of the mass of peasant farmers and some of the craftsmen of the towns. Originally the term '*raya*' applied to all subjects of a Muslim ruler, but it was later limited to those non-Muslims who, unlike the Muslims, paid the poll tax. Since they formed the great majority of the population in the empire's European provinces, they provided the bulk of its revenues. They were organized into *millets* or self-governing communities headed by their patriarch or bishop, who was responsible for their good behaviour. They lacked any political power within the structure of the empire, and they were not allowed to join the army or the civil service, but in time they gained increasing commercial and economic influence.

The Muslim Arabs who formed the great majority in the empire's Middle Eastern and North African provinces were not treated as second-class citizens in this institutionalized manner, but in Syria/Palestine and Iraq an Ottoman ruling class of governors and administrators was imposed upon them. A large military garrison and a staff of civil officials was established in the principal cities. The members of this ruling class not only remained Turkish-speaking but also, in contrast to their Mamluke predecessors, failed to put down roots where they were living. There was no Turkish colonization of the land. Officials were frequently moved to other provinces of the empire, which might not be Arabic-speaking, and they normally expected to retire to the Turkish heartland. At the same time, there was no attempt to turkify the non-Turkish Muslims who were Ottoman subjects. Only a very small minority adopted Turkish as their first language and entered the Ottoman ruling class; the vast majority carried on their lives much as before. Only a few Turkish words entered their language, mostly related to the army or cuisine. Mount Lebanon, inhabited by Maronites (a small Christian sect in union with Rome) and Druze, remained especially untouched. Here the Ottomans recognized the Lebanese emirs in their hereditary fiefs and allowed them the same autonomous privileges as they had enjoyed under the Mamlukes. Hence Lebanon was the only part of the empire in which something similar to European feudalism flourished. Charles Issawi, the noted economic historian, has suggested that this is why the Lebanese alone among the Arabs have made a marked success of capitalism.

There was some difference in the administration of Egypt as an Ottoman province. Selim the Grim had been prepared to leave the last Mamluke sultan as governor provided he accepted the status of vassal. But the sultan rebelled and was executed, and Selim appointed an Ottoman governor, or pasha. However, he left Mamluke emirs in charge of the twelve *sanjaks* or provinces of Egypt and they enjoyed a high degree of autonomy, which enabled them to treat their territories as personal fiefs, collecting taxes and commandeering supplies for their troops. There was a constant struggle for power between the pashas and the Mamluke aristocracy of emirs and beys, in which the Mamlukes frequently gained the upper hand before Istanbul again imposed its authority. During the three centuries of direct Ottoman rule in Egypt more than a hundred pashas came successively as the sultan's viceroy.

The conditions for the ordinary Egyptians were even worse than in the last years of anarchic Mamluke rule before the Turkish occupation. They could expect neither security nor justice. Ottoman administrators and Mamluke beys competed to squeeze them for taxes by use of the *kurbaj* (whip). No public works were carried out, the irrigation canals silted up and famine and disease were rampant. The population drastically declined. It is no surprise that Egyptians look on this period as a dark age. But Egypt suffered more than other Ottoman provinces. Because of its unique dependence on the Nile and the population's confinement within the narrow space of the Valley and Delta, Egypt's prosperity since the time of the Pharaohs had derived from a strong and wise central government controlling the waterway and providing security.

Syria, with its naturally autonomous mountain and desert regions, fared rather better. Mesopotamia was a remote and stagnant backwater of the empire with little to recall its former glory. A pasha with his court ruled in Baghdad, and there was little attempt to incorporate the tribes who occupied most of the land into the state. But at least the Janissaries secured the province from external dangers until the revival of the Persian threat in the eighteenth century.

The achievement of the Ottoman Turks, recent descendants of uneducated nomadic warriors from the Asian steppes, in building and administering their vast empire should not be underestimated. The trouble was that the institutions they created, while initially more effective and enduring than those employed by the empires which had preceded them in the region, could not be developed and transformed to meet changing needs and circumstances. An obvious example is that of the Janissaries. The idea of selecting young Christian slaves to be compulsorily converted to Islam and trained to form the core of the Ottoman army was original and certainly had no equivalent in any western Christian army. The Janissaries were not only a superb fighting force in the campaigns against the sultan's enemies: they also maintained the internal security of the entire empire. It was probably inevitable that they should in time become not only an autonomous power but also one that was fiercely opposed to any change in the system. As the clear Ottoman superiority in military skills over the empire's enemies declined, the Janissaries rejected all attempts to reform the army along the new lines that had been developed in the West. Whenever they felt that their privileges were being curtailed or that they were being superseded by their principal rivals, the *sipahis* or cavalrymen, they rose in rebellion, leading to acts of atrocious violence and barbarity on both sides. Eventually they were suppressed, but by then it was too late for Ottoman military power to catch up with that of the West.

Another rigid institution was the sultanate itself – a despotism which never contemplated any sharing of power. It had a fierce sense of self-preservation. When Bayezid I succeeded his father Murad in 1389, his first act as sultan was to order the strangulation of his younger brother, a potential rival. He thus instituted a tradition of imperial fratricide. There was some basis for his action in the Islamic principle that anything is preferable to sedition, and Mohammed the Conqueror a century later gave the practice the force of law. Selim the Grim had not only his two brothers strangled but his five orphaned nephews as well.

The elimination of rivals in the imperial family avoided the disastrous civil wars of the Mamlukes and can be said to have preserved the Ottoman dynasty for five hundred years. But it was at a terrible price. The sultan's palace became a cauldron of mistrust and fear which increased as he aged and the mothers of his sons intrigued, in most cases in vain, to preserve the sons' lives. Sometimes it was the least able son who succeeded, as when Sulaiman the Magnificent was succeeded by Selim the Sot. In moral terms the practice of executing royal princes for potential rather than actual sedition aroused horror in western Christendom and seemed to justify the denunciations of Turkish inhumanity. When an heir apparent had been clearly designated, he was kept under virtual house arrest in the seraglio in a small room known as the 'cage', to preserve him from possible rivals, with the result that on his succession he lacked any experience in government. He was also often in poor health or even physically deformed from his long confinement. The Safavid shahs of Persia had a similar system of immuring the heir apparent in the palace compound, and the dynasty suffered accordingly.

The fear of sedition extended outside the royal family throughout the imperial system. Grand viziers and governors were regularly disgraced or executed if they appeared to be gaining too much power. Under Selim the Grim this happened so regularly that it became astonishing that anyone was still prepared to accept the highest offices. Even the humane Sulaiman, under the influence of his ambitious wife Roxelana, had his outstanding grand vizier Ibrahim executed. With a system based on mistrust, sultans increasingly came to rely on a vast web of espionage centred on Istanbul to watch over their subjects. It was not a situation that helped to foster talent and initiative.

The well-being of the empire depended overwhelmingly on the character and ability of the sultan. When he was inadequate, the state suffered disastrously, unless the sultan was prepared to delegate the powers of government to a grand vizier of outstanding capacity. This occurred in the second half of the seventeenth century, when a series of grand viziers of the Koprulu family temporarily arrested the empire's long decline. On the other hand, after a period in which the central government had been weakened by incompetence or neglect, an incoming sultan found it necessary to restore his authority through measures of ruthless severity. These were accepted as necessary for the empire's preservation.

From the empire's foundation, its vital spirit was one of holy war for the furtherance of Islam. For at least two centuries it was militarily superior to its opponents, and the Ottoman devotion to military ideals could be justified. But, in contrast to the Abbasids in the Golden Age of Islam, Ottoman militarism was combined with a contempt for industry and commerce. The consequence was that when the empire was still in its heyday it was already being overtaken in material strength by the more innovative and industrializing economies of the Christian European states. Soon this was reflected in the military balance of power.

One factor in the empire's economic decline could not be avoided. In 1497 the Portuguese rounded the Cape of Good Hope and opened a new route to India and the Far East which outflanked the traditional link between Europe and Asia through Egypt and the Red Sea. Soon the Portuguese, followed by the French and the British, were competing for control of the parallel route through the Gulf. The influence of this factor should not be exaggerated. Its most disastrous effect was on Egypt. Syrian merchants concentrated on the land route from Alexandretta (the modern Iskenderun) through Aleppo to Baghdad and Basra, and a flourishing transit trade to and from the East survived. However, much of this trade came to be dominated by non-Muslim foreigners who were granted special legal and financial privileges for their protection when the empire was strong which they were able to exploit as it weakened.

More important than the diversion of trade was that the economy of the Muslim Middle East as a whole was transformed from the commercial and monetary economy that it had been in the Middle Ages and which could quite easily have continued to match that of Europe to one of military feudalism based on subsistence agriculture. This did not, however, immunize the empire from the economic scourge which affected the whole Mediterranean region in the sixteenth century. This was the huge influx of bullion from the Spanish Americas, which caused the depreciation of the Ottoman silver currency, leading to high inflation and increased taxation. The government was already beset with problems in financing its vast military expenditure. The lack of flourishing industrial and financial sectors in the Ottoman economy in contrast to those of western

Europe greatly contributed to the shift in the balance of power over the years.

It is far from correct that the Ottomans were always hostile to learning and the arts, as their later reputation suggested. Sulaiman the Magnificent was a man of the Renaissance. Certainly the Arabs regard their Ottoman centuries as years of cultural stagnation, but this is largely because of the downgrading of Arabic combined with the loss of political self-confidence. What is undeniable is that, as the empire weakened and declined, its leaders – sultans, pashas, generals and men of religion – turned in upon themselves to become increasingly hostile and outwardly contemptuous towards innovation, originality and external influences of all kinds. Muslim national pride demanded that attempts should be made to match the European powers by adopting some of their ideas and techniques, but these could succeed only if the rigid and reactionary Ottoman system was reformed from within. Efforts to achieve these reforms, although sincere and far-reaching, ultimately came to nothing.

The second Ottoman failure to take Vienna, in 1683, marked a decisive stage in the long decline of Ottoman power in Europe and the enforced shift in the empire's centre of gravity in the east. At the end of the seventeenth century, a new rival and enemy emerged in the form of aggressive and expansionist imperial Russia. Tsar Peter the Great was bent on making Russia a great European and Asian power, and the Ottoman Empire was his principal obstacle. Two centuries of intermittent Russo-Turkish wars, separated by periods of hostile peace, had begun.

Although the Ottoman Empire was more often than not on the defensive, its withdrawal from Europe was slow and irregular. The Ottoman armies were still brave and formidable, and they benefited from rivalries between the Christian powers of Europe. In the first half of the eighteenth century some lost ground – the Grecian Morea, Belgrade – was recovered. At the end of the century, Empress Catherine the Great failed in her declared aim of dismembering the Ottoman Empire and making Constantinople the capital of a New Byzantium. Nevertheless, under the Treaty of Küchük Kainarji in

1774, Sultan Mustafa III lost not only his control over some of his Christian subjects but also his suzerainty over the Muslim Tartars of the Crimea. As he claimed to be the Caliph of Islam, this was a greater blow than his conceding to Catherine a virtual protectorate over his Orthodox Christian subjects.

2. Islam on the Defensive, 1800–

At the end of the eighteenth century, the balance of power between the European Christian states and the Islamic world represented by the Ottoman Empire had swung decisively against Istanbul. The progressive retreat from Europe meant that the focus of the empire moved eastwards. In the first three centuries of its existence, the weight of Ottoman interest was directed towards the conquest and control of Christian lands – the spread of the world of Islam towards the West. It was from this that the empire's power and glory derived. Possession of the vast territories inhabited mainly by Muslim Arabs – including the Islamic holy places in Arabia and the great Muslim cities with a prestigious past such as Cairo, Damascus and Baghdad – was important but might be said to have been taken for granted. The Arabic-speaking provinces, economically stagnant or declining, enjoyed a large measure of autonomy under local dynasties such as the Mamlukes in Egypt and Mesopotamia or the Druze emirs in Mount Lebanon.

In the nineteenth century the Ottoman Empire had become the Sick Man of Europe in Western eyes. In reaction, successive Ottoman sultans placed greater emphasis on their leadership of Islam: the Sick Man of Europe could still be the Strong Man of Asia. The title of 'Caliph of Islam' – disused for five centuries – was revived and, through a false analogy between the caliphate and the papacy, the sultan's representatives began to claim spiritual authority over all Muslims, even when they were under non-Muslim rule.

The expansionist and colonizing empire of the first centuries was becoming an Islamic fortress under siege. The world of Islam did not face a frontal assault of the kind it had confronted seven hundred years earlier, in the First Crusade: it was being penetrated in a more subtle and insidious manner. The foreign non-Muslim trading communities had originally been granted their privileges and immunities, which came to be known as the Capitulations, in order to benefit the empire's economy. The first were given to the Genoese in the Galata suburb of Constantinople immediately after the capture of the city in 1453. The most famous were probably those granted to Francis I of France by Sulaiman the Magnificent in 1535 as a reward for French co-operation with the sultan against the Christian Habsburgs. The Capitulations were not only commercial: they granted full religious liberty to the French in the Ottoman Empire and, more significantly, the right to guard the Christian holy places. What amounted to a French protectorate was established over all the Latin Catholics in the Levant. In the mid eighteenth century these privileges were confirmed and extended as a reward for French diplomatic support in negotiations with Austria. The extraterritorial privileges created by the Capitulations were remarkable. Special consular courts had complete jurisdiction over the nationals of the countries concerned. Non-Muslim foreign nationals living in Turkey were not subject to Ottoman law, however grave the crime they might have committed.

France was ahead of its European rivals, but not by far. Russia claimed similar protective rights over Orthodox Christians in the empire. England's special ties were only with the smaller religious minorities such as Jews and the Druze, but these were supported by England's growing maritime and commercial dominance in the world.

By the end of the eighteenth century, British sea-power and trading ambitions formed another threat to Ottoman sovereignty in the world of Islam, on the eastern fringes of the empire. The English were not the first Europeans to arrive in force in the Persian/Arabian Gulf: the Portuguese came some thirty years before the Ottomans and, to further their aim of building a great empire in India and the East, attempted to dominate the Red Sea and the Gulf. They attacked and pillaged the eastern Arabian coast from Muscat to Bahrain, leaving forts and garrisons to dominate the indigenous Arab trading and pearling communities. Throughout the sixteenth

THE OTTOMAN EMPIRE IN 1792

Approximate limits of the Empire

North African States under Ottoman suzerainty

Areas under autonomous and tribal rulers

Lands lost, 1774 - 1792

| 0 | | | 1200 km |
| 0 | | | 800 Miles |

MOROCCO

ALGIERS

TUNIS

TRIPOLI

Algiers

Tunis

Tripoli

MEDITERRA

AUSTRIAN

BOSNIA

Belgrade

MONTENEGRO

ALBANIA

To Venice

Source: Bernard Lewis, *The Emergence of Modern Turkey*, Oxford University Press, 1961

century the Portuguese controlled the waters of the Gulf and the Straits of Hormuz. Occasionally the Turks, with the help of local tribes, were able to challenge their supremacy and drive the Portuguese out of Bahrain and Muscat, but it was Portuguese naval supremacy which counted.

The Portuguese presence was also a deep affront to the Persians on the northern side of the Gulf. Shah Ismail I, founder of the Safavid dynasty which ruled from 1501 to 1736, protested vigorously but, owing to his life-and-death struggle with the Ottoman Turks, he could do little more. In fact, throughout the sixteenth century it was the presence of Persia as a hostile neighbour on the Ottoman Empire's eastern border which reduced the power of the Turks to expand into Europe. In 1599 the English even attempted – unsuccessfully – to persuade the Persians to ally themselves with the Christian powers against the Turks.

The real challenge to the Portuguese came from two rival powers: England and Holland. By the end of the sixteenth century, English and Dutch adventurers (or pirates) were competing with the Portuguese for the spice trade. Shah Abbas I of Persia (1571–1629), a great military leader and administrator, encouraged the English and Dutch East India companies to establish special branches in Persia, giving the fledgeling companies special privileges. In 1602 he was able to oust the Portuguese from their foothold on the Persian mainland north of the island of Hormuz, and twenty years later, with the aid of the fleet of the English East India Company, he ousted the Portuguese from Hormuz itself. In gratitude he gave the Company special privileges in the port which bears his name, Bandar Abbas. Although a powerful ruler and a passionate defender of the Shiite branch of Islam, Shah Abbas, like the Ottoman sultan Mohammed the Conqueror, set a precedent for the granting of concessions to non-Muslims which was to provide the opportunity for foreigners to gain control over a large share of the economic life of Islam.

However, this Western penetration of the material world had little effect on the minds and beliefs of Muslims in the empire.

Secure in the knowledge of the superiority of Islam, they showed no interest in the ways of non-Muslim people. The contrast with the Golden Age of the first Islamic Empire, which had not hesitated to benefit from the wisdom and knowledge of other civilizations, was striking. Only a few individuals pondered on the reasons for the advances in Christian power. As might be expected, the most serious efforts to adopt Western innovations were in the military and naval fields, and these brought with them some revival of interest in mathematics, navigational sciences and cartography. In the early eighteenth century the mild and pleasure-loving sultan Ahmed III introduced some French manners and architecture into the capital, but the effect was entirely superficial. Almost incredibly, there was a total ban on printing in Turkish or Arabic. Printing was known because Jews, Armenians and Greeks began to introduce it from Europe from the late fifteenth century and to set up their own presses, but the religious authorities maintained the ban for Muslims. In 1727 reluctant permission was given for the first Turkish press to print books on subjects other than religion. By the time it was closed in 1742 it had printed seventeen books on language, history and geography. It was not allowed to reopen until 1784.

The practice of employing non-Turkish converts as high officials had changed since the early days of the empire, and officials were now mainly Turkish. But they were usually illiterate and both unable and unwilling to learn foreign languages, having little interest in the rest of the world. The empire thus depended on Christians and Jews as interpreters. The Greek chief dragoman, or interpreter, was an individual of power and responsibility.

Thus it was that the great movements of ideas in western Europe from the Renaissance through the Reformation and Counter-Reformation left the Ottoman world almost untouched. *A fortiori* the same applied to Safavid Persia.

In the Arab-speaking provinces of the Middle East and North Africa, where Muslims were the great majority, Turkish leadership of the Muslim *umma* or nation was accepted. Where local dynasties achieved considerable autonomy, as in Egypt, Tunisia and Mesopotamia in the eighteenth century, they nevertheless stopped short of challenging Ottoman sovereignty or attempting to establish an independent nation on a territorial basis – a term which had no meaning at that time. Similarly the Christian minorities, organized in their self-governing *millets*, accepted the overall structure of the empire. Their loyalties were religious rather than political, but they were resigned to their subordinate status.

The most notable exception to Muslim acceptance of Turkish leadership of Islam came from Arabia. In the middle of the eighteenth century in Nejd in the centre of the peninsula, a remarkable religious reformer named Muhammad Ibn Abd al-Wahhab appeared spreading the essential doctrine of *Tawhid* or the uniqueness of God, denouncing the prevalent backsliding and idolatry, and calling for a return to the purity of early Islam. Abd al-Wahhab formed a formidable alliance with an outstanding local tribal dynasty, the House of Saud (and thus planted the seed which nearly two centuries later grew into the kingdom of Saudi Arabia). In the second half of the eighteenth century the Wahhabi warriors spread northwards to the Gulf and into Mesopotamia, where they sacked the Shiite holy places of Kerbala and Nejaf. They then turned westwards and in 1806 took the Hejaz with the Islamic holy places of Mecca and Medina. They destroyed many of the saints' tombs and stripped the Kaaba – Islam's holiest shrine, in the Mecca Great Mosque – of its ornaments, which outraged their fierce puritanism. The emir Muhammad al-Saud had the public prayers read in his name instead of that of the Ottoman caliph/sultan – he did not regard the Ottoman Turks as worthy guardians of the holy places.

However, all this still lay in the future; as the eighteenth century drew to its close, the caliph's authority over Sunni Islam was still largely intact. In 1789 two events occurred which helped to crack the Ottoman insulation – the outbreak of the French Revolution and the accession as sultan of the reforming Selim III. The French Revolution introduced the novel concepts of political liberty and equality. It also created the basis of nationalism as it has been known in the last two centuries – derived from dedication and loyalty to a nation-state. The most important element was that the movement was secular; it was not only non-Christian but, at least initially, anti-Christian. As such it did not provoke the immediate Muslim hostility which would have been aroused by anything in the nature of a crusade.

More than any of his predecessors Selim III was interested in fresh external ideas and the possibilities of restoring the strength of the empire through reform. He had been conducting a secret correspondence with King Louis XVI before the Revolution, and he greatly admired French culture. He was not deterred by the regicide of the revolutionaries. Indeed the triumphant success of French arms against the Revolution's adversaries encouraged him to import French instructors into his new military and naval schools, where French was made a compulsory subject. A whole new class of young Turkish officers began to emerge – familiar with Western ways and prepared to learn from Western technical superiority. As part of the opening to the West, Sultan Selim for the first time allowed the establishment of embassies in five leading European capitals on a reciprocal basis.

It was even more significant that Selim III tried to apply his reforms to the internal administration of the empire. When he heard of his army's defeat by Catherine the Great of Russia, he called a council which enumerated the causes of defeat and disaster and proposed reform as the only remedy. He also insisted that the people should elect their own mayors and councillors without the interference of his governors, and he attempted to end illegal extortion and tax-farming (the practice of allowing local governors or tax-collectors to take a cut of the tax revenues).

Sultan Selim's reforms, however, did not extend to the Arab provinces of the empire, where power was largely in the hands of local rulers. Damascus for most of the eighteenth century was ruled by governors of the Azm family, who remained loyal to the sultan but independently managed the province's affairs. Sidon district, on the Syrian coast, was governed on similar lines by a ruthless Bosnian, Ahmad al-Jazzar, and his band of Mamlukes. They controlled the

Janissaries and kept the predatory beduin at bay. But while the cities prospered, the countryside was insecure and derelict. Squeezed for taxes, the peasant farmers flocked into the cities. Agriculture flourished only in the mountainous areas controlled by local Maronite and Druze emirs.

The situation in Mesopotamia was similar. Here there was constant strife between a series of contenders for power, but the contrast was even greater than in Syria between the rich courts of the pashas of Baghdad and Basra and the backwardness and poverty of the ruined countryside. The great food-producing region of medieval times was on the brink of starvation.

In the vital province of Egypt the situation was rather different. The productivity of the Nile Valley and Delta – perhaps the richest agricultural land on earth – could not be destroyed. With a minimum of secure and effective government, Egypt could export coffee, wheat and rice to the empire. The artisans of the towns produced fine textiles. For a few years (1768–72) an outstanding Mamluke, Ali Bey, provided the strong central government the country needed, but on his death the long-standing struggle between Ottoman officials and Mamluke beys was resumed. They competed to wrest more money from the unfortunate *fellahin* or peasants. The population had sunk to less than two million, compared with an estimated seven or eight million in Roman times, but the land of Egypt was still a glittering prize.

Apart from its natural fertility, Egypt enjoyed a remarkable geo--strategic position at the hinge of the Asian and African continents, guarding the principal route to India and the East. In 1798 the 29-year-old Napoleon Bonaparte, the aspiring dictator of France who had defeated Austria in a series of brilliant campaigns, saw the occupation of Egypt as a means of striking at the source of wealth of France's remaining arch-enemy, Britain, and of controlling the route to India. And his ambitions went further. Talleyrand represented his views to the Directory who then ruled France: 'Our war with this Power [England] represents the most favourable opportunity for the invasion of Egypt. Threatened by an imminent landing on her shores she will not desert her coasts to prevent our enterprise. This further offers us a possible chance of driving the English out of India by sending thither 15,000 troops from Cairo via Suez.' Such an achievement would have destroyed Britain's nascent world empire.

After landing near Alexandria in July 1798, Bonaparte marched up the Nile and defeated the Mamluke army at the battle of the Pyramids. The two Ottoman-appointed Mamluke beys fled to Upper Egypt, leaving Bonaparte to set up his own military government of occupation. This momentous event marked the first non-Muslim invasion of the heartlands of Islam since the time of the crusades. Bonaparte went out of his way to show his respect for Islam. He even told the shaikhs of the great Islamic university mosque of al-Azhar that he was a disciple of Muhammad and that he and his army were under the Prophet's special protection. The shaikhs were not impressed and wondered why he and his soldiers did not become Muslims. Bonaparte also tried to convince the Egyptians that his quarrel was not with the Ottoman sultan but with the Mamlukes, from whose tyranny he had come to deliver them. He treated the Egyptian shaikhs and notables as political leaders, appointing them to *diwans* or councils to administer the large cities, with a French commissary as chairman and adviser. It was an enlightened form of indirect colonial rule. But he notably failed to win the hearts and minds of the Egyptians. Al-Jabarti, the shaikh of Al-Azhar and a historian who left an account of the French occupation, described it as the beginning of the reversal of the natural order. Like his fellow-Muslims, he was alarmed by the promotion of Christian Copts and Greeks as officials and tax-collectors, and at the training of Christians for the army. The French were still regarded as intruders, and their claim to be upholding the authority of the sultan was not believed.

Despite his tendency towards Caesarism, Bonaparte was a product of the eighteenth-century Enlightenment, and he brought with him to Egypt a party of 165 scientists, artists and men of letters. This mission of savants set up Arabic and French printing-presses in Cairo and founded the Institut d'Égypte in imitation of the Institut National in Paris. Its members studied the antiquities and languages of ancient Egypt and laid the foundations of Egyptology. They also examined the economy and society of contemporary Egypt and made a survey for a future Suez Canal. The magnificent twenty-volume *Description de l'Égypte* which was the result of their work aroused Europe's interest in both Pharaonic Egypt and the contemporary world of Islam, which was mysterious and unknown. Orientalism in the West received a wholly new impulse.

Learned Egyptians, such as Shaikh al-Jabarti, visited the Institut and the printing-press and watched chemical and scientific experiments. Al-Jabarti saw a balloon launched at Cairo's Ezbekiyah Square. But while the Egyptians were politely curious about these displays of Western technology, their fundamental beliefs were unshaken.

With regard to its strategic objectives, Bonaparte's expedition to Egypt was a failure. Sultan Selim formed an alliance against him with France's enemies England and Russia. The destruction of Bonaparte's fleet in Abukir Bay by Nelson on 1 August 1798 placed his only line of communication with France at their mercy. When he advanced into Syria to forestall a Turkish invasion, he was turned back at Acre and forced into a disastrous retreat. In August 1799 he abandoned Egypt and with a handful of followers slipped back to Paris, where a crucial struggle for power was taking place. His successors in Egypt held on for another two years, facing sporadic insurrections in Cairo and attacks by Anglo-Turkish troops to enforce their withdrawal. Although they successfully repulsed these more than once, their weakening situation finally forced them to capitulate and evacuate Egypt.

Bonaparte's invasion was a brief episode in the long history of Egypt, but it had lasting significance. It not only aroused in the West a wave of interest in the Arab/Islamic regions of the Ottoman Empire; it also marked the opening of a prolonged struggle between the powers of Europe for influence and control over these territories. The struggle lasted a century and a half. It primarily involved

England and France, but Russia was also concerned with the Middle East region on its southern borders, and in the latter part of the nineteenth century the newly united states of Germany and Italy also began to intervene.

Britain responded to Bonaparte's threat to its vital interests by helping the Ottoman sultan to expel the French from Egypt. Anglo-French rivalry also extended to the Gulf and the Indian Ocean. After the outbreak of war between France and England in 1793, France sent various missions to Istanbul and Tehran to try to secure a friendly alliance between Turkey and Persia against Russia, and to revive French influence in Persia. French agents also appeared in the Gulf, studying the movements of British shipping between the Arabian waters and India. French intervention received a wholly new impulse with Bonaparte's invasion of Egypt. Attacks on British merchant shipping were stepped up by French war vessels and privateers based in Mauritius. A 'Napoleonic era' in the region lasted until the French were expelled from Mauritius in 1810.

The first British reaction to Bonaparte's arrival in Egypt was the East India Company's signature of a treaty with the sultan of Muscat. In the 1820s, similar treaties were signed with other local rulers along the Gulf coast. These treaties developed into annually negotiated truces through which Britain endeavoured to establish a Pax Britannica over the waters of the Gulf. At this stage British ambitions in the region were maritime/commercial rather than imperial. There was still no question of challenging the authority either of the Ottoman and Persian empires or of the independent Arab rulers who were outside Ottoman control. Provided these rulers did not make concessions to Britain's rivals, Britain's concern was only that they should help to suppress piracy.

3. Muhammad Ali's Egypt: Ottoman Rival

The Napoleonic episode had minimal direct effect on Egypt; but, through the defeat of the Mamluke beys and the weakening of their hold on the country, it had important indirect influence. When the French departed, the beys came out of hiding and attempted to reimpose their authority. At the same time, Sultan Selim III tried to oust them and restore direct control from Istanbul. But he failed, as the British who still occupied Alexandria took the side of the beys. When the British departed in 1803, they left a situation in which neither the Turkish governor nor the beys were strong enough to prevail, and two years of chaos and civil war ensued. The situation worsened when the Albanian Ottoman troops rebelled against the governor, and power shuttled between the sultan's representatives, the uncontrollable soldiery and the beys (who were split into two factions).

In the midst of this anarchy Muhammad Ali, the commander of one of the Albanian contingents which had landed with the Anglo-Ottoman expeditionary force in 1801, came to prominence as an ally of some of the Mamluke leaders against the nominal Ottoman governors. On 13 May 1805 the *ulama* (Muslim scholars), leading merchants and other notables who were regarded by the people of Cairo as their spokesmen and representatives, asked Muhammad Ali to be their ruler.

Understandably, Sultan Selim was suspicious of Muhammad Ali's intentions. There is little doubt that he helped to intensify the anarchy which led the Egyptians to appeal to him as their saviour. In an attempt to remove him from Egypt, the sultan had appointed him *wali* (governor-general) of Jeddah in Arabia. The Cairo notables, with the backing of the people, united to declare that they wanted Muhammad Ali to replace Khurshid Pasha, the existing Ottoman governor. After a few more months of chaos, Sultan Selim bowed to reality and confirmed Muhammad Ali as *wali* of Egypt.

In this way one of the remarkable figures of the nineteenth century came to control Egypt. His dynasty was to rule, either in reality or nominally, for a century and a half, until his great-great-grandson Farouk was ousted from the throne in 1952.

Born on the Aegean coast of Macedonia, Muhammad Ali was the rare combination of a soldier and a political leader of genius. Although almost illiterate, he was no narrow-minded bigot. Having worked as a tobacco merchant in his youth, he was accustomed to dealing with non-Muslims and Europeans. His sharp intelligence was quick in absorbing new facts and analysing their importance. Ruthless, fiercely ambitious and capable of harsh cruelty, he could also charm, and foreign visitors, however exalted, would quail at his piercing gaze before remaining to admire.

Muhammad Ali did not regard himself as an Egyptian or an Arab and he never spoke Arabic. But in 1805 he had already decided to make Egypt the basis of his power, and to do this he had to turn the Ottoman province into the nation-state which in a sense it had been in the time of the Pharaohs. Having done this, he came close to overthrowing the Ottoman Empire itself.

His appointment as *wali* did not give him control of Egypt; the Mamluke beys still dominated the countryside outside Cairo, and Britain continued to intervene on their behalf. With a mixture of cunning and ruthlessness he set about the destruction of the Mamlukes; but first he had to deal with the British threat. In this he was helped by the fact that, while Britain and Russia were competing to force Selim into an alliance against France, the sultan had reconciled himself with Bonaparte. Selim still admired the heirs of the French Revolution, and French officers continued to train his artillery. No doubt he was also impressed by Bonaparte's new victories over Austria. He recognized him as emperor of the French. Outraged, Britain and Russia stepped up their bullying pressure. In 1807 a British fleet under Admiral Duckworth sailed into the Sea of Marmara to demand the surrender of the Ottoman fleet, failing which, he said, he would burn the fleet and bombard Istanbul. With the help of Sebastiani, a French soldier/ambassador, the sultan organized his capital's defences and drove the British fleet away. Duckworth then sailed to Alexandria and landed an expeditionary force to forestall an expected new French offensive in the Mediterranean.

However, the British were rebuffed. Al-Jabarti records that Muhammad Ali's officials told them that they had no interest in letting them land to protect Egypt from the French, for this was the sultan's territory. The Mamlukes refused the British offer of support because they would not join Christians to fight Muslims. Popular resistance was aroused and inflicted a sharp defeat on the British at Rosetta. Muhammad Ali astutely avoided a full confrontation with the British at Alexandria and agreed on lenient terms for the withdrawal of their naval and military forces. He retained a permanent suspicion of British intentions towards Egypt, and ultimately Britain would be his nemesis — but that was many years in the future.

Muhammad Ali still had to face the Mamluke challenge to his rule, and his campaign against the beys lasted several years. It was no simple matter as, despite their unpopularity, they were entrenched in Egyptian society and his own Ottoman troops were unruly and demanding. He persuaded some Mamluke beys to settle on the outskirts of Cairo, where he could supervise them. Some remained in Upper Egypt, which they tried to make their stronghold. Muhammad Ali then defeated them in a series of small engagements. There remained a rump of beys in Cairo of whose loyalty he was justifiably uncertain. On 11 March 1811 he invited them to a reception at the Citadel, where he had them massacred. Tradition has it that only one escaped — by leaping with his horse from the Citadel.

The way was now open for Muhammad Ali to realize his dream of turning Egypt into a powerful centralized state which, while nominally an Ottoman province, would in reality be independent. Several factors were favourable to his aims. Although the Egyptian people had become accustomed to instability after more than two centuries during which the Mamlukes had struggled for power both among themselves and with a series of Ottoman governors, they longed for the security on which the country's prosperity depended. Although the *ulama* and other notables had played an important role in bringing Muhammad Ali to power, few of them had any relish for official responsibility. Moreover, Egypt – 'the gift of the Nile', as Herodotus observed – lends itself to centralized rule: anyone who could control the river and its delta would dominate the country. All the aspiring despot needed was to dispose of his rivals.

Muhammad Ali made liberal use of the sword and the gallows to stamp out the lawlessness which had plagued the country for many decades. The natural commercial and agricultural wealth of the country was then at once displayed. He set up a highly centralized administrative bureaucracy with the aim of raising revenues and combating the corruption and tax-fraud which had become endemic. At the same time he tried both to modernize and to expand the economy. The growing of high-quality long-staple cotton and sugar was introduced during his reign. He was prepared to seek advice and technical expertise from any quarter, including Christian merchants in Egypt and Europeans. As an admirer of France he invited French engineers to Egypt and with their help built dams and canals and introduced in the Delta a system of perennial irrigation to replace the ancient basin irrigation using the Nile flood. One million new acres of land were brought under cultivation. Hitherto, Egyptian industry had been confined to the manufacture of textiles; he now established a range of factories, protected with heavy tariffs against imports. The factories were crude and primitive, but they were the first of their kind in Egypt.

Muhammad Ali learned to read only at the age of forty-seven, but he understood the importance of education. He sent several hundred young Egyptians to Paris (and a few to London) to study industry, engineering, medicine and agriculture. In Egypt, where teaching until then had been confined to the Koranic schools, his French advisers helped to establish a system of state education which at least on paper was highly impressive. French doctors helped to found hospitals and a rudimentary system of public health.

His ambitions went far beyond turning Egypt into the most
advanced province of the Ottoman Empire in European terms. For
Egypt to act beyond its borders required the creation of an independent army and navy, and the major part of his energies were
devoted to this end. His concentrated drive to increase revenues
served this purpose. One of his first actions had been to order a
much needed cadastral survey of all land in Egypt, and within a few
years he had settled about two million acres or one-third of the
cultivated area on a small class of big landowners drawn from
members of his family (he had thirty children), senior army officers,
village shaikhs and beduin chiefs. But the greater part of the
increased revenues accrued to the central government, so it has been
said that he converted most of Egypt into a huge farm under the
direct administration of the government.

The new industries that he created were also directed mainly to
providing the land and naval forces with weapons and equipment,
although they also turned out non-military goods such as machine
tools, pumps, clothing, paper and glass.

The Egyptian *fellahin* or peasants had never been thought of as
promising military material, but properly trained and led they
proved that they could fight with discipline and courage. They were
at their best in defensive positions; they lacked the panache in attack
of the Sudanese. On the other hand, unlike the Sudanese, their
health stood up remarkably well to campaigns in colder climates.
Virtually all the officers and non-commissioned officers were non-
Egyptian. Some of the Mamluke officers came over to Muhammad
Ali's side but, when the Ottoman sultan banned all further export
of Mamluke recruits to Egypt, other officers were recruited from
among local Turks and Albanians. After 1820 Muhammad Ali reorganized the armed forces entirely with a *nizam al-jadid* or 'New
Order'. His eldest son, Ibrahim (1789–1848), proved to be an
outstanding general and leader of men. At its height in the 1830s,
the Egyptian army amounted to a quarter of a million men and was
the most formidable force in the Middle East.

In consolidating his personal power and the independence of

Egypt, Muhammad Ali was helped by a weakening in authority at the centre of the empire. In 1807 the Janissaries, in rebellion against the reforms and European innovations introduced by the New Order of Selim III, deposed the sultan and replaced him with his cousin Mustafa, who promptly abolished all the reforms. Fourteen months later Mustafa was assassinated, and his brother – the last surviving male of the House of Osman – succeeded as Mahmud II. He was a reformer like Selim, and ultimately he went much further than Selim in his long reign of thirty-one years, but in the first decade he had to proceed cautiously in order to consolidate his own power. It was not until 1826 that he was able to confront the problem of the Janissaries and destroy them in a massacre.

During this period Muhammad Ali was able not only to resist interference from Istanbul but also to make the new sultan dependent on him for holding the empire together. In 1807 he was asked to send an expeditionary force to the Hejaz to recover the holy places of Islam from the Saudi/Wahhabi invaders. He succeeded in procrastinating for four years while he was consolidating his hold on Egypt, but in 1811 he dispatched his second son, Tussun, with an army. Tussun was an indifferent general; he recovered Mecca and Medina but suffered heavy casualties and more than one defeat at the hands of the Wahhabi warriors. The indisciplined behaviour of the Albanian officers no doubt helped Muhammad Ali to decide on the subsequent remodelling of his armed forces. He went personally to the Hejaz to share the command with Tussun, and on his return to Cairo to deal with pressing domestic problems he replaced Tussun with the much more able Ibrahim as commander-in-chief.

Making full use of his cavalry and artillery, Ibrahim carried the campaign against the Saudis into their Nejd homeland. In May 1818 the Saudi capital Daraiyya (twelve miles from Riyadh) fell after a six-month siege in which the Turco-Egyptian army suffered heavy losses. Abdullah Ibn Saud, the Saudi ruler, was sent to Egypt where he was treated with honour and then to Istanbul where he was summarily executed. The first Saudi state had come to an end. However, the Egyptian garrisons remained only a few years in Nejd.

In 1824 the Saudis established their second state with their new capital in Riyadh and successfully resisted further attempts to conquer them. However, Muhammad Ali and Ibrahim had their prize in the Hejaz. This enabled them not only to reopen the sea-routes from Egypt to the Indian Ocean but also to monopolize the entire Red Sea trade. The *wali* even exacted an annual tribute from the imam of Yemen. He brushed aside a British proposal for Anglo-Egyptian co-operation in pacifying southern Arabia to protect the sea-routes to India against attacks by local tribesmen; instead he sent his own ships to occupy all the western Arabian seaports as far as Aden. Britain was obliged to concentrate on the Gulf region, where in 1820 it succeeded in concluding a General Treaty of Maritime Peace in perpetuity with the small shaikhdoms of the Trucial Coast (the United Arab Emirates of today). The British did not occupy Aden and found a colony there until 1839.

Sultan Mahmud was duly grateful to Ibrahim for the recovery of the Islamic Holy Land and promoted him to the rank of pasha with three tails as well as governor. This in theory made him super-ior in rank to his father, and it is probable that the sultan – by now alarmed at Muhammad Ali's ambitions – hoped to estrange him from his son. But Ibrahim remained loyal and continued to defer to his father throughout his life.

Sultan Mahmud sharply rebuffed Muhammad Ali's suggestion that he should be given the permanent governorship of Syria, but the *wali* of Egypt was not yet ready for a direct challenge to Istanbul.

The vast lands lying to the south of Egypt, known to medieval Arab writers as Bilad as-Sudan or the 'country of the blacks', provided a different opportunity. Islam and the Arabic language had advanced more slowly than in the Middle East and North Africa, but by AD 1500 the great majority of the inhabitants of the north and centre of today's republic of Sudan were Muslim and Arabic-speaking. For the past three centuries these lands had been dominated by the kingdom of the Fur – a people of uncertain origins – but there had been frequent incursions by Mamlukes from Egypt in search of slaves and gold. A group of them in flight from Muhammad Ali's repression had set up their own state in Dongola, on the west bank of the Nile, and were interfering with the river trade.

Muhammad Ali therefore had both political and commercial motives in attempting to conquer the Sudan. An additional motive was the provision of suitable employment for his unruly Albanian troops. In 1821 he sent an army commanded by his third son, Ismail, followed in the next year by two more under Ibrahim, victor of the Hejaz, and his son-in-law Muhammad. Between them they conquered an area half the size of Europe, nominally on behalf of the Ottoman sultan but in greater reality to add to his Egyptian viceroy's domains. In some ways the conquest was a disappointment. Muhammad Ali's dream of creating his own army of black slaves failed because they were too few in number and their health deteriorated when they were brought to Egypt. The gold mines were poorer than anticipated, and there was no breakthrough to the fabled wealth of tropical Africa. When Ismail was ambushed and killed by a resentful local chieftain, Muhammad Ali ordered a massacre which left its memory in Sudanese minds.

However, Muhammad Ali's conquest laid the foundations of the modern Sudan. The addition by his successors of the three Negro and tropical provinces in the south created the giant of Africa – part Arab and Muslim and part Christian and pagan and black. Even when, after sixty years, Turco-Egyptian rule came to an end, Egypt and Sudan remained inextricably linked.

The acquisition of Sudan had not been completed before the opportunity arose for expansion northwards, into the eastern Mediterranean. Sultan Mahmud invited Muhammad Ali to help put down the uprising in 1821 of his Greek subjects, who were demanding independence. The weakened and demoralized Ottoman troops were proving incapable of dealing with the rebels. Muhammad Ali's troops landed first in Crete and then in Cyprus to quell the uprising. But the heart of the rebellion was in the Morea on the mainland. The sultan hesitated to order him there because he rightly feared that Muhammad Ali's well-organized and disciplined forces might threaten his own authority. However, he finally had no alternative.

In 1825 Ibrahim moved with his fleet to the Morea, landed troops and two years later captured Athens.

When the Greek rebellion broke out, the powers of Europe paid little more than lip-service to the principle of Greek Christians breaking away from the Ottoman Empire to form an independent nation. They were deeply suspicious of each other's intentions. Russia did not favour the birth of a new Christian state in the Levant unless it would be under tsarist control. The other powers, led by Britain, were equally determined to prevent such Russian domination; however, they would probably not have been spurred into action if the Greek nationalists, who engaged in piracy when they were not fighting the Turks, had not begun to interfere with the Levant trade. An equally alarming development was the appearance of Muhammad Ali's forces to defeat the Greeks. With his control of the Morea, he would be able to dominate the region – raising the unwelcome possibility of the establishment of a new Muslim power in the eastern Mediterranean.

France had sympathetic ties with Muhammad Ali but was eventually induced to join Britain and Russia in the Treaty of London of 6 July 1827. Through this, the three powers aimed to mediate between the Ottoman government and the Greek patriots in order to bring about an armistice which would lead to the establishment of Greek autonomy under the suzerainty of the sultan. An additional purpose was to make Ibrahim's presence unnecessary and bring about his withdrawal.

When the sultan prevaricated, the Russian and French fleets joined the British fleet at Navarino and on 20 October blew the combined Turkish and Egyptian fleets out of the water.

The sultan broke off relations with the three powers and summoned his Muslim subjects for a *jihad* or holy war. But there was little he could do. In the previous year he had destroyed the Janissaries, and the reconstruction of the Ottoman army had hardly begun. His best protection was that Britain and France wanted neither the dismemberment of his empire nor the aggrandizement of Russia. Five years later, on 7 May 1832, in accordance with a new

Treaty of London, Greece became an independent kingdom under
the Bavarian prince Otho. All the powers of Europe could claim a
share in this settlement, and it had not led, as the sultan had feared,
to the disintegration of the empire.

Muhammad Ali's forces had suffered severe losses, and the financial strain on Egypt was heavy. But the disaster of Navarino had not
dampened the ambitions of the *wali* or his son. Muhammad Ali
believed he had been promised the pashalik of Syria as a reward for
his help against the Greeks, but Sultan Mahmud said that he would
have to be content with the pashalik of Crete. Muhammad Ali therefore decided to seize Syria for himself. While rebuilding his fleet,
he dispatched Ibrahim at the head of an army which routed the
Ottoman forces near Homs and again near Aleppo. Ibrahim then
passed through the Taurus range into Anatolia and defeated the
sultan's army at Konya. When he reached Bursa, he was poised to
take Istanbul and overthrow the Ottoman Empire.

A desperate Sultan Mahmud appealed to Britain to send the Royal
Navy to the Dardanelles and Alexandria. Palmerston, the British
prime minister, was in favour, but the majority in his cabinet refused.
The sultan was therefore obliged to turn to Russia. (Palmerston
later wrote that 'No British cabinet at any period of the history of
England ever made so great a mistake in foreign affairs.') The
Russians sent ships and landed troops; Ibrahim prudently agreed to
negotiate. By now alerted to the danger of Russian ascendancy in
the eastern Mediterranean, Britain and France intervened to insist
on a Russian withdrawal in return for the sultan's agreement to make
concessions to Muhammad Ali – the sultan granted him the pashalik of the whole of Syria. The Russians did withdraw, but the sultan
was obliged to accept an agreement known as the Treaty of Hunkiar
Iskelessi, which bound him to an alliance with Russia. This included
a secret clause which allowed Russian warships to pass freely through
the Dardanelles if Russia should be at war but made a similar concession to other powers conditional on Russian consent. Palmerston's
regrets are easy to understand.

Muhammad Ali's ambition to build a predominantly Arabic-

speaking empire on the ruins of Ottoman power no longer seemed
fanciful. He controlled the Nile Valley, the Red Sea and the eastern
Mediterranean. He even thought of making a bid for the caliphate.

However, his dream was a chimera. The pan-Arab idea did not
exist in the consciousness of the people, and the Albanian Muhammad Ali could not be its inspiration. Ibrahim could conceivably have
provided such an inspiration. Unlike his father, he spoke Arabic,
regarded himself as Egyptian and was prouder of his Egyptian
private soldiers than of their Ottoman officers. But he never challenged his father's authority and, although he was more cultivated
and civilized, he was not equal to Muhammad Ali's formidable
political abilities.

Ibrahim was placed in charge of Egypt's new Syrian possessions.
But, although he had a powerful army under his command, his task
of imposing a strongly centralized and modernizing administration
was not easy. The various sects of Syria – Sunni and Shia Muslims,
Druze and Maronites – had become accustomed to a high degree
of autonomy, whether under local dynasties, such as the Azms in
Damascus or the Shihabs in Lebanon, or Ottoman *walis* who
remained only for periods too brief to establish their authority.
Ibrahim was confronted by a variety of vested interests who had no
desire to be incorporated into a centralized economy based on the
type of government monopolies Muhammad Ali had instituted in
Egypt. The Ottomans had had their monopolies, but the system
was inefficient and could easily be subverted. In Syria and Lebanon
there were flourishing cotton and silk textile industries, although
they faced increasing competition from European imports, and the
Levantine merchants prospered on the transit trade to the East. They
resented Egyptian interference, as did the Druze landowners growing cereals on the Hauran plains of southern Syria.

Ibrahim was faced with various acts of rebellion, which he
suppressed with his customary ruthlessness. Nevertheless his
achievements during the decade of his governorship (1831–40) were
considerable. He streamlined the administration, reformed the tax
system and began the process of expanding and improving educa-

tion. His aims accorded with those of his father in Egypt, who guided and directed his actions: to lay the foundations of a strong state with a self-sustaining economy. Eventually he hoped that Syria's manufacturing industries would compete with those of Europe.

His plans would have been over-ambitious even if he had had more time to realize them. The Syrian merchants and landowners could be dynamic and enterprising, but they were not ready to be moulded into an alien system. Ibrahim did succeed in expanding and improving trade with Europe and in increasing the area under cultivation, but this was through more efficient government rather than the encouragement of local initiative. For all Ibrahim's attempts to identify with his subjects, he remained a foreign occupier. (Many of the same problems beset the next Egyptian attempt to rule Syria, 120 years later.)

As part of Ibrahim's policy of modernization, Christian missionaries were for the first time allowed to open schools. These missionaries were principally American Protestants and they founded several schools, including one for girls. They also established the first Arabic printing-press in Syria. Ibrahim went further to attempt to establish the principle of equality between Muslims and Christians. Within the Ottoman Empire this meant favouring Christians at Muslim expense. In Egypt Muhammad Ali had always made use of talent and expertise wherever he found it, and he did not hesitate to employ Europeans or to promote local non-Muslims when he deemed it necessary. In Syria this policy meant favouring the Christian merchants, who had the best contacts with Europe (and frequently held *berats* or patents granted by European consulates). Ibrahim imposed a special poll tax on the Muslims of the cities, which equated them with the non-Muslims who had always paid such a tax.

Not unnaturally, the Muslims were not in favour of this innovation. Their resentment greatly increased when Muhammad Ali insisted that Ibrahim begin conscripting Syrians into the Egyptian army. Ibrahim, who was much closer to identifying himself with his Arab subjects than his father, protested that this was unwise; but Muhammad Ali insisted.

However, Muhammad Ali and Ibrahim might have been able to subdue opposition and hold on to their east-Mediterranean/Arabian empire if they had not incurred the implacable opposition of the European powers, led by Britain. Muhammad Ali could defy his nominal master the Ottoman sultan Mahmud – and indeed could contemplate his overthrow – but Britain preferred that a weakened Ottoman Empire should survive rather than be dismembered and swallowed by one of its rivals. Britain was still less enthusiastic that the empire should be replaced by a dynamic and expansionist Muslim power; but it was precisely this possibility which alarmed the powers of Europe.

This was the period in which the Palmerstonian doctrine of imperialism was developed. It was directed not towards the acquisition of colonies – that was to come later in the century – but to the instant protection of British interests wherever they were threatened. As the world's leading industrial and commercial power, Britain saw these interests as largely economic. British manufactured goods were flooding eastwards to Asian markets by the Gulf and Red Sea routes. The era of the steamship had arrived, and Muhammad Ali had greatly eased the passage to India by developing the overland route between Alexandria and Suez. But although British trade was expanding throughout the eastern Mediterranean, it was severely obstructed by the system of monopolies in the Ottoman Empire. Palmerston directed all his powerful diplomacy with the Ottoman Empire towards having these removed. In 1838 he succeeded when an Anglo-Turkish treaty was signed giving Britain and the other European powers the right to trade throughout the Ottoman Empire in return for a tariff of only 3 per cent.

At one stroke Palmerston's treaty had opened the way to foreign commercial domination of the Ottoman Empire. It had also removed a principal source of the sultan's revenue from the state monopolies. Muhammad Ali rightly regarded the terms of the treaty as disastrous for his ambitions, and he refused to apply them to Egypt. He had done everything in his power to protect and facilitate British trade across Egypt, but he could not allow Britain to destroy the sources of his independence. A few weeks before the signature of the treaty, he had announced his decision to declare Egypt and Syria an independent, hereditary kingdom and had offered to pay the sultan the high sum of 3 million pounds as the price for his acceptance of this. Palmerston immediately registered his strong disapproval and made it clear that, if war should ensue between Muhammad Ali and the Ottoman Empire, Britain would be on the side of the sultan.

Britain was determined to foil Muhammad Ali's ambitions. It had become seriously alarmed by the spread of his power along the whole eastern coast of the Red Sea from Bab al-Mandab to Mecca. He had even seized the Tihama coast of Yemen, bought the city of Taez from its corrupt governor (an uncle of the imam of Yemen) and gained control over its valuable coffee trade. The vital route to India seemed to be threatened at a time when the importance of the Arabian coast had been increased by the arrival of steamships and the need for secure coaling-stations. 'I think that it will be absolutely necessary to have a possession of our own on or near the Red Sea,' wrote the Governor of Bombay, Sir Robert Grant, in 1837.

The opportunity to acquire such a possession soon arose. The sultan of Lahej, in whose territory on the south-eastern corner of Arabia lay the tiny port of Aden, was accused of permitting the molestation of British shipping. In January 1839 Commander Haines of the Bombay Marine landed with a small force and seized the town, inaugurating 130 years of British rule in Aden and increasing influence in the tribal hinterland. The Aden settlement was attached to the Bombay presidency, emphasizing its importance to India, and so remained until it became a Crown Colony.

A *de facto* alliance against Muhammad Ali was now in existence between Palmerston and Sultan Mahmud. In the summer of 1839, the sultan declared war on his ambitious viceroy and sent an army across the Euphrates into northern Syria. In spite of the new training of the Ottoman forces by the German military mission headed by Moltke, at the battle of Nazib they were once again soundly defeated by Ibrahim. (He successfully bribed some of the Ottoman troops to desert.) At the same time the admiral of the Ottoman navy, which had been ordered into action, decided to sail the entire fleet to Alexandria and surrender to Muhammad Ali.

Sultan Mahmud died suddenly, before the news of the Nazib disaster could reach him, and he was succeeded by his 16-year-old son Abdul Mejid. The boy sultan and his government were at Muhammad Ali's mercy.

Ibrahim wanted to consolidate his victory by advancing into the Anatolian heartland. There was nothing to prevent him, but his father commanded restraint. He understood that the destruction of the Ottoman Empire would provoke the powers of Europe. He still hoped that they would accept his more limited ambition of holding on to his possessions in the Levant, North Africa and Arabia. However, this was no longer possible. Palmerston had come to regard him as a dangerous menace. 'I hate Mehemet Ali,' he wrote to the British ambassador in Paris, 'whom I consider as nothing better than an ignorant barbarian who by cunning and boldness and mother wit has been successful in rebellion . . . I look upon his boasted civilization of Egypt as the arrantest humbug, and I believe that he is as great a tyrant and oppressor as ever made a people wretched.'

Palmerston had his own share of humbug. He knew that the Ottoman sultan was no less tyrannical than Muhammad Ali or Ibrahim and had a rather worse record for his treatment of minorities. The difference was that the Egyptian dictatorship was relatively effective while a weak sultan could be manipulated. Palmerston set about organizing the five powers of Europe (Britain, France, Prussia, Austria and Russia) behind a move to expel Muhammad Ali from the Levant. France was his greatest problem, because it still regarded Muhammad Ali as a valuable ally whose naval power – particularly in combination with that of France – would act as a counterpoise to Britain in the eastern Mediterranean. Palmerston used a masterly combination of diplomacy and bullying to overcome French resistance. Although half his own cabinet was afraid that he might be provoking a European war, Palmerston played on the fact that King Louis-Philippe of France was even more cautious because of his fears of an attempted *coup d'état*.

At the Conference of London in July 1840 the five powers, including a reluctant France, agreed to the 'Pacification of the Levant' under which Muhammad Ali would be obliged to withdraw all his troops from Syria and to restore the Turkish fleet to the sultan. His family would be recognized as hereditary viceroys of Egypt, but would not inherit his viceroyship of Syria.

When Muhammad Ali indignantly refused these terms, a British fleet under Admiral Napier appeared off the Syrian coast and sent out emissaries calling upon the population to revolt. All the resentment against conscription, high taxation and Ibrahim's flouting of local traditions found expression in rebellions which broke out all over the country. After failing to bribe Ibrahim's governor of Beirut to defect, the British fleet bombarded the city and an Anglo-Turkish force landed. When Napier sailed on to Alexandria, Muhammad Ali realized he was beaten. His French allies had deserted him and he could not fight the European powers alone.

Through the terms of the Treaty of London of 1841, the powers of Europe cut back Muhammad Ali's ambitions and restored his vassal status within the Ottoman Empire. He was stripped of all his possessions except the Sudan, which meant that Crete, Syria and the Hejaz were restored to direct Ottoman rule. At the same time he was obliged to reduce his armed forces, which at one time had approached a quarter of a million men, to 18,000. The instrument of his expansionism was removed, and he no longer could threaten to seize Constantinople.

His consolation was that his position as hereditary pasha of Egypt was confirmed. Although this had been the limit of his original ambitions, his horizons had subsequently expanded. But now he could no longer hope to dominate the trade routes to Asia or challenge the growing hegemony of the European powers in the eastern Mediterranean.

A semi-independent Egypt was still a country of some political and economic importance. Although tired and elderly (he was seventy-two at the time of the Treaty of London) Muhammad Ali was not entirely broken in spirit. Maintaining his enormous army had imposed an impossible burden of taxation on the Egyptian people. (As Palmerston typically observed, 'Like all countries Egypt has rich and poor. The rich is Muhammad Ali and the poor is everyone else.') He had already been seeking ways of retrenchment before the Treaty of London, and the enforced reduction in military spending could have brought relief. The trouble was that the focus of his entire economic policy – the *raison d'être* of his industrialization programme – was the servicing of the needs of his military power. Without demand for their products, the military factories would collapse.

It could be argued that Muhammad Ali's attempt to industrialize Egypt was already a failure. Unlike the European countries, led by Britain, which were achieving a rapid industrial revolution in the first half of the nineteenth century, Egypt had no natural resources of coal or timber to produce steam power and no steel industry. The 40,000 industrial workers, helped by camels and donkeys, produced nearly all their own power. The imported machinery was badly serviced and continually broke down. It was even more of a disadvantage that no class of independent entrepreneurs or trained managers was developing under Muhammad Ali's authoritarian regime. Although he sent some young Egyptians for training in Europe, it was mainly members of the Turco-Circassian officer class that he placed in charge of the factories. Crucial hydraulic and other engineering works were in the hands of foreign technicians, and commerce was increasingly controlled by European merchants.

It is possible, as some Egyptian economic historians have argued, that without European interference the mistakes could have been rectified and Egypt might have achieved a genuine industrial revolution in the wake of Europe. But the auguries were poor, and it would have required a successor to the aged Muhammad Ali of equal forcefulness and ability but greater enlightenment. Ibrahim might conceivably have filled the role and, with his health and reason failing, Muhammad Ali delegated his powers to his son in 1847. But in little more than a year Ibrahim succumbed to a fever, and Muhammad Ali followed him within a few months, on 2 August 1849, without realizing that his son was dead.

In accordance with the terms of the Treaty of London, Muhammad Ali was succeeded by his eldest male descendant – his grandson Abbas, the son of Tussun. Abbas was a gloomy reactionary who repudiated the European influences introduced by his grandfather and uncle. He dismissed the foreign advisers and closed the secular schools. However, he was far from being an Egyptian patriot and had no love for the Egyptians. Because he detested the French, he showed some favour towards the British and allowed them to build the Cairo–Alexandria railway – the first in Africa or Asia – which greatly enhanced Britain's imperial route to India. But Abbas was essentially a xenophobic Ottoman, loyal to the sultan. He had no imperial ambitions of his own. Moreover, a provision of the Treaty of London was that appointment of senior officers in his much diminished army must be approved by Istanbul. This ensured that the high command was in the hands of the Turco-Circassian ruling class rather than native-born Egyptians.

Abbas ruled only five years before he was murdered by two of his Albanian slaves. His uncle Said, who succeeded, was nine years younger than Abbas, corpulent, amiable and Francophile. His contrasting character did not, however, mean that he regarded himself as an Egyptian or cared for the interests of the Egyptians. His liberal attitude towards trade and enterprise resulted in the rapid growth in the size and importance of the foreign communities, and his friendship with the French engineer Ferdinand de Lesseps led to the building of the Suez Canal, which, under foreign ownership, was to be a prime cause and justification of Egypt's subjection to European control.

In his classic work *The Arab Awakening* (first published in 1938) the Palestinian writer George Antonius describes the development of the concept of an Arab nation in modern times. His chapter on Muhammad Ali and Ibrahim is entitled 'The False Start'. He quotes one of their contemporaries as observing that Muhammad Ali's genius 'was of a kind to create empires, while Ibrahim had the wisdom that retains them'. The suggestion is that, if Ibrahim had survived his father and the Western powers led by Britain had not combined against him, a revived Arab empire controlling the Nile Valley, the Red Sea and the Levant could have replaced the Ottomans as the world's leading Islamic power.

Such a development is hard to conceive. Muhammad Ali had no vision of Arab national regeneration. When he considered claiming the caliphate from the sultan it was not to restore it to Arab hands. He remained an Albanian/Turk who never learned to speak Arabic. Ibrahim, it is true, chose to regard himself as an Egyptian – much to his father's disgust. He spoke Arabic and could identify with his Arab soldiers. He dreamed of a revived Arab empire and sometimes rallied his troops with references to Arab historical glory. But none of this amounted to much. Centuries of Turkish political and military dominance in the Muslim world could not be erased. Neither Muhammad Ali nor Ibrahim had time to create new institutions which would last. Their dynasty survived, but their descendants were much lesser men.

4. The Struggle for Reform, 1840–1900

When 16-year-old Sultan Abdul Mejid I (1839–61) succeeded, his empire was in mortal danger. The reforms of his father, Mahmud II, had disrupted the old order while their benefits were still to be realized. The Janissaries, the core of the armed forces, had been repressed, but the training and weaponry provided by Moltke's military mission had yet to prove effective, as the ignominious defeats by Ibrahim's *fellahin* army had proved. The reforms in education – the new medical, engineering, naval and military schools staffed by foreign instructors; the student missions to European universities; and the creation of the first basis for compulsory primary education – were only beginning to produce a new generation of young Ottomans who could understand and cope with the great technical and scientific advances of the nineteenth century.

The young sultan lacked his father's force of character, although for a time he was backed by his formidable mother, but he decided to continue and extend the reforms. Mustafa Reshid Pasha, the outstandingly able foreign minister who was on a mission to London when Mahmud II's death was announced, was brought back to the capital to take charge of the reform programme and on 3 November 1839 the historic Noble Rescript of the Rose Chamber was promulgated – the first of a series of edicts which are known collectively as the *Tanzimat* or Reorganization. More than once, Mustafa Reshid fell from power, only to be restored again. Others carried on his work after his death in 1858. Conservative opposition was powerful, because the reforms were revolutionary in purpose and content. Although their achievements fell well short of their intentions, they initiated notable changes in the way the empire was governed and administered.

Two of the changes were truly revolutionary, in that they broke with the Islamic principles by which the empire had always been governed. The mere declaration of these changes, which were closely related, was shocking to traditional opinion. One was that all Ottoman citizens were to be perfectly equal before the law, regardless of race or creed. The other was the introduction of a new legal code which was distinct from that of the Islamic *sharia* administered by the *qadis* or Islamic judges.

Equality of all citizens before the law was a secular non-Islamic principle derived from the European Enlightenment and the nationalist ideals of the French Revolution. Islamic tradition and law prescribed tolerance and protection for non-Muslim subjects of the state, and it was according to these principles that non-Muslims were allowed a substantial degree of autonomy under the *millet* system. But this did not mean that the members of these minorities were equal to the Muslim majority.

The new concept of equality inevitably affected the supremacy of the Islamic *sharia*. Once again it was a principle which was at stake. Muslim rulers since the earliest days had in practice encouraged or allowed the creation of tribunals in which their own administrative decisions or customary law was applied. But these were on the fringes; the *sharia* courts were dominant, and nowhere more so than in the Ottoman Empire. Now the first steps were being taken towards the demotion of the *sharia* by creating a new body with powers of drafting legislation. The change was not immediate. The religious authorities fought against it and they were able for a time to prevent the introduction of a new commercial code outside the *sharia*. Nevertheless the process of secularization of the world's leading Islamic power had begun.

Because the sultan and his reformist advisers always claimed that the changes were in accordance with Islam, the mass of the population was not aware of their importance. They were none the less revolutionary. Turks and Arabs of today, depending on their point of view, would regard them as either milestones on the road to catastrophe or as steps towards the modernization of the Islamic world which were essential if it were to resist the encroaching power of Christian Europe.

The other reforms of the *Tanzimat* were aimed at this central purpose of regenerating the empire's strength. Sultan Mahmud's policy of opening new military schools with foreign instructors was greatly extended. Of greater importance was the new recruiting law, reducing military service from its hitherto indefinite period to a fixed term of five years followed by seven in the reserves. A body of civil police, or gendarmerie, was also instituted.

Modernizing the armed forces, although requiring time and energy, was simple compared with the task of raising educational standards. Mustafa Reshid understood that this was a prerequisite for the success of all the other reforms. The only existing educational institutions were the Koranic schools maintained by the *ulama* with private donations. A vast programme was launched for the creation of a state university and a centralized network of primary and secondary schools. A Ministry of Education was established. Although religion was proclaimed as having primacy in the new curriculum, in effect a system of secular education was being created. Many fewer schools were founded than had been hoped, but it was the principle that mattered.

Because these reforms were expensive, they were related to the single greatest weakness of the empire and the primary reason for its failure to match the power of Europe – finance. In the first great Ottoman centuries, the empire's vast resources had fed its conquering armies, although even then successive sultans had found that shortage of funds placed limits on their ambitions. By the mid nineteenth century the balance of economic strength had shifted wholly in favour of western Europe – and especially Britain and France, as they passed into the second stage of the industrial revolution which Turkey had barely begun. The European powers were able to use their political and economic power to force the empire to allow its economy to be incorporated into the nineteenth-century liberal capitalist system. British, French and Austrian textiles and other manufactures began to pour into the Middle East from the early years of the century. Facing the onslaught of Muhammad Ali's armies, the sultan was in no position to resist Europe's demands. As we have seen, the Anglo-Turkish treaty of 1838 removed all restrictions on European imports.

Free trade was by no means entirely harmful to the empire. As European manufactures flooded in, the traditional handicrafts and textile industries suffered, but there was a huge growth in demand for raw materials such as Syrian silk, Egyptian cotton and Anatolian wool. Production of cereals and fruit also expanded to meet the needs of the growing cities. The merchant class prospered and with it the capitalist institutions of banks, insurance and limited commercial companies began to develop for the first time in the empire. However, there were two drawbacks for the rulers of the empire. One was that so much of the newly created wealth accrued to foreigners, who benefited from the Capitulations, rather than to Ottoman subjects. The other was that the ending of the traditional system of government monopolies eliminated the principal source of state revenues.

Mustafa Reshid and his colleagues were aware of the dangers of the traditional policy of debasing the currency to meet the empire's chronic deficits. They took steps to avoid this by withdrawing the old coinage and issuing a new currency on European lines, consisting of a gold pound divided into 100 piastres. This ensured monetary stability for a period. However, at the same time they took the unavoidable but potentially disastrous course of issuing treasury bonds as a means of raising revenue. Before long these bonds were circulating as a form of currency, causing alarming inflationary pressure. The temptation to resort to Europe for state loans in order to withdraw the treasury bonds became overwhelming. The banking institutions now existed through which the savings of the willing European middle classes could be channelled into foreign investment. In 1851 Mustafa Reshid signed an agreement with a British and a French bank for a state loan of 55 million francs. This was the first step on the road which led to the bankruptcy of the empire two decades later.

Because the Ottoman armaments factories were inefficient and outmoded, new equipment had to be imported from Europe. Even in time of peace the effort to restore the military balance with the West placed a heavy strain on the empire's finances. At this point it became involved in war with its traditional European enemy – Russia. The Crimean War was not of its own choosing; it was more the consequence of rivalry between the powers of Europe.

Russia was mildly concerned at the prospect of a reformed and revived Turkey; however, the autocratic and ambitious Tsar Nicholas I believed that the collapse of the empire was a more likely outcome of the reform programme. In 1844 he proposed to the British government a plan for the empire's partition: Britain would have Crete and Egypt, Istanbul would be a 'free city', and the Balkan states would be autonomous under Russian 'protection. The tsar denied that he entertained Catherine the Great's dreams of restoring the Byzantine Empire – he said that Russia was in the fortunate position of requiring no more territory – nevertheless, Britain remained extremely suspicious of his intentions. It was still the policy of Britain – as well as of France and Austria – to keep the Sick Man of Europe alive as long as possible, to prevent any of his vital organs from falling into Russian hands. The British response to the tsar was guarded.

The empire might have been left in peace had it not been for a dispute between France and Russia over the control of the holy places in Palestine. In 1740 Sultan Mahmud I, through the Capitulations agreement signed with France, had granted privileges to the Roman Catholic monks in the holy places and had placed the French pilgrims as well as those of other Latin Catholic nations under the protection of the French flag. However, under the secular influence of the French Revolution, French interest in the holy places declined, and Russia took the opportunity to enlarge the privileges of the Orthodox Church in the Holy Land at Latin Roman Catholic expense. In 1850 Louis Napoleon, needing the support of the French Catholic Church in his struggle for power, decided to reassert Catholic rights in Palestine and made a formal demand in this respect to the sultan. When the tsar refused to relinquish any of the rights that Russia had acquired, the Ottoman government proposed a compromise through which both sides would retain their privileges but the sultan would undertake the protection of the holy places and the Christian pilgrims. Both France and Russia rejected this.

Britain was naturally concerned. Unlike Russia and France it was not spoiling for war but, disliking Russian ambitions towards the Ottoman Empire more than those of France, it was inclined to side with France and Turkey. The British government endeavoured to keep the peace, but it became clear that Russia was aiming to secure a protectorate over not only the Orthodox monks but also the twelve million Orthodox Christian subjects of the empire. This was something the sultan was bound to refuse. When the Russians occupied the Danubian principalities of Moldavia and Wallachia, Turkey declared war. Ottoman troops crossed the Danube and secured four initial victories. Although vast, the Russian armed forces were as much in need of modernization as the Turkish, and it seemed at first as if the Ottoman reforms were achieving results. The British and French fleets entered the Dardanelles strait. Britain hoped that this would be enough to cause the Russians to withdraw, but Tsar Nicholas was not deterred. The Russian fleet bombarded the Black Sea ports and destroyed a Turkish squadron. On 27 March 1854 Britain and France declared war on Russia, with strong support from public opinion at home.

The war lasted less than two years and ended when Austria threatened to intervene against Russia. If the hostilities revealed serious defects in both the British and the French armies – in some respects they were still fighting the Napoleonic wars – the Russians were in even worse condition. Although the war was fought over the internal affairs of the Ottoman Empire, Turkish troops played an insignificant role. After their initial successes on the Danube, only one Turkish division was involved.

The terms for the ending of the war were negotiated in the Treaty of Paris of March 1856. Russia abandoned its claims to the protection of the Ottoman Christians, and the exclusive Russian protectorate over the Danubian principalities was replaced by a joint protectorate of the powers of Europe. Free navigation on the River

Danube was entrusted to the supervision of an international commission and the Black Sea was neutralized.

Under the treaty, the Christian powers undertook to respect the independence and territorial integrity of the Ottoman Empire and to maintain it, if necessary, by armed intervention. This could be regarded as the admission of Turkey into the so-called Concert of Europe, but the manner in which it was done was highly patronizing. In effect the Christian powers were claiming the right to interfere in the internal affairs of the empire if they felt that their interests were threatened by one of their rivals. At the same time, the powers were expressing their approval of Turkey's essentially westernizing reforms. A new charter or Imperial Rescript was announced as a prelude to the Treaty of Paris, reaffirming the *Tanzimat* and carrying the reforms a stage further. This had been drafted in collaboration with the representatives of the powers, notably the energetic British ambassador Stratford Canning. On the insistence of the powers, the terms of the charter were incorporated into the Treaty of Paris.

The Imperial Rescript reiterated in stronger and more specific terms than ever before the full equality of all Ottoman subjects 'without prejudice of class or creed' in all matters relating to taxation, ownership of property, education and justice. If applied in full, this concept would have amounted to the dismantling of the Islamic order which was the basis of the empire. This was only very partially achieved, but the charter did have some important consequences: new commercial, maritime and penal codes, which were largely based on French law, were introduced, and the holy *sharia* ceased to be dominant in many areas of life.

However, the measure which had the most immediate and far-reaching effect on Ottoman society was the new land law, based on Western practices which it was hoped would enable the empire to catch up with Christian Europe. The traditional system, in which the land was the property of the state but the cultivators had a variety of established rights in return for the payment of a regular tax (the *miri*), was replaced by one which was based on individual freehold landownership with full rights of disposal and succession.

Such a revolutionary reform could not be fully applied. It was often circumvented, and many traditional practices survived. The results were highly discouraging. The old system was harsh and inequitable in many respects – the practice of tax-farming had been monstrously abused, and it was a long-standing aim of the Ottoman reformers to abolish it – but the practical result of the new land code was to turn many of the more influential tax-farmers into freeholders and the bulk of the cultivators into sharecroppers or hired labourers. A powerful new landlord class was thus created. Very few of the new class of large landowners were enlightened or progressive farmers. A prosperous peasantry on the Western model – investing in and developing its own property – was not created. Well-intentioned efforts by the reformers to increase agricultural output by the distribution of free seed and to create a network of rural co-operative banks to provide the farmers with cheap and easy credit were failures – the necessary administrative system and technical expertise were lacking. The only minor success was in the settlement of some hundreds of thousands of refugees from Russia on hitherto uncultivated lands in Anatolia.

Similar problems beset all the efforts of the Ottoman reformers to increase the productive capacity of the empire's economy as an essential means of raising revenues, as Western ambassadors in Istanbul were urging. In fact it was the liberal free-trade principles that had been imposed by Europe which prevented the reformers from providing the Ottoman infant industries with the protection they needed in order to survive.

The truth was that there was no prospect of a 'great leap forward' in the Ottoman economy which would have enabled it to compete with those of the industrialized powers of western Europe. The main features of advanced nineteenth-century capitalism and the expertise to manage them were lacking, and it would take much more than a generation to develop them. Moreover, the system of Capitulations meant that much of the more progressively managed parts of the economy were in foreign hands and therefore outside

Ottoman control. In 1867 an amendment to the land code for the first time allowed foreigners to own land in the empire.

The reformers did attempt to develop the backward infrastructure of the Ottoman economy – roads, railways and ports. But every effort in this direction only increased the burden of government debt. Despite some improvement in the collection of taxes, expenditure always outran revenues. Soon the Ottoman government was forced to take the fatal step of using receipts from foreign loans to meet the growing deficits. Finally, in October 1875, the government issued a public declaration that only half the amount needed to service the foreign debt could be paid in cash; the remainder would be covered with a new issue of government bonds. This was equivalent to a declaration of bankruptcy. Although twentieth-century experience has shown how debtor nations can skilfully exploit their position with their creditors, this was an appalling position in which the proud Ottomans found themselves.

Sultan Abdul Mejid had died in 1861, at the age of thirty-eight. If he had been a more forceful character and had given more support to Reshid Pasha and his successors, Ali and Fuad Pashas, it is possible that the reforms would have produced more concrete results. But this is extremely doubtful. There was a narrow limit to what decisions taken at the centre could achieve in trying to transform society in such a vast empire. Through the new schools and academies, the most lasting accomplishment was to further the process, begun much earlier in the century, of developing an Ottoman élite which for the first time in centuries was open to the outside world, could speak foreign languages and could absorb fresh ideas. By its very nature this process could only be gradual, but it was also difficult for reactionaries to reverse. Towards the end of the century the results were apparent in the emergence of a substantial class of educated young Turks with a real understanding of their country's needs. The reformers were no longer a tiny band of lonely men.

The changes at the heart of the empire had their negative aspect, however. Partly as a means of initiating reforms, Sultan Mahmud had greatly increased his autocratic powers. He had suppressed the

Janissaries and reduced the power of the feudal dynasties and local magistrates in the provinces. The process was reinforced by the reduction of the authority of the *ulama* over matters of religion, education and law. Sultan Abdul Aziz, who succeeded his brother Abdul Mejid in 1861, emphasized his title as caliph, which hitherto had been purely nominal; he claimed to be the spiritual as well as the political head of the empire. One by one the various countervailing forces with which even the greatest of the earlier sultans had to contend had been removed. But it was inevitable that eventually the Western concepts of constitutional government and the separation of legislative, executive and judicial powers which had penetrated the new Ottoman élite should be turned against the sultan's despotism.

Abdul Aziz had a more muscular personality than his brother but was of more limited mental capacity. Although initially declaring himself a reformist, he soon showed his sympathies with the reactionaries. However, he was incapable of reversing the process of reform. He was under constant pressure from the powers of Europe, led by France, and given the empire's weak financial condition he was in no position to resist. Grudgingly, he allowed Ali and Fuad Pashas to pursue the legal and educational reforms.

By 1871 Ali and Fuad Pashas were both dead. France, the inspiration of liberal reformist ideas, had been defeated by Prussia. External pressures were reduced and there were no men of standing to pursue the reforms. However, it was at this time that internal pressures began to emerge from a lower level.

Until the nineteenth century, hardly any Ottoman Turks were even aware of the immense technical and material advances achieved by Christian Europe. They neither spoke foreign languages nor travelled abroad, and their education and upbringing helped to convince them of the inevitable superiority of the world of Islam. By the middle of the nineteenth century this situation had changed, however. It was not so much that Western concepts of freedom and equality derived from the Enlightenment and French Revolution had penetrated the empire through the reformed educational system and the new printing-presses; indeed, these concepts were enshrined in the imperial charters which were the basis of the *Tanzimat*. It was much more that the young Ottomans who were now familiar with these concepts were travelling abroad in increasing numbers and were able to see for themselves what had happened in the countries where such ideas flourished. They reacted with shame and anger that Ottoman society had become so backward and impoverished in comparison with the West. Some of them concluded that the first necessity was to introduce Western concepts of constitutional government, although they always maintained that these were compatible with the Islamic faith. For others the solution was to revive and restore the true principles of Islam, which had been allowed to decay. These opposing trends exist throughout the Muslim world in the present day. But in the 1860s the supporters of both approaches agreed on the urgent need to reduce the despotic powers of the sultan.

In 1865 a secret revolutionary society was formed which became known as the Young Ottomans. In effect this was the first political party in the Ottoman Empire. Its intellectual inspiration was provided by a new literary movement which was strongly influenced by French writing and ideas but also intensely patriotic. Namik Kemal and Ziya Pasha were poets and dramatists of high quality. When exiled for their political agitation, they continued to publish opposition journals and pamphlets in European capitals and smuggled them into Turkey.

The empire had suffered a series of new humiliations at the hands of the European powers. In 1861, following civil war in Lebanon between Maronite Christians and Druze, Napoleon III, as the protector of the Christians, landed troops in Beirut. The sultan had to accept autonomy for Lebanon under a Christian governor to be chosen by the European powers with the consent of the sultan. When the Serbs revolted in the 1860s, Western pressure forced Turkey to withdraw its troops from the area. Then the Cretans rebelled and declared their union with Greece. Although the Ottoman forces were able to quell the revolt, the Western powers convened a conference in Paris at which Turkey accepted Crete's autonomy under Christian governors.

Personally extravagant and capricious, Sultan Abdul Aziz helped the empire to sink further into debt. The situation was worsened by a world-wide economic depression. In 1876 a revolt by Bulgarian peasants was suppressed with outstanding ferocity. The atrocities committed by the Turks helped to turn public opinion in the West even further against the Ottomans.

The sultan appointed and, after a few months, dismissed a series of grand viziers. One of these was to prove his undoing. Midhat Pasha, the greatest Turkish statesman of the late nineteenth century, was a closet constitutionalist who shared the opinions of the Young Ottomans. In 1873 he had told the British ambassador that the only way to avoid the imminent destruction of the empire lay in making the sultan's ministers responsible, especially in matters of finances, to a national popular assembly which would have to be truly national by avoiding all distinctions of class and religion. The empire would also have to be decentralized by the establishment of local provincial control over the governors.

As the political and economic crisis deepened, with Russia threatening war over the Balkans, a mass demonstration of theological students before the seat of government in Istanbul forced the sultan to recall the dismissed Midhat to office. He succeeded in persuading his fellow-ministers of the necessity for constitutional change, and they persuaded the chief mufti to issue a *fetwa* announcing the sultan's deposition on the ground of his 'mental derangement and ignorance of public affairs'. In the face of a show of force by troops and naval vessels, Abdul Aziz offered no resistance. But it was student power which had initiated the *coup d'état* – setting an ominous precedent.

High hopes were placed in the new sultan, Abdul Aziz's nephew Murad, who had a reputation for liberal constitutionalist sympathies. But Murad proved already to be suffering a nervous breakdown. He had to be instantly replaced by his younger brother, Abdul Hamid.

Abdul Hamid II, whose thirty-three-year reign (1876–1909) led to the final stages of the Ottoman Empire, was the last sultan of consequence. In many respects his complex character was strikingly different from that of most of his predecessors. Austere and pious in his personal life, he was ferociously hard-working. Before his accession, which he had not expected, he managed a farm and learned something of finance by investing in the Istanbul stock exchange. He could be ruthless, but he was not gratuitously cruel or vindictive. His considerable energies were dedicated to the survival of the empire, and his method was to pursue those modernizing reforms which might strengthen its defences and restore its power while maintaining an archaic personal despotism.

Inclination and necessity made him supremely devious in his dealings both with his own people and with overbearing foreign powers. He began his reign by deceiving both. The Balkans were in a state of acute crisis as a warlike Russia continued to support Serbian and Montenegran rebels against the sultan and to claim the right to protect Ottoman Christian subjects. In an effort to avert war, the British government led by Disraeli, and as anxious as its predecessors to prevent the destruction of the Ottoman Empire, called a conference in Istanbul to discuss the outstanding problems. As the conference made slow but real progress during December 1876, the young sultan promulgated a new constitution. Devised by Midhat Pasha and based on the Belgian constitution of 1831, this provided for an elected parliament and embodied the principle that men of all creeds should be treated as equals. It was the first of its kind in any Muslim state. As was intended, it deflated the Istanbul conference because it seemed to provide for the kind of reforms for which the European powers had been calling. The parliament assembled in March 1877 and promptly passed a resolution declaring that there was no need for Russian protection of Ottoman Christians. Frustrated and exasperated, Russia declared war on the Ottoman Empire, having arranged Austria's neutrality by means of a secret agreement which divided the Balkans into their respective spheres of influence.

Initially the Ottoman forces gave a good account of themselves, winning several victories against vastly superior numbers. But over-confident tactics led to disaster. An army surrounded in Plerna was forced to surrender. Slav troops rose in rebellion in all parts of the Balkans. One Russian army occupied the Armenian areas of eastern Anatolia, and another advanced on Istanbul. Abdul Hamid was obliged to sign the humiliating Treaty of San Stefano, which specified the virtual dismemberment of his empire in Europe through the creation of two enlarged and independent Slav states of Bulgaria and Montenegro.

Disraeli was appalled. As he saw it, the sultan had been 'reduced to a state of absolute subjugation to Russia'. He contended that all the powers had rights and interests in the Balkans under the terms of earlier treaties. However, Disraeli had to act carefully. He had the support of the Russophobe Queen Victoria (who regarded the Russians as 'the retarders of all liberty and civilization that exists'), but half his cabinet was opposed to any war on Turkey's behalf. British public opinion, which had been aroused by the oratorical denunciations of Turkish atrocities by the Liberal opposition leader William Gladstone, was also generally anti-Turkish. But, the British public was fickle. As the Russians continued to advance on Istanbul despite the armistice, Disraeli succeeded in rallying his cabinet and the nation behind a threat to intervene.

The Congress of Berlin, which in 1878 brought the powers together under the chairmanship of the German chancellor Bismarck, effectively annulled the Treaty of San Stefano and repartitioned the Balkans to take account of the interests of the powers of Europe other than Russia. The independence of Romania, Serbia and Montenegro were recognized, but the large Bulgarian state which Russia had provided for in the Treaty of San Stefano was reduced and divided into two provinces, one of which became a Turkish self-governing province called Eastern Rumelia. Bismarck commented, 'There is once again a Turkey in Europe.'

It was the persistence of Disraeli (now ennobled by Queen Victoria as Lord Beaconsfield) which enforced this Russian retreat. He also enabled the sultan to regain large Armenian territories in eastern

Anatolia which had been occupied by the Russians, in return for clear undertakings made to the Congress of Berlin of reforms in the interests of the Armenian population and guarantees of their security from attack by Muslim Circassians and Kurds. The *quid pro quo* for Britain's assistance in protecting substantial parts of the Ottoman Empire from Russia was a secret Anglo-Turkish agreement two months earlier by which Britain was allowed to occupy and administer the island of Cyprus – 'the key to western Asia' in Disraeli's imperial conception. To allay France's fears that this gave Britain too much hegemony in the eastern Mediterranean, France was allowed to understand that it could have a free hand in Tunisia, where Britain had hitherto entertained strong ambitions. Three years later France took Britain at its word by invading Tunisia and declaring it a French Protectorate, but this made it more difficult for France to protest when Britain invaded and occupied Egypt in the following year.

Abdul Hamid pursued with some skill his diplomatic policy of playing off the mutually suspicious European powers against each other, and he prevaricated over the implementation of the terms of the Treaty of Berlin as much as he could. But there was a limit to what he could do. In 1885 the Bulgars of Eastern Rumelia rose in rebellion. The two Bulgarian provinces were united, and the sultan appointed Prince Alexander of Battenburg, the prince of Bulgaria, as governor of Eastern Rumelia as a diplomatic way of accepting the annexation. Abdul Hamid was more successful with Greece. He resisted ceding to Greece the area of Epirus inhabited by Muslims, and he succeeded in holding on to Crete. Nevertheless, the Ottoman Empire in Europe had virtually ceased to exist.

In the empire's Anatolian heartland the situation was different. In Armenia there was agitation for the reforms promised in the Treaty of Berlin to be carried out. But, inspired by the series of independent non-Muslim governments which had been founded in succession to the empire in Europe, Armenian nationalists went much further and demanded national independence.

Abdul Hamid had no intention of allowing the Christian powers to dictate the way in which he ruled what was left of his empire. As soon as the 1876 Constantinople Conference had ended he had dismissed Midhat Pasha – the prime force behind the liberal constitution which he had accepted – and had sent him into exile. (In 1878 he was appointed governor of Syria, but in 1881 he was again banished. Allowed back into Turkey after British pressure, he was put on trial on a charge of plotting against the sultan. He was sentenced to life banishment and was later quietly murdered in prison in Arabia.)

As we have seen, Abdul Hamid allowed the Ottoman parliament to meet in March 1877. Despite the limits to its powers, the parliament showed worrying signs of independence – to the extent of demanding that some of the sultan's ministers should appear before it to answer charges. Abdul Hamid responded by dissolving the assembly after a session of three months. Six months later he recalled it, hoping that in the continuing international crisis created by the Russian menace it would be more docile. But, once the Treaty of Berlin was concluded in January 1878, parliament renewed both its accusations against certain ministers and its demands that they should answer them. This time Abdul Hamid felt strong enough to dissolve parliament and suspend the constitution indefinitely. The suspension was to last for thirty years. The reform movement of the Young Ottomans was crushed and destroyed.

The young sultan built up his own remarkable system of autocracy. Gradually he reduced the powers that had been delegated to the grand vizier and reinforced his personal bureaucracy, which reported directly to him. His deeply mistrustful nature caused him to rely on an elaborate system of espionage with Istanbul as the heart of the spider's web of imperial intrigue. He had no friends and trusted no one. His fears of abduction or assassination became paranoid to the extent that he always extracted his own teeth and prepared his own medicines. His emissaries not only reported on individuals or groups in the provinces who showed signs of becoming too powerful or ambitious but also acted on the sultan's orders to promote local rivalries and antagonisms. He preferred the use of the silken cord to the sword.

While Abdul Hamid had no sympathy for constitutionalism or democracy, he was not a hidebound reactionary. In contemporary terms he was a modernizer rather than a westernizer. Like certain of his predecessors, he accepted the need to learn from Europe in order to stand up to its power. In the early years of his reign he was prepared to fulfil the *Tanzimat* reforms and went some way towards carrying them through.

His first grand vizier, Mehmed Said Pasha – known as 'Ingiliz Said' because of his Anglophile tendencies – declared in a lengthy memorandum on the subject of reform that 'the advancement of a state can only be secured through knowledge and uprightness.' The people must be better educated; the state must be more just and less corrupt.

Public education was the field in which reform was most successful – especially at the higher level. The Mulkiye, or civil-service training-college, and the Harbiye, or war college, were greatly expanded and improved and some eighteen new higher and professional schools were established. The long-delayed project for the University of Istanbul – described as 'the first truly indigenous modern university in the Muslim world' – was carried through, although it was not until 1900 that it opened its doors.

Elementary and secondary education were also expanded. New schools were needed to supply the training-colleges with pupils. They still served only a small minority of the population, and a truly public education system was still a distant goal; nevertheless, the new Turkish élite, trained in modern languages and disciplines, had become much more numerous by the end of the century. The spread of literacy, the growth of higher education and the expansion of printing transformed the intellectual and cultural life of the cities. However, under Abdul Hamid the censorship which already existed was tightened to an absurd degree. Although newspapers multiplied, they were emasculated by the censor. Because the sultan was terrified of assassination, no report of the violent death of a head of state could be published. When the King and Queen of Serbia were murdered in 1903, Turkish newspaper-readers were informed that they had died of indigestion.

The ban on political activity and discussion limited the new generation of Turkish intellectuals to literary or academic writing. But there was no way in which they could be insulated against revolutionary or secular ideas. Political feelings were merely driven underground.

Discontent was fed by the constant, humiliating erosion of Ottoman power at the hands of Europe, despite all the efforts of the sultan and his grand vizier. Since the Capitulations were one of the most obvious manifestations of Ottoman weakness, the Ottoman government endeavoured to bring them under control. The privileges of the Capitulations had been granted to non-Muslims within the empire in the sixteenth century, when Ottoman power was at its height. In order to stimulate trade and industry, they exempted non-Muslims from taxes and gave them the right to be tried in their own consular courts. As Ottoman power declined, these privileges were reinforced and became flagrantly abused. The foreign communities were not only privileged and protected; they were virtually above the law. The European powers argued that, in spite of the reforms introduced in 1869, the Ottoman legal system was in no way suitable to be applied to their nationals in the empire.

In the first few years of Abdul Hamid's reign an effort was made to meet these objections. A newly established Ministry of Justice was given control first over the commercial courts and then over all non-religious courts. A new law attempted to regulate the mixed courts which had been created earlier in the nineteenth century to try cases between Muslim and non-Muslim Ottoman subjects. All these efforts were a failure. The European powers brusquely refused to recognize the new regulations. The extraterritorial privileges were unassailed and continued to flourish. The impetus behind all legal reform was removed, and in 1888 the sultan disbanded the official drafting committee which had been set up by his predecessor to prepare the new laws.

The fact that the extraterritorial privileges of the powers of Europe remained unscathed was bad enough; it was far worse that the empire itself was bankrupt and forced to submit to a measure of outside financial control.

Bankruptcy had in effect been declared in 1875, in the last year of the reign of Sultan Abdul Aziz, when his government announced that, in view of the size of the budget deficit, it would service only half of the external debt in cash and would make up the rest by a new issue of treasury bonds. The deficit was caused partly by a series of disastrous harvests in Anatolia but much more by the heavy military spending involved in the suppression of Balkan rebels and the war with Russia. The rival European powers had difficulty in co-ordinating their policies towards Istanbul but they moved inexorably towards imposing their financial conditions on the empire. The Congress of Berlin made the situation much worse by forcing the sultan to give up his richest Balkan provinces. A committee representing European holders of Ottoman bonds attended the Congress to press their claims, and they secured warm support from their governments.

In his desperate need to satisfy his European creditors, Abdul Hamid in 1881 issued the Decree of Muharrem, setting up a Council of the Public Debt in agreement with the bond-holders to ensure that the Ottoman debt would continue to be serviced. The Council was to include both bond-holders and Ottoman representatives. Although it was not a full international commission with official foreign-government representatives, as the powers had proposed at the Congress of Berlin, and the sultan could deny that it infringed Ottoman sovereignty, it was difficult to disguise the fact that the empire had submitted to a large measure of foreign financial control, and this became increasingly apparent over the years. Several of the more economically backward European states – not to mention the Latin American countries – had defaulted on their debts and the powers had given their bond-holders varying degrees of support to resolve the situation. But it was a wholly different matter for the caliph/sultan – the leader of the only Muslim great power – to accept such humiliation.

European manufactured goods had already begun to flow into

Turkey in the first half of the nineteenth century as the Ottoman efforts at protection collapsed. European financial control assisted the flood of imports. Three major foreign-controlled banks – the National Bank of Turkey, the Imperial Ottoman and the Deutsche Bank – as well as the foreign embassies were always ready to provide support for the policies of the Council of the Public Debt. However, the European powers were not attempting to stifle local Turkish industry – on the contrary, they encouraged the Ottoman reformers' efforts to increase production as the best means of raising the taxable capacity of the population and hence the ability of the Ottoman government to pay its debts. Both Abdul Aziz and Abdul Hamid were aware of the dangers of increasing economic dependence on Europe, and the *Tanzimat* reforms attempted to address the problem. But the measures were half-hearted and incompetently administered. New infant industries not only lacked protection but also, amazingly, still suffered from Ottoman internal taxes on the movement of goods which were only gradually and grudgingly removed. Existing local industries were unable to compete with the imports of increasingly sophisticated products from Europe – armaments factories, for example, found themselves confined to producing small arms, ammunition and military clothing.

Attempts to increase agricultural output and exports were rather more successful. Much of this success was not due to the government. The rising prosperity of industrializing western Europe had already increased the demand for exports of Turkish crops. British imports in particular received a powerful boost from the repeal of the Corn Laws in 1841. The American Civil War created a boom for Turkish cotton which did not entirely disappear when the war ended. The richer agricultural areas of the coastal plains and the Anatolian river valleys prospered.

The trouble was that the twin objectives of the nineteenth-century Ottoman reformers were contradictory: the creation of a prosperous class of peasant freeholders was incompatible with the desire for a powerful centralizing government which would re-establish the rights of the state wherever they had been eroded.

Inevitably the progress of reform was extremely slow and, equally inevitably, wherever freehold rights were established they went to the richest and most powerful or to those with the best connections.

A new factor in the situation was the right granted to foreigners to own land and property, under the reform law of 1867. The Ottomans had hoped and expected that, in return, the Europeans who acquired estates in the empire would forgo their privileges under the Capitulations. They were disappointed: the Europeans insisted on retaining their rights to immunity from police interference or the payment of Ottoman taxes.

Ottoman reformers and their European advisers were under no doubt that the biggest single obstacle to the improvement of the Turkish economy was the poor communication systems. When Abdul Hamid came to the throne there were only a few hundred miles of railway; the road system was rudimentary and the ports were primitive. The costs of moving farm produce across the country for export were prohibitive.

Road-building schemes were largely a failure because those roads that were built were not maintained and soon fell into disrepair. Railway building, largely by foreign concession-holders, achieved more results, and from the 1880s a boom in railway construction linked the regions of Anatolia with Europe and extended from Turkey to the Arab provinces of the empire. The length of track in this vast region was still modest by European standards, but the railway was of huge symbolic importance. In August 1888 the first Istanbul Express left Vienna.

It can be seen that much of the nineteenth-century development of the Ottoman Empire's heartland was due to the privileged foreigners. Railways were built by Europeans; banking and finance were largely in foreign hands; and foreign entrepreneurs were even responsible for the investment and installation of machinery that turned cotton into Turkey's most successful export industry. However, there was one aspect of nineteenth-century technical progress which Abdul Hamid and his ministers were determined to keep in Turkish hands; this was the telegraph. When Abdul Hamid came to the throne, in 1876, a French concessionnaire had already linked the entire empire to Istanbul with a telegraph network. Initially the system was operated by foreigners using the French language, but from the 1860s onwards the Ottomans made a special effort to turkize the system and place it under the control of a new Ministry of Posts & Telegraphs. Abdul Hamid immediately recognized the importance of the telegraph as a means of maintaining his despotic and centralized control over the empire. He could issue immediate orders to his officials in the most distant provinces, who found that they could no longer act as if they were semi-autonomous. Foreign ambassadors of despotic rulers were soon to make the same discovery.

Turkish indebtedness and relative military weakness forced Abdul Hamid to use intrigue and diplomacy to keep the powers of Europe divided in their Eastern policies. He had enjoyed some success in this following the Congress of Berlin in 1878. Although the powers were shocked to varying degrees by the sultan's reneging on his promises concerning the treatment of his Armenian subjects, joint action was prevented because Bismarck, chairman of the Congress, said he would co-operate on any matter except the imposition of Armenian reform on the sultan.

The Armenian situation drastically worsened during the following two decades. As Abdul Hamid made use of the Kurds, who coveted much of the same territory, to suppress the Armenian rebellion, the Armenians intensified their organized political activities. They raised their demands to seek a fully independent homeland in eastern Turkey and internationalized their movement by forming branches in western European capitals. Its most extreme form was the Hunchak (or 'Bell'), established in Geneva in 1881, which was the first revolutionary socialist movement in the Ottoman Empire. In 1890 the Armenian Revolutionary Federation was founded at Tiflis (the modern Tbilisi) in Russian Georgia, and armed bands began to make raids into Ottoman territory. The sultan responded by encouraging increased anti-Armenian activities among the Kurdish tribesmen, whom he trained and formed into cavalry regiments.

There was no attempt to conceal the fact that their role was to suppress the Armenians.

The response of the inflamed Armenians was an exceedingly unwise attempt to stir up a revolt among the sultan's Muslim subjects in Anatolia. This gave Abdul Hamid the excuse to incite a series of horrific massacres which took place throughout 1895 and 1896. Both regular Turkish troops and Kurdish irregulars took part. In some places the ordinary Muslim population was incited by rumours that the Armenians were about to murder them while they were at prayers in their mosques. Sometimes the Armenians sought refuge in their churches and asked for protection, but this was of no avail. The sound of a bugle was a signal for the massacres to begin. Most of eastern Turkey was affected, and perhaps a hundred thousand Armenians were murdered or died from subsequent disease and starvation.

It was possible to keep the scale of these massacres hidden from the outside world. News only trickled out and was often dismissed as exaggerated rumours. But in August 1896 a group of Armenian revolutionaries with characteristic foolhardiness took their struggle into the heart of Istanbul, where they raided and occupied the Ottoman Bank with the declared purpose of drawing the attention of the European embassies to the plight of their people. In the inevitable reprisal, the Istanbul mob led by religious fanatics was allowed to murder and pillage through the Armenian quarter. Now the powers of Europe could not ignore what was happening. In a series of joint notes they denounced the massacres and made clear their view that these were not spontaneous communal disturbances but had been deliberately provoked by the sultan and his agents. They made veiled threats of intervention by suggesting that the survival of the sultan and his dynasty was at stake.

Abdul Hamid's replies were evasive and unsatisfactory. The rumour spread through the capital that the British fleet would force the Dardanelles and land troops. But once again the sultan was saved by the jealous rivalry of the powers. In England the aged William Gladstone might rage against the 'unspeakable Turk' as a 'disgrace to civilization' and demand that Britain should if necessary act alone, but he was in opposition and the prudent prime minister Lord Salisbury, who like his monarch Queen Victoria always detested and feared the Russians more than the Turks, had no intention of doing such a thing. Public opinion might be aroused against the empire throughout Europe, but the governments of the powers still had no desire to see it dismembered. Russia did not want to see a powerful independent Armenia on its borders. France did not wish to risk its huge investments in the Ottoman Empire, which were now much larger than those of Britain. Germany had its own ambitions for political and commercial expansion to the east which could succeed only through an alliance with the sultan and his government. An international conference on the Armenian question in 1897 ended in failure, and the collapse of the empire was again forestalled. The Armenians, whose aims had never been realistic, were left to their fate.

Since his accession Abdul Hamid had regarded Germany, recently united under Bismarck, with the greatest favour among the powers of Europe. It not only lacked Britain, France and Russia's imperial ambitions towards the Muslim world but also acted to restrain them. Backed by its rising industrial strength, which was soon to outstrip that of Britain, and allied with Austro-Hungary, imperial Germany created a new focus of power in central Europe. But there were strict limits to Bismarck's ambitions: his own view was that the concept of eastwards expansion was a futile dream. One of his most notable observations was that the whole Eastern Question was 'not worth the bones of a single Pomeranian grenadier'.

However, Germany's foreign policy dramatically changed when, in 1888, the young Kaiser Wilhelm II acceded to the throne on the early death of his father. Intelligent but unstable, autocratic and ambitious, Wilhelm — although half-English through his mother, the daughter of Queen Victoria — was a passionate German nationalist. Against Bismarck's advice he was easily persuaded by Marshal von der Goltz, who headed the German military mission in Istanbul, that Asiatic Turkey was ripe for the growth of German influence.

The policy of '*Drang nach Osten*' (or 'drive to the east') was born. Abdul Hamid, always suspicious of liberal influences emanating from London and Paris and seeing nothing equivalent in Berlin, welcomed the new German interest. In 1889 he gave a lavish reception to the young kaiser and kaiserin when they made their first visit to Istanbul.

German engineers and scientists now joined the military experts in the difficult task of modernizing the Ottoman Empire. The principal German contribution was the building of the railway across Anatolia to Baghdad, with the prospect of extending it through Basra to Kuwait on the Persian Gulf. In 1898 the kaiser, who by now 'dropped the pilot' and dispensed with Bismarck's services, made a second visit to Istanbul of much greater significance. This time he went on from Turkey to the Arab provinces of the empire. With doubtful symbolism he entered Jerusalem dressed as a crusader knight, after praying on his knees outside the walls of the Holy City. But he went on to Damascus where, in a memorable speech at the tomb of Saladin, he swore Germany's disinterested protection for the 300 million subjects of the sultan/caliph.

The foundations had been laid of an Ottoman–German alliance which two decades later was to result in the destruction and dismemberment of the empire. But it was wholly understandable that Abdul Hamid should have clutched at Germany as an ally to help preserve from British and French imperial ambitions his Arab Asian dominions which were virtually all that remained of his empire. Morocco had never been Ottoman, Algeria was lost to France in the 1830s and Tunisia in 1881. Turkish governors still ruled the desert provinces of Libya, but, partly through accident and bungling, Egypt had come under lasting British control.

5. Britain in Egypt, 1882–1914

In 1841, combined European and Ottoman pressure had forced Muhammad Ali of Egypt to abandon all his dreams of empire except for possession of Sudan. However, he nevertheless left his successors a cohesive semi-independent state whose strategic position gave it considerable importance in the eastern Mediterranean. They also inherited gigantic problems which they were ultimately incapable of managing.

Some of these problems closely mirrored those of the Ottoman sultan. The abolition of Muhammad Ali's system of monopolies and the opening up of Egypt to European trade and enterprise (equivalent to the *infitah* or open-door policy of President Sadat more than a century later) not only removed the basis of the state's revenues but also made it impossible for the rulers of Egypt to maintain control over the country's economic development. There was no question of Egypt becoming an industrial power.

There were also important differences from Turkey, however. The enforced reduction of the armed forces to 18,000 men, under the 1841 Treaty of London, removed the need for high military spending, which had bled the country. But this also meant that Egypt was no longer a military power of any consequence, even though the Ottoman sultan was neither willing nor able to offer protection against occupation by a European power.

Egypt's open-door policy promoted a more intensive and comprehensive economic development than was taking place in Turkey. In area Egypt is the size of France and Spain, but only 3 per cent of this was inhabited, its population being less than one-tenth of what it is today. Good communications and a modern infrastructure were relatively easy to install, and by the 1870s the inextensive but intensely fertile lands of the Nile Valley and Delta were producing valuable crops for export, of which cotton was the most important.

Unfortunately this did little to improve the lot of the mass of Egyptians, for two reasons. One was that the foreign entrepreneurs who were responsible for so much of the new development made little contribution to Egypt's revenues; under the protection of the Capitulations, they paid virtually no taxes. Secondly, while the trend towards the granting of freehold property rights was more advanced than in Ottoman Turkey, the principal result was that more and more land was concentrated into vast estates owned by the Turco-Circassian ruling class, and especially the numerous members of the family of Muhammad Ali. At the same time, many of the small farmers – the *fellahin* – actually lost control over lands that their families had farmed for generations. The *kurbaj* (whip) might no longer be used to force them into the ranks of Ibrahim Pasha's armies, but it was employed to conscript labour among the landless peasants.

Abbas, Muhammad Ali's immediate successor (1844–54), was an embittered reactionary who dismissed his grandfather's French advisers and willingly closed schools and halted public works. But though generally xenophobic he was curiously Anglophile, and he allowed James Stephenson to build the Cairo–Alexandria railway in 1850–1, the first railway in Africa or Asia. Despite his meanness, Egypt's lack of revenues forced him into borrowing. On his murder by two household slaves (possibly as an act of revenge by his aunt, Princess Zohra, whom he had banished for amorous activities), he was succeeded by a man of very different temperament, his genial and Francophile uncle Said (1854–63). Said launched a vastly expensive new programme of public works – digging new canals, repairing dams and expanding both the railways and steamer transport on the Nile. He set a precedent by negotiating a loan from Fruhling and Goschen of London at 8 per cent. As European entrepreneurs, supported by their consuls and protected by the Capitulations, extracted expensive and one-sided concessions from the Egyptian government, Egypt's debts mounted dangerously.

The consequences of this extravagance were overshadowed by

one decision which was to be fateful for Egypt. As a youth, one of Said's closest European friends had been Ferdinand de Lesseps, a young engineer who was son of the French political agent. De Lesseps was interested in a scheme to cut a canal from the Mediterranean to the Red Sea across the isthmus of Suez. This was not a new idea. Napoleon had wanted to do it in order to gain control of the Red Sea for France, but his engineers had told him it was impossible because of the different levels of the Mediterranean and Red Seas. This was contradicted by a British engineer in the 1830s, and Muhammad Ali and his French advisers favoured the project. Palmerston, however, was strongly opposed – especially if the canal was to be built by French engineers. British interests would make control of the canal imperative, and this would mean the occupation of Egypt. As he famously remarked,

We do not want Egypt or wish it for ourselves, any more than any rational man with an estate in the north of England and a residence in the south would have wished to possess the inns on the road. All he could want would have been that the inns should be well-kept, always accessible, and furnishing him, when he came, with mutton-chops and post-horses.

Britain preferred the trans-Egyptian route to the East to be opened by extending the Cairo–Alexandria railway to Suez.

One of Said's first actions on his accession was to sign a canal concession agreement with de Lesseps. The terms were hugely unfavourable to Egypt: it had to provide a corvée of 20,000 unpaid labourers a year, pay for all the extensive ancillary works and abandon its rights to the land on both banks of the canal. In addition, when nearly half the shares in the Suez Canal Company were left unsold by public subscription, de Lesseps persuaded Said that he must purchase them.

Britain still opposed the scheme, and endeavoured to use its influence with the Ottoman sultan. But Said was sufficiently independent, and de Lesseps had the enthusiastic support of Napoleon III. In April 1859 the work began. The Canal was half completed when Said died and was succeeded as viceroy by Ismail, son of Ibrahim Pasha. Ismail was a man of ambition, intelligence and enterprise, but his failings were to destroy Egypt's hopes of independence. Work on the Canal was pushed ahead and was completed by 1869, when Ismail played the lavish host to the Empress Eugénie and other European royalty for the official opening. The cost to Egypt was gigantic. The sultan, encouraged by Britain, had maintained his right to veto the concession. Although de Lesseps persuaded him to refer the dispute to Napoleon III for arbitration, the French emperor's award, which was intended finally to determine the status of the Suez Canal Company, placed an unbearable burden on Egypt. Ismail had to pay the Company the extortionate sum of 130 million francs to relinquish its rights to land, navigation and free labour under the original concession. The sultan issued his firman of approval, but Egypt was rapidly approaching bankruptcy.

The Suez Canal was the most important single expense for Egypt, but there was much more. During Ismail's reign, 8,400 miles of canal were dug and the railway system was extended from 275 to 1,185 miles. Telegraphs, bridges, docks and lighthouses gave Egypt the infrastructure of a modernizing nineteenth-century state. In a remark which is still remembered in Egypt, Ismail claimed that 'My country no longer belongs to Africa; it is part of Europe.' Even *The Times*'s correspondent concurred when he wrote in 1876 that 'Egypt is a marvellous instance of progress. She has advanced as much in seventy years as many other countries have done in five hundred.' The cultivated area was extended by some 15 per cent, and between 1862 and 1879 the value of exports and imports nearly tripled.

There were two disastrous weaknesses in this apparent prosperity. One was that it depended so heavily on the export of a single primary product – cotton. Manufactured goods were mostly imported. Like Turkey, Egypt benefited from the effects of the American Civil War on cotton output from the southern states. The boom encouraged Ismail to further extravagance but swiftly faded. The other weakness was the mountain of debt on which the apparent prosperity was based. Within five years of Ismail's Canal concession he had borrowed over £25 million at rates of interest nominally varying between 7 and 12 per cent but in reality amounting to between 12 and 26 per cent. One of his troubles was that as viceroy appointed by the sultan, rather than an independent sovereign, he had no legal power to pledge the revenue of the state, so the terms on which he could borrow were proportionately more expensive. In 1867 he managed to secure from the sultan the style and title of khedive together with the right to change the law of succession in favour of his direct descendants instead of succession passing, as previously, to the eldest surviving member of the House of Muhammad Ali. In 1873 he obtained an Imperial Rescript which made him virtually an independent sovereign with the right to raise loans and secure concessions without reference to the sultan. All this was achieved only with heavy bribes, but it meant that what had previously been the personal liability of the viceroy now became that of the Egyptian state and ultimately of the long-suffering *fellahin*.

By 1875 Ismail's debts were so great that he was obliged to sell his 44 per cent of the Suez Canal Company's shares to the British government for the modest sum of £4 million. The prime minister, Disraeli, who had once supported Palmerston in his opposition to the building of the Canal, arranged for a loan to make the purchase through the London House of Rothschild. Gladstone, leader of the Liberal opposition, saw it as 'an act of folly fraught with danger' to involve Britain so intimately in Egyptian affairs. The French, of course, were furious.

The sale of Canal shares was not enough to save Ismail or Egypt from bankruptcy. Moreover the financial collapse of the Ottoman Empire was imminent and, despite Egypt's relative independence, this had a disastrous effect on Egypt's international credit. In fact Egypt's formal declaration of bankruptcy, in April 1876, followed that of Turkey by only seven months.

The consequences for Egypt were similar to those for Turkey but more profound. Whereas with Turkey and other defaulting countries the British government confined itself to moral support for the bond-holders and refused to become directly involved, Egypt was different because it lay across the route to India. As Palmerston had foreseen, the way in which Egypt was governed had become of vital interest to the British Empire.

When Ismail asked Britain for help, the British government sent out a high-level mission headed by a cabinet minister. The hope of the bond-holders and the British public was that Britain would now impose a form of financial control over Egypt. But the French were quite unprepared to allow the British to monopolize the external intervention in Egypt's affairs, and they sent out their own financial mission. Britain and France each proposed solutions which were favourable to their respective bond-holders and, after some diplomatic wrangling, a compromise was reached under which a Caisse of Public Debt (or *Caisse de la Dette*) would be established through which Egypt's total debts would be consolidated with repayments fixed at 7 per cent, absorbing some two-thirds of the state's revenues. The British and French governments were each represented by an independent executive controller-general. Anglo-French dual control of Egypt had begun. The English commissioner in the Caisse was a former secretary of the Viceroy of India, Captain Evelyn Baring, who was to set the tone for Britain's special relationship with Egypt during the next generation.

The controllers-general set about proving their worth and, through a variety of additional taxes, Egypt began to pay its debts at the rate that had been imposed. But the British and French officials in Egypt soon realized that the strain on the population was becoming intolerable. A low Nile flood and cotton pest added to the sufferings of the *fellahin*. Even liberal use of the *kurbaj* could not squeeze any more taxes from them. The controllers-general concluded that an international commission of inquiry was needed to examine the khedive's financial management. Reluctantly, the khedive accepted. As expected, the commission concluded that the source of Egypt's problems lay in the khedive's unlimited authority and that he must delegate some of his powers to 'responsible ministers'. Ismail agreed, in the spirit of his contention that Egypt was now part of Europe. He appointed a cabinet with the wily Armenian Nubar Pasha as prime minister, a British minister of finance and a French minister of public works.

But Ismail had no real intention of becoming a constitutional monarch. When his 'European' government took unpopular measures, as it was bound to do in view of Egypt's financial condition, he refused to share responsibility. He showed his authority by sharply suppressing a mutiny of officers who had not been paid for eighteen months and then dismissing Nubar as incapable of maintaining public order. Britain and France were still unprepared for direct military intervention, partly because the general public in their countries was not very sympathetic towards the bond-holders; they still vainly hoped to persuade Ismail to retain constitutional government. Partly at Ismail's own instigation, a coalition of army officers, pashas and *ulama* had formed something resembling an Egyptian national party, determined to prove that Egypt could govern itself. Conceivably a balance between the khedive and some form of representative institutions could be achieved. Ismail shrewdly chose Sherif Pasha, a leading constitutionalist, as his new prime minister.

Intervention came from an unexpected quarter. Germany and Austria were indignant at the measures Sherif's government proposed to reduce the burden of the floating debt to the bond-holders, most of whom were of German or Austrian nationality. They persuaded the by now exasperated British and French that Ismail must go, and together they put pressure on Sultan Abdul Hamid to use his residual powers to force Ismail to abdicate in favour of his son Tewfik. Ismail sailed into exile. He left few defenders. His real achievements were forgotten because of the disasters his reign had brought: after consolidating Egypt's independence, he had destroyed it through his extravagance.

The new young khedive lacked Ismail's courage and determination, but he had no wish to accept any form of liberal constitution. However, the political situation in Egypt was no longer simple to control. Although the rising national movement consisted of several disparate and incompatible elements, it was now formidable as they were temporarily united against the dangers of foreign domination and arbitrary government.

The ideological strand in the movement consisted of the politico-religious reformers who were disciples of Jamal al-Din al-Afghani, a formidable Iranian of obscure origin who was one of the most power-ful intellectual influences in nineteenth-century Islam. Al-Afghani preached the need for the restoration of true Islamic principles, but he also declared the need for national and Islamic unity as a defence against Christian European intervention. However, he had no faith in the Ottoman caliphate and opposed its power. He favoured consti-tutional government. Exiled, not surprisingly, from Turkey in 1871, he came to Egypt where he was tolerated by Ismail. Tewfik expelled him shortly after his accession – almost certainly with the encourage-ment of the Anglo-French dual control – but his influence survived. Later he lived in Paris, where he founded a secret society and published a journal dedicated to Islamic reform.

The second strand in the national movement consisted of the pashas, *ulama* and other notables who favoured constitutional reform. Many of them were Turco-Circassians who had to some extent come to identify themselves with Egypt and the aspirations of its people. But they were also wealthy owners of property who were easily frightened by the spectre of radicalism or a popular uprising.

The third element in the national party consisted of the genuine Egyptian or *fellah* (as opposed to Turco-Circassian) officers in the army. Ismail had blatantly favoured the non-Egyptians, who held all the highest military posts, and the *fellah* officers were in a state of seething discontent. They found a leader in Colonel Ahmed Arabi, the son of a small farmer of Lower Egypt. Although poorly educated, he had succeeded in rising to command the Fourth Regi-ment. Courageous and dignified, he was neither brilliant nor decisive but he appealed to the mass of Egyptians because he remained in touch with them and could express their grievances in terms they could understand.

The unpopular and ultra-reactionary Circassian war minister, Osman Rifky, attempted to have Colonel Arabi and some of his colleagues arrested and court-martialled for mutiny. But Arabi had the support of the key regiments in the capital and the manoeuvre failed. The government was forced to capitulate and dismiss Rifky.

Arabi and his friends became the natural leaders of a movement which rode on a swell of popular support. As *The Times* pointed out on 12 September 1881, 'The army, we must remember, is the only native institution which Egypt now owns. All else has been invaded and controlled and transformed by the accredited representatives of France and England.'

The situation was still capable of peaceful resolution. Neither Arabi nor those like the Islamic reformer Shaikh Muhammad Abduh, al-Afghani's disciple, who joined his ranks, were firebrand revolutionaries. Still less so were the landowners in the national movement. The British government – now headed by William Gladstone, with his long reputation for anti-imperialism – was still reluctant to intervene. The British representatives in Egypt, although often ill-informed about the true nature of popular feeling in the country, believed that the situation could still be saved if the khedive acted firmly but with wisdom and restraint according to their advice. Unfortunately, Tewfik was quite inadequate for the task. While appearing to show some sympathy for Arabi's demands, such as that the size of the Egyptian army should be increased and that the number of Europeans employed in Egypt should be reduced, together with their inflated salaries, his real objective was to be rid of the rebellious colonel. He even sent an emissary to Sultan Abdul Hamid to tell him that Arabi aimed to form an Arabian Empire with the agreement of Britain. But Abdul Hamid was more than a match for Tewfik in double-dealing. He informed Arabi that he was satisfied with his loyalty and commanded him at all costs to defend Egypt from invasion, lest it should share the fate of Tunisia, which had recently been occupied by France.

In fact Gladstone's government would have preferred the sultan to have taken responsibility for restoring the authority of the khedive. But it was also Gladstone's policy to maintain a close *entente* with France in the face of Bismarck's growing ambitions in Europe, and the French were totally opposed to any Turkish intervention, being nervous that Abdul Hamid might, through Egypt, be planning to raise a pan-Islamic resistance movement which would endanger their hold on Tunisia. Nevertheless, Britain was still hoping that no intervention at all would be necessary when, in December 1881, the French government fell and was replaced by one led by Gambetta, the arch-nationalist hero of France's resistance to Prussia in 1871. Gambetta insisted on strong action and forced Britain's lethargic foreign secretary, Lord Granville, into the dispatch of an Anglo-French Joint Note addressed to the British and French consuls-general in Egypt. The menacing Note in effect demanded the restoration of the *status quo ante* and the maintenance of the khedive on the throne 'on the terms laid down by the Sultan's Firmans and officially recognized by the two Governments, as alone able to guarantee, for the present and future, the good order and development of prosperity in Egypt, in which France and Great Britain are equally interested.'

The consequences of this high-handedness were predictable. National feeling in Egypt was further aroused. Arabi was appointed under-secretary of state for war and the quasi-parliament (the Chamber of Notables) demanded some control over Egypt's budget, which was in the hands of the Anglo-French financial controllers. Gambetta fell from power after only two months and was replaced by the more moderate De Freycinet, but the damage had been done.

The Egyptian army now dominated the nation, and the mass of the people gave it their enthusiastic support. The *fellahin* naïvely hoped that Egypt would henceforth be ruled by Egyptians and they would no longer be squeezed for taxes. Some of the notables shared these feelings, but many were alarmed by the threat of social upheaval and wavered in their support. Meanwhile the nervous and resentful khedive continued to intrigue against Arabi but did not dare to confront him openly, and Sultan Abdul Hamid maintained his policy of giving both sides the impression that he supported them.

As Egyptian national feelings hardened, so too did those of the British and French governments and their representatives in Egypt. The latter reported that the country was dissolving into anarchy, although this was far from being the case – Egypt was effervescent but not in chaos. Members of the British cabinet, preoccupied by a state of near rebellion in Ireland, convinced themselves that native Egyptians were incapable of governing themselves – only the Ottoman Turks were considered a natural governing race – and that vital British interests were at stake. Even Gladstone – anti-imperialist and notoriously anti-Turk – accepted this view. Later he told the House of Commons, 'It has been charitably believed, even in this country, that the military party was the popular party, was struggling for the liberties of Egypt. There is not the smallest rag or shred of evidence to support that contention.' This blatant untruth was an apparent attempt to satisfy his conscience.

Still hoping for Turkish intervention, although under Anglo-French supervision, Britain and France sent a powerful joint naval force which stood off Alexandria. Shortly afterwards an event took place which seemed to justify all the fears of the alarmists: a major riot in Alexandria left several hundred killed or injured, including some fifty Europeans. Relations between Europeans and Egyptians had certainly deteriorated as the oratory of Muslim shaikhs whipped up national feeling and every European came under suspicion of hoping for a European invasion, but that the riot had been instigated by the military, as European officials on the spot at first claimed, was highly improbable if only because it would have provided justification for European occupation. In fact the rioting started with a brawl and then spread, but it was the presence of the Anglo-French squadron which inflamed the situation. The action of the interventionists was self-justifying. Fearful Europeans evacuated Alexandria in thousands.

The attitude of the British government was now harder than that of the French. British suspicions that De Freycinet was planning a secret deal with Arabi were confirmed when the French premier refused a British proposal for Anglo-French protection of the Suez Canal on the ground that the only danger to the Canal came from outside intervention. When, on 19 July 1882, the British admiral issued an ultimatum to Arabi that Alexandria would be bombarded unless he dismantled the fortifications he was erecting around the city, De Freycinet withdrew the French fleet. A joint Anglo-French invasion of Egypt no longer remained a possibility.

The cabinet council, presided over by the khedive and attended by the sultan's representative, decided it would be dishonourable not to reject the ultimatum. Both Tewfik and Abdul Hamid were still uncertain whether Arabi's forces could resist and were hedging their bets. The British fleet bombarded Alexandria for ten hours, destroying all the forts and part of the city. Arabi evacuated his forces, leaving Alexandria in flames.

Sultan Abdul Hamid at last accepted the principle of sending Turkish troops to restore order, but he still prevaricated as he bargained with the British ambassador about the terms under which he would intervene. As he had not abandoned all hope of appearing to the Egyptians as their protector against the infidel, he failed to declare Arabi a rebel. Arabi still enjoyed popular support in the country and was maintaining a reasonable degree of order and security.

Meanwhile the mood in Britain was becoming increasingly jingoistic. Gladstone and some of the cabinet were still against invasion, fearing the consequences. France and the other European powers were not unhappy with the bombardment of Alexandria but they were totally opposed to any unilateral British occupation of Egypt. In the end the imperialists in the cabinet, supported by the British public, prevailed. Gladstone's request for funds for an expeditionary force was overwhelmingly endorsed by the House of Commons. He justified his action by claiming that Arabi and his followers were anti-Christian militarists who cared nothing for the liberties of the people. The insecurity of the Suez Canal was only a symptom, for 'the seat of the disease is in the interior of Egypt, in its disturbed and its anarchical condition.'

Arabi was no great military leader and he was dilatory in manning Egypt's defences – partly because he still believed that Britain would come to terms. Also he honestly believed that Britain would respect the neutrality of the Suez Canal, and he accepted the urgent appeals of the aged de Lesseps that he should do the same. He failed to cover his eastern flank. British warships appeared at Port Said and Suez and closed the Canal. Arabi's 10,000 regular troops and a rabble of hastily recruited *fellahin* were no match for the 30,000 troops of the British expeditionary force. At the battle of Tel el-Kebir, on 13 September 1882, the Egyptians were surprised and routed. Ten thousand Egyptians were lost, compared with the fifty-seven British dead and twenty-two missing. The British commander wrote in his official report on the battle, 'I do not believe that in any previous period of our military history have the British Infantry distinguished itself more than upon this occasion.'

British troops occupied Cairo. Arabi and his associates surrendered, and the khedive's authority was formally restored as the council of ministers made submission. In a laconic decree, Tewfik announced that the Egyptian army had been disbanded. But it was not possible to return to the previous *status quo*; for all his failings, Arabi had permanently changed Egypt through his unsuccessful movement. For the first time, a subject oriental people had attempted to throw off the domination of a privileged minority to establish its own form of constitutional representative government in defiance of the European powers. As one of his admirers, General Gordon, remarked, 'He will live for centuries; they will never be "your obedient servants" again.'

The fact that most of Arabi's former political allies now deserted to the khedive could not disguise the reality that the khedive was now a British puppet. The national party had been destroyed, but his real authority had gone with it. He was not even allowed to shoot Arabi without trial as a rebel: Britain insisted that the colonel should have a fair trial, and his costs were paid for by liberal-minded British sympathizers. (He was eventually sentenced to exile in Ceylon, where he spent eighteen years.)

Britain now faced a dilemma. Despite dark French and Ottoman suspicions that it had always intended to seize control of the Suez Canal and the Lower Nile, Britain knew that the acquisition of Egypt and its incorporation into the empire was out of the question. For one thing it would almost certainly have provoked a European war for which the British government, with its small army and its continued preoccupation with Irish affairs, was quite unprepared. A month after Tel el-Kebir, in response to a question in the House of Commons as to whether Britain contemplated an indefinite occupation of Egypt, Gladstone replied, 'Undoubtedly, of all things in the world, that is a thing which we are not going to do.' On the other hand, immediate evacuation was also out of the question, as the puppet khedive's regime could hardly have survived and vital British interests were at stake. The Gladstone government sent Lord Dufferin, a sophisticated statesman (a former governor-general of Canada and a future viceroy of India), to Cairo to recommend a solution. He roundly concluded that 'The Valley of the Nile could not be administered from London as it would arouse the permanent hatred and suspicion of the Egyptians.' He rejected both direct rule as in the colonies and indirect rule through a British resident as in the princely states of India. But Dufferin's own well-intentioned solution was vague: it was a matter of persuading the Egyptians that all Britain wanted was to help them to govern themselves 'under the uncompromising aegis of British friendship'.

In the end the Egyptians got neither direct nor indirect rule but a unique and curious hybrid. Egypt was not incorporated into the empire but it became the most important link in Britain's imperial system – a situation which lasted until the Second World War. British power in Egypt was overwhelming, but it always had to be exercised with apparent restraint. For one thing the other European powers, led by France, were bitterly jealous of Britain's control of the Nile and the Canal and retained important rights. Anglo-French dual control was abolished but the Caisse of Public Debt, the Capitulations and the international status of the Canal remained.

The person chosen to manage this unprecedented type of relationship between two countries was Evelyn Baring, who had returned to India after his first service in Egypt on the Caisse but was now brought back with the misleadingly modest title of British agent and consul-general in Egypt. Despite his unusual position, Baring – later Lord Cromer – was to become the archetype of the British imperial proconsul at the zenith of the empire. He was upright and dedicated, if quietly arrogant (being nicknamed 'over-Baring'). His genuine sympathies for the Egyptians – especially the *fellahin* – were always patronizing. In his twenty-four years as the real ruler of Egypt, he never learned any Arabic (leaving that to his oriental secretary). He had no love for Egyptian nationalists who believed that their people were capable of governing themselves. He acquired extraordinary influence in London – British foreign secretaries came and went, but Cromer remained.

When Cromer (as he will now be called) arrived in 1883, he believed he could set up a stable regime with British advisers which would make it possible for British troops to be withdrawn – provided the British government could end all interference by other European powers. But this was quite impractical, as he soon realized. Moreover, Egypt was under serious military threat from the south. Muhammad Ali's quasi-empire in the Sudan had remained under Turco-Egyptian rule for some sixty years until in 1881 it was destroyed by a rebellion under the inspired politico-religious leadership of Muhammad ibn Abdullah – 'the Mahdi'. Egyptian garrisons were overwhelmed and then in the spring of 1883, just as Cromer was arriving in Egypt, an entire Sudanese-Egyptian force led by British officers was wiped out by the Mahdi's troops. Egypt itself was under threat.

The Gladstone government was now fully aware of what it had taken on in Egypt. Britain had not only to stabilize the regime but also to protect it. There was no question of recovering the Sudan from the Mahdi with the forces available so, with Cromer's approval, an evacuation policy was forced on the reluctant khedive and his ministers. Cromer did not, however, approve of the government's decision to send the eccentric General Gordon to oversee the orderly evacuation of the remaining scattered Egyptian garrisons. This had huge public support in Britain – Gordon was a popular hero who had served in various parts of the empire as well as acting as governor-general of Sudan in the time of Ismail, vainly attempting to put down the slave trade. 'Chauvinists and humanitarians', in Cromer's words, now combined to pursue a more forward Sudanese policy. As Cromer had suspected, when Gordon was appointed, rather than carrying out the evacuation policy, he stayed on in beleaguered Khartoum in the belief that he could come to terms with the Mahdi and end his rebellion. A relief expedition from Egypt failed to reach him in time, and in January 1885 Khartoum was overwhelmed by the Mahdist forces and Gordon was speared to death on the steps of Government House.

The Mahdi himself died during the siege, but Sudan now came under the rule of his successor, the Khalifa, for thirteen years until it was slowly and painfully recaptured by an Anglo-Egyptian army under General Kitchener.

The Sudanese question was now temporarily shelved. The Mahdist forces were unable to penetrate Upper Egypt, as had been feared. The British troops in Egypt, who had begun to reorganize the Egyptian army, were capable of seeing to the country's defence, but there could be no question of their immediate withdrawal. However, the British government – now led by the cool and calculating Tory Lord Salisbury – was still prepared to try to reach an agreement with the sultan and the European powers which would allow a British evacuation within a few years provided Britain's interests were safeguarded. Salisbury sent Sir Drummond Wolff as his representative to Istanbul to negotiate with the Sultan, and Wolff and the sultan's envoy went to Egypt to arrange a settlement which would allow the British troops to withdraw from Egypt 'in a convenient period'. But the other powers, led by France and Russia, were bitterly opposed to Salisbury's insistence that Britain should have the right to return to Egypt whenever it pleased. As Sultan Abdul Hamid characteristically prevaricated, Salisbury's attitude hardened. While he continued to give priority to the maintenance of a European balance of power, he foresaw the coming scramble for Africa and also Egypt's crucial importance as both the gateway to India and the outlet of the Nile. While he had not abandoned the belief he had inherited from Disraeli that the survival of the Ottoman Empire was the best protection against Russian encroachment in the eastern Mediterranean, he was beginning to look on it as fatally diseased and to consider Egypt as a substitute.

In May 1887 Wolff and the Turkish envoys provided for the evacuation of the British garrison, leaving Egypt a neutral territory. However, Article 5 of the draft Anglo-Turkish Convention stipulated that British troops would not withdraw 'if there was any appearance of danger in the interior or without'. Abdul Hamid was faced with a dilemma. If he ratified the Convention it would set a precedent for other powers to occupy parts of his empire and then claim the right of re-entry before leaving. If he refused to ratify it he would in effect be abandoning even his nominal suzerainty over Egypt. In the event he decided to reject the Convention, and the most important part of the Arab world was lost to his empire.

Cromer was delighted with the sultan's decision – he felt he had managed to obtain a grip on Egyptian affairs and was restoring the country to solvency. As he characteristically wrote in his retirement, 'All history was there to prove that when once a civilized Power lays its hand on a weak State in a barbarous or semi-civilized condition, it rarely relaxed its grasp.' The British occupation of Egypt, which was to last seventy-four years, had happened almost by accident – it was neither planned nor foreseen. However, although Britain periodically affirmed its intention to withdraw (one calculation was that various ministers declared withdrawal to be imminent no fewer than seventy-two times during those years), the British came increasingly to take Egypt for granted. It was not coloured red on the map, but every British schoolboy somehow perceived that it was. It was inconceivable that Britain should give up control of the gateway to its empire in Asia and Africa.

However, as we have seen, Britain's control over Egypt was far from absolute. Annexation was out of the question as the European powers, led by France, had made clear that this could lead to war.

The Caisse of Public Debt and the Capitulations remained the instruments of international control over Egypt's finances. It was twenty-two years before the 1904 Entente Cordiale between Britain and France settled a number of outstanding differences between the two colonial powers in Africa and Asia (and also prepared the way for the Anglo-French alliance against Germany in the First World War). In particular, the Entente provided that Britain would renounce its rights and interests in Morocco (preparing the way for France's occupation of Morocco a few years later) while the French did the same for Egypt, accepting that no time-limit should be fixed for the British occupation. The Caisse of Public Debt was not abolished but its authority was much reduced.

Lord Milner, another great British imperial proconsul, called British rule in Egypt 'the Veiled Protectorate' – a system by which Cromer ruled from behind a screen provided by the khedive and his cabinet, whose members all had British advisers in their ministries. There were two main strands to Cromer's thinking: in politics he was an arch-imperialist, and in financial and economic matters he was a Gladstonian *laissez-faire* liberal. Fortunately, in Egypt the two ideologies were easy to combine. He had no belief that the Egyptians were capable of governing themselves, or ever would be. To use one of his own favourite phrases, they were a natural 'subject race', in contrast to the supreme Anglo-Saxon example of a 'governing race'. The Turkish aristocracy had the remnants of a capacity to rule, but its members were hopelessly decadent and corrupt. Like many of his colleagues, he had a patronizing affection for the hard-pressed *fellahin*, but he saw no point in training them to manage their own affairs – money spent on their education above the very lowest level was a dangerous waste. He had no doubt that Egypt would benefit from the europeanization of every aspect of life, although he realized with regret that this was impossible.

Egypt's commitments to repay Ismail's debts absorbed more than half its revenues, requiring the utmost financial prudence (which in any case fitted Cromer's Gladstonian principles). Fortified by his experience in India, Cromer believed in the thesis of John Stuart

Mill, which had been adopted by Gladstone, that taxation should be as low as possible, to allow money to 'fructify' in the pockets of the producing classes. Accordingly there were no tax increases (the public could hardly have borne them) with the significant exception that, on the free-trade principle, countervailing duties were imposed on the products of Egyptian industries to equalize their prices with those of foreign imports. This virtually wiped out the Egyptian tobacco industry.

Slowly and painfully the economy recovered, and by the 1890s the budgets were showing small surpluses. The mainstay of the recovery was the increase in the output of agricultural crops – principally cotton, but also cereals, beans and rice. This was greatly assisted by one of the only kind of public works that Cromer was prepared to countenance – irrigation. British engineers, most of them with previous experience in India, set about repairing the great Delta barrages and canals built under Muhammad Ali and Ismail and expanding the system. Their crowning achievement was the building of a new dam at Aswan in Upper Egypt. Completed in 1902 and raised further in 1907 and 1912, this saved vast quantities of water by evening out the flow of the Nile between the autumn flood season and the rest of the year.

Unable to reduce taxes, as they would have wished, Cromer and his advisers set about improving the lot of the *fellahin* by replacing the corvée with paid labour and preventing the use of the *kurbaj*. This was gradually achieved during the first decade of British rule.

There was no doubt that Egypt was now better administered than before. Government decisions were normally carried out; an effective and reasonably uncorrupt civil service was being created. One of the most important factors in this was that the British officials in the Anglo-Egyptian service were collecting the kind of statistical information without which effective government is impossible. In this respect Egypt was unique in the Ottoman Empire.

With the exception of a few Liberal and Radical MPs at Westminster, the British people, encouraged by the evidence of the tens of thousands of tourists who poured into Egypt every winter, had no doubt that the Egyptians should be wholly grateful for Cromer's efforts on their behalf. The reaction of the Egyptians was inevitably more various and complex. The khedive and his ministers, together with the Turco-Circassian ruling class from which they almost exclusively came, were happy that their power had been restored and that a radical nationalist upheaval had been averted. Their view was shared by those who had been temporarily swept by enthusiasm for the Arabi revolt. Shaikh Muhammad Abduh, the most important of Arabi's civilian supporters, decided to collaborate with the British occupiers when he was allowed to return from exile in 1884. He agreed to become a judge and began to work for the reform and modernization of Islamic education in Egypt. Cromer liked and respected him but felt that his task was impossible.

If the Egyptian ruling class temporarily accepted the presence of British troops, however, it was much less enthusiastic about what Nubar Pasha, the first prime minister after 1882, called the 'administrative occupation'. Nubar tried to retain Egyptian control over the civil police, but failed. His successor, Riaz Pasha, was equally unsuccessful in preventing European supervision of the legal system – European inspectors were appointed to the native courts. On both these matters Cromer was adamant. The truth was that inside every Egyptian, however much he had benefited materially from the British occupation, there was some degree of resentment against rule by a Christian European power. Inevitably, this resentment would grow over the years.

In the early years of the British occupation there was a remarkable growth in rural unrest and acts of brigandage. This both alarmed and mystified Cromer, who had a passion for good order. It was partly a grass-roots rejection of the occupation but it also reflected the breakdown of the traditional system whereby the *omdehs* or village mayors, appointed by the government, maintained law and order in the countryside in collaboration with the Islamic *qadis* or judges. Although the *omdehs* were sometimes arbitrary and cruel, they generally reflected the local viewpoint. It was a system that the *fellah* could understand.

It is true that European secularist principles of law had already been introduced into Egypt long before the British occupation. Muhammad Ali had started the process, which was extended by the introduction of the new Ottoman penal code, based on French law, in 1863. By 1880 the Islamic *sharia* law was confined to matters of personal status (divorce, inheritance etc.) and homicide. The trouble was that these principles were now being applied much more widely – to matters of government as well as law – under the aegis of a Christian colonial power. At least this was the theory.

In 1883 Lord Dufferin actually persuaded Tewfik to issue an Organic Law granting the right of universal suffrage to male Egyptians over twenty years of age. But Cromer saw to it that the elected legislative and provincial councils remained powerless. As we have seen, he had no faith in the capacity of Egyptians to govern themselves, and he considered representative institutions to be entirely unsuitable for the government of a 'subject race'.

Nor did Cromer believe there was any purpose in training an élite of native Egyptians to take over the higher executive positions – in fact, during his twenty-four years in Egypt, their numbers in the higher ranks of the government service actually declined, while those of Englishmen and other Europeans increased. Accordingly, he had little interest in the spread of education above the elementary level. From his experience in India he had concluded that the expansion of Western-style higher education manufactured a class of discontented and place-seeking demagogues who were divorced from their own people. As he wrote shortly before his retirement, 'I am doing all I can to push forward both elementary and technical education. I want all the next generation of Egyptians to be able to read and write. Also I want to create as many carpenters, bricklayers, plasterers etc., as I possibly can. More than this I cannot do.' Unfortunately, even these efforts were not very successful. On his retirement, about 1.5 per cent of the population was receiving primary education as compared with 1.7 per cent in 1873, and the vast majority remained illiterate.

Cromer reversed Muhammad Ali's and Ismail's policy of providing free education in state schools and colleges. His *laissez-faire* principles told him that it was not the state's duty to provide education, and this also accorded with his general aim to economize. The result was that higher education became the prerogative of the wealthy. Like the great majority of his British colleagues in Egypt, Cromer was unsympathetic towards proposals to establish a university, which he believed would foster dangerous nationalism. However, he did not interfere with the higher institutes of learning which had survived from Ismail's reign: the schools of medicine, engineering and law. Since the reformed Egyptian legal system was based on French law, the teachers in the law school were French and it was this, in the absence of a university, which became the focus of nationalism.

The obverse side of the neglect of education under Cromer was that there was no systematic attempt to impose English culture on Egypt in the manner in which the French aimed to produce a Gallicized élite in their North African possessions. The educational system was only partially and gradually brought under British control and Anglicized. Although the use of English inevitably became more widespread, and ambitious young Egyptians needed to acquire it, the Egyptian upper classes remained francophone. This was partly because of the limitations of the Veiled Protectorate and partly because Cromer would have regarded the effort to turn the native Egyptians into pseudo-Englishmen as futile; he had nothing but contempt for the few Egyptians who managed to acquire a university education abroad and became europeanized.

It was therefore natural that Cromer should make no attempt to interfere with the Islamic system of education which existed in the village *kuttabs* or Koranic schools and the *madrasas* attached to the mosques which served for secondary education. This would have provoked a most hostile reaction. Again the principle of *laissez-faire* served all his purposes. But while he respected the laws of Islam, he expressed the view that as a progressive social system it was a total failure. He often said that Egypt could never have a genuinely civilized society under Islam – the position of women alone making this impossible – but he had no wish to see Egyptians abandon their

religion. He felt that the europeanized Egyptian he so despised was
'generally an agnostic'. But while he sympathized with the efforts
of Muhammad Abduh – who had become grand mufti of Egypt
– to reform and modernize the education system at the great
al-Azhar mosque in Cairo, he was sure they were fruitless because
'reformed Islam is Islam no longer.'

Cromer's authoritarianism was so often negative rather than positive in its expression. He favoured *laissez-faire* rather than firm
government action. He considered that Egypt was a natural agricultural country and that the *fellah* was a good farmer – better than
his Indian equivalent – who with enough land and low taxation
would produce well. He considered Muhammad Ali's ambition to
turn Egypt into a manufacturing country as unrealistic, as it would
have required heavy protective tariffs and an expensive programme
of industrial training for Egyptians, to which he was naturally
opposed.

With prudent financial management Egypt was prosperous at
the turn of the century, and real *per capita* income was probably
higher than at any subsequent period. But this concealed some real
weaknesses. The level of dependence on a single crop – cotton – was
dangerous, and there were technical problems in overflooding from
irrigation through lack of drainage and a variety of cotton pests
which the parsimonious government was hesitant to tackle. Moreover, although Cromer hoped for the creation of a large class of
Egyptian small farmers who would act as a conservative bulwark to
society, only the most vigorous government action could have
prevented the new prosperity from accruing to those who were
already economically powerful – the big landowners – while the
fellahin sank deeper into debt. After twenty-four years of Cromer-
ism, 80 per cent of those who owned land in Egypt possessed less
than 25 per cent of the whole, while at the other end of the scale 1
per cent owned more than 40 per cent of the whole.

Egyptian nationalists would later claim that Cromer deliberately
planned to make Egypt a vast cotton plantation, producing cheap
raw material for the Lancashire cotton mills. But he had no such

conscious intention – to him this was a natural role for a 'subject race'. Moreover, although he would not have liked to admit it, he was in many respects continuing the policies of Ismail.

In 1892 Khedive Tewfik died and was succeeded by his 17-year-old son Abbas Hilmi, who was being educated in Europe. Cromer at first thought that Abbas would be as pliable as Tewfik, but he was intelligent and forceful – more in the mould of his grandfather Ismail than his father. Soon he attempted to assert himself by rejecting Cromer's choice of ministers and criticizing the standard of the British-trained Egyptian army. Since his succession coincided with the first new stirrings of nationalist feeling since the collapse of the Arabi revolt, Abbas began to see himself as leading a challenge to British rule. Cromer was thoroughly alarmed.

His fears were unnecessary. Abbas was hoping for help from Istanbul – Egypt was still nominally part of the Ottoman Empire. But, as usual, Sultan Abdul Hamid gave no more than verbal promises of support, as he was quite unprepared to risk his relations with Britain or the other European powers, which might have no love for the British occupation but equally had no wish to see any revival of Egyptian independence. Abbas had also hoped that the return to power of Gladstone's Liberal government in Britain would help him, because the Liberals professed greater understanding of Egyptian nationalism than the Tories. Unfortunately, Gladstone's foreign secretary was Lord Rosebery, a Liberal imperialist who gave his full support to Cromer. Seeing that he could be forced to abdicate, the humiliated Abbas capitulated. The Veiled Protectorate continued, with Cromer pulling the strings behind his screen.

When Abbas challenged the quality of the Anglo-Egyptian army, a furious Kitchener, its *sirdar* or commander-in-chief, threatened to resign. Since the army's dissolution in 1882, British officers had trained a new force of some 15,000 which included five black battalions of southern Sudanese tribesmen. (The cost was borne by the Egyptian budget, with an additional contribution towards the stationing of the British occupying troops.) The first purpose of the new army was to help defend Egypt's borders, but by 1892 both Cromer and the

British government had come to regard the reconquest of the Sudan as vital. Italy had penetrated Ethiopia and was threatening to gain control of the waters of the Upper Nile, and, as Cromer wrote to London, 'Whatever Powers hold the Upper Nile Valley must, by the mere force of its geographical situation, dominate Egypt.'

Reconquest began in 1895. Cautiously and economically, Kitchener's army, strengthened by 8,000 British troops, advanced up the Nile and finally routed the Mahdist forces outside their capital, Omdurman.

The difficult question arose as to the future status of the Sudan. The reconquest had been directed by Britain but it had been carried out in the khedive's name mainly by Egyptian troops at Egypt's expense. But there was no question of restoring the *status quo* of before the Mahdist revolt. In Salisbury's words, the British government had every intention of keeping 'a predominant voice in all matters connected with the Sudan'. The result was the decision to establish an Anglo-Egyptian condominium. Hailed as a masterpiece of British pragmatism, this worked reasonably well for some years. One advantage was that it prevented the system of Capitulations from being extended to the Sudan. But the theoretical equality of Britain and Egypt in the government of Sudan was no more than a façade: the higher levels of the administration were all in British hands, and the governor-general, who was appointed by the khedive on British advice, was always an Englishman. Egyptians had not abandoned their claim to rule Sudan and as they recovered their independence from Britain this became the most contentious issue between Britain and Egypt.

The nationalist renaissance in Egypt, on which Khedive Abbas had vainly hoped to capitalize, gathered strength in Cromer's last years, before his retirement in 1907. It found its leader in a slender and passionate youth named Mustafa Kamel, who, like several other nationalists, had studied law in Cairo and in France, where he had received encouragement for his views. Cromer was inclined to dismiss the nationalists as insignificant, and it was true that they had all the characteristics of salon intellectuals – powerfully eloquent but weak in practical proposals to meet the needs of ordinary Egyptians, from whose feelings they were divorced. These weaknesses were partly due to their style of education but also arose because the Veiled Protectorate denied them any prospect of taking a part in government.

The nationalists were also confused in their aims. Kamel was attracted to the pan-Islamic movement as the best weapon against the British occupation, and he received some secret encouragement and funds for his National Party from the sultan. But the illogicality of combining pan-Islamicism with Egyptian territorial nationalism was exposed in 1906 when Abdul Hamid, who was building a railway across Arabia to Medina, landed a force at the head of the Gulf of Aqaba and laid claim to the whole of the Sinai peninsula. Kamel and his party launched a vigorous campaign in his support. It was left to Cromer to insist that Sinai belonged to Egypt. His concern was to protect the Suez Canal from the Turks, but it was he rather than the nationalists who championed the cause of Egyptian territorial integrity.

Cromer allowed a free press to flourish in Egypt. He had a liberal streak, but principally he did not think that fiery nationalist editorials (Kamel founded his own paper in 1900) were a threat to his order. The ironic consequence was that there was greater freedom of the spoken and written word in Egypt than in the Arab Ottoman provinces. Two leading newspapers were founded in Cairo by Arab Christians from Syria.

The press was by no means exclusively anti-British, nor were all politically active supporters of Mustafa Kamel nationalists – some were more collaborators, who were doing well out of the British occupation and saw no advantage in bringing it to an end. But there were moderates to whom Cromer gave headmasterly approval as 'the Girondists of the Egyptian national movement'. These included Shaikh Muhammad Abduh, who died in 1905, and his spiritual disciples in the Umma or People's Party. They doubted Kamel's political judgement, especially during the Aqaba incident. Another moderate was Saad Zaghloul, a young lawyer. Cromer allowed him to become head of the newly created education department and, when Cromer left Egypt, warmly commended him as the ideal type of moderate nationalist. But Zaghloul was to become the representative of uncompromising nationalism and Britain's implacable enemy.

In 1906, despite Kamel's powerful charisma, his movement was losing ground. Then an event occurred which united the national feelings of all Egyptians. Although hardly momentous in itself, it was a turning-point in the British occupation and its effects may be compared with the effect on the Indian independence movement of the Amritsar massacre in 1919. At Denshawai, a small Delta village, a shooting-party of British officers was set upon and beaten by outraged *fellahin* who believed that the British were killing the pigeons which were the local staple diet. An officer who went for help died of concussion and heat-stroke. A *fellah* who tried to help him was found by a party of British soldiers who, assuming he had murdered the officer, beat him to death.

Cromer and his colleagues, backed by the British press, saw the incident as a symptom of the xenophobic fanaticism that was sweeping the countryside, fanned by the nationalists. Exemplary punishment was required. A special tribunal sentenced four to hang, seventeen more to prison or flogging. The sentences were carried out on the site, and the villagers were compelled to watch.

This was not an atypical act of colonial repression – the horrified reaction of educated Egyptians may be taken as a tribute to the general physical mildness of the British occupation. But the shock and outrage, even among those who had come to accept the British presence, gave a lasting impetus to the national movement. When Cromer retired in the following year, the silent Egyptian crowds watched him on his route to Cairo station from behind British troops with fixed bayonets.

Cromer's reputation remained high in Britain and his own self-congratulatory account of his achievements was generally accepted, although some close observers felt that he had become increasingly out of touch, surrounding himself with nonentities like any autocrat. In 1906 a reforming Liberal government had swept to power in Britain, however, and it was clearly time for a change.

The choice of successor fell on Eldon Gorst, a senior diplomat who had spent nearly twenty years in Egypt and, as financial adviser to the Egyptian government, had led the negotiations with France over the 1904 Entente Cordiale. Small, highly ambitious and academically brilliant, his outward sense of superiority concealed an inner lack of self-confidence. He lacked Cromer's presence but, unlike Cromer, he spoke excellent Arabic. He was not much liked by other Anglo-Egyptian officials.

Gorst was thrilled with his appointment. He wrote, 'Throughout the British Empire there is no place in which the occupant enjoys greater freedom of action than that of British Agent and consul-general in Egypt. The consul-general is *de facto* ruler of the country, without being hampered by a parliament or by a network of councils like the viceroy of India . . .' But, having stepped into Cromer's shoes, he felt that a change of direction was needed:

I wanted [he said] to render our rule more sympathetic to the Egyptians in general and to the Mohammadens in particular by preventing the British element riding roughshod over the Egyptians, by putting a check on the annual British invasion of new recruits, by giving great encouragement to the Egyptian official class, and last, but not least, by giving a more national character to the educational system.

Gorst was trying not to end the British occupation but to make it more acceptable and, by so doing, to subdue the nationalist ferment. To the fury of his British colleagues he set about reducing their powers in favour of the Egyptian *mudirs* (district officers) and he tried to blow life into the moribund provincial councils to act as the *mudirs'* advisers. But Gorst's principal strategy was to restore the authority of the khedive, which had been emasculated by Cromer. His rapprochement with Abbas allowed the khedive to replace the ministers who had been subservient to Cromer with others more to his liking. But the khedive was no democrat: he shared Gorst's aim of reducing the influence of the nationalists who challenged his authority. As happens so often, however, the modest degree of liberalization merely fuelled the nationalist demands. Agitation increased, and the press heaped an avalanche of abuse on Egyptian ministers as well as the English occupiers. Gorst found himself restoring the repressive press law of 1881 which Cromer had never found it necessary to use because he despised the native press and regarded it as a useful outlet for young Egypt to let off steam. In the countryside there was an alarming new crime wave which partly reflected the rebellious spirit of the nation. Gorst introduced a Relegation Law allowing suspected brigands to be imprisoned without trial in a new penal colony in the Kharga Oasis.

In common with not a few of the academically brilliant, Gorst lacked political imagination. His next error, in 1910, was to attempt to extend the Suez Canal Company's original ninety-nine-year concession, due to expire in 1968, by forty years in return for an annual share of the profits. He persuaded the shadowy general assembly to approve the Company's offer, but even this gathering of elderly and conservative notables was unable to accept something which so outraged Egyptian public opinion. The Canal Company was already regarded as a foreign 'state within a state'. Only one assembly member dared to vote in favour of acceptance. Gorst was obliged to let the matter drop.

Two days later Boutros Ghali, the Coptic grandee whom the khedive had chosen as prime minister, was assassinated by a young Egyptian nationalist. Ghali was unfairly regarded as a British stooge and, as minister of justice, he had presided over the Denshawai trial. When Gorst refused to reprieve him from execution, the assassin became a hero in the streets of Cairo.

Gorst's policies appeared to be in ruins, and there was uproar in Britain. Arthur Balfour, leader of the Conservative opposition in the House of Commons, used the occasion to deliver a philosophical address on the general unsuitability of self-government for 'orientals'. The former US president Theodore Roosevelt, who passed through Egypt on his return from an African hunting-trip, told the British to 'govern or get out'.

Although he did lack political flair, the well-intentioned Gorst was also unlucky and he faced the obstructive opposition of most of his British colleagues. His term of office began with a financial collapse and an acute recession. He might have recovered the situation if he had retained his energy and interest, but he was facing an agonizing death from cancer of the spine. In 1911 he had to go.

In some respects Kitchener, the hero of Omdurman, was the obvious successor. Deprived by the Liberal government of his ambition to become viceroy of India, where he had been commander-in-chief, he was glad to accept what he regarded as the almost equally important post of British agent in Egypt. He was soon entertaining visions of the annexation of Egypt to Britain, with himself as the first viceroy of Egypt and Sudan. He shared the dream of Cecil Rhodes – an Africa coloured red on the map from Cairo to Cape.

The British government warned that, while order must be restored, there must be no simple replacement of civilian rule by the military. Kitchener's style was much closer to that of Cromer than that of Gorst. He once again emasculated the role of the khedive, his old opponent. He restored the power of the British advisers and increased their numbers. His personal ascendancy – semi-regal in style – was even greater than that of Cromer, who expressed alarm from his retirement. The protectorate's veil had virtually been removed.

With a series of repressive measures, Kitchener succeeded in scattering the nationalists (whose morale had not recovered from Mustafa Kamel's premature death in 1908), but he did not rely merely on coercion. Like Cromer, he showed sympathy with the *fellahin*, but he took more practical steps to try to help them, attempting to familiarize himself with their problems in a series of quasi-royal visits to the countryside. He ordered the belated establishment of Egypt's first Ministry of Agriculture. He tried to tackle the problem of acute overflooding in the Delta by means of drainage, and that

of *fellahin* indebtedness with a new law which made it impossible
to recover in the courts any money lent to a *fellah* who owned less
than five *feddans* (a *feddan* being about one acre), that is 90 per cent
of all *fellahin* The economics of this measure were doubtful, as it
undermined the new Agricultural Bank which had been founded
to relieve the *fellahin* from the grip of the usurers. But it at least
temporarily raised the morale of the *fellahin*, who showed reasonable content with Kitchener's policies.

Having pacified the countryside – the Egypt which mattered in
the view of both Kitchener and Cromer – he felt he could ignore
the despised urban intelligentsia. In 1913 he even felt confident
enough to allow some constitutional changes, to satisfy both the
Liberal government at home and the moderate nationalists in Egypt.
A new partially elected legislative assembly was given some powers
over taxation and the right to interrogate ministers. This was a cynical exercise, because Kitchener had no more belief than Cromer or
Balfour in the value of representative institutions for orientals, but
he felt it would be a useful palliative and that those he dubbed the
'noisy extremists' would be excluded. But he was wrong. Saad
Zaghloul, now emerging as a truly intransigent nationalist, was
elected first vice-president of the new assembly. Zaghloul showed
himself a skilled parliamentarian and under his leadership the assembly so criticized and discredited government ministers that they
were delighted when the parliamentary session ended. The start of
the First World War before the next session was due to begin brought
the tentative exercise in constitutional government to an end.

Kitchener claimed credit for restoring order to Egypt, but later
experience shows that he was fortunate and his luck would not have
lasted. If it had not been for the war, which gave Britain the excuse
to clamp down on political activity, the new nationalist ferment
could not easily have been contained.

When the First World War brought Britain, France and Russia into
conflict with Germany and Austro-Hungary, Britain hoped that
Turkey would remain neutral and that Egypt could be kept out of the
war. Britain's sole strategic concern was the security of the Suez Canal.

When Turkey decided to join the Central Powers – Germany and Austro-Hungary – in November 1914, Egypt's status became a problem, for it was still nominally part of the Ottoman Empire. There were strong voices in the cabinet (in which Kitchener became minister of war) in favour of annexing Egypt and abolishing the Muhammad Ali dynasty. But the remaining British officials in Egypt demurred at the prospect of direct rule and, at a time when Germany was being accused of tearing up international treaties, the Foreign Office was opposed to breaking the countless undertakings not to annex Egypt.

The typical British compromise was to declare a protectorate, in December 1914, and simply to remove the figment of Ottoman suzerainty. The pro-Ottoman Khedive Abbas was conveniently on a European tour and was informed that he had abdicated. A replacement was found in his elderly and amiable uncle Hussein Kamel. There were still problems: Hussein Kamel could hardly be given the same title as his new suzerain King George V of England, so a compromise was reached on 'Sultan', to be addressed as 'Hautesse' instead of 'Majesté'. The new sultan died in 1917 and was replaced by his younger brother, Prince Ahmed Fuad. Fuad was not satisfactory, however – although no Anglophobe, he had been educated in Italy, where he lived with his exiled father Khedive Ismail, he spoke little Arabic and he made no attempt to hide his lack of sympathy for Egypt and its problems.

Still unresolved was the question of whether Egypt had become part of the British Empire and the Egyptians British subjects. Cromer, in retirement, considered that Egypt was now in the empire, but in fact the matter was left in abeyance. The protectorate declaration merely said that all Egyptian subjects 'will be entitled to receive the protection of His Majesty's government'. Egypt remained officially neutral, with Britain responsible for its defence, but Egyptians were expected to contribute to the war effort. Egyptian troops helped to defend the Suez Canal against the first and only Turkish attack. Over 20,000 Egyptians served in the camel transport and labour corps in Palestine and in France, and suffered heavy casualties.

The disadvantage of failing to annex Egypt was that Britain was unable to abolish the Capitulations and all the other international commitments. On the other hand, the fact that Britain never col--onized Egypt as France colonized Algeria meant that the eventual Egyptian independence was not bought at the cost of a long and bloody war.

The British remained ambiguous about the concept of an Egyptian nation – as did many Egyptians, although for different reasons. Cromer had described Egypt as a 'nondescript country'. Since a 'true Egyptian' was indefinable, an 'Egypt for the Egyptians' policy was nonsense. When Egypt ever achieved a self-governing body, he said, all the communities should have to have representation, and since the Europeans and Levantines (Italians, Greeks, Maltese etc.) – those whom Cromer called the 'Brahmins of Egypt' – contributed by far the most to the country's wealth, these should be represented out of proportion to their numbers. During the war, these ideas were codified by the British judicial adviser in a proposed constitution which would have given the British advisers and the foreign communities permanent control over all legislation. But by then such ideas were not only insensitive but quite unrealistic. The spirit of Egyptian nationalism, although forced underground during the war, emerged with renewed vigour when the war ended. The existence of an Egyptian nation became undeniable.

6. Turks and Arabs

Greek independence followed by the enforced Turkish withdrawal from most of the Balkans during the nineteenth century, caused the centre of gravity of the Ottoman Empire to shift inexorably eastwards. Because the sultan/caliph no longer ruled over millions of Christian Europeans, he was no longer a threat and a challenge to the powers of Europe. But he could aspire to leadership in Asia.

The shift towards Asia was increased by the loss of control over Arab North Africa, which had already achieved a large degree of independence. Algeria and Tunisia went to the French in 1830 and 1881. The great prize of Egypt, whose al-Azhar mosque/university underpinned the caliph's spiritual authority, was lost almost unnecessarily to the British in 1882. Tripoli, the last Ottoman foothold on the North African coast, was seized by the Italians in 1912, as Lord Kitchener in Cairo ensured Egypt's neutrality in the Turkish-Italian war.

However, Sultan Abdul Hamid still controlled the Arab heartland and the first great centres of Arab/Muslim civilization, from Mecca and Medina to Baghdad, Jerusalem, Damascus and Aleppo. Turkey controlled most of the hinterland of the Arabian peninsula — although the British had a colony in Aden, dominated the waters of the Persian Gulf and were establishing special treaty arrangements with the coastal shaikhdoms. Ironically, the opening of the Suez Canal had made it easier to send troops to re-establish the Ottoman Empire's hold on Yemen.

The Ottoman hold over this vast territory, with its plains, mountain ranges and river systems, varied in form and intensity. In many areas hereditary local dynasties, strengthened by their geographical remoteness in mountains and valleys, were allowed substantial autonomy in return for maintaining adequate forces, pacifying the surrounding countryside and collecting taxes. In some cases, as in northern Mesopotamia, they were needed to protect the empire's frontiers against the rival Persian Empire. In others, as in Mount Lebanon where they were indigenous rather than a Mamluke military caste, they were the most effective rulers because they had the loyalty of their people. But there were also large areas of steppe and desert which were dominated by powerful groups of nomadic tribes, such as the Shammar or Bani Sakhr, who could not be prevented from plundering the traditional trade and pilgrimage routes.

Life in the great cities was fairly stable and secure, but in the countryside it changed considerably and frequently according to the competence and authority of the local governors. It was into this variegated system that, from 1820 onwards, an attempt was made to introduce the reforms of the *Tanzimat* in order to centralize and streamline the administration of the state. The overall aim was to modernize and strengthen the empire in the face of the European threat.

Being based on an ideal rather than on reason, these reforms inevitably had indifferent results. They changed much over fifty years and they also disrupted. Since they introduced modern secular ideas, such as citizenship and universal equality before the law, they were opposed by the powerful religious authorities. They undermined delicate relationships which had stood the test of time between the many minorities which composed the Asian empire. Moreover, the disruption allowed the European powers, which were steadily increasing their economic influence throughout the Levant and Mesopotamia in the nineteenth century, to extend their political influence too. Two processes were therefore at work which were ultimately bound to conflict – Ottoman centralization and European penetration.

Mount Lebanon, with its large Maronite Christian population, provided the most suitable theatre for European intervention. The local rulers – the Shihabi emirs – had converted from Sunni Islam to become Maronites at the end of the eighteenth century. The outstanding Emir Bashir II played off the Maronite peasantry against the Druze peasantry and allied himself with the Egyptians during the period of Ibrahim Pasha's rule (1831–40).

When Ottoman rule was restored, the Shihabi princes were removed and, in the face of open Maronite/Druze conflict, Mount Lebanon was divided by the Ottomans, with strong encouragement from the European powers, into two administrative units – one for the Maronites and one for the Druze. Lebanon had its first government on a confessional basis. But this did not work. For one thing, the Maronites formed a majority in the Druze 'qaimaqamate'. Moreover, the whole region was in a state of disruption, as the traditional economy disintegrated under the invasion of Western products which began under Ibrahim Pasha.

The instability and tension increased until civil war broke out in 1860. The Druze landlords of Mount Lebanon wished to curb their Maronite tenants, who were increasing in numbers and wealth, and attacked and massacred them in thousands. This sparked off a wave of persecutions of Christians in other parts of Syria. France, which with varying degrees of encouragement from the Ottoman sultan had long regarded itself as the protector of its Maronite fellow-Catholics, landed troops in Beirut and invaded the Druze stronghold of the Shuf. A conference of European powers which had signed the Treaty of Paris following the Crimean War – which included the Ottoman Empire – met in Beirut to consider how Lebanon should be governed. The conclusion was the creation of the autonomous *sanjak* or province of Mount Lebanon, with a Christian governor chosen by the sultan from outside Lebanon and assisted by a Maronite-dominated council chosen on a confessional basis. This was to be under the protection of the six powers – Britain, France, Russia, Prussia, Austria and Italy.

Autonomous Lebanon covered only part of the present-day Lebanese Republic. It excluded Beirut, Tyre and Sidon on the coast and the Bekaa Valley to the east, and it was heavily dominated by the Maronites, who formed 90 per cent of the population. Although it prospered for the next half century, its creation was a first step towards undermining the *millet* system – the ancient network of

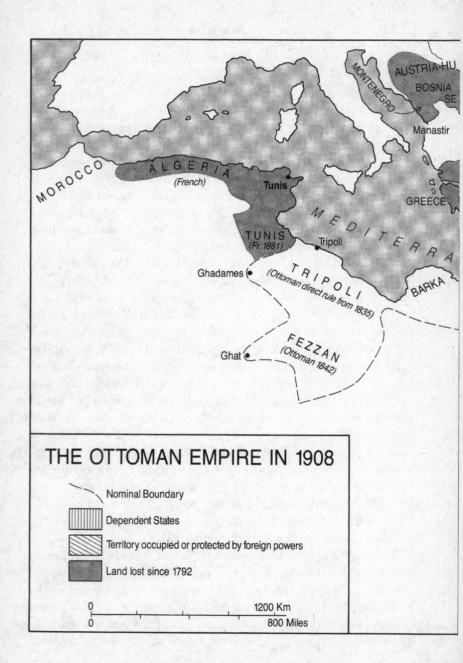

MONTENEGRO

AUSTRIA-HU

BOSNIA
SE

Manastir

MOROCCO

ALGERIA
(French)

Tunis

GREECE

M E D I T E R R A

TUNIS
(Fr. 1881)

Tripoli

Ghadames

T R I P O L I
(Ottoman direct rule from 1835)

BARKA

F E Z Z A N
(Ottoman 1842)

Ghat

THE OTTOMAN EMPIRE IN 1908

Nominal Boundary

Dependent States

Territory occupied or protected by foreign powers

Land lost since 1792

0		1200 Km
0		800 Miles

NGARY

RUMANIA

RBIA

BULGARIA

• Plevna

Sofia

• Seroz

• Edirne

Istanbul

Salonika

• Bursa

Ankara

• Sivas

Crete

• Izmir

• Kayseri

(Autonomous 1898)

• Aydin

• Konya

N E A N

CYPRUS

(Brit. Prot. 1878)

• Adana

Nizib

Aleppo

S E A

Beirut

•Damascus

Alexandria

•Jerusalem

Cairo

Suez Canal

EGYPT

(British Occupation 1882)

R U S S I A

BLACK SEA

CASPIAN SEA

• Trabzon

Erzurum

• Kars

P E R S I A

Baghdad

Basra

KUWAIT

(Brit. Prot. 1899)

AL HASA

D

HIJAZ

R E D

• Medina

• Mecca

Jedda

Suakin

S E A

ASIR

YEMEN

Massawa

• Sanaa

Aden

Source: Bernard Lewis, *The Emergence of Modern Turkey*, Oxford University Press, 1961 communities through which the religious minorities shared in the administration of the empire.

France was the chief patron of the Roman Catholics in the Arab Levant, and Russia of the Orthodox Christians. Britain was left as protector of the Druze and of the small community of Jews, who formed about 4 per cent of the people of Palestine. The unfortunate Armenians in the heartland of the empire lacked any effective outside patron. There were hardly any Protestant Christians in the empire, but American Protestant missionaries played a crucial role in the penetration of Western cultural influence. The founding in 1866 of the Syrian Protestant College – later the American University of Beirut – helped to stimulate alarmed French Catholics to found the Université Saint-Joseph in 1874. The two institutions would play a leading role in the cultural renaissance of the region.

In Palestine – the region known to the Christian West as the Holy Land, which in the twentieth century was to be given defined borders – European rivalries were peculiarly intense, as might be expected, but their effects tended to neutralize each other. Arab Christians were a minority, although a substantial one, and intercommunal relations between Muslims, Christians and Jews were generally harmonious. From the ending of Egyptian rule in Syria in 1840, the Ottomans were able to pursue their centralizing reforms of the *Tanzimat*. These meant reimposition of Turkish military control and the reduction of the powers of the local feudal lords, who had become virtually independent – levying their own taxes and fighting among themselves. The effects of the reforms were generally beneficial. Security improved, the population increased and the economy prospered. Jaffa became a household name in Europe through exports of oranges from the great plantations around it.

Although the direct power of the feudal families had been reduced, many of them were allowed to retain considerable influence. With economic progress and expansion, the trend was to increase the importance of the towns, and town councils were dominated by representatives of these families – Nimrs, Tuqans, Khalidis and Husseinis. Despite the centralizing policies of Istanbul, the Palestinian notables retained considerable freedom to manage their affairs. Jerusalem, because of its crucial importance, was in 1874 made an 'independent' *sanjak*, with the result that the governor of Jerusalem was directly answerable to the sultan in Istanbul.

It was not only in Palestine that improved security helped the economy to prosper as the population increased. In the vast plains of western and northern Syria, European late nineteenth-century travellers reported seeing limitless fields of golden corn where only a few years earlier had been barren waste.

The progress was not without setbacks, however. Even the lands of the ancient Fertile Crescent were dependent on an uncertain rainfall, and the 1870s saw a series of disastrous harvests. Ottoman bankruptcy affected the ability of the wealthier classes to invest. Finally, many able-bodied young Syrians and Palestinians were forcibly recruited into the Ottoman armies during the Russian and Balkan wars. However, by the 1880s the situation had improved. The Ottoman Empire had turned eastwards from the Balkans, and the coming of the railways vastly improved communications. Exports of silk, fruit and wool from Syrian ports steadily increased at the turn of the century.

Mesopotamia, or Iraq, remained the most backward and illgoverned of the Arabic-speaking provinces of the Turkish Empire. Its vast resources were left untapped. After 1831, when direct rule from Istanbul was reimposed under the *Tanzimat* reforms, the Ottoman *walis* or governors were unable to make much headway in pacifying the rebellious tribes and Kurdish hill-chiefs to settle the countryside and improve communication. The most was achieved by the enlightened Midhat Pasha, who arrived in 1869. He enforced conscription, founded municipal authorities and established schools and hospitals. He attempted to dredge the Shatt al-Arab waterway – the joint outlet of the Tigris and Euphrates rivers to the Gulf – and to open the Tigris and Euphrates to regular steamer navigation. But there was a limit to what he could do in the three years of his governorship. Baghdad, once the glory of the Golden Age of Islam, remained a squalid and impoverished city compared with Cairo, Aleppo or Damascus, which retained much of their former greatness.

In spite of Mesopotamia's poverty and backwardness, however, the powers of Europe were fully aware of its potential importance. In particular, Britain – which already dominated the waters of the Persian Gulf – saw it as the gateway to India and helped to establish telegraph and postal services linking Baghdad with Istanbul, the Gulf and India. Gradually it came to regard central and southern Mesopotamia as a British sphere of influence. But other powers were probing the region. France had an interest in Mosul in northern Mesopotamia; Russia looked towards the warm waters of the Persian Gulf; and, by the end of the century, imperial Germany, the sultan's new ally, had appeared on the scene.

Britain already controlled the waters of the Gulf and in 1861 it established a land base when it signed a treaty with the ruler of Bahrain to protect his island from external claims (from Persia and Turkey) in return for British suzerainty and the exclusion of all other powers. But from the mid nineteenth century the Ottomans set out to absorb into the empire and its reformed administrative system all the independent Arab principalities of Nejd (central Arabia) and the Gulf coast. Ottoman suzerainty had lapsed in this region since the withdrawal of the Turkish fleets in the seventeenth century. In 1819 the Egyptian forces of Muhammad Ali had conquered the Saudi/Wahhabi state in Nejd on behalf of the sultan, and Turco-Egyptian authority was extended to the coastal region of al-Hasa. But the Egyptian forces remained only until 1840, when Muhammad Ali's own quasi-imperial ambitions were cut short. The Saudi state, based on its new capital, Riyadh, revived.

A new opportunity for the Ottoman Turks arose in 1865, when the long and peaceful reign of the Saudi emir Feisal bin Turki came to an end and a violent feud over the succession broke out between his two sons. Midhat Pasha accepted the offer of vassaldom from one of them in return for Ottoman support, and in 1871 a Turkish force was dispatched by sea to establish garrisons along the Gulf coast. However, the principal result was thoroughly to alarm the

British government. Britain did not at this stage interfere in the internal affairs of the Arab shaikhdoms, but it had come to regard the Gulf as a British lake, and the reappearance of the Turkish navy in however modest a form was a cause for concern. The British-controlled government of India, which was especially involved, wondered whether the local Arab chiefs or the Persians might be stimulated into acquiring their own naval force to challenge British supremacy. But there was little need to worry: the Turks confined their attention to the mainland, and Britain strengthened its treaty with the ruler of Bahrain to forestall both Turkish and Persian ambitions.

The status of the emirate of Kuwait, with its great natural harbour at the strategic head of the Gulf, was a cause for concern. Since its foundation by the Sabah family from Nejd in the mid eighteenth century, it had grown and prospered as a pearling and trading centre under a succession of able rulers and it was a strong focus of British interest. However, the Sabahs were able to remain virtually independent in return for a nominal acceptance of Turkish suzerainty. It was only in 1899 that Britain finally accepted the request for formal British protection from the Kuwaiti emir, Mubarak the Great (1895–1916), and this was not to repel the Turks but to forestall the German plan to extend the Berlin–Istanbul–Baghdad railway to Kuwait. Under the Anglo-Kuwaiti Treaty, Mubarak accepted, in terms similar to other agreements with Arab Gulf rulers, not to 'cede, sell, lease, mortgage or give for occupation or any other purpose any portion of his territory to the government or subjects of any other power'.

The most prized of all the Arabic-speaking provinces of the Ottoman Empire was the Hejaz in western Arabia. It was the least developed economically, but it contained the Holy Cities of Islam – Mecca and Medina. Here Turkish control was maintained after the expulsion of the Wahhabis in 1811–19 but it was far from secure, even after the opening of the Suez Canal made it easier to dispatch troops from Istanbul. The Ottoman *walis* shared power with the prestigious Arab Grand Sharifs of Mecca, who by long tradition came from the Bani Hashem, the most noble of Arab clans, who traced their descent from the Prophet's daughter. Public order was badly maintained, foreign consuls were frequently murdered and the unfortunate Muslim pilgrims had little defence against marauding bandits.

As we have seen, Sultan Abdul Hamid, after the loss of most of his Christian subjects in the Balkans and the better part of his North African empire, determined to assert his leadership over what was still the greatest Muslim power in the world. He was prepared to make use of the *Tanzimat* reforms where they served his purposes in improving the administration of the outlying provinces, but the concepts within these reforms of the rights of citizens and equality before the law were even more distasteful to him than to his predecessors. He aimed at unfettered autocracy, but he pursued his aims by skilful diplomacy, intrigue and manipulation rather than brute force.

The Ottoman sultans in the eighteenth century had revived the title of caliph, and although it had little of its original meaning – the Prophet's successor and spiritual/political guide and leader of all Muslims – the world had generally acknowledged the title, as a form of diplomatic politeness. Abdul Hamid set out to assert himself as the sultan/caliph and world leader of Sunni Islam and to spread the doctrines of pan-Islam. This would serve the double purpose of strengthening his position within what was left of his empire and mobilizing its human resources against the increasing penetration by the Christian West. Unlike many of his predecessors, he was naturally pious and sober, and he emphasized these aspects of his court. He lavished money on mosques and Islamic foundations throughout the empire. He surrounded himself with the most learned Muslim scholars, and he established a missionary school to spread the news of Istanbul's rejuvenated faith and piety throughout the Muslim world.

Abdul Hamid had little need to worry about the loyalty of the mass of Anatolian peasants to their sultan/caliph, but his suspicious nature caused him to doubt the wholehearted acceptance of his leadership by his more numerous Arabic-speaking subjects. He became convinced that there was a movement to restore the Arab caliphate. There was little evidence for this. It was true that some non-Turkish Muslim thinkers in the empire blamed the last centuries of Ottoman domination for the current decadence of the Islamic world. Disciples of Jamal al-Din al-Afghani, like the Egyptian Muhammad Abduh and the Syrians Rashid Rida and Abdul Rahman al-Kawakibi, were passionately concerned with the revival and reunification of the Muslim *umma* or nation as a means of resisting the domination of the West and its ideas. They felt that this regeneration could come only through the Arabs among which Islam originated. But although these men founded newspapers and published pamphlets in Paris or Cairo (where they were under British protection), they were intellectuals rather than political activists.

Political dissent within the empire at that stage scarcely followed national/racial lines. The Egyptian nationalist leader Mustafa Kamel in the 1890s looked to the sultan as the natural leader of the pan-Islamic movement which he espoused against the British. Arab resentment and hostility against the Turks was only beginning to stir; indeed, the term 'Arab' was still generally reserved for the semi-nomadic people of the Arabian peninsula. Men like Rashid Rida believed that it was in Arabia that the movement for the regeneration of Islam would have to start, and in fact the first practical effort to oust the Ottomans as unfit rulers of the Islamic homeland was made by the Saudi Wahhabi forces at the beginning of the nineteenth century. But they had been defeated, and their challenge was to be renewed only when the empire was on the point of collapse.

Sultan Abdul Hamid's fears and suspicions of subversion among his non-Turkish subjects caused him to pursue a twin-headed policy. He promoted some to high positions in his government and lavished gifts and hospitality on visiting Arab dignitaries; at the same time, he constantly intrigued to prevent local political leaders from becoming too powerful. When necessary, he encouraged rivalry and antagonism between clans and tribes. He kept himself informed through his vast network of spies and the new telegraph system, installed by French and British engineers, which reached the most distant provinces. Any potentially dangerous local leader or possible trouble-maker was eliminated, if necessary by force. One of these was Hussein Bin Ali, a member of the family of the Grand Sharifs of Mecca – that is, a Hashemite. Because of his eminence, he had to be treated politely. Accordingly, in 1893 Abdul Hamid issued him with an invitation which he could not refuse: to come to settle with his three small sons, Ali, Abdullah and Feisal, in Istanbul. Abdul Hamid's instinct was correct, for Hussein and his sons would become one of the principal instruments for the downfall of the empire.

The most outstanding of the Arabs whom Abdul Hamid promoted was the Syrian Izzet Pasha. In the later years of the sultan's reign he rose to a position of great power and influence in which he was the principal force behind the single most important instrument of Abdul Hamid's pan-Islamic policy – the building of the Hejaz Railway. This ran from Damascus to Medina, but a planned extension to Mecca was never completed. Built by engineers from the sultan's new ally Germany between 1901 and 1908, the railway cost some £3 million and, because it was presented as a supreme instrument of Muslim piety – to reduce the dangers and arduousness of the pilgrimage to Mecca – a third of the cost was raised by volunteer contributions from throughout the Muslim world, to which were added special taxes imposed in the empire. The project added immensely to the pious sultan/caliph's prestige as the leader of Sunni Islam, but it had the important additional political/strategic advantage of bypassing the British-controlled Suez Canal and making it possible to send troops from Syria to the Hejaz within a few days.

Despite all Abdul Hamid's efforts to secure the loyalty of the Muslim faithful, in the Arab provinces there were stirrings of opposition to Ottoman Turkish rule. Some local leaders or clans had specific cause for resentment when the sultan favoured their rivals, and there was more general dislike of his despotic and unprincipled methods of government. Among the Arab Christian communities centred on Maronite Lebanon there was especially powerful anti-Ottoman feeling, fostered by cultural and commercial contacts with the West, the spread of literacy and education and the knowledge of French protection. But precisely because Arab Christians were a minority and their resentment arose from their sense of holding permanent second-class status in the empire, there was no question of their combining forces with their Muslim fellow-Arabs in a movement of rebellion. The concept of an Arab nation was confined to a few intellectuals, while that of a common Ottoman citizenship based on the principle of equal rights, which had originated in the *Tanzimat* reforms, had made little headway under Abdul Hamid's pan-Islamic order. Religious loyalties were still much stronger than Western secularist ideas. Syrian Arabs did not think in terms of overthrowing the empire which had been the champion and protector of the Islamic *umma* for four centuries.

The real rebellion against Abdul Hamid came from a wholly different source, which lay much closer to Istanbul. The most genuine and effective body of reforms which Abdul Hamid had taken over from his predecessors was the improvement and expansion of civil and military education. This had produced a substantial new educated middle class. The Young Ottomans who wished to end the sultan's despotism were effectively scattered and suppressed in the first years of his reign, but their ideals survived and re-emerged towards the end of the century in a revolutionary movement known as the Young Turks. This spread rapidly among the students in the military, medical and law colleges in the capital and the provinces. Talaat Bey, a law student who was also chief clerk at the Salonika post office, and Rahmi Bey, a local notable, together with a few associates, founded a secret society which they called the Committee of Union and Progress (CUP) to emphasize the ideal of the unity and equality of all races and creeds within the empire. This ideal attracted the support of Freemasons and Jews, who came to play a leading role in the movement. Links were established with the Turkish exiles in Paris.

Although the Young Turks staged an abortive coup in 1896, this was easily suppressed. The sultan had little idea of the danger that threatened, and his spy network seems to have been less effective close to home. The revolutionaries were appalled by the sultan's mishandling of the affairs of Macedonia, the last substantial Ottoman province in Europe, and outraged by the empire's abject weakness in relation to the powers of Europe. In 1908, provoked by reports that Edward VII of England and Tsar Nicholas of Russia were planning the partition of Turkey at their meeting in Tallinn, army officers such as Enver Bey, Jemal Pasha and Mustafa Kemal (the future Kemal Atatürk) joined the new movement, bringing to it the command of military units in the Macedonian army. It was in the spirit of saving the fatherland that in 1908 the Young Turks raised the standard of revolt in Salonika, the Macedonian capital, which had become the headquarters of the CUP. The rebellion spread rapidly, even to the Albanian units which Abdul Hamid had regarded as securely loyal.

The Young Turks, led by Major Enver Bey, demanded the restoration of constitutional rule. Discovering that both the Shaikh ul-Islam – the senior religious authority – and a majority of his own ministers sympathized with the revolutionaries, Abdul Hamid was forced to give way. The short-lived constitution he had abolished forty years previously was restored.

On behalf of the Young Turks, Enver Bey proclaimed the end of arbitrary government and the principles of the new order: 'Henceforth we are all brothers. There are no longer Bulgars, Greeks, Romanians, Jews, Muslims; under the same blue sky we are all equal, we glory in being Ottomans.'

The announcement was received with wild popular rejoicing in Istanbul. The wily Abdul Hamid did not lack resource. Affecting enthusiasm for the liberal constitutionalism he had so speedily discarded after his accession, he reopened the parliament which had been closed for forty-one years. The crowds lining the streets cried 'Long live the constitution', but they also chanted 'Long live the sultan.'

The Arabs in Istanbul and the notables in the Arab provinces also welcomed the new era. They hoped that the declared spirit of racial equality would mean the end of Turkish domination and of the imposition of Turkish language and culture on the Arabs in the empire.

A brief Turco-Arab honeymoon ensued, but for several reasons it could not last. In the first place the spirit of Ottomanism enshrined in Midhat Pasha's constitution took no account of racial equality among Muslims. Enver Bey in his declaration had referred to 'Muslims' rather than Arabs or Turks. The electoral system ensured the massive predominance of Turks in parliament – where they numbered 150 out of a total of 243, compared with 60 Arabs – despite the fact that Arabic-speaking Ottoman citizens almost certainly outnumbered the Turks in the empire. Secondly, the army officers who had taken over the leadership of the Young Turks were no liberal democrats. Their professions of faith in unity and equality as the spirit of Ottomanism were not hypocritical, but they did not go deep. They detested Abdul Hamid's rule for its corruption and inefficiency rather than its despotism. Faced with his appalling legacy of misgovernment – the empty treasury, the relentless pressure of the European powers in the Balkans and later the Italian invasion of Libya, the last Ottoman province in Africa – the Young Turks had little time to apply the principles of constitutional freedom. Moreover, unlike the Young Ottoman intellectuals, they had no interest in political theories – their approach to government was practical and empirical and their overriding aim was to strengthen the empire's defences. If they paid tribute to the ideals of the French Revolution, it was because they believed that the slogans of 'Liberty, Equality and Fraternity' had welded the people of France into the potent force which overwhelmed the Revolution's enemies. The citizens of the Ottoman Empire would no doubt behave similarly.

Their immediate problem was an attempt at counter-revolution. While avowedly accepting the new constitution, Abdul Hamid secretly encouraged the disgruntled and reactionary elements who opposed the new order. In April 1909, troops of the Istanbul garrison mutinied, massacred their officers and raided parliament. When Abdul Hamid pardoned the leaders of the revolt and formed a new cabinet, the Young Turks sent an army from Salonika to restore order, punish the insurgents and restore the authority of the CUP. Three days later parliament met and announced the abdication of Abdul Hamid. His brother Reshad was proclaimed sultan, with the title of Mohammed V. This mild and self-effacing 64-year-old was quite prepared to accept the role of constitutional monarch.

The CUP wisely decided to spare Abdul Hamid's life, and he was interned in a private villa in Salonika. His former subjects have extraordinarily mixed impressions of his long reign. For Turks, the record of the modernizing reforms he achieved in some limited areas is outweighed by his inability to prevent the final humiliation of the House of Ottoman which had once been a great European power. But a different impression has remained among the non-Turkish Muslims in the empire. In some cases they were peoples or tribes whom he had favoured over their rivals – Kurds against Armenians, Sunnis against Shiites in Mesopotamia. But over a longer period it is the record of his pan-Islamic policies which has survived. It matters less that these were often used to further his despotic ends than that he is seen as the last ruler to champion the cause of the Islamic *umma*. In the late twentieth century, Arabs will almost invariably refer to the fact that it was Sultan Abdul Hamid who refused the request of the Austrian Dr Theodor Herzl, the founder of political Zionism, to lease part of Palestine as a national home for the Jews. In fact Abdul Hamid was inclined to accept the request in return for substantial loans from international Jewry, but he was persuaded by his ministers that this would be disastrous for his pan-Islamic policies and his prestige among his Arab subjects. It is the sultan's refusal which is remembered.

If in 1908 there were scarcely any Arabs who thought of separation from the Turkish heart of the empire which remained the sole protector of Sunni Islam, there were undoubtedly many who hoped for decentralization, autonomy for the Arab provinces and the acceptance of Turco-Arab equality. The Young Turks, on the other hand, did not so much insist on Turkish domination as take it for granted. It was only when they felt threatened by increased national feeling among the remaining non-Turkish elements in the empire

– Greeks, Armenians and Kurds as well as Arabs – that they turned to a specifically Turkish nationalism. In its narrower form this aimed at the consolidation of the Turkish nation within Anatolia (or approximately the borders of the present Turkish Republic). But there was also a wider movement – the pan-Turanian – of which the ideologist was the writer Zia Gokalp. This called for the union of all Turkish-speaking peoples, including those of central Asia where the Turks had originated. Although the CUP did not formally adopt the pan-Turanian programme, the concept was highly attractive to some of its leaders such as Enver Bey. Romantic and historically dubious in its expression, it was essentially racist. It was also anti-Islamic, in that it called for a return to an era before the Turks adopted Islam.

The dominant outlook in the CUP was therefore secular and nationalist, rather than pan-Islamic. Most of its leaders were Freemasons, and they were closely associated with the Jews of Salonika, who played an important role in the Young Turk movement. But this did not mean that they were either able or willing to abandon the empire's role of leadership of the Islamic world which, after four centuries, was still acknowledged by both its Christian and its Muslim subjects.

Talaat Bey recognized the problem that this presented for the Young Turks' objective of an empire which would be both centralized and 'ottomanized' to a far greater degree than under Sultan Abdul Hamid. In a secret speech to the Salonika CUP in August 1910, he said that, while the constitution provided for equality of 'Mussulman and Ghiaur [i.e. non-Muslim]', they all knew that this was an unrealizable ideal.

The Sheriat [i.e. *sharia*], our whole past history and the sentiments of hundreds of thousands of Mussulmans and even the sentiments of the Ghiaurs themselves, who stubbornly resist every attempt to ottomanize them, present an impenetrable barrier to the establishment of real equality. We have made unsuccessful attempts to convert the Ghiaur into a loyal Osmanli and all such efforts must inevitably fail, as long as the small independent States in the Balkan Peninsula remain in a position to propagate ideas of separatism among the inhabitants of Macedonia.

These independent states – Greece, Serbia and Bulgaria – were indeed afraid that an Ottoman Empire rejuvenated by the Young Turks might try to recover its hold over the Balkans. Without any encouragement from the European powers – except for Russia – they formed a secret alliance, and in October 1912 they launched a war against Turkey. By December, they had seized Salonika and western Thrace, forcing the CUP to move its headquarters to Istanbul. The Turkish army retreated to lines defending the capital. When the Balkan allies fell out over the division of the spoils and fought each other, Turkey was able to recover a portion of Macedonia and the key city of Edirne, but Crete and most of the Aegean islands were ceded to Greece. Turkey's role in Europe had almost been eliminated.

The Young Turks did not expect ottomanization of the empire's Muslim subjects to present the same problems. The trouble was that, for them in their newly invigorated spirit of Turkish nationalism, ottomanization really meant 'turkification'. (It hardly needs to be said that pan-Turanian ideas were unlikely to appeal to Ottoman Arabs.) Turkish had always been the language of Ottoman officialdom, but Arabic held its place among the mass of Ottoman Arabs. As the language of religion, Arabic was also predominant in education. The Young Turks now aimed to turn the heterogeneous empire into a nation with a single language. Turkish was made a compulsory subject in every school. It was required to be used in the law courts, and even the street names in the cities were turned into Turkish, although it was incomprehensible to the vast majority of the population in the Arab provinces.

The result of these turkification policies was a profound stimulus to the consciousness of their Arabism among the Ottoman Arabs. This was still a long way from the secular Arab nationalism which emerged later: it was rooted in their pride in Arabic as the language in which God spoke to the world through the Prophet, and in the unique place of the Arabs in the history of Islam. This Arab awareness had been submerged but in no way eliminated by the acceptance of Turkish political and military leadership during many centuries.

One of the Arab responses to the concept of a Turkish master race was the founding of various societies or parties dedicated to the protection of Arab rights and the achievement of Arab autonomy within the empire. In Beirut, Baghdad and Basra these societies had to remain underground, but the most important of them – the Young Arab Society or al-Fatat – was established by a group of Arab students in Paris, and this secretly gathered support throughout the Arab provinces.

Within the empire, the Arab leader who was best placed to challenge Ottoman domination was the Grand Sharif of Mecca. As custodian of the holy places of Islam and supervisor of the Muslim *hajj* or pilgrimage, he was hardly a subject for 'turkification'. The powers in Istanbul had to treat him with a certain respect. The post was now occupied by Hussein Bin Ali, the troublesome member of the hereditary sharifian Hashemite family whom in 1893 Sultan Abdul Hamid had 'invited' to settle in Istanbul, where his activities could be kept under observation. As a gesture of goodwill during the brief Turco-Arab honeymoon after the 1908 revolution, the CUP appointed him Grand Sharif, ignoring the shrewd warnings of Sultan Abdul Hamid. They soon had cause for regret. Now in his mid-fifties, the venerable, white-bearded Sharif Hussein was powerfully ambitious. His mild and courteous manner concealed a will of steel which sustained his sense of his own destiny. But he was also naturally cautious, and he did not immediately cause trouble with the Turks. He even conducted a successful expedition on their behalf to suppress a rebellion in the Asir province of southwestern Arabia. In return, the Ottoman government encouraged him to extend its authority into the interior. This involved him in conflict with a formidable Arab rival – the House of Saud – which would cause the downfall of his Hashemite family in Arabia, just as the Hashemites would be the instrument for the overthrow of Turkish rule in the Arab provinces of the empire.

The House of Saud had recovered from its internal divisions in the 1860s, which had allowed the Turks to occupy eastern Arabia, but had then suffered defeat at the hands of its long-standing rivals in northern Nejd, the Rashids. In 1891 Abdul Rahman, the head of the House of Saud, was forced to flee from Riyadh and take refuge with the emir of Kuwait. He was accompanied by the eldest of five sons, the ten-year-old Abdul Aziz, commonly known by his patronymic Ibn Saud, who was to prove to be one of the outstanding figures in the modern history of the Middle East.

By the time he reached manhood, Ibn Saud dominated his companions with his physical presence and personality. In 1902 he succeeded in recapturing the Saudi capital of Riyadh with a tiny force, and he set about restoring the former Saudi/Wahhabi state. Rashidi power was in decline; he reconquered Nejd and in 1913 went on to occupy the eastern Arabian province of al-Hasa, which had been barely held by the Turks. He was recognized by Britain as 'Sultan of Nejd and its Dependencies', but he could not go further as the entire Persian Gulf coast from Kuwait to Oman was under Britain's exclusive influence.

In western Arabia, he suffered a setback. Sharif Hussein succeeded in taking Ibn Saud's favourite brother, Saad, hostage and Ibn Saud was forced to accept a nominal Ottoman suzerainty in order to ransom him. He swore revenge against the Hashemites.

Sharif Hussein, having made himself indispensable to the Turks, set about asserting the rights and dignity of his office against the Ottoman *wali* of the Hejaz. But he was looking further – to making the Hejaz an autonomous Arab province which could then be the nucleus for the independence of all the Arab provinces within the empire.

Hussein's sons, by now grown to manhood, shared his ambitions. Abdullah, the second and cleverest, was deputy for Mecca in the new Ottoman parliament, and he caused the CUP the greatest suspicion. They tried to win him over by offering him the post of governor-general of Yemen, where Ottoman authority had recently been reasserted, but he cannily refused. Less cautious than his father, in February 1914 he visited Cairo to sound out the British agent, Lord Kitchener, and his oriental secretary, Sir Ronald Storrs, on the possibility of the British government supporting his family's ambitions on behalf of the Arabs. But although Britain by this time did not see how war with its great rival imperial Germany could be avoided, it did not see an Ottoman alliance with Germany as inevitable. The traditional policy of regarding the survival of the Ottoman Empire as favourable to British interests remained. Kitchener was therefore non-committal to the point of being discouraging, and Abdullah came away disappointed.

After Sultan Abdul Hamid's unsuccessful counter-coup in 1909, the CUP were in sole command in the empire and free to pursue their illiberal and centralizing policies. They at once prohibited the formation of political associations based on ethnic or national groups and closed down minority clubs and societies. They made much wider use of the death penalty than Abdul Hamid would have considered. The CUP's policies did not, however, go unchallenged. In the Young Turks movement there had always been a different, liberal, tendency which favoured decentralization of power and saw ottomanization not as the imposition of Turkish political and cultural dominance but as the creation of a pluralist and multi-denominational empire in which the autonomous rights of the religious and national minorities would be respected. In its most explicit form, this tendency was represented by the Ottoman Decentralization League of Prince Sabah al-Din, a nephew of Abdul Hamid, who had gone into exile in Paris to escape his uncle's despotism. With his programme for the devolution of power to autonomous provinces under the Ottoman flag and for protection of the Ottoman army, he appealed to Arabs as much as to liberal Turks. Branches of his League sprang up throughout the empire. It was dissolved as subversive by the CUP shortly after the 1908 revolution, but it continued to survive underground and in 1912 it emerged as the Ottoman Administrative Decentralization Party, which was formed in Cairo under British protection by a group of prominent Syrian *émigrés*.

Although the Prince's League was suppressed by the CUP, there were many more in the new Ottoman parliament who favoured both constitutional government and some degree of decentralization. They feared that the CUP was proving even more despotic in its methods than Abdul Hamid. They received support from respected liberal elder statesmen from the Hamidian era.

All these groups and individuals combined in 1911 to form a single opposition front: the Liberal Union. This soon demonstrated that it had widespread popular support. The CUP acted promptly by dissolving parliament and using all means of pressure in the subsequent election – known as the 'big-stick election' – to ensure that out of 275 members only six belonged to the opposition.

This high-handed action only provoked a more dangerous opposition to the CUP from within the armed forces. A group called the 'Saviour Officers' demanded the withdrawal of the army from politics and, with the support of Albanian units, used threatening troop movements to carry out a bloodless coup which forced the resignation of the CUP-controlled government and its replacement by one led by the veteran liberal Kamel Pasha.

The liberal interregnum lasted only a few months. The Balkan war was reaching its most disastrous stage, with the enemy at the gates of Istanbul. It was the occasion for the CUP to recover power. On 23 January 1913, Enver Bey and a group of officers forced their way into the cabinet room and shot dead the minister of war. A CUP government was restored, and Turkish liberalism went underground for a long period.

The empire was now effectively ruled by a triple dictatorship of Enver, Talaat and Jemal Pashas. Enver, the youngest of the three, was brave, vain and flamboyant – still the popular hero of the Young Turks. He commanded adoration in the army and concentrated on the revival and improvement of the Ottoman military forces, whose morale was at a low ebb following the Balkan disasters. His admiration for the military power of Germany, which was helping to train the Ottoman army, made him the most pro-German of the triumvirate. In contrast to Enver, Jemal Pasha was cool and calmly self-assured, but his aristocratic politeness concealed a streak of coarse ruthlessness. Talaat, the only civilian, was the ablest and most intelligent – a man of ideas. He was charming and humorous, but quite uncompromising in his fierce Turkish patriotism.

By 1914 the CUP had been in charge of the empire for barely six years. The liberal interregnum had been too brief to affect its policies. In the Arab provinces these had caused a serious deterioration in Turco-Arab relations, but in the Turkish homeland there were some substantial achievements of the kind that are often associated with effective modernizing dictatorships which are little concerned with constitutional liberties. Provincial and municipal government were greatly improved; the cities were made cleaner and safer and public transport was organized. Javid Pasha, the brilliant finance minister, of Jewish origin, was able to do little to ease the empire's burden of foreign debt – especially as costly wars were being fought – but he successfully reformed the tax system to improve revenues. (The CUP failed in its efforts at liquidating the Capitulations; that had to wait until Turkey joined the Great European War.)

Perhaps the Young Turks' greatest achievement was in expanding education. Building on the efforts of the nineteenth-century reformers, they went much further in creating a modern progressive system at all levels, with new teacher-training colleges and specialized institutes. They were the first rulers of an independent Muslim country to create a state education system which was open to girls; previously the daughters of only the wealthiest classes had been educated, privately. The way was opened for Turkish women to enter public life as lawyers, doctors and administrators.

Enver Bey's degree of success in rejuvenating the Ottoman armed forces is difficult to evaluate. The armed forces were of enormous size; one million men were under arms when the Young Turks came to power, and this number was increased by the introduction of military conscription. But it was the raising of military standards and the modernization of weapons which were most required. The German general Liman von Sanders was appointed inspector-general of the Ottoman army, and the British admiral Sir Arthur Limpus was given the task of reorganizing the navy. When war came,

Turkey's opponents, who had never doubted the courage of the Turkish soldiers, certainly found them better prepared for modern warfare than they had expected.

In its foreign policy the CUP was by no means unresourceful. The overriding aim, as in everything else, was the preservation of Turkey's Asian empire and the strengthening of its defences. The intense rivalry between the European powers left opportunity for manoeuvre. Both Talaat and Jemal were anxious to secure an alliance with the Triple Entente of Russia, France and Britain which aimed to hold the balance of power in Europe against the ambitions of the Central Powers – imperial Germany and Austro-Hungary. Russia was the most eager to respond, as it was by now thoroughly alarmed by the dominant position Germany had acquired in Istanbul and feared that it would gain control of the Dardanelles straits. Although Britain and France had shown some benevolence towards the Young Turks' revolution, they were unprepared to include the Balkan states in any territorial guarantees for Turkey's remaining position in Europe. They both expected Turkey to remain neutral in any forthcoming war and that their interests would thus remain secure. Britain no longer regarded the survival of the Turkish Empire as a matter of great concern; the alliance with Russia provided sufficient protection for vital British interests in the Persian Gulf.

Despite Talaat's and Jemal's repeated efforts, they were unable to achieve an alliance with the Triple Entente. Feeling that there was an urgent need for protection from one of the powers, they accepted Enver Pasha's view that this should be Germany. On 2 August 1914 – five days after the assassination of the Austrian archduke Francis Ferdinand at Sarajevo, which led directly to the First World War – Turkey signed a secret alliance with Germany which allowed Turkey to remain neutral unless Russia intervened in the Austro-Serbian conflict which had just broken out. On 4 August Britain declared war on Germany. Yet even then all was not lost. Talaat still favoured neutrality. Diplomatic relations with Britain were satisfactory. The British naval mission headed by Admiral Limpus and the British ambassador Sir Louis Mallet were of high standing. In

London the Ottoman ambassador, Hakki Pasha, had by the summer
of 1914 succeeded in negotiating a series of agreements which satis-
factorily resolved all the outstanding differences between Turkey
and Britain, France and Germany over their railway interests in
Mesopotamia and Syria and navigation on the Tigris and Euphrates.
An Ottoman–British agreement defined the borders between
Kuwait, Nejd and Iraq.

Turkey ultimately abandoned neutrality because Enver – the
dominant member of the triumvirate – was convinced that Germany
would win the coming war. Any doubts about taking Germany's
side were removed when Britain commandeered two Turkish battle-
ships which were on the point of completion in British shipyards.
This high-handed action caused a wave of anti-British feeling
throughout Turkey. As Germany poured ships and men into Istanbul, the British fleet blockaded the Dardanelles and demanded that
Turkey affirm its neutrality by expelling the German mission. On
28 October the German admiral took the Turkish fleet into the Black
Sea to bombard Russian ports, and on 3 November the British fleet
shelled the Turkish ports at the entrance to the Dardanelles.
Although they had been reluctant to join the war before having
time to mobilize, Enver and his colleagues could not retreat. Turkey
declared war on the Allies on 5 November.

7. The Persian Factor

The only great schism in Islam – between Sunnis and Shiites which followed the death of the Prophet – led to a prolonged struggle for dominance in the Muslim world between the two branches of the religion. For some four centuries it was possible or even probable that Shia Islam would prevail, and it reached the height of its power in about AD 1000. But first the Seljuk Turks who came to dominate the Islamic heartlands in the eleventh century and then their Ottoman successors four hundred years later were fiercely Sunni. Shiism continued to survive and flourish in Persia and Mesopotamia, but henceforth it constituted a declining minority of the Islamic *umma*.

There is no great doctrinal difference between Sunni and Shiite Islam: they agree on the absolute centrality of the Prophet in the religion and on most of the historical details of his life; there are no major differences in ritual; and on theological matters there is a broad consensus. The division is historical and political. The Shiites believe that the Prophet should have been succeeded by his cousin and son-in-law Ali and that the succession was then reserved for the direct descendants of Muhammad through his daughter Fatima and her husband Ali. The successor, or imam, who was also the infallible interpreter of Islam, was generally nominated by the previous imam from among his sons. Most Shiites believe that there were twelve imams – Ali, his sons Hassan and Hussein, and nine in line of descent from Hussein. The last was Muhammad, born in 873, who disappeared mysteriously or went into occultation. The 'Twelver' Shiites, who in the twentieth century form the great majority of Shiites in the world, believe that Imam Muhammad is only hidden and will reappear as the Mahdi or 'Rightly Guided One' to restore the golden age. (Another Shiite sect, the Zaydis, is confined to Yemen, while offshoots of Shiism, such as the Druze,

Alawites and Ismailis, are numerically small although they may have strong local political importance.)

Shah Ismail I of Persia, who ruled from 1501 to 1524 and founded the Safavid dynasty (1501–1736), established Shiism as the state religion. It is probable that a majority of his subjects were Sunnis, but he skilfully used the new faith to bind his disparate peoples together. Shia Islam became the foundation of a proud and even xenophobic Persian nationalism which still flourishes in the modern age, as for the past four centuries Persia (renamed Iran in 1935) has been the only nation-state of significance in which Shiism is the official religion.

Ismail had wider aspirations for his religion, and when the ardently Sunni Ottoman sultan Selim I persecuted his Shiite subjects, he attempted to come to their aid. His ill-trained troops were no match for the Ottoman Janissaries and he was defeated, but he was able to prevent the Turks from seizing any of his territory and he even held on to the districts of Mosul and Baghdad which he had won in earlier campaigns. He also held off the Sunni Uzbeks in Turkestan to the north-east. Persia was on the defensive, but the menace of Sunni enemies helped the process of welding the nation together.

The struggle between the rival Sunni Ottoman and Shiite Persian Empires lasted more than two centuries along their common frontier which stretched for some 1,500 miles from the Black Sea to the Persian Gulf. The battle for Mesopotamia wavered back and forth and was finally decided in the Ottoman favour only at the end of the seventeenth century. Even then, Mesopotamia was far from secure from Persian attack. Persia's western frontiers have remained roughly unchanged until the present day.

The need to guard against the hostile Persian presence on the Ottoman Empire's eastern borders acted as a brake to Turkish western expansion, earning Persia the gratitude of the Christian states of Europe. Equally, the Ottoman Empire served to isolate the Persian Empire from the West.

Except for relatively brief periods of recovery, the Safavid dynasty went into a long secular decline on the death of its founder. The apogee of the dynasty was the reign (1587–1629) of Shah Abbas the Great. With the help of the English adventurer Sir Robert Sherley, he carried out much-needed reforms of his army, establishing an élite cavalry corps which was comparable to the Turkish Janissaries, and his reign was a period when the stuggle went against the Ottomans. He was a capable administrator, and a builder of genius. He made his capital the city of Isfahan, which became one of the masterpieces of Islamic architecture. He fostered trade and industry and, although an ardent Shiite Muslim, encouraged Christian Armenians to inhabit a quarter of the capital. Isfahan grew until his English visitors noted that it rivalled London in size.

When Shah Abbas died, he left his country immeasurably stronger than when he had come to the throne at the age of sixteen. European penetration of the Persian Empire had hardly begun. With the help of the fleet of the British East India Company in the Gulf, he was able to evict the Portuguese, who, a century earlier, in the time of Shah Ismail, had obtained a foothold on the island of Hormuz and on the adjoining mainland. In return for its help, he granted the Company valuable privileges at the port of Bandar Abbas, which was named after him. But British domination of the Gulf still lay well in the future.

Envoys of the European powers to Abbas's court were politely received but he resisted their suggestions that he form an alliance with them against the Ottoman Turks – Persia's isolation from the West was the best guarantee of its empire's integrity.

Abbas left his country one fatal legacy: he instituted the practice, which closely resembled that in the Ottoman court, of immuring the heir apparent and other royal princes in the harem, for purposes of security. The result was that the heir and princes were physically weakened and totally inexperienced in the art of government. His successors were not only cruel and despotic but also incompetent, and the court eunuchs secured excessive power and influence.

In 1709 the Sunni Afghans rose in rebellion, and, repeatedly defeating the badly led Persian forces sent against them, succeeded in capturing Isfahan and forcing the shah to flee. The Afghans controlled only part of the country, and a majority of the people remained loyal to the Safavids.

Persia was in a gravely weakened condition. Tsar Peter the Great of Russia had for long been seeking ways of establishing a trade route to India across the Caspian Sea and beyond. Using as a pretext the attacks on some Russian merchants in northern Persia during a tribal uprising, he invaded the country in 1722. His action alarmed the Ottoman Turks, who now also invaded Persia, to prevent Russia from gaining control over territories on their borders. War between Russia and Turkey was avoided by the settlement of 1724, under which the two powers agreed to partition northern and western Persia between them, leaving the rest to the Afghan usurpers in the centre and the Safavids in the east. Russian pressure was henceforth a permanent feature of Persia's existence.

In 1729 the Safavids were restored to the throne. However, this was accomplished only with the help of Nadir Quli Beg, a member of the Asfar tribe, who had formerly been a leader of a gang of robbers but turned out to be a brilliant general. In 1736 he deposed the young Shah Abbas III, bringing the Safavid dynasty to an end, and placed himself on the throne with the title of Nadir Shah.

Before he ascended the throne, Nadir Shah's military skill had already succeeded in forcing both the Ottoman Turks and the Russians to relinquish their conquests. He recaptured Kandahar from the Afghans and thus restored Persia's previous borders. But this enormously ambitious man was not content with this. He turned eastwards with his armies to invade India, which, under the Mogul dynasty, was sunk in corruption and decline but still vastly wealthy. Bypassing the well-defended Khyber Pass, he defeated the Mogul emperor Mohammed Shah and in March 1739 entered Delhi in triumph. The booty was on a gigantic scale. An Indian historian remarked that 'the accumulated wealth of 348 years changed owners in a moment.' One captured item was the Peacock Throne, which Nadir removed to Persia where it served for the coronation of future shahs.

Nadir had succeeded where Alexander the Great had failed. However, he did not attempt to hold India but restored the bulk of Mohammed Shah's lands to him, while keeping the provinces on the southern banks of the River Indus which had belonged to the Persian Empire of Darius the Great.

His appetite for conquest was still unsatisfied. He turned against the Uzbek states of Turkestan to the north-east and captured Samarkand and Bokhara. He drove into the Caucasus to hold back the advancing Russians. By 1740 he had not only restored and extended the borders of Persia but also established the country as a great military power. However, his genius was purely military; he had no concern with the just and efficient administration of the empire. He was a Persian Bonaparte without a Code Napoléon. Harsh, cruel and suspicious, he came to be hated by his subjects, and in 1747 his murder by a group of his own officers was little mourned. Some fifty years of relative chaos ensued as the throne was disputed between rival claimants. In 1794 Agha Mohammed of the Qajar tribes defeated his enemies and made himself shah. Although a eunuch (he had been made one when taken captive as a youth), he was the founder of the Qajar dynasty, which lasted until 1925. After capturing the city of Tehran he made it his capital. On his assassination in 1797, Agha Mohammed was succeeded by his nephew Fath Ali, who reigned until 1834.

By the beginning of the nineteenth century Persia's long isolation from the West had come to an end. The Ottoman Empire, which though hostile had acted as a barrier of protection from the West, was in irreversible decline. Britain was in possession of India, and its navy controlled the waters of the Gulf. The Russian Empire was continuing the great colonial expansion eastwards into Asia that had begun under Peter the Great. Throughout the nineteenth century Persia was caught in the pincer-like pressure of these two powers.

However, it was France – and specifically the remarkable ambitions of Napoleon Bonaparte – which was instrumental in bringing Persia into the orbit of European politics. Having failed in his attempt to use Egypt as a springboard for an attack on the British in India, in 1800 Napoleon planned an invasion of India via Afghanistan in alliance with Tsar Paul of Russia. The plan may have been wholly impractical, but it thoroughly alarmed the British rulers of India. It was aborted by the assassination of Tsar Paul in 1801, but the French menace remained. When the advancing Russians annexed two provinces of Georgia and in 1805 declared war on Persia, seizing Derbent and Baku, the Persian shah Fath Ali turned to France for help. By the Franco-Persian Treaty of Finkenstein in 1807, Bonaparte undertook to recover the territories Russia had seized. But Bonaparte almost immediately made peace with Tsar Alexander, and Persia was left to face Russia alone.

By the 1813 Treaty of Golestan, which ended a hopeless war, Persia ceded Georgia, Baku and other territories to Russia. But the struggle was not ended: three frontier districts remained in dispute, and when Russia arbitrarily occupied them in 1827 the shah was compelled by outraged public opinion to declare war. After initial successes, this war also ended in disaster for Persia, mainly because the shah refused to pay his troops during the winter. Under the humiliating Treaty of Torkaman in 1828, Persia not only gave up all claims to Georgia and other territories lost in the earlier war but also paid a heavy indemnity and granted extraterritorial rights (similar to the Ottoman Capitulations) to Russian citizens on Persian soil. This and a simultaneous commercial treaty providing for free trade between Russia and Persia provided the basis for future relations between Persia and other European powers.

Britain's principal concern in the region in the early nineteenth century was to maintain Afghanistan as a barrier to French and Russian ambitions towards India. In 1800 Britain sent a mission to Persia, the first since the time of King Charles II. Headed by a young Scots officer, Captain Malcolm, it aimed to persuade the shah to bring the ambitious Afghan emir of Kabul under control to counteract any possible designs of the French or Russians and to sign a political and commercial treaty. The mission was successful, but the treaty lapsed in 1807 when Britain refused to provide help against Russian aggression on

Persia's north-western borders. The British interest remained, however, and in 1814 another treaty was signed whereby the shah agreed not to sign treaties or co-operate militarily with countries hostile to Britain; in return, Persia was to receive a subsidy of £150,000 a year which would lapse if Persia engaged in any war of aggression. The subsidy was withdrawn in 1827, when Persia was technically the aggressor in its second disastrous war with Russia.

When Fath Ali died, he was succeeded by his grandson Mohammed Shah (1834–48). The young shah was determined to win fame by recovering some of Persia's lost territories. He was wise enough to see he could do nothing to stem the Russian colonizing drive through Turkestan which, only temporarily halted by the Crimean War, was pursued relentlessly throughout the mid nineteenth century. Instead, with Russian encouragement, he turned eastwards to try to conquer the province of Herat in north-western Afghanistan and territories beyond. Britain was instantly alarmed. France was no longer a threat to India, but expansionist Russia seemed highly dangerous. The Persian–Russian treaty of 1828 gave the Russians the right to appoint consuls throughout Persian territory. Britain gave help to the Afghan rulers of Herat and exerted pressure on the shah by occupying Kharg Island in the Gulf. Mohammed Shah was forced to abandon his siege of Herat.

Nasir al-Din Shah, who succeeded his father Mohammed in 1848 at the age of seventeen and reigned for forty-eight years, pursued the same policy of attempting to recover territories to the east, with Russian encouragement. Britain protested and imposed a treaty on Persia under which the shah undertook to refrain from any further interference in Afghanistan. When, despite the treaty, in 1856 Nasir al-Din obtained control of Herat through an Afghan nominee, Britain again seized Kharg Island and, near Bushire, landed troops which advanced inland to defeat a strong Persian force. The British then withdrew and sailed up the Shatt al-Arab waterway at the head of the Gulf to capture the port of Mohammereh. Under a treaty concluded in Paris in 1857, Persia then agreed to withdraw from Herat and to recognize the kingdom of Afghanistan.

In the 1870s and 1880s, Russia completed its conquest of central Asia and bordered Persia on the north-east as well as the north. The 1,200 miles of common frontier stretched from Mount Ararat and around the Caspian Sea to the borders of Afghanistan. Given its weakness, Persia's only means of resisting Russian pressure was to seek Britain's backing, and this required the granting of a series of concessions to British commercial interests.

Throughout the nineteenth century the Persian shahs ruled as despots with little restraint on their personal power. Only the nomadic tribes – about a quarter of the population, who inhabited the mountain ranges along Persia's eastern and western borders – retained a sense of independence, regarding the monarchy with some disdain. The great majority of the rest of the population consisted of illiterate peasant farmers living close to subsistence level in small mud villages. Although legally free, in practice they were tied to the land. Most of the landlords (who measured their wealth by the number of villages they owned) were absentees, living in the larger cities and leaving the management of their villages in the hands of an agent. Despite their wealth and power over the peasantry, they did not form a cohesive feudal class which was capable of challenging the absolutism of the throne, and, as the ultimate owners of the land, the shahs did not hesitate to confiscate an individual landlord's property when they were in need of funds.

There was no European type of bourgeoisie or professional class. In Shiite Persia, the religious hierarchy, made up of mullahs, with a better-educated upper class of *mujtahids*, learned in Islamic law, was much larger than its equivalent, the *ulama*, in Sunni Islam. But, despite its influence with the people, it rarely chose to defy the authority of the throne. The nearest equivalent to a middle class was formed by the *bazaaris* or merchants, who ranged from itinerant pedlars to wealthy exporters of the carpets and textiles which were virtually Persia's only manufactured goods. However, their lack of cohesion meant that their political influence was very limited.

The most serious challenge to the shahs came from the leaders of religious sects. In the 1840s a rebellion broke out led by the Agha

Khan, spiritual head of the Ismailis, and then another by the Babi movement, created by Mirza Ali Mohammed, son of a Shiraz merchant, who after making the pilgrimage to Mecca declared himself to be the *bab* (gateway) to the divine truth. His movement spread and became so strong that in 1850 Nasir al-Din Shah was obliged to have him executed. Two years later a Babi attempt to assassinate the shah led to the fierce persecution of the sect, and most of the survivors fled the country. However, an offshoot of the Babis – the Bahais – continued. This never threatened the shahs but was still held in suspicion.

The closest equivalent to a reform movement in nineteenth-century Persia was instituted by Mirza Taqi Khan, the capable and honest vizier appointed by the young Nasir al-Din when he came to the throne. Impressed by the *Tanzimat* reforms in Ottoman Turkey, he persuaded the shah to reorganize the armed forces and ensure that they were properly paid and to end the sale of titles and offices and various other abuses. He was also responsible for the founding of the École Polytechnique or Dar al-Fanun in Tehran and the first Persian newspaper. But the reforms were short-lived. The shah's formidable mother persuaded him that Taqi Khan was becoming too powerful, and Nasir al-Din ordered his execution.

Despite his occasional acts of cruelty the shah was generally a humane ruler, but his liberal and reformist inclinations, which had been encouraged by Taqi Khan, did not last. He was affected by the failure of the constitutional movement in Ottoman Turkey and Abdul Hamid II's speedy reversion to autocratic rule in 1878. In the last years of his reign he ruled as despotically as any of his predecessors. His greatest achievement was to establish security throughout the empire. There was some very limited modernization in the form of paved roads and the electric telegraph (installed by the Indo-European Telegraph Company, acting on behalf of the British government of India to serve its imperial interests). The Dar al-Fanun in Tehran taught science and engineering on modern lines, and there was a modest growth in the publishing of newspapers and books. In general, however, the systems of administration, education and justice (which applied both Islamic and customary pre-Islamic law) remained on medieval lines. The shah enjoyed travelling to Europe but prevented the Persian upper class from educating their children abroad, in case they should be infected with Western ideas.

The shah and his court were extravagant and demanding. To protect the throne, he maintained substantial armed forces which, although ill-paid, corrupt and inefficient, were costly. Since there was so little economic growth or development, and the returns from the sale of government offices were limited, state revenues were minimal. The shah therefore had recourse to the granting of concessions to foreign interests. The most remarkable of these was the concession awarded to Baron Julius de Reuter, a naturalized British subject, in 1873. Covering all Persia, this gave the Baron a seventy-year monopoly on the construction and operation of all Persian railroads and streetcars and on the exploitation of all mineral resources and government forests, including all uncultivated lands; an option on all future enterprises connected with the construction of roads, telegraphs, mills, factories, workshops and public works of every kind; and the right to collect all Persian customs duties for twenty-five years. In return, de Reuter was to pay the Persian government 20 per cent of the railway profits and 15 per cent of those from other sources. Lord Curzon commented that this represented 'the most complete and extraordinary surrender of the entire industrial resources of a kingdom into foreign hands that has probably ever been dreamt of, much less accomplished in history'.

The shah naïvely believed that he had both ensured some revenues and delegated his country's economic regeneration to Britain. Russia's furious reaction forced him to cancel the concession, but in 1899 British pressure forced him to grant a more limited concession which enabled de Reuter to establish the Imperial Bank of Persia, with the right to issue its own banknotes, and to search for oil.

Largely because of his willingness to mortgage the country's resources in this way, Nasir al-Din lost popularity in his later years and a liberal reformist movement began to emerge. Although Persia was much more isolated from the West than Ottoman Turkey, there was some penetration of Western ideas and methods via the foreign military missions, consular and bank officials and the Christian missionaries who were permitted to found schools and hospitals. The reform movement had a more potent stimulus from another source – the reformer and preacher of pan-Islamic ideals Jamal al-Din al-Afghani. The shah was attracted by al-Afghani's writings in his Paris exile and in 1886 he invited him to Persia, where he became an honoured member of the Royal Council. However, he soon began to preach subversive and revolutionary ideas – to the alarm of the shah and his ministers – and, when in 1890 he led the popular denunciation of the granting of a tobacco concession to a British group, he was deported from Persia. His movement survived, and in 1896 one of his disciples assassinated Nasir al-Din.

The reform movement gathered strength during the reign of Nasir al-Din's weak and ailing son Muzaffar al-Din, who exceeded his father in extravagance. A new reformist leader was Malkom Khan, the Persian ambassador in London, who campaigned against the shah's chief minister. When dismissed, he published a newspaper *Qanun* ('Law') calling for a fixed code of laws and the assembly of a parliament. Although banned in Persia, the paper nevertheless had a wide circulation in the country.

In 1903 the shah appointed his able but ultra-reactionary son-in-law Prince Ayn-u-Dula to assume control of government affairs. His actions provoked further opposition, and matters came to a head in 1905. A group of merchants, outraged by the extravagance and corruption of the court and the country's increased indebtedness which had led the government to introduce an onerous new customs tariff, took *best* or sanctuary in a Tehran mosque, in accordance with an ancient custom, in order to voice their protests. They were joined by some prominent mullahs. When the shah promised to meet some of their demands but then prevaricated and intensified the repression, a larger group combining many of the country's notables – merchants, bankers and clerics – took *best* in the grounds of the British legation to persist with their demand for the introduction of a legal code and also, for the first time, a constitution. In October 1906, now in desperately bad health, the shah complied – with extreme reluctance. A Majlis or parliament was convened which drafted a Fundamental Law of the constitution.

The Constitutional Revolution, as it is known, received the support of virtually the whole nation and was a milestone in Persian history. Subsequent shahs attempted to reverse it, but none was wholly successful and some form of constitutional and representative government has survived to the present day.

The constitutionalists received some inspiration from the attempt by their Russian counterparts in 1905 to end the autocratic role of the tsar. A different kind of stimulus came from the Russo-Japanese War of the same year, in which for the first time a modernizing Asian state defeated one of the great European powers. (This was also an inspiration for the Egyptian nationalist leader Mustafa Kamel in the same period.) However, with its blend of the secular and clerical, the reform movement had a strongly Persian character.

Muzaffar al-Din was succeeded in 1907 by his son Mohammed Ali, who reigned for only two years, amid continuing unrest. Like his father, he repeatedly promised to accept reforms only then to ignore them. At one point he bombarded the Majlis, which he had attempted unsuccessfully to dissolve, and killed or wounded many deputies. This led to a serious uprising in Tabriz which his troops were unable to quell. Russian troops intervened, ostensibly to protect Russian nationals. The nationalist forces gathered strength and marched on Tehran. Unable to resist, the shah took refuge in the Russian legation. As he went into exile in Russia, the Majlis decided that his 11-year-old son Ahmed Mirza should succeed him.

Popular feeling had been stirred up not only by the shah's action but also by the Anglo-Russian agreement of August 1907, which was designed to settle all outstanding differences concerning Persia and Afghanistan between Russia and Britain. The two powers were already expecting the coming struggle with imperial Germany, in which there were strong chances that Ottoman Turkey would be Germany's ally. In effect the agreement divided

Persia into Russian and British spheres of interest, with Russia taking the north and centre, Britain the south-east, and the south-west remaining a 'neutral' zone. Persian opinion was dismayed and angry when the agreement was made known. Britain especially had been thought to have sympathized with the constitutionalist revolution. The European powers' wider strategic interests did not concern the Persians: Russia and Britain were henceforth regarded as the two imperial powers which sought to destroy Persia's independence.

Britain might be said to have had the worst of the 1907 agreement, because south-eastern Persia consists mainly of desert. However, British interests in Persia were about to receive a powerful boost. De Reuter had abandoned his mineral concession after two years, having failed to find oil, but in 1901 Shah Muzaffar al-Din granted an Englishman, William Knox D'Arcy, a sixty-year petroleum and gas concession covering the whole of the Persian Empire. The British government had lobbied strongly in D'Arcy's favour through the legation in Tehran, and the Persian grand vizier, who had been won over, successfully kept the deal secret from the Russians until it was signed.

D'Arcy looked for oil for several years without success, until his funds were nearly exhausted and he began to look around the world for new investors. At this point the British Admiralty intervened. The First Sea Lord, the dynamic and independent-minded Admiral John Fisher, had long ago determined that the British navy should convert its ships from the use of coal to oil. This, he reckoned, would increase its fighting capacity by 50 per cent. But 90 per cent of the world's oil was then produced in the United States and Russia, and the rest was already covered by concessions. The world market was dominated by Standard Oil and Royal Dutch Shell. It was urgently necessary to find an independent source under British control. In 1905 the Admiralty persuaded the British Burmah Oil Company to link up with D'Arcy and provide new funds. In 1908 D'Arcy's engineers, at the point of abandoning the search in despair, drilled into one of the world's largest oilfields at Masjid-i-Sulaiman in south-western Persia. The Anglo-Persian Oil Company was formed, and shares were sold to an enthusiastic public.

There were still difficulties. The oilfields were situated not in the British sphere of influence but in the neutral zone. The semi-independent Arab shaikh of Mohammereh regarded the area as his territory. Marauding tribes threatened the pipeline needed to export the oil to the Gulf. Accordingly Britain signed an agreement recognizing the shaikh and his successors as the lawful rulers of Mohammereh in return for an annual rental. The shaikh undertook to protect the oil installations.

In 1911 the young Winston Churchill became First Lord of the Admiralty in Britain's Liberal government, and a huge and expensive three-year development programme for the navy was launched. In addition to Persia's vital strategic significance for the British Empire, Persian oil was of crucial military importance. In June 1914, just two months before the outbreak of the First World War, Churchill presented the House of Commons with an agreement under which Anglo-Persian would guarantee oil supplies for twenty years while the British government would buy a controlling interest in the company (later the Anglo-Iranian Oil Company and ultimately British Petroleum) for £2.2 million. Despite a few members' misgivings that this would provoke the Russians and further weaken the Persian government, the agreement was overwhelmingly approved. Churchill later estimated that the investment brought savings of £40 million and paid for the gigantic expansion of the British navy without any cost to the British taxpayer.

With the 11-year-old Ahmed Mirza on the throne, Persia's internal situation became more chaotic. The victorious nationalists split into two parties – revolutionaries and moderates. The Russians sent troops to Kazvin in Tehran province, against British protests, on the familiar pretext of protecting their nationals. The lack of administrative experience of the new regime showed the urgent need of foreign advisers but, since neither Britain nor Russia would agree to the appointment of the other's nationals, it was necessary to look elsewhere for these. Belgians were placed in charge of the customs.

An appeal was made to the United States, and President Taft recommended an experienced lawyer and civil servant William Shuster, who in 1911 was placed in charge of Persia's finances with full powers for a three-year period. Although the United States was in no way an imperial power in the Middle East at that period, the Russians vigorously protested, and persisted with their opposition to the point of threatening to occupy Tehran. The regent Nasir al-Mulk thereupon carried out a *coup d'état*, dissolved the Majlis and acceded to the Russian demands by expelling Shuster and his colleagues in January 1912. Shuster's efforts had just begun to show results, but the country was now left in even greater confusion.

Protests from the US government and liberal opinion in Britain were in vain – the need to accommodate Russia in the face of the expected war with Germany was paramount for Britain's Liberal government. When the war did break out and Turkey allied itself with Germany, the Turkish threat to Russian territory and to the oilfields in the south caused Russia and Britain to occupy part of Persia in spite of its declaration of neutrality.

8. The Sick Man Dies: 1918

In November 1914 the fate of the Ottoman Empire was sealed when Turkey joined Christian Europe's civil war in alliance with the Central Powers of Germany and Austro-Hungary against Britain, France and Russia. As we have seen, the powers of Europe, with the intermittent exception of Russia, had preferred to maintain the integrity of Asiatic Turkey and its Arab dominions. They interfered to bring pressure on successive sultans to further their interests, but they did not consider partitioning the empire. Britain's single-handed occupation of Egypt in 1882 was reluctant and almost accidental – the restoration of Ottoman authority in Egypt would have been preferable but was impractical. However, once the action was taken, Egypt became a vital link in Britain's world-wide imperial system which could not be abandoned.

Apart from their war strategy, all three Allies had to consider the reactions of the millions of Muslim subjects in their empires – Arabs in French North Africa and Muslim peoples in British India and in Russian central Asia. Would they be willing to fight for their Christian rulers against the sultan/caliph? It was a popular belief that any Muslim was only waiting for the call to *jihad* or holy war to slaughter the infidel. The triumvirate who ruled Turkey hastened to issue such a call.

Britain had two immediate strategic concerns in the Middle East – the protection of the Suez Canal and the protection of the Gulf. Both were vital links with India: the Canal had to be kept open for the transport of Indian troops to Europe, and the Gulf region now had the additional value of the oil installations at Abadan.

Jemal Pasha was the member of the Ottoman triumvirate who took command in Syria. As he stepped onto the train in Istanbul he declared, 'I shall not return until I have entered Cairo.' Jemal was an able general and he was assisted by a brilliant German chief of staff, von Kressenstein. Egypt was denuded of British troops, who had been sent to France, and was defended only by hastily assembled Australian and Indian units supported by Egyptian artillery and two French cruisers which happened to be in the Canal. Jemal's first assault on the Canal, in January 1915, was repelled. His hopes that the Egyptian populace would rise against the British occupiers were belied. However, with the help of Sinai beduin tribesmen, von Kressenstein kept British forces tied to the Canal for two years. The Germans also succeeded in stirring up the warlike Senussi tribesmen in Cyrenaica and, although they posed no serious military threat, these also kept substantial British forces tied to the frontier.

As soon as the war with Turkey broke out, an Indian brigade was landed at Basra, which it took without difficulty, and began the advance towards Baghdad. Britain suffered a dangerous setback when a large Anglo-Indian force was surrounded at Kut and was forced to surrender, but Baghdad fell in March 1917 and by the end of the war British troops were in control of most of modern Iraq.

The war began disastrously for the Turks as, contrary to German advice, Enver Pasha, who was both commander-in-chief and minister of war, launched his troops against Russia in the Caucasus in the hope of raising a revolt among the Muslims of central Asia to help fulfil his pan-Turanian dreams. The Russians recovered from the initial onslaught and the Turkish troops suffered from the fearsome cold. Moreover, throughout eastern Anatolia the Turks were threatened by the insurrection of their embittered Armenian subjects, who disrupted communications and formed volunteer groups to help the Russians. Others joined the Russian Armenian forces. The Turks took a terrible revenge by ordering the deportation of the entire Armenian population from eastern Anatolia to northern Syria. Hundreds of thousands were killed, and many more died of hunger, exposure and disease. Between one and a quarter and one and a half million perished. Armenian nationalists still seek revenge against representatives of the Turkish state.

Despite the reverses on the Caucasus front, Turkey was far from defeated. With the war bogged down in France and the Russian advance held by Germany and Austria, Britain attempted to eliminate Turkey from the war by landing a large force (including Australasian contingents) on the Gallipoli peninsula to threaten Istanbul. The German inspector-general Liman von Sanders was in command of the Turkish defences, and his second in command was Mustafa Kemal (the future Kemal Atatürk). Despite a munitions shortage, the Turks fought tenaciously and neither side succeeded in dislodging the other. But by the winter it was Britain which accepted failure and withdrew its forces. Turkey's morale improved; by a huge recruitment drive, its forces were increased to fifty-two divisions or 800,000 men. However, successes against Britain in Mesopotamia were offset by continued advances of the Russians into eastern Anatolia. The Turkish forces were widely spread over several fronts.

The role of Egypt in the Gallipoli campaign was as a vast military camp and hospital for the Allies. The Egyptian people responded with their customary stoical friendliness to the invasion of tens of thousands of uninhibited Allied troops, even though the troops provoked a crippling rise in prices. An auxiliary labour corps of some three thousand Egyptians was sent to the Dardanelles, where they proved an outstanding success at digging trenches.

In the summer of 1916, von Kressenstein launched his final offensive against the Suez Canal. He was beaten back, and the British forces under General Murray were then in a position to sweep the Turks out of Sinai. By December 1916 they had reached El Arish before Gaza.

The Egyptian people were forced into political quiescence by the vast weight of British military power. The *fellahin* could show only passive resistance to increasingly insistent demands by the military government that they should surrender their firearms and volunteer for camel transport or the auxiliary labour corps. Several thousand did eventually serve in Palestine and France and suffered casualties.

The pro-Turkish and pan-Islam feeling which Britain had feared was almost non-existent. The oriental secretary in Cairo, Sir Ronald

Storrs, wrote, 'Pious Muslims shake their heads and say, "We wish the Turks all success – from afar." ' In the Canal zone it was only some Muslims in two Indian battalions of the Canal Defence Force who deserted to the Turks. They were caught and shot and the trouble was prevented from spreading. A succession of Indian Muslim ruling princes was brought in to help stiffen the morale of the troops.

That pro-Turkish feeling was subdued did not mean that Egyptian nationalism was dead. Although leaderless and confused, the students were fervently nationalist and their clubs seethed with bitter opposition to the occupation. Secretly they applauded two unsuccessful assassination attempts on the life of Sultan Hussein Kamel. However, the British government handled the situation with some skill. When the sultan died in the summer of 1917, it resisted the demands that Britain should annex Egypt which came from some MPs and which were supported by Sir Reginald Wingate, the new high commissioner in Cairo; Britain was still concerned with the reaction of other Mediterranean powers. Instead the 49-year-old Prince Ahmed Fuad, a son of the khedive Ismail, was brought in to replace Hussein Kamel.

While pro-Turkish sentiment presented little problem for Britain in Egypt, there was a possibility that anti-Turkish feeling could be encouraged in the Ottoman Arab dominions. It was known that the Arabs had good cause for resentment against their rulers – especially in the aftermath of the brief Arab–Turkish honeymoon which followed the Young Turks revolution – but detailed intelligence was lacking.

Six weeks before Turkey entered the war, Lord Kitchener, at Ronald Storrs' suggestion, approached Sharif Hussein in Mecca to find out which way the Arabs would turn if Turkey allied itself to Germany. The sharif was as cautious as Kitchener himself had been with the Emir Abdullah eight months earlier. He hinted that he might bring the Hejazis out in revolt against the Turks if he was ensured of enough British support. A further message from Kitchener (who by now was minister of war in the British cabinet) promised Hussein that, if he would come out against Turkey, Britain would guarantee his retention of the title of Grand Sharif and defend him against external aggression. It hinted that if the sharif were declared caliph he would have Britain's support, and it included a general promise to help the Arabs obtain their freedom.

The message was enough to cause Sharif Hussein to contemplate the much wider objective of a general revolt against the Turks, under his leadership. But for this he required much more specific assurances from the Allies, and the year 1915 was spent trying to elicit them from Cairo while he continued to sound out the other leading Arabs in the peninsula with whom he was in contact.

The British cabinet for its part had no clear policy towards the Arabs or for the future of the Ottoman provinces in Asia after Turkey's defeat. It was obviously desirable that Turkey should be knocked out of the war as soon as possible, but this was primarily to give Britain and France access to Russia and Romania to encircle the Central Powers. This was the strategy behind the Gallipoli campaign. There was an assumption that the Turks would have to give up Constantinople/Istanbul and the Dardanelles strait and that 'in the interests of Islam' (according to the foreign secretary, Sir Edward Grey) there should be an independent Muslim political unit somewhere else. Its centre would naturally be the Muslim holy places and Arabia, but it remained to be settled what else it would include.

Britain's Arab policy evolved in a way that the British considered pragmatic but which the Arabs came to regard as unprincipled. Sir Percy Cox, the chief political officer of the Mesopotamian Expeditionary Force, which occupied Basra at the beginning of the war, was aware of the importance of winning Ibn Saud, the new power in central Arabia, to the British cause. He sent Captain W. H. I. Shakespear as British representative at the Saudi court. Shakespear had already made friends with Ibn Saud during his heroic journeys of exploration in Arabia, and he was the Englishman whom the Wahhabi ruler most admired. However, Shakespear was killed in a skirmish with the Saudis' Rashidi enemies in January 1915. His death eliminated the possibility that Britain might invest in the Saudis, who had long demonstrated their independence from the Turks, as the leaders of an Arab revolt.

To the Arab Bureau – the group of high-level British experts gathered in Cairo – there were sound political reasons for looking to the Hashemites from the Hejaz to lead the Arabs. Sharif Hussein's position as keeper of the Islamic holy places made him the obvious person to counter the Ottoman call for a *jihad* against the infidel. But at that stage Britain had little knowledge of the state of opinion in Mesopotamia (Iraq) and Syria, although it was in a position to sound the feelings of leading Arabs in Cairo. Moreover, Britain had to consider the interests of its principal allies, Russia and France. In 1915 there was already a fear that huge Russian losses were causing the Russian people to lose enthusiasm for the war. France, which was bearing the brunt of the war on the western front, had a claim to a special position in Syria, based on long-standing cultural and political ties that had been acknowledged by Britain before the war. During 1915, Britain began secret negotiations with its two allies on the future of all the Ottoman lands. Although British, the government of India also had its own interests and means of pressure on London, and it regarded Mesopotamia, the Gulf and the Arabian peninsula, as its special concern. It is hardly surprising that Britain lacked a coherent policy towards the Arabs.

The British government negotiated the agreement with Sharif Hussein to launch his revolt against the Turks by a correspondence which took place between July 1915 and February 1916, being conducted through Sir Henry McMahon, the British high commissioner in Egypt.

The sharif's aim was to secure British support for Arab independence in all the Arab provinces of the Ottoman Empire from Mersin in the north, the Persian frontier in the east, the Mediterranean in the west, and the Red Sea and the Indian Ocean in the south. The only temporary exception he was prepared to make was Aden. Doubtless he knew that Britain would not accept all his demands, but he was setting out his maximum negotiating position.

McMahon's crucial letter is his second, dated 24 October 1915, in which he pledged British support for Arab independence in the areas proposed by the sharif subject to certain reservations:

The districts of Mersin and Alexandretta, and portions of Syria lying to the west of the districts of Damascus, Homs, Hama and Aleppo, cannot be said to be purely Arab, and must on that account be excepted from the proposed delimitation.

Subject to that modification, and without prejudice to the treaties concluded between us and certain Arab Chiefs, we accept that delimitation.

As for the regions lying within the proposed frontiers, in which Great Britain is free to act without detriment to the interests of her ally France, I am authorized to give you the following pledges on behalf of the Government of Great Britain, and to reply as follows to your note:

That subject to the modifications stated above, Great Britain is prepared to recognize and uphold the independence of the Arabs in all the regions lying within the frontiers proposed by the Sharif of Mecca.

In other passages in the same letter, McMahon said it was understood 'that the Arabs have already decided to seek the counsels and advice of Great Britain exclusively; and that such European advisers and officials as may be needed to establish a sound system of administration shall be British'. He added that he considered it was agreed that

as regards to the two Vilayets of Baghdad and Basra the Arabs recognize that the fact of Great Britain's established position and interests there will call for the setting up of special administrative arrangements to protect those regions from foreign aggression, to promote the welfare of their inhabitants and to safeguard our mutual interest.

The ambiguity in some of these phrases was no doubt deliberate, and the shrewd sharif was aware of the reasons. He protested vigorously about the exemption of the Syrian Mediterranean coast from the area of Arab independence, saying that the vilayets of Aleppo and Beirut could not be regarded as anything but Arab provinces. He reluctantly agreed to shelve the problem for the duration of the war but declared his trust that Britain would subsequently persuade 'her ally France' to hand them over to the Arabs. He was more ready to compromise on the Iraqi provinces, recognizing the existing reality of the British military occupation, but he pointed out that, because they were part of the former Arab Empire, the seat of the caliphs and the first centre of Arab culture, it would be 'impossible to persuade or compel the Arab nation to renounce the honourable association'. He agreed that the end of the occupation would be determined by negotiation, but 'without prejudice to the rights of either party or the natural wealth and resources of these parts'.

The ambiguity which sowed most trouble for the future concerned Palestine. The name was not mentioned in the correspondence because Palestine was not an Ottoman administrative division, although it was a geographical expression employed throughout the Christian world. British cabinet ministers certainly referred to Palestine in their discussions. By no stretch of the imagination could McMahon's exemption of 'portions of Syria lying to the west of the districts of Damascus, Homs, Hama and Aleppo' – which was a vague attempt to accommodate French interests in Lebanon – have referred to the *sanjak* of Jerusalem, which covered two-thirds of Palestine and lay well to the south. It may be argued that the sharif either understood or should have been aware that Palestine was excluded, but there is no proof and he never accepted it. Britain could easily have clarified the situation by saying that Palestine must have a special status because it was sacred to Judaism, Christianity and Islam, but it chose not to do this. Clarity was not an objective.

The sharif's weakness lay in the fact that his claim to leadership was far from being acknowledged by the Arabs outside the Hejaz. Apart from the imam of Yemen (who remained pro-Turkish), the Arab shaikhs on the fringes of the Arabian peninsula (who were in treaty relationship with Britain) and Ibn Saud in the interior (who was the sharif's hostile rival), the Arabs of Mesopotamia looked forward to their own independence, while the sharif had little contact with the Arabs of Syria, who were under iron Turkish rule. When Jemal Pasha first arrived in Syria to command the Fourth Army, he curbed his naturally despotic nature and declared a policy of 'clemency and tolerance towards the Arabs'. 'I am in a position to assure you that the Turkish and Arab ideals do not conflict,' he said in Damascus in January 1915. 'They are brothers in their strivings, and perhaps their efforts are complementary.' However, after his failure to invade Egypt and his intelligence services reported the scale of Arab anti-Turkish activities, he resorted to a policy of repression. First he took every opportunity to send Arab units of the Ottoman army out of Syria and replace them with Turks, and then he put on trial a number of prominent Arab civilians who had been implicated in treasonable activities by documents seized in the French consulates. Eleven were publicly executed in August 1915 and twenty-one more the following May in the central squares of Damascus and Beirut.

However, if the Syrians were feeling increasingly anti-Turkish, they by no means saw their salvation in France. Hostility towards the possibility of French rule surprised even British intelligence, which attributed it to aspects of French colonial policy in northwest Africa. Only the Maronites of Mount Lebanon looked to France as a protector.

By the spring of 1916, Sharif Hussein knew that he had to act, as a large Turco-German force was about to arrive in the Hejaz on its way to Yemen. On 16 June he raised the flag of the Arab Revolt and seized Mecca from its small Turkish garrison. He had hoped for a simultaneous landing by Allied troops at Alexandretta (Iskenderun) to promote an uprising against the Turks in Syria, but this was rejected by the British war cabinet, despite strong support from the military, because of French opposition to any landing in Syria other than by French troops. For the time being the Arab Revolt remained confined to the Hejaz. On 2 November 1916 Sharif Hussein was proclaimed 'King of the Arab Countries' by his followers, but this was not acceptable to Britain and France. A compromise was reached, and in January 1917 they both recognized him as King of the Hejaz.

Britain had never specifically promised to acknowledge Sharif Hussein's claim to leadership of all the Arabs, although it had encouraged him to believe that it would. The truth was that Britain's secret negotiations with France on the future of the Arab Ottoman dominions had already resulted in an agreement early in 1916. The two allies had previously accepted, with some misgivings, that Russia should have Constantinople and the Dardanelles. The task of negotiating had been delegated to Georges Picot of France and Sir Mark Sykes of Britain, and the Sykes–Picot agreement which they concluded partitioned the whole of Syria and Iraq and a large part of southern Turkey into spheres of direct or indirect French and British influence. France's area corresponded to the future states of Syria and Lebanon, and Britain's to Iraq and Transjordan. France's area of direct control would be the Mediterranean coastal regions, and Britain's the vilayets of Basra and Baghdad (in addition to the ports of Haifa and Acre). In the hinterland, which would be under the indirect control of the two powers, France and Britain were prepared 'to recognize and uphold an independent Arab state or confederation of Arab states under the suzerainty of an Arab chief'. In addition there was an area including Jerusalem and most of Palestine which was to be under some form of international control. Only the area comprising the present-day Saudi Arabia and North Yemen was to be left independent. (Britain had Aden and retained its exclusive relationship with the Arab Gulf shaikhdoms.)

For understandable reasons, Britain and France chose to keep the details of their agreement secret. Sharif Hussein had some suspicions of the Allies' intentions, and in early 1917 Sir Mark Sykes was sent to Jedda by the British Foreign Office to allay his fears. But although they discussed the question of French arms in Lebanon and the Syrian coastal regions, with Hussein maintaining the principle that these regions were as much Arab in character as the interior, Sykes did not inform him of the broader aspects of the Sykes–Picot agreement.

Meanwhile, although the Arab Revolt launched by the sharif aroused little response in Mesopotamia and Syria, which were still firmly under Turkish control, it made an important contribution to the war in the Middle East. It immobilized some 30,000 Turkish troops along the Hejaz railway from Amman to Medina and prevented the Turco-German forces in Syria from linking up with the Turkish garrison in Yemen. There could have been the most serious consequences for the Allies if the enemy forces had made contact with the Germans in East Africa and succeeded in closing the Red Sea to Allied shipping. The Arab forces, who were mainly armed tribesmen with only a small core of regular troops, were under the command of Emir Feisal, the sharif's third son. Feisal lacked the subtle intelligence of his elder brother, Emir Abdullah, but with his imposing appearance and restrained dignity he seemed to Colonel T. E. Lawrence, one of the British officers sent by the Arab Bureau in Cairo to help the revolt, to possess the right qualities for leadership.

In the spring of 1917 the British offensive against Turkey in Syria/ Palestine was going badly. In April, General Murray's expeditionary force was heavily repulsed in Gaza and held up for three months. Then, at the end of June, Murray was replaced by General Allenby, a brilliant and forceful commander (nicknamed 'the Bull'), who at once moved GHQ from Cairo to Palestine and speedily raised morale. At the end of October he launched his offensive and drove on towards Jerusalem.

Morale was also high in Emir Feisal's camp. In July his forces captured the port of Aqaba with a daring stroke. The Arabs were making an important contribution to Turkey's defeat. However, as Allenby was advancing, the Bolsheviks seized power in Russia, discovered documents referring to the Sykes–Picot agreement among the imperial archives, and informed the Turks about these. Jemal Pasha lost no time in passing the details on to the Arabs, as proof of treachery against the Muslim peoples of the Ottoman Empire by the Christian powers. Sharif Hussein at once asked for an explanation from Sir Reginald Wingate (who had succeeded

McMahon in Cairo). Wingate represented the Petrograd documents as referring to provisional exchanges between the British, French and Russian governments, rather than to any hard agreement, and suggested that the success of the Arab Revolt and the withdrawal of Russia from the war had created an entirely new situation.

This last point was true, but its principal consequence was to relieve the Allies of their promise of Constantinople and the straits to Russia. The success of the Arab Revolt had scarcely improved Sharif Hussein's bargaining position *vis-à-vis* the Allies. Their mutual and independent interests remained unchanged. With its huge base in Egypt, Allenby's armies in Palestine and control of Mesopotamia (Baghdad had fallen in March 1917), Britain was much the stronger power in the region. Its priority was the security of the British Empire, both in the present and in the future. But France was Britain's only major partner in the total war with Germany. It had suffered colossal casualties in Europe – far greater than Britain's – and in 1917 its determination was wavering. Britain was not going to frustrate the Middle East ambitions of its ally for the sake of the Hashemites, who were heavily dependent on British money, arms and military advice.

Allenby drove on to take Jerusalem on 9 December. Tactfully he walked rather than rode into the Holy City. He was then held up by the severity of the winter and the stiffening of the Turco-German forces under the command of General Liman von Sanders, who were benefiting from Russia's removal from the war. But in September 1918 Allenby resumed his advance to drive the Turks out of Syria. Damascus fell on 1 October. The first Allied troops to reach the city were a body of Australian cavalry, but Lawrence arranged for Feisal's Arab forces to make the triumphant entry and install their own governor.

Liman von Sanders was recalled, and it fell to Mustafa Kemal, who had halted the Russian advance in Anatolia in 1916, to extricate the Seventh Army. He brought it back to Aleppo and finally managed an orderly retreat across the Taurus Mountains. Aleppo fell to the Allies on 26 October, and two days later the Ottoman government abandoned the struggle and signed the armistice agreement at Mudros.

The revelation of the Sykes–Picot agreement was not the only reason for Arab doubts about Britain's intentions for the future of the Arab provinces of the Ottoman Empire. On 2 November 1917 – a few days before Jemal Pasha informed Sharif Hussein of the secret Anglo-French accord – a letter from the British foreign secretary, Arthur Balfour, to a leading British Zionist Jew, Lord Rothschild, was published:

His Majesty's Government view with favour the establishment in Palestine of a National Home for the Jewish people, and will use their best endeavours to facilitate the achievement of this object, it being clearly understood that nothing shall be done which may prejudice the civil and religious rights of existing non-Jewish communities in Palestine or the rights and political status enjoyed by Jews in any other country.

This apparently unsensational document, known as 'the Balfour Declaration', planted the seeds of a conflict which has lasted almost a century and is unlikely to be resolved before another century has passed. Although few were aware of this at the time, it was the result of a compromise between British and Zionist aims. Its consequences have been greater than those of the Anglo-French agreement, which were eliminated by the demise of British and French imperial power within a few decades.

Since the failure of the last attempt to restore Jewish independence in Palestine in AD 134, the Jews had become scattered throughout the world. Only a few thousand religious Jews remained in Jerusalem, and there were tiny communities elsewhere in the Holy Land. The Jews in the rest of the world experienced varying degrees of persecution and prosperity, discrimination and tolerance, but from the eighteenth century they benefited from the economic expansion of western Europe and the movement towards religious toleration. During the nineteenth century, liberalism and assimilation appeared to be steadily gaining ground in western Europe, particularly in Russia and Russian Poland, where the concentration of Jewish population was greatest. Just as anti-Jewish movements, influenced by the nationalist temper of the nineteenth century, began to emphasize race rather than religion, so the Jews themselves, under the influence of their environment and the pressure of persecution, began to think in terms of a new Jewish nationalism. However, it took nearly two thousand years to develop the idea of a mass return of the 12 million Jews in the world to Palestine to re-create a Jewish state – the Jewish prayer 'Next year in Jerusalem' was the expression of a spiritual or Messianic ideal rather than a political slogan.

In the second half of the nineteenth century, there was a steady movement of Jews from eastern Europe to settle in Palestine. Supported by Jewish philanthropy, they went mainly to found colonies to work the land. They were the pioneers of 'practical Zionism'. They were very much fewer than those who went to western Europe and the United States, but by 1914 there were about 80,000 Jews (including the indigenous communities) in Palestine, compared with about 650,000 Arabs.

'Political Zionism', or the concept of turning Palestine into a national Jewish state, was founded by Theodor Herzl, a prominent Austrian political journalist who in 1896 published his book *Der Judenstaat* (*The Jewish State: An Attempt at a Modern Solution of the Jewish Question*), in which he declared that the Jewish question was neither social nor religious but national. Although himself an assimilated agnostic Jew, he maintained that assimilation had not worked. Anti-Semitism was growing. He did not believe that all Jews should be forced to go to the new Jewish state; the important thing was that Jews should enjoy sovereignty over a piece of territory to suit their national requirements. If it were in Palestine, the European Jews would help to civilize the surrounding region.

Herzl organized the first Zionist Congress, at Basle in 1897, where the delegates called for the colonization of Palestine by Jewish agricultural and industrial workers and *the organization and binding together of the whole of Jewry*.

For tactical reasons, the early Zionists spoke of a 'home' rather than a 'state' in Palestine, although they still had to secure Ottoman consent for this. As we have seen, Herzl's request was rejected by Sultan Abdul Hamid. Herzl then considered Sinai and Cyprus (inhabited by Greeks and Turks), but these were denied him by Cromer of Egypt and the British Colonial Office. In 1903 the British government made a lukewarm offer of territory in Uganda, which Herzl reluctantly agreed to consider, but this was rejected by the sixth Zionist Congress shortly before his death in 1904.

There followed a decade of frustration for political Zionism. The World Zionist Organization, based in Vienna, was established on a sound footing, and it was possible to step up the process of practical Zionism as the Young Turks allowed some relaxation of Jewish immigration into Palestine. A Jewish National Fund to buy land in Palestine was founded in 1901. But the objective of turning Palestine into a national home for all the Jews seemed as far away as ever. World Jewry had still to be won over to Zionism. Many of the most prominent and wealthy Jews in central and western Europe were opposed to what they saw as a disruptive movement. American Jews still showed little interest. Religious leaders were divided, with the chief rabbi of Vienna declaring that Zionism was incompatible with Judaism.

The weight of support for Zionism came from the mass of east-European Jews. However, in the years leading up to the First World War the Zionist organization moved the focus of its attentions to Britain, where it could act most freely and where, according to Herzl, there was least anti-Semitism. Two of Herzl's leading east-European lieutenants – Chaim Weizmann and Nahum Sokolov – were now living in England. By 1914 Weizmann, as president of the English Zionist Federation, was familiar with half the British cabinet. Such Zionists fully understood the importance of securing the support of the most powerful Gentiles as well as world Jewry. In some important cases they had little or no need to persuade.

Many different individuals contributed to the genesis of the Balfour Declaration. The British Gentiles among them were guided by a remarkable mixture of imperial *Realpolitik* and romantic/historical feelings. It was a Jewish member of the British government, Herbert Samuel, who in January 1915 first proposed to the cabinet the idea of a Jewish Palestine which would be annexed to the British Empire. But it was not until after David Lloyd George took over the conduct of the war at the end of 1916, as the leader of a National Coalition of Liberals and Conservatives, that the Zionist cause made real headway. The prime minister, a close friend of the Gentile Zionist editor of the *Manchester Guardian* – C. P. Scott – was an easy convert, as were other members of his cabinet – Balfour, the foreign secretary; Lord Milner, the former imperial consul in Africa; and a large group of Foreign Office officials and government advisers which included Sir Mark Sykes. These were non-Jews who saw huge advantages in a Jewish Palestine as part of the empire. But underpinning their imperial convictions was the romantic appeal of the return of the Jews to Zion, which, founded on Old Testament Christianity, was part of their Victorian upbringing. (Zionism also had this twin attraction for Churchill, who was not in the cabinet in 1917 but would return to it.) The British cabinet had already veered away from the commitment in the Sykes–Picot agreement to international control for Palestine. 'Britain could take care of the Holy Places better than anyone else,' the prime minister told C. P. Scott, and a French Palestine was 'not to be thought of'.

It was ironical, but in the circumstances not surprising, that the only Jew in the cabinet, Mr Edwin Montagu, secretary of state for India, should also be the most outspoken opponent of the Balfour Declaration. Montagu was a member of the highly assimilated Anglo-Jewish aristocracy, many of whom feared the effect of Jewish nationalism on their own position. Montagu had his counterparts in other countries – Henry Morgenthau Sr, a former US ambassador to Turkey, was a pronounced anti-Zionist, for example. Nevertheless the British cabinet was convinced that world Jewry was overwhelmingly in favour of Zionism and gave credit to Britain for supporting the cause. It believed that this had helped to bring the United States into the war in April 1917 and to maintain its enthusiasm thereafter. The British may have had an exaggerated view of the wealth and influence on Washington of American Jews at that period, but it was their belief in these that mattered. Moreover, the Germans were aware of the possibilities to be gained by winning Jewish sympathy, especially among the many American Jews of east-European origin who hated the Russian government. Germany was trying to persuade the Turks to lift their objections to Zionist settlement in Palestine, although so far without success. Finally, it was hoped that Britain's adoption of Zionism would win over the Russian Jewish socialists who were trying to influence the Kerensky government to take Russia out of the war.

All these strands of practicality and idealism came together in making the Balfour Declaration. The British cabinet believed it was a finely balanced document. When Balfour asked Rothschild and Weizmann to submit a draft, it said that 'Palestine should be reconstituted as the National Home for the Jewish people.' This was too strong and the final draft, as we have seen, said only that the British government favoured 'the establishment *in* Palestine of a National Home for the Jewish people'. It also added the provisos concerning 'the civil and religious rights of existing non-Jewish communities in Palestine' and 'the rights and political status enjoyed by Jews in any other country'.

Even this cautious wording greatly increased Sharif Hussein's alarm about the Allies' intentions. This time Commander D. G. Hogarth, the head of the Arab Bureau, was dispatched to see him in Jedda. Hogarth pressed the case for the return of the Jews to Palestine, but Sharif Hussein – now King of the Hejaz – was already showing perceptive anxiety that the Balfour Declaration might foreshadow a Jewish state in Palestine. Hogarth reported, 'The King would not accept an independent Jewish State in Palestine, nor was I instructed to warn him that such a state was contemplated.' Hussein accepted the assurances and ended by showing enthusiasm for the advantages that Jewish immigration would bring to the Arab countries.

The British government lost no time in implementing the terms of the Balfour Declaration. Soon after Jerusalem's capture from the Turks, Weizmann arrived at the head of a Zionist Commission and established its headquarters there. The Commission found that the Arabs of Palestine were already thoroughly alarmed – they took it for granted that Palestine should remain a purely Arab country. Before the war they had begun to resent the activities of the Zionist colonists and their establishment of exclusive Jewish communities, but these had not presented a serious threat as the Ottoman authorities had kept their expansion to a minimum. Now, in 1918, the Arabs believed the Zionists aimed to take over the country and place them in subjection. After all, although the Arabs formed about 90 per cent of the people of Palestine, the Balfour Declaration referred to them as the 'existing non-Jewish communities' whose civil and religious rights – but not political rights – were not to be prejudiced.

Weizmann and the Commission felt that the British military authorities were not doing enough to bring home to the Palestinian Arabs Britain's determination to implement the terms of the Balfour Declaration. British officials in Palestine, for their part, thought the Zionists should do much more to reassure the Arab majority of their real intentions. The question is, what were these real intentions?

Although the Zionists were prepared to make tactical compromises of the kind which produced the Balfour Declaration, there can be no doubt that their true aim was to turn Palestine into the national home for the Jews to which most of the Jews in the world would want to emigrate. They might have differed over its precise borders, but in their view Palestine was to become a Jewish national state with a substantial Jewish majority. However, they had come to realize how difficult it might be to achieve this. Weizmann was surprised by how 'non-Jewish' Jerusalem and Palestine had become. He left after a few months, believing that it might be impossible to prevent Palestine from becoming an Arab state.

The attitudes of British ministers were more complex. Although they had more than an inkling of the true Zionist objectives, most of them were quite ignorant of the real situation in Palestine and the sentiments of its people, although few regarded these as of great importance compared with the interests of the British Empire. They certainly could not foresee that they were helping to create one of the least soluble political problems of the twentieth century. Some were disturbed when the incompatibility between Zionist aspirations and the overwhelming feelings of the indigenous Arabs became apparent from the reports of British officials on the spot. The author of the Balfour Declaration had no such doubts. A year after the war he wrote, 'The four great powers are committed to Zionism and Zionism, be it right or wrong, good or bad, is rooted in age-long tradition, in present needs, in future hopes, of far profounder import than the desires and prejudices of the 700,000 Arabs who now inhabit that ancient land.'

The doubts that had been raised about the intentions of the Allies did not prevent the wild Arab rejoicing which greeted the liberation of Syria. The civil population had suffered fearfully from the war, because a plague of locusts, combined with the normal disruption of war and the corruption of Turkish officials and Syrian merchants, had caused widespread famine. Between 300,000 and 500,000 people died, out of a total population of 4 million.

Although it was Allenby's policy wherever possible to allow Emir Feisal's troops to enter the captured cities in triumph and to take over the administration, the entente with France was clearly Britain's first consideration, and when France objected to the display of Feisal's flag in Beirut Allenby ordered its removal. The French hastened to land troops in Beirut at the end of the war, and the whole coastal area from Tyre to Cilicia in Asia Minor came under French military administration. The British Occupied Enemy Territory Administration South (OETA South) covered Palestine, while the main towns in the Syrian interior were under Feisal's authority but with an attachment of British officers (OETA E East) on whom the Arabs, with their limited experience in administration, were heavily dependent. Mesopotamia was maintained as a single unit under an Anglo-Indian administration. The Sykes–Picot agreement, modified to reflect the realities of the situation, was already being applied.

Allenby and his military administrators faced a prospect of immense difficulty, which was not helped by the frequently conflicting instructions they received from Whitehall. Apart from France and the Zionists, with their demands, the new American ally had entered the scene. The fact that the United States had no imperial ambitions towards the Middle East greatly added to the moral force of President Wilson's sermon-like speeches about the post-war settlement. He chose to take Britain at its word. When a group of seven prominent Arabs living in Cairo presented a memorandum asking for a clear definition of British policy, Britain's reply – known as the Declaration to the Seven, and given wide publicity – was that the future government of Arab territories liberated by the action of Arab armies would be based on the principle of the 'consent of the governed'. Wilson included this phrase among his Four Ends of Peace which, under his influence, were later incorporated in the Covenant of the League of Nations. It was later given even greater force by an Anglo-French declaration of 7 November 1918 – that is, in the week between the signing of the armistice agreements with Turkey and Germany – which said that the goal of the British and French governments was the complete and final liberation of peoples oppressed by the Turks and the setting up of national governments and administrations which should derive their authority from the free exercise of the initiative and choice of the indigenous population.

Even allowing for American pressure, it is difficult to see why Britain and France should have felt that such barefaced hypocrisy was necessary. Turkey had already been defeated, and there was no need to sustain the Arab Revolt. There was no intention in London or Paris of allowing the indigenous population in the former Ottoman territories the free choice of their rulers. Even 'the consent of the governed' was an empty phrase.

9. The Anglo-French Interregnum, 1918–1939

Partition of the Arab East

The end of four centuries of Turkish rule in the Middle East was sudden and complete. Since Turkish rule had been accepted as the natural order for so long, it is hardly surprising that its removal left the vast majority of the population feeling confused and disorientated. The Ottoman ruling class had provided the leaders of Arab society – even in Egypt, which had been under British control for nearly forty years.

As we have seen, Ottoman governments and their representatives in the Arab provinces sometimes gave reason for them to be detested, but this did not mean that Turkish political leadership of the heart of the Islamic world had come to seem unnatural. Despite some later rewriting of history, the concept of a separate Arab nation – still less the doctrine of secular Arab nationalism – had scarcely begun to develop. The Hashemite claim to Arab leadership had been born almost haphazardly in the circumstances of war. It was far from being accepted by all the Arabs and would always suffer from its sponsorship by Britain. But the total Ottoman collapse did give Britain and France a brief period in which they felt that they could act largely as they pleased. This was something that would otherwise have been unimaginable for two invading Christian powers.

The Turkish heartland of the Ottoman Empire only narrowly avoided its own dismemberment – largely through the indomitable leadership of one man, Mustafa Kemal. After the signing of the Mudros armistice agreement, the new sultan, Mohammed VI (Mohammed V had died in July 1918), dissolved the Turkish parliament and formed a new government of men who were ready to accept the terms of the Allies. Apart from an Allied administration of Istanbul, the French were occupying Cilicia and Adana, British forces had taken over the Dardanelles strait and the Italians, the fourth of the western Allies, had landed at Antalya. Only the Russians had no claim. Under the Treaty of Brest-Litovsk (9 March 1918, after the Bolshevik Revolution), Turkey had regained all the territories lost to Russia in the war, as well as those ceded in 1877. But this would mean little if Turkey ceased to exist.

The Committee of Union and Progress had collapsed and its leaders had fled. The sultan then decided to crush the remnants of the Young Turks. Mustafa Kemal, who already enjoyed high prestige in Turkey, was causing the sultan and his government trouble by organizing resistance to the Allies in Istanbul, so Mohammed VI appointed him inspector-general of the Ninth Army, based on Samsun, with orders to disband the remainder of the Ottoman forces.

Mustafa Kemal landed at Samsun on 9 May 1919, but instead of disbanding the army he gathered supporters for the declaration of a Turkish state free from foreign control. The Allies, determined to fight resurgent Turkish nationalism, allowed a large Greek force to land at Izmir and occupy the surrounding district. Greek ambitions extended to the whole of western Anatolia, in which there were large Greek minorities – the former Christian Empire of Constantinople might be restored.

While the sultan ordered the Turkish troops not to resist the Greeks, Kemal was rapidly gathering support for the cause of Turkish independence. Although exhausted by eight years of almost continuous warfare, the Turkish people were roused to pursue the struggle by the Greek advance into the Anatolian heartland. They rejected the harsh terms of the Treaty of Sèvres of August 1920, which would have left Turkey helpless and deprived of some of its richest provinces, and the sultan, now little more than a puppet, was increasingly discredited.

The Graeco-Turkish war lasted two years, from 1920 to 1922. At first the Turks were unable to halt the Greek advance, but in 1921 the tide turned with a great Turkish victory on the River Sakayra. In 1922 the Greeks, weakened by dissension at home, were in headlong retreat, and in September 1922 Mustafa Kemal occupied Izmir. When his forces crossed the Dardanelles to drive the Greeks out of European Turkey too, a direct clash with Britain was only narrowly averted. The Allies gave way and by the terms of the armistice, to which Greece also adhered, they recognized Turkish sovereignty over Istanbul, the straits and eastern Thrace.

The peace conference which followed culminated with the Treaty of Lausanne of 24 July 1923. This recognized full Turkish sovereignty in nearly all the territories which are now those of the Turkish Republic. The long-suffering Armenians lost their hopes of independence in the process. After the Bolshevik Revolution, eastern or Russian Armenia declared its independence. Hopes of the western or Turkish Armenians of joining the new republic were destroyed by the advance of Mustafa Kemal's forces, and in December 1920 the government in the Armenian capital, Yerevan, handed over power peacefully to the Bolsheviks. The remnants of the Turkish Armenians fled mainly to Lebanon and Syria, where after a few years they were offered citizenship.

The Kurds suffered a similar bitter disappointment. The Treaty of Sèvres recognized an independent Kurdish state of Kurdistan, but this was cancelled by the 1923 Treaty of Lausanne. The Kurdish problem remained to destabilize the politics of the three countries in which Kurds form important minorities — Turkey, Iran and Iraq.

Although a considerable body of Turkish opinion favoured the retention of a constitutional monarchy, Mustafa Kemal was determined to get rid of the sultan, and his prestige and authority were such that he had his way. On 1 November 1922 the National Assembly passed a law abolishing the sultanate, and Mohammed VI fled into exile. On 29 October 1923 Turkey was proclaimed a republic, with Kemal as president.

The Islamic caliphate attracted as much loyalty as the sultanate and, although Mustafa Kemal would have liked to abolish the offices of sultan and caliph together, he bowed to the popular will in this matter. He agreed that Mohammed VI's nephew Abdul Mejid should become the spiritual head of Islam. But, although the caliph

S E A

Y

Aleppo

Hama
Homs

SYRIA

Damascus

TRANSJORDAN

SAUDI
ARABIA

Mosul

Kirkuk

IRAN

R. Tigris

Baghdad

IRAQ

R. Euphrates

THE LEVANT IN 1939

Countries under French Mandate

Countries under British Mandate

Borders

| 0 | | | 400Km |
| 0 | | | 250 Miles |

Source: Nicholas Bethell, *The Palestine Triangle*, André Deutsch, 1979 was shorn of all political power, his court became the centre of monarchist intrigue, and when two prominent Indian Muslims, Emir Ali and the Agha Khan, published a declaration calling upon the Turkish people to preserve the caliphate, Mustafa Kemal took advantage of the unfavourable Turkish reaction to this foreign interference and abolished it. A bill to this effect was passed by the National Assembly on 3 March 1924.

The title of caliph has not since been revived. In May 1926 a caliphate congress, held in Cairo, was attended by delegates from thirteen Muslim countries (not including Turkey), but its deliberations were inconclusive. Since then, the caliphate has not been an issue in the politics of the Muslim world.

Mustafa Kemal was a secular nationalist who believed that all the inheritance of the Ottoman Empire should be abandoned and Turkey should be transformed into a modern European state. This involved less of a sudden break with the past than might appear. The *Tanzimat* reforms had laid the foundations of a secular state, and the Young Turks, even while attempting to preserve the empire, had given a powerful impetus to the cause of Turkish nationalism. During the war years, the secularization of education had proceeded and the universities and public positions had been opened to women. Certain of the law courts under the control of the religious authorities had been placed under the Ministry of Justice. A law in 1916 had reformed marriage and divorce.

Mustafa Kemal carried the process much further. A new legal code, based on a variety of European systems, was substituted for the Islamic *sharia*. In 1928 the constitution became officially secular with the deletion of the clause reading that 'the religion of the Turkish state is Islam' and 'laicism' was established as one of the six cardinal principles of the state. A Latin-based alphabet replaced the Arabic script of Ottoman Turkish and finally, in 1935, surnames on the European model were introduced. Mustafa Kemal took the name of Atatürk or 'Father of the Turks'.

Because of Kemal's extraordinary ascendancy over his people, these reforms were profound and far-reaching; however, they did not mean that the Turkish people as a whole renounced Islam. Though the authority of the *ulama* was destroyed, the Turkish masses, who remained peasant farmers, preserved their Islamic faith. Even the intelligentsia would have ridiculed the idea that they had ceased to be Muslims – in their view there had only been a Turkish reformation of Islam.

What the creation of the Turkish Republic and the abandonment of the empire did mean was that Turkey abruptly ceased to be a factor in the political development of the Middle East (only territorial disputes involving the vilayets of Mosul and Aleppo remained, and these were settled in the 1920s and 1930s – with Britain and France). Atatürk's success in developing a strong national state capable of dealing with the European powers on equal terms influenced both Arab and Persian nationalists – especially the latter – but their differing circumstances meant that Turkey was more of an inspiration than an example. They neither wished nor could hope for their countries to become part of Europe, although Turkey could nurse this aspiration, even if to some it appeared unrealistic.

After the abolition of the sultanate and caliphate, Atatürk organized the new republic as a secular parliamentary democracy. The 1924 constitution guaranteed equality before the law and freedom of thought, speech, publication and association. In theory sovereignty lay with the people and was exercised in their name by the single-chamber parliament – the Grand National Assembly – which elected the president of the republic, who chose the prime minister. Ministers were supposed to be responsible to parliament.

Democracy remained severely restricted, however. Atatürk used his immense prestige to override the constitution whenever he chose. In 1924 he organized his supporters as the Republican People's Party (RPP). This dominated political life, as all members of the Assembly belonged to it, and the RPP ruled Turkey for twenty-seven years. Yet, despite his authoritarianism and arbitrary methods, Atatürk planted the seeds of liberal constitutional government. The Assembly had real powers, and Atatürk tried to have his way by persuasion rather than by force.

In the economic field, Atatürk concentrated on developing Turkey's rich mineral resources, industry and communications. With a lively memory of Ottoman Turkey's subservience to European financial and economic control through the Capitulations, he instituted an *étatist* policy of large-scale state enterprises to exercise close control over planning and development. Although increasingly bureaucratic and inefficient, these enterprises made considerable progress towards industrializing Turkey between the two world wars and, because they had no Marxist ideological basis, their eventual liberalization did not present insuperable difficulties.

After Atatürk's death in 1938, opposition to the elected dictatorship gained ground and his successor, Ismet Inönü, partly under the influence of the democratic ideals of the Western Allies in the Second World War, allowed the establishment of a multi-party system. The Democratic Party emerged as the chief rival to the RPP, advocating free enterprise and a multi-party system, and it steadily gained popularity until it won a resounding victory in the 1950 elections. The genuineness of Turkey's secular democracy was demonstrated when Inönü allowed a peaceful transfer of power.

The experience of Turkey's former Arab subjects was wholly different.

At the end of the First World War the principal concern of the four Western Allies, as they prepared for the peace conference to be held in Paris, was the post-war settlement in Europe following the defeat of Germany and the Austro-Hungarian Empire. The future of the Middle East was not high on the conference agenda. As a consequence of its defeat of Turkey, Britain had acquired supreme power in the region, subject only to its obligations to its French ally. The war in the desert had caught the imagination of the British public, as the well-publicized romantic exploits of T. E. Lawrence provided relief from the squalid horrors of the trench warfare on the western front.

The possibility of annexing the former Ottoman Arab provinces as colonies was not seriously entertained except by a few Arabist officials – the age of European imperial expansion was already at an end. But the Arabs, who for so long had been ruled by Turks, were regarded as one of the 'subject races' rather than a 'governing race', to employ Cromer of Egypt's categorization of humanity. (The 'noble and independent' Arab beduin were different, but they did not occupy territory of political or economic significance.) The conflict between the undertakings to Sharif Hussein and to France concerned only a small minority of specialists, such as T. E. Lawrence himself, who were almost unanimously Francophobe. In general it was felt that the Arabs should be grateful for their liberation from the Turks – as indeed most of them were. Although in theory the new doctrine of self-determination, based on President Wilson's ideals, was the guiding principle of the post-war settlement, its effect was quite underestimated.

It was Egypt – the country which had already been under British control for nearly forty years – which provided the first shock. Compared with the Syrians, the Egyptians had suffered little from the war. With the huge rise in cotton prices, Egypt's natural wealth had actually increased. Large profits were made from the supply of goods to the Allied troops. But the prosperity concealed powerful social grievances. Although supposedly voluntary, recruitment of the *fellahin* and their camels and donkeys to the labour and transport corps was in effect compulsory under martial law, and was deeply resented. The new wealth accrued to the big and medium-sized landowners, who possessed 75 per cent of the cultivated area, and to a small new capitalist class in the cities. The reality for the rest of the population was a steep rise in the cost of living. The government's lack of any social and economic policy allowed the large landowners to abandon food-growing for cotton-growing, thus creating a near-famine and a sharp rise in the death rate, which actually exceeded the birth rate during the war.

The fermenting nationalism which had merely been submerged by martial law came to the surface. The British high commissioner, Sir Reginald Wingate, had allowed the formation of a commission headed by the British judicial adviser to consider legislative reform

and Egypt's political status after the war. This reached the conclusion that Egypt should have a legislature of two chambers, of which
the Upper House would be the more important. This would include
Egyptian ministers, British advisers and representatives of the
foreign communities elected by special electorates. The judicial
adviser's view was that, since Egypt's financial interests were largely
in foreign hands, the Egyptians had no right to a dominant voice in
legislation affecting them.

These proposals, when leaked in November 1918, were a provo-
cation to Egypt's nationalist leadership. They were fully aware that
the Wilsonian doctrine of self-determination for the people freed
from Turkish rule had been endorsed by the Allies. Already the
Arabs of Arabia, whom the Egyptians regarded (with some justice)
as being more backward than themselves, were preparing to send a
delegate to the Paris peace conference. Two days after the Armistice,
Zaghloul Pasha presented himself at the British Residency at the
head of a delegation (*wafd* in Arabic – the name that was to become
attached to Zaghloul's supporters) to say that the Egyptian people
wanted their complete independence and to request proceeding
to London to present their case. Zaghloul had been kept out of
the government by Wingate, but he was the undoubted leader
of the nationalist movement. Balfour, Britain's foreign secretary,
who was already looking forward to the Paris peace conference,
brusquely rejected the visit and when Rushdi Pasha, the prime
minister, proposed that he should come to London instead he
repeated the refusal, saying in a dispatch to Wingate that while the
British government 'desire to act on the principle which they had
always followed of giving the Egyptians an ever-increasing share in
the government of the country . . . as you are well aware, the stage
has not yet been reached at which self-government is possible.' Britain had no intention of abandoning its responsibilities for order and
good government in Egypt 'and for protecting the rights and interests both of the native and the foreign populations of the country'.

Zaghloul seized his chance. Pointing out that even Egypt's prime
minister had been spurned, he organized a nation-wide campaign

of protest to back his claim to be Egypt's true representative. Balfour relented to the extent of inviting Rushdi to London, but he rejected Rushdi's insistence that Zaghloul should accompany him. Rushdi and his cabinet then resigned on 1 March 1919, with the full approval of Sultan Fuad.

Although Zaghloul stepped up his agitation, the high commission believed the trouble would die down and recommended that Zaghloul be deported. Balfour agreed, and Zaghloul and three of his colleagues were bundled on a train to Port Said and taken on a British destroyer to Malta.

The public reaction was immediate and severe. Rioting students in Cairo were supported by strikes among government officials, doctors and lawyers and the capital came to a standstill. To British astonishment, the trouble spread to the provincial towns and the countryside, to take the form of a national uprising which Egyptian nationalists later called their 1919 Revolution.

Stern military action, with the use of flying columns into the countryside and bombing raids on suspect gatherings, brought the uprising to an end in a few weeks. But the British government understood that repression would not suffice. News of the uprising had been as unwelcome as it was unexpected at a time when the government was concerned with the Irish troubles nearer home as well as involved in the affairs of the Paris conference. The prime minister, Lloyd George, with one of his rare intuitive flashes, decided that General Allenby, who had arrived in Paris to give his views on Syria, was the right man to restore the situation in Egypt, and in March 1919 Allenby was instantly dispatched to replace Wingate.

Allenby's brief was to restore law and order and do anything required 'by the necessity of maintaining the King's protectorate over Egypt on a secure and equitable basis'. However, behind the bluff and sometimes brusque military exterior of Allenby 'the Bull' lay an acute political mind with liberal tendencies. He had already, in Paris, argued against the imposition of French rule in Syria against the clearly expressed wishes of the inhabitants, and he at least half-believed in the principle of self-determination – which was 50 per

cent more than the British and French politicians who had publicly
adopted it.

Immediately on his arrival, Allenby assured the Egyptians of his
intention to redress their justifiable grievances. Using all his prestige he forced a reluctant Lloyd George to agree to the release of
Zaghloul and his colleagues – an action which horrified Anglo-
Egyptian officials. Zaghloul unrepentantly resumed his demand
for an end to the protectorate, and some of the strikes and agitation
were resumed. Allenby acted firmly, as London expected, but he
already understood, as the British government did not, that the
protectorate would have to go. He now welcomed the decision to
send out a high-level mission headed by the colonial secretary, Lord
Milner, although again the mission's brief was to study the cause
of the disorders and to recommend the form of the constitution
which *under the protectorate*, 'will be best calculated to promote
[Egypt's] peace and prosperity, the progressive development of
self-governing institutions and the protection of foreign interests'.
In prescient words, Balfour told the House of Commons on 17
November that '. . . the question of Egypt, the question of the
Sudan, and the question of the Canal, form an organic and indis-
soluble whole' and England was not going to give up any of its
responsibilities. 'British supremacy exists,' he said; 'British supremacy is going to be maintained.'

The truth was that the course of the First World War had
appeared to justify the British occupation of Egypt and the change
in focus of British Middle Eastern policy from Istanbul to Cairo
which had occurred almost accidentally in the nineteenth century.
It was hardly surprising that in 1919 no British statesman was
prepared to contemplate abandoning control of Egypt.

When the British government's intentions were made known,
Zaghloul ordered a boycott of the Milner mission, which spent
three disheartening months in Egypt and was everywhere met by
hostile demonstrations and demands for Egypt's complete independence. However, the mission reached some firm and realistic
conclusions: that, since it had never been part of the British Empire,

Egypt could not be annexed in the post-war world and had to be recognized as an independent constitutional monarchy. The preservation of British rights and interests would have to be secured by an Anglo-Egyptian treaty to replace the protectorate. This raised the question of who would sign on Egypt's behalf. Adly Pasha, the prime minister, was a politician of standing but he knew he could not carry the nation without Zaghloul's support. Adly persuaded Zaghloul to go to London with his mission to work at the details. After several weeks' discussion, during which both sides made concessions, the basis for a treaty had been reached. Egypt would be independent, with its own diplomatic representatives. Britain would defend Egypt in case of war and, although it would have the right to keep forces on Egyptian soil for the protection of its 'imperial communications', this 'would not constitute in any manner a military occupation of the country or prejudice the rights of the Government of Egypt'.

Zaghloul and his Wafd had achieved most but not all of their aims. Now Zaghloul showed his fatal lack of statesmanship. Unwilling to admit that he had failed to achieve Egypt's total independence, he refused to urge the mass of his supporters in the country to accept the terms of the treaty. When, as prime minister, Adly Pasha went to London in July 1921 to conclude the treaty (without Zaghloul, who had insisted that he should lead the delegation), he did not dare to make the concessions demanded by Lloyd George's cabinet, which was hardening its position. Adly knew that Zaghloul could bring out 'the street' to denounce him for treachery. When Adly returned from England empty-handed, Zaghloul and his followers stepped up their protests with strikes and violent demonstrations.

Allenby now acted firmly by ordering Zaghloul's second deportation – this time to the Seychelles – having ensured with a heavy use of force that there would be no repeat of the 1919 uprising. He then proposed that Britain should make a unilateral declaration of Egypt's independence while reserving its vital interests. The British cabinet was divided between moderates led by the foreign secretary, Lord Curzon, and hardliners represented by Winston Churchill, the new young secretary of state for the colonies. Allenby stormed into London threatening to resign if his proposals were not accepted. Lloyd George gave way, and on 28 February 1922 Britain published a declaration recognizing Egypt as 'an independent sovereign State' but reserving to its discretion four points to be the subject of Anglo-Egyptian negotiations in the future. These were 'The security of the communications of the British Empire in Egypt; the defence of Egypt against all foreign aggression or interference, direct or indirect; the protection of foreign interests in Egypt and of minorities; and the Sudan.'

Two weeks later Sultan Fuad assumed the title of King Fuad I. A constitutional commission produced a constitution based on the Belgian model, providing for a Senate and an elected Chamber of Deputies. Although this gave the king considerable powers – including the right to dissolve parliament and to appoint some of the senators – these were not as great as the king would have wished, and Allenby had to intervene to prevent the establishment of a royal dictatorship. The ultimate consequence was that for the next thirty years Egypt was governed by an uneasy and ultimately unworkable balance of forces: the palace, where the powers of the Muhammad Ali dynasty had been partially restored; parliament and the politicians, among whom the Wafd party was usually but not always dominant; and the British residency (which, despite independence, was still not an embassy). Repeated efforts to negotiate an Anglo-Egyptian treaty to settle outstanding differences broke down because Britain's minimum demands were unacceptable to Egyptian national pride. The most enduring of these differences concerned the Sudan, which the monarch and the Wafd united in claiming for Egypt – a claim which Britain resolutely rejected. Indeed it was the Sudan problem which caused a final break between Britain and Zaghloul. The 70-year-old leader, allowed back from exile, won a sweeping victory for his Wafd in the first parliamentary elections. As prime minister, he pressed Egypt's claim to the Sudan. There was a full-scale mutiny by Sudanese military cadets, who were Sudanese nationalists but ready to co-operate with their Egyptian counterparts against Britain. Anglo-Sudanese officials naturally blamed Egypt for the disturbances. In this fevered atmosphere in the summer of 1924, Sir Lee Stack, *sirdar* of the Egyptian army and governor-general of the Sudan, was murdered by a group of ninety Egyptian terrorists. An outraged Allenby drove to the Egyptian parliament with a cavalry escort to deliver a harsh ultimatum which included the banning of all demonstrations, the payment of a heavy indemnity and – most important – the withdrawal from the Sudan of all Egyptian troops. Rejecting the ultimatum, Zaghloul resigned. Although still Egypt's national leader, he never regained power. He died in 1927. The king dissolved parliament and was able for a time to establish a royal semi-autocracy with weak ministers, but his powers were insufficient for this to last and the unstable façade of parliamentary democracy survived.

In Egypt, Britain had already been effectively governing the country for nearly forty years, but it was there dealing with a people who had constituted a nation for some 5,000 years, even while under the rule of a series of empires. In the rest of the former Ottoman provinces the victorious Allies were confronted with a very different situation. With the exception of the remote and mountainous kingdom of Yemen, there were no nation-states. Sharif Hussein's ambitious claim to become ruler of a unified kingdom was summarily rejected by the Allies and he was confined to the weak and impoverished kingdom of the Hejaz.

Despite strong French opposition, Hussein's son, Emir Feisal, secured a place at the Paris peace conference, although it was made clear to him that he represented only the Hejaz and not the Arabs as a whole. From this weak position in Paris, he attempted to retrieve what he could of Arab aspirations. Taking his stand on the various declarations by the Allies in favour of self-determination, he proposed that a commission of inquiry be sent to Syria and Palestine to examine the wishes of the inhabitants. President Wilson enthusiastically accepted the proposal, and his suggestion that the commission should consist of French, British, Italian and American representatives was endorsed by the conference. But in reality the French were strongly hostile to the commission, while the British were lukewarm, and eventually all the parties except the Americans withdrew. The American appointees, Henry King and Charles Crane, decided to go on their own, and their report fully explains British and French hostility towards the commission.

They found that the inhabitants of Syria/Palestine overwhelmingly opposed the proposal to place them under great-power mandates which were a thinly disguised form of colonial administration. They acknowledged the need for outside assistance, provided it came from the United States or, as second choice, from Britain. On no account did they want assistance from France. The King–Crane commission started out strongly favourable towards Zionism but soon concluded that the Zionist programmes would have to be greatly modified if the promises of the Balfour Declaration to protect the rights of the non-Jews in Palestine were to be upheld. After discussion with Zionist leaders in Jerusalem, they had no doubt that the Zionists looked forward 'to a practically complete dispossession of the present non-Jewish inhabitants of Palestine'.

The King–Crane report was ignored by the Allies. It was clearly repugnant to Britain and France; and the United States, after raising so many expectations, was about to retreat into twenty years of isolationism. But a serious rift between the Allies also seemed possible, as the British government regarded French ambitions in Syria as excessive – a view that was strongly held by all the leading British Arabists, such as T. E. Lawrence. Britain also felt some obligation towards the Hashemites – a sentiment that was in no way shared by the French. When France wanted to garrison Syria with French troops, Britain refused to agree.

Meanwhile, after Emir Feisal's return from Paris in May 1919, his supporters organized elections wherever they were possible throughout Syria (although they were blocked by the French in the coastal regions). A General Syrian Congress, meeting in Damascus, called for recognition of the independence of Syria (including Palestine) and Iraq and for the repudiation of the Sykes–Picot agreement, the

Balfour Declaration and the mandatary system. But the realities of power soon reasserted themselves. Britain persuaded Feisal that he must compromise with France. In November 1919 he went to Paris and reached an agreement with the French premier, Clemenceau, providing for French occupation of the coastal areas and a French monopoly of assistance to the fledgeling Arab state in the interior.

Feisal was quite unable to persuade his followers to accept the dismemberment of Syria, and on 8 March 1920 the General Syrian Congress in Damascus passed a resolution proclaiming the independence of Syria/Palestine with autonomy for Lebanon. At the same time a similar meeting of Iraq's leaders declared Iraq's independence, with Emir Abdullah as king.

Britain and France responded swiftly. Refusing to recognize the Damascus resolution, they hastily convened a meeting of the Supreme Council of the League of Nations, which announced its decision on 5 May 1920. Syria was to be partitioned into the two French mandates of Lebanon and Syria and the British mandate of Palestine, while Iraq was to remain undivided as a British mandate. The British mandate for Palestine carried with it the obligation to carry out the terms of the Balfour Declaration.

Aroused by these decisions, the Arabs of Syria urged Feisal to declare war on the French. Aware of his military weakness, Feisal allowed his hot-headed younger officers to attack French positions on the Lebanon border. The French commander-in-chief, General Gouraud, sent an ultimatum on 14 July demanding that French forces be allowed to occupy Aleppo, Homs, Hama and the Bekaa plain. Feisal accepted the ultimatum but the action was pointless because the French had already decided to seize Syria. A French column, including Senegalese and North African Arab troops, advanced and took Damascus on 25 July. Brave resistance by Feisal's ill-trained troops could do little against French tanks and planes. France invited Feisal to leave Syria, and he was received in exile by an embarrassed British government. The colonial secretary, Winston Churchill, told the Imperial Conference in 1921 that French operations against Syria had been 'extremely painful' but 'we have these

strong ties with the French and they have to prevail, and we were
not able to do anything to help the Arabs in the matter . . .'

Having been awarded the mandates for Syria and Lebanon, one
of France's first acts was to enlarge Lebanon at Syria's expense.
France's intention was to make Lebanon the headquarters for its
Middle Eastern operations. The Maronites of Lebanon traditionally looked to France as their protector, whereas Syria had become
a focus of Arab nationalism. In his decree of 31 August 1920,
General Gouraud declared the creation of *le Grand Liban*, consisting of the former autonomous *sanjak* of Mount Lebanon plus the
Bekaa plain to the east and the coastal towns of Tripoli to the
north and Sidon and Tyre to the south. The population of *le Grand
Liban* had a small Christian majority, but this was threatened by
the stronger Christian tendency to emigrate and the higher Muslim
birth rate.

The Allies' decisions on the partitioning of the Ottoman Empire
were not carried out peacefully. Apart from the fighting in Syria,
there was an uprising against the Jews by the Arabs in Palestine,
whose alarm intensified as the objectives of the Zionist leaders
became clear. In Iraq, where Arab hopes had been thwarted by the
establishment of an Anglo-Indian administration on colonial lines
with virtually no Arab participation, the tribes of the middle
Euphrates rose in a rebellion which was put down only at heavy
cost.

The urgent need for post-war economy caused the British
government to act. Churchill, with T. E. Lawrence as adviser, held
a conference in Cairo in March 1921. No Arabs were present, but
the meeting was attended by the high commissioner for Iraq, Sir
Percy Cox, and the newly appointed high commissioner for Palestine, Sir Herbert Samuel, who had first put forward the Zionist idea
to the British cabinet. It was decided to carry out the arrangement
already prepared in London to make Feisal King of Iraq. The future
of Emir Abdullah created a problem. Disappointed in his hopes of
becoming King of Iraq, he had arrived from the Hejaz at Maan near
Aqaba in November 1920 at the head of tribal forces, declaring his

intention of attacking the French in Syria to avenge his brother Feisal.

From Cairo, Churchill travelled to Jerusalem, with the joint purpose of reassuring the Palestinian Arabs that there was no intention of allowing Palestine to become a Jewish state and of conferring with Abdullah. He rejected Abdullah's various proposals for the incorporation of Transjordan (that is, the east bank of the River Jordan) into either Iraq or Palestine under an Arab administration, but a provisional arrangement was reached whereby Britain agreed to recognize Abdullah as emir of Transjordan with an annual British subsidy until Britain could persuade France to restore an Arab state in Syria with Abdullah at its head. Since the French were adamant against this, the provisional arrangement became permanent, and the state of Transjordan came into existence until, following the first Arab–Israeli war (1948–9), it was incorporated with the West Bank of Jordan to form the Hashemite kingdom of Jordan.

The mandates for Palestine, Syria, Lebanon and Iraq were formally approved by the Council of the League of Nations in July 1922 and became effective in September 1923. In 1924 the United States, which was not a member of the League of Nations, gave its approval to them. Transjordan was added to Britain's Palestine mandate, but the mandatary was permitted to exclude it, and in fact did exclude it, from the area of Jewish settlement.

The dismemberment of the Ottoman Empire thus resulted in the creation of five new states – Syria, Lebanon, Transjordan, Iraq and Palestine. All of them were under the tutelage of Britain or France, which had also been chiefly responsible for establishing the shape of their frontiers. With the Treaty of Mudros (1918), Turkish suzerainty over Yemen, which had never been very effective, finally came to an end. The country's remoteness and inaccessibility, reinforced by the wishes of its rulers, ensured that it remained backward but independent. Another new state – the kingdom of the Hejaz, the residue of King Hussein's dream of an independent Arab federation

under Hashemite rule – was short-lived. In the rest of Arabia, Ibn
Saud, 'Sultan of Nejd and its Dependencies', was extending his rule.
Having finally subdued his Rashidi enemies to the north, in 1920
he sent his 15-year-old son Feisal to the south-western Arabian highlands of Asir to secure the allegiance of its people. He did the same
with the Jawf region on the borders of the newly created emirate
of Transjordan. But Ibn Saud was faced with a recurring problem:
his undisciplined and ferocious tribal warriors, who had no regard
for international frontiers, launched raids deep into the territory of
Transjordan and Iraq. British planes and armoured cars joined the
local tribesmen to drive them back with heavy losses.

The boundaries between Nejd and both Kuwait and Iraq were
still not properly defined. Ibn Saud regarded border demarcation
as ludicrous in an area where the nomad inhabitants lacked any
sense of nationality and were accustomed to wander over huge
stretches of desert to find pasturage for their flocks. But the British
protectors of Iraq and Kuwait were determined to establish a frontier beyond which Wahhabi power would not be allowed to expand.
At Uqair, the sea-port of al-Hasa on the Gulf, Sir Percy Cox, high
commissioner of Iraq, reached an agreement with Ibn Saud whereby
a large slice of territory claimed by Iraq was allocated to the new
kingdom of Iraq. In order to placate Ibn Saud, some two-thirds of
the land that had been considered to belong to Kuwait at the time
of the 1913 agreement with the Ottoman government became part
of Nejd. An embarrassed Cox later explained to the emir of Kuwait
that nothing could be done to prevent Ibn Saud from taking the
territories if he wished.

Britain was less successful in arranging an accommodation
between Ibn Saud and his old rival and enemy King Hussein of the
Hejaz, to which all Wahhabi ambitions were now directed. The
embittered old king refused to sign the 1921 draft treaty, which
would have meant accepting the accomplished fact that Syria, Lebanon and Palestine were all lost to the rule of his family. His annual
subsidy from Britain had been discontinued. However, he still aimed
to assert himself. He demonstrated his authority over his family by

making a state visit to Aqaba, where he was received with due deference by his son Abdullah, the new emir of Transjordan. He then
made a fatal error. Since Mustafa Kemal of the new Turkish Republic had just abolished the institution of the Islamic caliphate, Hussein
declared himself to have assumed the title of 'Prince of the Faithful
and Successor of the Prophet'.

Early in the war Britain had supported the idea of a restored Arab
caliphate, but now it was no longer interested. In the Muslim world
as a whole, apart from some Hashemite loyalists in Palestine and
Syria, reaction to Hussein's declaration ranged from indifference to
anger. Among Ibn Saud's Wahhabi warriors there was rage. It was
at this moment that Britain decided to end the £60,000 subsidy it
had been paying Ibn Saud since 1915. He therefore no longer had
any motive for restraining his warriors, who at once fell upon the
Hejaz. Hussein, who, whatever his faults, remained dignified and
courageous to the last, wanted to fight to the end, but the Hejazis
persuaded him to abdicate in favour of his eldest son, Ali, who had
retreated to barricade himself with his forces in Jedda and might be
able to sue for better terms from the Wahhabis. Hussein sailed away
to an embittered exile in Cyprus, taking with him what remained
of his treasures.

Ali held out in Jedda for a year until he surrendered and abdicated.
Ibn Saud's forces soon overran the rest of the Hejaz, but he took
care to restrain his Ikhwan warriors, reports of whose excesses terrified the local population. Ibn Saud gave priority to security. He
reopened the Islamic pilgrimage route and set out to demonstrate
that he could ensure the security of the holy places after centuries
of disorder. An English Muslim who made the *hajj* (pilgrimage) in
1925 wrote of Ibn Saud, 'He is probably the best ruler that Arabia
has known since the days of the four Khalifas.'

With Ali's abdication in December 1924, Ibn Saud became ruler
of the whole Hejaz, except that in the extreme north-west the
British authorities in Palestine retained some territory by sending
troops and armoured cars to occupy the strip of land between Maan
and Aqaba, on the grounds that, as part of the former Ottoman

vilayet of Damascus, it should now be included in the British mandate for Palestine. The reality was that it was considered essential for Emir Abdullah's emirate of Transjordan to have an outlet to the sea. Ibn Saud never accepted the *fait accompli*, but he was unable to prevent it.

Ibn Saud now controlled the holy places of Islam. The question was, how would the Muslim world respond? The great majority of Muslims, who were not Arabs, were likely to be sceptical that a tribal leader from central Arabia should succeed in protecting and securing the holy places when the sharifian rulers and Ottoman Turks had so manifestly failed. Already they were alarmed by the Wahhabi destruction of the tombs of Muslim saints.

Ibn Saud acted with skill and caution. He appointed his second son, Emir Feisal, as his viceroy of the Hejaz and Abdullah Damluji, an experienced Iraqi in his service, as director of foreign affairs. Delegates of eminent Persian and Indian Muslims visited the Hejaz and reported favourably. The people of the Hejaz were also impressed by Ibn Saud's ability to maintain security and by his willingness to adjust to their more sophisticated urban ways. On 8 January 1926 the Hejaz notables approached him with a formal request to accept their loyalty as King of the Hejaz, and he agreed to rule, with God's help, through the holy *sharia*.

As well as being their king, Ibn Saud was the people's imam, which meant that he led them in prayers and set them an example in religious devotion. But he went no further than this – unlike Sharif Hussein, or King Farouk of Egypt at a later date, Ibn Saud never aspired to the title of caliph; he was only resolutely opposed to anyone else taking the title.

The Soviet Union was the first of the powers to recognize the new Saudi regime, followed rapidly by Britain, France and the other European powers. The United States was to wait another decade before it showed any interest in Arabia. The Soviet Union saw Ibn Saud as an independent anti-imperialist force and hoped to use his new state as a channel for political and commercial penetration of the Middle East, which was otherwise under British or French

control. By 1938 the Soviets realized their error and the Soviet legation in Jedda was closed. Most of the staff were liquidated in the
Stalinist purges.

Problems with Britain remained, as Ibn Saud refused to recognize
the British mandates in Iraq, Palestine and Transjordan until his
claim to the Maan–Aqaba territory was accepted. Under the 1927
Treaty of Jedda this matter was shelved, but Britain recognized 'the
complete and absolute independence of the dominions' of Ibn Saud,
who in return agreed to respect all the British treaties of protection
with Arab Gulf shaikhdoms.

He was still faced with the task of unifying and administering
his vast but thinly populated territories – some two-thirds the size
of India. He had appointed his eldest son, Saud, viceroy of Nejd
with Feisal as viceroy of the Hejaz, but he also needed outside help
and this he confined to Muslim Arabs – Iraqis, Syrians and Egyptians.
His policy was to make each tribal chief responsible for security in
his own area and accountable to him, while the Wahhabi army
remained in the background as the ultimate sanction. He also
contracted several dynastic marriages with the daughters of the leaders of important tribal confederations, which partially explains why
forty-four sons survived him and today there are some four or five
thousand Saudi princes in direct line of descent from the king.

He showed wisdom in many respects. Although he remained
the supreme ruler, with overwhelming prestige, he never ignored
public opinion. He was determined that his kingdom should have
those Western inventions which would make life easier for his
people, provided these did not undermine their way of life. He did
not try to force the pace but used persuasion where possible. A
gathering of religious shaikhs was convinced that the telephone
was not the instrument of the devil when they heard on it a voice
reciting the Holy Koran. (A generation later his son, King Feisal,
used the same methods to overcome objections to television and
to girls' education.)

Despite his tact and political skill, in 1929–30 Ibn Saud was faced
by a full-scale revolt among some of his Ikhwan warriors, who

denounced his Western innovations and demanded the right to raid across the borders into Transjordan and Iraq, whose people they regarded as infidels. Eventually Ibn Saud took the field against them and put down the rebellion. His authority was now unchallenged throughout his territories, and on 8 September 1932 the kingdom of the Hejaz and the sultanate of Nejd were officially united as the kingdom of Saudi Arabia.

The desert boundaries of the new kingdom with the Arab Gulf shaikhdoms remained unsettled, but this would only present problems later, in the oil era. On the other hand, a dispute with the Imam Yahya, ruler of the ancient kingdom of Yemen, concerning the Asir coastal region on the Red Sea, led to a brief Saudi–Yemeni war in 1934. After a Saudi force under Emir Feisal had occupied the Yemeni port of Hodeida, Ibn Saud ordered a halt. In the peace negotiations he behaved with generosity and magnanimity, abstaining from any demands on Yemeni territory. A treaty of 'Muslim Friendship and Arab Fraternity' was the basis of untroubled relations between the two countries for the next thirty years.

In the first three decades following the break-up of the Ottoman Empire, Saudi Arabia and Yemen were the only states of the Mashreq or Arab East which were fully independent. Under its imam Yahya, who ruled from 1904 to 1948, mountainous Yemen kept itself virtually impenetrable to the outside world and hardly impinged on the politics of the region. Saudi Arabia, because it included the holy places of Islam and had in Ibn Saud a ruler of unique prestige, exerted more influence. However, it remained the least developed part of the region – proud but intensely poor. The improved administration of the *hajj* pilgrimage increased revenues in the 1920s, as the number of pilgrims increased to 100,000 a year and each pilgrim paid a fee of £5 in gold. However, the number of pilgrims declined drastically in the 1930s as a consequence of the Great Depression, falling to only 20,000 in 1933. In 1931 Ibn Saud's finance minister was forced to declare a moratorium on all the kingdom's debts and to commandeer for ready cash the gasoline stocks of two private companies in Jedda. With some reluctance, in 1933 Ibn Saud granted an oil concession for the kingdom's eastern territories to Standard Oil of California. Oil was discovered in commercial quantities in 1938, in what was to prove to be one of the largest oilfields in the world, but, because the Second World War intervened, it was only in the 1950s that the kingdom became the major producer in the region and began to acquire vast wealth.

The Inter-war Years

(a) Egypt

Britain's unilateral declaration of Egypt's independence in 1922, with significant reservations protecting British imperial interests, gave Egypt an unstable and anomalous political framework. The British residency was no longer the only real centre of power in the country but one of three, alongside the palace and the Wafd. As long as British troops remained in occupation, British power could always be exerted, but it was exercised with increasing difficulty and diminishing effectiveness.

The same pattern of events was repeated several times. The king, who had considerable powers under the constitution but wished that they were greater, would dissolve parliament and try to rule without it. When he could do so no longer, an election would be held in which, provided the elections were substantially free, the Wafdists always won a sweeping victory. In later years the Wafd was seen to have lost its cohesion and sense of purpose as it became riddled with faction and corruption, but in the 1930s it was undoubtedly the political expression of Egypt – comparable to the Congress Party in India during the years of struggle for independence from British rule.

In 1925 Britain's Conservative government replaced Allenby as high commissioner with Lord Lloyd, a close friend of Winston Churchill who, like Churchill, refused to acknowledge that the empire was in decline. Lloyd accepted the constitutional position in Egypt and used his influence to prevent King Fuad from attempting to exclude the Wafd from power. But he was adamant on maintaining Britain's reservations to Egypt's independence, and for this he considered it necessary that the numbers and authority of both civilian and military Anglo-Egyptian officials should not be reduced beyond the point which he considered to be the essential minimum. In particular he resisted Wafdist efforts to expand the armed forces and replace the British high command with Egyptian officers. Fearing a repeat of the Arab Revolt, Lloyd was always prepared to summon a British warship to Alexandria in times of crisis.

In general Lloyd had his way, but he felt angrily frustrated. As he wrote to a friend,

... our present position is impossible ... We cannot carry on much longer as we are. We have magnitude without position; power without authority; responsibility without control. I must insure that no foreign power intervenes in education, aviation, wireless communications, railways or army (where all seek to do so), and I must achieve this without upsetting the parliamentary regime which we forced upon the country against the king's wishes ...

Lloyd's analysis of the anomalies of the British position in Egypt was correct. The British government's aim remained to secure an Anglo-Egyptian treaty of alliance in which, in return for some concessions, Egypt would accept the limitations to Egyptian independence which Britain considered essential – including the abandonment of the Egyptian claim to sovereignty over Sudan. When King Fuad paid a state visit to London in 1927, the British Foreign Office attempted to initiate negotiations for a treaty with the Egyptian prime minister, Sarwat Pasha, without Lloyd's knowledge. Lloyd had the satisfaction of seeing his prediction vindicated that any Egyptian prime minister would be either unwilling or unable to sell such a treaty to the Egyptian parliament. When Zaghloul Pasha died later in the year, Nahas, his successor as leader of the Wafd, was anxious to show that he was as fervent a champion of unfettered Egyptian independence as his predecessor. After weeks of aimless political manoeuvres, the Egyptian parliament rejected the proposed treaty.

When Ramsay MacDonald came to power in Britain at the head of a Labour government, Lloyd was replaced. His romantic right-wing brand of Toryism had been too much even for Stanley Baldwin's Conservative government. Another attempt was made to reach a treaty agreement, and this time success seemed in sight as Britain was even prepared to withdraw its troops from the Suez Canal zone, but – not for the last time – negotiations broke down over Egypt's demand for the revision of the 1899 Anglo-Egyptian condominium agreement on the Sudan. The Sudan was a question which was capable of arousing the whole country, as even the illiterate *fellahin* were aware of the importance of the Nile flood on which their lives depended.

King Fuad had not given up hope of reducing the Wafd's domination of Egypt's political life. When he refused to give his assent to two bills presented to parliament by the Wafd, Nahas resigned in the belief that the king would be unable to resist the Wafd's popular strength. The king turned to Sidky Pasha, an autocratic millionaire who had held office with ability in various governments but always followed his own path. Sidky was not a king's man, but he was quite prepared to inaugurate a quasi-dictatorship under royal auspices. With the help of British troops he suppressed public demonstrations and went on to amend the 1923 constitution and the electoral law to increase the king's powers and ensure the defeat of the Wafd in the 1931 elections.

Sidky's position was immeasurably strengthened by the fact that he was clearly no puppet of Britain, the palace or anyone else. He muzzled the press and deflated the Wafd by preventing it from using its most powerful weapon – control of the streets. At the same time he used the political moratorium to exhibit his talent for finance. Sidky had been one of the original promoters of Egyptian capitalist enterprise during the First World War; his abilities were suited to dealing with the consequences of the world depression and shielding Egypt from them as far as possible. His regime marked the beginning of the move away from free-trade liberalism, installed under Cromer, towards the egyptianization of the economy.

In opposition, the Wafd was more than ever the popular party. When in 1933 Sidky was forced to abandon the premiership after a stroke and was succeeded by lesser men, the Wafd was able to rouse the country with demands for the restoration of the 1923 constitution which would inevitably restore the party to power.

Britain faced a dilemma. The popular mood in Egypt was becoming dangerous. In November 1935 there was a huge pro-Wafd demonstration by students in Cairo. (The grave 17-year-old leader of the secondary students, named Gamal Abdul Nasser, was grazed on the forehead by a police bullet.) But Britain was still reluctant to see the return of a Wafdist government.

However, a solution was at hand. Although the Wafd had lost none of its appetite for power, it was now more prepared to compromise to achieve it. The Wafd had learned that it could never hold power for long against British opposition. At the same time, it shared Britain's growing alarm at Italian imperial ambitions in Africa, manifested by Italy's invasion and seizure of Ethiopia. Egypt was dependent on Britain for its defences.

As the Wafd abandoned its demand for an immediate and total British evacuation, its relations with the British high commission improved. Nahas became on good terms with the formidable Sir Miles Lampson, who, with more than a trace of the qualities of Cromer, had been appointed high commissioner in 1933 and was to remain in Egypt for thirteen years.

Even King Fuad, although still detesting the Wafd, was prepared to envisage its return, as this would give him some much needed popularity. In December 1935 he agreed to the restoration of the 1923 constitution. Four months later he died and was succeeded by his handsome and affable 16-year-old son Farouk, who returned from a brief and inadequate period of schooling in England.

The first important event of the new reign was the signing, on

26 August 1936, of the Anglo-Egyptian treaty of alliance, at which no fewer than six unsuccessful attempts had been made over the previous fourteen years. If the 1922 declaration had given Egypt semi-independence, the 1936 treaty went some of the rest of the way. Sir Miles Lampson became ambassador instead of high commissioner, and Britain sponsored Egypt's entry into the League of Nations. Britain undertook to bring the Capitulations to a speedy end and at the Montreux Conference in 1937 Egypt obtained full rights of jurisdiction and taxation over all residents from the Capitulatory powers.

The treaty was for a period of twenty years and both parties were committed to a further alliance in 1956, although Egypt would then have the right to submit to third-party judgement the question of whether British troops were any longer necessary in Egypt. The British occupation was formally ended, but British troops would only gradually be withdrawn to the Canal zone and Sinai, as Egypt's defence capability improved. Egypt gained control over its security forces for the first time since 1882. The British inspector-general of the Egyptian army was replaced by an Egyptian, and military intelligence was egyptianized. The numbers of Europeans in the police force were scaled down, although Russell Pasha remained at the head of the Cairo police force until his retirement ten years later. Egypt had to abandon most of its ambitions to recover control over the Sudan, though it is true that the terms of the Allenby 1924 ultimatum were reversed. Egyptian immigration into the Sudan was no longer restricted, and Egyptian as well as Sudanese troops were to be placed at the disposal of the governor-general. Egyptian officials were to be employed where no Sudanese were available. However, this did not mean that the pre-1924 situation in Sudan had been restored, because by this time a Sudanese national movement had developed and more Sudanese had become qualified. The Anglo-Egyptian condominium in Sudan was a fiction as Britain remained unequivocally the dominant partner.

As events turned out, all the treaty's concessions to Egyptian nationalist demands were largely nullified by the clause which gave

Britain the right to re-occupy the country with the unrestricted use of Egyptian ports, airports and roads in the event of Britain's involvement in war. Only three years passed before this clause was invoked. However, in 1936 the immediate reaction of the Egyptian crowds was favourable. The young king was wildly cheered in the streets – even Sir Miles Lampson was applauded. There were hopes of a new era, as the king gave the impression that he would take a special interest in the plight of the impoverished *fellahin*. Under his guidance the Wafd would institute some true reforms.

The reality was rather different. Farouk did not lack either intelligence or good intentions, but he had been badly trained for his task. Also, he shared his father's detestation of the Wafd and his taste for political intrigue.

The Wafd remained the party of the masses and the true expression of political Egypt. However, before the treaty, its 'anti-Britishness' was the only real plank in its political platform. Its ranks contained a whole spectrum of views, from arch-conservative to extremely radical, but its centre of gravity was well to the right. The vast majority of those who voted for it lived in the rural areas which were dominated by the large and medium-size landowners. Very few Wafdist members of parliament wanted any serious changes in Egypt's social or economic system; above all they did not want any reform in the fantastically unequal holdings of land, which meant that 6 per cent of the proprietors owned 63 per cent of the cultivated area. On the other hand, Egypt's small but growing industrial sector was the creation of a few wealthy Egyptians outside the Wafd, such as Sidky Pasha and Talaat Harb, who co-operated with a number of European industrialists and financiers in establishing an Egyptian Federation of Industries in 1924.

In one field – education – the Wafd could claim to have instigated reform to repair the neglect of the Cromer era. One of the first acts of the Zaghloul government in 1923 had been to declare education free and compulsory. The education budget was steadily increased in the 1920s and 1930s, and the number of pupils of both sexes rose rapidly. The expansion was most remarkable in secondary and university education. But there were serious defects. Since few new schools were built, the classes became overcrowded and standards declined. Also, no attempt was made to adapt the system to Egypt's needs and, as later became characteristic of many newly independent countries, a growing body of graduates from the state secondary schools and universities was unable to find employment. The problem was compounded by the existence of an entirely separate network of foreign secular and religious schools alongside the Egyptian state system. These had high prestige but they greatly accentuated class divisions, as the sons and daughters of the Egyptian upper class who were sent to them grew up speaking French and feeling little in common with the mass of their fellow-countrymen.

The students began to show increasing impatience and discontent with the Wafd and with Egypt's handicapped form of parliamentary democracy in general. Many of them regarded the Anglo-Egyptian treaty as a betrayal, and some of them looked to a new leader – an eloquent and charismatic former schoolteacher named Hassan al-Banna, who founded his Muslim Brotherhood in Ismailia in 1928.

In his early years al-Banna appealed most to the poor and illiterate, but in 1934 he moved his headquarters to Cairo and began to attract supporters from the better educated – students, teachers, civil servants and army officers. Branches of the Brotherhood sprang up throughout the country. Al-Banna's appeal was simple and idealistic. He called for an Islamic state based on the Holy Koran, the traditions of Islam providing everything that was needed for the new social order. But if the Brotherhood lacked a political programme, it had organization through its network of branches. Its youth groups began to receive paramilitary training.

The Brotherhood had rivals in its appeal to Egyptian youth. There was the Young Egypt (Misr al-Fitat) party of Ahmad Hussein, which was nominally socialist but which, with its uniform of green shirts modelled on Mussolini's Black Shirts, had a strongly fascist character. In response the Wafd organized a rival group of Blue Shirts, who fought a series of pitched battles with the Green Shirts in the universities. It was not long before a fascist-type royalist youth movement was formed and joined the fray. Egyptian political life was speedily deteriorating.

Although the Anglo-Egyptian treaty was unpopular with those who wanted to end all traces of the British occupation, it had one side-effect which helped their cause. The Egyptian army was now theoretically an ally of the British, so Britain was anxious to improve it; at the same time the Wafd needed to gain popularity. For the first time the Military Academy was opened to young men from classes other than the landowning aristocracy. Gamal Abdul Nasser, Anwar al-Sadat and a score of other ambitious young Egyptians were able to take up a military career and so play their part in the Free Officers movement which seventeen years later launched the 1952 revolution which brought both the monarchy and the British occupation to an end.

The Wafd was, however, in a slow but inexorable decline and no longer had the unrivalled control over the masses of Zaghloul's day. King Farouk, who now enjoyed the advantage over his father of being in control of his own secret police as well as the paramilitary youth movement, made the active independent politician Ali Maher his *chef de cabinet*. In December 1937 he felt strong enough to dismiss the Wafd 'for having violated the spirit of the constitution', and in the subsequent elections, which were partially rigged, the Wafd was heavily defeated. In August 1939, barely two weeks before the outbreak of the Second World War, the king felt able to appoint Ali Maher prime minister.

However, although the Wafd's power was in decline, the king still had to reckon with the British embassy, and this was now in *de facto* alliance with the Wafd. Although Lampson in theory no longer enjoyed Cromer's degree of authority, he behaved as if he did, and his treatment of the young king recalled Cromer's handling of the rebellious Khedive Abbas Hilmi forty years earlier. Lampson referred to him contemptuously as 'the Boy' and assured the Foreign Office that he was perfectly capable of dealing with him. Farouk, who had detested Lampson from the moment when Lampson arrived in Egypt, lacked the courage and strength of character to stand his ground against the British embassy on questions of genuine political importance; he could only irritate and provoke Lampson in minor matters, such as keeping him waiting for appointments.

Nevertheless, a *modus vivendi* would probably have been reached if it had not been for the outbreak of war in 1939. This vastly increased Egypt's importance to Britain as a military base and, at the same time, strengthened Lampson's hand in his dealings with the king.

(b) The Mandates

The system of mandates set up by the League of Nations under Article 22 of its Covenant was unprecedented. It was also a form of compromise. While the victorious powers in the First World War wished to retain the former German colonies and the territories of the Ottoman Empire which in most cases they had made great sacrifices to conquer, they had made frequent pledges that their inhabitants would not be handed back to their former masters. They had also made solemn undertakings that the annexation of territory was not their aim in war. The outstanding example was the Anglo-French declaration about the former Ottoman provinces of 5 November 1918.

The mandates were not colonies but a form of trust in which the mandatary power administered the territory under the supervision of the League of Nations through a Permanent Mandates Commission. The supreme council of the League defined the terms of the mandates and the boundaries of the territories. The United States was not a member of the League but, as one of the former Allies, insisted that its consent to the mandates was necessary, and all mandate proposals were therefore submitted to the United States, which approved them on condition that 'free and equal treatment in law and in fact was secured to the commerce of all nations.'

It must be said that some British and French statesmen regarded the distinction between mandates and colonies as no more than a

fiction. One of the frankest was the British foreign secretary, Lord
Curzon, who told the House of Lords on 25 June 1920,

It is quite a mistake to suppose . . . that under the Covenant of the League
or any other instrument, the gift of the mandate rests with the League of
Nations. It does not do so. It rests with the Powers who have conquered
the territories, which it then falls to them to distribute, and it was in these
circumstances that the mandate for Palestine and Mesopotamia was
conferred upon and accepted by us, and that the mandate for Syria was
conferred upon and accepted by France.

The mandated territories, which included the former German
colonies in Africa and the Pacific, were at varying stages of political and social development. Since the mandate principle was that
they should be brought to independence as soon as was practically
possible, they were divided in three classes. The former Turkish
vilayets of Mesopotamia (Iraq), Palestine and Syria, were included
in class A, for which early independence could be most easily fore-
seen. The mandates for them were issued to Britain and France
only when the Treaty of Lausanne came into force in August 1924,
by which time the two Allies had already made various *de facto*
arrangements for the establishment of boundaries and forms of
administration which the League of Nations was in no position to
reverse. Many *faits accomplis* had to be accepted.

The League was supposed to enjoy an unqualified right of supervision, and the mandatary powers were obliged to submit annual
reports on the exercise of their trusteeship. In addition the League
could receive petitions from inhabitants of the territories and other
interested parties. The weakest point in the system lay in the impossibility of independent verification of the mandataries' reports,
which varied in completeness and accuracy.

(1) IRAQ

The new kingdom of Iraq suffered from many problems related to
its national unity. The centrifugal forces were powerful. The large

and rebellious Kurdish minority in the north felt that it had been deprived of its hopes of self-determination by the post-war settlement. There were also substantial Turkoman and Christian Assyrian minorities. The Arab population was divided between Sunnis and Shiites, the latter being more numerous but the Sunnis being politically dominant.

However, Iraq was perhaps the most successful of the mandatary regimes. Although King Feisal I had been imposed on the country from outside, he proved to be an effective unifying force. Kurdish and tribal beduin lawlessness was gradually overcome, and the Shiite *mujtahids* or religious authorities (who were mainly Persian) were brought under control. Relations with Persia were not cordial but remained peaceful. The boundary disputes with Ibn Saud, exacerbated by Hashemite–Saudi rivalry, were more bitter, but a measure of reconciliation was achieved through British mediation. The relationship with the former Turkish suzerains was the most difficult. At the 1923 Lausanne Conference, the Turkish Republic demanded the return of most of the vilayet of Mosul, which was widely believed to be rich in oil. After two years of wrangling within the League of Nations, Turkey reluctantly but unequivocally accepted the award of Mosul to Iraq.

Following the defeat of those British officials in the immediate post-war period who favoured Iraq's incorporation into the British Empire, relatively liberal policies were pursued. The initially extensive powers of British officials were gradually reduced. A constituent assembly was convened in 1924 which, in the following year, approved an Anglo-Iraqi treaty and an Organic Law which made Iraqi ministers responsible to a two-chamber parliament. However, the treaty, which maintained important exclusive British rights in Iraq, was approved only under heavy British pressure against the radical opposition which demanded unfettered independence.

By the late 1920s Britain was prepared to end the mandate, provided British interests could be maintained, but a new treaty was long delayed because of the continued nationalist opposition to any

British tutelage in a concealed form. Some League of Nations members also insisted that Iraq was not yet ready for full independence. (France, in particular, was alarmed by the possible precedent for its own mandates.) Finally, an Anglo-Iraqi treaty was concluded in 1930, providing for a twenty-five year alliance during which the two countries undertook to consult each other in order to harmonize their common interests in matters of foreign policy. Britain would have the use of certain air bases in Iraq and existing means of communications and in return would provide a military mission to help train the Iraqi army.

In 1932 the British mandate formally ended; Iraq became independent and joined the League of Nations under British sponsorship. Only a strong body of Iraqi opinion remained dissatisfied, believing that the country was still under British hegemony. In their view this was aggravated by the power of the Iraq Petroleum Company, which monopolized Iraq's oil resources. In August 1933, an ominous prelude to independence was the massacre by an army unit of three hundred Assyrian villagers in northern Iraq. The massacre was applauded by most Iraqi opinion and the soldiers were never punished. A large part of the Assyrian community left for Syria.

King Feisal I died suddenly in 1933 and was succeeded by his son Ghazi. Handsome and popular, Ghazi had the reputation of being an Arab nationalist, but he lacked his father's authority. In 1927 oil had been discovered in commercial quantities near Kirkuk in the north, and production bringing in the first substantial revenues began in 1934. Irrigation, communications and the public services all made progress – the development of the country's vast potential resources had begun. However, the absence of King Feisal made the development of a viable political system more difficult. The country was served by some able and devoted ministers and officials who survived from the Ottoman period, of whom the most outstanding was Nuri al-Said. But parliamentary democracy failed to take root. No authentic political parties developed. Elections were largely controlled, with conservative, personal and class interests remaining dominant. A series of incompetent, reactionary and increasingly authoritarian cabinets succeeded each other in office. Politicians had no hesitation in organizing a tribal uprising, which could never be fully controlled, against the government of their rivals in office. The old-style politicians were opposed by an alliance of reformist middle-class intellectuals and young nationalist army officers inspired by the example of Kemal Atatürk. In 1936 these seized power under the leadership of General Bakr Sidqi. The movement ended, ten months later, as it had begun – with assassination and a military coup. It had failed because the reformist elements were soon set aside; the army was divided and the bulk of the population was alienated from the new rulers. But the coup was an event of great significance, because it established a precedent for military coups in the Arab world. Despite its failure, the Iraqi army had gained a new self-assurance and a taste for interference in political life.

The army faction which overthrew Bakr Sidqi remained in power behind the scenes, capable of making or unmaking cabinets. However, in 1938 this group, known as The Seven, was instrumental in bringing a civilian – Nuri al-Said – to power. Pro-British and conservative, Nuri was to dominate the Iraqi state for the next twenty years through his strong personality and political finesse.

(ii) Syria and Lebanon

Having enlarged Lebanon at Syria's expense, France based its policy in the two mandates on the strengthening and promotion of the traditionally Francophile Maronite Christian elements as against the Muslim Arab population. In both countries in the early years of the mandates France behaved in the manner of a colonial government backed by superior military power. The press was controlled, and nationalist demonstrations were instantly suppressed.

The terms of the mandates promised a constitution for both countries in three years. But France considered the creation of an independent unitary state in Syria to be a very distant goal. The French army regarded strategic control of the region as essential, and French politicians were always concerned with the potential effect of concessions on France's North African possessions.

Some members of the minorities and a small proportion of the Sunni Muslim majority accepted that French rule might bring advantages. But the vast majority, especially the educated élite, demanded immediate independence, and many went further to insist that the independent state should also include Palestine and Trans-jordan. France, on the other hand, with the unmistakable purpose of dividing Syria in order to rule it more easily, partitioned the country into separate autonomous districts: one in the Alawite (Nusairiyah) mountains in the north-east inhabited mainly by the sub-Shia Alawite sect, one in the Jebal Druze in the south where most of the people were Druze, and one in the rest of Syria with Damascus as the capital. Within the last a special status was given to the district of Alexandretta (now Iskenderun) with its mixed population of Arabs, Turks and Armenians. All three districts had autonomous administrations with French advisers, but there was an overall supervisory administration under the high commissioner for Syria and Lebanon in Beirut.

The fragile framework was soon shaken when in 1925 a revolt in the Jebal Druze, due to local grievances, led to an alliance between the Druze and the nationalists of Damascus, who had begun to organize themselves in the People's Party.

The Druze warriors penetrated Lebanon and even the suburbs of Damascus, provoking a two-day French bombardment. The rebellion continued sporadically for two years, leaving much bitter-ness, but the French were constrained to pursue a more conciliatory policy. In 1928 they allowed elections to be held for a Constituent Assembly. These were clearly won by the nationalists, who formed a cabinet. The constitution drafted by the assembly was, as expected, unacceptable to the French because it spoke of the unity of geographical Syria and failed to recognize French control.

In 1930 the French high commissioner unilaterally promulgated a new constitution which made Syria a parliamentary republic with France retaining control over foreign affairs and security. Desultory and unsuccessful negotiations followed to draw up a Franco-Syrian treaty which would be acceptable to both sides. However, by 1936 a new situation had arisen. A left-wing Popular Front government had come to power in France, and Britain had created precedents by granting independence to Iraq and reaching a treaty agreement with Egypt. Like their Egyptian counterparts, the Syrian nationalists, now organized in a National Bloc coalition, were concerned by the rising tensions in the Mediterranean region created by Italian imperial ambitions.

Negotiations now made progress, and in 1936 a treaty was signed providing for Syrian independence, with Franco-Syrian consultation on foreign policy, French priority in advice and assistance, and the retention by France of two military bases. The Druze and Alawite districts would be incorporated into Syria.

However, although the treaty was ratified by the Syrian parliament, it was never ratified by the French Chamber of Deputies and so remained inoperative. The Popular Front government fell from power and was replaced by a more right-wing cabinet which insisted on keeping control over the Levant states for strategic and economic reasons. There were prospects of the discovery of oil in northeastern Syria, and Syria and Lebanon lay across the air-routes to the Far East. With the renewed threat of war with Germany, the potential effect of Syrian independence on French North Africa had become even more important – France, with its 40 million population, could hope to balance Germany's 80 million only by drawing on the manpower of North Africa.

The prospect of war with Germany also led France to conciliate Turkey over the question of the district of Alexandretta, which was claimed by Turkey. In 1937 France gave the district a fully autonomous status, and after a Franco-Turkish commission had ensured a Turkish majority in parliamentary elections (although Arabs and Armenians outnumbered Turks in the population) France agreed to the absorption of the District of Alexandretta into Turkey in June 1939. The district was renamed the Hatay. Turkey in fact remained neutral during the Second World War but at least it did not become

Germany's ally as in the First. To the present day, official maps of the Syrian Arab Republic show Alexandretta as part of Syria.

By 1939 it had become clear that the French government had no intention of ratifying the Franco-Syrian treaty. On the eve of the Second World War the Syrian president resigned and the constitution was suspended.

France expected Lebanon, with its dominant Francophile majority, to be easier to govern than Syria. However, the creation of *le Grand Liban*, which included many Muslims and non-Maronite Christians, caused the balance of the population to change. Although the Maronites remained the largest single community, their narrow majority in the population was eroding as a result of their lower birth rate and higher tendency to emigrate than other communities. A constitution, which was drafted in Paris with little consultation with the Lebanese, was imposed in 1926. It provided for a bicameral parliament and a president. In an attempt to ease sectarian tensions, the principle was established that seats in parliament and the cabinet should be distributed on the basis of religious affiliation. The president was a Maronite, the prime minister a Sunni Muslim and the president of the Chamber of Deputies a Shiite. There would always be a Greek Orthodox and a Druze member in the cabinet. However, the president, who was elected for a six-year term and had the right to choose the prime minister, enjoyed the strongest powers and the Maronites remained politically and socially dominant in the country.

Emotionally, a large part of the Lebanese population both rejected French control and saw themselves as part either of Syria or of a wider Arab nation. The growth of a Lebanese national identity focused on the land within the borders of *le Grand Liban* was fragile and made more difficult by the sectarian basis of the political system, but it would be an error to suppose that such a national identity did not exist. The people of Tripoli, Sidon and the Bekaa were not unanimous in wishing to secede from the Lebanese Republic. The unity of the Lebanese nation could have been greatly strengthened and much more trouble avoided in the future if the Maronites had agreed to a more equitable sharing of power – by allowing, for example, the presidency to alternate between Christians and Muslims. Nevertheless, the prosperity of Beirut as a centre of trade and services helped towards the growth of a middle class of both Muslims and Christians with some common sense of a national interest which partly transcended sectarian loyalties. A nascent movement for independence, critical of excessive and undiminishing French interference in government, was joined by a number of prominent Maronites. In 1936 the Maronite patriarch published a collection of memoranda voicing these criticisms in detail. In the same year the French government proposed a Franco-Lebanese treaty similar to the one with Syria, but, just as with Syria, although this was promptly ratified by the Lebanese parliament, it was never ratified by the right-wing governments which succeeded the Popular Front in France.

Outside the political sphere, the achievements of the French mandatary in Lebanon and Syria were far from negligible. It introduced a relatively modern administrative system, customs organization and land registration based on a pioneering cadastral survey. It built many roads and improved urban amenities. In Damascus and Aleppo it initiated city planning. One of its finest achievements was the creation of a department of antiquities to preserve and administer the Levant states' unparalleled archaeological heritage. Some encouragement was given to agriculture, especially in northeastern Syria's Jazirah region, but the economic effects of the mandate were affected by the chronic weakness of the French franc on which the Syrian and Lebanese currencies were based. Also, considerable resentment was caused by the policy of granting monopolies to French companies whose profits were repatriated to France.

Education received a powerful stimulus, although in some respects the policy was controversial. The French language and culture were promoted. Arab children were taught a French interpretation of history and even learned to sing 'La Marseillaise'. Foreign mission schools were protected and in Lebanon much of the educational system and almost all higher education remained in

their hands, with teaching mostly in French or English. As a consequence the educational standards of the Lebanese people as a whole
were higher than anywhere in the former Ottoman Empire. On the
other hand, the lack of an adequate state education system did nothing to promote national unity. In Syria, where the mission schools
were much less important, a state educational system was constructed
under the mandate and the University of Damascus was established,
with its teaching mainly in Arabic.

(III) PALESTINE AND TRANSJORDAN

When the British government undertook the mandate for Palestine
in 1919, it was unaware that it was taking on an impossible task. Its
failure to solve the problems was to infect Britain's relations with
the Arabs for decades.

Article 6 of the Balfour Declaration, which was incorporated
within the terms of the mandate, stated:

The Administration of Palestine, while ensuring that the rights and position of other sections of the population are not prejudiced, shall facilitate
Jewish immigration under suitable conditions and shall encourage, in
co-operation with the Jewish Agency referred to in Article 4, close settlement by Jews on the land, including State lands and waste lands not
required for public purposes.

Britain's first high commissioner for Palestine, from 1920 to 1925,
was Sir Herbert Samuel, a Jew who had been the first to propose
the idea of a Jewish Palestine to the British cabinet in 1914. But he
had never been an active member of the Zionist movement, and
as high commissioner he made strenuous efforts to be fair to the
'other sections of the population', ultimately incurring the disappointment and even odium of the Zionists. He set up an
administration including Muslims, Christians and Jews and for a
time worked with an advisory council of similar composition
which he hoped would lead ultimately to a partly elected legislative
council for a joint community. But the Arabs, who fundamentally

rejected both the mandate and the Balfour Declaration, boycotted the elections and demanded a national government. Severe rioting ensued. On Samuel's insistence, the British government issued a White Paper declaring Britain's intention to hold the balance between the Arab and Jewish communities. However, the Arabs were convinced by this that the true intention was to wait to grant self-government until the Jews in Palestine had grown sufficiently in numbers and power to become dominant, and they continued to demand an immediate national government, citing the promises made to the Arabs during the war. They rejected Samuel's proposal for the formation of an Arab Agency to match the Jewish Agency.

One of Samuel's actions with good intentions towards the Arabs had fateful consequences. To maintain the balance between the two leading families in Jerusalem, he overturned the elections for mufti of Jerusalem in favour of a young nationalist, Hajj Amin al-Husseini. From this position, Hajj Amin, an uncompromising nationalist who singularly lacked political wisdom, was able to gain the leadership of the Arabs of Palestine.

However, the years 1923 to 1929 were relatively quiet, mainly because Arab fears were reduced by the drop in Jewish immigration. In 1927 there was nil Jewish immigration into Palestine and in 1928 the net immigration was only ten persons. The Zionists continued to consolidate their settlements and their political presence, but their hopes of dominance receded. The British mandatary authorities became complacent and drastically reduced the garrison, despite the warnings of the Permanent Mandates Commission.

In 1929 the situation sharply deteriorated. In August, Britain consented to the creation of an enlarged Jewish Agency in which half the members were recruited from Zionist sympathizers outside Palestine. The Zionists acquired a new sense of confidence. In the same month a dispute concerning religious practices at the Wailing Wall in Jerusalem led to widespread communal clashes, with severe casualties. Troops were rushed in and order was restored. Arabs massacred Jewish colonists in Hebron. Arab casualties were mainly caused by British soldiers.

Britain was fully confronted with the contradictions in the mandate. The new high commissioner, Sir John Chancellor (1928–31), proposed that the mandate should be reshaped to remove the special privileges of the Jews, restrict their land purchases (which were proceeding apace with the help of Zionist funds and sales by absentee Arab landlords) and give the Arabs a measure of self-government. A British technical report established that there was no margin of land available for new immigrants without substantial development funds which, at a time of world depression, the British government was quite unready to provide. In 1930 the colonial secretary in Britain's Labour government issued a White Paper which gave some priority to Britain's obligations to the Arabs by restricting Jewish immigration and ending Jewish land purchases. In the ensuing uproar the Zionists, who naturally saw their hopes of a Jewish Palestine vanishing, were able to use their sympathizers among all parties in the British parliament to cause Ramsay MacDonald's weak and nervous cabinet to rescind the White Paper. The Palestinian Arabs became convinced that recommendations in their favour would always be annulled at the centre of power. They began to attempt to organize their own international support. In December 1931 a Muslim Congress was called in Jerusalem, attended by representatives of twenty-two Muslim countries, to warn against the danger of Zionism. But although fellow-Arabs in neighbouring countries were beginning to be aroused by the plight of the Palestinian Arabs, there was little practical support they could provide. A boycott of Zionist and British goods called in 1933 was largely ineffective.

In the first half of the 1930s there was a sharp rise in Jewish immigration, from 4,000 in 1930 to 30,000 in 1933 and 62,000 in 1935. This was due partly to fears of Hitler's rise to power in Germany but much more to growing confidence in Palestine's future which, in spite of world depression, was enjoying something of a boom based on its citrus industry. In 1935 the Arab parties, although far from united, collectively demanded the cessation of Jewish immigration, the prohibition of land transfer and the establishment of democratic institutions. The British offered a legislative council of twenty-eight members on which the Arabs would have fourteen seats and the Jews eight, with the remaining six reserved for British officials. Most, although not all, Arabs rejected the proposal because they would not be represented in proportion to their numbers. The Jews bitterly denounced it because they believed it would provide the Arabs with a permanent stranglehold on the development of the Jewish national home. For this reason some Palestinians later came to regret their rejection.

The Arab rebellion of 1936–8 against the mandate, which at first smouldered and then burst into flame, was provoked by continuing fears that Jewish immigration would lead to Zionist dominance and the certainty that Britain would not effectively prevent it. The spark was provided by the knowledge that the Zionists were smuggling in arms for self-defence. In April 1936 the Arab political parties formed an Arab Higher Committee, under Hajj Amin, which called a general strike. This was maintained for six months. At the same time Arab rebels, joined by volunteers from neighbouring Arab countries, took to the hills and a full-scale national uprising began.

For not the first nor the last time, Britain sent out a commission of inquiry. Lord Peel's commission of 1937 concluded that Britain's obligations to Arabs and Jews were irreconcilable and the mandate unworkable. It therefore for the first time recommended the partition of Palestine into Jewish and Arab states, with Jerusalem and Haifa remaining under British mandate and with a 12,000 annual limit to Jewish immigration for the next five years. The tiny Arab state would be joined to Transjordan under Abdullah. The Zionists' response was ambivalent. Britain had for the first time spoken of a Jewish state and had proposed the forcible transfer of some of the Arab population. But they disliked the limitation on the size of the Jewish state, which would exclude Jerusalem, and the limit on Jewish immigration. They still hoped to become dominant in an undivided Palestine. The Arabs, on the other hand, were unanimously outraged (except for Emir Abdullah of Transjordan, who urged acceptance) and their rebellion intensified, in spite of the heavy use of British force and the outlawing of the Arab Higher Committee. Most of the Committee's members were deported to the Seychelles, but Hajj Amin escaped to Baghdad, from where he continued to exert some influence in favour of the maximum Arab demands.

The League of Nations then authorized the preparation of a detailed partition plan. However, the technical commission which reported in November 1938 declared the Peel commission's proposal to be unworkable. The British government agreed and called for a round-table conference, which was held in London during February and March 1939. This was a failure, as were the two bilateral conferences with Jews and Arabs which followed. (The conference with the Arabs included representatives of the Arab states, as an acknowledgement that Palestine was of interest to all the Arabs.)

The Arab rebellion gradually died down in the early months of 1939. Following the Munich crisis in 1938 and the postponed threat of immediate war, Britain had been able to pour in extra troops. The long and unsuccessful struggle left the Palestinian Arabs exhausted and demoralized.

The British government, however, was primarily concerned with the approaching world war, which now seemed inevitable. The priority was to secure at least the passive support of the Arabs who formed the vast majority of the population in the strategically vital Middle East region (including Palestine, where they were still some 70 per cent). It was assumed that the Jews would inevitably be on Britain's side in any war against Hitler. A new British government White Paper in May 1939 provided for the limitation of Zionist immigration to 75,000 over the next five years, with further immigration subject to Arab 'acquiescence'. The White Paper said that the object was the establishment 'within ten years of an independent Palestine State in such treaty relations with the UK as will provide satisfaction for all commercial and strategic interests of both countries'. It was clear that the Arabs would still then be in substantial majority.

Although this new policy was more favourable to the Arabs, the mufti's party rejected it – mainly on the grounds that experience showed that the British government could not be trusted to carry it out against Jewish opposition. More moderate Arabs shared these doubts. The Zionists, on the other hand, were appalled and angered because they considered it a death blow to their aspirations and a betrayal of the Balfour Declaration. They became even more determined to establish their own state in Palestine. Already the Jewish community in Palestine was largely self-governing through an elected assembly which levied its own taxes. Purely Jewish trade unions were united in a confederation, the Histadrut, which performed numerous other functions as banker, entrepreneur and landowner. Between 1922 and 1939 Jewish colonies had increased from forty-seven to two hundred and Jewish land-holdings had more than doubled. The Hebrew University on Mount Scopus in Jerusalem, opened in 1925, was playing the leading role in the training of the country's intellectual and academic leadership. The most significant development for the future was the creation of the Haganah, the secret but officially tolerated Jewish army. This gained experience in defending Jewish settlements against Arab attacks, and some of its members assisted British forces in suppressing the Arab rebellion.

The Jews in Palestine were a formidable force and they were determined to oppose Britain's new policy. But the odds seemed heavily weighted against them.

East of the River Jordan in the newly created emirate of Transjordan under the rule of Emir Abdullah, the problems were infinitely less complicated. Having secured the League of Nations' approval for Transjordan's exclusion from the policy of the Jewish national home, on 25 May 1923 Britain recognized Transjordan as an independent state, subject to British obligations under the Palestine mandate. Under French pressure, Syrian leaders who had taken refuge in Transjordan were ordered to leave.

All troops were placed under the command of a British officer, and with British help the fledgeling Jordanian forces were able to deal with some internal tribal dissension and the incursions of Wahhabi warriors from Nejd in the early 1920s.

The country was poor, undeveloped and thinly populated, but it acquired a social and political cohesion which Palestine lacked. Britain virtually dictated the terms of the 1928 treaty under which, through a British resident appointed by the high commissioner for Palestine, Emir Abdullah was to be guided by British advice in such matters as foreign relations, finance and jurisdiction over foreigners. There were a score of British advisers and a modest British subsidy (£101,000 out of a total state budget of £257,000 in 1925–6) and, in spite of the poverty, some slow and steady progress was made. Roads and schools were built, although it was fifteen years before the country had more than one secondary school.

In 1931, after ten years' experience in Iraq, Captain John Bagot Glubb (or Glubb Pasha, as he was later known) arrived to found the Desert Patrol as a special branch of the Transjordanian army (the Arab Legion) entrusted with the task of keeping order in the desert. Its novel aspect was that it used tribesmen to maintain security among their fellow-beduin. Glubb had remarkable success in gaining the confidence of the beduin and persuading them of the advantages of stability and order. In this way they became loyal to the Transjordanian state and many of them came to serve in the regular armed forces.

Faced with the problem of Palestine, Britain was happy to allow Abdullah increasing independence as the undisputed leader of Transjordan. Although his claim to rule was based on his Hashemite family's version of pan-Arabism, his remarkable political skills enabled him to secure the fierce loyalty of most of the local tribal leaders to himself and his family. In 1934 Britain agreed that the emir could appoint consular representatives in other Arab states, and in 1939 it approved the formation of a council of ministers in charge of government departments and responsible to the emir. In 1946 Transjordan became formally independent, although still relying heavily on British subsidy and support. Emir Abdullah took the title of king.

Although Transjordan was developing separately and differently, it was far from insulated from events in Palestine west of the River

Jordan. There were many ties of blood between the people of the two banks, and the higher levels of education among Palestinians resulted in some of them being recruited as officials for the fledgeling administration in Amman. Transjordanians felt emotionally involved in the unfolding tragedy of Palestine. However, an element of territorial nationalism was growing up in Transjordan as it did elsewhere in the former Arab provinces of the Ottoman Empire. (Here it was given some historical validity by the feeling that the Transjordanians were descended from the Nabataeans of Petra.) A feeling of 'Transjordan for the Transjordanians' was eventually translated into a law confining government posts to Transjordanians. This was opposed by Arab nationalists, who maintained that nothing should intensify the artificially imposed divisions between the Arabs, but in practical terms the separate development of Transjordan had the support of the great majority of the country.

Abdullah concentrated on building up his power base in Transjordan, which, though smaller and poorer than Palestine or Syria, had the advantage that he could rule it through his personal authority. But this did not mean that he had abandoned his Hashemite pan-Arab aspirations. These did not include Egypt or the Arabian peninsula, which by 1925 had been lost by the Hashemites to Ibn Saud, but he had never abandoned his family's claims in Greater Syria. He had little chance in French-ruled Syria, but Palestine was different. At the beginning of the British mandate he made a shrewd and realistic assessment of the Zionists' power and aspirations and was quite prepared to negotiate with them. He foresaw a time when the Palestinian Arabs might seek his protection and be prepared to accept his rule. It was for this reason that he urged acceptance of the 1937 Peel commission's proposal for partition and the joining of Arab Palestine to Transjordan.

Inevitably Abdullah's stand gave him many enemies among Arab nationalists who opposed the Hashemites, ranging from Hajj Amin's Husseini family in Palestine to republicans in Syria. He had his supporters in both these countries, but they did not predominate. His Hashemite cousins in Iraq were more friendlily disposed but were not prepared to accept his leadership. He was prepared to await events in Palestine.

Persia/Iran

Although Persia declared its neutrality at the outbreak of the First World War, it did not escape involvement. Turkey's violation of Persian territory in order to attack Russia and the Turkish threat to the Anglo-Persian Oil Company's oilfield and refinery in the south of the country led to the occupation of large areas of Persian territory by Russian and British troops. This increased sympathy among the Persian people for the German and Turkish side in the war. At the end of the war, Persia joined the League of Nations as an independent state, but the country was in chaos. Its armed forces were divided and the treasury was empty.

The defeat of Russia in the war and the subsequent Bolshevik Revolution helped to relieve Persia from Russian pressure for a time. This tempted Britain to bring Persia into its sphere of influence. The foreign secretary, Lord Curzon, wrote in 1919,

Now that we are about to assume the mandate for Mesopotamia, which will make us coterminous with the western frontiers of Persia, we cannot permit the existence, between the frontiers of our Indian Empire . . . and those of our new Protectorate, of a hotbed of misrule, enemy intrigue, financial chaos and political disorder. Further . . . we possess in the south-western corner of Persia great assets in the shape of the oilfields, which are worked for the British Navy and which give us a commanding interest in that part of the world.

Curzon instigated the Anglo-Persian agreement of 1919 which, while reaffirming Persia's independence and territorial integrity, provided for the appointment of British military and civil advisers, co-operation in the development of transport and a loan of £2,000,000. The agreement would have ensured British ascendancy in Persia and was strongly criticized by the United States. However, in consequence of the strength of feeling aroused in the country, the Majlis refused to ratify the agreement and the British advisers who had taken up their posts were sent home.

In contrast, on 26 February 1921 a Soviet–Persian treaty was signed by which the Soviet government renounced 'the tyrannical policy' of tsarist Russia, remitted all Persian debts and abandoned extraterritorial privileges for Russian nationals. The treaty also gave up all concessions then held by the Russian government or nationals, although the Soviet government secured under pressure the valuable concession of the Caspian fisheries, which had previously belonged to Russian nationals but had lapsed. This treaty was promptly ratified by the Majlis. Little attention was paid to a clause authorizing Russia to send troops into Persia if it judged that it had become a base for military action against Russia.

With a weak and corrupt government and an incompetent young shah, the internal situation further deteriorated. At this point the forceful and outstanding commander of the Persian Cossack brigade, Colonel Reza Khan, was persuaded by a group of reformers to march with his men on Tehran. He entered the capital on 21 February 1921. The cabinet resigned and a new government was formed with Reza Khan as minister of war and commander-in-chief. Shortly afterwards he took full control of the government as prime minister.

Reza Khan's first task was to reunite and build up the armed forces. He commandeered state funds to ensure that the troops were regularly paid. In this way he gradually created a relatively efficient and disciplined army of 40,000, through which he aimed to establish the authority of the central government throughout the country. In 1924 he suppressed a rebellion by the autonomous shaikh of Mohammereh (renamed Khorramshahr), in whose territory the Anglo-Persian Oil Company's concession lay. To help reorganize the country's disastrous finances he invited in a US financial expert, A. C. Millspaugh, who with a small group of advisers made considerable progress. In the inter-war years Persia became a major oil producer. Production rose from 12 million barrels in 1920 to 46 million in 1930, making Persia the fourth largest producer in the world, after the USA, Russia and Venezuela.

Because of public disillusion with the long experience of corrupt and incompetent monarchy, there was widespread support for a republic. The religious leaders, who feared the consequences of Kemal Atatürk's abolition of the caliphate and institution of a secular republic, opposed such a change, however. Reza Khan therefore decided to retain the monarchy and make himself shah. On 31 October 1925, by a large majority, the Majlis declared the end of the Qajar dynasty. A new constituent assembly then vested the crown in Reza Shah, with the right of succession to his heirs. He took the name of Pahlavi for his dynasty. In 1935 he officially changed the name of the country from Persia to Iran.

Although it was the mullahs who had helped to make him shah, he regarded most of them as backward and reactionary. In fact in many respects he modelled his regime on that of Atatürk as he embarked on a policy of westernization. He introduced a French judicial system which challenged the competence of the religious courts. Civil offices were opened for marriage, education was reorganized on Western lines and literacy steadily increased. The University of Tehran was established in 1935, with a number of Europeans on the staff. In 1936 women were compelled to discard the veil and European costume was made obligatory for both sexes. Reza Shah pursued his policy of pacifying and unifying the country – a task which had been beyond the competence of the Qajar shahs – by subduing the semi-independent tribes. The Bakhtiaris and Kashgars were placed under the rule of military officers.

Improved communications were vital for the unification of the empire's extensive territories. The German Junkers company organized an internal air service. Postal services and telecommunications were vastly improved. American and European engineers helped to build roads and railways. The construction of a Trans-Iranian Railway from the Caspian Sea to the Gulf was a project for which the shah aroused the enthusiasm of the whole nation.

Progress meant industrialization, and a range of new textile, steel, cement and other factories were established. Some of them were profitable.

Reza Shah's firm rule and national assertiveness raised Iran's international standing and increased its bargaining power. He denounced all treaties which conferred extraterritorial rights on the subjects of foreign powers. In a dispute with the Soviet government over the Caspian fisheries, he secured a compromise in the formation of a Persian-Russian company to exploit the fisheries. To achieve his aim of improving the meagre revenues from the Anglo-Persian Oil Company, he was prepared to take the risk of cancelling the concession in 1932. Britain referred the matter to the League of Nations, and the dispute ended in 1933 with a compromise under which Persia received substantially better terms.

Reza Khan's vigorous assertion of Persian national rights forced Britain to remove the seat of its authority in the Gulf to Bahrain on the western coast. Two British coaling stations on Persian territory were removed, and the Royal Air Force switched its route for flights to India from the Persian to the Arab shore. However, friction continued as Reza Khan periodically reasserted Persia's claim to Bahrain.

Reza Khan's successes had negative aspects. His lavish and authoritarian military rule left little room for personal freedom or initiative. The Majlis was preserved but became little more than a façade. Some of the economic policies were misconceived and wasteful. Agriculture was seriously neglected, and the policy of settling the nomads was an outright failure because no adequate provision was made for them to maintain their flocks in the areas of their settlement. Most seriously for Reza Khan's reputation, he acquired huge areas of the best land for himself either by confiscation on political charges or by methods of purchase which amounted in effect to expropriation.

Oil and the Middle East

The first oil to be discovered in the Middle East was in Persia, and for the first three decades of the twentieth century Persia remained the only oil-producing country in the region. Lord Curzon may have slightly exaggerated when he declared that 'the Allies floated to victory on a wave of oil' in the First World War, but nevertheless for Britain, with its controlling interest in the Anglo-Persian Oil Company, Persian oil was the major strategic and economic interest in the region alongside the Suez Canal.

However, even before the First World War there was little doubt that northern Mesopotamia was another potentially oil-rich area. Oil from surface seepages was taken by donkey to provide domestic fuel in Turkey. In 1904 Calouste Gulbenkian, a wealthy Armenian financier, wrote a report on the commercial possibilities of the oil of northern Mesopotamia which caused Sultan Abdul Hamid to transfer these state lands to his own privy purse. On the eve of the First World War, the Ottoman government granted a concession to the Turkish Petroleum Company (TPC) in which the Anglo-Persian Oil Company had a half interest together with Royal Dutch Shell and the German Deutsche Bank. The participants in TPC pledged themselves not to be interested directly or indirectly in the production or manufacture of oil in the Ottoman Empire in Europe and Asia except through the TPC with the exclusion of certain areas delimited on a map by a red line. This became known as 'the Red Line agreement'. Hence at the end of the war, Britain, with its troops occupying Mosul and having expropriated the German interest in TPC, was in a commanding position to control Mesopotamian oil. However, Britain had obligations to France under the secret 1916 Sykes–Picot agreement, which, in its original form, included Mosul in the French zone of influence. In 1919 Britain persuaded France to transfer Mosul to the British zone, in return for a guaranteed role in the development of Mosul oil.

France also agreed to the construction of two separate pipelines for the transport of oil from Mesopotamia and Persia through the French spheres of influence to the Mediterranean.

It was at this point that the United States government intervened. Although the USA was retreating into the political isolation which lasted until the Second World War, it was determined that, while accepting the Anglo-French mandates, an 'open-door' policy should be maintained in commercial matters in the mandated territories. This meant equal treatment 'in law and in fact to the commerce of all nations', but oil was the chief concern. The British government, on the other hand, felt that the USA already had enough oil of its own in Texas. A prolonged and sometimes acrimonious correspondence between the US State Department and the British Foreign Office ensued. The final upshot was that Iraq's oil industry became a monopoly of the Iraq Petroleum Company (IPC), the successor of the TPC, which was owned jointly in 23.75 per cent shares by the Anglo-Persian Oil Company (later BP); Royal Dutch Shell; an American group which was ultimately reduced to Standard Oil of New Jersey and Socony-Vacuum (later Mobil); and the Compagnie Française des Pétroles (CFP), with Calouste Gulbenkian holding the remaining 5 per cent. The US State Department had achieved an entrée for American companies into the Middle Eastern oil arena, but in doing so it was in fact accepting the provisions of the Red Line agreement which Britain considered to be still in force, excluding all other than IPC participants.

A major oilfield was discovered near Kirkuk in 1927, and by 1934 production was contributing substantially to Iraq's revenues.

Throughout the 1920s the Anglo-Persian Oil Company, which continued to dominate the Middle East oil scene, showed little interest in the oil potential of the territories on the western shores of the Gulf – that is in Kuwait, Bahrain or the Eastern Province of the future kingdom of Saudi Arabia. This was partly because the company's geologists were convinced that, despite the seepages of bitumen in Kuwait, only the eastern side of the Gulf would yield oil in commercial quantities. The western shores of the Gulf lacked the Oligocene–Miocene rock formations found in Persia and Iraq. However, this did not mean that either the British government or APOC was happy to see a concession granted to a non-British company on the western shore. On APOC's behalf the British government resisted US pressure to allow the emirs of Kuwait and Bahrain to grant concessions to non-British companies. In 1931 the emir of Bahrain granted a concession to Standard Oil of California, which organized the Bahrain Petroleum Company (Bapco) as a Canadian-incorporated subsidiary to maintain the fiction that it was British.

When Bapco found oil in commercial quantities in May 1932, after only six months' drilling, the situation was transformed. The potential of the western shores of the Gulf was apparent. Standard Oil approached King Ibn Saud for a concession and the king, in desperate need of funds, responded. Anglo-Persian sent a representative to make a counter-bid but, since the company already had more than enough oil on its hands and its primary concern was only to exclude competitors from the region, he was authorized to offer an advance payment of only £5,000, whereas Standard Oil, after some hard bargaining, offered £50,000. On 29 May 1933 Standard Oil of California's concession was signed, covering all the eastern parts of the kingdom.

In this way the foundations were laid for the close relationship between Saudi Arabia and the United States which has profoundly influenced the modern history of the Middle East. The king, although far from being anti-British, was probably inclined to favour the US company, apart from its more generous offer, because the United States had no imperialist record in the Middle East. As the ruler of an entirely independent state, he was fortunate in being able to make a free choice.

Standard Oil of California later sold shares in its concession to the Texas Company, and in 1944 the company operating the concession took the name Arabian-American Oil Company (Aramco). The fact that American oil companies developed Saudi Arabia's major natural resource had an important influence on the kingdom. Aramco was never a simple instrument of US foreign policy – in fact it was often at loggerheads with Washington – but the company helped to train young Saudis and a trend began which led to the great majority of a new Saudi élite receiving at least part of their education at American universities. It was natural that US companies, among which Bechtel Corporation was outstanding, should

play the major role in the development of the kingdom's new infrastructure. As it came to be realized that Saudi Arabia possessed about
one quarter of the world's proved oil reserves, the Saudi–US
connection became even more significant.

Kuwait's shrewd ruler, Emir Ahmad, had been conducting
prolonged negotiations over an oil concession with both APOC
and the American Gulf Oil company. But the bargaining had become
desultory because the oil companies were cutting back on their
investments during the world depression. Britain's insistence on
excluding non-British companies was also a stumbling-block.
However, in 1932, following the precedent set in Bahrain, Britain
finally succumbed to intensive US pressure to an 'open-door' policy
for US oil companies in Kuwait. With the discovery of oil in Bahrain
and the conclusion of the Saudi agreement with Standard Oil in the
following year, the pace quickened. After lengthy negotiations
behind the scenes, APOC and Gulf Oil agreed to bury their differences and form an alliance to negotiate jointly as equal partners for
a concession. For this purpose they formed the Kuwait Oil Company
(KOC) on a fifty–fifty basis. After further negotiations, in which
Emir Ahmad fought successfully to limit the amount of political
control which Britain insisted on maintaining over KOC through
a separate agreement it reached with the company, a concession
agreement for seventy-five years covering all Kuwaiti territory was
signed in December 1934.

The remaining Arab shaikhdoms on the western side of the Gulf
all had exclusive treaty agreements with Britain. But the British
government was still alarmed at the possibility that the precedent
of King Ibn Saud granting a concession to a purely American
company might be followed by one of the fiercely independent
rulers. A company called Petroleum Concessions Ltd, in which
Anglo-Dutch, US and French companies held shares in the same
proportion as in the Iraq Petroleum Company, was therefore formed
to negotiate. The ruler of Qatar granted it a concession in 1935, but
the rulers of the six Trucial States (so called since the 1853 truce with
Britain under which they undertook to abjure sea warfare) proved

more difficult. They bargained and prevaricated for better terms, and various forms of pressure – including threats to confiscate their pearling fleets, on the grounds that they were still engaging in the slave trade – had to be used until they gave in. The last to succumb – in 1939 – was the eccentric but wily ruler of Abu Dhabi, Shaikh Shakhbut, who had become something of a legend in the Gulf since, after his succession in 1928, he succeeded in restoring stability to Abu Dhabi following twenty years of fierce family strife. He was convinced that there was oil in his territory – bubbles of oil had been seen around some of Abu Dhabi's two hundred islands – and the oil men agreed that it was the most promising of the Trucial States. He therefore drove a hard bargain for the concession. He had to wait twenty years before he was proved right, but oil was then found in enormous quantities.

In Saudi Arabia, Kuwait and Qatar, oil on a commercial scale was discovered shortly before the Second World War but its development had to be postponed until after the war. However, in 1939 it was already apparent that the territories surrounding the Persian Gulf would become of enormous strategic and economic importance. In fact by the second half of the century their reserves of oil and natural gas amounted to some two-thirds of all those that had been discovered.

10. The Second World War and Its Aftermath

The Middle East was as heavily involved in the 1939–45 conflict – the culmination of what has been aptly described as Europe's thirty-year civil war – as in that of 1914–18. The Turkish Republic was neutral. The new semi-independent nation-states which had been formed from the Arab provinces of the Ottoman Empire were non-belligerent, but they were under British or French occupation and therefore lay within the zone of war. Political life was largely frozen for the duration of hostilities.

As in the First World War, the retention of India was of supreme strategic and political importance to Britain. The protection of oil supplies from Iran was also a considerable secondary concern. Once again Egypt became Britain's great Mediterranean base. With a neutral Turkey and Iran, the Middle East region seemed fairly secure. The British realized with relief that, as a result of the 1939 White Paper on Palestine, the Palestinian Arabs were not going to embarrass them while they were at war with Germany.

The situation was transformed by Italy's entry into the war on Germany's side in June 1940. British forces in Egypt were engaged against the Italians in Libya, and British forces in the Sudan fought the Italian garrisons in Eritrea. Italian aircraft raided Egypt, and the country expected a full-scale Italian invasion. As in 1915, reinforcements were brought in from Australia, New Zealand and South Africa. Britain's determination to keep the Axis powers out of the eastern Mediterranean caused it to divert tanks from the home front to Egypt even when the danger that Hitler would invade Britain was at its height.

The battle in Egypt's Western Desert rolled backwards and forwards. In September 1940 the Italians entered Egypt and reached as far as Sidi Barrani; by the end of the year some spectacular British

victories had driven them back into Libya. But, with German reinforcements, the Axis forces, now commanded by General Rommel,
re-entered Egypt in April 1941. In the following month the Germans
captured Crete, and the British hold on the eastern Mediterranean
became perilous.

The danger for Britain was compounded by the situation in Syria
and Iraq. Although Iraq broke off relations with Germany in
September 1939, an Anglophobe nationalist group of civilians and
military became increasingly dominant, encouraged by Germany's
victories over France. In March 1941 they seized power in a putsch,
and Rashid Ali al-Gailani became prime minister in a government
with pro-Axis leanings. The regent, Nuri al-Said and other leading
politicians had to flee the country. The government's refusal of a
British request to move troops across Iraq under the terms of the
Anglo-Iraqi treaty led to open, if subdued, hostilities. Iraqi troops
surrounded the British base at Habbaniyah. But Iraqi opinion was
divided and uncertain, and promised Axis help for the rebels was
too little and too late.

A small Indian force was landed at Basra, to be joined by Arab
troops from Transjordan under Glubb Pasha. The revolt collapsed
after a few weeks; the Rashid Ali government fled and the regent
returned. Successive Iraqi governments co-operated with the Allies
for the rest of the war.

Following the fall of France in 1940, Syria and Lebanon came
under the control of the Vichy government. Britain promptly
declared that it would not allow a German occupation of the two
Levant states, but the Vichy government – anxious to secure as many
concessions as possible from Germany – instructed the high commission in Beirut to collaborate fully with the Axis. The climax came
in June 1941 when German aircraft *en route* to help Rashid Ali in Iraq
were allowed to use Syrian airfields. On 8 June 1941 a mixed force
of General de Gaulle's Free French and British troops launched a
three-pronged invasion from Palestine. Despite some stiff resistance
by the Vichy forces, the fighting lasted only six weeks, at the end
of which an armistice agreement was signed. Vichy troops were

given the choice of joining the Free French or of repatriation to France.

The Soviet Union's entry into the war in July 1941, followed by that of the United States in December, provided reassurance that the Allies would prevail in the end. In the winter of 1941–2 the Axis forces were again pushed back into Libya. But the darkest hour for the British in the Middle East was still to come. With Japanese victories in the Far East threatening Malaya and India, it became the turn of the British forces in the Western Desert to be deprived of tanks, which were diverted eastwards. In January 1942 Rommel again began to advance towards Egypt.

Among the Egyptian people, attitudes towards the war were mixed. The great majority of the politicians were against declaring war on Germany, either because they felt it was not Egypt's war or because they were far from certain that the Allies would win. On the other hand, Egypt more than fulfilled its obligations under the terms of the Anglo-Egyptian treaty. German nationals were interned and German property was placed under sequestration.

King Farouk had no special affection for Germany, but many of his closest circle were Italian, and Ali Maher, his favoured prime minister, was known to have pro-Axis sympathies. When Maher failed to take action against Italian nationals, Britain's ambassador Sir Miles Lampson pressed the king to dismiss him. Farouk reluctantly complied and replaced Maher with two successive prime ministers who were much more sympathetic to the Allied cause. In August 1941 Egyptian troops took over guard duties in the Suez Canal area.

However, there were many in Egypt, apart from the king, who remained so doubtful about the outcome of the war that they felt Egypt should have a more neutral government as an insurance against an Axis victory. Others went further, believing that Egypt should entirely assist such a victory – these included General Aziz al-Masri, the Egyptian chief of staff, and a young captain, Anwar al-Sadat. Sadat was caught working for the pro-German underground by British Intelligence and was interned.

The British prime minister, Churchill, had never had much patience with Egyptian nationalist feelings and had none in time of war. He complained continually that the Egyptians were taking insufficient action against enemy agents who 'infested' the Canal zone. As soon as Churchill became aware of the doubtful loyalty of the Egyptian army to the Allied cause, he insisted that Egyptian troops be sent back from the Western Desert to the Delta and that General Aziz al-Masri should be dismissed. Any possibility of allowing King Farouk to bring Ali Maher back to power was ruled out.

The crisis between Britain and the king reached its climax early in 1942. Under Allied pressure the government decided to break off relations with Vichy France. The king, who was absent from Cairo and not consulted, was furious and forced the prime minister to resign. To have replaced him with Ali Maher would have been too provocative, but he showed his intention of having Maher as a member of a cabinet in which he would hold the real power. Lampson, on the other hand, wanted to see a Wafdist government installed. Rommel was advancing in Cyrenaica, and the cry of 'Long Live Rommel' was heard in the streets of Cairo. Lampson knew that, while it still enjoyed widespread popularity, the Wafd would provide the most effective support for the Allies. He also knew that Farouk would resist the return of the Wafd he detested.

Lampson secured the support of the British government and military chiefs for the use of force. He delivered the king an ultimatum that if he refused to ask Nahas Pasha to form a government by 6 p.m. the following evening (2 February) he would have to 'face the consequences'. When the ultimatum expired with no reply, Lampson had the Abdin Palace surrounded by British troops and armoured cars and forced his way in to see the king, bearing an instrument of abdication. After hesitation, the king capitulated at the thirteenth hour and agreed to call Nahas. Lampson was dismayed because he had hoped to be permanently rid of Farouk.

This humiliation of the monarchy was a seminal event in the modern history of Egypt. For all his faults, the king still personified Egypt, and nationalist opinion was outraged. One senior officer,

General Muhammad Neguib, requested the king's permission to resign from the Egyptian army. The 24-year-old Lieutenant Gamal Abdul Nasser, then stationed in Sudan, was one of a group of young officers who began to dream of taking action to restore Egypt's army.

At this crucial point in the desert war, Britain was concerned only with securing the Egyptian domestic front. Rommel's forces continued their advance, to reach within sixty miles of Alexandria. Exhausted and low in morale, some thousands of British troops deserted and hid in the Delta. As the British embassy burned its files, the British civilians in Egypt came close to panic. Women and children were sent by train to Palestine. But Nahas and his government, having thrown in their lot with Britain, kept their nerve. They interned all suspected Axis sympathizers, including Ali Maher, and refused to accept the inevitability of German occupation even when Rommel's radio was triumphantly announcing his imminent arrival in Cairo.

In August 1942 Churchill came to Cairo and it was agreed that General Montgomery should take over the Eighth Army. On 23 October the battle of Alamein, a turning-point in the war, marked the beginning of the Axis decline in the Middle East. Within seven months the remaining German and Italian forces had evacuated North Africa. The war receded from Egypt, but the country became an even vaster war base for the Allies, with some 200,000 troops either stationed, in transit or on leave in Egypt. An American presence made itself felt, and the Anglo-American Middle East Supply Centre made Egypt the focus of the Allied war effort in the Middle East and North Africa.

Reza Shah of Iran was less fortunate than Farouk. His country was strategically as important as Egypt to the Allies, and the huge German advances after the invasion of the Soviet Union in June 1941 raised the possibility of a German occupation of Iran and its oil-fields. Since Russia and Britain had long been the aggressive imperialist powers in Iranian eyes, nationalist sentiment, especially among the ruling class and senior army officers, tended to be pro-German.

The Nazi regime had begun seizing the advantage before the war. German companies played a leading role in Iranian industrialization, German propaganda was vigorous and Nazi agents were active throughout the country.

As soon as the Soviet Union entered the war, it began to demand that German agents and saboteurs should be curbed. Reza Shah appealed to the United States to support Iran's neutrality but the United States, although still not a belligerent, was already bound by the Lend-Lease Act of 1941 to help Britain to supply the Soviet Union with arms through Iran. Washington was unsympathetic and urged Reza Shah to help the Allies 'to stop Hitler's ambition of world conquest'.

The crisis came to a head when the Iranian government officially rejected a joint Soviet and British request to send arms supplies across the country to the Soviet Union. On 25 August 1941 Soviet and British troops invaded Iran simultaneously from the north and south. Iraq provided a convenient base for the British invasion following the replacement of the Rashid Ali government by a pro-British regime. Iranian troops could offer little resistance, and on 16 September Reza Shah abdicated in favour of his 23-year-old son, Mohammed Reza Pahlavi. In January 1942 a tripartite treaty of alliance was concluded with Britain and the Soviet Union, both of which undertook 'to respect the territorial integrity, sovereignty and political independence of Iran' and 'to defend Iran by all means at their command from aggression'. Britain and the Soviet Union defined their respective zones, with the British occupying the south, centre and west and the Russians holding the three northern provinces of Azerbaijan, Gilan and Mazandaran.

The Russians claimed the right of intervention under the terms of the Persian–Soviet treaty of 1921. However, the new agreement stated that the Soviet and British forces permitted to remain on Iranian soil did not constitute an occupation and would be withdrawn not later than six months after the end of the war. In return, Iran undertook to render non-specified military assistance to the Allies. In September 1943 Iran declared war on Germany. In December, Stalin, Roosevelt and Churchill, after holding their first joint meeting in Tehran, issued a declaration expressing their desire for the maintenance of the 'independence, sovereignty, and territorial integrity' of Iran.

The US role in Iran steadily increased during the war, and by 1945 there were 30,000 American troops in the country, although they were non-combatants employed in dispatching supplies to Russia and managing the Trans-Iranian Railway, and they operated as part of the British forces, who were responsible for law and order.

Middle East Reactions: Nationalism, Pan-Arabism and Islam

Italy's surrender in 1943 and the removal of the threat of a German invasion of the Middle East enhanced Britain's position in the region. However, the new situation also meant that Britain was less able to use the overriding exigencies of the war to maintain control over political developments. The minority of Middle Easterners – Arabs and Iranians – who had calculated on an Axis victory to secure their nationalist demands had been disappointed. This did not mean that the majority abandoned their aim of securing the removal of European domination.

The situation in Syria and Lebanon was unusual in that Britain had helped Charles de Gaulle's Free French to oust the Vichy regime in 1941 on the understanding that France would recognize the two countries' independence. This was declared by General Catroux, de Gaulle's representative, before the invasion of the Free French force and was underwritten by Britain with the somewhat ambiguous formula that Britain would recognize that France had a predominant position over the other European powers once the promises of independence had been carried out.

De Gaulle, however, did not believe that the Free French had liberated Syria and Lebanon in order to give them up. He wished to secure treaties based on the 1936 agreements which fell well short of independence. The Syrians almost unanimously rejected the idea of a treaty, hoping to bring matters to a crisis while British troops were still present.

Even in Lebanon, in spite of the traditional Maronite reliance on French protection, the desire for independence was dominant. The new mercantile classes, both Christian and Muslim, felt strong enough to stand by themselves without French protection and they disliked the mandate's limitations on their activities. In 1943 an unwritten 'National Pact' was reached between certain Christian and Muslim leaders to the effect that Lebanon should remain independent within its existing frontiers but should follow an independent Arab foreign policy. Elections held in the same year led to the victory of those opposed to the mandate, and the new government proposed to remove from the constitution those clauses which safeguarded French control. The French replied by arresting the president of the republic and most of the government. Faced with popular disturbances, world-wide protests and a British ultimatum, the French gave in. The ministers were released and the constitution amended.

Elections in Syria in 1943 also produced a clear victory for the nationalists. Gradually and reluctantly, the French began to transfer the mandates' powers to the two governments. But they had not given up all hope, keeping the local Lebanese and Syrian armed forces under the control of the French high command as a means of securing post-independence treaties. When in May 1945 a contingent of Senegalese troops landed in Beirut, the Syrians correctly concluded that France aimed to maintain military control after the departure of the British. Fighting broke out in Damascus and the French bombarded the city. Another British ultimatum forced the French troops to return to barracks. Although these troops remained for one more year, France's rule in the Levant had come to an end. In 1946 Syria and Lebanon joined the United Nations as independent states.

The United States and the Soviet Union, having recognized Syrian and Lebanese independence, were not prepared to accept

France's continuing predominance, but it was Britain that France held responsible for its exclusion. Twenty years later General de Gaulle secured some measure of revenge by vetoing Britain's entry into the European Economic Community.

Egypt was the centre of Britain's power in the Middle East but, following the installation of the Wafd government, the country's internal politics were not a major British concern. The Wafd, although still confident that it was the expression of the popular will, was sensitive to charges that it had been placed in power by the British. It claimed to champion the cause of the egyptianization of the state. To the extreme irritation of the British and other foreign communities, it made the Arabic language compulsory for all official correspondence and commercial accountancy. But the reality was that Nahas was still dependent on Lampson's support to prevent the vengeful king from dismissing him. In fact the Wafd, riddled with corruption and public scandal, was losing its mastery. Extra-parliamentary forces, of which the Muslim Brotherhood was the most significant and dangerous, were growing in strength. Rampant inflation, exacerbated by the presence of Allied forces, caused increasing public discontent with the government. The land-owning class was growing richer and, as in the First World War, a new wealthy class of merchants and industrialists had grown up by supplying the foreign forces with goods and services. But the great majority of Egyptians were sinking further into poverty.

In October 1944 the king seized the chance of Lampson's absence from the country to dismiss Nahas and replace him with Ahmed Maher, Ali Maher's genial and very different brother. The new prime minister insisted that Egypt should at last declare war on Germany, in order to ensure its membership of the projected United Nations Organization. On 24 February 1945 Ahmed Maher announced Egypt's declaration of war to parliament; as he left, he was assassinated. Almost certainly the act was planned by the new terrorist wing of the Muslim Brotherhood. Political murder was about to become a feature of Egyptian life.

Egyptians of all political parties felt that, as a reward for Egypt's contribution to the Allied war effort, Britain should evacuate the country entirely and accept the unity of Egypt and the Sudan. But although they hoped that the Labour Party, which had just come to power in Britain, would be more sympathetic to Egyptian national aspirations, the new Labour government was chiefly concerned with maintaining Britain's dominant military position in the Middle East and was not prepared for a revision of the 1936 treaty, which it felt had stood the test of time. Ubiquitous British troops in Cairo reminded the Egyptians of the continuing occupation. The Wafd, in opposition, anxious to renew its nationalist credentials, encouraged anti-British agitation. In February 1946 strikes and demonstrations led to violent rioting in which Muslim Brothers and communists as well as the Wafd all played a role.

The aged but still formidable Sidky Pasha was recalled to power. He acted to control the demonstrations, although some attacks on British soldiers and civilians continued. He insisted that Britain should negotiate, and by now the Labour government was ready to respond. The British military and the Conservative opposition, led by Winston Churchill, maintained that Egypt was an essential Western base for a regional defence system. A crisis with the Soviet Union over Iran had already marked the onset of the Cold War. But the foreign secretary, Ernest Bevin, was prepared to agree to the principle of total evacuation provided the Suez base could be reactivated in the event of renewed war in the Middle East (which by now to the Western powers meant a Soviet invasion of one of the countries in the region). Field Marshal Montgomery, who visited Egypt in the summer of 1946, agreed that Britain could evacuate the Suez base provided it maintained troops in Palestine, Libya and Cyprus. But he also ominously insisted that Britain 'must remain strong in the Sudan, in case of difficulties with the Egyptians'. It was necessary 'to control the Nile, the life-blood of Egypt'.

The old obstruction to the ending of the British occupation of Egypt remained. Although Sidky swiftly reached agreement with

Bevin on a total British evacuation in three years, they glossed over the Sudan issue, saying that the 1899 condominium agreement would remain until, after consultation with the Sudanese, a new common agreement could be reached on the Sudan's future status 'within the framework of the unity between the Sudan and Egypt under the common Crown of Egypt'.

The Egyptians understandably interpreted this as meaning that Britain had accepted Farouk as king of Egypt and the Sudan. But the British government, with strident support from British officials in the Sudan, soon made it clear that it had no such intention. Instead it began to institute moves towards Sudanese self-government. Anglo-Egyptian relations remained as bad as ever. Britain did unilaterally fulfil part of the terms of the Sidky–Bevin agreement, as all troops were withdrawn from the Delta to the Suez Canal zone; however, there were over seven times as many as the 10,000 stipulated in the 1936 treaty.

In March 1945 the League of Arab States had been established, with Britain's blessing. It had its headquarters in Cairo and an Egyptian secretary-general. But the founding members, who were the seven Arab states which had achieved independence – Egypt, Iraq, Saudi Arabia, Transjordan, Yemen, Syria and Lebanon – ensured that the League was in no way a federation. Each member retained its full sovereignty, and decisions taken by the Arab League Council were binding only on those members which had voted for them.

Although the League was theoretically inspired by the doctrine of pan-Arab unity, this remained a fragile and undeveloped ideology. As long as the Ottoman Empire remained in existence, the great majority of Arabs, whatever their grievances against the Turks, assumed that the empire would remain the leader of the Muslim world. Only Christian Arabs of the Levant, who felt no such loyalty, thought seriously of secession, but they found little response among their Muslim fellow-Arabs. A few intellectuals such as Rashid Rida or al-Kawakibi argued that the Turks had forfeited their right to Muslim leadership and that Islam would be best served by a return to an Arab caliphate. But this hardly amounted to a programme for political action.

The pan-Arabism preached by Sharif Hussein when he launched his Arab Revolt was haphazard and rudimentary and derived strongly from his personal and family ambitions. His claim to be King of the Arabs was recognized by no more than a few. In the exultant but brief period when Emir Feisal was established as King of Syria, he attempted to keep the pan-Arab idea alive. 'We are one people,' he said in May 1919, 'living in the region which is bounded by the sea to the east, the south, and the west, and by the Taurus mountains to the north.' Most significantly, he was also fond of saying 'We are Arabs before being Muslims, and Muhammad is an Arab before being a prophet.' This was the germ of a secular Arab nationalism. But within a year Feisal was expelled from Syria and, although the British installed him in Iraq, the Arab peoples of whom he spoke were divided by new national frontiers.

In the years following the First World War, therefore, there were two contrary trends among the eastern Arabs. One of these trends was the development of territorial nationalism in the new nation-states as they became involved in a struggle for full independence from Britain and France. This required the creation of a national identity, and it was sustained by the ambitions and rivalries of the national leaders. The House of Saud was hostile and suspicious towards the Hashemites, and there was rivalry between the Hashemites of Iraq and Transjordan.

The opposing trend was the aspiration towards Arab unity based on the feeling, to which all Arabs subscribed to some extent, that they had been artificially divided in order to weaken them and keep them under Western tutelage. Unity was necessary for Arab self-protection and renaissance. This tendency received a powerful impetus from the events in Palestine. The growing awareness that the Zionists, with the help of the West, aimed to seize as much of Arab Palestine as they could was the strongest factor in mobilizing Arab opinion, which was frustrated but not restrained by the fact that so little that was effective could be done to help the Palestinian Arabs.

Islam was and remains a uniquely potent element in Arab nationalism. Muslim militants, such as the Muslim Brotherhood, maintained that nationalism and Islam were incompatible since all Muslims of all races from China to Morocco were members of the same great Islamic nation or *umma*. Pan-Arab intellectuals attempted to demonstrate to the contrary that Arabism and Islam are mutually inclusive. As Abdul Rahman Azzam, the Arab League's first secretary-general, said in a lecture in 1943, the ideals of Islam were the same as those of modern Arab nationalism and of the Arab nation which aimed to take its rightful place in the world and resume the mission which Muhammad had inaugurated. But the debate was largely artificial. Muslim militants in the Arab countries made their appeal for Islamic revival to their fellow-Arabs. Arab nationalism, on the other hand, could never be secular in the style and to the degree of Atatürk's Turkish Republic (or even the Iran of Reza Shah) for the simple reason that Islam is an integral part of Arab civilization and culture. Hence Michel Aflaq, the young Syrian Christian school-teacher who was the ideologist of the Arab Baath (Renaissance) Party which he founded in Damascus in the 1940s, maintained that Islam was a permanent tendency in the life of the Arab nation. 'Muhammad was the epitome of all the Arabs, so let all Arabs today be Muhammad,' he told his followers. On the other hand, the representatives of the House of Saud, keepers of the holy places of Islam, have never had any problem about reconciling their Arab and Islamic aspirations, invariably mentioning them in the same breath.

In the 1920s and 1930s, Egypt largely excluded itself from any pan-Arab movement, with the approval of its fellow-Arabs. There was a conflict between the patriotism of an ancient nation-state (in Egypt known as 'Pharaonism') and the ideals of pan-Islam. An extreme view was put forward by the great Egyptian writer Taha Hussein, who said that though Egypt might be part of Europe by virtue of its present culture, it was Pharaonic in its traditions – it was certainly not part of the Muslim East. But most Egyptians had mixed feelings and managed to remain Egyptian patriots while finding inspiration in the concept of Islamic unity at the same time. Mustafa Kamel, Egypt's nationalist leader at the end of the Cromer era, was of this kind. But pan-Arabism did not appeal. Zaghloul interrupted Azzam Pasha, who was speaking to him of Arab unity, with the question 'If you add one zero to another, and then to another, what sum will you get?'

The situation gradually changed from the late 1930s onwards. A growing body of Egyptians, among whom Azzam was outstanding, could see the potential role in the Middle East for Egypt once it was freed from British control, and there were other Arabs who were reaching the same conclusion. Sati al-Husri, an Aleppo-born writer who had followed Emir Feisal from Syria to Iraq and was to do more than anyone to popularize the idea of Arab unity, argued in 1936 that nature had endowed Egypt with all the qualities which made it incumbent upon the country to assume the leadership of the Arab national movement.

The shift towards a view of Cairo as the nucleus of pan-Arabism was not shared by Arab leaders or the Arab masses, including the Egyptian people themselves. It was by no means agreed that the Egyptians should even be regarded as Arabs. In December 1942 Nuri al-Said put forward a scheme for the unification of Syria, Lebanon, Palestine and Transjordan with 'semi-autonomy' for the Jews in Palestine, as a first step towards Arab unity. Egypt was not included. Another scheme, which was proposed by King Ibn Saud's friend and adviser the British Arabist H. St John Philby, was for the Saudi monarch to head an Arab federation with an autonomous Jewish state in Palestine. This found favour with the Gentile Zionist Winston Churchill and the Zionist leadership. Again Egypt was excluded. However, despite Ibn Saud's high prestige, which caused both Churchill and Roosevelt to imagine him as 'King of the Arabs', all such schemes were impractical because of the enmity between the Saudis and the Hashemites – neither would ever accept the others' leadership.

However, the British Foreign Office was in favour of closer ties between the Arab states, provided that Western interests could be maintained. A major factor was the hope that it would be easier to solve the Palestine problem within a broader Arab framework. From May 1941 onwards, Anthony Eden, the British foreign secretary, made repeated statements that Britain favoured any scheme that commanded general approval among the Arabs for strengthening the cultural, economic and political ties between the Arab states. Britain now accepted that Egypt – the site of the Middle East Supply Centre and focus of the Allied war effort in the region – would make the best headquarters for any Western-sponsored Arab federation. Moreover the Wafd government led by Nahas, in wartime alliance with Britain, had begun to be attracted by the concept of an Egyptian-led Arab union. King Farouk was equally determined that Egypt should not be left out. Reluctantly Nuri al-Said and the other Arab leaders came to accept the inevitable: there was no alternative to Egypt. The last act of the Wafd government before it was driven from office in October 1944 was to sign the Protocol of Alexandria with the six other independent Arab states which led to the foundation of the Arab League in the following year.

While Arabs and Iranians in their overwhelming majority sought the removal of European tutelage and domination in the aftermath of the war, there was one group in the Middle East which had different priorities: the Zionist Jews. When the war began, their dream of an independent Jewish state in Palestine had faded as a result of the change in British policy embodied in the 1939 White Paper. Their anger and bitterness were deep. Yet there could be no question of not helping Britain in the war against the Nazis. David Ben Gurion, the Zionist leader who was to become Israel's first prime minister, coined the slogan that the Jews would fight the White Paper as if there were no war and the war as if there were no White Paper. Some 27,000 Palestine Jews enlisted in the British forces during the war, but others believed they could best serve their cause by building up the Haganah, the semi-secret Zionist army in Palestine. The war gave a powerful impetus to the development of a Jewish munitions industry, which supplied the British forces in

1942–3 but could strengthen the Zionists in the future. The British
continued to reject Zionist demands for the formation of a Jewish
army, flying the Zionist flag, to fight alongside the Allies.

As the danger of German invasion passed with Rommel's defeat
at Alamein, and at the same time news began to leak out from Europe
of Hitler's unspeakable atrocities against the Jews, the Palestine
Zionists turned decisively against Britain. Enraged by Britain's
deportation of the few illegal immigrants who managed to reach
Palestine, they blamed Britain alone for the failure to rescue European Jewry. Anti-British acts of resistance multiplied. A splinter
group from the mainstream Haganah joined hands with the even
more extreme Stern Gang in widespread attacks which culminated
in the murder of Lord Moyne, British minister of state in Cairo, in
November 1944. An outraged Churchill, a close friend of Moyne,
temporarily abandoned his long-standing pro-Zionism.

The war also marked a decisive move of the headquarters of
international Zionism from Britain to the United States. Chaim
Weizmann still believed that the Zionists' best hopes of achieving
their aims lay in Britain, but he was overtaken by a new generation,
represented by David Ben Gurion, which looked to the coming
American superpower to force Britain's acquiescence. At a conference, in which all shades of Zionist opinion were represented, at
the Biltmore Hotel in New York in May 1944, a programme was
adopted providing for unrestricted Jewish immigration and the
establishment of Palestine as a Jewish commonwealth 'integrated
in the structure of the new democratic world'.

The Palestine Arabs, on the other hand, remained largely quies-
cent during the war. Some 12,000 joined the British forces. Hajj
Amin al-Husseini escaped from Baghdad after the fall of Rashid Ali
and went to Germany, where he tried to mobilize Muslim world
opinion for the Axis cause. But he had little impact.

The coming to power of a Labour government in Britain in 1945
raised the hopes of the Zionists, because the Labour Party had
opposed the 1939 White Paper and in conference in 1944 it had passed
a resolution suggesting that the Arabs should move out of Palestine

as the Jews moved in. But once in power the Attlee government was faced with complex and daunting realities. Britain was nominally one of the Big Three which had won the war, and the Labour government had no more intention than the Conservative opposition that Britain should relinquish its position at the top table. In the Middle East region, where it had been the undoubted victor, Britain appeared to be the paramount power. In fact, exhausted and impoverished by the war, Britain was already facing a decline in its role, and the Labour government's momentous decision to grant independence to India in 1947 would undermine Britain's position as a global power. At the same time it was beset by problems in Europe, caused by the expansion of the Soviet empire in eastern Europe and by the breakdown of the wartime alliance with Stalin, which marked the outbreak of the Cold War. In the Middle East, Britain was confronted by Egypt's demands for an end to the British occupation. Alternative military bases could be found in the eastern Mediterranean, but this was no answer to the by now insoluble problem of Palestine.

The prospect offered by the 1939 White Paper – that Palestine would become an independent binational Arab/Jewish state with the Arabs dominating the government – had been destroyed by Hitler. He had been defeated, but there was now overwhelming pressure that the survivors of the Holocaust should be allowed to take refuge in Palestine. Neither the Western countries, such as the United States, nor the Zionist leadership wanted them to go elsewhere.

The British foreign secretary, Ernest Bevin, still believed that a solution might be found by negotiation. He unwisely told the House of Commons that he would 'stake my political future' on solving the Palestine problem. But he wanted to make the United States share responsibility. As soon as the war ended, President Truman cabled the British government to demand the immediate entry of 100,000 Jews into Palestine. The US Congress wanted unrestricted immigration. In November 1945 Bevin announced the formation of an Anglo-American commission of inquiry. In April 1946 this recommended the continuation of the mandate and a unitary state, repeal of restrictions on land sales and the immediate admission of 100,000 Jews – in effect a return to the 1922 policy. The commission criticized the existence of the Jewish underground forces, which it estimated at 65,000, and it recommended that they should be disarmed.

The British government found these proposals impracticable as they stood but approved some discussions on Jewish and Arab autonomy. As Britain continued trying to prevent illegal Jewish immigration, the Zionist underground stepped up its activities, which reached a peak with the blowing up in July 1946 of the King David Hotel in Jerusalem, containing British civilian and military offices.

Meanwhile, the seven independent Arab states were attempting to act to prevent an Arab disaster in Palestine. Their heads-of-state meeting in Egypt in May 1946 reaffirmed the Arab character of Palestine, and another meeting in June in Syria passed secret resolutions threatening British and US interests in the Middle East if Arab rights in Palestine were disregarded.

The British government faced an impossible dilemma. Public opinion in Britain was divided between Zionist sympathizers and those outraged by Zionist atrocities. In the Middle East, all British interests in the Arab world would be threatened if the Zionists were allowed to seize Palestine, but Britain was under relentless pressure from the US to allow massive Jewish immigration and, in the aftermath of the war, Britain was financially dependent on Washington. (In support of the so-called Truman Doctrine of overseas US involvement, set out in an address to Congress on 12 March 1947, President Truman asked Congress for aid, which Britain could no longer afford, to enable Greece and Turkey to maintain their independence against the Soviet threat.) After one more futile attempt to obtain Arab and Jewish agreement on a joint plan, Britain handed the problem over to the United Nations in February 1947.

In August 1947 a majority report of a UN Special Commission on Palestine (UNSCOP) recommended the partition of Palestine into Arab and Jewish states, which would still be economically unified, with Jerusalem and its environs to be international. By a vote of 33 to 13 with 10 abstentions, these recommendations were substantially adopted by the UN General Assembly in its Resolution 181 of 29 November 1947. This resolution was passed because both the USA and the Soviet Union, which then dominated the UN, voted in favour and were prepared to use pressure. The Soviet Union at that time regarded the Zionist struggle in Palestine as one of liberation against imperialism. Only the Islamic Asian countries voted against the resolution. An Arab proposal to question the International Court of Justice on the competence of the General Assembly to partition a country against the wishes of the majority of its inhabitants (there were 1,269,000 Arabs and 678,000 Jews in Palestine in 1946) was narrowly defeated.

The Zionists welcomed the partition because it recognized a Jewish state which, although including a large area of desert in the south, the Negev, covered 55 per cent of a country in which Zionist land-holdings still amounted to less than 8 per cent of the total. The Arabs, as always, bitterly opposed partition but they were especially outraged because the proposed Jewish state would include almost as many Arabs as Jews.

Britain had already, in September 1947, announced its intention to give up the Palestine mandate on 15 April 1948. The United Nations had made no proposals as to how the partition of Palestine should be carried out or financed, and Britain refused to implement a policy which was not acceptable to both sides or to participate in the UN Palestine Commission which was supposed to supervise the transitional period. Britain merely handed over power to whichever community was locally in the ascendant and, since Arab cadres, in contrast to Jewish cadres, were generally lacking, order was better maintained in the Jewish areas. Communal fighting broke out immediately and soon developed into full-scale civil war as the British administration was dismantled.

Faced with this disaster, the US retreated and declared its opposition to forcible partition. On 30 March 1948 it called for a truce and the further consideration of the problem by the UN General Assembly. But the Zionists, anxious about the American shift in policy, redoubled their efforts to establish their state. The extreme Zionist Irgun and the Stern Gang were now collaborating with the Haganah, and the master-plan, known as Plan Dalet, for the seizure of most of Palestine was put into effect. Operations were launched against strategically situated Arab villages. An Arab Liberation Army of some 3,000 volunteers from outside Palestine had some initial successes but could do little against greatly superior Zionist forces. Arab civilian morale crumbled in the face of the onslaught and a psychological offensive which exploited reports of the massacre on 10 May by Irgunists of 250 inhabitants of the village of Deir Yasin. Tiberias, Haifa, Acre, Jaffa and much of Arab Jerusalem fell, and some three to four hundred thousand refugees streamed in terror towards the neighbouring Arab countries.

On 14 May the last British high commissioner left Palestine and the mandate formally ended. The Zionists immediately proclaimed the state of Israel and within hours they had received the *de facto* recognition of the Soviet Union and the United States.

Early on 15 May, units of the regular armies of Syria, Transjordan, Iraq and Egypt crossed the frontiers of Palestine in the hope of restoring the situation for the Arabs.

This apparently determined action by the independent Arab states masked their fatal disunity. It was a unanimous decision of the Arab League to intervene in Palestine, but the unity was no more than a façade. There was no effective liaison between the Arab armies and they did not act in concert. Their military capacity did not reflect the overwhelming Arab superiority in numbers, with 40 million Arabs confronting some 600,000 Zionist Jews. In fact to take the field Egypt had some 10,000 regular troops, Transjordan's Arab Legion 4,500, Syria 3,000, Lebanon 1,000 and Iraq 3,000. Their arms were British or French and, in the case of Transjordan, the commander-in-chief General Glubb and senior officers were British. One surviving Arab statesman recalls that the Arab armies were useful only to perform ceremonial parades. They were confronting some 60,000 Jewish troops who, although never officially recognized by the mandate, were armed and trained and many of whom already had battle experience.

Some of the Arab leaders, especially in Syria and Iraq, were so ignorant of the situation that they expected a walk-over. King Abdullah had the most realistic appreciation of Zionist strength. For some time he had been in secret negotiation with the Zionist leaders and he had formed with them what amounted to a strategic alliance which would enable him to take over the Arab part of Palestine and exclude the Palestine nationalist leaders, such as the Husseinis, who were hostile to the Hashemites. The Egyptian prime minister Nokrashy Pasha, who lacked the flamboyant confidence of the more ambitious Nahas, also had doubts about an Arab victory and had no illusions about the adequacy of the Egyptian armed forces. But Egyptian public opinion had been roused. The Muslim Brotherhood wanted to fight for Palestine, and Hajj Amin al-Husseini, who was now in Egypt, exerted a powerful influence. Of greater importance was King Farouk's determination that the Egyptian army should enter the war.

If Zionist resistance had collapsed there is little doubt that even King Abdullah would have been obliged to continue until the state of Israel had been strangled at birth. But the declared objective of the Arab governments was only to restore order and to protect the 45 per cent of Palestine which had been allotted to the Arabs under the UN partition plan.

At first all went well for the Arabs as they occupied areas which were not yet controlled by the Jews. The Egyptians entered Gaza and Beersheba and linked up with the Arab Legion near Bethlehem. The Legion, with its Iraqi allies, held the central section of Palestine and attempted to blockade Jewish west Jerusalem, although, disastrously for the Arabs, they were unable to cut the road from Tel Aviv to Jerusalem.

The UN mediator, Sweden's Count Folke Bernadotte, secured a four-week ceasefire from 11 June and put forward proposals for a settlement which were rejected by both sides. When the fighting

resumed, the Jews broke the siege of west Jerusalem and made lightning gains in nearly all sectors, capturing Nazareth and western
Galilee, which had been allotted to the Arabs. A second ceasefire
called on 18 July was ineffective, and when the fighting finally ended
in January 1949 the Jews had occupied all the Negev up to the former
Egypt–Palestine border except for the Gaza Strip on the coast. The
Iraqis and Jordanians held a slice of territory to the north and south
of Jerusalem. Only 21 per cent of Palestine remained in Arab hands.
The number of Arabs within the area held by Israel had decreased
by between 700,000 and 750,000.

Between February and July 1949 the new UN mediator, the
American Ralph Bunche, succeeded in securing separate armistice
agreements between Israel and Egypt and the Arab states (except
Iraq, which nevertheless withdrew its troops). It was broadly agreed
to fix a temporary frontier where the lines had been at the start of
the negotiations, while certain border areas were demilitarized.
Jerusalem was divided between the Arab east and Jewish west. The
Gaza Strip came under Egyptian administration.

No peace treaty was signed. In December 1948 the UN General
Assembly appointed a three-member conciliation commission to
promote a final settlement and to arrange an international regime
for Jerusalem, but all its efforts were frustrated. The Arab states
refused to consider a peace treaty unless the Israeli government
agreed to accept all Arab refugees wishing to return to Israel. Resolutions demanding that the refugees should be given the option of
return or compensation for their property were constantly reaffirmed
by the UN General Assembly, and it was on this basis that Israel
was admitted to the UN on 11 May 1949. But Israel maintained that
the future of the refugees could be discussed only as part of a general
peace settlement. The impasse was complete. Half of the Palestinian Arabs had become refugees. Neither the new state of Israel nor
its Arab neighbours could expect even a minimum of security and
stability.

11. The Entry of the Superpowers and the Nasser Era, 1950–1970

The repercussions of the Palestine disaster (*al-Naqba* in Arabic) were felt throughout the Arab East. Blame was divided between Britain, the United States and the Arab leaders whose incompetence and divisive rivalries had contributed to the miserable Arab performance. Arab opinion in general was radicalized. In Syria, a military *coup d'état* took place even before the truce was signed. Although it was soon overturned and a form of constitutional parliamentary government restored, the Syrian armed forces had acquired a taste for political power which was never to diminish. Syria became a byword for political instability.

The Transjordanian monarchy, although at the eye of the storm, survived with the support of a loyal army. King Abdullah was able to carry out his ambition of uniting what was left of Palestine in his newly proclaimed Hashemite kingdom of Jordan. The majority of the inhabitants of the enclave, defenceless and in imminent danger of being swallowed up by the Zionists, saw no alternative and in December 1948 a conference of some 2,000 Arab notables at Jericho invited King Abdullah to unite Palestine and Jordan. The move was bitterly opposed by the other Arab states, who attempted unsuccessfully to block it. They tried to revive the UN resolution for the internationalization of Jerusalem but, since this was unacceptable to Israel, they failed. King Abdullah remained in control of the Arab Old City.

Jordan had acquired a Palestinian population twice as numerous as the Transjordanians, and half a million of them were destitute refugees. The Palestinians accepted King Abdullah's annexation as the consequence of *force majeure*, but most of them had reservations about being ruled by Transjordanians, whom they regarded as less advanced than themselves. A minority actively detested the Hashemites.

King Abdullah handled this delicate situation with practised ambiguity. He and his government tried to carry out the political integration of the new population and Jordan was the only Arab state to offer the refugees full citizenship, but, like the others, it continued to maintain that the refugees were primarily an international political and economic responsibility and would never abandon their right of return. Thus Jordan aimed both to combat Palestinian separatism and to maintain its right to speak for the Palestinians while proclaiming that one day an Arab Palestine would be restored. This 'Jordanian paradise' was to last for nearly thirty years. It created acute political difficulties but the Jordanian monarchy survived, through a combination of good fortune, external aid, divisions among its enemies and the flexibility and determination of its rulers. Abdullah was assassinated by a Palestinian youth as he entered the al-Aqsa Mosque in Jerusalem on 20 July 1951. His son, Tallal, proved to be mentally unstable and abdicated a year later. Tallal's sixteen-year-old son Hussein (1952–99), then at school in England, succeeded and, against all the odds, became the longest-surviving Arab head of state.

Egypt was the Arab country in which the Palestine disaster had the most momentous long-term effects. The younger officers who served in the war became convinced of the criminal incompetence of the men ruling Egypt. Food and medical supplies were inadequate, while arms were obsolete and in some cases worthless. Senior officers gave contradictory and meaningless orders, while some showed downright incompetence. (An outstanding exception was Major-General Muhammad Neguib, who was severely wounded in the fighting.) Gamal Abdul Nasser, recently promoted to major, was wounded and distinguished himself in a defensive engagement, but his most vivid memory was the words of one of his most admired superiors shortly before he was killed: 'Remember, the real battle is in Egypt.'

For several years there had been a clandestine movement among the younger nationalist officers. Nasser – grave, thoughtful and reticent in manner, but with considerable charismatic charm – had emerged as its natural leader and organizer. Many of his closest colleagues served with him in Palestine, and on their return they stepped up their activities, more than ever convinced of the urgent need for a radical change in the regime. The military coup in Damascus in March 1949 started a chain reaction which affected all the Arab states. In Egypt the Free Officers, as they now called themselves, formed an executive committee of which Nasser, now a colonel, was formally elected president. They established a chain of cells throughout the armed forces and began to distribute mimeographed tracts denouncing the regime.

Egypt's parliamentary democracy was already crumbling as the extra-parliamentary forces gathered strength. Of these the Muslim Brotherhood was the most visible and had gained new prestige from its members' brave actions as volunteers in Palestine. In November 1948 Nokrashy Pasha made use of martial law to declare the Brotherhood dissolved and its branches closed. A month later Nokrashy was assassinated, and two months after this Hassan al-Banna, founder and Supreme Guide of the Brotherhood, was himself shot down – almost certainly by a wing of the state counter-terrorist police.

King Farouk was steadily losing what remained of his youthful popularity. A combination of glandular disorder and self-indulgence had transformed the handsome boy-king into a cartoon-satire of middle-aged debauchery. His divorce of his popular Egyptian wife Farida at the height of the Palestine war had not helped his reputation, and the frivolous luxury of his life in Mediterranean resorts during Egypt's troubles seemed a callous insult to his impoverished subjects.

Although Farouk's humiliation by Britain had made him increasingly cynical, he had not abandoned his inherited taste for political intrigue or the desire to hold on to power. In January 1950 he recalled his old enemy Nahas and allowed a general election in which the Wafd was still able to gain its customary sweeping victory. Both parties in this improbable palace–Wafd alliance hoped in this way to preserve their share in Egypt's ramshackle system of government.

Britain also hoped for an improvement in Anglo-Egyptian relations, pending the still elusive final agreement, and made some conciliatory gestures. The British government had been working to set up a combined Middle Eastern command with the US, Turkey and France, which it hoped Egypt would join. This was essentially a Cold War move, aiming to keep the Soviet Union out of the eastern Mediterranean, but already it was doomed to failure. Neutralist feeling was nascent in the Middle East, where most of the population regarded the old imperial powers as a more serious threat than Soviet communism. When Britain presented the plan to Egypt in October 1951, it was flatly rejected. In fact the Wafdist government had already decided to abrogate the 1939 Anglo-Egyptian treaty and unilaterally to declare Farouk King of Egypt and the Sudan.

Faced with mounting criticism and exposure of its corruption, the Wafd was anxious to restore its credentials for uncompromising nationalism. But although its move was wildly popular in the country, it was dangerous because in its struggle with Britain the Egyptian government had to enlist the support of all the forces in the country which were aiming for the overthrow of the constitutional regime. Nahas not only declared a state of emergency and took steps to cut off supplies of food and Egyptian labour to the British troops in the Canal zone but also went further and encouraged the formation of volunteer 'Liberation' squads to carry out sabotage and guerrilla attacks. For these the obvious recruits were Muslim Brothers, communists and any other groups with valuable terrorist experience. Some Free Officers helped to train these groups behind the scenes.

In Britain the Conservatives won the October 1951 elections. They were to remain in power for the next thirteen years. Churchill returned as prime minister and Eden as foreign secretary. Egypt retained its prime importance in their eyes, but there was no obvious solution to the crisis. The Suez base was maintained by importing labour from East Africa, but it had been rendered useless as the 80,000 British were occupied in defending the base against sabotage. The alternative was the reoccupation of Cairo, which was something that even the imperialist Churchill was unwilling to contemplate.

As the guerrilla attacks were stepped up, the British extended their countermeasures and arrested suspects – who included the Egyptian police. Then on 25 January 1952 a strong British force surrounded the police headquarters at Ismailia at dawn and called upon its occupants to surrender. The minister of the interior ordered them to resist, which they did with great courage until some fifty were dead and many more injured.

The next day – since known as Black Saturday – a frenzied mob burned the centre of Cairo. Special attention was paid to British property but also to shops, hotels and restaurants owned by foreigners. Responsibility was never clearly established, but the Muslim Brotherhood, the quasi-fascist Young Egypt organization and other militant groups led the mob. The government may have connived in the first attacks but did not expect them to spread so dangerously. The king, who was entertaining senior officers to lunch, did not attempt to intervene. It was not until the evening that regular troops were called in to bring the city under control. The king and the government subsequently blamed each other for the delay.

The belated move to call in the army was prompted by the very real fear that British troops might intervene from the Canal zone. No Egyptian had forgotten that the British occupation in 1882 had been prompted by riots in Alexandria. In fact the British had a plan to intervene to protect British lives and property, but the rioting had ended before any decision to implement it could be taken.

The king used the government's mishandling of the crisis to dismiss Nahas. He recalled his favourite, Ali Maher, but he only lasted five weeks and Egypt then had four different governments in as many weeks. It was increasingly difficult to find anyone with enough authority to form a cabinet.

The Free Officers realized that the regime was crumbling. Before the crisis, they had planned to move into action in 1954 or 1955. Because they needed a senior officer with a well-known name who would act as their figurehead and give their movement weight and respectability at home and abroad, they had brought in Major-General Muhammad Neguib, who was known to be sympathetic, and he became president of the Free Officers' Executive Committee in January 1952. But secrecy was imperative. The king detested Neguib and, in the same month, was enraged by his election as president of the Army Officers' Club against the king's own nominee. Despite their efforts, the Free Officers knew that the state security police were coming close to uncovering their secret organization. But fortunately the king still believed that the great majority of the army remained loyal, and in July he departed as usual to his summer palace in Alexandria.

On the night of 22–23 July, army units loyal to Free Officers seized all the key points in the capital, against only token resistance, and Anwar Sadat announced the success of the revolution over Cairo Radio. Convinced that Britain might intervene to save the king, the Free Officers moved swiftly to take control of Alexandria. Nasser overcame the demands of some of his colleagues that Farouk should be put on trial and executed; instead, the king was allowed to abdicate and go into exile with his new queen, Narriman, and their infant son. This enhanced the reputation of the revolutionaries – not least because the ex-king's behaviour in exile added to the discredit of the monarchy.

The avuncular, pipe-smoking figure of General Neguib was reassuring to interested foreign powers, which were swift to recognize the new regime. The Free Officers transformed their Executive Committee into a Revolutionary Command Council (RCC), with Neguib as its president. It was more than a year before it became apparent to the outside world that the tall, impressive but rather sombre 34-year-old Colonel Nasser was the true leader of the revolution.

The Free Officers had been planning their revolution for a decade and had a clear concept of what they wanted to do – rid the country of foreign (mainly British) influence, eliminate the power of the landlords and the monarchy, and end the corruption of political life. But they had no developed political ideas, let alone a political programme. A few of them had sympathies with the Muslim Brotherhood and a few were Marxists, but the majority could only be described as nationalist. They moved swiftly to consolidate their power. The Wafd remained a threat because, under the old constitution, it could still win any parliamentary election. The leading Wafdist politicians and the ex-king's cronies were put on trial and, charged with plotting with a foreign power and corruption, were sentenced to various terms of imprisonment.

In January 1953 the RCC felt able to dissolve all the political parties and confiscate their funds. A provisional constitution was promulgated which placed supreme power for the next three years in the hands of the RCC. From there it was only one short step to the abolition of the monarchy – the Egyptian Republic was officially proclaimed on 18 June 1953. The old Ottoman titles of bey and pasha were abolished. As Neguib commented, 'The world's oldest monarchy became, for the time being, the world's youngest republic.' Neguib did not regard himself as a figurehead: he felt he had been called upon to command, and he insisted on taking the posts of president and prime minister. Nasser for the time being contented himself with the posts of deputy premier and minister of the interior.

The RCC adopted one important social political measure in the first weeks after the revolution – land reform. In 1952 less than ½ per cent of the landowners between them owned over one third of all cultivable land, while 72 per cent of cultivators owned less than one *feddan* (about one acre) each, amounting to only 13 per cent of the land. Before 1952 several Egyptian economists and politicians had made detailed proposals for land reform, some of which had even reached parliament as draft laws before being quietly quashed. The RCC's agrarian reform limited land holdings to 200 *feddans* and redistributed the confiscated land to the *fellahin* in lots of two to five *feddans*. Legal rents were also drastically reduced. The reform was radical rather than revolutionary, and Marxists called it 'American-inspired'. Only about 10 per cent of the *fellahin* benefited from the redistribution. However, because it was generally successful in avoiding drastic falls in output, it served as a model for other developing countries. Above all, it succeeded in its prime objective of reducing the overwhelming political power of the big landowners who had successfully blocked social and political reforms for generations.

The former regime was not the only threat to the RCC; the principal challenge came from the Muslim Brotherhood and the communists. Of the two the Brotherhood, with its nationwide organization, was much the more formidable and, having played a leading role in undermining the monarchy, it felt it was entitled to at least a share of power in the new regime. But the Brothers were outmanoeuvred and defeated by Nasser, who proved himself a masterly political tactician.

During 1953 Nasser was involved in a power struggle with both Neguib and the Brotherhood. Although honest and popular, Neguib was far from being a natural revolutionary leader. Conservative in temperament, he felt his office entitled him to exercise authority over the hot-headed young officers in the RCC. He was also politically naïve. Nasser appeared to give way to him, and he allowed himself to be placed in a position in which he seemed to be advocating a return to the pre-revolutionary political system, which was something that the army in particular would not tolerate. In April 1954 Neguib capitulated to Nasser, who became prime minister. Neguib lingered on as president, without any real power.

Its tendency to violence was the Brotherhood's undoing. An assassination attempt on Nasser in October 1954 provided grounds for suppressing the organization, and because Neguib was proved to have connections with the Brotherhood, although it was never suggested that he was implicated in the assassination attempt, he was removed from office and placed under house arrest.

By the end of 1954 Nasser was in undisputed control of Egypt, and he would remain so until his death in 1970. He was the first true

Egyptian to rule the country since the time of the Pharaohs. His father, who came from a poor *fellah* family of Upper Egypt, had earned the primary school certificate which enabled him to enter the Egyptian white-collar class as a post office official. Nasser had passed through secondary school to enter the military academy when it was opened to the sons of other than pashas and beys as a result of the Anglo-Egyptian treaty. He had shown early his qualities of leadership and his passionate devotion to Egypt. Wide reading of Arab/Islamic and Western history and biography convinced him that the Egyptian people had innate qualities waiting for national redemption after centuries of submission to oppression.

In 1954 Nasser's freedom of manoeuvre was greatly enhanced by the recent settling of the two outstanding political questions which had beset Egypt for over fifty years – the British military occupation and the Sudan. Failure to settle the latter had long prevented a solution of the former, and the RCC's decision on taking power to separate the two went halfway towards resolving both of them.

The Sudan problem was tackled first, and an Anglo-Egyptian agreement for immediate Sudanese autonomy followed by self-determination after three years was reached on 12 February 1953. In a sense both parties were bluffing – neither was able to reject the principle of sudanization and self-government when the other proposed it. The Egyptians hoped and expected that an independent Sudan would opt for union with Egypt. The British were counting on Sudanese elections resulting in a pro-British (and anti-Egyptian) regime under the conservative Umma party. The British were shocked when the pro-Egyptian parties won the elections, but the RCC was equally taken aback when the new Sudanese government decided on complete independence and against union with Egypt. Sudanese independence was declared on 1 January 1956.

The RCC was bitterly disappointed over the Sudan, but the agreement made it possible to begin negotiations over the British Suez base. Talks continued intermittently throughout 1953 and early 1954. A basic obstacle to the agreement was that Britain still regarded Egypt as part of the Western sphere of interest, but negotiations were made easier by the fact that Egypt was no longer the centre of British Middle East policy – Turkey had joined NATO in the autumn of 1952, and the British joint armed forces HQ had been moved from Suez to Cyprus in December 1952.

Nasser rejected a British demand to keep 7,000 servicemen in Suez, but he agreed to the reactivation of the base in the event of an outside attack on any Arab state or Turkey. As the negotiations dragged on, he allowed guerrilla attacks on the base area as a means of putting pressure on Britain. Finally, in July 1954, agreement was reached on the basis of a British proposal to evacuate all British troops and maintain the base on a seven-year lease with a cadre of civilians on contract to British firms. In accordance with the agreement, the last British troops left Egypt on 31 March 1956. *The Times* correspondent wrote on 2 April 1956, 'Their departure was almost as silent and devoid of ceremony as presumably was the nocturnal disembarkation of General Wolseley's forces which captured Port Said 74 years ago.'

At the signing of the agreement in Cairo, Nasser had spoken of a 'new era of friendly relations . . . We want to get rid of the hatred in our hearts and start building up our relations with Britain on a solid basis of mutual trust and confidence which has been lacking for the past seventy years.' These hopes were not fulfilled. The British government – and especially the foreign secretary, Anthony Eden, who replaced Churchill as prime minister in April 1955 – had developed an antipathy towards Nasser during the frequently acrimonious negotiations over Sudan and the Suez base. As Nasser's prestige and popularity grew throughout the Middle East, he seemed to present a threat to all British interests in the region. Britain's hostility was exacerbated by the fact that the Egyptians, despite their noble heritage, were still regarded as one of Lord Cromer's 'subject races' – the leadership of a desert aristocrat such as Ibn Saud was acceptable, but not that of an Egyptian colonel of *fellah* origins.

In his little book *The Philosophy of the Revolution*, published in 1954, Nasser had already shown his awareness of the kind of role that Egypt could play. He wrote of its location at the coincidence of three circles – the Arab Circle, the African Circle and the Islamic Circle. Still in hazy terms, he saw Egypt as the focus of a vast movement of resistance to the imperialism of the West. Initially, he did not see the Arab Circle in terms of pan-Arab unity – indeed, he was suspicious of the Arab League, which he regarded as a fraudulent imperialist conception, and he reduced its influence by removing from office the League's eloquent pan-Arabist secretary-general, Abdul Rahman Azzam. But he did see the Arab states as potential allies in ending Western hegemony. Unfortunately, the only other independent Arab state which had the makings of a stable autonomous power – Iraq – was led by a man whom Nasser regarded as the imperialist West's chief ally – Nuri al-Said. To make matters worse, he was a man of real stature and personality. It was this bitter rivalry with Nuri (which was much more than a mere clash of personalities) that was the main factor in involving Egypt deeply in the politics of Arab nationalism.

Matters came to a head in 1955 with the conclusion of a series of military agreements between Iraq, Turkey, Iran and Britain which became known as the Baghdad Pact. The idea of this patently anti-Soviet alliance had originated with the United States, which had dropped it on realizing that the Arabs were much more concerned about Israel than about any Soviet threat. Britain had joined the pact as a means of maintaining some part of its dominant position in the area. Nasser tried every means to prevent Iraq from joining, because he saw the Pact, with its NATO links through Turkey, as an instrument of continued Western domination. But he failed to persuade the indefatigably pro-Western and anti-Soviet Nuri al-Said. The great mass of articulate Arab opinion was on Nasser's side in this matter, and his influence was enough to prevent Jordan from joining, although the young King Hussein was in favour. But as Nasser's popularity with the Arabs grew, the hostility he aroused in the West increased.

Nasser's horizons were broadening. A crucial influence on his thinking was Pandit Nehru, the figurehead of India's independence, who visited him in Cairo in February 1955 and agreed with him to oppose all military alliances such as the Baghdad Pact. Nasser also developed a warm admiration for President Tito's Yugoslavia. While Nehru had succeeded in pursuing an independent non-aligned policy while remaining a member of the British Commonweath, Tito had defied Soviet leadership of the communist bloc (even under Stalin) and accepted American aid without renouncing communism. Nehru, Tito and Nasser would come to be regarded as the founding members of the club of non-aligned states. In April 1955 Nasser headed Egypt's delegation to the Afro-Asian Conference at Bandung in Indonesia – an event of immense contemporary importance since it symbolized a concerted attempt by the great majority of the developing world to throw off the hegemony of the white Western nations. The importance of Egypt and its revolution was acknowledged as he was treated as an equal by Asian statesmen such as Nehru and the Chinese premier Chou En-lai. Some of the credit for this was due to his personal qualities – for one so young and inexperienced he acted with remarkable skill and assurance.

Nasser was well on his way to becoming the hero of Arab nationalism; his picture appeared on display throughout the Arab East. But hero status brought new dangers and responsibilities, for he was beginning to arouse huge expectations among the Arabs. Since he was championing the cause of neutralism in the Cold War, he began to arouse the suspicion and hostility of the United States. At the same time Israel was coming to regard Nasser's Egypt as its principal external challenge.

Although Britain appeared to remain the principal Western power with Middle Eastern interests in the decade following the Second World War, in reality its position was being rapidly overtaken by the United States, for two reasons: the onset of the Cold War and US sponsorship of Israel.

US involvement began in Iran. At the end of the war both Britain and the United States withdrew their troops from Iran, as stipulated in the 1942 treaty, but the Soviet Union refused for several months to evacuate the northern provinces. When the Soviet army finally withdrew, the Soviet Union sponsored a puppet socialist regime in Azerbaijan which it aimed should secede from Iran and join the Soviet Union. Unexpectedly firm action by the Iranian government suppressed the Azerbaijani separatists, but the Soviet Union continued to exert pressure on Iran through the autonomy movements in Azerbaijan and Kurdistan and the powerful communist Tudeh Party in Iran. The so-called Truman Doctrine of March 1947, under which the USA offered Greece and Turkey aid (which Britain could no longer provide) to maintain their independence, was soon extended to Iran. In October 1947 the Iranian Majlis plucked up its courage and annulled a highly unpopular Soviet–Iranian agreement for joint exploitation of the oil reserves in the northern provinces.

Britain and the Anglo-Iranian Oil Company remained the principal targets for the powerful force of Iranian nationalism, of which a veteran aristocratic politician, Mohammed Mossadegh, became the spokesman. In 1949 the Iranian government launched an ambitious and much needed seven-year development plan based on the country's revenues. But whereas between 1944 and 1950 AIOC's profits had increased more than tenfold, Iran's revenues had increased only fourfold. Negotiations started with the company in 1948 to increase Iran's share were frustrated by Mossadegh and his followers in the Majlis, who insisted on Iran's right to regain control over the country's principal natural resource. Public opinion was so roused that in May 1951 the young shah was forced to appoint Mossadegh as prime minister and give his assent to a bill nationalizing the Iranian oil industry.

The measure was not only wildly popular in Iran; it inspired the Arab man-in-the-street. Mossadegh's name became legendary in the Middle East as Nasser's would become a few years later. But Mossadegh was unable to carry through his revolution, both because of the strength of the forces opposing him and because of his own inadequacies as a revolutionary leader. The AIOC withdrew from Iran and, in pursuit of their common interest, the major international oil companies successfully imposed a boycott of Iranian oil. Britain resorted to economic pressures and military threats in an attempt to have the nationalization reversed and appealed to the International Court of Justice, which ruled against it, and to the UN Security Council, which refused to intervene. The US government unsuccessfully attempted to mediate. But Iran's revenues dwindled to a trickle.

Mossadegh's popularity among the poor Iranian majority increased with his intransigence against the West. He demanded and received authoritarian powers. He broke off diplomatic relations with Britain and closed its consulates. But in many respects his social and political outlook was reactionary. As a member of the land-owning class, he opposed the breaking up of the large estates in favour of peasant proprietors and he stopped even the shah's modest land-distribution scheme. As the doubts about him grew among Iranian politicians, the shah took courage to challenge his actions and appoint the loyalist General Zahedi prime minister. The shah's attempt failed and he had to flee the country in August 1953, but six days later he returned and Mossadegh was overthrown in a counter-coup which was planned and organized by the CIA, with substantial assistance from British intelligence.

Relations with Britain were restored, but it was the USA which now took over as the principal Western influence in Iran. A group of US, Dutch and British oil companies formed a consortium in which AIOC had a 40 per cent share and negotiated an agreement with the National Iranian Oil Company that had been formed to take over AIOC's assets in Iran to resume operations. The agreement was for twenty-five years. In August 1955 the Iranian government signed a treaty with the United States. With this and its joining the Baghdad Pact in the following year, against strong Soviet protests, Iran indisputably joined the Western camp in the Cold War.

In 1952, when the Eisenhower administration replaced that of President Truman, the United States still had only a peripheral interest in the politics of the Arab world. It had scant sympathy for what remained of the imperial aspirations of Britain and France. It had good relations with the young revolutionaries in Egypt, and it urged Britain to come to terms over the military occupation. But it had no desire to take Britain's place. As we have seen, when Eisen-hower's secretary of state John Foster Dulles realized that Egypt and the other Arab states were uninterested in joining an anti-Soviet Middle East Defence Organization, he left Britain as the only West-ern member of the Baghdad Pact while he concentrated on strengthening the 'northern tier' of states confronting the Soviet Union – Turkey, Iran and Pakistan.

However, the United States did have a close interest in Israel, largely for domestic political reasons. Zionist political influence in the United States went far beyond the American Jewish community. The US Congress was overwhelmingly supportive of the young Zionist state in the Middle East and, although he was the least inclined of any post-war US presidents to relinquish the executive's control of US foreign policy, Eisenhower could not ignore these sentiments.

Although the concept of direct superpower rivalry between the United States and the Soviet Union for influence in the Middle East had come to seem part of the natural order in the 1950s, the history and development of Russian and American interest in the region were totally different. The very concept of the Middle East as a geopolitical entity was new to Russia.

Historically, Russia had more reason for interest in the Muslim world as a whole than any of the Western powers. For 250 years Russia had been ruled by Islamized Mongols. After its restoration to Christendom, Holy Russia absorbed millions of Muslim subjects. By the end of the nineteenth century, following the great tsarist expansion eastwards, the Russian Empire not only contained some 15 million Muslims but also shared some 2,000 miles of frontiers with the only Muslim states which could be regarded as truly sover-eign – the Ottoman Empire and Persia.

The Russian Bolsheviks retained the tsarist empire and created the six Muslim Soviet Republics to form the southern fringe of the USSR. Pre-revolutionary Christian Russia always regarded Islam as hostile but the fact remained that its southern population from the point of view of culture and religion and to a large extent of race remained part of the Middle East. All had belonged to the Muslim East of the caliphates.

This was the reality that the Soviet Union inherited. Lenin's policy was to renounce all tsarist imperial ambitions in the Middle East and to consolidate the Soviet hold on the Muslim republics. The communists were as hostile to Islam as the tsars, regarding it as a counter-revolutionary force. They maintained a fiction that it was being artificially maintained as an anti-Soviet instrument by Western imperialist intrigue, but over the years they could not fail to realize the prevalence and staying power of Islamic culture both outside and inside the borders of the Soviet Union.

Initially, Soviet policy in the Middle East was based on the assumption that the peoples of the region who had been dominated or exploited by Ottoman, British and tsarist imperialism would be attracted by the ideals of the Bolshevik Revolution. The Soviet leaders believed that they had a good chance of gaining control over the secular nationalist movements which were developing in the area. But for the time being the Arab countries remained under British or French control, and the main hopes of the Soviet Union were concentrated on Turkey and Iran, which were always the principal focus of Russian interest. The Soviet misunderstanding of nationalism soon brought disappointment. In Turkey, Mustafa Kemal and his colleagues were quite prepared to accept Soviet arms and money in their struggle against the West, but before long they made clear both that they detested communism and that they still regarded Russia as Turkey's traditional enemy. Moreover, whereas Lenin at least favoured the idea of supporting bourgeois nationalism, even if it meant the collapse of local communist movements, on the ground that nationalism would enforce the retreat of imperialism and hence prepare the way for the eventual downfall of capitalism, his policy was to a large extent reversed by Stalin. Stalin believed that local communist parties should be the spearhead of Soviet policy and that Soviet interests could best be served by a programme of subversion and, where it seemed appropriate, by direct action.

In Iran this policy was especially disastrous. The Soviet Union's support for the establishment of the communist Tudeh Party, its attempt to exploit mutinous movements in the army, and constant efforts at subversion through its consulates, commercial organizations, clubs and propaganda agents served only to rally all the anti-Russian feelings of Iranian nationalism in a way which was no different from the days of the tsars. By 1934 Reza Shah had closed down all the Soviet trade agencies and clubs and all but one of the consulates.

In the Arab countries of the Middle East the communist parties were minuscule and dominated by intellectuals who generally came from the religious and ethnic minorities. The Soviet Union tried to gain a political and commercial entrée into the Arab world through the newly created kingdom of Saudi Arabia, but this was a failure and Stalin closed down the legation in 1938.

Until the Second World War the Arab countries were hardly aware of the existence of the Soviet Union. Its entry into the war in 1941 transformed the situation. The Soviet Union's epic resistance to Hitler's armies gave it new prestige. As an ally of the Western powers, its diplomatic representation, which had hitherto been confined to Turkey and Iran, was extended to most of the Arab states. The Soviet military occupation of northern Iran was made in agreement with Britain and the United States.

However, in the immediate post-war period Stalin's neo-imperialist policies were soon rebuffed. Iran and Turkey remained the focus of Soviet interest, but their hostility was provoked by the disastrous attempt to establish a separatist pro-Soviet Iranian Azerbaijan and by a demand for the return of the provinces of Kars and Ardahan, which were ceded to Turkey in 1921. In 1952 the pro-Western government of the kingdom of Iraq broke off relations with Moscow and the moves began which united Iraq with Turkey, Iran and Pakistan in the anti-Soviet Baghdad Pact. Soviet policy in the Middle East suffered a blockade.

The situation began to be transformed with the death of Stalin in March 1953. Under Khrushchev's leadership of the Soviet Communist Party, the Soviet Union, instead of lending support to the small and uninfluential communist parties in the Arab states, reverted to Lenin's policy of backing popular national leaders who were prepared to show independence from the West. Nasser of Egypt was such an Arab leader *par excellence*. Daniel Solod, the exceptionally active Middle East expert who was Soviet ambassador in Cairo, laid the foundations of a *de facto* alliance between the Soviet Union and the Egyptian revolution.

Nasser's growing popularity among the Arabs and his espousal of neutralist policies had two inevitable consequences: one was that his relations with the Western powers deteriorated and the other was that Israel began to regard Egypt as its biggest external challenge. The Zionist state had greatly increased in power and confidence since its birth. Under the 'Law of Return', which gives any Jew the right to emigrate to Israel and settle there, nearly 700,000 Jewish immigrants had poured into the country – first from eastern and central Europe and then from Yemen, Iraq and the Arab Maghreb states. Their absorption, combined with a determination to achieve full employment, a high level of social services and a European standard of living, presented formidable difficulties – especially as the new state was cut off from its natural markets by the total economic boycott which the Arab states attempted to impose and also felt the need to exceed the combined military strength of all its Arab neighbours. Although Israel's economy remained vulnerable, the obstacles were largely overcome through the economic skills and enterprise of the population and the enormous flow of foreign aid, much of it in the form of grants rather than loans, from world Jewry, West Germany (as war reparations) and the United States.

In the absence of any prospect of peace negotiations leading to an Arab–Israeli settlement, Israel from the outset initiated a policy of overwhelming reprisal for any border violations or acts of infiltration – whether these were carried out by individual Palestinian farmers whose lands had been bisected by the armistice lines or by trained *fedayeen* (commandos), the Israeli military response was much the same. In one incident in October 1953, Israeli forces killed some fifty villagers in Qibya on the West Bank.

When Nasser came to power he had every reason to avoid involvement with Israel. Not only was he confronted by major domestic and foreign problems, but also the Palestine war had exposed the weaknesses of the Egyptian armed forces. The West would sell him arms only in tiny quantities, and he was not yet prepared to turn to the East. When Israel's first premier, the militant David Ben Gurion, temporarily withdrew from politics in December 1953 and was succeeded by the moderate Moshe Sharett, there was a period of relative Egyptian–Israeli *détente*. But in February 1955 the scandal of the Lavon affair – the failure of a plan by the Israeli secret service to force the British to stay in Egypt by simulating Egyptian outrages against British institutions – brought Ben Gurion back to power. One week later the Israeli army carried out a massive reprisal for the *fedayeen* attacks in a raid on Egyptian headquarters in Gaza, inflicting heavy casualties. The action was a milestone in the history of the Arab–Israeli conflict.

Nasser could not ignore this humiliating exposure of Egyptian military weakness. His immediate response was to unleash more *fedayeen*, who tried to penetrate deep into Israel and blow up installations. Egypt suffered world-wide condemnation, but at least Nasser had staved off all demands for an immediate all-out war with Israel, for which he knew that Egypt was not prepared.

It was more important that Nasser began secret negotiations for the purchase of arms, culminating in the announcement on 27 September 1955 – another landmark in recent Middle East history – of a deal with Czechoslovakia for the supply of very large quantities of arms, including Soviet aircraft and tanks, in exchange for rice and cotton. This was the first deal of its kind by any Arab country. The West was outraged, while Arab public opinion was delighted.

Western hostility and Israeli concern reached new heights. France had joined the ranks of Egypt's enemies, mainly because it was convinced (incorrectly) that the rebellion in Algeria which had broken out in 1954 was stimulated and financed from Cairo. A Franco-Israeli alliance which was to last for more than a decade was formed, and news of a secret deal to supply Israel with French weapons added to the urgency of Nasser's search for arms. The British government's detestation of Nasser was approaching its climax. Anthony Eden, the prime minister, held Nasser responsible for every manifestation of Arab anti-Western feeling, including the young King Hussein of Jordan's dismissal of the British commander-in-chief of the Arab Legion, General Glubb. Eden had already decided that Nasser's overthrow was essential. Moreover, Britain and France's colonial empires in black Africa were yet to be disbanded, and Egypt had begun to play the role in the African Circle which Nasser had predicted. Cairo Radio gave vigorous and often vituperative support in various languages for anti-colonial liberation movements throughout Africa. The United States, which still had fewer direct interests in the Arab world than Britain or France, was chiefly concerned with the Cold War aspect of Nasser's neutralism. Pro-Zionist congressmen joined the chorus of those who were saying that Nasser's aim was to unite the Arab states by force and turn them into Soviet satellites. US–Egyptian relations deteriorated further when in May 1956 Nasser recognized communist China, the object of US detestation. Apart from demonstrating his independence, Nasser had the additional motive of evading a possible UN embargo on Middle East arms supplies (China not being a UN member).

The Western powers had, however, not entirely given up hope of keeping Egypt within their orbit. The new Egyptian regime had set its heart on the building of a giant dam on the Nile, near Aswan. By increasing the cultivated area by 30 per cent, providing year-to-year water storage to prevent flooding and drought, and enormously increasing the hydroelectricity supply, this would form the cornerstone of Egypt's development programme. In February 1956 a provisional agreement was reached whereby the World Bank would loan $200 million on condition that the United States and Britain loaned another $70 million to pay the hard-currency costs. The USA and Britain imposed conditions which Nasser found difficult, since they involved some Western control over the Egyptian economy. When he finally made up his mind to accept, however, the

USA abruptly announced that the offer was being withdrawn, because Egypt's economy was too unstable for so large a scheme.

The USA and Britain believed that, even if Nasser did not fall from power, he would become more pliable. They were not convinced that the Soviet Union would make good its hints that it was prepared to finance the dam. They were surprised and outraged when Nasser chose the fourth anniversary of the Egyptian Revolution, 26 July 1956, to announce to vast cheering crowds in Alexandria and, via Cairo Radio, to the rest of the Arab world that he was nationalizing the Suez Canal Company and creating an Egyptian Canal Authority to manage the Canal. The entire Third World was thrilled. There existed no more potent symbol of Western colonial domination than the Suez Canal. But there was apprehension about the consequences – the West would surely not allow Nasser to succeed.

Three months of negotiations in London and New York followed, in which Britain took the lead in trying to enforce some international control of the Canal. They failed largely because the US Eisenhower/Dulles administration refused to consider the use of military force to coerce Egypt. But the British and French governments were determined to use force. The secret Franco-Israeli alliance devised a plan for a joint invasion of Egypt with Britain. Eden finally agreed to this, with reluctance due only to his fear that the collusion with Israel would be discovered, with disastrous consequences for Britain's remaining interests in the Arab world.

On 29 October 1956 Israel invaded Sinai, and on the following day Britain and France issued a joint ultimatum (seventy-six years after their Joint Note threatening Arabi Pasha) calling on Egypt and Israel to cease fighting and to withdraw their forces ten miles from the Canal. Israel, as part of the plan, accepted the ultimatum, although its forces were still much more than ten miles from the Canal. Nasser rejected it and ordered his troops which were suffering heavy losses in Sinai to return across the Canal. When the ultimatum expired on 31 October, British and French planes began to bomb Egyptian airfields, destroying almost the entire Egyptian airforce except for those planes which had been sent to Syria for safety. On 5 November an Anglo-French force, assembled in Cyprus, landed near Port Said and, after capturing the city, advanced southwards along the line of the Canal, which the Egyptians had already blocked with sunken shipping.

World opinion was overwhelmingly hostile to the tripartite invasion. The threatened break-up of the British Commonwealth, Soviet warnings and especially the opposition of the United States, which refused to provide help and to relieve the alarming drain on sterling, all contributed to Britain's decision to halt its Suez action. The UN General Assembly decided on 4 November to create a UN Emergency Force (UNEF) to supervise the cease-fire it was calling for and which Britain and France accepted on 6 November. Israel could not continue alone. Britain and France had made two major miscalculations: one was that the Egyptians would be incapable of managing the Canal on their own and the other was that as soon as hostilities began there would be a popular uprising against Nasser. In fact after nationalization the Egyptians showed that they could manage the Canal efficiently, and Nasser's popularity in Egypt and among Arabs elsewhere reached new heights. Egypt suffered military defeat against overwhelming force but scored an almost total diplomatic victory. An angry President Eisenhower compelled the Israelis to withdraw from Sinai and Gaza early in 1957, leaving Egypt in full control of the Canal and its immense quantities of British military stores. With US assistance the Canal was cleared and reopened in April 1957. All British and French property in Egypt was sequestered. About 3,000 British and French nationals were expelled, and many thousands more left because of the loss of their livelihood. Britain and France attempted to retaliate by imposing an economic blockade of Egypt, but the gesture was futile.

The century of Anglo-French domination of the Arab world was finally drawing to a close. Two years later Britain's remaining substantial Arab ally, the Iraqi monarchy, was swept aside by a popular army-led coup and the Baghdad Pact collapsed. The British quasi-colonial role in the Gulf and southern Arabia would last another decade until its dismantlement was forced by financial constraints. France, although apparently more firmly installed in the Arab West, withdrew even earlier when it conceded Algeria's independence in 1962 after a prolonged and futile attempt at repression.

The years 1956 to 1959 marked the high tide of Nasserism as he seemed to sweep all before him. His appeal to the Arabs – and especially to the younger generation, who formed the majority – was overwhelming. They saw him as a modern Saladin who would unite them in order to drive out the Zionists – the crusaders of the twentieth century. The danger for Nasser was that he was raising expectations which neither he nor Egypt could fulfil. He was aware of Arab military weakness, which it would take time for Soviet help to remedy, but he could not regulate the tide of Arab fervour. His personality transcended Arab doubts about Egypt's commitment to the cause of Arab unity, which were shared by the Egyptians themselves.

In June 1956 a new Republican Constitution was promulgated and approved by a 99 per cent affirmative vote. This declared Islam as the religion of the state, recognized Egypt as part of the Arab nation, and provided for government by a president and a council of ministers and a single legislative chamber. Nasser was confirmed as president for a six-year term. Political parties were replaced by a similar political organization, the National Union. Nasser's hold on power was thus formalized. Although he gave high executive positions to some of his outstanding former colleagues in the RCC, he made sure that no rival centres of power developed. The only partial exception, which ultimately proved disastrous, was that he allowed Abdul Hakim Amer, the defence minister, a large measure of independent control over the armed forces. Amer had charm and presence but lacked self-discipline and was an incompetent military commander.

Nasser's political mastery of Egypt could not easily be translated to the other Arab states. His appeal among the masses was immensely powerful but the rulers of most independent Arab states, in addition to Nuri al-Said in Iraq, were basically pro-Western and conservative and therefore hostile to Nasserism. They used what means they could to oppose the alarming trend. In Jordan, King Hussein had swum with the tide in dismissing General Glubb and allowing the formation of a pro-Nasser government which, in October 1956, terminated the agreement under which Britain subsidized the Jordanian army. But when in April 1957 the government proposed to establish diplomatic relations with the Soviet Union and King Hussein heard that a nationalist military coup was being planned against him he reacted with the support of ultra-loyal beduin elements in the army and dismissed the government. He was helped by the reality that his overthrow would almost certainly lead to Israel's occupation of the West Bank. The harsh realities of Jordan's perilous position helped to develop the king's mastery of political combat. His courage and shrewdness also played their part.

In Lebanon the ambitious and resourceful President Camille Chamoun used the strong powers of the Maronite presidency to ensure that an overwhelming majority of his pro-Western supporters were successful in parliamentary elections. Lebanese Arab nationalists – who were mainly, but not exclusively, Muslims – could only protest.

The Saudi Arabian attitude towards the rise of Nasserism was more ambiguous. King Saud, who succeeded Ibn Saud in 1953, was affable and physically impressive like his father but a lesser man in other respects. He was wildly extravagant and foolish. Although he delegated some powers to his able and experienced brother, Crown Prince Feisal, he maintained a system of largely personal rule with the help of a group of frequently corrupt advisers. He lacked the wisdom to cope with either the new flow of oil wealth or the increasingly complex demands of the twentieth century.

His Arab policy was initially guided by the long-standing rivalry between the House of Saud and the Hashemites. This brought him closer to Egypt, despite the incongruity between Saudi traditionalism and the Egyptian Revolution. In 1955 Saudi Arabia agreed to join Egypt and Syria in a joint military command system which was clearly directed against the Baghdad Pact. In 1957 King Saud also accepted that Saudi Arabia should help Egypt and Syria to replace the British subsidy to Jordan.

In the power struggle which was developing in the Arab East, Syria was the key. It was the country in which the desire and need for Arab unity was felt most passionately, but it lacked any strong central authority representing Syria's identity. Since the fall of Colonel Shishakli, who dominated the country from 1950 to 1954, the old political parties from the days of the French mandate contended for power under the parliamentary constitution. Conservative pro-Western Iraq was not without influence, but the trend in Syria was inexorably leftwards, towards the radical neutralist position of revolutionary Egypt. In 1956 Syria followed Egypt in acquiring arms from the Soviet Union and in recognizing communist China. The leftwards tendency was closely associated with the increase in power and influence of the Baath Party. Although founded as little more than a debating society a decade earlier by two Damascus school-teachers – Michel Aflaq and Salah Bitar – the Baathists succeeded better than any other group in focusing popular feeling. Aflaq, the party ideologist, although shy and uncharismatic, acquired a substantial following for his pan-Arabist ideas among the younger generation. The Baathists won few seats in parliament, but they had supporters in key areas and they were on close terms with a group of officers who were strongly neutralist in feeling and were dominant in the army. From 1956 they were indispensable elements in any government.

The Suez War inflamed popular feeling in Syria and accelerated the leftwards trend. The government multiplied its ties with the Soviet Union.

The possibility that the entire Arab East might be moving into the Soviet camp intensely alarmed the United States, which saw the world in Cold War terms. The credit it had earned among Arab nationalists for its role in blocking the tripartite aggression against Egypt was quickly dissipated when it joined the Anglo-French economic blockade of Egypt. The USA openly and covertly attempted to rally all the anti-Nasser and pro-Western forces in the Arab world. In January 1957 the president issued what became known as the 'Eisenhower Doctrine', which named 'international Communism' as the greatest threat to the Middle East and promised financial aid to any government which helped to resist it. Iraq and President Chamoun of Lebanon accepted such aid, as did Saudi Arabia, although in ambiguous terms. King Saud was by now thoroughly alarmed by the radical pro-Soviet trend in the Arab world, but he was not yet ready to join the camp of his old Hashemite enemies in Baghdad. He sent some troops to Jordan as a token support for King Hussein's regime following the king's dismissal of his nationalist government. In an improbable attempt to build up the Saudi monarch as a rival to Nasser in the Arab world, or even as an 'Islamic Pope' – a self-contradictory concept – the Eisenhower administration invited him on a state visit to the USA. In Lebanon, assistance by the US embassy and the CIA for the pro-Chamoun forces in the parliamentary elections was a badly kept secret, as were their botched attempts to encourage a pro-Western coup in the Syrian army.

In general, these US actions did more to strengthen the nationalist/neutralist trend in the Middle East than to reassure the pro-Western elements. The Soviet Union, which had undertaken to help build the Nile High Dam and to resist the Western economic blockade of Egypt, gained new friends. Cairo's *Voice of the Arabs* radio programme poured out propaganda, which was often unscrupulous but nevertheless highly effective, against the United States and the 'reactionaries' who were its allies in the Arab world.

As the Middle Eastern Cold War developed, the nervous and vulnerable Syrian regime felt the pressures most strongly. As the United States declared its alarm that Syria was moving into the Soviet camp, the Soviet Union issued a warning to the West against intervening in Syria. In September 1957 Syria accused Turkey of massing troops on its frontier. The threat was insubstantial, but Nasser sent a token body of troops to Damascus to express support.

Although the government was normally dominated by Syrian

politicians of the old school, who would have preferred to keep Syria in the pro-Western camp, real power lay in the hands of the Baath. But the tide of pro-Soviet feeling meant that the communists were also gaining ground – especially in the army. Faced with relentless US pressure but also the prospect of sharing power with the communists – or even a communist takeover – the Baath decided that the best policy was a union between Syria and Egypt which would secure Nasser's protection. The conservative politicians were forced to swim with the popular tide. On 2 February 1958 the Egyptian and Syrian presidents jointly announced the complete merger of their two states into a United Arab Republic.

The West and its Arab allies were predictably hostile and alarmed. In reaction, the Hashemite monarchies of Iraq and Jordan announced their own federal union. On the other hand the ultra-reactionary and isolationist Imam Ahmed of Yemen decided it was a wise insurance to join the United Arab Republic in a shadowy confederation to be known as the United Arab States, which was also declared in February 1958.

From then on events moved swiftly – 1958 was a momentous year for the Middle East. In March, King Saud was forced to relinquish powers to his brother Feisal after the Syrians revealed details of a plot by the king or one of his advisers to assassinate Nasser and so prevent the union of Syria and Egypt. Feisal was regarded as less pro-Western and more pro-Egyptian than his brother. In May the dangerous political polarization of Lebanon between Lebanese and Arab nationalists, which had been intensified by the Suez crisis, developed into a muted civil war which simmered on throughout the summer with Syria, now part of the United Arab Republic, aiding and encouraging the Arab nationalist rebellion against President Chamoun and his pro-Western government.

It was his decision to help Chamoun which in July 1958 led to the downfall of Nuri al-Said of Iraq. Although always a masterly politician, he and his colleagues were dangerously out of touch with popular opinion – especially among army officers. An Iraqi version of Egypt's Free Officers organization had been formed under Brigadier Abdul

Karim Kassem. When the government ordered a brigade stationed near Baghdad to move to Jordan – almost certainly with the aim of exerting pressure on Syria to destroy the union with Egypt – the troops used the opportunity to seize the capital, overthrow the regime and declare a republic. Opposition was minimal but, in contrast to Egypt's bloodless coup, the young King Feisal II, his uncle the crown prince and all but one member of the royal family, as well as the premier Nuri al-Said himself, were murdered. A government was formed with Kassem as prime minister and minister of defence and army officers in other key positions. The new republic of Iraq declared its close alignment with Egypt.

Nasser and Nasserism were triumphant. Not only were they ruling in Syria – the vital Arab heartland – but in Iraq their strongest single opponent in the Arab world and the only effective remaining instrument of pro-Western policies had fallen. It was true that the immediate consequence of the Iraq revolution was that the United States, fearing the final collapse of the pro-Western camp in the Middle East, landed 10,000 marines in Beirut at President Chamoun's request, while British troops were flown into Jordan. But the marines did not help to keep Chamoun in power – the US wisely encouraged the compromise whereby the Lebanese settled their crisis themselves. General Fuad Chehab, the army commander who had kept the armed forces neutral in the political struggle, was constitutionally elected to succeed Chamoun. The rebels achieved much of what they wanted, since Lebanon became more neutral and less stridently pro-Western than under Chamoun. The short-lived Jordanian–Iraqi federation had collapsed, and it did not look as if a few British troops would be enough to keep King Hussein on his throne.

Though Nasser was at the apogee of his power in the Middle East, a decline from the summit was almost inevitable. In reality Nasser's extraordinary successes – which were partly due to the mistakes of his opponents and their failure to understand the true nature of his appeal to the Arab masses – had concealed the underlying weakness of his position. Suez and its aftermath had given

Egypt an international status which it could not hope to sustain.

Arab expectations of the imminent triumph of the cause of unity were at their highest – like the German or the Italian states in the nineteenth century, the members of the Arab League could unite as a single entity. But there were a host of geographical and political reasons why Bismarck's role could not be Nasser's. The political societies of the Arab nation-states – some of them new, like Syria and Iraq; some of them ancient, like Egypt and Yemen – were vastly different and their common culture and the emotional euphoria of pan-Arabism were not enough to unite them.

Nasser's immediate problem was the government of the United Arab Republic. He said later that when the Syrian leaders came to Cairo to ask for union he felt it would be better to start with a loose federation for a transitional period. When they insisted on a full merger it was his turn to insist that, if he was to have the responsibility, the UAR should be ruled from Cairo. But although Nasser had a remarkable capacity for self-education – and in his lengthy public speeches he always sounded like his people's teacher – he had not learned enough about Syria. It was wealthier, less populous and more pluralistic than Egypt, and its political society was much less mature. Above all, it was a supremely difficult country to govern.

On their side the Syrian Baathists, who were the force behind the merger, had deceived themselves. They had come to feel that Nasser shared many of their ideals and aims. As they saw it, he had adopted Michel Aflaq's slogans of 'Freedom, unity and socialism' and 'One nation with an eternal mission'. There was some truth in this, but what Nasser was not prepared to do was to allow the Baath to rule Syria under the umbrella of his authority and prestige. He soon brushed the Baathist leaders aside, into sullen exile or bitter opposition. The post-independence parliamentary constitution was replaced by a single political organization on the Egyptian model. Nasser appointed two Syrian vice-presidents for the UAR and several Syrian ministers in the central government, but he kept most of the executive and legislative power in his own hands.

Some of the Egyptian officials who went to work in Syria were of high calibre, but many were not. Inevitably, Syrians began to feel that they were in the position of junior partners to Egyptians whom they were inclined to regard as less able and energetic than themselves. In particular the Syrian army suffered from wounded pride, while Syrian merchants, businessmen and landowners who had a long tradition of dynamic activity in a generally free economy watched with growing apprehension as Egypt imposed its state socialist principles upon them. In Egypt the move in the economy away from the capitalist West towards the Soviet bloc, the drive towards rapid industrialization and the building of massive public works including the Nile High Dam had made a huge expansion of the public sector almost inevitable. The 'Arab socialism' which Nasser was developing may have been restrained by pragmatism in Egypt, but it was not adapted to Syria. The Syrian left was equally hostile. While the Baath had been ousted, the communists were given short shrift – as they were in Egypt.

To make matters worse, Syria's basically agricultural economy suffered three consecutive years of disastrous drought between 1958 and 1960.

As Syrian disaffection with the union increased, the new revolutionary government in Iraq soon belied the high hopes of the pan-Arabists. Before the end of 1958 Kassem had arrested and jailed his principal collaborator in the military coup, Colonel Aref, who favoured an immediate Iraqi–Egyptian union. He blamed an abortive Arab nationalist revolt in Mosul in February 1959 on Nasser. During 1959 he allowed the Iraqi communists to strengthen their position at the expense of the Arab nationalists (led by the Iraqi Baathists), and for nearly four years he succeeded in maintaining a precarious balancing act by preventing either group from taking over the state. Despite this, Nasser distrusted him and was convinced that Iraqi communism was a danger to the whole Arab world. Kassem, an unstable and inordinately vain man, developed a bitter and jealous hatred of Nasser.

To meet the declining situation in Syria, Nasser in 1960 sent his closest colleague, Field Marshal Abdul Hakim Amer, to Damascus as his proconsul with instructions to alleviate the causes of growing Syrian opposition to the union. But although Nasser retained much of his personal popularity among the Syrian people and drew wildly enthusiastic crowds on his visits, he had manifestly failed to discover a satisfactory method of governing Syria. On 28 September 1961 a group of Syrian army officers rebelled. They arrested Field Marshal Amer, put him on a plane to Cairo and announced Syria's secession from the United Arab Republic. A new government was hastily formed from conservative Syrian politicians.

Nasser initially contemplated intervening, but changed his mind when all resistance to the coup rapidly faded. A few days later he said it was not imperative for Syria to remain part of the UAR but he would not oppose its re-entry into the United Arab States.

It was a time for Nasser's many enemies both in the Middle East and elsewhere to triumph. Western governments were delighted, but equally the leaders of Iraq, Jordan and Saudi Arabia did nothing to conceal their pleasure.

Nasser himself told the Egyptians, 'We must have the courage to admit our mistakes.' But his own analysis was that he should have been more vigorous in imposing Egypt's socialism on Syria. Three months before Syria's secession a series of laws had been decreed in Egypt nationalizing cotton export firms, banks, insurance companies and 275 major industrial and trading companies as well as cutting maximum land holdings by half and sharply increasing income tax. Nasser was convinced that Syria's secession was simply the counter-attack of the Syrian bourgeoisie against such a sharp move to the left. Believing that Egypt's bourgeoisie might be planning similar action, he launched his own precautionary counter-offensive in which the property of more than a thousand of Egypt's wealthiest families was confiscated.

He knew that this was insufficient and that he had to give his Arab socialism a clearer ideological definition. He spent the winter of 1961–2 in preparing his 30,000-word Charter of National Action before summoning a National Congress of Popular Powers attended by labour unions, professional associations and other

community groups to debate its terms. Although influenced by
Marxism (especially the Yugoslav model) and European welfare-
state socialism, he attempted to adapt these to his view of the
special needs of Egyptian and Arab/Islamic society. The Charter
was secular but not anti-religious. It started from the assumption
that Egypt's pre-revolutionary parliamentary democracy based on
Western models was a 'shameful farce' because 'political democracy
cannot be separated from social democracy.' The vote was meaningless unless the citizen was free from all exploitation, had an
equal opportunity with his fellows to enjoy a fair share of the
national wealth and was assured of an adequate living-standard.
Although the Charter endorsed the nationalization of all public
services and most of industry and the export—import trade, it ruled
out land nationalization and allowed the private ownership of
buildings, subject to supervision. It distanced itself from Soviet
practice by rejecting the priority given to heavy industry at the
expense of the production of consumer goods.

The Charter provided for a new and unique political organization, to be known as the Arab Socialist Union, with a pyramid form
based on 'basic units' in villages, factories and workshops and rising
through elected councils at the district and governorate levels to the
National Executive headed by the president. The National Assembly was retained as the ASU's legislative branch. In this, as in all the
ASU's elected bodies, half the seats had to be reserved for workers
or farmers (defined as anyone owning less than twenty-five *feddans*).
Nasser believed that his intention was clear: to create a social democracy in which the mass of the Egyptians would for the first time
genuinely participate. But such a system can hardly flourish when
it is created instantly from above – it was significant that the National
Congress approved his Charter without amendment.

Nasser's absorption with his National Charter and the fact that
he was no longer concerned with the problems of governing Syria
– which he said had taken up three-quarters of his time for three-
and-a-half-years – did not mean that he was turning his back on
the Arab world or abandoning his claims to Arab leadership. These

were not his intentions – even if they had been, circumstances would not have allowed them. He remained by far the dominant figure on the Arab scene, and expectations in him remained high among ordinary Arabs. To symbolize his attitude, he retained the name of United Arab Republic for Egypt.

Hostile Arab governments poured out invective. The Saudis concentrated their attack on Egyptian socialism, which they said was atheistic. Even Imam Ahmed of Yemen – ailing, but still awe-inspiring to his subjects – contributed to the anti-Egyptian chorus; the shadowy United Arab States of the UAR and Yemen was dissolved. The most violent abuse emanated from Syria, where a series of highly unstable governments elected under the old constitution replaced each other in rapid succession. Syrian spokesmen accused Nasser and Egypt of oppressing Syria with a reign of terror, as well as embezzling funds of the Syrian state. Cairo's response was louder and more effective than all these criticisms, because Egypt's propaganda media were more developed than those of any other Arab state. Nasser's theme was that there could be no compromise between Arab socialism and 'reaction'. One of his favourite phrases was that 'unity of ranks is no substitute for unity of aims.'

Yet Egypt was to some extent on the defensive. After a flaming row with the Syrians at an Arab League council meeting in Lebanon, Nasser announced that Egypt was withdrawing from the Arab League. Then, one year after Syria's secession, events in distant Arabia enabled him to regain the initiative. On 28 September 1962 some pro-Egyptian officers in the Yemeni army revolted against Imam Badr, who had just succeeded his father Ahmed, seized the main towns and declared a republic. The royalist cause was not lost, however, because Badr escaped and his uncle, Emir Hassan, returned to Saudi Arabia from the United States to rally support among Yemeni tribesmen against the new republic. Nasser at once decided to answer the revolutionaries' call for help, and a substantial Egyptian expeditionary force sailed up the Red Sea to the Yemeni port of Hodeida. The resulting prolonged involvement in the Yemen – described as 'the Egyptian Vietnam' – cost Egypt dear. Its troops

were ill-prepared for guerrilla tribal warfare in mountainous territory. The intervention was unpopular among those of the Egyptian
public who were directly affected by it and a matter of indifference
to most of the rest. Yet the fact of a Nasserist coup in Yemen raised
Egypt's morale at the time and increased its prestige in the rest of
the Arab world. In mounting the expeditionary force to Yemen,
Nasser showed conclusively that Egypt's armed forces were the only
ones in the Middle East about which Israel needed to worry. It was
Nasser's opponents who were now on the defensive. The defection
to Cairo of seven of Saudi Arabia's precious officer pilots in October
1962, followed shortly by the commander of the Jordanian Air Force
and two Jordanian pilots, showed that the loyalty of the armed forces
in the two Arab monarchies was dubious.

Pan-Arabist emotion was a powerful factor in a further coup in
Iraq, on 9 February 1963. An army revolt, in which Baathist officers
played the leading role, overthrew and killed General Kassem. Colonel Aref was installed as president and immediately declared his
pro-Egyptian sympathies.

Syria's fragile government could not long resist the joint pressure
from Cairo and Baghdad. Exactly one month after the Iraqi revolt,
a military coup in Damascus swept aside all the men who had been
in power since the break-up of the Syrian–Egyptian union, and a
new Revolutionary Command Council pledged itself to support
'the new movement of Arab unity'. The Baathists had not led the
coup, as they had in Iraq, but they were the only civilian organization outside the old regime which was capable of forming a
government. Within a week, Iraqi and Syrian ministerial delegations
were in Cairo to discuss plans for the unity of Syria, Iraq and Egypt.

This seemed like another moment of great triumph for Nasser.
But disillusion came even more swiftly than with the Syrian–Egyptian
union as the mutual mistrust between Nasser and the Baathists came
to the surface. Nasser felt he could get along with the Iraqi Baathists
– who had borne the brunt of the struggle with Kassem, were in
firmer control than their Syrian counterparts and had no heritage
of rancour with Egypt – but he had no confidence in the Syrian

Baath. For their part, a few idealistic Baathists in both Syria and Iraq had a genuine doctrinal disagreement with Egypt in their demand for democratic freedoms and collective leadership. But most Baathists simply believed that salvation for the Arabs could come only through the Baath party and to this end were prepared to use methods which were quite as totalitarian as anything in Egypt.

The tripartite unity talks were not helped by the fact that Nasser dominated them with his personality and his long experience of power. (He later made cruel fun of the shy and stuttering Michel Aflaq, who was incapable of expressing his views clearly.) Although a form of agreement on a tripartite federation was reached on 17 April, the union was stillborn. During May and June the Syrian Baathists were purging the army of non-Baathist officers and suppressing Nasserist demonstrations. Following the ruthless suppression of an attempted pro-Nasser coup in Syria in July, Nasser openly attacked the Baath for the first time, describing the Syrian regime as 'secessionist, inhuman and immoral' and revealing that Egyptian intelligence had uncovered an Iraqi–Syrian alliance against him.

As Egypt's relations with Iraq and Syria worsened, Nasser had some satisfaction when in November the Iraqi Baathists, who had already made themselves unpopular by their violent methods and who had renewed the exhausting war with the rebellious Kurdish minority which had so weakened Kassem's regime, split into two factions and were ousted by President Aref (whom they had tried to keep as a figurehead) and some senior non-Baathist officers. True to his simple-minded notions, Aref renewed pressure for an immediate union with Egypt. But experience had made Nasser cautious. He suggested to the Iraqis that they should first ensure their own national unity, which among other things meant finding a solution to the Kurdish problem.

Although Nasser regarded Arab political union as impossible for the foreseeable future, he saw the urgent need for some kind of joint Arab action. The Israelis had completed the diversion of some of the waters of the River Jordan to the Negev Desert, though this was something he and other Arab leaders had rashly sworn to prevent. This was no time to insist on 'unity of aims' before 'unity of ranks'. In the Arabs' divided condition there was little hope of their taking effective common action, but there was a very real danger that one Arab state – Syria, where the most irresponsible ultra-left elements were in the ascendant – would act on its own and plunge the others into a war with Israel for which they were not prepared. Nasser therefore issued an invitation to all Arab kings and presidents, which he knew they would find it difficult to refuse, to meet in Cairo in January 1964, setting a precedent for the holding of regular summit meetings. He used the occasion to mend his bridges with pro-Western Arab leaders such as King Hussein, the ailing King Saud, and President Bourguiba of Tunisia and to emphasize the isolation of the Syrian Baath. A second summit was held in Alexandria in September. The Arab heads of state agreed to set up a Unified Arab Military Command under an Egyptian general, and also a Palestine Liberation Organization (but not a government in exile), with its own army, to represent the Palestinian people. They all agreed, although with little enthusiasm, on the choice of the verbose and flamboyant Palestinian lawyer Ahmed Shukairy to head the PLO. King Hussein made clear that the PLO would not have any authority inside Jordanian territory. The heads of state also decided on plans to divert the sources of the River Jordan in Arab territory, in order to forestall Israel's irrigation schemes.

The pressing problem of how to satisfy Arab public demands for action over Palestine without provoking a potentially disastrous war with Israel had been postponed rather than solved. Arab opinion was deluded in thinking that some positive action was at last being taken. Lebanon and Syria were reluctant to carry out the diversion of the Jordan tributaries in their territory without more adequate protection than the Arab states could provide, and the mutual trust which was essential if the Unified Arab Military Command was to function was lacking.

During 1965 and 1966 the division deepened between the radical Arab camp (led by Egypt) and the conservative (led by Saudi Arabia).

In December 1964, King Saud had abdicated and had been succeeded by his brother Feisal. Although Nasser agreed publicly with Feisal on the need to settle the disastrous royalist/republican civil war in Yemen, neither was prepared to make the necessary compromise.

In Feisal, Nasser for the first time since the death of Nuri al-Said faced a rival star-personality, although one of a very different kind from himself. The most they had in common was the puritanical restraint of their private lives. Reserved, dignified and reflective, Feisal commanded immediate respect. Like Nuri, Feisal made little appeal either to the intelligentsia or to the urban masses, but he was the custodian of the holy places of Islam and the ruler of an Arab state which, however backward and underdeveloped, had never been under imperialist control and therefore lacked the complexes of the colonized. As a diplomat and statesman he was in a different class from his brother Saud: while refusing any kind of liberal constitutional reform, he was encouraging a much more rapid and intelligent social and economic development at home. This made it all the easier for him to rally to his banner those elements in the Arab world afraid of or antagonistic towards Nasserism.

Feisal's appeal was naturally more Islamic than nationalist. In December 1965 he went on a state visit to Iran, and in his address to the Iranian Majlis he suggested the need for Islamic unity against subversive alien influences from outside. Although he was deliberately unspecific, no one doubted that he was referring to Egypt's Arab socialism. Feisal had embarked on creating a conservative 'Islamic Front' against Nasser.

Nevertheless, it was Nasser who continued to play the commanding role on the world stage. His differences with the Soviet Union, which had arisen over Nasser's hostility towards the Iraqi communists, had been overcome and Moscow still regarded Cairo as the focus of its Middle East policy. The relationship was symbolized in the much publicized visit to Egypt in May 1964 by the Soviet premier Khrushchev for the inauguration of the second stage of the building of the High Dam – the gigantic project which not only aimed to change the face of Egypt but was also the flagship of Soviet aid to the Third World. On the other hand, the United States also accepted the inevitability of Nasser's Arab leadership. Towards the end of the second Eisenhower administration, the US State Department came to the conclusion not only that Nasser was not a communist but also that in reality he promised the best defence against communism in the Middle East. This revised attitude was consolidated by President Kennedy, who came close to establishing cordial and confident relations with Nasser and was warmly admired by him in return. Between 1958 and 1964 the USA provided Egypt with over a billion US dollars in aid – mostly in cheap long-term loans.

Kennedy's death came as a shock to Nasser and to all the Arabs, who felt they had lost the first American statesman with some sympathy for their point of view. Nasser was not reassured when President Johnson, who had much less interest in foreign affairs than Kennedy, gave evidence of being much more sensitive to the concerns of US Zionists. Nasser's relations with Washington deteriorated sharply over the question of the Congo (Zaïre), where Egypt was giving increasing support to the rebels against the government of Moise Tshombe which the US wanted to sustain in power. Nasser reacted angrily and defiantly when he concluded that the US was trying to use its supplies of cheap food to Egypt as a means of pressuring him to change his policies. However, when the US House of Representatives passed a resolution to stop all further aid to Egypt, President Johnson and his secretary of state, Dean Rusk, refused to accept that the hands of the United States should be tied in the Middle East in this way. The president exerted all his influence to have the vote reversed in the Senate.

For reasons of language, racial and religious affinity and strategic interest, Nasser had not given the same priority to his African Circle as to his Arab Circle, but Egypt had acquired important influence throughout black Africa, where most of the states had only just acquired independence. In July 1964 Nasser was host to the second conference of the Organization of African Unity. His position as a leader of the non-aligned movement was taken for granted, and in

October 1964 fifty-six heads or representatives of heads of non-aligned countries held their summit meeting in Cairo. The concept of non-alignment might have been incapable of precise definition but it had real meaning to most countries in the Third World, which to some extent identified it with Nasser and his policies.

Nasser's function as a world statesman could not solve his domestic difficulties or avert the looming threat of a new war with Israel. Egypt's commitments were dangerously over-extended. Although his policies of industrialization and rapid economic expansion had achieved a commendable growth rate over the past decade, some of the projects had been ill-conceived and the burden of debt had risen to alarming levels. He had successfully exploited Egypt's strategic role to secure aid from East and West, but Western aid was tailing off, the country's credit was being destroyed and foreign exchange was desperately short. Although the Egyptians' acceptance of his leadership still appeared overwhelming, to an extent which could not be explained solely by the police methods which the regime undoubtedly used, in the summer of 1965 Nasser, in uncharacteristically depressed mood, announced the discovery of a nation-wide conspiracy by a revived Muslim Brotherhood, revealing ideological and political dissatisfaction at many levels of society.

The responsibilities of Egypt's assumed role of Arab leadership were more immediately dangerous. The continuing civil war in Yemen not only added to Egypt's economic burdens but also tied down some 40,000 of its best-trained troops. At the same time, events were moving rapidly towards the tragic denouement of a third Arab–Israeli war.

In February 1966 the Syrian regime, which had begun a rapprochement with Egypt, was overthrown by the radical wing of the Baath. The new Syrian rulers had no love of Nasser, but they were more strongly hostile towards the Arab kings and, if possible, even more bellicose than their predecessors towards Israel. While King Hussein was trying to prevent Palestinian *fedayeen* from operating from his territory, Syria gave them encouragement and support and accordingly Israel's threats of heavy retaliation were principally directed against Syria. Nasser could not reject a Syrian appeal for help, and in November 1966 he signed a comprehensive Syrian–Egyptian defence pact. He had a commitment to Syria without the power to control it.

A few days later, three Israeli soldiers were killed by a mine explosion near the Jordanian frontier. Although Syria was clearly the main source of Palestinian sabotage attacks, Israel launched its customary heavy retaliation raid against a West Bank village. Protesting against their inadequate protection by the Jordanian army, the West Bankers rose in a revolt which was quelled only with difficulty. King Hussein angrily attacked Nasser for his criticism of Jordan's handling of the affair and taunted him with hiding behind the protection of the UN Emergency Force (UNEF), which had kept the Egyptian–Israeli front quiet since 1956.

Tension rose to a new height the following spring, as Israeli leaders issued increasingly severe warnings to Syria. Soviet, Syrian and Egyptian intelligence combined to warn Nasser that an Israeli attack on Syria was imminent. Nasser's response on 18 May was to ask the UN secretary-general U Thant to withdraw the UNEF from Sinai (where, on Israel's insistence, it was stationed only on Egypt's side of the border). When U Thant complied, the road to war was wide open. Nasser ordered troops into Sinai and, with the eyes of the Arab world upon him, announced the closure of the Straits of Tiran to Israeli shipping. King Hussein, realizing that he would be unable to stand aside from the inevitable war that was coming, flew to Cairo on 30 May to sign a defence pact with Egypt. Egypt now had defence agreements with both Syria and Jordan, but there was no real co-operation between them and no semblance of an Arab joint command.

The Arab countries were now in a state of emotional self-intoxication as the belief became widespread that final victory over Israel was imminent. Even Nasser abandoned his usual doubts about Arab military capabilities, although he had exaggerated faith in his own military commander, Field Marshal Amer. He also believed that it was possible that the United States would restrain Israel from attacking and that he could score a tactical victory without fighting. He himself promised the Soviet Union that Egypt would not strike first. However, experience should have told him of the high probability that Israel would act if international pressure was not going to reopen the Straits of Tiran to its shipping. Any last doubts should have been removed when the activist General Moshe Dayan joined the Israeli cabinet on 1 June.

On 5 June 1967 Israel attacked all seventeen of Egypt's military airfields, destroying most of its airforce on the ground, and on 6 June Israeli forces advanced rapidly into Sinai. The seven Egyptian divisions in Sinai were defeated, and an estimated 10,000 Egyptian soldiers were killed or died of thirst in the struggle to return across the Suez Canal, which Israeli forces reached on 9 June. After destroying the Egyptian airforce, Israel could turn against Jordan, which had entered the war as Egypt's ally. By the evening of 7 June, with the Old City of Jerusalem and the West Bank occupied, Jordan accepted the UN Security Council's demand for a cease-fire. Egypt accepted on the following day. Israel was now free to turn against Syria, which had confined itself to probing attacks. Israeli troops stormed up the Golan Heights and occupied the key town of Quneitra on the Syrian plateau. Syria accepted the cease-fire on 10 June.

The swift and shattering course of the Six-Day War had many immediate and long-term consequences. The Zionist state of Israel had gained military control over all Jerusalem and the remaining 21 per cent of Palestine. Some 200,000 more Arab refugees crossed the River Jordan to the East Bank. Israel had occupied the whole of Sinai and its forces were on the banks of the Suez Canal, where this time they intended to stay. In seizing the Golan Heights, Israel had removed Syria's strategic advantage.

While Israel's victory had been too swift for the Soviet Union to help its Egyptian and Syrian friends, Western governments and public opinion were almost unanimously hostile towards the Arabs and favourable towards Israel. The only notable exception was France's President de Gaulle, who during both the war and its aftermath showed some sympathy with the Arab position and warned against Israel's domineering tendencies. Egypt's break with Britain and the United States was complete. At the outset of the war, on the basis of information from King Hussein that Jordanian radar stations had detected approaching from the sea a large flight of aircraft which could come only from British and US carriers, Egypt broke off relations with the US and Britain and expelled all US and British citizens.

Nasser's heavy share of responsibility in the disaster was clear, and his position, both in Egypt and among the Arabs, was irreparably damaged. In dark tones on the third evening of the war he announced on Cairo Radio his acceptance of full personal responsibility and his intention to resign and hand over power to his vice-president, Zakariya Mohieddin. He also dismissed his right-hand man Field Marshal Amer. Whether or not Nasser had expected it, the reaction was an overwhelming public demand that he should remain in office. The extraordinary dominance which he had achieved in Egypt, and his position as the generally well-loved father figure of a nation accustomed to paternalistic rule, meant that he was not allowed to abandon the presidency at a time of such desperate crisis. His health was deteriorating – he suffered from 'black diabetes', which caused defective blood circulation – and there is little doubt that the 1967 disaster shortened his life. But in one sense Egypt's situation made his position easier, since those who might have challenged his power were restrained by their lack of any practical alternative to his policies. In August 1967 he was faced with a conspiracy to restore Field Marshal Amer as head of the armed forces, and in 1968 and 1969 there were serious outbreaks of student and industrial unrest, but he overcame these with a mixture of firmness and mild concessions. While there was considerable dissatisfaction, especially among the professional classes and intelligentsia, because the old power structure had not been radically changed, the continuing state of emergency with Israel provided a powerful argument for postponing fundamental reforms.

The Soviet Union at once showed its readiness to repair Egypt's enormous military losses, and Soviet arms and equipment poured into the country. But although Nasser's public speeches were defiant and even bellicose in tone, in reality he accepted that Egypt's military options were extremely limited. In November 1967 he accepted the UN Security Council Resolution 242 calling for an Israeli withdrawal from the occupied territories in return for Arab *de facto* recognition of Israel, and he publicly agreed with the Soviet leaders on the need for a political settlement in the Middle East.

As Egypt's armed forces recovered, in 1969–70 Nasser allowed them to conduct a 'war of attrition' against Israel along the Suez Canal. The Egyptians scored several successes, which raised public morale, but Israel exacted a heavy cost by bombarding Egypt's Canal cities and conducting commando raids deep into Egyptian territory. Nasser asked the Soviet Union to step up its aid, and the number of Soviet military advisers in Egypt was increased from about 3,000 to 10,000. But Nasser still had not abandoned hope that a political solution to the Arab–Israeli conflict could be achieved through US pressure on Israel to withdraw from occupied Arab territories. On 1 May 1970 he made what he called a 'final appeal' to President Nixon to withhold support for Israel so long as it continued to occupy Arab lands, and on 23 July he announced Egypt's acceptance of the Rogers Plan, sponsored by the US secretary of state William Rogers and based on UN Resolution 242, which led to a cease-fire in the Suez Canal area on 7 August.

The burden of Arab leadership had finally proved too heavy for Egypt. It would be an exaggeration to say that the Nasser era in the Middle East came to an end during the six fateful days in June 1967, although it began an irreversible decline then. In fact Arab shame and humiliation caused by the catastrophe intensified the anti-Western trend in parts of the Arab world. In South Arabia (the former British Aden Colony and Protectorate) left-wing extremists took power when Britain withdrew in 1967 and created the People's Democratic Republic of Yemen. In 1969 the conservative parliamentary regime in Sudan was overthrown by radical socialist army officers led by Colonel Jaafar Nimeiry, who moved the country leftwards towards closer relations with Egypt and the Soviet Union. A few months later

the aged King Idris of Libya was ousted in a coup led by a passionately
Nasserist young beduin colonel named Muammar Qaddafy. The
events in Sudan and Libya were a boost for Nasser in his decline; they
offered the prospect of strategic depth for Egypt's armed forces and
of economic help through Libya's oil wealth. On Qaddafy's insistence,
Libya, Sudan and Egypt began to discuss plans for a federation. But
Nasser's experience could not make him enthusiastic about such a
prospect, and in 1969 neither Sudan nor Libya could be of much help
in Egypt's immediate difficulties.

The support of Sudan and Libya could not outbalance two greater
realities which tended to diminish Egypt's role in the Arab world.
One was the fact that Egypt's defeat greatly enhanced the position
of King Feisal, the leader of the conservative and fundamentally
pro-Western oil states of Arabia. At the Khartoum summit meeting
which followed the 1967 war, Feisal secured Nasser's agreement to
withdraw all his troops from Yemen. Although the Arab leaders at
the summit reached the apparently intransigent conclusion that there
should be no peace, no direct negotiations and no recognition of
Israel, the reality was that, in return for substantial economic aid
which would continue 'until the traces of aggression are removed',
Nasser agreed that the Arab oil states could lift the half-hearted
boycott they had imposed on Britain and the United States during
the Six-Day War.

King Feisal was now in a stronger position to press his view that
Islamic unity was at least as important as Arab unity. In 1969 he
secured the holding of the first conference of Islamic heads of state
at Rabat, before the Arab summit for which Nasser was pressing.
The Islamic summit was a triumph for Feisal as it agreed to the
founding of the Organization of the Islamic Conference (OIC)
with its permanent headquarters in Jedda. When the Arab summit
did take place a few months later, Nasser failed to secure Feisal's
agreement that the Arabs should devote all their resources to
supporting Egypt in its struggle with Israel. It was a tired and disillusioned Nasser who accepted the US-sponsored cease-fire on the
Suez Canal a few months later.

The other major consequence of Egypt's defeat was that the Palestinian Arabs no longer looked to the Arab regular armies led by Egypt to liberate Palestine. Neither the Palestine Liberation Organization created by the Arab heads of state nor the Palestine Liberation Army, excluded from Jordan, played any role in the Six-Day War. On the other hand, al-Fatah, the largest of the unofficial Palestinian guerrilla organizations, had since 1965 been carrying out operations against Israel from Jordan and Syria. After the 1967 war it chose one of its leaders, the small and dynamic Yasir Arafat, as its spokesman. Guerrilla operations against Israel faced formidable difficulties and made little military impression, but in the wake of the war they aroused enormous public enthusiasm. In 1969 al-Fatah and its allies succeeded in ousting the discredited Ahmed Shukairy from the leadership and Arafat was elected chairman of a new PLO executive. The PLO could never be wholly independent of the Arab states as it could only operate in their territory, but it was not controlled by any one of them. A genuine new political entity in the Arab world – the embryo of a future Palestinian state – had emerged.

The radical anti-Western trend among the Arabs which followed the Six-Day War ran counter to the increased influence of Saudi Arabia. But the Palestinian guerrillas, and the Baathists who controlled Syria and Iraq, were no more inclined to accept Egyptian leadership than King Feisal. Nasser could still act as a mediator, however. When in Jordan in September 1970 a civil war broke out between the Jordanian armed forces and Palestinian resistance organizations, which had bitterly criticized his acceptance of the US peace plan, he was able to call the Arab heads of state to an emergency summit in Cairo at which he succeeded in bringing Yasir Arafat and King Hussein together. It was his last political act. On 28 September, as his guests departed, he died – exhausted – of a heart attack.

Gamal Abdul Nasser has sometimes been compared to Muhammad Ali. Like the pasha, for a time he dominated much of the Middle East from Cairo and gave Egypt a power and influence in the world beyond its natural strength. He also for a time successfully exploited the rivalries of stronger powers, but ultimately ended in failure. But the comparison does not go very far. Unlike Muhammad Ali, Nasser was a native Egyptian – the first to rule Egypt for more than 2,000 years – with a passionate love for his country. But he was an Egyptian who developed a genuine belief in the movement to unite the Arabs, of which he saw Egypt as the natural leader. His attempts to modernize and industrialize Egypt and to carry out social and economic reforms were as much intended to create a better educated and fairer society for the mass of Egyptians as to add to the country's strength. After their long period of humiliation, he gave them a new sense of pride and dignity which by no means entirely disappeared after his downfall.

Yet Nasser was essentially a man of his time – that of the decolonization of the Arab world – who, as he perceived himself in his early tract *The Philosophy of the Revolution*, fulfilled a role that was waiting to be filled. His influence was in decline before his early death at fifty-two, and 'Nasserism' – a term he personally disliked – could not long survive his disappearance. In a sense, the way in which he came to personify the Arabs in the eyes of the world gave the Arab East an unnatural and temporary unity following the dismemberment of the Ottoman Empire. After his death, underlying forces came to the surface and soon revealed how fragmented the Middle East had become.

12. The Years of Turbulence

With the ending of the Nasser era, the trends which had been apparent since the Arab disaster of 1967 asserted themselves more strongly. There was a further shift in power and influence towards the oil-producing states of the Middle East. At the same time, Israel, which had suffered a period of economic crisis and self-doubt before the Six-Day War, gained new confidence as the indisputably dominant military power in the region. On the other hand, the Arabs of Palestine, whose suffering and oppression had intensified, began the process of asserting their own national identity.

In the two key states of the Arab East – Syria and Iraq – younger leaders emerged in Hafez al-Assad and Saddam Hussein, who, against powerful opposition, succeeded in dominating their country's affairs till the end of the century. Neither could hope to don Nasser's mantle of Arab leadership, if only because of intense rivalry between them, but they were able to make the Syrian and Iraqi nation-states become regional powers of significance. They were helped by the fact that Anwar Sadat, Nasser's successor, effectively abandoned Egypt's claim to Arab leadership by setting out on his own course which led to a separate peace with Israel. The tragic victim of the variety of conflicting religious/political and socio-economic forces in the Middle East was the tiny republic of Lebanon, which from 1975 was devastated by a 15-year civil war.

The post-Nasser era was marked by a sharp decline in the influence of the Soviet Union in the Middle East and some improvement in relations between the United States and most of the Arab regimes, although these relations were always endangered by the virtually unswerving US support for Israel. By the end of the 1960s Britain had withdrawn from the Gulf and southern Arabia, and the quasi-imperial British role in the Middle East had been finally liquidated.

The Rise of the Oil States

Before the Second World War, the Middle East countries – principally Iran and Iraq – produced less than 5 per cent of the world's output of crude oil. By 1949, as Kuwait and Saudi Arabia joined the ranks of the big producers and western Europe was ravenous for oil to fuel its post-war recovery, the proportion rose to 12 per cent and a decade later to 25 per cent. As Middle East oil was uniquely plentiful and easy to produce and the economies of the rich industrialized states continued to expand, the upward trend seemed inevitable. By 1970 the Middle East was producing half the oil of the non-communist world.

The Middle Eastern oil-producing states began to become relatively wealthy in the post-war period. In 1950 the oil companies' practice of making modest royalty payments for each tonne of crude oil extracted was abandoned for a new system of a fifty–fifty division of net profits between the oil companies and the ruler or government of the producing state. Since output was also increasing steadily, government revenues rose rapidly. In Iraq they went from £13.9 million in 1951 to £51.3 million in 1953. In Saudi Arabia, where revenues were barely half a million dollars before the Second World War, they reached $56 million in 1950 and over $200 million by 1956.

This new wealth transformed the outlook for these previously impoverished countries and enabled them to embark on the building of schools and hospitals and the creation of an economic infrastructure. But their needs were great and their income was still limited in relation to their population and extensive territories. Iran, which had enjoyed some oil income for two generations, had the largest population – about 20 million in 1960. The exception was Kuwait, whose population of fewer than 200,000 was gathered mainly in Kuwait City at the head of the Gulf. Kuwait's oil revenues increased astronomically – from £3 million in 1949 to £60 million in 1952 – making it the first of the oil city-states (to be followed a decade later by the emirates of Abu Dhabi and Dubai), and it was possible for the modest but exceptionally wise Emir Abdullah Salem al-Sabah (1950–65) to envisage Western living standards for his people within a generation.

In the 1950s Kuwait was still tied to Britain by the Anglo-Kuwaiti treaty of 1899. To the outside world, and especially to the other Arab states, it appeared as little more than a British colony. For Kuwait to become fully independent was difficult, because of the lack of educated Kuwaitis who would be capable of running the administration. However, in 1961 the Kuwait government asked for the abrogation of the treaty, and Britain complied. The risks were immediately apparent when the unstable Iraqi dictator Abdul Karim Kassem revived a long-standing claim to Kuwait and threatened to occupy it by force. The emir appealed to Britain, which landed troops – the Macmillan government seeing an opportunity to redeem the shame of the Suez episode – but two months later they were withdrawn and replaced by an Arab League force. Kuwait had skilfully demonstrated that, though the other Arab states might formerly have regarded Kuwait as an artificial entity, they now wanted its independence. This was the best guarantee for the country's future.

The Kuwaitis wisely adopted a position of resolute neutrality between the conservative and radical camps in the Arab world. They declared their non-alignment in the Cold War by immediately establishing diplomatic relations with the Soviet Union.

Nothing did more to enhance Kuwait's position than efforts it made to share its new wealth with its less fortunate fellow Arabs. In the year of independence it set up the Kuwait Fund for Arab Economic Development to provide long-term low-interest loans for vital development projects in the other Arab states. The Fund was a pioneer of its kind in the developing Third World.

The rulers of the other Arab Gulf states who were in treaty relationship with Britain – Bahrain, Qatar and the tiny emirates of the Trucial Coast – still saw neither the need nor the possibility of abandoning British protection for full independence. In 1958 oil had been found in vast quantities in Abu Dhabi, which was called a 'new

Kuwait', but its population was less than a quarter of Kuwait's and it seemed too small even to become another oil city-state. When the British Labour government decided in 1966 to abandon South Arabia, including the Aden military base, it was assumed that it would reinforce its military base in Bahrain. The British prime minister Harold Wilson still dreamed of a British quasi-imperial role east of Suez. However, in 1968 a drastic British financial crisis caused a sudden volte-face and Britain informed the ruling Arab emirs that it would be finally withdrawing from the Gulf by 1971. This so concentrated the rulers' minds that for the first time they discussed subsuming their rivalries in a federation. Bahrain and Qatar, with the bare minimum of income and population to remain unattached, opted for independence, while the seven shaikhdoms of the Trucial Coast formed the federation of the United Arab Emirates with their capital in Abu Dhabi, the largest and richest of the members. Abu Dhabi's shrewd and able ruler Shaikh Zaid became president of the federation, which has survived into its fourth decade in the face of considerable scepticism.

The wealth of the Arab Gulf states and their role in the international oil industry has given them a significance in the affairs of the Middle East and the rest of the world out of all proportion to the size of their populations. However, this does not mean that the oil-producing states of the Middle East – including those like Iran or Iraq with much larger populations – acquired any significant role in world affairs in the 1950s and 1960s as a consequence of their increasing revenues. They had only a minor share of control over the export and marketing of their crude oil and gas – their largest, and in some cases their only, national resource. Control remained in the hands of the major international oil companies, and the example of the failure of Mohammed Mossadegh's attempt to acquire full control of Iran's oil industry through the act of nationalization served as a potent warning. In 1956 and 1967, attempts by the Arab oil-producing states to use oil as a bargaining counter against Western support for Israel were half-hearted and ineffective and were speedily abandoned. However, this did not mean that these countries abandoned all hope of acquiring more power over their major national resource by means other than nationalization – they all felt a strong sense of grievance. In the 1950s and 1960s, the great flow of cheaply produced oil from the Middle East actually caused the price of oil to fall in absolute terms and even more in real terms. In 1959 the major oil companies twice cut crude oil prices in Venezuela and the Middle East without consulting their host governments. The exasperated reaction of the governments of Iraq, Iran, Kuwait, Saudi Arabia and Venezuela was to form the Organization of Petroleum Exporting Countries (OPEC), which was pledged to restore prices and to force the oil companies to consult OPEC members before any future price changes.

As all the major producing countries joined OPEC, its members accounted for 90 per cent of oil exports outside the communist world. But OPEC was in no way an effective cartel, as its members lacked both the means and the determination to impose pro-rationing – that is, the limiting of production on a quota system – which would have been the only way to raise prices. This still did not mean that they had abandoned their objective of gaining sovereignty over the development of their natural resources. They soon realized that the key was the acquisition of knowledge and experience in the oil industry by their own nationals. Despite the failure of Mossadegh's adventure, Iran, with much the oldest oil industry in the Middle East, had the advantage of a surviving National Iranian Oil Company which from 1957 onwards gained valuable experience in partnership with the Italian state oil company AGIP outside the principal oil-producing areas controlled by the consortium of major American, British and French companies. Iraq, Kuwait and Saudi Arabia all followed Iran's example by establishing their own national oil companies in the 1960s. In 1961 Kassem of Iraq made an ill-advised attempt to make a short cut to control of the country's oil resources by issuing Law 80 expropriating without compensation all the Iraq Petroleum Company's concession area except for the 0.5 per cent of this area in which it was already operating. The company refused to accept the unilateral decision and drastically cut back production and exports so that Iraq, like Iran in 1952, lost its position among the major Middle East oil producers.

However, the oil companies were not to remain triumphant and contemptuous of OPEC for long. In the late 1960s there was the first complete reversal in the international oil market in favour of the oil-producing countries. The closure of the Suez Canal (from 1967 to 1975) and the intermittent closure by the Syrians of the pipeline across their territory caused a shortage of some 25 million tonnes of oil for Europe. This placed a premium on the oil of Libya, where the young anti-Western Colonel Qadaffy replaced the elderly and conservative King Idris in 1969. Libya could exploit the fact that it was dealing with small 'independent' US oil companies outside the magic circle of the major companies. Libya secured an increase in price; it was modest, but a new trend had been set. As the oil companies feared most, what they called a 'leap-frog' effect took place as the three biggest Middle East producers – Iran, Saudi Arabia and Iraq – negotiated through their experienced and Western-trained oil ministers the Tehran agreement of 1971, which secured a further small increase. The agreement was supposed to run until 1976, but in 1973 the fourth Arab–Israeli war broke out (see below, page 331), the Arab states declared an oil boycott of countries supporting Israel – the first remotely effective use of the 'oil weapon' – and in the ensuing sellers' market caused by a panic fear of shortages among the industrialized nations the price of oil increased at a pace that previously would have seemed unimaginable. By the end of 1974 the price had quadrupled – from about $3.5 a barrel to $15.

This huge shift in income – and hence of power and influence – to a few Middle Eastern states had important political and economic consequences. The symptoms appeared immediately, as within a few days of the ending of the war the nine countries of the European Economic Community and Japan issued a joint declaration on the Arab–Israeli problem which was unprecedentedly favourable to the Arab standpoint.

The shift in power was most immediately apparent in the case of

Iran, with its ambitious westernizing shah and its population comparable only to that of Egypt in the region. Although Iran was not involved in the Arab–Israeli war or the Arab oil boycott which triggered the new price rises, it took the lead in exploiting the situation within OPEC, demanding even higher increases in oil prices to compensate for the inflation (partly caused by the price increases themselves) in the prices of industrial goods imported from the West. The shah greatly extended his aim of establishing Iran as a regional superpower, declaring in various press interviews that Iran would become one of the half-dozen leading industrial powers in the world by the end of the century. He dramatically increased the already high spending on Iran's armed forces (the USA having none of the reservations about supplying weapons to Iran that it felt about Israel's Arab neighbours). As part of his determination to impose a 'Pax Iraniana' on the Gulf region and to exclude radical pro-communist elements, he sent some 3,000 troops to Oman to help its sultan against left-wing rebels in Dhufar supported by the quasi-Marxist state of South Yemen. At the same time the original estimates for state expenditure under Iran's fifth five-year plan, for 1973–8, were more than doubled, with the emphasis on the development of the infrastructure and industrialization.

The effect of the price rises on Saudi Arabia was equally spectacular, if somewhat different. Before the oil boom Saudi Arabia, like Iran, had been spending heavily on economic infrastructure, education and health, while about a quarter of its revenues were devoted to defence. Under King Feisal's wise and prudent leadership, the kingdom had moved in a decade from being in debt to having a large surplus. Although it still had huge development needs and much of the population was still living on the edge of poverty, there was no way in which the pace of development could keep pace with the increasing revenues. Similarly, despite the high spending on the armed forces, Saudi Arabia was still a long way from being a significant military power. The kingdom was faced with the novel problem of having to dispose of its surplus income. The quadrupling of oil prices in 1973 raised this problem to a quite different level.

Revenues rose from $2.7 billion in 1972 to just under $25 billion in 1975. The Saudi state was receiving every hour as much as its revenues for an entire year in the 1930s.

The pace of Saudi development was enormously accelerated. The second five-year plan, for 1975–80, called for the spending of $142 billion, or ten times that envisaged by the first plan in real terms. The prospect of completing all the main infrastructure projects – roads, airports and sea-ports and power stations – by the end of the decade was now attainable. But the fundamental objective, which had already been decided in the early 1960s, was to make use of the country's gigantic oil and gas resources as the basis for a variety of other industries. The centrepiece of this plan was the creation of two entirely new industrial cities – one at Jubail on the Gulf and the other at Yanbu on the Red Sea. The cost was initially estimated at $70 billion, which was more than that of putting a man on the moon. It was undeniably the biggest single industrial project in history.

Despite these astronomical costs, it was still possible to bring immediate benefits to the Saudi people through a variety of subsidies and the abolition of the few existing taxes.

Saudi Arabia also became one of the world's biggest aid donors, through either its own Saudi Development Fund, created in 1974, or a variety of international agencies. In the 1970s the Saudi Arabian aid programme accounted for more than 10 per cent of the kingdom's GDP – a far higher proportion than that of any of the major industrialized countries. But, despite this massive spending, Saudi Arabia by 1975 had accumulated greater financial reserves than those of the United States and Japan combined.

In less than a generation the impoverished desert kingdom had acquired immense international responsibilities as a financial superpower. It was a key member of the International Monetary Fund and the World Bank. Because it was by far the biggest non-communist oil exporter, with one-third of the proved reserves in the non-communist world, it became OPEC's 'swing' producer, which meant that by raising or lowering its level of output it could influence the international price of oil. The Saudi oil minister, Ahmed Zaki Yamani, became in the 1970s one of the best-known personalities on the world scene.

The assassination of King Feisal in April 1975 by a deranged nephew was a tragic loss for the kingdom which he had brought through a period of peculiar difficulties into an era of international prominence which brought new problems. However, the succession of his brother Khaled was smooth. The new king was in poor health and had little appetite for government. Crown Prince Fahd, an able man with an easy-going temperament but a powerful appetite for administration, took over the main responsibility for running the government (as he continued to do when he succeeded on King Khaled's death in June 1982). The replacement of the austerely aristocratic Feisal by the affable Fahd meant a change of style rather than substance; essentially, Saudi policies remained the same. At home the breakneck pace of economic development was combined with extreme conservatism in social mores. Abroad, Saudi diplomacy was quiet, cautious and generally conciliatory, even when championing the cause of Islam and the Arabs.

In Iraq – the third major oil-state in the Middle East – the Baathists recovered power in 1968, through a military coup after five years in the wilderness. In time they succeeded in gaining a firm grip on the country, largely due to the efforts of the civilian vice-president of the Revolutionary Command Council, Saddam Hussein, a natural leader of ruthless determination who established control over the internal security services and the military wing of the Baath to emerge as the strongman of the regime. President Bakr had little power. In June 1972 Saddam Hussein took the bold step of nationalizing the Iraq Petroleum Company. Times had changed in the twenty years since Iran's attempt to nationalize and the ten years since Kassem had expropriated most of the company's concession area. IPC's parent companies had been losing heavily through their cutback in Iraq's production. After vigorously protesting, they accepted the act of nationalization in return for fair compensation.

The breaking of the twelve-year impasse in its oil industry

combined with the quadrupling of prices in 1973–4 transformed Iraq's economic outlook. Revenues rose from $584 million in 1972 to $7.5 billion in 1974. The prospect of realizing the country's huge natural potential, which had been hampered for so long by political instability, seemed more easily attainable. However, Iraq's perennial problem with its large Kurdish minority, which had threatened its stability since its foundation as a nation-state, remained. In 1970 Saddam Hussein hoped that this problem had been laid to rest when he reached an agreement with the veteran Kurdish leader Mullah Mustafa al-Barzani and his followers, providing for the appointment of a Kurdish vice-president in the central government and the creation of a Kurdish Autonomous Region in the north-east where the Kurdish language would have equal status with Arabic. But although relations improved for a time, they deteriorated again during the four-year proposed transitional period, and in March 1974 Barzani rejected Baghdad's offer of autonomy as hypocritical and inadequate and rose once again in rebellion. The war between Iraqi forces and Kurdish irregulars was renewed with customary ferocity.

The Kurds conducted their war with support from Iran and from sanctuary inside Iranian territory. Relations between the shah's government and the Iraqi Baath, with territorial disputes and mutual charges of subversion, had been bad for some years and at times on the brink of war. Saddam Hussein decided on drastic action. In March 1975 he accepted public reconciliation with the shah at an Algiers summit meeting of OPEC states. According to the terms of the ensuing agreement, the shah cut off his aid and closed his borders to the Iraqi Kurds. The Kurdish revolt collapsed and Barzani went into exile. However, in return, the Iraqis had to concede that the Iran–Iraq frontier on the Shatt al-Arab waterway – the joint outlet of the Tigris and Euphrates rivers to the Gulf – should pass along the *thalweg* or median line rather than the eastern shore, as had been agreed in 1937 when Iraq had been diplomatically supported by Britain. The resentment felt by the Iraqi Baathists over this concession to its larger neighbour at a time of weakness rankled deeply and would return to the surface in a few years.

The end of the Kurdish rebellion was only temporary, but with the greater feeling of security and vastly increased revenues Iraq was able to play a more prominent role on the Arab stage, where it had been marginalized for some years. Saddam Hussein, who succeeded as president in August 1979, used harsh and dictatorial methods but he showed considerable qualities of leadership. In accordance with his pan-Arab ideology, he invited tens of thousands of Egyptians to settle in Iraq and assist in the country's accelerating development. He also went out of his way to conciliate Iraqi Shiite Muslims who, although numerically superior, had always been dominated both politically and socially by the Sunnis. The sense of Iraqi nationhood received a powerful boost among its Arab population. The new, more dynamic Iraq, with its radical ideology, began to cause some alarm among its more conservative neighbours in the Arabian peninsula.

The intensification of the rivalries between the oil-producing states of the Middle East did not alter the fact that collectively they had gained immensely in world importance as a consequence of the sudden transformation of the international oil industry. In the first place they had formed the vanguard among Third World countries in fulfilling the 1966 UN General Assembly resolution which called for all states to acquire permanent sovereignty over their natural resources. Iraq and Algeria were the first to succeed in nationalizing their oil industries. The more conservative states, such as Saudi Arabia and Kuwait, preferred the course of acquiring increased state participation in the companies operating in their territory. The result was the same: within the decade from the mid-1960s, the role of the international oil companies had been reduced to one of drilling for oil, producing it and marketing it on contract to the owner states.

Within the Arab world, the shift in weight and influence from the traditional political power centres of Cairo and Damascus eastwards to the Arabian peninsula, which was already perceptible in the 1960s, now became fully apparent. Not only manual workers but also those with high skills and professionals from the Levant states and Egypt looked to the eldorado of the Arab Gulf countries as a means of transforming their living-standards.

However, it was their enhanced role in the world economy which gave the oil-producing states their new international status. The decisions of OPEC – in which the Middle East countries were overwhelmingly dominant – were headline material; the investment of the 'petro-dollars' of its members' huge and growing surpluses affected not only international currency markets but the business climate in many of the advanced industrial countries.

There was a reverse side to all this. In the first place the oil states – invariably personified in the Western media as 'the Arabs' – became the target of widespread hostility and resentment. The wealthier industrialized countries blamed them for the global inflation of the 1970s; Third World states without oil of their own saw their development plans shattered by the huge increase in the price of imported fuel. Where the Arab oil states were able to use their increased influence to secure some improved international appreciation of the Arab position on Palestine, those hostile to their cause attributed this to 'oil blackmail'. Israel understandably did everything to encourage this view.

The OPEC states soon discovered the limitations to their power. At the time of the 1973 war the Arab states declared that they would continue their embargo of Western countries supporting Israel until Israel had withdrawn from all occupied Arab lands. But the real fear that the United States and its allies, faced with disaster to their industrialized economies, might invade and occupy their oilfields forced the Arabs to lift the embargo in March 1974. As this fear receded, it became apparent that the quadrupling of prices was leading to a reduction in the rate of consumption and that this, combined with the increase in output, would soon result in a world oil surplus. The industrialized countries, having been startled into awareness of the dangers of dependence on cheap oil, began to seek to conserve their own resources and to exploit alternative sources of energy such as coal, nuclear power or oil-bearing shale deposits. The threat of a collapse in oil prices showed that OPEC was far from being a monolithic bloc – there was a huge difference in outlook between those countries such as Iran or Algeria whose needs exceeded their revenues and those such as Kuwait, Libya or Abu Dhabi, with small populations, which could afford to cut back production in order to maintain prices. This placed additional responsibility on Saudi Arabia as the OPEC 'swing' producer, responsible for one-third of OPEC's output and, with its immense spare capacity, capable of doubling or halving its production in order to reduce or raise prices on the international market.

As a sharp and sometimes acrimonious debate continued within OPEC, it seemed at times that the organization might break up, and its demise was regularly foretold by some international economists. But this did not happen. When disaster threatened, the necessary minimum agreement on the sharing of output was reached. Much of the credit for this was due to Saudi Arabia's willingness to use its power to stabilize the market. OPEC even survived a new and potentially disastrous surge in oil prices in 1979–81 caused by a panic among consumers on the outbreak of the Iraq–Iran war. The artificial boom, which took prices as high as $34 a barrel, was followed by a prolonged glut in the 1980s, during which OPEC with difficulty maintained prices at around $18 a barrel.

OPEC's share of world oil exports fell from its height of 90 per cent when the organization was founded to about 40 per cent as production from non-OPEC sources such as the North Sea, Alaska and Mexico was stepped up. Faced with increasing budget deficits, Saudi Arabia and Kuwait had to begin drawing on their foreign reserves. The enormous material losses caused by the Gulf War meant that Iran and Iraq could no longer be regarded as among the more affluent of Third World countries. However, the underlying fact remained that more than 60 per cent of all the proved reserves of crude oil in the world were in the territory of the states bordering on the Persian/Arabian Gulf, easily accessible and cheap to produce. Hence the relative decline of these countries' importance in the world economy from its high point in the 1970s was likely to be temporary. The creator of the universe gave Arabs and Persians an instrument of power which was discovered and realized in the twentieth century and will no doubt continue to be wielded in the twenty-first.

Egyptian Initiatives

In 1970 the death of Nasser, who had dominated Egypt's political life for sixteen years, left a vacuum. However, when, in declining health, Nasser had left Egypt for an Arab summit meeting in Morocco in 1969, he had appointed Anwar Sadat as his sole vice-president to manage the country's affairs in his absence. Sadat was the same age as Nasser and a former fellow-officer and conspirator (although a civilian at the time of the 1952 revolution); he came from a similar moderately prosperous village background. Although Sadat had been a member of the original Revolutionary Command Council, Nasser never appointed him to ministerial office but he made him the speaker of parliament after 1956 and occasionally used him on important diplomatic missions. The public did not regard him as a political heavyweight; he was the butt of many of the famous Cairene political jokes. However, as the sole vice-president, his election as president was a foregone conclusion under Egypt's constitution.

Initially Sadat promised only to follow in Nasser's footsteps, but a change of emphasis towards more 'Egypt first' policies soon emerged. Relations with Turkey, Iran and some European states which had long been hostile were repaired and improved. There was a perceptible relaxation in the atmosphere of public life.

In April 1971 Sadat made more decisive moves to stamp his mark on the regime. He dismissed his vice-president, Ali Sabry, formerly one of Nasser's closest aides, who had challenged his policies in the Arab Socialist Union, and when, two weeks later, seven ministers and officials resigned *en bloc* he had them arrested and charged with attempting a coup. They had been hoping to maintain a collective leadership with Sadat as little more than a figurehead, but Sadat was popular with the general public, who wanted firm leadership, and he had the support of the army.

Sadat was announcing that the Sadat era had begun. In his speeches he increasingly denounced the errors of the Nasser period. He promised that the police-state apparatus would be destroyed, that the rule of law would be restored and vigorously applied, and that genuinely free parliamentary elections would be held. He called this his Corrective Movement.

But although these moves enhanced his popularity, he was threatened by the lack of any progress in the Arab–Israeli dispute. The US government showed no willingness to follow up the Rogers Plan of 1970 by enforcing an Israeli withdrawal from Sinai. Sadat's offer in February 1971 to reopen the Suez Canal in return for an Israeli withdrawal to the Mitla and Geddi passes in central Sinai received no response. On the other hand, the Soviet Union rejected Egypt's repeated appeals to supply the types of arms that made the crossing of the Canal a feasible alternative. The two superpowers were becoming increasingly interested in their own *détente*. President Nixon and his national security adviser, Henry Kissinger, were not unhappy that a closed Canal should hamper communist supplies to North Vietnam. On the other hand, Secretary-General Brezhnev did not want to risk another Middle East war on the very doubtful assumption that it would mean Egypt's recovery of the Canal and of Sinai. Israel was naturally content with the *status quo*.

At home Sadat had to face an increasingly restive people. Left-wing students demonstrated against the impasse. The morale of the army, paralysed on the Canal, sank lower. Sadat's repeated promises that action would shortly be taken to recover lost territory aroused increased scepticism.

In July 1972 President Sadat made what seemed like a desperate throw to restore his popularity when he ordered the withdrawal of all the 15,000 Soviet military advisers and service personnel from Egypt. The move was popular because the Soviet presence was widely disliked, especially by the army, but at that stage Egypt had no real alternative to Soviet aid. The West's relations with Egypt were improving but not to the extent of providing arms. Popular impatience exploded in fiercer rioting in January 1973, raising doubts as to whether the Sadat regime could survive.

In fact by this time Sadat had already decided that he had no alternative but to launch against Israel a war of limited objectives which would oblige the West and the Soviet Union to reassess the situation. The risks were enormous, but inaction was no longer possible and he was helped by the fact that Israel and the superpowers contemptuously assumed that he could not possibly succeed.

In preparing the ground, his objective was to secure Syria as his military ally and Saudi Arabia as his diplomatic and financial ally. Relations with the Saudi kingdom had been transformed for the better since Nasser's death, but Syria presented greater difficulty. Its leader, Hafez Assad, was twelve years younger than Sadat and came from Syria's Alawite minority, the sub-Shia sect of Islam which had traditionally formed the Syrian underclass but was disproportionately represented in the armed forces. Assad had risen rapidly in the ranks of both the air force and the Baath Party, in which he belonged to the radical wing in opposition to the more moderate elements such as the veteran Baathist leader Salah Bitar who favoured conciliation of the Syrian middle class. When the radicals or neo-Baathists ousted their opponents in a coup in 1966, Hafez Assad became defence minister. Salah Bitar and Michel Aflaq, the original founders of the Baath, went into exile.

The new regime survived the Palestine catastrophe of 1967 with difficulty. But the experience served to broaden Assad's horizons, and he began to show his masterly aptitude as a political strategist. Seeing that the somewhat faceless men of the regime who belonged to the civilian wing of the Baath were leading the country to disaster by stridently rejecting all political solutions to the Arab–Israeli conflict without being capable of any military initiative, he moved in 1970 to impose the authority of the military wing, secure in the support of the Syrian armed forces. He became prime minister, and in 1971 he took over the presidency with a revised constitution which gave him supreme executive power. Despite the drawback of being an Alawite in predominantly Sunni Syria, he succeeded in creating a highly personified rule which was not under serious challenge. Briefly he became Anwar Sadat's ally, but he would soon become his most formidable opponent. The two men mistrusted each other, and there was a fundamental difference in their war aims. Assad hoped to drive Israel out of Syrian territory and to inflict a sharp military defeat on the enemy. Sadat wanted victory for the essential purpose of obliging the West — especially the United States — to revise its view of the Middle East conflict; he hoped that Washington would take Egypt as seriously as it took Israel.

The Syrians and Egyptians co-ordinated their plans during the summer of 1973 and launched their attack simultaneously on the night of 6 October, the Jewish feast of Yom Kippur. Their initial success was stunning. Within twenty-four hours the Egyptians had put 90,000 men and 850 tanks across the Suez Canal, seized Israel's fortified Bar–Lev line and established bridgeheads along the Canal. Israel lost some 300 tanks. At the same time, three Syrian divisions and an armoured brigade broke through Israel's defences in the Golan Heights and were poised to descend on to the plains of Galilee.

The Arabs' strongest weapon was the element of total surprise, which was helped by Israel's complacency. In the Egyptian forces improved training and officer–men relationships and the high quality of logistical planning helped to maintain morale. Israel's qualitative advantage in air power and armour over Egypt was partially neutralized by the Soviet-supplied missile defence system and by anti-tank 'suitcase missiles' capable of being held by a single infantryman.

Egypt and Syria had deliberately excluded Jordan from joining the offensive because, lacking Soviet missile air defences, Jordan would have been unable to prevent a potentially disastrous Israeli thrust through its territory into southern Syria. But Jordan did send two armoured brigades to Syria after the war began. Iraq contributed three divisions and three fighter squadrons, which suffered heavy casualties on the northern front, while 1,800 Moroccan troops were involved in bitter fighting around Mount Hermon on the first day. The main contribution of the Arab oil-producing states, led by Saudi Arabia, was the use of the oil weapon in declaring an immediate cut in production and a boycott of countries supporting Israel. However, this could not affect the military outcome.

Israel's military recovery was swift, helped by an immediate and massive airlift of the most sophisticated arms from the United States. Israel struck first at Syria, which directly threatened its territory, and by 12 October had pushed the Syrian forces back to their main defensive lines until the front was stabilized some thirty miles from Damascus. (It is possible that Israel feared Soviet intervention if it tried to advance on the Syrian capital.) It was now able to turn its full weight against the Egyptian forces in Sinai, where its initial counter-attacks had been thrown back with further heavy losses. Shortly after the American aid to Israel, the Soviets began an airlift of arms to Egypt. However, on the night of 15 October an Israeli force led by General Ariel Sharon succeeded in crossing to the west bank of the Canal in a gap between the Egyptian armies and establishing a bridgehead. The Egyptian high command, reluctant for reasons of prestige to withdraw forces from Sinai to deal with the threat, reacted too slowly. The Israelis broke out of their bridgehead and came within fifty miles of Cairo. Egypt's Third Army was surrounded and cut off in Sinai.

The United States and the Soviet Union jointly sponsored a Security Council resolution calling for an immediate cease-fire, the implementation of UN Resolution 242 of 1967 and negotiations for a peace settlement 'under appropriate auspices'. This became UN Resolution 338 on 22 October 1973. Egypt and Israel accepted, as did Syria after twenty-four hours' delay. The cease-fire was due to come into force on 22 October, but it immediately broke down. At this point the superpowers came as close as ever before to a direct clash over the Middle East. The Soviets threatened to respond unilaterally to an Egyptian request for US and Soviet troops to be sent to the Middle East to enforce the cease-fire, and the US responded by placing its forces on Defence Condition Three in the early hours of 25 October. The Soviet Union backed down and agreed instead to the formation of a UN Emergency Force in the Middle East from which the troops of the permanent members of the Security Council would be excluded.

The consequences of this fourth Arab–Israeli war (or fifth if the 1968–70 war of attrition along the Suez Canal is included) were substantial and far-reaching, but they were not all immediately apparent and took time to have their full effect.

Israel had snatched a stunning military victory from initial defeat, but the cost was heavy and the psychological effects were deep. Losses in tanks and planes were much heavier than in previous wars; 2,521 Israelis were killed and 7,056 were wounded – about half of them permanently maimed. Arab losses were greater but much less as a proportion of the population, and the performance of the Arab armies had been sufficient to destroy the myth of Israeli military invincibility. The Israeli public, led by the press, launched a form of witch-hunt to apportion blame, focusing on the Labour coalition cabinet of Mrs Golda Meir and especially the defence minister, Moshe Dayan, who was known to have lost his nerve on the initial surprise Arab assault. The Israeli Labour Party had effectively governed the country since the foundation of the state, with the support of the more affluent and better educated Ashkenazi Jews of European origin, but it now began a slow but inexorable political decline. The gainer was the right-wing ultra-nationalist Likud Party, led by Menachem Begin. This had previously been regarded as unelectable, but it now won widespread support from the mass of Sephardic or oriental Jews, who resented the political and social dominance of the Labour establishment. In elections in March 1977 the normal Labour vote of about 40 per cent sank below 25 per cent, while the Likud won 33.4 per cent. Begin became prime minister, and the prospects darkened for any settlement of the Arab–Israeli dispute.

The near defeat in 1973 reinforced Israel's determination to ensure its military superiority over the combined forces of the Arabs and to use this as the main instrument of its diplomacy. With massive

US aid and support, Israel's forces by the end of 1974 were proportionately larger than in October 1973 and qualitatively much improved.

In contrast Egypt's near-victory in Sinai had a harmful effect on President Sadat's diplomacy. Whether or not he totally believed it, he continued to claim that it had indeed been a glorious triumph, and this fiction weakened his hand in subsequent negotiations. On the other hand, he had achieved his most immediate aim of breaking the Middle East impasse and causing a reassessment of US policy in the region. The basis of the Egyptian president's policy was his declared view that the United States always holds 99 per cent of the cards in the Middle East. Immediately following the war he renewed diplomatic ties with Washington after a break of seven years and established a close working relationship with Dr Henry Kissinger (who had been confirmed as secretary of state just two weeks before the outbreak of the war). Through Kissinger's tireless mediation, Sadat secured two military disengagement agreements with Israel – Sinai 1 in January 1974, under which Israeli troops withdrew from the east bank of the Suez Canal and light Egyptian forces occupied a six-mile strip along the shore, and Sinai 2 in September 1975, which took the Israeli forces behind the key Mitla and Geddi passes in Sinai. Early-warning stations manned by US civilians were set up on the passes. The disengagement enabled Egypt to clear and reopen the Canal by June 1975, to start work on the rebuilding and repopulation of the Canal cities and to recover its oilfields in Sinai.

The obverse side to these achievements was that they finally shattered the wartime alliance with Syria. President Assad's mistrust of Sadat turned to bitter contempt as he believed that the Egyptian was ready to opt out of the Arab front against Israel in order to embrace the United States and concur with its wishes. He regarded Egypt's acceptance of US manning of the early-warning stations in Sinai as proof of this. Assad was prepared to end Syria's long diplomatic breach with the United States and to respond to Dr Kissinger's diplomacy as the secretary of state shuttled relentlessly between Middle East capitals, but the Syrian was much more wary than the outgoing and uncomplicated Sadat.

Assad too accepted a disengagement agreement with Israel, engineered by Kissinger in May 1974, under which Israelis withdrew from a small band of territory in the Golan, including its capital, Quneitra, which they first destroyed. But he hoped and believed that it was the United States' intention to proceed to an overall Arab–Israeli settlement based on UN Security Council Resolutions 242 and 338 through the reconvening of the Geneva Middle East peace conference under UN auspices. Later he came to believe that, through his lack of experience in international diplomacy, he had allowed himself to be deceived by Dr Kissinger, who had no intention of trying to persuade Israel to withdraw to its 1967 borders or to agree to Palestinian aspirations. The secretary of state's overriding aim was to exclude the Soviet Union from the Middle East.

President Sadat had no reluctance about excluding the Soviet Union from the Middle East. While his relations with Moscow, which halted all military supplies to Egypt early in 1973, deteriorated to breaking-point, he turned increasingly to the United States and the West. The reversal of alliances corresponded to his deepest political instincts and was reflected in many aspects of his domestic policy. The political opening to the West was matched by an economic and financial open-door policy (*infitah* in Arabic) to encourage non-communist investment in Egypt through tax holidays, freedom to repatriate profits and guarantees against nationalization. Liberalization of the economy brought some results, but the *infitah* policy was often mishandled and critics complained that it failed to treat the real needs of the people. A new-rich class and the old-rich who had recovered their property flaunted their wealth. As foreign banks and businesses opened branches in Cairo, the price of property and services rose steeply. The country's huge indebtedness received some relief from the Arab Gulf states, which were not averse to Egypt's Westward leanings.

Sadat had partially fulfilled his promises to relax the political repression of the Nasser era and to restore the rule of law, but government remained authoritarian. Although he allowed political parties to operate again, the electoral system ensured that the government party dominated parliament totally and the opposition was marginalized. A little criticism was tolerated, but an overwhelmingly pro-government press was ensured. When severe rioting broke out in all major Egyptian cities in January 1977 in protest against sharp price rises for essentials, President Sadat blamed the disturbances exclusively on the left. The rioters had chanted Nasser's name, but he declared that Nasser and Nasserism had been dead since 1967. From then on he was openly critical of all aspects of the Nasser era except for the immediate achievements of the revolution in which he had participated. At the same time he gave quiet but effective support and encouragement to the Islamic militant trend as the best barrier against Nasserism and the left. One consequence of the surge in Islamic feeling was that relations between Egyptian Muslims and the Christian Coptic minority deteriorated to an extent that had not occurred in Nasser's time.

The need for a peace settlement with Israel in order to relieve Egypt's disastrous economic difficulties seemed even more acute. The election of Jimmy Carter to the US presidency in 1976 raised the hopes of all the Arab states, as Carter and his secretary of state, Cyrus Vance, showed that they were prepared to launch a serious new initiative through the reconvening of the Geneva peace conference. President Carter spoke openly of the need for Israel to withdraw from occupied Arab lands and became the first US president to refer to the need for a Palestinian 'homeland'. He met all the principal Arab leaders (including President Assad) and convinced them of his sincerity. However, hopes of resuming the Geneva conference always came up against the same obstacle: the refusal of the Israelis, which still had US backing, to have dealings with the Palestine Liberation Organization, which the Arab states had committed themselves to recognizing as the sole legitimate representative of the Palestinian people. The election of a Likud government headed by Menachem Begin in March 1977 further dimmed the prospects of any progress towards peace. President

Carter continued to persevere and some hopes were raised on 1 October when a joint US–Soviet statement on the Middle East outlined the principles and objectives for a full Arab–Israeli peace settlement and a common approach to Geneva. This was the first superpower accord on the Middle East of its kind, and the first occasion on which the US officially subscribed to the term 'the legitimate rights of the Palestinians'.

The superpower agreement seemed like a milestone; but it was not to be. President Carter, taken aback by the harshness of the reaction of Israel and its Zionist supporters in the US, emphasized that all US moves would be co-ordinated with Israel – the United States still felt committed to Dr Kissinger's undertaking to Israel that it would never expect it to deal with the PLO.

Meanwhile, President Sadat had been planning his own dramatic initiative without the knowledge of his foreign minister and most of his advisers. Having sounded out the Israeli government's reaction through mediators in Romania and Morocco, on 9 November 1977 he announced to an astonished Egyptian parliament that he would go to Jerusalem to address the Israelis directly in the Knesset. Mr Begin warmly responded to this proposal and the visit was fixed for 19 November.

Sadat was impatient, and the high theatre of his action appealed to him. He was also happy to take a road to peace which excluded the Soviet Union he detested. But while most of the rest of the world was delighted and admiring, the Arab states were generally dismayed. Some were simply shocked at the gesture of speaking directly to the enemy in of all places the Holy City of Jerusalem, but all sensed that Egypt, despite Sadat's vigorous denials, was starting on the road towards a separate peace with Israel. That was the accusation from an angry President Assad when Sadat vainly tried to reassure him.

Sadat's speech to the Knesset caught the imagination of millions around the world who watched the spectacle on television. He spoke with eloquence and dignity, invoking the spirit of tolerance in Islam and the equality of Jews, Muslims and Christians in the sight of

God. But he also spoke of Palestinian rights and his rejection of Israel's annexation of Jerusalem. The occasion revealed the immense gulf between him and the Israeli leaders. In his polite but intransigent reply, Begin said that the Jews were back in their God-given land of Israel by right and there was no question of it being divided. He was not specific about territory but left the clear impression that Judaea and Samaria (i.e. the West Bank) were part of Israel and that the 'Arabs of the Land of Israel' (i.e. the Palestinians) at best were tolerated guests.

Peace negotiations between Egypt and Israel began almost immediately. The United States had not been privy to Sadat's initiative, but President Carter now committed his country to 'full partnership' in the peace process. His attempts to persuade other Arab states to revise their attitude were in vain. Libya, Algeria, Syria, the PLO, South Yemen and the Yemen Arab Republic formed a 'Front of Steadfastness' to oppose Sadat. (Iraq shared their views but failed to join because of its regime's antagonism towards Syria.) Saudi Arabia and Jordan were apprehensive but prepared to await events.

Sadat repeatedly affirmed that he had no intention of abandoning the Palestinian cause, despite PLO ingratitude, but his assertions carried declining conviction. He threatened to break off the negotiations with the United States and Israel, but he could not afford them to fail, as the Israelis well knew. A proud and inordinately vain man, he was infuriated by Arab criticisms. He broke off relations with the Front of Steadfastness states and closed down the PLO offices in Cairo. He had promised his poverty-stricken people that there would be no war and had hugely raised their expectations. Moreover, he had aroused a spirit of Egyptian nationalism based on a feeling that Egypt had made the greatest sacrifices in blood and treasure on behalf of the Arabs, who were now showing their ingratitude.

In September 1978 President Carter succeeded in bringing Sadat and Begin together at his Camp David retreat where, after twelve days of negotiations, two agreements were signed: 'a framework for peace in the Middle East', which was intended to deal with the

Palestinian question, and 'a framework for peace between Israel and Egypt'.

The second of these was fairly straightforward – providing for the restoration of Egyptian sovereignty over its territory (except for the partial demilitarization of Sinai) and the normalization of relations between the two countries. The former was more complex, providing for a transitional period in the occupied territories of a maximum of five years during which a local 'self-governing authority' would be established to provide 'full autonomy' for the inhabitants. The 'final status' of the occupied territories would be decided before the end of the transitional period. There were loopholes and ambiguities. It was unclear who would represent the Palestinians in the negotiations; Jordan was expected to take part, but Jordan had not accepted and was refusing to speak on the Palestinians' behalf. Nothing was said about the vexed question of the future of Jewish settlements in the occupied territories. Above all there was nothing to link the two agreements on peace between Israel and Egypt and a solution of the Palestine problem. On this crucial point Sadat gave way on the last day of the negotiations when he was threatening to leave. He said it was a response to the urgent pleading of President Carter.

Egypt was now set on the inevitable course towards a separate peace with Israel which President Assad and others had predicted. No serious obstacles to this remained. The most difficult obstacle was the presence on Egyptian territory of Jewish settlements which had been established since 1967, but Israel saw the neutralizing of Egypt – the biggest Arab military power – as a far greater prize. Ironically, it was some politicians of the more moderate Israeli Labour Party who were anxious about giving up a strategic hold on Sinai. For Mr Begin, what mattered most was that Israel could consolidate its hold on 'Judaea and Samaria'. He never concealed his belief that Israeli sovereignty extended over them, even if for tactical reasons he refrained from declaring this officially. (Israel did, however, on 30 July 1979 declare the whole of Jerusalem, including the Arab eastern part, to be part of the united and eternal capital of

Israel. As a result the slim chance that the Palestine part of the Camp David agreements might achieve anything disappeared.)

The Treaty of Washington was signed on 26 March 1979, bringing to an end thirty-one years of the state of war between Israel and Egypt. Ambassadors were exchanged in 1980, and Israel finally evacuated Sinai on schedule in March 1982. The borders were open, but relations were hardly those normal for neighbouring states. Trade and economic exchange remained minimal and, although Israeli tourists began to come to Egypt, hardly any Egyptians went to Israel. Three decades of hot and cold wars were replaced by a cold peace. Yet the treaty endured, because it was greatly in Israel's interest and cancellation was scarcely an option for Egypt. Israel made clear it would regard cancellation as a *casus belli*, and Egypt, having turned to the West and renounced its friendship with the Soviet Union, was heavily dependent on the United States, which was Israel's ally.

Egypt was not only tied to the United States: it faced isolation from nearly all the Arab states. At a Baghdad summit meeting in November 1978, following the Camp David accords, they decided to move the headquarters of the Arab League from Cairo to Tunis. They agreed to impose sanctions on Egypt if the accords led to a peace treaty, which Saudi Arabia, Jordan and the moderate states still hoped would not happen. After the signing of the Treaty of Washington in March 1979, they closed their embassies and broke off trade and diplomatic relations with Egypt. The Arab oil states cut off the aid and investment which was crucial to Egypt. A Tunisian lawyer, Chedli Klibi, was elected secretary-general of the League – the first non-Egyptian to hold that post in the twenty-four years of the organization's existence.

For a whole decade Egypt stood outside the mainstream of Arab politics – no longer the centre of gravity of the Arab world. But its isolation could never be complete. Most of the hundreds of thousands of Egyptians working in the Arab oil states remained. Cairo was still the greatest Arab city, and a major centre of Arab cultural life. Fewer Arabs visited Egypt, but a range of private contacts continued. But the fact remained that the political decisions made in Cairo were no longer of major importance in the affairs of the Middle East.

For their part the Egyptian people had mixed feelings about the trend of events. While there was relief that there was to be 'no more war', as Sadat had promised, there was disappointment that peace had brought fewer benefits than had been hoped, except to the small class of beneficiaries of the *infitah*. Although US aid to Egypt now came close to matching that to Israel, it made much less difference to Egypt's larger population. But the doubts went deeper than this.

Sadat had touched a chord of Egyptian nationalism and resentment against the other Arabs. Some of the country's leading intellectuals, who had once been supporters of the Nasser Revolution and its pan-Arabism, rationalized these feelings by talking of an Egyptian identity and destiny which were separate from those of the other Arabs. Yet Egyptians could not easily abandon their feeling that Egypt was naturally placed for Arab leadership and for a major role in the wider Islamic world. Sadat's declarations that the Arabs must first beg for Egypt's forgiveness if Egypt was to help them were taken seriously only by a small group of sycophants. There were growing doubts about the president's eagerness for Egypt to replace Israel as the United States' principal surrogate in the Middle East.

As Sadat's natural vanity was fed by the adulation of the West's media, he became increasingly intolerant of criticism at home. His earlier reputation for liberalism was destroyed by new repressive laws to restrict political life and muzzle freedom of expression. Islamic activists, whom he had originally encouraged as a bulwark against the left, now turned outspokenly against him because of his peace with the Zionist enemy and his contemptuous hostility towards the Islamic Revolution in Iran. In September 1981, imagining a concerted move to overthrow him, Sadat ordered the arrest of 1,500 personalities covering the whole political spectrum and including Muslim divines and Coptic bishops. One month later, during a Cairo military parade, he was assassinated by a small group of Islamic extremists within the army. The great majority of Egyptians did not approve of the murder, and there was no general uprising of the Muslim population as the assassins had hoped, but neither did the Egyptian public grieve. The crowds in the Cairo streets were unusually silent.

The succession of Vice-President Husni Mubarak, who was slightly wounded in the attack, proceeded smoothly. A former head of the air force, Mubarak was regarded as honest and straightforward, if uninspiring. He lacked the very different kinds of political charisma of his two predecessors, but he showed both wisdom and common sense. He released Sadat's political prisoners and established a dialogue with the opposition. There was no question of the presidency abandoning its authoritarian power, but he successfully calmed the domestic political scene. At the same time he halted the media attacks on Egypt's fellow-Arabs and began his country's rehabilitation in the Arab world. The process was gradual, and restrained by the necessity of maintaining the peace treaty with Israel and the dependent relationship with the United States, but it was helped by the inescapable fact that Egypt's isolation had drastically reduced the Arabs' political strength in the world. With the notable exception of Syria, the Arab regimes had good reason to want Egypt back in the Arab fold.

Israel/Palestine and the Lebanese Victim

Israel's devastating victory in the June 1967 war and the catastrophe suffered by the Arab armies provoked the rise of the Palestinian guerrilla organizations as an independent force in the Arab world. However, their significance was political rather than military. Israel was not seriously concerned by guerrilla activity on its new borders – casualties had been considerably heavier on the Suez Canal front during the 1969–70 war of attrition. The Israeli defence minister, Moshe Dayan, exercised virtually complete control over the occupied territories of the West Bank and Gaza, and he adopted a policy of consolidating Israel's economic and political hold over them while awaiting a time when the Arabs would be ready to make peace on Israel's terms. Israel wanted direct negotiations leading to peace treaties with the neighbouring Arab states, and it did not consider it had any prior obligation under UN Security Council Resolution 242 to withdraw from all the occupied territories. In fact it envisaged only a partial withdrawal and continued military control of the occupied territories even in the event of peace. The permanence of the occupation was underlined by the launching of a colonization drive in 1968 with a series of military settlements which were established along the Jordan Valley. Most of these were later handed over to civilian settlers. There was no question of negotiating with leading Palestinians for the establishment of an autonomous Palestinian state on the West Bank, although this idea was entertained by some prominent Israelis outside the government.

General Dayan's method in the occupied territories was to deal firmly with opposition and unrest while making the occupation as inconspicuous as possible. An 'open-bridges' policy which allowed Arabs of the occupied territories to travel to Jordan and other Arab states was maintained.

For their part the Palestinian guerrilla organizations, grouped together in the reconstructed Palestine Liberation Organization, did not at this stage foresee the establishment of a small Palestinian state alongside Israel any more than the Israelis. The Palestinian National Covenant, which was adopted in 1968 by the Palestine National Council (the Palestinian quasi-parliament in exile) looked forward to the total Arab liberation of Palestine and the disappearance of the state of Israel. Palestine would be for the Palestinians, who were defined (Article 5) as 'the Arab citizens who were living permanently in Palestine until 1947' and 'whoever is born to a Palestinian Arab father after this date'. Jews who were living permanently in Palestine 'until the beginning of the Zionist invasion' would also be considered Palestinians (Article 6), but by implication this excluded the majority of Israeli citizens.

Despite their failure to cause Israel any serious military problem, the Palestinian guerrilla organizations enjoyed high prestige. Their morale reached a climax with the battle of Kerameh in the Jordan Valley in March 1968, when the Jordanian army and Palestinian commandos co-operated in a major engagement against an Israeli reprisal raiding force which inflicted heavier losses on Israel than on previous occasions. But the increasingly independent activities of the Palestinian organizations, which brought heavy Israeli reprisals against Jordanian territory, threatened Jordan's stability. The Jordanian civilian and military authorities were divided between those who wished to accommodate the commandos and those who wanted to restrict and control their activities. Both King Hussein and the PLO chairman Yasir Arafat favoured compromise, but the king had to contend with increasing anti-Palestinian resentment in his army, especially among ultra-loyalist elements of beduin origin, while Arafat was unable to control and discipline the smaller extremist groups in the PLO. Under pressure, the king agreed to the formation of a provisional military government.

The spark of civil war was lit in September 1970 when the left-wing Popular Front for the Liberation of Palestine hijacked three Western airliners to a deserted airstrip in east Jordan. From 17 September fighting was general between army units and guerrillas until on 25 September a cease-fire was arranged by an inter-Arab mission representing Arab heads of state who had hastily met in Cairo at President Nasser's invitation (shortly before his death). King Hussein and Arafat reached a fourteen-point truce agreement providing for a return to civilian rule. Although the guerrillas still held some strongholds in north Jordan and certain quarters of Amman, they had been fatally weakened by the fighting. The king made prime minister one of his closest advisers, Wasfi Tel, who adopted an uncompromising attitude towards the guerrillas.

Gradually the full weight of the Jordanian army was used to expel the guerrillas from the country, and by July 1971 their last military bases in Jordan had been eliminated. Other Arab states expressed outrage but could do little to help the guerrillas, and Jordan, although isolated, stood firm. The frustration and despair of the

Palestinians gave rise to the self-styled 'Black September' movement, a shadowy and undisciplined group bent on revenge. In September 1971 Wasfi Tel was assassinated in Cairo. Black September was responsible for a series of incidents – mainly outside Israel – involving hijacking, bombing and attempts to take hostages. The most sensational, during the Olympic Games in Munich in September 1972, led to the death of nine Israeli athletes who had been taken hostage by Black September terrorists. The world reacted with horror, but the Palestinians, with nothing left to lose, felt that their cause was at least attracting public attention.

The expulsion of the Palestinian guerrillas from Jordan caused the PLO to concentrate its activities in the one remaining Arab country where they could enjoy some freedom of action – Lebanon. While many Lebanese – especially the Muslims – had some sympathy for the Palestinians' struggle, the majority of Lebanese Christians were hostile and the Maronite political leaders demanded that the guerrillas be excluded from Lebanese territory. But the Lebanese state, built on a delicate political compromise, was weak and unable to defend its interests. All Lebanese were sharply aware of their country's defencelessness in the face of Israeli reprisals against Palestinian guerrilla activities.

For a time the clashes between the guerrillas, the Lebanese army and armed civilian groups of various loyalties were prevented from deteriorating into a general conflict through a series of patched-up compromise agreements achieved through Arab mediation. But such mediation became increasingly difficult after 1971, when the PLO transferred its headquarters from Jordan to Lebanon, where it had the last opportunity for building up a 'state within a state'.

The 1973 Arab–Israeli war and its aftermath brought some benefits to the case of the Palestinians on the international level. The feeling that Israel was no longer invincible, the improved performance of the Arab armies and the great increase in wealth and influence of the Arab oil states were reflected in a new awareness of the Palestinian struggle for self-determination. West European states inclined more strongly towards the Arabs, while Cuba and twenty-seven

African states, several of which had been friends of Israel, broke off
diplomatic relations with Israel by the end of 1973. In September
1974 the UN General Assembly for the first time agreed to include
'the Palestine question' as a separate item on its agenda and then
invited the PLO to take part in the debate, and on 13 November
Yasir Arafat, accorded the honours of a head of state, addressed the
UN General Assembly. 'I have come bearing an olive branch and a
freedom fighter's gun. Do not let the olive branch fall from my
hands,' he said. The PLO now had quasi-official status in various
international organizations.

After the UN's action the Arab states felt they could do no less
in recognizing the PLO. At their summit meeting in Rabat in October 1974, King Feisal of Saudi Arabia took the lead in persuading a
reluctant King Hussein to accept a resolution endorsing the right
of the Palestinian people to establish an international authority
under the direction of the PLO 'in its capacity as the sole legitimate
representative of the Palestinian people'. Subsequent attempts to
dispute this title by proposing an alternative Palestinian leadership
consistently failed.

Yet there was a weakness at the heart of the PLO's position, as
Arafat could not fail to be aware. The 1973 war had helped its cause,
but the Palestinians had played no part in the decision to go to war
and had fought only minor actions on the Lebanese border. World
recognition of the justice of Palestinian claims depended heavily on
Arab diplomacy, and the key Arab states (notably Egypt) wanted
peace. The prospect of recovering Palestine for the Arabs was as
remote as ever.

This paradox was reflected within the Palestine Liberation Organization. Some of the Palestinian leaders, including Yasir Arafat, had
reached the conclusion that Palestinian aims should be scaled down
to the creation of a Palestinian 'mini-state' in the West Bank and
Gaza and that the PLO should seek a settlement in co-operation with
Egypt through a UN-sponsored conference at which they would be
represented. This was bitterly opposed by others – the rejectionists
– who refused to abandon, even temporarily and tactically, the goal

of making the whole of Palestine a 'democratic, non-sectarian state'. Arafat and his colleagues did not admit that they had abandoned that aim, which was the theme of his speech to the UN General Assembly, but, as he said later, it was a dream and 'Is it a crime to dream?' The reality was that the Palestinian mini-state was now the objective, and the formula that was successfully adopted was to have the Palestine National Council pass a resolution calling for the establishment of a 'national authority' on any Palestinian territory that might be liberated.

However, as Israel, with the support of the United States, stood by its refusal to grant any recognition to the PLO, the chances of recovering even a small portion of territory to set up a PLO state seemed remote. The PLO concentrated on building up its shadow state in Lebanon. Here the situation was rapidly deteriorating and the Palestinian presence was far from being the only reason. The Shiite Muslims who were the majority of the population in southern Lebanon and had traditionally been the country's social and political underclass had found a charismatic new leader in Imam Moussa al-Sadr, a cleric of Iranian origin, who organized a Movement of the Disinherited with its own armed militia – Amal ('hope'). The deprived southerners suffered most from Israel's reprisal raids against the Palestinian guerrillas, and some fled their homes to the relative safety of the suburbs of south Beirut. The social and economic disparities in Lebanon, always dangerously strong, were being increased by the effects of the great Middle East oil boom, which brought added prosperity to the country's affluent business classes. Meanwhile the plethora of armed militias representing Lebanon's many sects and political trends acted with increasing independence in open defiance of the inadequate Lebanese armed forces.

In 1975 the unrest developed into full-scale civil war. At first it was mainly a conflict between the right-wing Christian militia and an alliance of leftists under the leadership of the Druze politician Kemal Jumblatt. The conflict was fuelled from outside by the supply of arms and money from various quarters, including Israel, some

Arab states and very probably the CIA. The Palestinian leaders initially tried to keep out of the civil war but were dragged in remorselessly, until by January 1976 they were fully engaged on the side of the leftists. After initial successes, the leftist-Palestinian alliance gained control of some 80 per cent of the country, but at this point Syria began to intervene in force, fearing that Lebanon would be partitioned into a tiny Christian state, which would be in alliance with Israel, and a remainder in the hands of Lebanese Muslims and Palestinians, outside Syria's control. President Assad, like any Syrian leader, regarded Lebanon as a vital Syrian interest. He also saw the Palestinian cause as the responsibility of all the Arabs – and especially of Syria, as the leading front-line state with Israel. He did not believe the PLO should act independently, and his personal relations with Arafat were characterized by deep mutual distrust.

Syria's intervention led to a bizarre alliance with the right-wing Lebanese Christians which, although short-lived, was sufficient to turn the tide against the leftist-Palestinian coalition. The Arab states reluctantly endorsed the presence of Syrian troops in Lebanon as the main body of an Arab peace-keeping force. The civil war died down, leaving some fifty thousand dead and many more injured, while about one million Lebanese were driven from their homes. As in all such wars, atrocious acts of massacre, kidnapping and murder were committed by both sides.

With their usual vigour the Lebanese set about restoring their economy. Trade and banking revived; the Lebanese currency remained strong and it seemed that Lebanon could not easily lose its commercial pre-eminence in the region. But it was soon apparent that the civil war had subsided rather than ended. The fears and hatreds which had been intensified by the war remained, and the Syrian forces were incapable of disarming the sectarian militias and pacifying the whole country. The Lebanese Christians, who had welcomed them in 1976, soon came to detest the presence of Syrian troops and demand their withdrawal. But Syrian domination was opposed by some in the opposite camp, too. In March 1977 the Druze leader Kemal Jumblatt was assassinated, almost certainly by

Syrian military intelligence. Moreover, the continuing presence of the Palestinian quasi-state in Lebanon meant that Israel always found cause to intervene. The alliance between Israel and various branches of the Christian militia, which had begun during the civil war, continued to develop.

Since Israel's earliest days, its leaders had seen the advantages of promoting Christian separatism in Lebanon and the creation of a Maronite-dominated Christian state which would be in alliance with Israel. In southern Lebanon the Israelis had an opportunity to make a start by helping to establish a friendly border enclave controlled by a Lebanese Christian officer who had their full support. By Israeli–Syrian mutual agreement, mediated through the Americans, Syrian forces kept a substantial distance from the Israeli frontier. Lebanese southerners now crossed the 'open border' into Israel for refuge or medical treatment. The great majority were Shiites, and some of them, embittered by their suffering and antagonized by the frequently domineering and insensitive attitude of the PLO fighters towards them, joined the Christian militia.

The situation became more dangerous with the advent to power in Israel in May 1977 of a right-wing government headed by Menachem Begin. The virtual certainty that Israel need no longer be concerned about war with Egypt after President Sadat's visit to Jerusalem in November meant that Israel was free to concentrate on its northern front. In March 1978 it launched its first full-scale invasion of south Lebanon, with the aim of destroying the Palestinian guerrilla bases. The Palestinians melted away northwards and it was mainly the Lebanese who suffered. On this occasion, firm UN Security Council action, backed by President Carter, secured an Israeli withdrawal by June and the installation of a UN International Force in Lebanon (UNIFIL). But Israel continued to maintain and support the friendly border enclave over which UNIFIL had no control.

The years 1979–81 were a period of uneasy stagnation in the Arab–Israeli conflict. It became fully apparent that the conclusion of a separate peace between Egypt and Israel was not going to lead to any comprehensive settlement; in fact it made this more difficult in that Israel, faced with an Arab front in disarray from which the strongest member was excluded, was even more determined not to yield to the demands of Palestinian nationalism. In June 1980 the members of the European Community issued what was called the Venice Declaration, in which they said that the PLO should be 'associated' with any Middle East peace negotiations. But Israel could afford to ignore such suggestions as long as the Europeans still accepted President Sadat's view that the United States held 99 per cent of the cards in the Middle East.

In July 1979 the Israelis formally annexed east Jerusalem and declared the united city their permanent capital. In August 1981 the Saudi Arabians put forward their own plan, to be guaranteed by the UN, providing for Israel's withdrawal from the Arab territories occupied in 1967 and the creation of a Palestinian state in the West Bank and Gaza with east Jerusalem as its capital. All states in the region, including Israel by implication, should be able to live in peace. But Saudi Arabian influence, although strong, was not enough to secure Arab endorsement. A new disturbing factor had emerged in the outbreak, in 1980, of full-scale war between Iran and Iraq. This diverted attention in the Middle East and the rest of the world away from the Arab–Israeli conflict and caused further division among the Arab states.

During this period, Lebanon hardly enjoyed peace. Violence between sects and within sects, with their inevitable reprisals, and massive Israeli retaliation for Palestinian guerrilla attacks resulted in many thousands of dead and injured. Some partial respite was achieved when, in September 1981, the PLO arranged an unofficial cease-fire with Israel through US mediation. But Israel had not abandoned its aim of finally destroying the Palestinian quasi-state in Lebanon. An assassination attempt on the Israeli ambassador in London by young Palestinian extremists provided Israel with a pretext: on the following day – 6 June 1982 – it launched another full-scale invasion of Lebanon but this time it did not halt at the River Litani, some twenty miles from the border, but went on to besiege Beirut for two months. Thousands died and tens of thousands were made homeless in the capital and the cities and villages of the south.

The Arab states were appalled, but frustrated and humiliated because of their inability to influence events. Many Lebanese Christians greeted the Israeli invaders as friends and deliverers, while even some Muslims showed that they had come to detest the Palestinian presence in their country. Syrian forces put up some resistance but, after Israel destroyed their missile sites without losing any planes, Syria agreed to a cease-fire. The Israelis secured a stranglehold on the PLO headquarters in Beirut but the Palestinians, supported by some Lebanese allies, were able to demonstrate that what would have been Israel's first occupation of an Arab capital would be extremely costly. Faced with tremendous odds, Palestinian fighters put up a fair resistance, although they lacked an effective strategy.

The Arab gains from this – which might be called the sixth Arab–Israeli war – were negative but important. The heavy civilian casualties among Lebanese and Palestinians, the huge destruction of property and the callous saturation bombardment of Beirut all helped to swing world opinion against Israel, and began to divide public opinion inside Israel itself.

President Reagan, responding to desperate appeals from King Fahd of Saudi Arabia, began to show public disapproval of Israel's actions and to exert pressure for restraint. Through US mediation an agreement was reached whereby Israel would stay outside Muslim west Beirut and Yasir Arafat and 13,000 Palestinian fighters would be evacuated under US military supervision. The evacuation began on 22 August. On the following day Bashir Gemayel, the young leader of the combined Christian militias, was elected president under the shadow of Israeli guns. But on 14 September, before he could take office, he was assassinated – almost certainly by Syrian agents – and Israeli troops, against vigorous but vain US protests, entered west Beirut 'to maintain order'. Two days later atrocious massacres of Palestinian civilians by Lebanese rightist militiamen took place in the Sabra and Shatila refugee camps – in areas now under Israeli military control and without any Israeli attempt to foresee or prevent them. The event provoked huge protests by the peace movement in Israel. The frustrated Arabs could only denounce the USA for breaking its promise that Palestinian civilians would be protected after the fighters had been withdrawn.

Nevertheless, there seemed for a time to be a chance of a new understanding between the United States and the Arabs. On 1 September 1982 President Reagan announced comprehensive proposals for a Middle East settlement which for the first time showed equal concern for Arab and Israeli interests. Although he ruled out the creation of a Palestinian state, he said that permanent Israeli control over the occupied territories was unacceptable and proposed instead the establishment of an autonomous Palestinian entity linked with Jordan. While Mr Begin angrily rejected the Reagan plan, the response of the Arab states was more conciliatory. At a summit meeting in Fez, they put forward their own plan – which was in fact identical with the Saudi proposals of the previous year. Although it differed from the Reagan plan in important respects – notably in demanding the creation of an independent state – the US and the Arab proposals were not too far apart for their reconciliation to be inconceivable. On the other hand, US–Israeli relations were distinctly cool.

However, this was only one of many false dawns in United States relations with the Arabs. It was not only that the US government in reality still supported Israel in its rejection of Palestinian self-determination; the more immediate problem was that US strategy in the Middle East ignored the role of Syria and, by extension, that of Syria's ally, the Soviet Union, which had more than replaced the Syrian weapons lost in the fighting with Israel. The Kissinger Doctrine of excluding the Soviet Union as far as possible from Middle East diplomacy still held.

In September 1982, US marines returned to Lebanon to form part of an international peace-keeping force with similar Italian and French and much smaller British contingents. United States declared policy was to secure the evacuation of all foreign troops – Israelis,

Syrians and the remaining Palestinians – to enable the new Lebanese president, Amin Gemayel, to establish the authority of the Lebanese state throughout its territory. Vigorous US mediation between Lebanese and Israeli negotiators finally produced, on 17 May 1983, an agreement between Israel and Lebanon which fell short of a peace treaty but which was clearly intended to establish normal relations between the two countries in every respect. But President Assad, who was outraged at this attempt to remove Lebanon from Syria's influence and link it with Israel, had the means of aborting the agreement. Neither the United States nor Israel was able to force him to withdraw his troops, and the Lebanese state was far too weak. In November, suicide-bombers blew up the US marine headquarters and that of the French contingent, leaving more than three hundred dead. Although the United States attributed the direct responsibility to extremist Shiite militia, it considered that Syria must have approved and backed the action. The United States identified Syria, with its Soviet backers, as the obstacle not only to a settlement of the Lebanese problem but also to peace in the whole area. Its response was to move closer to Israel – with Israel's actions in invading Lebanon forgotten and forgiven – by adopting a common strategy towards an Arab–Israeli settlement and greatly increasing military and economic aid.

The United States was forced to accept that its strategy for Lebanon had failed. The American public would not have accepted any deeper involvement of US troops in the hopeless cause of pacifying Lebanon. In February 1984 the US marines were withdrawn from Beirut, and the other, European contingents soon followed.

Israel also found that the objectives of its invasion of Lebanon were far from achieved. The PLO structure in Lebanon had been destroyed and its fighters scattered, but Arafat and the PLO survived and eventually made their headquarters in Tunis. Israel's dream of having a friendly neighbour to the north, dominated by Christian Maronites, had rapidly faded. The Israeli forces were quite unable to control the multi-factional civil war that was raging and turning Lebanon into a partitioned country with shifting internal borders.

In southern Lebanon the mainly Shiite population, who had not initially resisted the Israeli invasion because of their sufferings caused by the Palestinian presence, turned bitterly against the Israelis, who too often behaved as conquerors. The Israeli forces faced increasing attacks from Lebanese fighters, who now included members of Hizbollah ('the party of God') – Shiite extremists supported by revolutionary Iran. As Israeli casualties mounted, Israel's intervention in Lebanon became increasingly unpopular at home.

In September 1984 the Israeli Labour leader Shimon Peres became prime minister of a Labour/Likud coalition after a tied election.

The Labour Party had not been responsible for the invasion of Lebanon, although it had not effectively opposed it. By June 1985 Peres was able to secure the withdrawal of Israeli forces from Lebanon. However, Israel kept military advisers with the South Lebanon army, composed mainly of Christians in a ten-mile buffer zone along the border, and to this extent could still interfere in Lebanon's internal affairs. But it had abandoned its opportunity to influence directly the character of Lebanon's regime.

It seemed to many that, although Arafat and his PLO colleagues had survived the siege of Beirut, their organization's effectiveness was ended. Moreover a worse blow was to come in April 1983 when a rebel movement within the PLO, supported by Syria, declared Arafat's leadership to be corrupt and denounced what was seen as his intention to abandon the armed struggle in favour of diplomacy in collaboration with Jordan. Expelled from Syria by President Assad, Arafat made his headquarters in Tripoli in north Lebanon, where he faced attacks by the rebels backed by Syrian and Libyan troops. After lengthy negotiations, Arafat and 4,000 loyalists were evacuated by Greek ships flying the UN flag.

This was surely the end. The PLO's fighters were scattered to the farthest corners of the Arab world, and its headquarters was 2,000 miles away from Palestine in Tunis, at the opposite end of the Mediterranean. But in fact these disasters caused most of the four million Palestinians, whether in the diaspora or in Palestine, to cling more tightly to Arafat and the PLO as the only effective symbols of national identity. To the outside world the pudgy and half-shaven figure of Arafat seemed to lack appeal, but to his own people he had powerful charisma and magnetism, especially when speaking in his Arabic tongue rather than coping with Western interviewers. There was still no real alternative to him as 'Mr Palestine', as Israel acknowledged by attempting to destroy him and his headquarters in an air raid on Tunis in October 1985. He was also a subtle politician. He infuriated Western well-wishers by refusing to state clearly what they knew to be true – that he was ready to recognize Israel and abandon the armed struggle in return for an independent Palestinian state – and he opened himself to the charge of changing his words to suit his audience, but he knew that he had first to convince the great majority of Palestinians or their movement would shatter and dissolve. It was to prevent internal differences from emerging that he consistently refused, despite the urging of outside sympathizers, to form a provisional government-in-exile whose policy decisions would have had to be binding on all its members.

The PLO survived as an organization, and Arafat pursued a diplomatic offensive as he shuttled between the many capitals of the world that were ready to receive him, but Western governments remained wary and the United States continued to back Israel's refusal to have any dealings with the PLO. Both countries still hoped that the Palestine problem could be solved through an agreement with Jordan which would leave the Palestinians in the occupied territories under some form of Jordanian–Israeli condominium. In February 1985 the stalemate appeared to be broken when King Hussein and Arafat agreed on a joint Palestinian–Jordanian peace initiative, based on the exchange of territory for peace. But a year later the initiative collapsed, for reasons which had become familiar: the Jordanian monarch felt that Arafat had reneged on his undertaking to declare his willingness to recognize Israel, while Arafat refused to give up this last Palestinian card of negotiation or even to negotiate without at least securing United States recognition of the Palestinian right to self-determination and hence the right to establish an independent state.

The impasse was broken by a development which none of the parties to the Arab–Israeli conflict – including the PLO – had fore-seen. In December 1987 the Palestinians in the occupied territories began an uprising against the Israeli occupiers. The uprising or *inti-fada* – an Arabic word which was to become as much part of the international vocabulary as the Russian *glasnost* – was unexpected because, although there had been days or even weeks of sporadic unrest, the Israeli occupiers had faced a relatively easy task for two decades. Guerrilla attacks had never been a serious military problem; internal resistance had not been prolonged or organized. When a hostile political leadership had looked like emerging, its members were imprisoned or deported. In December 1987, however, a minor incident in Gaza sparked off a resistance movement which, although unplanned and at first unorganized, refused to die down. The half of the population who had not yet reached twenty years of age had known only foreign occupation. As the occupiers seized more land and water and planted new Jewish settlements on their territory they saw a future that could only become darker. Some 200,000 crossed each day into Israel to work, but it was generally to perform menial and unskilled tasks – the Palestinian economy was entirely colonial in kind. The despair of the people of the occupied territo-ries was increased by the fact that the Arab states appeared to have lost interest in them. For the first time ever at a meeting of Arab heads of state, in Amman in August 1987, the Palestine problem had been displaced from the head of the agenda by a different question – the Iraq–Iran war.

The *intifada* took the form of demonstrations, tyre-burning, the illegal raising of the Palestinian flag and strikes. Its characteristic feature was the hurling of stones at Israeli soldiers by Arab adoles-cents and even children. A significant innovation was that an anonymous National Unified Command of the Uprising emerged which, through pamphlets and a secret radio station on Syrian terri-tory, gave some effective organization to the demonstrations and strikes.

The Israeli authorities, surprised by the intensity and persistence of the uprising, responded with mass arrests and deportations, curfews, beatings and the various forms of plastic bullet, which were often lethal or caused grievous wounds. In the first two years there was an average of about one Palestinian death each day.

After two years some 50,000 Palestinians had been arrested, 7,000 wounded and more than 500 killed. About half of those arrested were under the age of eighteen. The rebels rarely resorted to arms – their uprising was called the 'Stone Revolution' – but as its second year progressed it became increasingly bitter as the Palestinians began killing anyone suspected of collaborating with the Israeli secret police, and Islamic fundamentalists opposed to any political compromise came to the fore.

For Israel, the effort to suppress the *intifada* was costly and damaging – both to the morale of its troops, mostly untrained in putting down civil resistance, and to Israel's international reputation. There was no question that it was capable of opposing the insurrection militarily and economically – it was the political dimension that was important. Despite defiant assurances by Israeli political leaders that the rebellion would be ended, it became an accepted international truism – shared by the United States government and much of the Israeli public – that any purely military solution would be ineffective. Israel was faced with the prospect of a *de facto* Palestinian state being created west of the River Jordan.

The success of the uprising merely in staying alive gave a wholly fresh impetus to the PLO. Although it had neither timed nor organized the internal rebellion, and the amount of support and direction it could provide from outside was very limited, the Arabs under occupation left no doubt that they regarded the PLO as their representative and Arafat as their leader. Everywhere they displayed his picture as the symbol of their defiance. Paradoxically, this demonstration of the spirit of Palestinian nationalism enabled the PLO leadership to adopt a more overtly moderate position which emphasized the common interest of Palestinians and Israelis in peace and security. At the same time it persuaded King Hussein of Jordan to destroy once and for all the credibility of the 'Jordanian option' –

that is, the belief then entertained by many Israelis and some Western governments that Palestinian nationalism could remain under joint Jordanian and Israeli hegemony. In July 1988 the Jordanian monarch announced that he was finally abandoning all Jordan's responsibilities for the West Bank. From there it was only one step for the PLO to declare, through its quasi-parliament meeting in Algiers in November, the establishment of an independent Palestinian state with Arafat as its president. But simultaneously the Palestine National Council for the first time unambiguously declared its acceptance of UN Security Council Resolution 242 of 1967 – the step which the United States had long been demanding as a demonstration that the PLO was willing to recognize Israel. It also declared that it was renouncing all forms of terrorism.

Arafat spelled this out more clearly in other world capitals. He was advocating a 'two-state solution' – that is, a small independent Palestinian state living alongside Israel. This had been his objective for years, but he had never felt confident enough to declare it unambiguously for fear that abandoning the dream of liberating all Palestine from Zionism would divide his people against each other.

Israel's leaders denounced the PLO's new stand as false and treacherous. The threat to their position was underlined when for the first time the United States declared that it was prepared to begin a dialogue with the PLO through its ambassador in Tunis.

However, Palestinian hopes of rapid rewards for their new concessions were not realized. In March 1990 Yitzhak Shamir, the Israeli premier from 1988 to 1990, dismissed his Labour partners in his coalition and eventually succeeded in forming a right-wing Likud government. Although the United States showed increasing impatience with Shamir's stubborn rejection of any plausible formula for Palestinian autonomy it was still unprepared to exert concentrated pressure on its Israeli ally to change its attitude. An increasingly disillusioned Arafat, faced with a growing Islamic fundamentalist element in the *intifada* that rejected any two-state solution in favour of the old slogans of total liberation, began to look towards President Saddam of Iraq, who was posing as the champion of the Palestinians and threatening Israel with its missiles. After a botched terror raid on an Israeli beach by a PLO splinter group, almost certainly promoted by Iraq, the United States broke off its listless dialogue with the PLO.

Consequently, Arafat showed some evident sympathy with Saddam's invasion of Kuwait in August 1990, though formally advising an Iraqi withdrawal, while ordinary Palestinians in Jordan and the occupied territories cheered Saddam as a hero. Powerful anti-Palestinian feelings were aroused among the Gulf Arabs, and Western governments declared that the PLO had marginalized itself in the Gulf conflict. But this was premature and unrealistic. The *intifada* had superficially subsided in the first half of 1990, partly through exhaustion and partly through a more restrained Israeli policy of repression, but in October a renewal of violence enhanced extremism on both sides and further envenomed relations between Arabs and Jews. In these circumstances there was no way that either the United States or Israel could promote an alternative Palestinian leadership to the PLO.

Forty years after the triumph of Zionism in the creation of a Jewish state, a new stage had been reached in the Palestine problem that this had created. This emphatically did not mean that the problem had been solved, or even that it was nearer a solution – a 'solution' that would be satisfactory to all the parties concerned is in any case inconceivable. The original concept of the partition of Palestine into an Arab and a Jewish state – approved by the United Nations in 1947 with so little concern for its consequences, and so bitterly rejected by the Arabs of Palestine at the time – had come to be accepted by a new generation of Palestinians and much of the rest of the world. But, after twenty years' occupation it was no longer accepted by Zionist Jews, except for a small, albeit growing, minority. Some, represented by Israel's prime minister Yitzhak Shamir, saw the West Bank (or Judaea and Samaria) and Gaza as part of the Land of Israel and could not contemplate abandoning it to an Arab sovereignty. Others, represented by the Labour leader Shimon Peres, although ready to give up some land for peace, still could not face the prospect of an independent neighbouring state governed by the PLO under President Arafat. In this rejection of an independent Arab Palestine, Israel had the support of the world's most powerful state, and experience had shown on multiple occasions that the United States government, however much it disapproved of certain Israeli acts or attitudes, would exert pressure to change them only on the rarest occasions and never for long. It remained a cardinal principle of the US–Israeli alliance that the United States would sustain Israel's military machine and economy to ensure that Israel remained the most powerful state in the Middle East.

Syria's crucial role in trying to restore peace and unity to the Lebanese state was grudgingly acknowledged by most of the world after the withdrawal of Western and Israeli troops in 1984 and 1985. But if Syria was dominant in Lebanon, it was far from all-powerful. Even President Assad's supreme abilities as a political tactician could not resolve the multifarious conflicts of Lebanon. It proved impossible to secure the essential minimum of an agreement among the factions to reunite the country. While Syria had some friends among the Maronites, these were outnumbered by its bitter enemies who controlled the strongest militia, the Lebanese Forces. Even Syria's allies in Lebanon – the Druze, the Shiite Amal militia and the extremist Hizbollahis – were far from obedient and sometimes fought each other. An additional factor was that some of the Palestinian fighters, now fiercely anti-Syrian, had returned to Beirut and the south and had become engaged in fighting with the Amal militia who besieged the Palestinian refugee camps. By sending their forces into Muslim west Beirut, the Syrians were able to reduce the fighting between the militias, but Christian east Beirut and the Shiite southern suburbs remained outside their control.

When President Amin Gemayel's six-year term of office ended in September 1988, the anti-Syrian Maronites prevented the parliamentary deputies from electing a successor who would have been acceptable to Syria. After the failure of every alternative, Gemayel's last act as president was to appoint General Michel Aoun, the

Maronite commander of the armed forces, as prime minister. Since Muslims refused to serve in his cabinet and the previous Sunni prime minister declared himself still in office, Lebanon had two half-governments and no head of state. It seemed as if the little republic of Lebanon was doomed to final destruction after less than seventy years of existence. The Lebanese economy, which had survived the first decade of civil war with amazing resilience, was on the point of collapse.

However, the peculiar circumstances of Lebanon, with its shifting balance of internal forces and external pressures, do not favour final solutions or dissolutions. The Arab states, backed by all the outside powers concerned with the region, made unsparing efforts to hold Lebanon together. This required an accommodation between Syria and its Lebanese Christian opponents which was difficult to achieve. General Aoun, who suffered from minor Napoleonic delusions, was uncompromisingly defiant. He was buoyed up by a vague and unwarranted belief that the Western powers would come to the aid of the Christian Lebanese, although he also received real help in money and arms from Syria's arch-enemy Iraq. He was unable to fulfil his boast of driving the Syrians out of Lebanon, but equally the Syrians and their allies lacked the power and will to overrun the Christian fortress enclave. In the summer of 1989 the two sides poured shells on to each other, causing atrocious suffering mainly to civilians.

Against most expectations, Arab mediators secured a cease-fire in September 1989 and persuaded the surviving and elderly deputies of the Lebanese parliament to meet in Taif, Saudi Arabia's summer capital, where they hammered out an agreement on a new political structure for Lebanon, through which the Maronites, who had been politically dominant since the French creation of Greater Lebanon, would relinquish some of their powers. Since it was a compromise, many were dissatisfied. The Christians had not secured Syria's immediate departure and the Shiites, now more numerous than Lebanese Sunnis, felt that they should have a more influential role. But the agreement made it possible for the deputies to meet in Syrian-controlled north Lebanon to elect on 5 November 1989 a new president – Rene Muawwad. General Aoun defiantly declared the election illegal and claimed that he was still Lebanon's constitutional leader.

Two weeks later Muawwad was assassinated by a car bomb in west Beirut. Under Syrian protection the deputies then elected yet another Christian president, Elias Hrawi, whom the rebel general found equally unacceptable. Although Hrawi was recognized by the Arab states and the rest of the world Aoun maintained his defiance. But his authority over Christian Lebanon was challenged by the Christian militia group in the Lebanese Forces. A bloody conflict ensued, causing atrocious suffering to the people of east Beirut and leaving General Aoun in control of only one third of the Christian enclave. The *de facto* partition could not be permanent and the issue of a death certificate for the Lebanese Republic was still postponed.

Aoun's nemesis was not long delayed. In October 1990, as world attention was diverted towards the Gulf and the containment of Iraq (which had supported Aoun in his hostility towards Damascus) the Syrians were able to overrun the general's fortress enclave in alliance with Lebanese forces loyal to President Hrawi and bring about his surrender. The Syrians now dominated all of central Lebanon but their first aim was to extend the Lebanese government's authority throughout the one hundred square miles of greater Beirut, ensure the withdrawal of the rival militias and reopen communications. If the Lebanese heartland could be secured, even under Syrian hegemony, the Lebanese Republic still had a chance of survival.

Islamic Reassertion, Revolution and War

With the decline and defeat and dismemberment in 1918 of the Ottoman Empire – the last Muslim great power in global terms – the world of Islam was on the defensive. In the nineteenth and early twentieth century the Arabs came under some form of Western colonial domination. The Muslims of central Asia were absorbed into the Russian Empire, the Muslim former rulers of India became part of the British Raj, and the Persian/Iranian Empire suffered a joint Russian–British hegemony. It was only in Turkey, the former heartland of the Ottoman Empire, that a nation-state which was strong enough to remain independent of the European colonial powers was forged, by the political and military genius of Kemal Atatürk. But his cause was secular Turkish nationalism and not Islam.

The Arab and Iranian response to European domination differed from Turkey's in that it was neither purely secular nationalism nor an Islamic counter-offensive but a combination of both. The Islamic cultural element was supremely important. As Frantz Fanon, the Martiniquais intellectual who joined the Algerian revolution against France, pointed out in his classic work *The Wretched of the Earth*: whereas European colonizers thought of black Africans in essentially racial terms, their attitude towards the Arab world was different. Here they were confronted by a specific and unified, if not homo-geneous, culture which was derived from its Arab/Islamic tradition. Beyond doubt it was the indestructibility of this culture which prevented France from not only colonizing Algeria but also turning it into a permanent European dependency as at one time seemed perfectly feasible.

However, to say that Arab resistance to European domination drew its inspiration from Islam and its heritage does not mean that in this respect it was pure and uncompromising. The great nine-teenth-century and early twentieth-century Muslim reformers such as al-Afghani, Abduh and Rida reached the conclusion that the world of Islam began to decline when the Turks took over its lead-ership from the Arabs. Although this was not their intention, their ideas provided the intellectual basis for Arab nationalism. The Arabs of the Middle East formed an alliance with the European colonizers to overthrow Ottoman Turkish rule, but when this succeeded they were left with weak Arab nation-states under European domination. The pan-Arab nationalist movement which developed in the 1920s and 1930s was given a powerful fresh impetus by the loss of Arab Palestine in the 1940s and reached its peak in the 1950s under Gamal Abdul Nasser of Egypt, who aimed to overcome this weakness and throw off European hegemony. But although Arab nationalism was not purely secular, neither was it wholly Islamic. Unlike the nationalism of Atatürk, it could not be entirely secular for the obvious reason that for any Arab – even a non-Muslim – to cut himself off from his heritage of Islamic civilization would be to deny his own identity. But equally the pan-Arab movement could not be purely Islamic in its ideology, in the sense of regarding Islam as the sole path to the true self-determination of the Arab peoples. This was not only because some of the leading exponents of pan-Arabism, such as the Baath ideologist Michel Aflaq, were Christians: its Muslim leaders were also strongly influenced by European and American concepts of secular nationalism. Many had been educated at Western institutions or trained by European officers. However grudgingly, to some extent they accepted Atatürk's belief that it was reactionary Islam which had allowed the West (and the Zionists) to defeat and dominate the peoples of the Middle East – Turks, Persians and Arabs.

Among the Arabs who most fiercely resisted Western domination there were indeed some who saw nothing of value outside Islam. These were Muslim nationalists rather than Arab nationalists; today they are called fundamentalists. They had, and have, a utopian view that if Muslims were to set up an Islamic order in which the holy *sharia* would be the only authority, all the internal problems of government and society and the external problems of un-Islamic domination and influence would be solved. While their dedication and readiness for martyrdom made them formidable, they remained a minority in the Arab struggle for full independence from the West. Their refusal to compromise and their willingness to use violence against anyone who did not wholly share their views alienated potential allies. Whenever there seemed a chance that they might gain power, they deeply alarmed the majority. Their first organized movement in the modern Arab world – the Muslim Brotherhood, in Egypt – believed that it was on the point of overthrowing a corrupt monarchy but was then, as we have seen, swept aside by the Nasser Revolution.

A seeming exception to the rule that militant Islamic fundamentalists are unlikely to be successful in winning control of an Arab state in the twentieth century occurred in Arabia. Here the puritanical Wahhabi reformers, allied to the House of Saud, had in the eighteenth century been the first Arab movement to challenge the authority of the Ottoman sultan/caliph and to denounce the religious backsliding of their fellow-Muslims. Defeated in the early nineteenth century by the secular power of Muhammad Ali, the Ottoman governor of Egypt, they finally triumphed in the 1920s through the political and military genius of Ibn Saud. Here at last the uncompromising forces of Islam were in power. But King Ibn Saud knew his limitations. Although he enjoyed prestige as the custodian of the holy places of Islam, his new kingdom was remote, desperately poor and militarily weak. It was in no position to spread its puritan revolutionary movement northwards to the great centres of Arab population – Cairo, Damascus and Baghdad. Moreover – and most important – the grinding poverty of the people of Saudi Arabia caused Ibn Saud and his sons who succeeded him to ally themselves with the West – especially the supremely secular United States – to relieve the country's economic backwardness. Ironically, the puritanical Saudis subsequently proved to be endowed with unimaginable natural wealth, but, although the Saudi kingdom then acquired prestige and influence in the councils of the world, it needed non-Muslims even more – for the development and protection of its newly discovered resources. The alliance with the West deepened with the added spur of the Saudi fear and detestation of communism.

So it was that, although the Saudis were amazingly successful in preserving their identity through the retention of their system of government and laws and their conservative social mores, their inter-relationship with and dependence on the West was also undeniable. Saudi Arabia might take the lead in creating international bodies and organizations to increase the links between the Muslim states, and it lavishly endowed Islamic missions and mosques throughout the world – all of which powerfully assisted the reassertion of Islam in modern times – but the militant Islamic fundamentalists were not satisfied. They wanted to exclude the West from the world of Islam. In 1979 the House of Saud was made brutally aware of their existence even inside the kingdom when a group of young fanatics, denouncing the corruption of their rulers, seized and held for a time the Great Mosque at Mecca – the holiest shrine of Islam.

After the Arab catastrophe in 1967, volatile world opinion seized on the possibility of an Islamic fundamentalist revolution sweeping through the Arab countries. In the heyday of pan-Arab nationalism in the 1950s and 1960s, the importance of Islam as a political force was grossly underestimated by the majority of Western journalists and academics – and, indeed, by much of the Arab intelligentsia. A common view was that the Arabs were determined to catch up with the West's material and technical progress, and for this Islam had nothing to contribute. After 1967 there was a sudden reversal of this opinion. Secular Arab nationalism had been proved a failure and was dead; the masses would reject Western progress and turn to fundamentalist Islam as their only hope.

Both views were misleading. Islam had never ceased to be a supremely powerful underlying force; it was only reasserting itself more openly in the wake of the Arab defeat. On the other hand, nationalism was far from dead, even if it had to modify its form. All the regimes of the Arab states – even in Saudi Arabia – still subscribed to the notion that the Arabs form a single nation which should be more closely united. There was no question of breaking up the League of Arab States. At the same time, it was apparent that there had been a strengthening of territorial nationalism – the local patriotism that had grown up around the flag and capital of the individual Arab states (however artificial their creation by the West may have been) and that supported their particular interests. There was no likelihood that an Islamic revolution would be able to sweep all this away.

The Islamic revolution which did occur took place not in the predominantly Sunni Muslim lands but in Shiite Iran. All but a very few of the closest observers were taken by surprise.

Since the overthrow of Mossadegh in 1953, Iran had come to be seen as an example of the progress and development which were widely held in the West to be synonymous with westernization. In the 1950s, elections to the Majlis were carefully controlled to ensure that acceptable candidates were elected. The National Front ceased to function as an organized political force and the communist Tudeh Party was proscribed. Power was increasingly concentrated in the hands of the shah. However, the task of the shah's loyalist governments was not easy. Their hope was that economic growth would dampen opposition to the control of political life but, although oil revenues expanded, the large-scale projects to develop the infrastructure took time to mature and there was widespread corruption and inefficiency. Anti-Western nationalist feelings, inflamed during the Mossadegh crisis, were by no means extinguished. They gained strength from the regime's close identification with the Western camp, symbolized by Iran's adherence to the anti-Soviet Baghdad Pact in 1955.

In 1961 the unrest obliged the shah to appoint as prime minister Ali Amini, a wealthy aristocrat with a reputation as a liberal reformer. He tackled government extravagance and corruption and relaxed controls on the National Front and left-wing opposition. He brought into the cabinet as minister of agriculture Hassan Arsanjani, a radical politician committed to land reform and the break-up of the large estates consisting of scores of villages. Amini persuaded the shah to allow him to dissolve the Majlis and rule by decree to push through his reforms. But his reformist experiment was short-lived. He aroused opposition on all sides – from the landowners and the army as well as the politicians who demanded the restoration of the Majlis. Within a year he had been forced to resign and the shah reasserted his authority.

The shah nevertheless pursued and even intensified some of the reform measures – notably land reform, which was extended to the

Islamic *waaf* properties (whose revenues were used for the upkeep of mosques or charitable works), while the large landowners were limited to the holding of one village. Female suffrage was introduced, and women's rights were legally extended. A Literacy Corps was founded to enable high-school students to teach in village schools as an alternative to military service. In this way the shah's government retained the initiative. The National Front declared that it favoured the reforms but said that they were 'unconstitutional', while the mullahs, whose most effective spokesman was Ayatollah Khomeini of Qum, denounced them as 'un-Islamic' as well as unconstitutional. In 1963 the National Front was disbanded by the government and then disintegrated. Khomeini and other religious leaders were arrested, and a year later Khomeini was sent into exile and took up residence in the Shiite region of southern Iraq. The religious opposition resorted increasingly to underground activity and violence, but this was ineffective and the government was able to denounce both the nationalists and mullahs as reactionary opponents of reform.

For more than a decade the shah could rule without serious opposition pressure. He reconvened the Majlis and allowed it to function with officially sponsored political parties and an opposition which consistently voted for government bills. Outside parliament the ubiquitous SAVAK secret police relentlessly suppressed dissent.

The shah showed increasing self-confidence and a vaulting ambition to make his country the indisputably dominant regional power. The West was always ready to provide him with the most sophisticated modern weapons. Although remaining in the Western camp, however, he improved relations with the Soviet-bloc countries and signed with them a series of large-scale industrial agreements. He secured greatly improved terms from the oil companies, which amounted to the National Iranian Oil Company taking over control of operations. In 1967 he amended the constitution so that the queen would automatically become regent in the event of his death before the crown prince reached his majority, and in the twenty-sixth year of his reign he and the queen were crowned in a wholly un-Islamic ceremony. In 1971 he celebrated the two-thousand-five-hundredth anniversary of the Persian monarchy with colossal extravagance at the ancient capital of Persepolis.

The huge increase in Iran's oil revenues in 1973–4 drove the shah's ambitions to the border of megalomania. He began to proclaim that his country would be among the six most advanced industrial countries of the world by the end of the century. In fact – in spite of the real industrial progress, the extension of education and literacy, and the growth of the professional and business class – many of the standards of Iranian society remained those of the Third World. With hindsight it is possible to discern that the sudden vast increase in government revenues was the nemesis of the regime. The huge growth in spending which followed placed intolerable strains on the country's social and economic fabric. When overspending led to retrenchment and recession combined with continuing inflation, even the members of the new middle class who had benefited most from the shah's policies became disaffected, while the mass of the population tended to see the hasty westernization and un-Islamic modernization of the country as the source of all evil.

The shah, in common with most Western observers (including ambassadors), still underrated the opposition. He saw only an opportunistic alliance between the extreme left and the mullahs, and referred contemptuously to 'Islamic Marxists'. In fact it was the mullahs who were best able to articulate the discontent of the majority.

As the tide of unrest gathered momentum, it became apparent that popular opposition was massive and deep-seated. The huge coalition of discontent found its voice in Ayatollah Khomeini. After being ousted from his Iraqi exile by an embarrassed Iraqi government (which wanted stable relations with Iran), he took refuge in Paris, from where he issued uncompromising demands for the shah's abdication. As strikes and demonstrations spread, the shah attempted a series of measures, mixing concessions with firmness, in an effort to secure his power. But these were ineffective. The armed forces remained apparently loyal, but the shah had finally lost the will and determination to hold on to power through the massive repression which would have been necessary – his arrogant demeanour had always concealed a certain lack of decision. He was also suffering from the cancer which was to kill him two years later. Without the will to retain his throne, neither his loyal followers nor his US allies could help him. On 16 January 1979 he left Iran with his queen, ostensibly on holiday but never to return. His departure from Tehran was cheered by two million supporters of Ayatollah Khomeini. Twenty-five centuries of the Persian monarchy had ended.

Two weeks later the frail 76-year-old ayatollah showed that he could inspire millions of his people to frenzied enthusiasm when he returned in triumph to declare that, with his Islamic Revolution, a truly Islamic republic would be established.

This momentous event was soon to be compared in importance with the French Revolution of 1789 and the Bolshevik Revolution of 1917. For the comparison to be sustained it was necessary for the Iranian Revolution's influence to spread far beyond Iran's borders, and especially to the Muslim peoples of the Middle East. Khomeini and his clerical associates left no doubt that this was their intention. They proclaimed that all the regimes of Muslim countries in the region were corrupt, unworthy and un-Islamic and therefore deserved to be overthrown. They also denounced these regimes' association with the West. Khomeini declared that a true Muslim country should have no truck with either East or West, but his special hatred was directed towards the United States – 'the Great Satan', the former ally of the shah. Anti-American rage swept Iran and, when President Carter allowed the shah to travel from his retreat in the Bahamas to the United States for medical treatment, a crowd of militants stormed the US embassy in Tehran, seizing some fifty US hostages and all the embassy documents. This outrage against all the norms of diplomacy, which even the most radical and revolutionary regimes usually accepted, provoked the United States, with the support of its allies, to declare Iran an international outlaw. Khomeini was not displeased. His uncompromising defiance of the

West provoked admiration among all the Muslim masses to whom he wished to appeal. This was reinforced by his adoption of the cause of Palestine. He reversed the shah's *de facto* alliance with Israel and invited Arafat to Tehran, where he was greeted as a hero.

At home, Ayatollah Khomeini set about consolidating clerical rule under his leadership. His authoritarianism provoked the opposition of the secular nationalist and left-wing elements who had supported his revolution, but they were no match for the hold he had gained over the Iranian people. In fact the most serious opposition to his rule came from more senior Islamic clerics who challenged his religious authority. But even this he was able to contain. He had political genius, which they lacked. He based his rule on the doctrine of *velayat-e faqih* – that is, 'government of the Islamic jurist' – which he had expounded in lectures in exile. This holds that the true Islamic state must be based on the Koran and be modelled after the Prophet's Islamic community in the seventh century, and that it should be administered by the clerical class as the Prophet's heirs. As the self-appointed governing Islamic jurist, Khomeini was able to hold supreme power above that of the president, prime minister and elected parliament, which were all provided for in the new Islamic constitution. Under his authority, mass trials of the shah's former supporters were organized, leading to many executions. The educational system was purged of non-Islamic influences. Squads of young Muslim militiamen enforced a strict Islamic code of conduct. Educated Iranian women, who had reached an advanced stage of emancipation before the revolution, had their role in public life sharply reduced and all had to envelop their heads and bodies in Islamic dress in public,

The success of the Khomeini Revolution and its declared desire to export itself caused serious alarm among Iran's Arab neighbours, but nowhere more than in Iraq. With its secular pan-Arabist ideology and its large Shiite population with little share in political power, Iraq was a vulnerable target. Tehran Arabic broadcasts poured hatred and contempt on the Iraq regime and called on the Iraqi people to overthrow it.

Iraq's president, Saddam Hussein, decided to act first. Although Iran has immense resources and three times Iraq's population, he believed that the Khomeini Revolution could be overthrown by a swift blow. The Iranian regular armed forces were demoralized. Iran's large minorities – the Kurds in the north-west, the Turkomans of the Caspian plain and the Arabs of Khuzestan in the south-west – saw their religious and cultural identities threatened by the Shiite fundamentalist policies of the Revolution and were demanding autonomy and threatening revolt. The economy, facing a Western boycott, was in dire condition. Almost certainly, exiled royalist Iranian officers helped to convince President Saddam that it was time to move. On 17 September 1980 Iraq, alleging various minor acts of Iranian aggression, denounced the 1975 agreement with the former shah and invaded Iran.

The eight-year war which ensued was on an epic scale, with colossal casualties, massive material destruction and mutual rocket attacks on Baghdad and Tehran in 'the war of the cities'. Iraq initially advanced deep into Iranian territory, but its invasion soon proved the danger of attacking a revolution. Iranian morale was higher than expected, and the Arab Iranians of the south-west did not rise to support the invaders. Within a year Iraq had been forced back, and by May 1982 Iran had recaptured nearly all its territory. All Iraq's outlets to the sea were cut off. A prolonged stalemate ensued, interspersed by large-scale offensives which, as in the First World War, left many dead but the battle lines scarcely changed. Iraq, which could obtain arms from both East and West, had the advantage in weapons – especially tanks and artillery. Iran, lacking fresh supplies of its American weapons, was forced to turn to sources such as North Korea or the international black market in arms. It used its numerical superiority to launch human-wave assaults which often involved thousands of teenage youths imbued with the characteristically Shiite readiness for martyrdom.

For some time the Gulf War directly involved only Iraq and Iran. Initial world alarm caused a further steep rise in oil prices, but the reaction of the world outside the Middle East could be summed up in a possibly apocryphal comment ascribed to Dr Henry Kissinger: that the best result would be for both sides to lose the war. The war was prolonged because, while Iraq was prepared to settle for a return to the old frontiers, Iran demanded nothing less than the downfall of Saddam Hussein.

The six Arab Gulf states – Saudi Arabia, Kuwait, Qatar, Bahrain, the United Arab Emirates and Oman – supported Iraq with varying degrees of enthusiasm and openness, and as the war progressed they helped to sustain Iraq with money and supplies. They were appalled at the prospect of an outright Iranian victory. The threatening situation, aggravated by the Soviet invasion of Afghanistan in 1979, acted as a catalyst for them to join together in self-defence in May 1981 to establish the Gulf Co-operation Council. This looked forward to a staged process of political and economic fusion, somewhat along the lines of the European Community.

Among the other Arab states, Jordan and Egypt declared their support for Iraq in the war even more openly. Jordan's Aqaba port became the principal route for Iraqi imports of war materials; Egypt supplied arms and ammunition. But President Assad of Syria declared himself Iran's ally in the war and closed Iraq's oil pipeline across Syrian territory. Although this bizarre friendship between a professed Arab nationalist and an Iranian Shiite fundamentalist might have had something to do with the fact that Assad came from Syria's sub-Shia Alawite minority, from his view it was primarily a strategic alliance against the detested rival Baathist regime in Iraq. Syria benefited from the supply of a regular quota of free Iranian oil and from the pro-Iranian sympathies among the Shiites of Lebanon. President Assad rejected all the repeated attempts by other Arab states to persuade him to change sides. The ideological cynicism of the Syrian–Iranian alliance was underlined when, in February 1982, the Syrian army ruthlessly repressed an armed rising in the city of Hama by the Muslim Brotherhood, whose aims were closely similar to those of Iran's Islamic Revolution.

While the fears of the Revolution among most Arab regimes were real enough, the danger that it could reach out to topple them

receded as the war progressed – even when Iran appeared to have
the advantage. Khomeini emphatically wished to appeal to all
Muslims, not only to the Shiite minority, and he scorned any
concept of nationalism within the Islamic *umma*. But he could not
prevent the war from widening the ancient Persian–Arab rivalry
or the Sunni–Shiite division. In the Arab Gulf states, any initial
popular enthusiasm for the Islamic Revolution was soon confined
to the Shiite minorities. This caused their Sunni rulers serious
concern, but increased their determination to stand firm, and the
bloodthirsty repression of all opposition in Iran also helped to
antagonize their Sunni subjects. In Iraq, with its Shiite majority,
territorial nationalism showed itself to be the stronger force. Just as
the Arab-speaking Iranians had refused to side with Iraq, the great
majority of Iraq Shiite Arabs remained loyal and showed no eagerness to be occupied and ruled by the Islamic Republic. It was Iraq's
Sunni Kurds who gave the regime serious trouble.

In countries more remote from the Gulf War – in Egypt, Sudan
and the Maghreb states – the Khomeini Revolution's defiance of
both West and East retained it some prestige among Muslim militants who had no love for the Iraqi regime. But the Ayatollah's
influence was symbolic. There was no question of accepting his
political leadership – the Muslim Brothers of Egypt and Sudan had
begun their own struggle long before the Iranian Revolution.

The murderous stalemate in the Gulf War continued from 1982
to 1987. 'The war of the cities', with rockets and shelling, was
pursued sporadically at heavy cost. The Iranians alternated human-
wave assaults with attacks on a smaller scale at varied points along
the frontier to wear down Iraqi morale, but this was higher now
that Iraqi troops were defending their own territory. In 1986 the
Iranians captured Iraq's Faw peninsula on the Gulf coast but failed
at heavy cost in an attempt to seize Basra. The focus of the war
moved to the waters of the Gulf, where Iraq's air superiority could
be used against Iran's vital oil exports but Iran's naval superiority
enabled it to blockade Iraqi supplies. The danger that the tanker
war might intensify and spread at last attracted the serious attention

of the superpowers. In 1987 the United States offered to reflag Kuwaiti tankers to provide protection (following a similar offer by the Soviet Union), and by mid-year the USA was in full-scale naval confrontation with Iran. On 20 July the UN Security Council unanimously passed Resolution 598 calling for an immediate end to all hostilities. Iraq accepted this but Iran refused, on the grounds that at the very least President Saddam's responsibility for the war should be internationally accepted.

In 1988 the war took a new and final turn. Between May and June the Iraqis recaptured Faw and drove the Iranians out of other key areas on the frontier. With the numbers of willing Iranian martyrs declining and economic collapse looming, the closest supporters of the infirm octogenarian Khomeini persuaded him that there was no alternative to accepting the UN cease-fire. He told his people that taking the decision 'was more deadly than taking poison'.

The cease-fire held, with the help of the UN observers, but it was still only an armed truce. UN-sponsored peace talks failed to achieve a peace agreement to settle the outstanding border disputes, or even an exchange of prisoners. The two regimes remained deadly enemies, although they had to accept that renewed war was impossible for some years. They began to rearm even as they set about reconstructing their ruined economies.

A triumphant President Hussein declared that Iraq had won the war – which in a sense it had, even if he had not achieved his original war aims of overthrowing the Islamic Republic. He had won by not losing, just as Khomeini had lost by not winning.

On 4 June 1989 Khomeini's long-expected death finally occurred. The succession passed smoothly in spite of an underlying struggle for power between those, including Khomeini's son Ahmed, who wished to pursue his uncompromising hostility towards the West and those who sought to normalize Iran's relations with the world as an essential means of restoring the economy, while insisting that the Ayatollah's legacy would remain unchanged.

It was the pragmatists who won. The Assembly of Experts swiftly appointed the mild-mannered former president Khameini as the new spiritual leader. Two months later the speaker of the Majlis, Ali Akbar Rafsanjani, a man of high political skill, succeeded in having himself elected president with greatly increased powers and promptly ousted the leaders of the hardline faction from the cabinet.

For the millions of Iranians who mourned Khomeini's death there was no one who could replace the man whom many of them had come to regard as God's embodiment on earth, even if anyone had wished to try. In the decade since the Revolution, hundreds of thousands had died and the economy had been ruined in a war which had ended in failure. Dissidence had been harshly repressed, and a large proportion of the skilled and educated had fled into exile. Yet the scowling figure of Khomeini, so deeply unattractive to most of the rest of the world, still represented to his intensely proud people a spirit of unyielding defiance after centuries of humiliation by stronger powers.

The question was, how much of Khomeini's legacy would survive? While clerical rule had been institutionalized and seemed likely to last for a time, Rafsanjani, with modest religious credentials, was essentially a secular figure. But he was not all-powerful – his hardline opponents had been bypassed but not subdued. He had to move cautiously towards calming and moderating the Islamic Republic's policies towards the rest of the world, in order to reconstruct the economy and encourage the urgently needed exiles to return.

Only one thing seemed certain: Iran's Islamic Revolution would not permanently change the face of the Middle East. This had proved beyond Khomeini's power, and it was certainly impossible for his successors. As the representative of militant Shiite Islam, Iran could count on the open allegiance of many Lebanese Shiites and the covert sympathy of Shiite minorities in the Arab Gulf states, but little more. With its fifty-five million people, and occupying a strategic position, it was still a major power in Middle Eastern terms and all states with interests in the region were therefore anxious to have dealings with Tehran. But its power to influence events outside its borders was no greater than in the time of the shah.

Iraq's World Challenge

The ambitions of President Saddam Hussein of Iraq, who had been the effective ruler of his country since 1968, were not exhausted by his eight-year struggle with his larger neighbour. Despite mountainous debts and an economy in desperate need of reconstruction he still maintained a huge military machine with nearly one million men under arms, and he poured vast sums into developing advanced weapons. During the summer of 1990 he threatened Kuwait because of its reluctance to allow Iraq secure access to the Gulf through its territory. He also blamed Kuwait for the fall in the price of oil by producing in excess of its OPEC quota — a fall which he claimed was losing Iraq a billion dollars a month in revenues. In late July he massed troops on Kuwait's border. But despite this and the failure of Saudi Arabia's efforts to mediate there were few — except the Iranians — who expected his next move. On 2 August he invaded and occupied the whole of Kuwait on the spurious assertion that there had been a pro-Iraqi uprising against Kuwait's Emir. The Emir and his ministers fled to Saudi Arabia where they set up a government-in-exile. A week later Saddam announced the annexation of Kuwait as Iraq's nineteenth province. He declared that the child had been restored to its mother, regardless of the fact that the Kuwaiti emirate had been born some two centuries before its supposed parent — the Iraqi state.

If Saddam had successfully taken the world by surprise, he had also miscalculated the extent of its opposition. The UN Security Council unanimously imposed mandatory sanctions against Iraq that, following a series of resolutions, became almost totally effective in blocking Iraq's foreign trade and freezing its foreign assets. The first major crisis of the post-Cold War era offered the extraordinary spectacle of a country of eighteen million people defying the two superpowers and most of the world. As Iraqi troops advanced to the Saudi Arabian border there arose the alarming prospect that Saddam would seize the Saudi oilfields which, in conjunction with those of Iraq and Kuwait, would make him master of more than half the world's oil reserves. The United States, which had regarded an Iraqi victory in the Gulf War as preferable to the triumph of Ayatollah Khomeini, now denounced Saddam Hussein as an international outlaw. President Bush immediately responded to King Fahd of Saudi Arabia's urgent invitation to send troops to defend the kingdom. Even after the initial threat had receded with the arrival of airborne forces, there was a continued build-up of naval, land and air forces totalling some six hundred thousand personnel, and carrying the most advanced weapons. The great majority were American but Britain and France sent substantial contingents and no less than fifty-four countries contributed either military forces or financial support. Of the greatest political importance to the United States was the addition, apart from the troops of Saudi Arabia and other Gulf states, of Arab forces from Egypt, Syria and Morocco, and others from Muslim Pakistan and Bangladesh. It was vital to demonstrate that this was not one more Western crusade against the Arabs and Islam.

In fact opinion among the Arabs was divided and confused on the issue. While the governments of the Arab League declared with varying emphasis that Iraq should withdraw from Kuwait, there were those, such as Jordan, Sudan, Libya and Algeria as well as the PLO, that showed some degree of sympathy with the Iraqi position. These governments gave priority to announcing the danger to the Arabs and Islam presented by the huge influx of infidel Western armies. King Hussein of Jordan and Yasir Arafat tried urgently to negotiate an 'Arab solution' to the crisis.

All Arab leaders had to take some account of public opinion, which often tended towards a simplistic view of Saddam Hussein as a twentieth-century Saladin who would defy the West and unite the Arabs. The great majority of Arabs who are poor felt little sympathy for the Gulf Arabs with their vast recently inherited wealth. Demonstrators in Jordan and the Israeli-occupied territories cheered Saddam as a hero while even some Islamic militants who had known him as a ruthless secular dictator felt some response to his appeal for *jihad* or Islamic holy war against the Western invaders.

President Saddam acted with some guile but also made gross miscalculations, which were partly due to his ignorance of the world and partly to his insulation from the advice and criticism of his colleagues, whom he had so intimidated. He shrewdly linked the Gulf crisis with the Palestinian cause by contrasting the West's instant reaction to his seizure of Kuwait with its failure to end Israel's occupation of Arab lands. He made some headway with his appeal to popular Arab and Islamic sentiment, although he would never overcome the suspicion and hatred of those who had direct experience of his ruthlessness, such as the hundreds of thousands of Egyptian *fellahin* who were forced to leave their livelihood in Iraq. Two weeks after the invasion he took the risk of offering peace to Iran and formally abandoning all the aims for which he had gone to war, in order to ensure Iran's neutrality. This enabled him to withdraw vital troops from the Iranian border and reinforce his Kuwait defences. The Iraqi people seemed to accept the necessity for this drastic action.

Saddam's efforts to win over opinion outside the Middle East were grossly misconceived. Outrage was caused by his detention of hundreds of foreigners as hostages, mostly Westerners caught in Kuwait or Iraq; some were used as human shields by being confined close to potential military targets. Bad feeling was not assuaged by the release of selected groups of women, children, the sick and aged in a charade of humanitarian gestures. As news trickled out of the Iraqi troops' pillage of Kuwait and atrocities committed against the remaining third of the Kuwaiti population that had not fled, there were calls in the West for Saddam to be tried as a war criminal and for Iraq to pay war reparations.

In spite of the overwhelming array of force deployed against Iraq, the United States and its allies were faced with an acute dilemma. Their prime objective was clear: to force Iraq to withdraw from Kuwait to enable the legitimate government to be restored. But from the outset it was clear that other decisions would be necessary. There was a question whether, even in the event of an Iraqi withdrawal, it would be reasonable to leave Saddam with his formidable military machine intact (including chemical weapons) and with the continuing capacity to threaten the Middle East with his power. It also had to be considered whether the destruction of this power would not drastically unbalance the region. A more immediate decision had to be made as to how long it would be possible to wait to see if the sanctions decreed by the UN would be enough to weaken Iraq and force its withdrawal, before using military force. There was a danger that, as the weeks stretched into months, the motley coalition of the international force opposing Iraq would break apart – especially if Iraq were to offer a compromise such as a partial withdrawal from Kuwait or propose that the Palestine problem should be solved simultaneously with that of the Gulf. But the unity of the international force might be even more strained if a lightning strike to destroy Iraq's air force and cut off its forces that were dug in behind formidable defences should fail in its objective and lead to a prolonged and costly campaign.

However, none of these immediate fears was realized. Saddam miscalculated the determination of his opponents and overestimated his own military power and ability to inflict on them unacceptable losses. When the US obtained UN Security Council authorization for the use of force if he failed to evacuate Kuwait by 15 January, he continued to prevaricate. He suddenly released all foreign 'guests' (i.e., hostages) but still gave no hint of leaving Kuwait. Shortly after the deadline the coalition launched a devastating air assault on Iraq and its forces in Kuwait. With its air force grounded or in refuge in Iran, Iraq was unable to respond except by firing Scud missiles against Saudi and Israeli targets. These caused some damage but failed in their chief objective of involving Israel in the war to split the West from its Arab allies.

The land attack launched after five weeks' bombing outflanked the 42 Iraqi divisions in the Kuwait field, and these were destroyed or immobilized. Before fleeing, the Iraqis sabotaged 90 per cent of Kuwait's oil wells in revenge, seriously damaging the Gulf's ecology. Saddam Hussein seemed doomed by his catastrophic defeat. Iraq's Kurds in the north and Shiites in the south rose in rebellion, seizing control of many towns. But they lacked strategy and heavy weapons, and with the remaining half of his armed forces Saddam brutally suppressed the uprisings. Hundreds of thousands of Kurds and Shiites fled for refuge to the Turkish and Iranian mountain borders.

Iraq was forced to agree to heavy and stringent peace terms, which included elimination of all its potential for weapons of mass destruction and payment of heavy reparations. The US and Britain insisted on Saddam Hussein's departure before the removal of UN sanctions and Iraq's resumption of normal relations with the world. But the motley Iraqi opposition groups failed to remove Saddam and no internal coup succeeded; Western powers were not prepared to occupy Baghdad. Promising to liberalize his regime, a weakened but still inadequately chastened Saddam seemed able to survive for a time the consequences of his colossal errors.

13. Pax Americana

The devastation of Iraq was proof – if proof were needed – that the collapse of the Soviet Union had left the United States as the unassailable global power. The struggle for the region had lasted about forty years – or a similar period to the Anglo-French interregnum which preceded it. But with the end of the East–West conflict, those Middle East leaders long seen as Russian clients rushed to realign with Washington, before they succumbed to the fate of their fellow-dictators in Eastern Europe. Those that refused to submit to the American yoke – Libya, Iraq and Iran – were punished with UN or US sanctions. The Soviet satellite in South Yemen, the People's Democratic Republic of Yemen, was wiped from the map altogether, and swallowed by its North Yemen neighbour.

The vacuum left by the collapse of the Soviet Union impelled Washington to a new activism in the region. For the next decade, the key official decisions affecting the Middle East would be taken either in Western capitals or at the UN headquarters in New York. In his victory address to Congress in March 1991, President George Bush unveiled a four-point plan to bring his new world order to the Middle East. The United States, he said, would strengthen its military ties to the Gulf, rid Iraq of its weapons of mass destruction, end the Arab–Israeli conflict on the basis of land for peace, and embark on a drive for 'economic freedom' and 'human rights'.

Buttressing what amounted to a programme for reformatting the region was the most powerful show of foreign armoury the Middle East had seen since the height of the British Empire. Bush had claimed that Washington's mobilization of half a million troops to the Gulf 'did not mean stationing US ground forces in the Arabian Peninsula' for the long term, but there was no rush to decamp. One decade after the Gulf War, the US still kept 25,000 troops in the region, 10,000 of them based in Saudi Arabia and Kuwait. Stashes of hardware were stockpiled in other Gulf emirates ready to equip an army ten times the size. In addition, the Pentagon positioned an armada in the Persian Gulf comprising two aircraft carrier groups armed with 15 warships and 350 fighter-jets. Several thousand more US troops and a squadron of US fighter planes were stationed in south-eastern Turkey at Incirlik Base, which for the next decade was to be one of the most strategically important footholds for the US in the Middle East. Incirlik lay in striking distance not only of Iran and Syria, but also the oil- and gas-rich former Soviet republics. In addition, Washington oversaw the supply of billions of dollars in military aid and arms to Israel, Egypt, Turkey and the Gulf states. In short, the United States had the Middle East encircled.

Initially, the prospects for Pax Americana looked good. In the absence of superpower rivalry, regional conflicts were widely predicted to crumble away. North Africa's Cold War rivals, Algeria and Morocco, embarked on a United Nations-administered peace process to end a twenty-five year conflict over control of the former Spanish colony of Western Sahara (with the expectation that Morocco's sandwall dividing the territory would wither as fast as the Berlin Wall). Arab and Israeli leaders took their seats round a negotiating table in Madrid. And across the Middle East, cafés bubbled with talk of the onward march of democracy, state accountability and human rights. But Middle Easterners quickly discovered that the readjustment from a bipolar to a unipolar world would not inaugurate the promised utopia. And from 1995 onwards, the history of the Middle East is of a clear pattern of uncoordinated but manifest dissent at US hegemony – from defiance in Iraq and resistance in Palestine, to the wildfire spread of militant Islam across the Sunni world.

Humbling Iraq

To the evident relief of Iraq's neighbours, the United States immediately set about neutering the Arab world's most powerful military.

Before the Gulf War, Saddam Hussein had presided over a million-man army and an arsenal that outstripped Egypt and Turkey. Some 30,000 Iraqi soldiers were killed in the 1991 allied air bombardment. Tens of thousands more were slain as the Iraqi army retreated on the road back to Basra. The bulk of the country's oil infrastructure, its refineries and pipelines, was pulverized by air strikes. Iraqi oil production plummeted from a high of over 5 million barrels a day prior to its war with Iran in 1980 to a few tens of thousand barrels after its retreat from Kuwait. The Arab Monetary Fund put the damage caused by the US-led bombing at $190 billion.

What war left unfinished, the armistice was designed to complete. One month after Iraq's surrender, the UN Security Council passed Resolution 687 assigning a UN Special Commission (UNSCOM) to search out and destroy Iraq's weapons of mass destruction and stipulating that sanctions should not be lifted until its mission had been completed. Fear of the Iraqi weapons programme was not without foundation – Iraq had repeatedly dropped chemical bombs on both its Kurdish rebels and Iranian troops. But the effects of sanctions on a country dependent on oil revenues to buy food were appalling. All imports, including food, were subject to a blockade by land and sea, as were pesticides and the fertilizer Iraq required to grow its own basics. Within months, inflation in Iraq had reached 2,000 per cent and average earnings had collapsed to a tenth of their pre-war level, roughly equivalent to the wages of Bangladesh. A teacher's monthly salary was barely enough to buy a kilo of meat. The UN reported that 'the majority of the population live on a diet of semi-starvation'. Because of a ban on chlorine, sewage was discharged untreated into the Euphrates. Cholera and typhoid, diseases Iraq had stamped out in the 1970s, returned.

At first, the pressure proved effective. The day UNSCOM began work, Baghdad admitted to a stockpile of over 1,000 tons of liquid nerve gas, and 11,000 chemical warheads. Anticipating UNSCOM's mission would be over in a matter of months, Iraq stood aside as the weapons inspectors uncovered the existence of an advanced nuclear programme replete with several kilograms of highly enriched uranium. One year into its work, UNSCOM declared it had destroyed all Iraq's medium- and long-range missiles (most of them supplied by Europe), and plentiful stocks of mustard gas. The problem was that the more UNSCOM's scientists exposed, the more questions their revelations begged: indications of a biological weapons programme, for instance, posed the possibility that Iraqi medical laboratories were doubling as plants to nurture germ warfare. And as the investigations became protracted, Iraq used armed protestors to block UNSCOM's work: on occasion Iraqi soldiers fired over their heads. Sometimes the shots were merely intended as delaying tactics to give Iraqi officials enough time to scurry documents away. Other times, they forced the UN's biologists and chemists to scarper altogether.

Several times it seemed that UNSCOM inspectors were on the verge of declaring their mission accomplished. After four years, UNSCOM informed the UN Security Council that Iraq's nuclear and chemical arsenal had been destroyed, but that the elimination of its biological weapons programme remained incomplete. Lured by the prospect of a speedy lifting of sanctions, Iraq confessed to concealing production of nearly half a tonne of anthrax and 1.7 tons of VX nerve gas, a poison ten times more potent than the sarin it had unleashed against Iranian troops. Baghdad claimed all its stockpiles of biological weapons had been destroyed in the Gulf War; UNSCOM demanded proof. The UN agency's doubts proved well-founded when in August 1995 Saddam Hussein's son-in-law defected to Jordan armed with crate-loads of military documents, which he promptly delivered to his UNSCOM and CIA interrogators. Hussein Kamil Hassan had variously served as Iraqi minister of oil, defence, arms procurement, and commander of the presidential guard, but most importantly, he was widely believed to be the architect of Iraq's biological weapons programme. He further testified that since his Gulf War defeat, Saddam Hussein had assigned his second son, Qusay, to conceal his weapons of mass destruction.

Hussein Kamil's defection was motivated less by a belated pang of conscience, than by a family feud. His standing as Saddam Hussein's most decorated relative had spurred the Iraqi leader's jealous eldest son, Uday, to fits of pique – following the Mamluke custom of eliminating family rivals he had shot his uncle, the minister of the interior, earlier that summer. Faced with the implosion of the presidential family (Hussein Kamil had also absconded with Saddam Hussein's two daughters), the Iraqi leader admitted that at the time of the Gulf War Iraq had twenty-five warheads primed with biological weapons with a range of 360 miles, and had embarked on a fast-track programme to manufacture a nuclear bomb within a year.

Despite the setbacks, five years after the Gulf War Saddam Hussein's grip on Iraq seemed firmer than ever. Immediately after the Gulf War, he had thwarted simultaneous popular uprisings by Shiites in southern Iraq and Kurds in the north after President Bush called on Iraqis 'to take matters into their own hands'. Shiites, who comprised a majority of Iraq's population, rose up with all the pent-up fury of decades of Sunni subjugation and seized control of the Shiite holy cities of Karbala and Najaf, butchering their Baath party officials in the process. As testimony to their Iranian sympathies, if not outright support, the rebels tore down murals of Saddam Hussein and pinned posters of the late Ayatollah Khomeini in their place. Meanwhile, Kurdish militiamen, or *peshmergas* (literally, 'those who face death') swept in an arc from the north towards Baghdad. Together the rebels controlled fourteen of Iraq's eighteen provinces. Sandwiched in central Iraq between Kurds and Shiites, Saddam Hussein sent his Republican Guard in helicopter gun-ships to re-establish central control.

That Saddam Hussein was defending his own rule was not surprising. That the Kurds and Shiites were left to his mercy after President Bush had called on them to revolt was. From the first the United States had declared that 'regime change' would be its price for the lifting of sanctions. But it soon became apparent that Washington was less than ready to see the immediate fall of its foe. State Department strategists in Washington warned that without the 'iron fist' of Saddam Hussein, Iraq would fragment into three: a Kurdish north, a Sunni middle and a Shiite south. Added to such concerns was pressure from Washington's two regional allies, Turkey and Saudi Arabia, chary of the United States' apparent penchant for dismemberment of Soviet satellites in the aftermath of the Cold War (in the USSR, Yugoslavia and Ethiopia). Ankara, already engaged in a guerrilla war with its own Kurdish rebels, the PKK, feared the emergence of the nucleus of a Greater Kurdistan on its southern flank. The prospect of democracy – which would hand power to a pro-Iranian Shiite majority – was even less appealing to the staunchly Sunni Saudis, whose own marginalized Shiite population bordered Iraq. Asked what he thought of the uprising, the US National Security Advisor, Brent Snowcroft, was unambiguous. 'We would have preferred a coup,' he said.

Accordingly, the US watched while Saddam Hussein counter-attacked. Some US troops used force to deny the rebels access to the arms depots in southern Iraq. Some 100,000 Iraqis died in Saddam Hussein's onslaught. Seventy thousand Shiites took refuge in Iran and 1.5 million Kurds – a full half of the Kurdish population – fled into the snow-capped mountains on the borders.

In a bid to stem the outcry over the humanitarian tragedy, the UN Security Council approved Resolution 688, sanctioning a 16,000-man US-led force to carve out a Kurdish – though pointedly not a Shiite – safe haven. The US further demanded Iraq withdraw its troops from its Turkish border, and Saddam Hussein obliged by vacating three provinces, including the northern cities of Irbil and Suleimaniya. Without seeking UN authorization, the United States, Britain and France also declared a ban on Iraqi aircraft flying north of the 36th parallel. Shielded by the air umbrella, Kurds returned to re-establish a Kurdish autonomous zone and rebuild towns razed by Saddam Hussein's military onslaughts over the previous two decades. Shiites had to endure a further year – and another cull of their clergy (reduced from 10,000 in 1979 to a few hundred by 1993) – before the Western powers declared a second air-exclusion zone in the south. Iraqis were not alone in suspecting that while the

justification for the no-fly zones was humanitarian, their purpose
was distinctly strategic: to box Saddam Hussein into the provinces
surrounding Baghdad. As its name suggests, Operation Southern
Watch offered Saudi Arabia and Kuwait a protective shield, while
to the north Operation Provide Comfort gave the CIA and Iraqi
opposition groups a northern safe haven from which to scheme
against Saddam Hussein.

Washington chose Ahmed Chalabi, a rotund London-based Shiite
businessman convicted in Jordan of embezzlement, to lead the Iraqi
opposition. In June 1992 Chalabi, under CIA tutelage, brought
twenty opposition groups to Vienna to launch the Iraqi National
Congress, or INC, which, modelled on the PLO, declared itself
the sole legitimate representative of the Iraqi opposition. It was a
motley, quarrelsome crew of intellectuals, Kurds and Shiites, but
its most powerful component was the Iraqi National Accord, a
movement embracing up to a thousand dissident army officers,
including some Sunnis from Saddam Hussein's home province of
Tikrit. The INC's only glue was a common desire to topple Saddam
Hussein, but in Vienna its constituent parts agreed on a charter to
form a liberation army to fight for democracy. The INC made a
base in Salahuddin, a safe-haven town, and began broadcasting anti-
Saddam Hussein propaganda across Iraq. At its height, its
Salahuddin headquarters had a staff of some 5,000 Iraqis and was a
magnet for deserters from the Iraqi army. The United States, in the
words of Saddam Hussein's highly critical biographer, Said Aburish,
seemed intent 'on turning the clock back and acting as arbiters of
the fate of Iraq in the manner of the victorious powers in 1917'.

The defection of Hussein Kamil to Jordan could have landed
American officials with just the military alternative to Saddam
Hussein they seemed to be looking for. But Kurds and Shiites were
loath to pay homage to a man remembered for his brutal suppression
of the 1991 rebellion. Distrusted by his foreign patrons and fellow-
Iraqis alike, a dejected Hussein Kamil incredibly fell for his
father-in-law's offer of amnesty, and in February 1996 donned military fatigues and drove back to Baghdad. Three days later he was

dead, in what Iraqi TV described as a family vendetta. 'We have cut off the treacherous branch from our noble family tree,' said his uncle General al-Majid beside footage of his bloodstained corpse.

As Saddam Hussein's family recovered its unity, loyalty in the opposition ranks tottered. Their momentum was sapped by the failure of a series of clumsy coup attempts and a wave of inner-city bombings that backfired. An INC attempt in 1995 to co-ordinate an offensive while British and American jets patrolled the no-fly zones ended in failure with hundreds of deaths, and one of many army purges. In an attempt to re-energize the rebel force, the US Congress in 1998 passed the Iraq Liberation Act, injecting almost $100 million dollars into military training. But instead of fighting Saddam Hussein, the opposition increasingly fought itself. Kurdish elections in the safe haven exacerbated the rivalry between the land-owning Kurdish Democratic Party (KDP) led by Masud Barzani and its rival, the Patriotic Union of Kurdistan (PUK), a self-styled left-wing peasant-based movement under Jalal Talabani. Together, the two leaders could have mustered 40,000 troops, and constituted the main armed threat to Saddam Hussein. But rival external backers increasingly wedged them apart. Iran armed the PUK while Iraq and Turkey supplied the KDP both with weapons and smuggling dues from the supply of cheap Iraqi fuel trucked by road to Turkey. Pitched battles erupted in the late spring of 1994, igniting a Kurdish internecine war that was to rage for the next four years. Only in September 1998 did the US finally broker a truce.

But by then, Saddam Hussein had reaped the benefits of his bickering foes. When the PUK routed the KDP, Barzani solicited the help of an eager Baghdad. In mid-1996 400 Iraqi tanks forged into the safe haven and within thirty-six hours had replaced the PUK flag over the Kurdish parliament in Irbil with the two emblems of the KDP and the tricolour of Iraq. Horrified at the advance, the CIA and INC fled their nearby base at Salahuddin and evacuated their 5,000 agents, leaving American plans for a bridgehead from which to topple Saddam Hussein in tatters. In what smacked of a parting shot, President Bill Clinton lobbed cruise missiles on southern Iraq — a revealing indication of where Washington's concerns really lay — and raised the southern no-fly zone to the perimeter of Baghdad. Iraqi tanks withdrew, but Saddam Hussein had proved that despite his Gulf War defeat, he remained a formidable military power commanding 380,000 men. International tears for the Kurds proved largely of the crocodile kind. As long as the Kurds had proved useful, the US had trumpeted their rights in Iraq. But it had long dismissed the Kurdish movement in Turkey, the PKK, as terrorists even though it was resisting a Turkish policy of cultural annihilation far more pervasive than that of Baghdad. In pursuit of the PKK, Ankara's troops and F-16 bombers invaded the safe haven in May 1997 with barely a whisper of criticism from Washington. US military aid continued to flow to Ankara, as did its supply of arms used in the killing of an estimated 23,000 people in Turkey's war with the Kurds.

With the Iraqi opposition an apparent spent force, Washington relied on sanctions and the United Nations to maintain the pressure. The UN Sanctions Committee in New York, which controlled all Iraq's imports and exports, banned the entry of textbooks, journals, newspapers and business mail in what the head of the UN aid agency in Baghdad, Hans von Sponeck, called a policy of 'intellectual genocide'. Even pencils were prohibited from what had been one of the most literate societies in the Arab world on the grounds that the graphite might be used for nuclear reactors. The food ban was similarly punitive. A widely circulated UN survey of Greater Baghdad claimed that over a quarter of children under five were 'severely malnourished' — a figure higher than in most African states. By 1997 some 7,000 children were dying each month of hunger and disease. The death toll was on a par with some of the worst post-war atrocities: according to UN estimates, sanctions cost the lives of over one million Iraqis.

If Western powers had intended that sanctions would feed popular unrest, they were disappointed. In fact, sanctions merely nourished Saddam Hussein's grip on Iraq. Far from breaking its backbone, the pauperization of Iraq aroused a revival of national consciousness and a collective determination to survive. Almost all the 134 bridges destroyed in the Gulf War bombing were restored within three years. Baghdad's soaring television tower, flattened in a cruise missile attack, resurfaced twelve metres taller than the original, crowned with a restaurant called Babil. Sanctions did spur a million Iraqis into exile, and in a remarkable reversal of urbanization, hundreds of thousands abandoned the cities for the land in a drive for food self-sufficiency. But the byproduct was that the middle class, which formed the rump of civil discontent, was more dispersed, impoverished and powerless than ever. Furthermore, the rationing of staples gave the Iraqi leader the ultimate tool of power: control over his people's bellies.

The result was that despite the Gulf War rout, Saddam Hussein's personality cult grew ever more Orwellian. Even the inner sancta of Shiite shrines bore his image, carefully refashioned from secular Baathist to religious martyr. And while a shortage of paper forced civil servants to ravage the files to reuse the blank side of old documents, the state printing press went into overdrive, churning out a nineteen-volume biography of Saddam Hussein. At the same time, in 1996 he went some way to alleviating his people's hunger by finally acceding to a UN proposal to allow Iraq to sell its oil through a UN-controlled bank account in Paris. Under the 'oil-for-food' deal, the UN became the effective proprietor of Iraqi oil and the spender of its revenues. Half the proceeds went on the Kurds, reparations for Kuwait and UN expenses, and the remainder on food and medicine for Iraq. After nearly five years of refusing to sign a deal that 'violated its sovereignty', Iraq buckled and accepted the terms. It took a further year for their food to arrive, but Baghdadis danced in the streets.

For Iraq, weapons inspections amounted to a further intrusion of sovereignty. Just when UNSCOM's chief, the Swedish diplomat Rolf Ekeus, had agreed a formula to complete its mission, the UN Security Council replaced him with a bullish and confrontational Australian, Richard Butler. He began his tenure by demanding no-notice inspections of the headquarters of Iraqi Special Security and the presidential palaces. Initially Iraq responded by submitting an 800-page document on its biological weapons programme, and then when its gesture of goodwill was spurned, declared 100 sites, including eight presidential palaces, off bounds to UNSCOM. After the UN Security Council demanded unconditional access to any and all Iraqi sites, Baghdad upped the ante, refusing to countenance further inspections until the UN set a deadline for lifting sanctions. In protest, in November 1997 Butler ostentatiously withdrew his staff from Iraq.

Shuttle diplomacy by the UN secretary-general, Kofi Annan, postponed the threat of American bombing, and UNSCOM returned to Iraq. But the UN agency had lost all pretence of neutrality and increasingly resembled an instrument of Western intelligence gathering. Under UN resolutions, American unmanned U-2 spy planes flew over Iraq on behalf of UNSCOM. Inspection teams, packed with American personnel, pried inside the country's most sensitive military positions. UNSCOM's cameras and sensors monitored 300 sites. Americans manned key positions in the UNSCOM hierarchy, most notably the deputy chairman Charles Duelfer and the chief weapons inspector Scott Ritter, an aggressive former US intelligence officer who on his own admission repeatedly liaised with Israeli intelligence. Israel, as well as the US, was party to UNSCOM's U-2 imagery, and provided surveillance equipment to tap communications from the office of the presidential secretary. Armed with the findings, President Clinton was able to lob cruise missiles with increasing accuracy, and avoid the embarrassment of the sort of 'collateral damage' that in earlier raids had blown up Baghdad's al-Rashid Hotel, the favoured lodging of visiting journalists. In an interview five years after stepping down as UNSCOM chief, Rolf Ekeus admitted that attempts were made to provoke crises that could 'form the basis for direct military action'.

It was little surprise then that Annan's intervention had merely delayed not resolved Iraq's standoff with UNSCOM. Amid ever more rancorous divisions among the five permanent members of the UN Security Council (the Anglo-Saxon couple, the United

States and Britain, pitted against the trio of China, Russia and France), Iraq again ordered UNSCOM out. In December 1998, without waiting for UN approval, President Clinton responded with a seventy-hour bombardment of Iraq named 'Operation Desert Fox' after a Nazi general. In the eyes of the American media, the timing had less to do with Iraq than with Clinton's cynical attempt to deflect attention from the impeachment debate in the US Congress over his affair with a White House intern, Monica Lewinsky. The raid failed either to prevent the debate or to force Iraq to allow back the inspectors. Bombings intensified twenty-fold over the following year, with the US and Britain flying two-thirds as many missions as the far more public NATO raids on Milosevic's former Yugoslavia. In December 1999, the UN Security Council voted to replace UNSCOM with a new body, UNMOVIC, the Monitoring, Verification and Inspection Commission. But despite a mandate sanctioning the use of force to implement its terms, come mid-2002 UNMOVIC had still not embarked for Iraq.

What US policy did achieve was a marked rise in Arab antipathy towards Washington. Asked on American television whether the starvation of 500,000 people was justified, US Secretary of State Madeleine Albright declared it was 'worth it'. The response evoked an outpouring of anger at the longest siege in modern history. To assuage popular sentiment, Saudi Arabia's new *de facto* leader, Crown Prince Abdullah, reopened its Iraqi border after a decade of closure and Egypt reappointed an ambassador to Baghdad. 'Iraq will soon be integrated into the Arab fold,' said President Hosni Mubarak. 'It is only a matter of time.' Following Russia's lead, one former Arab foe after another flouted the air embargo, dispatching planes to the newly opened Saddam International Airport, without notifying the UN Sanctions Committee. Syrian planes flew from Damascus to Baghdad for the first time in twenty years. So too did an Iranian airliner, bringing the Iranian foreign minister, Kamal Kharrazi, the highest-ranking Iranian official to visit Baghdad since the Iranian Revolution.

Iraq's escape from isolation was not quite complete. Saudi Arabia and Kuwait still provided US planes a base from which to bomb Iraq. But by the millennium's end, Iraq's improved regional relations had pushed the level of smuggling through Turkey, Syria and Iran up to 800,000 barrels of oil per day in revenue beyond UN control. With France and Russia disguising their own economic interests in moral indignation, the UN Security Council more than doubled Iraq's oil sales allowance back to its pre-Gulf War OPEQ quota of 3 million barrels a day. To boost production, it also allowed Iraq to spend $500 million repairing its wells.

Even the United States appeared resigned to Iraq's oil sector revival. Rapid growth in the global economy was pushing demand for oil and prices higher, and Washington was hunting for new sources of oil. Located atop known reserves of 100 billion barrels of oil, the second largest reserves in the world, Iraq made a tempting object of investment. Several of the companies engaged in multi-million contracts to rebuild the oilfields were American subsidiaries. And by 2001, Iraq had emerged as the fastest-growing supplier of American oil. The Clinton administration, which in its first term had derided the Iraqi regime as irredeemable, had by its close become a discreet business partner.

In drawing up a balance sheet ten years on from the Gulf War, Baghdad had much to celebrate. By the end of 1999, it had secured Security Council approval for a surge in oil exports, healed some of its shattered ties with its neighbours, including Kuwait, defeated two rebellions, and rid the country of its UNSCOM surveillance. Saddam Hussein's weapons programme had been seriously depleted, but many of the scientists responsible remained in their labs, and his conventional forces, on paper at least, remained the largest in the Arab world. Above all, sanctions had failed to unseat the regime. Saddam Hussein had challenged the world's only superpower and survived. By 2001, he even found the time to write a novel, *Zabibah and the King*, in which the king, representing Saddam, falls in love with a poor, married woman, symbolizing Iraq, and defends her from the other kings who become jealous and plot against him.

But Saddam's defence of his woman had come at a terrible price.

Iraq was crisscrossed with air-exclusion zones extending as far as Baghdad, and subject to regular bombing and sanctions. Nor had Saddam Hussein reckoned on the restoration of America's Gulf War cabinet. In December 2000, the United States returned its Gulf War leaders to power, with the election of George W. Bush, the son of Saddam Hussein's nemesis. Dick Cheney, the Gulf War defence secretary, became vice-president, and the 1991 chief-of-staff, General Colin Powell, secretary of state. Denouncing the Clinton years as the age of appeasement, the Bush administration returned to the unfinished business of the 1991 Gulf War and vowed to unseat the Iraqi leader by force.

Umpiring the Arab–Israeli Conflict

America's enforcement of UN resolutions on Iraq set the standard by which the Arab world judged international treatment of the region's other leading manufacturer of weapons of mass destruction and occupier of Arab land, Israel. Washington's round-the-clock air cover for Iraq's rebellious Kurds was contrasted with its reluctance to provide international peacekeepers to protect the Palestinians. And its readiness to use force to implement UN Security Council resolutions on Iraq was measured against its indulgence of Israel's continued occupation. Saddam Hussein himself had first made the link between Iraq and Israel a few days after his invasion of Kuwait when he offered to withdraw if Israel withdrew from the occupied territories, and Syria pulled out of Lebanon. The Bush administration rejected the proposal, but the secretary of state, James Baker, did recognize that come the end of the Gulf War, Arab allied support for ending one occupation might require US support for ending another.

In US eyes, the Gulf War created new possibilities. For the first time, Israel and Syria were publicly on the same side in a conflict; peace negotiations could take place unencumbered by Soviet bloc interests and power-games of superpower rivalry; and the Gulf War had shown that Arab states, not Israel, could defend US vital interests.

Six months after the Gulf War, Baker announced the staging of a Middle East peace conference in Madrid, using language markedly less sentimental than any of his predecessors. Negotiations, he said, would be based 'on total withdrawal from territory in exchange for peaceful relations'. Anxious to build on their nascent alliance with the world's sole superpower, Syria and Lebanon readily accepted. So, too, did the Jordanians and the Palestinians, both eager for an opportunity to return to favour with Washington after their perceived flirtation with Saddam Hussein during Iraq's 1990 invasion of Kuwait, even though the conference terms stipulated the exclusion of the PLO. Only Yitzhak Shamir, Israel's truculent prime minister, differed. In an attempt to scupper the talks, he drafted into his cabinet Rehavam Zeevi, a hardline Israeli general who advocated the forced deportation of Palestinians, and unveiled a programme to double the Jewish settler population in the West Bank and Gaza. President Bush responded by threatening to withhold loan guarantees vital for Israel to absorb a flood of Soviet Jews. Shamir buckled. On 30 October 1991, fourteen years after President Carter had first floated the idea of a Middle Eastern Versailles, Israel sat down to negotiate an end to its occupation of Syrian, Lebanese, Jordanian and Palestinian land.

The opening was hardly auspicious. The Syrian foreign minister, Farouq al-Shara, reminded delegates Israel was led by a terrorist once wanted in Britain for killing Count Bernadotte, the UN mediator to Palestine in the 1940s. 'This man,' said Shara, holding aloft a poster of the young Shamir, 'killed peace mediators.' Shamir directed the same charges at the Palestinian delegation, unlikely suspects given that its team was comprised of medics and academics. Shamir made it clear he was negotiating for negotiation's sake to buy time for more settlement building. 'I would have carried on autonomy talks for ten years,' he later admitted with remarkable presience, 'and meanwhile we would have half a million people in Judea and Samaria [the West Bank].'

If Shamir believed that time was on Israel's side through its continued West Bank colonization, his left-wing opponents were convinced the demographic clock was ticking against them. The collapse of the Soviet Union had resulted in a mass influx of Russian Jews, but even so the Jewish state stood to lose its Jewish majority if it held on to what Shamir called 'Greater Israel'. According to the widely circulated figures of an Israeli academic, Arnon Soffer, by 2002 Jews were already a minority in mandatary Palestine. By 2020, he estimated the combined Arab and Israeli population would have increased from 10 million to 15.5 million, of which Jews would comprise 40 per cent.

Faced with such predictions, the mood among the Israeli public oscillated between keeping a Jewish majority and keeping occupied land. In the run-up to the June 1992 elections, Labour Party leader Yitzhak Rabin promised to conclude an agreement on Palestinian self-government within a year, and freeze settlement building. Remarkably it was an election promise he nearly kept. Handsomely voted into office, the laconic former chief-of-staff spent the next three years negotiating the handover of the occupied territories he had conquered in 1967. To clear Palestinian decks of opponents he expelled over 400 Hamas activists to Lebanon, ended the thirty-year ban on contact with the PLO and entered into secret negotiations with Arafat's advisers who had spent the previous eighteen months in Tunis barred from the negotiating table. Arafat's authority had reached its nadir. He was isolated internationally for his perceived Gulf War support for Baghdad and internally by a grassroots leadership in the occupied territories which had waged the *intifada* and now basked in the spotlight of the negotiations. Aware that he was struggling for his political survival, Rabin calculated that Arafat might offer the best terms for peace for the minimum territorial price. In January 1993, two Israeli academics and Ahmed Qurei, the PLO treasurer better known as Abu Ala, began the first of fourteen rounds of secret talks in Oslo. On 13 September 1993, in one of the most abiding images of the twentieth century, President Clinton gathered the Middle East's leaders on the White House lawn and like a mother-hen stretched out his arms over Rabin and Arafat. (The US judged it propitious to ignore Norway's fundamental role: henceforth the US would make sure that subsequent agreements would be named after American locations, not European cities, and that they – not Europeans – would be effective intermediaries.)

The Oslo Accords were less a treaty than a timetable, beginning with a pull-out from Gaza city and Jericho within four months and leading at the end of a five-year interim period (May 1998) to Israel's withdrawal from all the West Bank and the Gaza Strip, excepting 'specified military locations', settlements and Jerusalem. For Rabin, the main advantage of Arafat's deal over that offered by the formal Palestinian delegation was that the most intractable issues of sovereignty over Jerusalem, settlements, water and refugees were deferred for five years without any Israeli commitment to compromise; that Israel gained formal Palestinian recognition of its sovereignty over three-quarters of mandatary Palestine, without any Israeli recognition of Palestine's right to a state; and that no sanction was written into the deal to prevent Israel from exploiting the clear asymmetry in the political, economic and military strength of the two sides.

That said, for all its failings, the Declaration of Principles on Interim Self-Government agreed in Oslo marked a seismic shift in Arab–Israeli relations and heralded the mutual recognition of two rival nationalisms that for a century had underpinned the Middle East conflict. In July 1994, Yasir Arafat was greeted back in Gaza with a hero's welcome after twenty-seven years in exile, and shortly after was elected president of the Palestinian Authority. Over the following six years, his administration received $3.5 billion in donor aid, took full or partial control of 40 per cent of the West Bank and full control of 70 per cent of the Gaza Strip, and acquired many of the trappings of independence, including uniformed police. In the process, Israel, too, look set to mature from its 45-year existence as a paranoid *shtetl* into a diverse, economically prosperous state. Internally, Israel's leaders advocated greater equality for non-Jews and investment for the country's marginalized Arab towns. The appointment of Israel's first Arab ambassador triggered a debate about the propriety of a national anthem which celebrated Jewish yearning for the East when a quarter of its 7 million people were not Jews. The Zeitgeist was characterized in the maturing of Rabin from a sullen general to a convinced apostle of Palestinian peace. In his last Knesset speech he made an admission which for a stalwart Zionist amounted to heresy: 'We did not come to an empty country.'

From the first, Oslo had its detractors. Livid at the Palestinian decision to abandon the principle of a comprehensive peace, Syria's Hafez al-Assad warned Arafat to take more care of his personal safety. Jordan's King Hussein, whose pre-1967 realm had included the West Bank, read the Oslo Accords as the last nail in the coffin of his dream to again be King of Jerusalem. He joined Assad in champing at Arafat's betrayal. But neither was entirely ingenuous. Jordan had privately agreed the terms of its treaty with Israel by October 1992. And before Oslo, Hafez al-Assad, bereft of Soviet backing, had begun his long-distance chess game with Rabin, with the self-effacing US secretary of state, Warren Christopher, relaying the moves. Syria demanded full withdrawal, Israel full peace including open borders and an exchange of ambassadors. The shuttle diplomacy continued throughout 1994, and by the end of the year, Syria's chief-of-staff, Hikmat Shihabi, was holding talks with his Israeli counterpart, Ehud Barak, in Washington. Not for the last time, Syria felt insulted at Barak's arrogant approach. But the talks continued, resulting in a draft agreement on security arrangements intended to take effect following Israeli withdrawal. Syria began preparing its public for what it called the strategic option of peace.

Tentative moves towards normalization between Israel and Arab states followed fast on the heels of agreements with the Palestinians. On his return from his reluctant White House handshake with Arafat, Rabin stopped over in Rabat to be publicly congratulated by King Hassan II of Morocco. And thereafter, with the exception of Libya and Iraq, all Arab states joined in the peace process, with even Hassan al-Turabi, the militant leader of the Sudanese Muslim Brotherhood, appealing to his Palestinian counterpart, Hamas, not to reject the Oslo Accords. President Clinton presided over another public signing ceremony at the White House between King Hussein and Rabin in June 1994, followed four months later with peace treaty festivities in the Arava desert on the Jordanian–Israeli border culminating in a release of balloons. Plans were announced for a joint Red–Dead Sea canal, integrated electricity grids and direct telephone links – all economic symbols of a warm peace that Israel had failed to secure from Egypt. Jordan was rewarded by having its US debts cancelled and, to Arafat's exasperation, by a formal Israeli commitment to respect Jordan's special role in the Muslim shrines of Jerusalem. Temporarily seduced by talk of peace dividends, the Arab League debated lifting the economic boycott. Qatar offered to supply gas to Israel, and joined Morocco, Tunisia and Oman in opening liaison bureaux in Tel Aviv. Rabin's old rival and foreign minister, Shimon Peres, peddled a romantic vision of a future Middle East common market, stretching from Marrakech to Muscat, modelled on the European Union. The United States offered backing, rallying Arab leaders and businessmen to a series of economic summits, of which the first in 1994 in the Moroccan city of Casablanca was to be the most elaborate. There was also a military component. Jordan agreed not to allow a third country to deploy forces in Jordan that could threaten Israel. And in February 1996, Turkey opened its airspace to the Israeli air force, in the process wedging Syria in a Turk–Israeli sandwich and ceding Israeli bombers a flight path to both Iran and Iraq.

By 1995, the United States had much cause for satisfaction at the stability of its post-Gulf War hegemony. Washington's policy of dual containment had successfully isolated Iran and Iraq in the region, just as it was integrating Israel into the fold. The family of Saddam Hussein seemed set to self-destruct, with the defection of his son-in-law, Hussein Kamil. And Israel had begun its withdrawal from the occupied territories. But from this high point in mid-1995, three events were about to rapidly upset the region's Pax Americana: the elimination of Hussein Kamil, noted above; the publication of a *fatwa* by Usama bin Laden; and three bullets fired by an Israeli zealot.

Israel's Missed Opportunity for Peace

In late 1995 an Israeli law graduate from Bar Ilan religious university attended a peace rally in Tel Aviv and shot dead its guest of honour, Israel's prime minister. Yigal Amir, the assassin, argued that Rabin had betrayed the Messiah by preparing for an end to Israeli rule of biblical land, and claimed his act had rabbinic blessing. The killing, he argued, was a logical outcome of religious Zionism, the officially propagated ideology that hailed the conquest of the West Bank – Judea and Samaria – as inaugurating the messianic age. For three decades, Rabin and his fellow Israeli leaders had fostered the religious settler movement, only for the movement to turn on him when he tried to dump it. From the first days of the Oslo Accords, a heady cocktail of Jewish settlers, Russian migrants and students from religious seminaries demonstrated by burning effigies of Rabin in SS uniform. Settler leaders announced the formation of militias and warned that the dismantling of settlements would trigger revolt. In February 1994, an American-born settler, Baruch Goldstein, gunned down twenty-nine Muslim worshippers in Hebron's shared shrine, known as the Tomb of the Patriarchs to Jews and the Ibrahim's mosque by Muslims, before being disarmed and beaten to death. The rabbi officiating at his funeral said the fingernail of a Jew was worth more than the lives of a thousand Arabs, and his grave at the neighbouring Kiryat Arba settlement became a carefully manicured park. In a court case, Baruch Goldstein's widow won the right to keep her husband's machine gun, with which she triumphantly decorated her mantelpiece. In Jerusalem, Jews staged anti-Palestinian riots.

Wildfire religious fanaticism among Palestinians was similarly destructive. For thirty years, the PLO had championed itself as the sole legitimate representative of the Palestinian people. But the *intifada* had spawned other contenders, most prominently Hamas. Denied a place in the peace process, they opted to spoil it instead. Tapping widespread public scepticism they topped polls in student

402   A History of the Middle East

and trade-union elections for the first time. And following Goldstein's Hebron attack, they launched their first bus bombings on Jerusalem and Tel Aviv.

Israel's response marked the antithesis of the normalization the peace process was supposed to deliver. Rabin ended normal movement between the occupied territories and Israel, the greatest single benefit of its post-1967 occupation. He established barriers and checkpoints which emphasized the military occupation the Oslo Accords were designed to lift, and at a huge economic cost prevented tens of thousands of Palestinians from working in Israel. Amid the economic downturn and increase in restrictions on movement, Arafat was ridiculed as an Israeli lackey. He grappled to maintain control internally, clamping down on opposition and in the process intensifying the opposition to the PLO's rule. Instead of a democratic state, the PLO established another regional autocratic regime, the Palestinian Authority or PA, dependent on 70,000 intelligence and security personnel, nearly four times the number stipulated under the Oslo Accords. A 1997 investigation revealed that a third of the Authority's $800 million budget, for the most part foreign aid, was either wasted or skimmed off by corrupt officials. 'It's a mafia state,' said Abdul Jawad Saleh, a former agriculture minister beaten by Palestinian police for leading an anti-corruption protest. As living standards for the majority plummeted, returning PLO exiles – Israel's new interlocutors – swooned in luxury. Palestinian security officers were rumoured to frequent the bar at a Jewish settlement in Gaza where fifty families occupied a piece of land the size of a neighbouring camp housing 100,000 refugees.

Rabin's assassination attenuated the declining confidence in the Oslo process. Even King Hussein of Jordan found his successor, Peres, slippery. Peres's vision of a New Middle East smacked suspiciously of a replacement of Israeli military might with economic hegemony, and Jordanians mocked the Arava treaty as the 'king's peace'. Among Israelis, Peres was seen as lacking the mettle of Rabin. In an attempt to counter his soft image ahead of early elections, he ordered the extra-judicial killing of Yahya Ayyash, the Hamas 'engineer' who had masterminded earlier bomb attacks. In the process Peres triggered a sickening cycle of violence. The suicide squads, which had lain dormant for the previous six months, blew up four buses in a week. Clinton and a host of Arab leaders desperate to preserve Peres in power staged an anti-terrorism summit in the Egyptian resort of Sharm al-Sheikh. But faced with Israeli jibes of appeasement, Peres looked north. For almost a decade, South Lebanon's population had been mere bystanders as a few hundred guerrillas from the Iranian-backed Hizbollah Shiite militia engaged in a carefully choreographed routine of tit-for-tat clashes with the Israeli army and their Christian militia occupying the south of the country. But when Peres unleashed his 'Grapes of Wrath' offensive, it was civilians who bore the price. Four hundred thousand Lebanese fled a blizzard of 25,000 Israeli shells, one of which fell in a UN compound near Qana village and killed over a hundred Lebanese who had gone there for shelter. Grapes of Wrath not only set back Lebanon's post-war reconstruction and restored Israel's reputation as a colonial bully; it also cost Peres the election. Arab Israelis boycotted the poll en masse and Peres, who had entered the campaign 20 per cent ahead in the polls, lost albeit by a minuscule margin. Six months after Rabin's assassination, Israelis elected Binyamin Netanyahu as prime minister – the man who as Likud leader had compared the Oslo Accords to Neville Chamberlain's appeasement of Hitler.

For the next four years, the peace process sunk into hibernation. Netanyahu had a degree in architecture, and the political ambition to rebuild Greater Israel. He revived the spirit of religious Zionism, putting Bible teaching and Jewish history at the core of the school curriculum. Jewish settlements sprouted atop West Bank hills, cutting hopes for a contiguous and viable Palestinian state into pieces. Palestinian protests were dismissed as terrorism, the Arab world was portrayed as the perennial enemy of the Jewish people, and Israeli tanks rolled up to the outskirts of Nablus. President Clinton pressured Netanyahu to sign the 1998 Wye River memorandum committing Israel to withdraw from a further 13 per cent of the West Bank, but Netanyahu reneged on the deal and pulled troops out of just 2 per cent, part of Hebron, a town in the Southern West Bank. Further raising tensions, he confiscated one of the last segments of open land outer Jerusalem still in Palestinian hands, announced the construction of the Har Homa settlement on its soil, and declared, 'the battle for Jerusalem has begun'. After five years of the peace process, Israel in Arab eyes was again resurfacing as a regional cancer, and US attempts to reshape the Middle East map were in disarray. Arab states backpeddled on normalization, and in Israel and the Arab world anti-Oslo voices stole the limelight. Netanyahu's high-profile release of Hamas's jailed spiritual leader, Ahmed Yassin, in exchange for Mossad agents caught in Jordan trying to assassinate a Hamas official resulted – deliberately or otherwise – in boosting Palestinian opposition to Oslo. The hysteria which greeted Yassin's return to Gaza upstaged Yasir Arafat's own triumphal return from exile three years earlier and revealed the dramatic growth in Palestinian popular support for the Islamist movement. Netanyahu's coalition partners on the religious right were equally dismissive of the Oslo process and, following his partial withdrawal from Hebron, threatened to withdraw from his coalition. Facing a vote of no confidence, Netanyahu went to the polls in May 1999 and lost.

On the eve of the millennium few would have predicted that the euphoria which greeted the victory of Labour leader, Ehud Barak, would so fatally and quickly turn to despair. In his post-election address, he promised ecstatic crowds to end Israel's 22-year occupation of Southern Lebanon within a year. And after an effusive exchange of compliments between Assad and Barak, Syria and Israel sent their delegates to West Virginia to resume negotiations from the point at which discussions in Maryland had ended four years before – full withdrawal for a full peace. Talks were followed by a meeting in Washington between the Syrian foreign minister, Farouq al-Shara, and Barak – the highest-level public encounter between the two states since the conflict began. Their differences narrowed down to Syria's demand to return to its pre-1967 borders lapping the shores of Lake Tiberias. Israel argued that in the intervening thirty years, over-usage by Israel had caused the lake to shrink several metres short of the pre-1967 border, and that Syria therefore had no claim to its shores. Even the charm of Clinton, who travelled to the ironic setting of Lake Geneva to meet an ailing Assad was unable to bridge the impasse. Since neither side would yield a metre, the talks collapsed.

Failure on the Syria track upset Barak's other initiatives. Syria forbade Lebanon, where it maintained 30,000 troops, to make peace with Israel until it had retrieved the Golan Heights. And without a green light from President Assad, the Lebanese army declined Barak's appeal to deploy along the Israeli border. Hizbollah instead filled the vacuum. Barak determined to push on regardless and present Syria with a *fait accompli*. But Israel's orderly withdrawal, scheduled for 7 July 2000 turned into a rout by the end of May. Under attack, Israel's proxy militia, the South Lebanon Army (SLA), abandoned their positions and weapons to Hizbollah and withered away to Israel, leaving only the running sore of the Shebaa farms, the Israeli-occupied foothills of the Golan Heights where the borders of Lebanon, Syria and Israel meet still in their hands. A massive Israeli bombardment of Lebanon's power stations failed to stem the Hizbollah advance. South Lebanese villagers joined the revelry by breaking down the doors of Khiam prison, a notorious torture centre, and freeing its inmates. Across the Arab world, Hizbollah's victory was hailed as proof that armed resistance by a tiny Islamist guerrilla force could defeat Israel, the most heavily armed state between France and India.

With his parliamentary coalition fast unravelling, Barak belatedly turned to the Palestinian track in a rush to conclude a deal. Barak sought to bypass the third phase of the Oslo agreement, which required Israel to withdraw from the West Bank and the Gaza Strip, and jump straight to negotiations on permanent status from which Israel had withdrawn in 1995. Much of the groundwork on settling the core disputes of Jerusalem, settlements, borders, water and refugees was completed in meetings in Stockholm over the summer of 2000. And on 11 July the two leaders arrived at the US presidential retreat of Camp David to spend a fortnight resolving a century-old dispute, while Bill Clinton, anxious to secure a final foreign policy coup in the twilight of his presidency, shuttled between them. The

Camp David setting evoked the dramatic breakthrough concluded by the earlier trio of Carter, Sadat and Begin twenty-three years earlier. As Palestinian chief negotiator Saeb Erakat acknowledged at the time, the negotiations marked the closest Israelis and Palestinians had yet come to a final settlement of their differences. The Israelis insisted they had offered more to the Palestinians than ever before. Indeed five years earlier, prior to Rabin's death, Palestinian negotiators appeared ready to accept far less, including a Palestinian capital outside the borders of Jerusalem. Why then did Camp David result in such a catastrophic collapse?

Details of the negotiations remain shrouded in recrimination. Palestinian delegates say Barak's proposals at Camp David amounted to Israeli annexation of the best Palestinian lands, a patchwork state of disjointed Bantustans, the perpetuation of Israeli control over much of East Jerusalem (the old city would have been more a Palestinian municipality than a capital), a continued Israeli military presence on Palestinian territory, Israeli control over Palestinian natural resources, airspace and borders, and the return of fewer than 1 per cent of nearly four million refugees to their homes, with no recognized right of return.

Israelis stress Barak's political bravery in breaking Israeli taboos. According to Israeli negotiators, Barak agreed to withdraw from all the Gaza Strip and all but 5 per cent of the West Bank including the Jordan Valley, which since 1967 had served as Israel's security border. Israel stated it had no plans to divide the territory into enclaves and that the only separation would be between Gaza and the West Bank with a safe passage attaching the two; according to Barak, Israel would also maintain a slither of land slicing through the West Bank from Jerusalem to the Jordan River, with Palestinians restricted to tunnels running underneath. On refugees, Barak proposed an annual drip into Israel of tens of thousands of refugees in the guise of 'family reunification', and a $20 billion compensation fund to settle the rest in the new state of Palestine, but flatly refused any 'right of return'. To the exasperation of Palestinians, Barak characterized Palestinian refugees as 'salmon', suggesting in the words of one negotiator, Hussein Agha, that Palestinian 'yearning to return to their land somehow is supposed to fade away in roughly eighty years in a manner that the Jewish people's never did, even after two thousand years'. On settlements, Barak accepted evacuation of all but a small group of settlements abutting the Green Line, where 80 per cent of settlers would reside; unlike Israel's withdrawal from Sinai, he offered to leave the remaining settlements intact to house returning refugees; finally, on Jerusalem, Israeli negotiators say Barak proposed transferring all East Jerusalem to Palestine, bar the Jewish quarter of the Old City, the Western Wall and the belt of Israeli suburbs built in East Jerusalem since 1967. Jerusalem would be an open city, and the capital of two states. Their key sticking point was sovereignty of the holy site that Muslims call the Dome of the Rock or al-Aqsa sanctuary and Jews the Temple Mount. As with Syria, negotiators were just a few square metres away from a peace treaty.

The negative chemistry cannot entirely explain their failure. Their predecessors at Camp David, Begin and Sadat, forged an agreement despite their equally mutual disdain. What was harder to reconcile was the deepening mistrust of their peoples for the Oslo process. Israelis saw seven years of concessions rewarded with suicide bombs and the Palestinian Authority's revolving-door policy of imprisoning militants one day and releasing them the next. Palestinians saw the subversion of their dreams into the creation of an Israeli puppet police state. Promised a post-Oslo boom, Palestinians had instead experienced a dramatic decline in living standards, sparked in part by 400 days of curfews and bars on access and movement between the occupied territories and Israel, which prevented Palestinian labourers from getting to work, and traders from getting their goods to market. The cycle of negotiations and the endless prevarications seemed little more than a cynical Israeli delaying tactic to build more checkpoints, roads and settlements in an attempt to scupper the creation of a viable Palestinian state. In the seven years between Oslo and Camp David the settler population of the West Bank doubled to 200,000. In Gaza, 6,500 Jews continued to enjoy the most fertile land and plentiful water resources while one million

Palestinians lived trapped in ghetto conditions. After a brief freeze under Rabin, there was a particularly intense period of construction under Netanyahu and his bullish infrastructure minister, Ariel Sharon. Engineers spread a web of highways across the West Bank – ostensibly to enable settlers to bypass Palestinian towns and villages, but in reality carving the territory into cantons. The rate of settlement under Barak was even faster than under Netanyahu (Barak explained he needed to mollify the right wing). For Palestinians, the language of negotiations for a two-strike settlement contrasted starkly with the intensifying colonization on the ground.

With dwindling popular support for the peace process, both sides sought to hide from rather than face the critics. Talks were held abroad and in secret, led by negotiating elites far removed from the festering resentment of the people they were supposed to represent. As much as the occupier, most Palestinians mistrusted the intentions of the self-styled honest broker, the US, which had repeatedly used its veto at the UN to protect Israel from criticism. There was also a gnawing doubt shared by many Palestinians that having won control over Nablus, Hebron and Gaza, they should now abandon for ever their claims to Nazareth and Haifa and much of Jerusalem. Despite Israel's outright victory in the regional arms race, guerrilla warfare in Lebanon had shown it could nullify Israel's overwhelming technological superiority. If Hizbollah could wage low-intensity warfare with success, why not the Palestinians' veteran armed militias? Struggling to balance the appeal of liberation and self-determination with the responsibilities of nascent statehood, Arafat returned from Camp David to Gaza as a Palestinian Saladin clothed in combat fatigues, chanting the Arabic for Jerusalem, 'al-Quds, al-Quds, al-Quds'.

Israel maintains that the uprising was premeditated and that Arafat was merely seeking a pretext. The *intifada*, Israel notes, erupted five years to the day after the signing of the interim agreement, which had stipulated a five-year period for a permanent settlement. Palestinians say the firelighter was Ariel Sharon, the new leader of the Israeli opposition Likud party. They saw his decision to parade on the al-Aqsa sanctuary, the third holiest shrine in Islam, with a 1,000-strong guard as a deliberate challenge to the delicate *status quo* prevailing atop the world's most fought-over piece of real estate. Four times over the previous decade, furious clashes had erupted in the cobbled courtyard that religious fire-brands of the three religions of the Book venerated as the holy fuse for Armageddon.

In the close confines of the sanctuary, Sharon's military entourage opened fire on stone-throwers, killing four Palestinians and trig-gering what was named the al-Aqsa *intifada*, but became the first Israeli–Palestinian war. Initially the resistance was fought much like the first *intifada*. One month into the fighting, Israeli troops had injured 4,000 Palestinians and killed 130, including a twelve-year-old boy, Muhammad al-Durra, whose death huddled in his father's arms on a Gaza street was broadcast worldwide on television. But where the first *intifada* had been waged with slingshots, increasingly the second was fought with bullets and suicide bombings. In the early weeks of the confrontation, the ratio of Palestinian to Israeli deaths was 25:1 as Israeli forces used what an official fact-finding commit-tee led by US Senator Mitchell reported were 'lethal means to control demonstrations of unarmed Palestinians'. After twenty months of fighting, the Palestinians had reduced the ratio to 2:1.

Ten years of pent-up frustration, misery and blame fed the belliger-ency. People on both sides were cooped up in their homes – Israelis for fear of inner-city bombings, Palestinians because of military curfews. A poll conducted in the heat of the violence in March 2002 showed 60 per cent of Israelis favoured the expulsion of Palestinians over the Jordan River. A Palestinian poll gave suicide bombers an 80 per cent approval rate, up from 10 per cent before the outbreak of fighting in 2000. Those who questioned the morality of suicide operations, such as the Palestinian Authority's Jerusalem represent-ative Sari Nusseibeh, were heckled. Within days of the uprising, the violence had spilled over to the Arab–Israeli villages of Galilee, where Israeli troops shot dead eleven Arab protestors, and a Jewish mob rampaged through the Palestinian streets of Nazareth, and torched an ancient mosque in Tiberias. As fighting flared, Israeli voters went to the polls in early 2001 to elect Sharon their prime minister.

While previous post-Oslo leaders had ordered Israel's tanks to the foothills of Nablus, Sharon sent them in, fighting Palestinian insurgents and the self-rule Oslo had delivered with fighter-jets and attack helicopters. Sharon prided himself on incremental reoccupations, noting that after a few months Israeli tank incursions, which had initially provoked a global outcry, barely raised an eyebrow. Israel bombed the international airport at Gaza, destroyed Arafat's helicopters, and knocked down the Palestinian radio and television masts. In March 2002, tanks destroyed the Palestinian headquarters in Gaza and a month later bulldozed the presidential compound in Ramallah, caging Arafat in the basement in a grisly re-enactment of Sharon's siege of the PLO in Beirut twenty years before. With Palestinian central government decimated, the refugee camp militias of the Islamist movements Hamas and Islamic Jihad had an increasingly free hand. To regain his grip on the uprising, Arafat's own movement, Fatah, formed the al-Aqsa brigades, which sought to regain local credibility by mimicking Hamas's suicide bombings. Sharon called up his reserves. On both sides, leaders incapable of making peace were sending their young to fight in a mutually reinforcing death cult.

Foreign mediation offered a more rational course to cool tempers, but the one superpower able to enforce a solution had a new president, George W. Bush, who appeared largely indifferent until faced with the need to secure regional cooperation for his war on Iraq. Fearing that Israel's re-invasion might undermine Arab support for his plan to overthrow Saddam Hussein, Bush publicly demanded Sharon pull back the tanks. In March 2002, Washington sponsored a UN Security Council resolution proposing the creation of a Palestinian state, and finally made explicit what had been implicit in a decade of mediation. In a 2002 speech to assuage mounting anger at US plans to invade Iraq, President Bush stated that a Palestinian state 'could' be achieved within three years, outlining a path which subsequently materialized into the 'Roadmap'. The efficacy of the undertaking, which could have been a Balfour Declaration for the Palestinians, was tempered by Bush's demand that Palestinians create a model democracy and at the same time replace Arafat, one of the region's few elected leaders.

Similarly seeking to divert regional attention from Iraq, Arab leaders weighed in with proposals of their own, including the eminently conciliatory initiative of Saudi Arabia's Crown Prince Abdullah which offered Israel a 'full normalization and normal peaceful relations' with the Arab world in return for a full withdrawal from occupied territory. Viewed from the battlefront, the offer was, in the words of Hizbollah, 'US ink written with Arab hands'. And when it came to a vote at the Arab summit in Beirut in March 2002, over half the Arab leaders – though not their delegates – stayed away, including President Mubarak, who feared Saudi Arabia was stealing Egypt's thunder as the regional peacemaker, and Libya's Qadaffy, who announced his preference for the creation of a single secular state named Isratine. Nevertheless, for the first time the Arab League offered Israel a full peace with its twenty-two members. 'No one expected,' said an astonished Jordanian foreign minister, Marwan Muahser, 'that all Arab states, including Libya and Iraq, would accept.'

Sharon never replied. His lack of courtesy at the time was blamed on the bombing of a Passover supper in a coastal Israeli hotel the night before the Arab League's declaration. Instead he pulverized the remaining skeletal infrastructure of Palestinian statehood. The education ministry was stripped of its computer hard-drives, and safes ripped from the health ministry. The northeastern quarter of Jenin refugee camp was flattened with a ferocity that participating Israeli soldiers were quoted as likening to Sharon's earlier part in the ravaging of the Beiruti refugee camps of Sabra and Shatilla. Initial claims of 500 dead were later revised down to fifty, of whom twenty-three were Israeli soldiers. But all told, the UN estimated that Israel inflicted $300 million of damage in its six-week operation. The popularity ratings of the two leaders among their own communities soared. Arafat again became a

symbol of his people's defiant struggle for a state; Sharon embodied the bunker mentality with which Israel would fight to preserve
itself. Ten years after the Madrid summit, Palestinians had no land,
the Israelis no peace, and the United States few pickings to show
for ten years of regional brokerage.

The Elusive Promise of Democratization

Of the elder George Bush's four pillars for a 'new world order', it
was perhaps his promise to build 'a world in which freedom and
respect for human rights find a home among all nations' which most
stirred the hearts of the congressmen. Here was the world's most
powerful state promising not only to project US military power,
but also its values of liberal democracy and free markets among the
world's most closed political systems. The wave of democratization
coursing through the communist empire in Eastern Europe only
intensified the momentum for the United States to promote a new
contract between ruler and ruled in the states for which it had just
gone to war. These included not just Kuwait, but also such Gulf
War allies as Syria's Hafez al-Assad, whose dictatorship seemed as
passé in the new world order as Nicolae Ceauşescu's of Romania.

As US troops amassed in the peninsula for the 1991 war on Iraq,
a group of Saudi businessmen and former ministers petitioned
King Fahd of Saudi Arabia to embark on the creation of a 'modern
Islamic state', equipped with an independent judiciary and elected
government. Later that month a convoy of Saudi women led by
a princess drove round Riyadh in protest at the kingdom's ban on
women drivers. The results were less than impressive. The women
were arrested and sent into internal exile, and the petitions politely
filed. But Saudi Arabia's neighbours were more open to glasnost.
King Hussein lifted martial law in 1991, licensed political parties
the following year, and in 1993 introduced a progressive press law
guaranteeing the individual's right to publish. In Kuwait, the
newly restored emir eventually consented to stage elections for a

parliament he had dissolved seven years earlier. Other Gulf principalities gingerly trod the electoral path. Even Saudi's King Fahd
appointed a *majlis al-shura*, Arabic for consultative council. Western
diplomats-cum-apologists noted that within a few decades of statehood the Gulf had embarked on a path to democracy that had taken
Europe centuries to realize. Critics said the changes were simply
cosmetic.

In the euphoria of the communist collapse, Western strategists
argued political liberalization would broaden the popular base of
the United States' Middle Eastern allies, bolster their legitimacy and
improve stability. They also assumed that the process might answer
the growing doubts over what sort of transition might follow the
demise of the Middle East's ageing coterie of rulers. But the received
wisdom that democracy was good for Western interests was sorely
tested by election results from Jordan, Yemen, Israel and Iran, the
four Middle Eastern states most advanced on the road to multi-party
democracy. All four elevated to parliament a bloc of religious
politicians, suspicious of and hostile to US foreign policy. The same
pattern was repeated even more starkly in Algeria. After adopting
a constitution legalizing independent political parties, Algeria staged
the first round of its first multi-party general elections in December
1991. The Islamic Salvation Front, FIS, won with a landslide, reaping
188 of the 231 seats contested. The National Liberation Front, the
FLN, the dirigiste secular party which had governed since independence was pushed into third place. Responding to appeals from
150,000 panic-stricken secular demonstrators, the Algerian army
staged a coup, cancelling the elections and appointing one of their
own head of state. With the acquiescence of Western capitals, tanks
moved on to the streets, martial law was declared, and the Islamist
party, FIS, banned.

The lesson from the plight of Algeria was three-fold. It shocked
Arab regimes into recognition of the harsh reality of the ice-thin
levels of their popular support and the mass enthusiasm for political Islam. It dissuaded Islamist politicians from pursuing a
democratic path to power, and goaded them to arms. And it turned

both Western strategists and local westernized elites off the idea of democracy. In the final count, concluded Washington's mandarins, pro-Western military tyrants were better guarantors of the new Middle East order than unpredictable, unstable democracies.

Algeria paid a terrible price for denying Islamists power. As clashes erupted across Algeria, thousands of FIS activists were incarcerated in to internment camps. Hundreds more fled to the mountainous hinterland from where they began an armed assault on key economic installations, as well as members of the security forces, politicians, intellectuals and foreigners. At least 100,000 Algerians were killed in the bloodshed, and millions displaced. But in some ways their recourse to violence enabled an intensification of military rule. It allowed the army elites, first in Algeria, and later in Egypt and Israel, to treat Islamist dissent as a security not a political problem, and thereby spare the establishment from sharing power. Algeria's generals – known as the *eradicateurs* – negotiated with the armed groups, but eliminated anyone found negotiating with the Islamist political wing, not least their own president, Mohammed Boudiaf, who was assassinated in June 1992. FIS politicians aspiring to make a comeback shared a similar fate. In 1999, Abdelkader Hachani, the most senior FIS leader to elude arrest, was shot during a dentist's check-up, spoiling the Algerian joke that the dentist was the one place an Arab could open his mouth.

While edgy Middle East regimes feared the spillover of Islamist revolt, the real impact of the violence was the militarization of the political domain. In Turkey, the armed forces brought down the country's first Islamist prime minister, Necmettin Erbakan, a year after he was elected to power in 1996. His party, Refah ('Welfare'), was banned, on the grounds it violated the country's secular constitution, and Erbakan sentenced to jail. The generals argued that they had intervened to preserve democracy rather than destroy it, and continued to take annual delivery of $800 million dollars of US military hardware.

Across the Arab world, rulers and generals used the fig-leaf of cosmetic elections and referenda to prolong their mandates and secure legality if not legitimacy with scores of more than 99 per cent of the vote. The result was that although twelve of the region's twenty states were embroiled in major revolts or violent upheavals in the 1990s, the political map of the Middle East barely changed. For the most part, voters boycotted North Africa's series of elections in 2002, unwilling to participate in what one observer called 'the parlour game indulged in by the Maghreb's ruling circles'. In Algeria, the FLN was restored to victory. In Tunisia, President Ben Ali amended his own constitution, awarding himself judicial immunity for life and allowing him to stand for a third term, and promptly won a 99.52 per cent yes vote from a 99.56 per cent turnout.

Their European and American backers shied from linking aid programmes to an improvement in the region's human rights record or the development of civil society, and the US State Department reined back its democracy programmes in the Arab world. The bulk of US aid to the region remained military rather than economic. Spared Western sanction, President Ben Ali banned Tunisia's Islamist party, al-Nahda, abolished human rights groups, shackled the press, and rigged elections. Tunisians, who boasted the Arab world's highest literacy rate and its largest middle class, were subdued by a system they called Khubzism (after the Arabic for bread, *khubz*), which roughly translated as 'eat and shut up'. For all that, Tunisia was implausibly defined by its US aid programme as a 'stable democratic country'.

Bereft of democratic transition, Western strategists began to hunt for an alternative means for the transfer of power following the autocrats' demise. A solution was a matter of urgency. By 1997, the majority of Arab leaders were in their seventies, and some, like President Hosni Mubarak of Egypt, had refused to name a successor. King Hussein ranked as the world's longest reigning absolute monarch, but even the average Arab leader reigned for two decades, twice the length of the region with the next most entrenched rulers, Africa. Across the Gulf, government was run much like a family business, with sons and brothers vying for the key positions of prime minister, ministers of defence, foreign affairs and interior, except in Oman where Sultan Qaboos held all four. In their dotage, Gulf monarchs were spending as much time in European sanatoria as in government, and their top-heavy decision-making process was rotten with *rukud*, Arabic for inertia. And yet their longevity in what was widely held to be one of the world's most troubled spots was remarkable. Following independence, the standard form of transition had been military coup. The first eight of Yemen's nine leaders were removed by the bullet and for the first decade after Syrian independence the average leader lasted three months. One generation on, Arab states had produced rulers who not only survived for decades, but could also expect to die in their beds. Would not dynastic succession, asked the policy-makers, be the most stable way of transferring power?

The first states to face the transition were the less problematic monarchies and Gulf tributaries, where the succession of crown princes was already an established tradition. In 1995, Shaikh Hamad ibn Khalifa al-Thani ousted his father, the emir of the tiny Gulf state of Qatar, in a bloodless coup assisted by French mercenaries. Four years later, three Arab heads of state (King Hussein of Jordan, King Hassan of Morocco and Emir Isa al-Khalifa of Bahrain, otherwise known to his people as Jack) followed each other to the grave in quick succession, and their thirty-something sons were smoothly enthroned in their place. Western foreign ministries rushed to pay homage to a 'new generation' of Arab monarchs their spokespersons hailed as reform-minded and dynamic.

The creation of hereditary republics proved harder to sell. For decades Syria had trumpeted its laurels as a Baathist revolutionary bridgehead, whose principles included a rejection of 'exploitative inheritance'. Hafez al-Assad had been born in a stone hovel in a mountain village that had no shop, café or mosque. But his sons had been raised in palaces and groomed to inherit the state. When the father died in June 2000 Syrians mocked that in place of *assad*, Arabic for lion-king, they got a shy Simba, but Western leaders, led by Washington, rushed with almost rude haste to herald Bashar al-Assad as Syria's new president. It was a sign of how reactionary the Arab world had become that there was no overt resistance. Assad became a trend-setter, and the rulers of Iraq, Yemen and Libya – the one-time ringleaders of the anti-royalist front – all promoted their progeny to positions as sons-in-waiting. Egyptian pundits universally derided the succession of Assad junior, hoping to avoid the imposition of a Mubarak junior. After a half-century of rivalry between the republican and royalist blocs, there was now very little difference between the two: as a rule they were all dynastic autocracies.

Keen to shore up their legitimacy, the new leaders promptly promised to usher in a new age of democracy and modernization. The result from Morocco to Bahrain via Syria was a Prague spring of glasnost. King Mohammed of Morocco sacked his father's brutal but faithful grand vizier, Driss Basri, and to cries of 'king of the poor' toured the rebellious Berber hinterland that his father had deliberately impoverished. Syria's President Bashar released hundreds of his father's political prisoners, nodded in the direction of a courageous democracy movement, and chose a wife from the Sunni Muslim majority, signalling his intent to broaden the base of his father's minority Alawite rule. Sheikh Hamad of Qatar abolished the ministry of information, and held the emirate's elections with universal suffrage, simply ignoring traditionalists (and neighbouring Saudi Arabia) who wanted women kept disenfranchised. The new leader of the nearby emirate, Bahrain, moved to resolve the violent uprising of the island's Shiite majority under his father by inviting back the exiled opposition, re-establishing an elected parliament after a 25-year suspension, and releasing political prisoners.

As if following a manual, the new generation of leaders snuffed out the yearnings for change as soon as they felt secure. Shaikh Hamad of Bahrain banned 'sectarian' (that is, Shiite opposition) websites and appointed himself king. King Abdullah of Jordan and Bashar of Syria restocked the prisons with fault-finding MPs, academics and journalists who dared voice concerns at corruption. The hosts of Syrian democracy forums – little more than evening discussion groups – were sentenced to prison for organizing secret societies. And King Mohammed appointed a new vizier with as great a zest for baton-beating human rights activists as Basri. It was not clear whether the return to rule by repression was the result of conviction, or because the new generation felt too fresh to challenge the old guard. But ultimately, the young leaders were all deterred from reforming the system that had installed them in power. All five sons continue to confuse royal coffers with public budgets, treat the judiciary as an arm of the executive, and make it illegal for journalists, let alone an electorate, to hold them to account. Some even suggested that the sons might be worse than their fathers. At least their fathers had had to struggle for their crowns, it was observed. The sons received theirs on a silver platter, having done little to merit the title.

The shift from one generation to another is still in mid-flow. The succession looks particularly uncertain in Saudi Arabia where the hereditary line passes not from father to son, but through a succession of thirty-six brothers in varying degrees of senility. In 1995, the tenth-in-line, Crown Prince Abdullah, took over after a stroke paralysed his epicurean half-brother, King Fahd. Abdullah revived popular support for the al-Saud monarchy with his pious image and an uncharacteristic streak of anti-American populism, but as he turned eighty in 2002 his rule seemed hardly a recipe for longevity.

Ironically the one country to buck the dynastic trend was Iran, the country most implacably opposed to US hegemony. Ayatollah Khomeini's legitimacy rested in his theology of *velayat al-faqih*, or rule by the expert in *fiqh*, or Islamic law; but his designated successor, his loyal president, Ali Khamenei, was regarded by many of his clerical contemporaries as lacking the necessary religious qualifications for the post. Following Khomeini's death in June 1989, the reformist parliamentary bloc proposed electing a successor, before acceding to a compromise which amended the 1979 constitution and stripped Iran's Supreme Leader of powers hitherto akin to a Jacobean divine right of kings. 'The Leader is equal to the rest of the people in the country in the eyes of the law,' read the amended constitution. 'He is not infallible, must accept his resignation, and be accountable.' The clause was designed to pave the way for the transfer of power from clerical exponents of Islamic law, who were accountable only to God, to parliamentary representatives, accountable to the people.

In some ways, the debate revived the rift between the *vox populi* that toppled the shah and the mullahs who hijacked his throne. Over the following decade the parliamentarians scored some noticeable successes over the Supreme Leader Ali Khamenei and his Council of Guardians. In the general elections of May 2001, the youth vote catapulted the reformist president, Mohammed Khatami, back to a second term in office with 80 per cent of the vote. But while the hardliners held only 20 per cent of parliamentary seats, they still controlled 80 per cent of the levers of power. Clerical appointees ran the judiciary, the army, radio and television, the key business conglomerations, and the Hizbollahi God-squads who saw themselves as the armed guardians of the Islamic Revolution. In an ongoing backlash, many newspapers – one of the few conduits open to the reformers – were closed, and writers and journalists imprisoned en masse. 'You may put the people in chains,' wrote one of them, Musani Kadivar, after serving a jail sentence, 'but you cannot kill freedom.'

The other spoonful of American medicine President Bush had promised the region in his 1991 victory speech to Congress was 'economic freedom'. With the dismantling of the Soviet Union's command economy, the possibilities for the spread of the free market to the non-capitalist world seemed unfettered. Yet again, however, Middle East leaders proved reluctant apprentices, judging that globalization and the transfer of control over finance, goods, people and information to the market might threaten their absolute rule. Governments paid lip-service to the initiatives of global financial institutions like the World Bank, but more often than not did their utmost to limit their impact. Instead of perestroika what the Middle East got was a regional variant of crony capitalism. Privatization, where it happened at all, became a byword for the

handover of profitable state industries to the rulers' family or
chums. Across the Gulf, the opening of all but the smallest business
normally required princely support, a euphemism for payment of
a commission to or partnership with a member of the royal family.
In monarchies and republics alike, members of the ruling family
used their influence to win the largest contracts, and blur the
boundaries between the leader's private purse and the state treasury.
Gulf rulers all proved unwilling to surrender their privileged access
to oil income, and though few know the exact sum, by the turn of
the millennium the Saudi state was reported to be paying the ball-
park figure of $14 billion a year to subsidize its 30,000-strong royal
household.

The positive consequence of continued state economic control
is that the region has been remarkably insulated from turbulent
global markets. The negative fallout is that the Middle East attracts
a dismal share of not just international but also local investment.
Arab financiers preferred to leave their vast financial reserves stashed
in Western banks, with Saudi nationals holding an estimated $700
billion in foreign vaults. Where it has been locally invested, there
have been striking successes. Within a generation, the Gulf emirates
turned their mud huts into skyscrapers, and their harbours for pearl-
diving dinghies into ports for tankers. A particularly shrewd and
far-sighted government in Dubai successfully converted the city-
state into an intercontinental hub for transport and trading between
Europe and Asia, and more radically into the region's cyberspace
nexus. But for the most part, innovation continued to be stifled by
the authorities' obsession with losing control. In 1992, Tunisia was
second only to South Africa as the promoter of the communications
revolution in Africa. But as the country's opposition groups took
refuge in cyberspace, President Ben Ali reined in his e-entrepreneurs,
priced the service out of the market, and arrested Tunisians logging
on to political sites. Ten years on, the president's relatives, including
his daughter, ran the country's two internet providers, and Tunisia's
place as a regional market leader had been overtaken by more liberal
African states.

Perhaps the lure of self-enrichment and absolute power would have mattered less if Middle Eastern economies had been less dependent on the vagaries of a single commodity, oil. OPEC's share of production shrank as investors sought regions more receptive to private-sector involvement and less prone to political turbulence. American and Russian oil companies tapped huge reserves in the Caspian basin. Non-OPEC countries, especially Russia, grabbed the chance to challenge Arab oil supremacy and displace OPEC as the key energy supplier to the West. Coupled with the reduction in OPEC's share of oil production was a gruelling decline in the price of oil, so that by 2002 a barrel of oil was worth less than before the first OPEC oil price hikes of 1973. In 2001 prices, the oil income of the world's largest producer, Saudi Arabia, had crashed from a peak of \$227 billion in 1981 to \$35 billion in 1998, before recovering to some \$60 billion.

The impact was exacerbated by the Middle East's mushrooming population. A UN Development Report on the Arab world published in 2002 estimated the population of the twenty-two states of the Arab world to be 280 million people, of whom 38 per cent were under fourteen. The region boasted the highest birth rates in the world and by 2020, it said, there would be 400–450 million Arabs. The surge was not just the result of traditional resistance and religious opposition to family planning. Some states, like Saudi Arabia, regarded a high birth rate as a strategic priority to boost their active populations to the levels of regional rivals, Iran and Iraq. But at such rapid rates, economic growth simply could not keep pace. Income in the region's lumbering giant, Saudi Arabia, slumped from \$19,000 per head in 1981 to \$7,000 in 2001 – a stunning reversal triggering huge social strain.

In a desperate attempt to sustain both living standards and the system of patronage, regimes ran up huge budget deficits and landed themselves with vast bureaucracies, often little more than white-elephant employment schemes. Some attempt was made to cut back on profligate arms deals: in the first flush of victory after the liberation of Kuwait, Riyadh awarded US companies a 'war tribute' worth $60 billion in contracts, and spent a further $33 billion on US arms, only to scale back drastically in the mid-1990s. The kingdom reacted to a decision from the European Investment Bank pronouncing that it could no longer extend loan guarantees to Saudi Arabia, by delaying the delivery of American F-16 fighter jets.

But such measures only partially addressed the long-term malaise. Older generations wistfully recall the time when oil gave their governments the financial clout to project their influence beyond their borders. But by the dawn of the twenty-first century, governments were struggling to provide for their own citizens. In most Arab states, a majority of young people was un- or under-employed, and in 2002 unemployment across the Arab world reached 60 million. With almost half the population is under eighteen, unemployment was set to balloon. Even where there were jobs, millions of graduates were priced out of the job market because of the Gulf's addiction to the cheap labour of Asian *gastarbeiters* (as well as by the natural disinclination of many American and British technicians to train themselves out of lucrative jobs). Creaking cot-to-coffin welfare systems faced severe strain. Seventy years after the discovery of oil, a third of Jeddah's four million residents had no running water, and across the kingdom power cuts were a regular occurrence. By the mid-1990s economic tensions in Bahrain – the poorest Gulf state and the only one with indigenous beggars – were fuelling an uprising that pitted the island's Sunni elite against its much poorer Shiite majority.

So far no other Gulf state has had to grapple with the same degree of disturbance, and even the Arab world's gloomiest economists still bank on the region's long-term prospects. Middle East states sit atop two-thirds of the world's bank of oil deposits. And while reserves in the rest of the world will last perhaps a few decades, the Gulf will still be pumping into the twenty-second century. At current rates of growth in the global economy, world demand for OPEC oil is predicted to triple to 60 million barrels a day by 2020.

The problem is that much could change in the interim. Major

discoveries outside OPEC coupled with a dramatic surge in alternative energy, particularly fuel-cell vehicles, could render Middle
Eastern oil if not obsolete then secondary at a time when the vast
bulk of Arab petroleum remains underground. The impact on
regimes almost entirely dependent on oil to lubricate their economies would be massive.

Arabs are desperate for answers as to why, when they were blessed
with the product that drives the world's economy, they so miserably
missed out on the global growth of the 1990s. In 1960, the average
North African was richer than the average South Korean; forty years
on, the South Korean is seven times richer, and the Arab world
experienced the world's lowest growth rate outside sub-Saharan
Africa. Arab leaders argue that were it not for terrorism targeted at
such vital sectors as tourism (on which one in ten Egyptians rely for
an income) their economies would be thriving. But in the minds of
many Arabs, economic stagnation is directly linked to political stagnation. Without deft management, the zest for a popular share
the region's political and economic power remains a recipe for instability.

The Growth of Muslim Liberation Theology

For all its symbolism and pious rhetoric, political Islam is less a religious tradition than a twentieth-century popular movement that arose
in response to the military humiliations, political depredations and
socio-economic discontents of recent history. Its followers were
attracted to its politics not because their childhoods had been steeped
in Koranic education, but because it proved to be the most potent
protest movement around. Unlike nationalism, socialism and liberalism, Islamic activism was the first home-grown ideology in the Arab
world. It gained wide currency in the late 1980s and throughout the
1990s because it thrived in the one non-governmental institution no
Arab regime dares ban: the mosque. Its discourse was couched in
the same sacred terminology that the region's regimes also used to

underpin their legitimacy, and as a consequence was similarly hard to proscribe. And it peddled its message by means of sermons recorded on cassettes that were out of earshot of even the most totalitarian state. For the first time since independence, taxi-drivers could spend the day tuned into dissident voices, not the president's men.

Like its ideological forerunners, Islamic activism was the creation not of the poor, but of frustrated middle-class students. It first gained a following not in the shanty towns hugging North Africa's cities, but on the campuses of universities and technical colleges. Arab students volunteered to fight the Afghan *jihad*, Arabic for 'just struggle', against the Soviet Union in much the same spirit as their left-wing European counterparts in the 1930s went off to fight the Spanish Civil War. Nor were they normally impoverished. The hijackers who knocked down New York's World Trade Center were Western-educated high-flyers, and over three-quarters of them came from the Arab world's wealthiest state, Saudi Arabia. Several of the Palestinian suicide bombers in 2002 were sons of Gazan millionaires. Usama bin Laden, one among scores of Arab-Afghan commanders, belonged to the richest non-royal family in Saudi Arabia. His cohort, a shy doctor named Ayman al-Zawahari, came from a gentrified family of lawyers and diplomats long resident in the upmarket Cairo suburb of Maadi. And their cohorts were almost entirely manned by graduates, among them the sons of former government ministers. This was no peasants' revolt.

Nor was its religious outlook especially traditionalist. Its fiercest opponents were the quietest divines of Sunni orthodox schools, the *ulama*, who opposed any *bida'*, Arabic for innovation, and in some notable instances still maintained the earth was flat. Unlike the clerics raised in religious schools, Islamist activists were schooled in the secular natural sciences, in particular medicine and engineering. Abdel Salam Faraj Atiya, the author of the *Just War – An Absent Duty* (the essay which sanctioned the assassination of Sadat) was an engineer, as was Usama bin Laden. They embraced Western tools of modern communications, and despite the orthodox prohibition on the human image (rigidly enforced by their hosts, the Taliban) Islamist activists had no problem with the mass-reproduction of bin Laden's icon and video sermons. Whereas Sunni orthodoxy had throughout the ages enjoined submission to secular authority, the Islamists wanted to usurp it and purge the loyal clergy who legitimized it. And like Protestant Christianity in the age of the Reformation, the Islamists challenged the *ulama*'s monopoly on exposition of the scriptures and their accretions of tradition. They reinterpreted the eternal message of the Prophet Muhammad afresh, as if they were the first generation of Muslims, or *aslaf*. Accordingly, Islamists saw themselves as neo-*aslaf*: they subscribed not to a reactionary mindset, but to an activist and revolutionary ideology they called *Salafia Jihadiya*, or zealous Salafism.

The movement rooted its grievances in the carve-up of the Sunni-led Ottoman Empire by Western powers, and the redistribution of its Arab heartland to non-Sunni sects. Following the Second World War, Britain and France bequeathed their mandates to the Jews in Palestine, a Maronite Christian president in Lebanon, and after much infighting to heterodox Alawites in Syria, whom key Sunni scholars considered non-Muslims. Even in the Ottoman core of Turkey, where the leaders professed to be Sunni, the ruling ideology adopted was avowedly secular. After 900 years of hegemony, Sunni elites found themselves booted from power, and subjugated.

Ever since Kemal Atatürk abolished the Ottoman caliphate in the 1920s, the Muslim Brotherhood had preached the millenarian restoration of a caliphate holding sway over a borderless pan-Islamic state. But its followers were divided on what means justified that end. The founder of the Muslim Brotherhood, Hassan al-Banna, sanctioned assassinating politicians, and was in turn assassinated. His successors participated in the Egyptian revolution in 1952, and Gamal Abdul Nasser offered their Supreme Guide, Sayyid al-Qutb, the post of education minister. But Qutb – a one-time literary critic – refused, and penned his most important tractate, *Milestones on the*

Way, which remains the Islamist primer. Writing in an Egyptian torture camp, he argued that the region's leaders had forfeited their membership of the Muslim community by dint of their corrupt rule and their refusal to apply God's law, the *sharia*. As such they had led their subjects back into the *jahiliya*, the pre-Islamic age of ignorance, were therefore apostates, and should be put to death. In response to three assassination attempts, Nasser had Qutb strung from the gallows in 1965.

Until Qutb, the Islamic movement in the Middle East had sought to propagate reform, if not reformation, by working within society. After his hanging, the Brotherhood split into a mainstream that preached non-violent opposition, and a revolutionary, clandestine sect dedicated to applying Qutb's 'liberation theology'. It was this avant-garde which emerged as the Egyptian Islamic Gihad. Unlike the Muslim Brotherhood, which sought to maximize its popular base, Gihad organized in secret cells to plot *coups d'état*. It espoused the subjugation of Christians, the use of force to impose the *sharia*, and the doctrine of *takfir*, the damnation of the ruling authority as apostates. Both the integrationists and the isolationists sought to establish an Islamic state, but the difference in their theology can be compared to the early Protestant debate between the broad church of Martin Luther and Calvin's narrow enclave of pure faith. In Protestant Islam, the Muslim Brotherhood considered all Muslims eligible for salvation and preached to the Muslim *umma*, or nation; the *jihadi* militias saw true belief limited to the cells of their *gamaa islamiya*, normally translated as 'Islamic group', but perhaps better rendered as an Islamic vanguard'. The *jihadis* disagreed over whom to put on their hit list of apostates. Some argued that anyone working for the state was an apostate, depicting any writer published by the Ministry of Culture as being as much of an infidel as Israel's Ariel Sharon. Others restricted *takfir* to just the ruler and his senior ministers.

Though they grabbed most of the most headlines, the *jihadi* groups never comprised more than a small minority of the followers of political Islam. The Islamic liberals of North Africa, who preached tolerance and denounced the use of violence against fellow-Muslims, attracted far greater support. But the authorities boosted the extreme fringe by banning Islamist dissent *in toto*, and treating all its manifestations as a single fundamentalist scourge. Arab governments themselves argued that political Islam was like drugs – exposure to its soft form was a slippery slope to hardcore terrorism. Usama bin Laden, they cited by way of example, had started his political career as a Muslim Brotherhood acolyte.

The *jihadi* ranks were undoubtedly swollen by the radicalism engendered by repeated bouts of police brutality against moderates from the Muslim Brotherhood. At the same time, both the Brotherhood and its more violent sister movement fed on the crushing defeat of secular Arab nationalism in the 1967 war with Israel, attributed in the words of a preacher in Mecca to Nasser's pursuit of war with 'an un-Islamic spirit'. Finally, throughout the 1970s, pro-US regimes across the region gave the Islamist movement a certain room for manoeuvre to counter what at the time appeared to be more threatening leftist dissent, often permitting the inflow of Saudi oil funds to their ranks. Successive Israeli governments fostered political Islam as an alternative to the Palestinian nationalist movement. In Egypt, Sadat released Muslim Brotherhood activists from Nasser's internment camps and allowed religious associations to organize on campus to counter socialist radicals. More broadly, the US encouraged the movement as a means to upset the underbelly of the Soviet Union in Muslim central Asia.

Egypt's flirtation with the Brotherhood came to an abrupt halt following Sadat's assassination in 1981. But the support for the global movement continued. For the next ten years his successor, Hosni Mubarak, ensured a relative peace in Egypt by jailing hundreds of militants, and then sending many of them, including Ayman al-Zawahari, the future leader of Islamic Jihad, to Afghanistan to wage *jihad*.

It is doubtful that the Egyptian government ever expected a rabble of errant Islamists to defeat the might of the Soviet Empire.

But in February 1989 the last Russian troops withdrew from Afghanistan, leaving the Arab mujahideen victorious and equipped with a battle-hardened core skilled in modern guerrilla warfare. The numbers of recruits was staggering. Over 15,000 Saudi volunteers went to train in Usama bin Laden's camps, many of them graduates and public-sector workers seeking a subsidized adventure holiday. Saudi Arabia, too, became a conduit for thousands from across the Muslim world, where on production of a *tazkia*, or personal reference from a Saudi imam, they would qualify for 75 per cent off a Saudi Airlines flight to Peshawar, the capital of Pakistan's North-West Frontier Province and gateway to Afghanistan. In 1980 Kamal Hassan Ali, Egypt's minister of defence, announced a training programme for Islamist revolutionaries in army camps, and advertisements in the official Egyptian press called on the young to 'join the caravan' travelling to Afghanistan. On arrival in Peshawar, they were assigned to recruitment centres run by Arab volunteers, of whom the most charismatic was the Palestinian Abdullah Azzam. His Maktab al-Khadimat, or Services Bureau, attracted over 20,000 Arab mujahideen and formed the mainstay of the Arab *jihad* in Afghanistan. In 1986 bin Laden opened his own recruitment office, al-Qaeda or 'the Base', together with an adjoining guest-house, Beit al-Ansar. It had beds for 150, and a khaki marquee in the garden to cater for the overflow. Saudi, Pakistani, British and American military intelligence – welcoming the cheap supply of cannon-fodder to confront the 'evil empire' – also trained and armed the recruits.

The Afghan campaign launched a worldwide network of Islamist militias tens-of-thousands strong and inspired millions more to believe in the seemingly God-blessed powers of the *jihadis* to vanquish worldly forces. If they could defeat the might of the Soviet Empire, they asked, what might they do to their own far weaker, unpopular and ungodly regimes? As Pakistan began disbanding the Arab recruitment centres following the Soviet withdrawal from Arghanistan, Middle East élites reeled in horror at the prospect of incoming hoards of mujahideen returning home on a mission to

establish *sharia* states. Portcullises came down across the Arab world
to keep out the returning 'Arab Afghans'.

The external Islamist threat to Arab regimes was compounded
by the rapid internal spread of political Islam. In Yemen, Sudan and
Saudi Arabia, Islamists had won a share of power, and in other states
religious societies were threatening to replace the state as providers
of education and welfare. Following earthquakes in both Algeria
and Egypt in the early 1990s, Islamists proved more effective than
the state in getting aid to the people, and whenever elections were
allowed to proceed without state interference, Islamists topped the
polls. In Egypt, they swept the board in elections for such key professional associations as the lawyers and engineers, and in Algeria, as
noted, the Islamist party, FIS, won an outright majority in the first
round of voting in December 1991. When the Algerian army
cancelled the second round, imposed martial law, and banned the
FIS, Islamists tried to instigate a mass uprising of Iranian proportions, and having failed fled to the hills. There they formed a
military wing, the Islamic Salvation Army (AIS), declared a *jihad*
and targeted state institutions. Hundreds more joined more extreme
cells, collectively called the Armed Islamic Group (GIA), which
struck at state and society alike. From the spring of 1993, the GIA
expanded their range of targets to include journalists, artists, musi-
cians and foreigners. As their popular base narrowed, terror attacks
grew increasingly random. Tactics such as the faux barrage, in which
guerrillas disguised as soldiers stopped buses and slaughtered their
passengers, paralysed normal life in Algeria. The GIA perpetrated
a series of massacres in the outlying suburbs of the capital, Algiers,
particularly during Ramadan, the holy month commemorating the
Prophet's victory at the battle of Badr against the infidels of Mecca.
But the attacks on civilians highlighted the militants' desperation
and undermined popular support. Frustrated in the armed struggle
and tempted by offers of a presidential amnesty, defections increased.
A weary AIS came down from the mountains after negotiating a
truce in January 2000, leaving a further 3,000 guerrillas from other
groups still prowling the hills and killing some hundred a month.

Fuelled by the clandestine return of Arab Afghans, *jihadi* groups elsewhere in the Middle East moved to emulate Algeria's armed rebellion. In neighbouring Libya, mujahideen fought a desperate war from their redoubts in the Green Mountain in the east of the country. Further east, *jihadi* groups launched their first attack on tourists in Upper Egypt in May 1992, and killed the country's leading secular author, Farag Fouda. Two groups led the violence: the Islamic Gihad, which targeted security force personnel and senior officials, and the less professional Gamaa Islamiya, whose targets in the name of Islam included civilians, particularly the soft but high-publicity targets of foreigners and Christians. The army retaliated with helicopter attacks and troop assaults targeting poor inner-city neighbourhoods suspected of harbouring the perpetrators. The increasingly lethal cycle of violence prompted militants to attempt the assassinations of the Egyptian president and several of his senior ministers. The violence only abated following popular outrage at the killing of fifty-eight tourists in the Valley of the Kings in Upper Egypt, abhorred even by the lawyers who for the past decade had acted as their clients' mouthpiece. A series of military trials resulted in the execution of over sixty leaders, and the detention of a further 20,000 suspects without trial. Further battered by an international crackdown in the wake of the US embassy bombings in East Africa in 1998, the armed groups were simply too militarily weak to repeat the triumph of the Afghan *jihad*, and after the loss of over 1,000 lives the rebellion petered out.

Much like Sharon's crushing suppression of the second Intifada, the waning of violence allowed the Mubarak regime to claim that there was a military solution to the threat of Muslim militancy. But their cries of victory were dubious for two reasons. First, while they had won the battle against Islamist militias they had lost the war against their programme. To deflect the charge of apostasy, Middle East leaders peppered their speeches with the sacred language of their opponents. Saddam Hussein, a Baathist, for instance, reinvented himself as an Islamic nationalist. Middle East governments also adopted much of the Islamist agenda, conceding ground on religious personal law, particularly on issues of minority rights and equality for women, provided it did not threaten their power. In Egypt secular women's organizations, like Nawal al-Sa'dawi's Arab Women's Solidarity Association, which sought to replace strict Islamic personal mores with Western standards of personal liberty, were banned. Local officials enforced unreformed Ottoman legislation that church restoration – even the repair of a church toilet – required a presidential decree; Coptic emigration increased from a trickle to a steady stream. In the face of Islamist opposition in Kuwait, a principality hitherto proud of its vibrant parliamentary system, the emir temporarily backed down on his Gulf War promise to introduce female suffrage. Shiites encountered tighter restrictions on entering the civil service and armed forces, though not to the extent of Saudi Arabia and Bahrain, which banned Shiites from the security forces altogether. And the Jewish communities in the Arab world, which dated back 2,500 years and numbered nearly a million on the eve of independence, were all but whittled away by the end of the second millennium. Rulers also sought to deflect their zeal abroad. Egypt's state media received a green light to increase coverage of the *intifada*; religious leaders appeared on television preaching the sanctity of suicide bombing. 'It is one of the highest forms of martyrdom,' broadcast Ahmed al-Tayyeb, a senior religious official. Students in Cairo demanded that the authorities open their borders with Israel to enable volunteers to join the *jihad*. The handful who were shot trying were hailed as martyrs. Children, educated throughout the 1990s to believe in reconciliation with Israel, were in the age of the second *intifada* raised expecting to fight Jews, and perhaps Americans too.

In the short term, the Islamization of divorce, clothing and family planning, coupled with the focus on holy struggles abroad, assuaged Islamist pressure, but longer term it fuelled their cause. Islamists led the crowds chanting angry denunciations not just of Sharon, but of their own passive leaders. Ten years after the outbreak of *jihadi* Arab revolts, the Middle East had become a more monochrome if angry place. As in Ottoman times, a person's religious sect, rather than their state, was their badge of identity, and as the swathe of veils was intended to prove, Sunni revivalists were again the ascendant group.

The Globalization of Islamic Jihad

There was another reason for mistaking the lull in local Islamist violence for victory, namely that the movement had been less crushed than chased abroad, where as in the early 1980s it set its sights on confronting a superpower. In the throws of the Afghan struggle in 1987, an imaginative young *mujahid*, Usama bin Laden, revealed his night-time 'vision' of the re-creation of an Islamic superstate. The Prophet Muhammad had defeated the two great empires of the day: first Persia, then Byzantium, he told his fellow brothers-in-arms; the Arab Afghans would overcome the Soviets, and then set their sights on America. Such foresight marked a radical departure from the norms of *jihadi* ideology. Hitherto, Qutb's followers had focused on the local overthrow of their own leaders, or 'Pharaohs', and their replacement with a puritan Islamic state. Evincing parallels with President Bush's speeches, bin Laden postulated the creation of a new (Islamic) world order in which Muslims were either with him, or against Islam.

Had the Arab Afghans been integrated in their homelands following their victory over the Soviets, bin Laden's reinterpretation of *jihad* might have been no more than the reverie of a dreamer. As it was, by 1993 the Arab veterans had dispersed to the four corners of the earth, where global reach fed the global idea. Hundreds of fighters found refuge in the poor warring peripheries of the Arab world, in Somalia and Sudan. In Yemen, President Ali Abdullah Salih recruited returning Afghan veterans in another anti-Marxist *jihad* against his leftist rivals in the former Soviet-backed state of South Yemen. But perhaps the largest number, an estimated 12,000, quietly slipped home to Saudi Arabia. Among them was bin Laden. He arrived in the kingdom shortly before the 1991 Gulf War, in time to watch Western forces of 'unbelievers occupy Islamic soil'.

He offered to mobilize his Arab Afghans to fight the Iraqi threat instead, and then, when spurned, returned in a huff to Afghanistan in spring 1991. Once again, he was chased out, this time by Afghans, who having rid the country of Soviet troops were less than enthused at the prospect of accommodating an arrogant foreign militia. He spent the next four years in Sudan, evading Arab secret police and an assassination attempt in his local mosque, before US and Saudi pressure persuaded Sudan to expel him. By now, his peregrinations had begun to echo those of Imru al-Qays, the wandering, mythical king of Arabian epic forced out of his ancestral valley into the harsh world of Byzantine–Persian superpower politics. In 1996, he arrived in Afghanistan as a guest of the newly ascendant Taliban and set about using his family wealth to revive al-Qaeda and build what one of his foot-soldiers later described as a '*jihad* camp for the world'.

The Muslim periphery was not the only sanctuary for *jihadi* exiles. Britain's reputation as a haven for foreign opposition groups, and for lax asylum laws, also made it an attractive destination. The first to arrive were injured Afghan veterans sent to Britain for rest and recuperation. But many mujahideen had grave misgivings about resorting to infidels to salvage their Islamic mission. In the summer of 1993, twelve *jihadi* scholars, including the Jordanian spiritual mentor of radical Islam, Abu Qatada, met in Peshawar to debate the question of whether Islamic law permitted a Muslim to seek asylum in a non-Muslim land. A few, including a preacher who had journeyed from London, argued that a non-Muslim society would tempt the true Muslim from the righteous path. But a majority consented, citing the precedent of the Prophet Muhammad's flight to the then Christian haven of Abyssinia. 'There's no difference between British and Arab governments,' Abu Qatada is said to have argued. 'None of them are Islamic. As a Muslim, you must go where you feel secure.'

Following this *fatwa*, or legal opinion, Arab Afghans flocked to London, initially flying British Airways direct from Karachi to London, until their false passports raised the suspicions of the British immigration authorities and they had to travel via the Gulf and

Sudan instead. They were the latest in an incoming wave of Arab political émigrés who by the 1980s had turned Britain into an Arab media centre free from the clutches of the Middle East's censors. Following suit, Arab Afghans dubbed London 'the intellectual capital of Islamic Jihad', and a plethora of Islamic groups, including bin Laden's, set up their media operations in London, and indulged in the oxygen of publicity afforded by the presence of so many Arab newspapers and satellite channels. So important was London as a *jihadi* centre that the records of bin Laden's satellite phone used as evidence in American court cases showed that by 1998 the bulk of his calls were made to Britain. In the mid-1990s, the Arab Afghans were joined by a fresh influx of Islamist politicians and fighters on the run from Middle Eastern governments. To the fury of Arab leaders, Britain dismissed official Egyptian, Saudi, Yemeni, Tunisian and Algerian requests for extradition as interference in its liberal traditions of asylum. But there is little doubt that at times London served as a logistical support base, as well as a soapbox, for the armed Islamist struggle, and some asylum seekers continued to illegally exit and re-enter Britain on false passports.

Western exile had a profound impact on the *jihadi* movement. It broadened its horizons and spawned a fresh formulation of its mission. For guerrillas in Egypt and Algeria, *jihad* had been essentially a local armed struggle, a second war of national liberation. For the exiles in London, *jihad* was global, ideological and curiously Anglocentric. They saw individual Arab rulers not as towering Pharaohs, but as American puppets, and their rampant repression and corruption as a symptom of a larger evil, namely Western neo-imperialism. Their target audience was not a nation-state, but the worldwide *umma*, or nation, of one billion Muslims, and their goal was to spark a global Islamic rebellion. The new ideology sparked a bitter doctrinal rift between the nationalist *jihadis* and bin Laden's 'cosmopolitans'. The roots of the dispute dated back to the rout of Soviet forces from Afghanistan, when bin Laden had opposed the doctrine of *takfir*, or excommunication, and the declaration of a *jihad* in Muslim countries. In an echo of his Muslim

Brotherhood roots, he argued that *jihad* was only legitimate when waged against non-Muslim rulers in the *dar al-kharb* ('land of war'). Former brothers-in-arms denounced him as a renegade *jihadi*, and one group tried to assassinate him.

The internal feud flared into the open in 1998, when to the shock of many of his followers, the exiled chief of Egyptian *jihad*, Ayman al-Zawahari, announced an alliance with bin Laden's al-Qaeda. The ideological partnership was signed with a joint *fatwa* declaring war on the United States and sealed with the marriage of the daughter of Zawahari's deputy, Muhammed Ataf, to bin Laden's son. Their *fatwa* called on all Muslims to 'fulfil their duty [*sic*] to kill Americans and their allies' — civilians and soldiers alike — 'in order to liberate the al-Aqsa mosque and the Holy Mosque [Mecca] from their grip'. Entitled 'Declaration of *Jihad* against Crusaders and Jews', it listed three *casus belli*: the US bases in the Arabian peninsula where 'the crusader armies are spreading like locusts', US 'dismemberment and destruction' of Iraq, and finally American backing for 'the petty state of the Jews'. The global movement wound up operations in Egypt, and opened new fronts against the non-Muslim *dar al-kharb* in Chechnya, Kashmir, the Philippines and Bosnia.

The depiction of Western powers as wolves in sheep's clothing struck a chord in the region. Following Desert Storm, the United States consolidated its military presence on a scale not seen in the region since the days of the British Empire. The US maintained it was protecting the Gulf states from the twin threats of Iran and Iraq, but the continuous footage of Western attacks on Palestine, Iraq and later Afghanistan convinced many that their supposed ally was in fact a foe. Nowhere was this view as deeply held as in Saudi Arabia, where the new prevailing mood of anti-Americanism attracted the interest of a powerful caucus of senior royals, apparently including that of Crown Prince Abdullah. Even during the Gulf War, he was reported to have expressed regret that his soldiers were being sent to fight Iraq, rather than joining Iraqis to 'reclaim our usurped rights in Palestine'.

Washington's failure to appreciate the resentment engendered by its military presence in Saudi Arabia showed a distinct lack of historical perspective. Only a generation earlier, neighbouring Yemenis had fought to expel British troops from Aden, and the mood was as militant in Saudi Arabia. For centuries, the ruling puritanical Wahhabi sect had defended the al-Sauds from outside predators, and their zeal had ensured that Saudi Arabia was the only Arab state to escape European colonization. The Western thirst for oil and the heady pace of modernization made their task all the more urgent. Through their control of the kingdom's education, media and mosques, ultra-orthodox prelates raised Saudi youth on a theological diet that taught good Muslims to combat *kufr*, or infidel, forces. Even in kindergarten, children learnt to recite the saying attributed to the second caliph, Omar: 'I will purify the Arabian peninsula of Jews and Christians.'

A showdown between the opposing forces was only a matter of time. In the aftermath of the Gulf War, a hundred prominent preachers presented King Fahd with the first in a series of increasingly vehement petitions attacking his 'illegitimate foreign alliances'. 'What is happening in the Gulf is part of a larger Western design to dominate the whole Arab and Muslim world,' warned one of their most prominent preachers, Safar al-Hawali, in a taped 1991 sermon for which he was jailed. The authorities oscillated between intermittent crackdowns in deference to their American allies and forbearance, noting that acceptance of a Western military presence had led to the downfall of Arab monarchies in Egypt, Iraq and Libya. In 1994, bin Laden was stripped of his Saudi citizenship, and soon after hundreds of his followers were imprisoned. Bin Laden replied with an open letter to King Fahd in which he admonished the Saudi leader for marrying his 'destiny to that of the crusader Western governments'. In late 1995 a car bomb destroyed the US military training mission in the centre of Riyadh: the opening shot in his war on America.

Islamist guerrillas in Algeria and Egypt had both attacked foreigners as part of their local armed struggle; bin Laden's *jihad* was the first to make them its primary objective. His targets were initially either military or official, audaciously simple and spectacularly high-profile. In 1996 a truck bomb devastated an American military barracks in the eastern Saudi city of Khobar, injuring or killing nearly 400 Americans (although Washington pinned the blame on Iranian-backed Shiite groups), and two years later the same method was used to destroy two US embassies in East Africa in simultaneous attacks on 7 August 1998. Saudi political columnists noted that the operation coincided with the eighth anniversary of the arrival of American troops in Saudi Arabia. For the first time, Washington hit back at bin Laden, lobbing cruise missiles at Afghan caves and Khartoum, which did little to damage al-Qaeda but wrecked a Sudanese plant manufacturing medicines. Two years later, al-Qaeda packed a motorboat with explosives and rammed it into the side of an American destroyer, USS *Cole*, docked off the southern Yemeni port of Aden. In what bin Laden interpreted as a sign of success, the United States abandoned the Yemeni refuelling depot for its Fifth Fleet and pulled its military personnel out of Aden.

Over the following months, Western expatriates in the peninsula continued to fall victim to small-scale attacks inspired but not planned by al-Qaeda. By now Washington was fully appraised of the threat, and bin Laden was named as the United States' most wanted terrorist. Under American pressure his cadres were chased from Yemen, Sudan and Britain back to the safe haven accorded them by the Taliban in Afghanistan. Armed with their laptops they wrote treatise after treatise of Islamist theory. One intellectual, Abu Walid al-Masri, typed his 100,000th page on the history of the *jihad* movement, and Zawahari finished his partially published opus, *Knights Under the Flag of the Prophet*, forewarning the onset of the final showdown with the 'evil empire' of the United States on its home turf.

14. Bellum Americanum

For *jihadis* who had long despaired of their impotency in the face of outside forces, al-Qaeda's coordinated crashing of hijacked planes into Manhattan's Twin Towers and the Pentagon on 11 September 2001 recaptured their imagination and revived respect for Islamist militancy. From Java to New Jersey, small groups of worshippers performed the *Qunut* – an additional supplication, accompanied by the words, 'May God destroy America'. At the same time it triggered horror, within the Muslim world as well as without, over the morality of a cause which claimed to act in accordance with divine will. Iran's President Khatami publicly denounced the killing of 2,976 people as a crime against humanity and its perpetrators as beyond the pale of Islam.

Washington's response – the war on terror – deepened the divisions where there was scope for healing. The Orwellian terminology was apt for a campaign which was multi-pronged, global and ongoing. In their own countries, Western powers swiftly cracked down on émigré Muslims, chasing *jihadi* support groups underground. Abroad, US planes waged war on Afghanistan, overthrowing bin Laden's hosts, the Taliban, and bombing his mountainous Tora Bora hide-out.

Middle Eastern regimes initially hoped to merge their own local struggles against their Islamist opposition with Washington's global campaign. Their leaders took succour from watching Western powers replace the civil liberties discourse they had advanced in the 1990s with that of counter-terrorism. Led by Washington, Western governments applied the same measures they had once berated Arab states for – military and in camera tribunals, internment, indefinite detention, guilt by association – and tightened asylum procedures. 'Join the approach that has long been charted by Syria,' Bashar al-Assad advised visiting American congressmen. Egypt's prime minister, Atif Obeid, called on the US 'to use our model to fight terror'.

The shifting Western focus allowed Arab regimes to back-pedal on democratic reforms and consolidate their security regimes. Jordan, a rare shining star of reform through the 1990s, suspended parliament, delayed elections, ruled by decree (promulgating a ban on the playing of religious cassettes in buses and taxis) and dispatched intelligence agents to take up editorial posts at the kingdom's newspapers. Israel, Egypt, Libya and Algeria all handed Washington and London lists of local Islamists, and by linking them to al-Qaeda garnered Western support for their campaigns against their exiled oppositions. After a twenty-year boycott, Libyan leader Qaddafy was rehabilitated as a new recruit to the war on terror, and Algeria's president was fêted at the White House in 2001, for the first time in fifteen years. '[Arab] dictators have never been so well regarded in the world as they have since September 11,' bemoaned Moncef Marzouki, a prominent Tunisian dissident forced into exile.

Washington, however, was rife with debate on the wisdom of tying its colours to the region's dictators. A vocal and increasingly prominent view argued that security regimes were less the panacea of global *jihad* than its cause. *Jihadi* violence was a product of internal and unaddressed ills inside the Arab world; had Arab regimes ruled less brutally and more equitably, they would not have exported their ills to the West. Regime-change, engineered externally, argued these ideologues known as neo-conservatives, would liberate populations from their current tyranny, install democracies, turn the population into stakeholders in their societies, and spread Western values. The neo-cons allied themselves with American imperialists and business interests inside the Bush Administration to plan the reconfiguration of the Middle East and its vast oil wealth.

The time was propitious for grand ventures. Flushed from its initial conquest of Afghanistan, Washington felt buoyed to tackle the region where the nineteen hijackers originated. Saudi Arabia initially seemed a fitting target since fifteen of the hijackers were Saudi citizens. The kingdom's alliance with the US – which had strengthened throughout the Cold War, when the Saudi brand of Islam had served to unsettle the Muslim underbelly of the Soviet bloc – faced severe strain. Post 9/11, US officials scoffed at their erstwhile allies as 'Arab Taliban', and wondered whether there might not be more reliable guarantors of US interests than the Al Sauds. The US–Saudi annual review of military relations was cancelled, and a $10 million gift from a Saudi prince to the victims of the World Trade Center less than politely returned.

Anger in the Arab world was also on the rise. Schoolchildren in the kingdom distributed lists of US goods to boycott. In a rare admission of vulnerability, the then Saudi ambassador to Washington, Bandar bin Sultan, defended the kingdom's reluctance to join America's anti-Taliban alliance. 'In a Western democracy, when you lose touch with your people, you lose elections,' he said. 'In a monarchy, you lose your head.'

All the same, rather than destabilize the world's prime energy supplier, Washington focused its sights on Iraq, a more tangential front of *jihad*. None of the hijackers were Iraqis; none of the hundreds of calls Western intelligence agencies monitored on bin Laden's satellite phone stemmed from Iraq. In fact, Iraq's programme of weapons of destruction, not its support for global *jihad*, was the US's *casus belli*.

That said, Iraq offered many attractions for a comparatively low cost. Ten years of sanctions had whittled away its former strength, leaving its military arsenal, so impressive on paper, wasting and obsolete. Iraq also made an apt starting point for instituting regional change, and rebalancing America's regional alliances away from autocrats and towards broader-based social forces. But, in the name of democracy, America opened the Pandora's box of sectarianism. By toppling Saddam Hussein and ousting his narrow powerbase rooted in a security force drawn from Iraq's central Sunni tribes, the US overturned four centuries of Sunni dominance of Shias.

While Sunnis comprised 85 per cent of Muslims worldwide, within the Middle East Sunni and Shia populations were more finely balanced. From the borders of Afghanistan to the Levant, Shias constituted 140 million people, or half the population. In Lebanon they were the largest single confessional group, officially estimated at 38 per cent. They formed 65 per cent of Bahrain's population; 42 per cent of Yemen's, 35 per cent of Kuwait's and 15 per cent of the UAE's. In Saudi Arabia, they numbered 1.6 million, or 10 per cent of the population. There were also substantial Shia minorities in Syria, Turkey and Pakistan. But the largest Shia population of all was in Iraq.

Under Saddam Hussein, Sunni Arabs exercised power through Iraq's security apparatus and the support they garnered from neighbouring Sunni Arab states who perceived Iraq as the Arab bulwark against Persian designs on the region. Yet Sunni Arabs comprised barely a fifth of the Shia majority state. Amid the rising sectarian rivalry, Shia populations around the world anticipated regime change as liberation from the Sunni yoke.

Sunni power brokers were less enthused, fearing Saddam Hussein's fall might trigger a domino effect. Ever since Napoleon Bonaparte first conquered the Nile Delta in 1799, Western colonial powers had chipped at more than a millennium of Sunni Muslim rule, divvying-up the Near East between non-Arab or non-Sunni satraps. In the carve-up that followed the First World War, Christians had won power in Lebanon and Jews in Palestine; a generation later Alawites had won power in Syria. Fearing further erosion, Jordan's King Abdullah warned that US policy would create a Shia arc extending horizontally from Iran west through Iraq, Syria and Lebanon to the Mediterranean, and vertically incorporating the world's largest oilfields from the Shia-majority Azerbaijan in the north via Iraq to the eastern Arabian coast.

At the Arab summit in Beirut in March 2002, Gulf leaders publicly embraced Saddam's deputy, Izzat Eddin Ibrahim. Visiting American officials preparing their war plans faced constant clamouring that the region's crisis was in Palestine, where Israel was suppressing the second *intifada*, not Baghdad. Financial anxieties fuelled their fears. Jordan's monarch feared for his oil supply which Iraq supplied for free, and UN agencies – which had served as the conduit for $60 billion of Iraqi oil expenditures – faced the loss of their largest ever cash cow.

Saddam Hussein was neither an Iraqi Nasser nor an Arab Bismarck, and still less a new Saladin as some Arabs vainly hoped (Mussolini was a more likely antecedent). But his supply of medicines for Palestine's wounded, his cry of '*Jihad* to liberate Palestine!', his largesse to targeted social sectors (he built a housing estate for Jordanian journalists), and his image as a Sunni standard bearer all struck a popular chord. Thus, rather than celebrate the toppling of the region's most brutal dictator, Arab demonstrators took to the streets to protest against it. Egyptian and Jordanian police opened fire to quell near daily protests. In Damascus and Riyadh, thousands flouted interior ministry bans to rally outside US consulates.

Inside Iraq, the mood was decidedly ambivalent. Washington was widely perceived as serving its own needs, not Iraq's. Amid the countdown to war, the UN Security Council dispatched dozens of UN monitors to rake Iraq for elusive weapons of mass destruction, but none for human rights abuses. Sanctions too were widely blamed for eroding the coping mechanisms of Iraq's people, while strengthening the regime by giving it control over the population's bellies. That said, after a decade of foreign sanctions and internal brutalization, many looked for any way out. Shias, in particular, welcomed US intervention. Washington's rhetoric of rescuing Iraq from tyranny dovetailed surprisingly with Shia millennial theology, which promised redemption from oppression. Democracy was all the more attractive if it could deliver majority (Shia) rule.

The speed of America's conquest of Iraq was aptly likened to the six days in June 1967 it took Israel to conquer Jerusalem, the West Bank, the Golan Heights and Sinai. Galloping 700 kilometres from the Kuwaiti border, US forces captured Baghdad in ten days, and the country in less than three weeks. Government forces largely fled. With remarkably few casualties, the invasion toppled the most militarized regime in the Arab world.

The pace of conquest, however, was illusory. As America's forces raced north, they bypassed most of Iraq's cities. The regime collapsed, but a plethora of well-armed local chieftains and religious leaders filled the vacuum. In Baghdad, mobs pillaged the assets of central government, stymieing the possibility of an immediate resumption of central control. The machinery of state – public records offices, prisons and courtrooms – was reduced to ash, and symbols of power, including the world's greatest Assyrian collection at the Iraq Museum, stripped. In the north, Kurdish *peshmerga* forces expanded their Kurdish autonomous zone southwards, into the territories of a purported ancestral Kurdistan, including the oil-rich town of Kirkuk. US generals, who weeks earlier had scorned Saddam Hussein's seventy-two gold-plated palaces, L is XIV furniture and private swimming pools gave free rein to their troops to delight in them, oblivious to the unfolding looting and warlordism raging outside the gates.

Two months after the invasion, Washington attempted to assert control by appointing Paul Bremer, a former US counter-terrorism department chief, to head its Coalition Provisional Authority (CPA) charged with running Iraq. Within days of his arrival, he quashed planned local elections and ruled as sovereign, issuing fiats that began, 'I hereby promulgate', and were designed to serve as the architecture of a model state. By the time of his hurried departure thirteen months later, he had issued 100 orders, 17 memoranda, 12 public notices and 12 regulations, whose cumulative affect was to gut Iraq of its security forces, bureaucracy, nomenklatura and nationalized industries.

But for all his grandiose ambitions, Bremer never really projected his authority much beyond the walled Green Zone that US forces carved out of central Baghdad. Corruption was rife. His skeletal staff – often composed of novices and non-Arabic speakers – administered billions transferred in pallets of cash. US corporations grabbed the largest contracts, and after taking huge service charges handed them on to subcontractors who took their slice and did the same. What little trickled into Iraq was used to hire migrant labourers, as in Arab Gulf states. Iraqi employees and products were considered too high-risk. By the end of his tenure, Bremer had spent all Iraq's oil revenues as well as the Iraqi assets which the UN had

A History of the Middle East

frozen and licensed for his disposal. Of the promised reconstruction, there was no sign.

His political architecture was similarly threadbare. In deference to local demands for representation, he appointed a 25-member Governing Council of Iraqis, divvying out posts on the basis of sectarian demographic weight. Though hailed as Iraq's most representative body because it awarded Shiites a majority, most of its members were long-term exiles. All but one of its nine rotating presidents lived abroad, five of them in London. Bremer's plans were similarly foreign. His blueprint for revamping Iraq was based on the Allied reconstruction of post-war Germany. In place of de-Nazification he imposed de-Baathification, disbanding the forces of law and order to the last traffic warden. But while he perfected his plans in his palace, other forces unleashed by the US invasion reshaped Iraq on the ground.

Iraq's Shia Conversion

Saddam's overthrow precipitated a wave of Shia triumphalism. By the time US tanks rolled into Saddam City, the capital's slum district which was home to two million Shiites, young clerics surfacing from years in hiding were already in control and fanning out through the city. By the end of April 2003, clerics controlled two-thirds of Baghdad's clinics and a third of its hospitals. Saddam City was renamed Sadr City, after the two leading Shia clerics who had opposed Saddam. Across southern Iraq vigilantes led by clerics imposed their version of Islamic law, lashing alcohol merchants and destroying gypsy encampments.

After decades of suppression and closure, the *husseiniya*, or Shia prayer hall, resurfaced as the hub of communal decision-making. Exuberant Shia crowds whitewashed Saddam's ubiquitous aphorisms and stencils from billboards and classroom walls, and replaced them with images of ayatollahs. They unearthed mass graves, where according to Human Rights Watch Saddam had buried 300,000

Shias. Shia seminaries, closed as part of Baath party policy as comprehensive as Henry VIII's dissolution of the monasteries, also resurfaced. For the first time in centuries, Shia flags flew over Iraq's institutions. In short, America's toppling of the Baath spawned a Shia renaissance.

The religiosity appeared to take the American newcomers by surprise. Paul Wolfowitz, the US deputy secretary of defence, had predicted Iraqi Shiites would be better friends for the US than the Saudis because they were 'secular'. But within months the US-appointed Governing Council had signed a Basic Law, or quasi-constitution, stipulating that Iraq's laws should conform to the Islamic canon.

That said, despite appearances, the clergy's ascendancy in Iraq bore significant differences to that in neighbouring Iran. Unlike Ayatollah Khomeini and his theory of the *velayat al-faqih*, or sovereignty of a single religious jurisprudent, Iraq's leading clerics did not aspire to create a theocracy, still less to run one, but rather to advise the ruling authorities. The leading religious party, Dawa, espoused the notion of *velayat al-umma*, or popular sovereignty, in which the people served as God's vice-regents and held legislative and executive power. 'Islamic theory rejects aristocratic regimes and proposes a form of government which contains all the positive aspects of the democratic system,' wrote their leading ideologue Mohammed Baqir al-Sadr in the 1970s before Saddam tortured him to death.

Foremost amongst Iraq's Shia clerics was Grand Ayatollah Sistani. He made an unlikely Iraqi liberator. Born 800 miles away in the Iranian shrine city of Marshad in 1930, he first visited Iraq aged thirty and was something of a recluse. And yet for over a year his *fatwas*, written in a pinched hand, flummoxed and ultimately unseated Bremer, carrying far more weight than the latter's edicts heavy with legalese. Though cloistered in his Najaf office, he was the dynamo that drove Iraq's transition to democracy. He gave elections a religious stamp of approval, declared voting an Islamic duty, and as spiritual leader of Iraq's largest community, kept Iraq's 15 million Shias from open revolt against US forces on the understanding that the US would stage free and fair elections and hand power to their victors.

To this end he galvanized demonstrations in numbers rarely seen in the Middle East except at funerals. Launched in January 2004 from the Basra mosque where Shia rebels had launched their 1991 revolt, the protestors marched north, gathering numbers as they moved up the Tigris. By the time they reached Baghdad, Bremer had begun to backtrack on his ambition to govern Iraq. In March 2004, he handed back the first ministry to Iraqi rule, and as he ended a visit to the health ministry officials unfurled a large black banner from its rooftop, proclaiming 'Hussein's Revolution'. Bremer furtively left Baghdad in June 2004, handing over to an unelected Interim Iraqi Government and a US ambassador. Despite mounting violence, Sistani continued to champion Iraq's first parliamentary elections, set for January 2005, turning his office into an election machine. He authorized a single Shia list, dispensed millions of dollars in campaign funds, and used the 2,500 mosques which followed his *fatwas* to broadcast voting instructions to the faithful. Defying the threat of massacres by Sunni rebels seeking to enforce a boycott and thwart a Shia victory, Shias turned out to vote in their millions.

Sistani did face challenges to his reformist creed. Muqtada Sadr was the young scion of Iraq's most prominent clerical family, with a reputation for siding with the Shia poor and dispossessed. Impatient with Sistani's constitutional approach, Sadr called for a popular revolution against both the US occupation and the mercantile elites allied with Sistani. After failing to spark a popular uprising in November 2003 with a creed steeped in millenarianism, he opted for military means. He assembled a 60,000-strong armed force, drawn largely from the lower, and predominantly Shia, ranks of Saddam's disbanded infantry. He named it the Mahdi's Army after the twelfth Imam of the Shiites, who according to Shia tradition would return as the Messiah, and made rapid gains. In March 2004 his forces swept through seven southern provinces, and overran police stations and a Coalition base from Basra to Kirkuk, procuring much-needed arms in the process. They also wrested control of Iraq's lucrative Shia shrine-cities, Karbala and Najaf, from Sistani's clerics. Though rapidly pushed back elsewhere in Iraq, they only abandoned Najaf after US-led forces, with Sistani's tacit assent, stormed the shrine in August 2004.

Amid growing intra-Shia rancour, forces professing loyalty to Sistani repeatedly clashed with Sadr's as they vied for control of Shia towns. Only loosely controlled by the clerics, the military wings repeatedly resorted to gangsterism. After heavy fighting for control of Basra in spring 2008, US–Iraqi forces attacked Sadr's heartland in Baghdad, Sadr City. Sadr disbanded his forces and fled to Iran to study religious jurisprudence in Qom, determined to renew his claim to political and religious Shia leadership at a later date.

The Sunni Counter-attack

As Saddam's Sunni hierarchy tumbled under the combined assault of Bremer's decrees and Shia supremacists, angry protests erupted led by the newly unemployed. For the most part, they closely mirrored Iraq's sectarian divide. Heavy-handed US responses, particularly in Fallujah, where US forces opened fire on demonstrators to lethal effect, fuelled the anger. Without a Sistani figure to harness dissent, Sunni opposition in central and northern Iraq fragmented into loosely coordinated cells of former soldiers, under the command of Saddam's generals, particularly those of the Republican Guard. Their targets were the newly ascendant Shia leadership, US forces, and the foreign mercenaries and Iraqis they employed.

An influx of *jihadi* groups, who trickled in from Afghanistan before the invasion and flooded from across the region and beyond soon afterwards, fuelled animosities. Hosted in Sunni areas, they made common cause – or in the words of US commanders 'a marriage of convenience' – with ex-Baathist cells. From their rear bases along the upper Euphrates and Tigris valleys, especially in the western province of Anbar, they conducted a wave of suicide bombings in Iraq's major cities. Initially focusing on foreign targets – the Jordanian Embassy and the Baghdad headquarters of the UN and Red Cross were amongst the first targets – they increasingly targeted Shia civilians.

The brutality of US counter-insurgency methods and the siege and subsequent storming of Anbar's main towns, Fallujah and Ramadi, only accentuated sympathies for the *jihadis*, further cementing the alliance with the local population. In contrast to Arab nationalism, *jihadi* ideology thrived on repression. 'Jihadi violence is like a virus,' noted an exiled ideologue. 'The more you bomb it, the more it spreads.'

Despite, or perhaps because of, Saddam's capture in December 2003, the revolt flourished. *Jihadi* cells were ever more in the commanding seat. The following month rebels dispatched their first platoon-sized Special Forces – operating under such names as 'Jihadi Earthquake Brigades', challenging US forces' hold on provincial capitals. In October 2006, an umbrella group of *jihadi* organizations in Mesopotamia declared an independent Islamic state covering Arab Sunni provinces across Iraq. US forces had some success co-opting Iraqi Sunnis by reviving military units Bremer had disbanded, but *jihadi* groups retained remarkable staying power. Six years on, they continued to jolt central government with a series of huge bombings against government offices.

Iraq's Civil War and Shia Victory

Iraq does not split neatly into Sunni and Shia parts. Iraqi tribes straddle the sectarian divide and most count tribesmen from both. In the north, a substantial minority of Iraq's Kurds are Shia; in the south a quarter of Basra is Sunni, and Baghdad is a communal patchwork. Or was.

Bremer's handover of formal control to Iraqis launched the communal race for control of Iraq. Shias fought with the demographic muscle of the ballot box, Sunnis with arms. At their peak, an average of six suicide bombings a day struck Baghdad, sometimes targeting Shias in their market places, other times their shrines. Guided by Sistani, Shias displayed remarkable restraint. But Shias were increasingly traumatized: rumours of a suicide bomber loose amongst pilgrims on a bridge linking Baghdad's two principal shrines precipitated a stampede in which nearly 1,000 people died – the single worst toll in post-invasion Iraq. As the bloodshed swelled, people on both sides looked to armed groups to safeguard their economic, legal and physical well-being.

The *jihadis'* destruction of Samarra's gold-topped İmam al-Asqari Shia shrine in February 2007 marked the tipping point. In its wake, Shia militants attacked over a hundred Sunni mosques and killed a dozen Sunni imams. Death squads armed with electric drills toured heterogeneous but predominantly Shia suburbs and satellite towns of Baghdad, torturing Sunnis to death. The predominantly Shia security forces – drafted by the Iraqi government under US supervision and commanded by a Shia interior minister and his appointees – exacerbated the terror. Sunni fighters, who had fared well against US troops, were increasingly on the defensive. Three-quarters of the 3,000 cadavers arriving in Baghdad morgues every month in 2007 were Sunni.

The revenge killings triggered a Sunni flight, emptying whole neighbourhoods of their non-Shia populations. As they fled, US forces erected concrete blast-walls and checkpoints, splitting the capital into cantons of separate sects and quarantined confessions. Baghdad's hotchpotch grew increasingly monochrome, with the east bank of the Tigris – Rusafa – almost entirely rid of its Sunnis. Similar scenes repeated themselves in other hitherto mixed parts of Iraq. By 2007 over two million mainly Sunni Iraqis had fled north or abroad: an average of 100,000 people per month. Many were middle class. In their absence sectarian warlords and tribal sheiks held ever greater sway.

When the civil war's dust settled in 2008 the result was a striking change in Baghdad's demography. A Colombia University survey revealed that of the capital's five million people, only a few hundred thousand were Sunni. Countrywide, the proportion of Iraq's Sunni Arabs fell from 20 to 12 per cent of the population. Washington claimed credit for the decline of the Sunni insurgency, attributing it to its increased troop 'surge', beginning in summer 2007. More accurately, the Shia counter-attack had shattered Sunni resistance. Many Sunni fighters jumped at the US offer to register for a Sons of Iraq programme, which allowed them to keep their guns and earn cash nominally fighting al-Qaeda, and salvage a little honour from the jaws of defeat. Having previously fought ballots with bullets, Sunni Arabs begrudgingly ended their boycott and insurgency, and accepted political integration into the post-Saddam Iraq. By 2009, the death-toll had dropped from a few thousand to a few dozen per month.

The costs of Shia victory were huge. Seven years on, 5 per cent of Iraq's 27 million people had been killed, wounded or uprooted. Twice as many Americans had been killed as had died on 9/11, and the estimated cost – according to a US Congressional report – topped $4 trillion. For all the talk of reconstruction, the only cranes on Baghdad's horizon pre-dated the war and were stationary. Oil production remained below pre-war levels. And power and water cuts in the oil-rich state were the norm.

The Region-wide Rise of Popular Movements

The colonial powers that carved countries out of the Ottoman Middle East had predicted that over time they would gain weight as independent states, acquire national identities and win the ensuing loyalty of their subjects in return. Eighty years on, they were struggling to keep afloat. People increasingly identified and expressed a sense of belonging to pre-existing tribal or other bonds, not their nation. Hybrid populations fractured according to ethnicity or sect.

Marriage between sects, once common, waned. Walls divided cities, mapping sectarian or ethnic boundaries.

Centrifugal forces were most striking in the once unified state of Iraq. Kurds turned their safe haven into a virtual protectorate, with their own flag, language and parliament; Shia factions campaigned for a nine-province autonomous zone in the south; and Sunni groups declared their own emirates. The same forces unravelling Iraq spilled into neighbouring states, tearing at their seams. Lebanon's 1990 Taif agreement, which ended the civil war and promised an abrogation of confessional politics, remained ink on paper.

Young Lebanese – more than their parents – grew up first and foremost Maronites, Shiites, Sunnis or Druze. Jewish irredentist parties in Israel campaigned to rid their state of many of its Arabs. Moments of crisis, such as the 2006 war with Israel, amplified Lebanon's communalism. Berber movements in Algeria and Morocco struggled against the ruling ideology of Arabism and clamoured for minority rights and recognition of their tongue, Tamazight, as an official language. Even Saudis began defining themselves not by their kingdom but by their region – the Hejaz coastal strip in the west, the Shia Hasa region in the east, and the tribal rump in the middle.

A key cause of the draw of transnational ideologies and the erosion of belief in a nation state was the failure of Arab regimes to meet the needs of their people. Mismanagement, inequalities, corruption and state violence eroded their credibility. Saddled with rapidly growing populations and archaic economies, they struggled to maintain patronage mechanisms and provide jobs. In many Arab states, oil exports cushioned the authorities from addressing the malaise as long as prices remained high. But when prices fell (for instance from $145 a barrel in July 2008 to $35 five months later) and the global economy slumped, governments were forced to slash subsidies. Iranian President Mahmoud Ahmadinejad failed to deliver promises to lift 14 million of his country's 70 million-strong population out of poverty, and faced mass urban opposition in 2009 when he stood for re-election. Syria struggled to deal with the loss of Gulf largesse, free Iraqi oil and Lebanese resources. Economic crisis in

Yemen, the Arab world's poorest state, sparked provincial revolts, as oil production levels almost halved in a decade across the region. Mounting corruption and human rights abuses further undermined confidence in the state's provision of law and order.

Overburdened central governments increasingly surrendered their roles as ultimate welfare provider, social safety net, judicial arbiter and protector to clan, confessional and ethnic movements. Tribal sheikhs and ayatollahs filled the vacuum left by ineffective heads of state. Local leaders derived further strength by rallying with kin or co-believers beyond national boundaries, creating supranational or transnational identities which further weakened the state.

A stream of refugees criss-crossing the region helped to transfuse the communalism, as well as in some countries tilt demographic balances. Shia communities expanded rapidly in the UAE, Jordan and Syria. Iraq's Sunni exiles, too, set up base in neighbouring states, carrying their animosities with them.

Sweeping media innovations further helped carry the trans-national identities to a mass audience beyond the reach of state media. The advent of fax, the internet and satellite television brought voices hitherto stifled by the regimes' monopoly on information and bans on public protest into the home. The initial challenges were costly and cumbersome: in 1993, Saudi dissidents – the Committee for the Defence of Legitimate Rights, or CDLR – fled to London and each week spent thousands distributing a newsletter alleging rampant immorality within the House of Saud. Electronic mail and the inter-net much reduced costs while raising awareness with targeted reports. Egyptian students and workers defied government efforts to thwart labour protests by organizing a general strike via internet chat-rooms; and tens of thousands of Saudis used Facebook to expose officials behind the bureaucratic failings which led to the deaths of hundreds in flash floods in Jedda in November 2009. Mobile phones and such web community sites as Twitter helped stoke Iran's countrywide protests following the contested 2009 elections.

Satellite television further enchanced the capablilities of transnational movements, and enabled leaders to reach the disenfranchised
and illiterate, who comprised a third of the Arab population.
Unencumbered by censorship restrictions, regimes that sent their
dissidents into exile soon found them beamed back by satellite. Saudi
dissidents demanding political liberalization, an end to a one-family
kingdom, and even the separation of religion and state went
from jail to the television studio. Iranian supporters of the deposed
Shah in Los Angeles brodcast calls for a royalist rebellion to the
disaffected in Tehran. Qatar's al-Jazeera, the most popular, innovative and earliest Arabic satellite station, gave the Muslim
Brotherhood's televangelist, Yusuf Qaradawi, his own prime-time
programme, *Sharia and Life*, and procured exclusive coverage of bin
Laden's homilies. In 1990, Saudi state radio suppressed news of the
Iraqi invasion of Kuwait for three days. Ten years on, such censorship was inconceivable. Much as the age of printing in Europe
challenged fifteenth-century Christian orthodoxy through unme-
diated access to sacred texts, so the information age enabled the
region's population to challenge the established order.

Initially, some governments sought to proscribe the medium.
Egypt confiscated satellite dishes on grounds of curbing porno-
graphy and upholding Islamic mores, and Teheran dispatched gangs
of religious vigilantes to rip them from rooftops. But they failed to
quell demand. Unable to silence the technology, the regimes
adopted it. Iran launched its own satellite channel in late 1997, as
well as a 24-hour Arabic-language station, al-Alam, broadcasting to
Shia communities in Iraq and the Gulf.

Struggling to bolster their legitimacy, some Arab regimes sought
to pin their national identities to transnational ones. Many Sunni
states launched heavily publicized campaigns against alleged Shia
missionaries, banned Shia places of worship and ran news bulletins
that reported Sunni suicide bombings in Iraq as legitimate acts of
resistance. In his eulogy, President Mubarak called Saddam a martyr,
and charged that, Arab or not, Shias were loyal to Iran. Muammar
Qaddafy commissioned a statue of Saddam to stand next to Omar

al-Mukhtar, the Libyan resistance leader hanged by the country's
Italian occupiers. Jordanian immigration police questioned Iraqi
refugees with the words, 'Muslim or Shia?' Shia politicians also let
barbs fly. Iraq's interior minister, Bayan Jabr, mocked the Saudi
foreign minister as 'a Beduin on a camel', after the latter warned of
rising Iranian influence inside Iraq.

Fuelled by the rhetoric, new regional blocs began to crystallize.
While Sunni Arab regimes shunned the Shia-majority Governing
Council, Tehran was the first to recognize its authority as Iraq's
representative body. It opened 'consulates' in Iraq's Shia shrine cities,
ostensibly to oversee the welfare of the thousands of pilgrims, and
facilitated the return of Iraqi exiles from Iran, some of them armed.
Several Shia militias, particularly the Badr forces, continued to
benefit from Iranian training and logistical support.

Fear of encroaching Iranian influence induced neighbouring
Sunni states to seek footholds inside Iraq. Jordan and Saudi Arabia
set up military field hospitals in the Sunni outskirts of the capital
and in Fallujah, the springboard of Sunni resistance. Turkey, nervous
of rising Kurdish clout on its borders, bolstered its pre-war presence
of 2,000 troops and forty tanks in northern Iraq with military 'liaison' offices, and opened a new office in Kirkuk. Fearing Shia
revanchism, Jordan and other Sunni Arab states for a time gave free
passage to Sunni *jihadi* fighters. ('We cannot prevent people from
choosing to commit suicide,' observed Jordan's information minister, Mohammed Adwan.) By 2005, half the thousands of foreign
jihadis in Iraq were Saudis. Yet while successful in rallying their
subjects around a common cause, Arab regimes' actions reinforced
the very non-state actors that eroded their sovereignty.

Shia Non-state Actors

Iraq's transformation galvanized Shiites across the region who were
seeking to shrug off their second-class status, and produced a new
benchmark for securing their rights. Released from the Baath's

shackles, the city of Najaf served as a dynamo energizing Shia movements, particularly in Iran where many considered Sistani their spiritual leader. In response to President Ahmadinejad's contested election victory in 2009, frustrated youth led by dissident clerics sympathetic to Sistani's school of Shiism took to the streets in the country's biggest political awakening in decades.

Ayatollah Sistani's religious endorsement of elections and mass demonstrations ignited similar protests in the Arab heartland. When Iraqis went to the polls in 2005, tens of thousands in Bahrain, the Gulf archipelago where Shias comprised a majority, staged protests demanding King Hamad ibn Isa al-Khalifa introduce similar reforms there. 'I think that Iraq could represent a democratic model for the Arab-Muslim world,' Ali Salman, a leading Shia politician and cleric in Bahrain told the crowds. After attempting to quell the protests with his security forces, the king agreed to hold parliamentary elections in November 2006. Despite gerrymandering, Shia opposition candidates won sixteen of the seventeen seats they contested, or 40 per cent of the total.

In Saudi Arabia, the authorities restricted Shia residency to particular zones, and barred them from working in the security forces and the courts. The Saudi embassy in Washington had no Shia staff, and some Saudi schools – a traditional Wahhabi domain – taught that Shia Islam was a Jewish heresy. Following Saddam's downfall and inspired by Najaf's ayatollahs, 450 Saudi Shiites presented a tractate to King Abdullah – entitled 'Partners in the Homeland' – demanding an end to religious discrimination and the establishment of a Shia religious authority to regulate their internal affairs. A month later, Abdullah announced municipal elections for spring 2005, the kingdom's first, granting Shias and Sunnis limited, but equal, electoral rights. There were numerous restrictions. Half the seats on the council were appointed, and both women and political parties were banned, but Shia leaders opted for political participation not boycott, citing Sistani's *fatwa* declaring voting a religious duty.

Candidates in the predominantly Shia Eastern Province played down calls for autonomy, and played up demands for equal rights to local civil service posts, hitherto staffed by Sunnis parachuted in from other provinces. The results were impressive. While Sunni Saudis trickled to the polls, Shias flowed. In the town of Qatif – where the bulk of Sistani's adherents lived – almost four-fifths of registered voters cast their vote, the highest turnout countrywide, compared to less than a third in the capital, Riyadh. Shias who had hitherto organized underground now campaigned publicly. And following the vote, the Saudi provincial governor eased restrictions on Shia religious activity.

Against the backdrop of increasing external intervention in Lebanon, many Lebanese, across the sectarian divide, also adopted Sistani's model of mass action. The catalyst was the assassination of former prime minister Rafiq al-Hariri, in February 2005. Hariri was a businessman who had hitherto worked closely with the Syrian regime, but amid mounting resentment at the continued presence of Syrian forces in Lebanon – particularly after Israel pulled its forces from southern Lebanon in 2000– the relationship had grown increasingly strained. In 2004, exasperated by Syria's logistical support for Iraqi insurgents, the Bush administration oversaw the passage of Resolution 1559 through the UN Security Council, demanding all foreign forces leave Lebanon and paramilitary forces disband – an unstated reference to Hizbollah. Sensing Syria was on the back foot, Hariri and other politicians voiced support.

To secure his silence, Syria responded with its time-tested formula of violence, and on Valentine's Day 2005 Hariri was killed by a car bomb. The assassination backfired, provoking mass anti-Syrian protests which military orders to disperse failed to deter. Met with flowers, Lebanon's security forces themselves beat a retreat. Sensing a sea change in the public mood, Assad recalled his forces, ending a three-decade presence. By April 2005, the last Syrian soldier had left. Lebanon's confessional factions rushed to fill the vacuum, literally, by calling on their followers to converge on public squares. On 8 March 2005 Shias – the country's largest but poorest sect – converged on Beirut's plush city centre, the showpiece of Lebanon's civil war reconstruction, and led by Hizbollah's leader, Hassan Nasrallah, demanded an end to the quota system which divvied-up

Lebanon's cabinet and government posts by sect and diminished their demographic weight. A week later Lebanon's other sects united to stage a counter-rally against a 'one person, one vote' electoral system they feared would create another Shia-dominated state. This rally was larger and certainly more colourful, bringing the kaleido-scope of Lebanon's cultures into Martyrs Square: Sunni preachers in white tunics, Druze in woolly white hats, coiffured Maronite dames with their Pekinese and Filipina maids in tow, and above all young Lebanese in Western dress and hairstyles. For years, the two marches referred to by their dates – 8 March and 14 March – defined the two Lebanese camps vying for power.

Lebanon held successive elections which took place peacefully, but although all sects participated and formed coalition govern-ments, both camps prepared for a showdown. Facing continued demands for it to disarm from a common alliance of non-Shia sects, Hizbollah – which maintained the country's only active militia – increasingly opted for violence. To justify its retention of resistance forces six years after Israel's withdrawal from Southern Lebanon, it launched a border attack on Israel in July 2006. Over the following month it fended off a counter-attack by the region's most powerful military. Its medium-range missiles repeatedly struck Israel's third largest city, Haifa, as well as an Israeli battleship, and its electronic intelligence penetrated Israel's mobile telephone network. Even on the last day of battle, it retained sufficient muster to fire hundreds of missiles.

Externally its regional political capital soared, salvaging some of the Arab honour lost when the US invaded Iraq. Unlike Saddam's army, no Hizbollah soldier surrendered, and Iran quickly replen-ished its arsenal. Internally, however, Hizbollah suffered at the ballot box, 1,500 Lebanese civilians were killed and hundreds of thousands displaced. On the defensive politically, but with its military prow-ess strengthened in the battle with Israel, Hizbollah increasingly put its forces to use internally as well. Car bombs killed and maimed 14 March politicians and activists, and rival militias fought street battles. The government tried to curb Hizbollah's state-within-a-state, but

overreached. In May 2008, it tried to size control of Hizbollah's
internal telecommunications system, prompting the militia to send
its forces into central Beirut, the seat of government. Lebanon's
army only averted a civil war by staying out of the fray. 'We wanted
the army to give us security. But what can the army do when
Hizbollah is stronger than the army?' grumbled Walid Jumblatt, the
Druze leader in the beleaguered 14 March camp, while gunmen
paraded outside his Beirut home.

The Doha agreement broke the stalemate: Hizbollah translated
its military presence into political gain – withdrawing from West
Beirut in return for enough seats in government to veto any unilateral move by the 14 March majority. Elections a year later resulted
in a surprising victory for the 14 March camp, but in backroom deals
Hizbollah and its backers continued to deny it power. After five
months in limbo, the parties announced a coalition restoring the
status quo ante. Hizbollah held a third plus one of the thirty cabinet
seats, giving it the veto power necessary to protect its militia. Unable
to rely on Obama's support to the same degree as the Bush administration's, one by one 14 March's leaders trooped to Hizbollah's
neighbouring backer, Damascus. Jumblatt, a longstanding bell-
wether of Lebanese politics, went there first. Prime minister Saad
Hariri, who had led the campaign to indict Syrians for his father's
death, followed soon afterwards. In his government policy statement
he recognized Hizbollah's right to maintain its resistance. Ultimately,
Hizbollah's power rested in its diplomatic and military clout as much
as its *vox populi*.

Perhaps the most remarkable Shia awakening was in northern
Yemen, where most of the population are Zaydis, a Shia offshoot.
Zaydi rites and practices are closer to Sunni Islam than the Twelver
Shiism predominant in Iran and Iraq, and until toppled by the
1962 revolution its Imam had ruled over both Sunnis and Shias in
Yemen for a millennium. Though himself of Zaydi origins,
Yemen's president, Ali Abdullah Salih, remained deeply nervous
of Zaydi stirrings. In the 1990s he posted Iraqi Baathists schooled
in suppressing Shiism to the northern provincial capital and Zaydi

heartland, Saada; later he encouraged Salafi veterans of the Afghan *jihad*, who were even more implacably opposed to Shiism, to settle, study Wahhabi doctrines and train in Damaj, a desert oasis nearby.

The influx of outside forces disturbed the region's traditional social balance between Zaydism and Sunni orthodoxy. Fearing a religious assault, Zaydis took up arms in 2004 led by a young Najaf-trained Yemeni cleric, Hussein Badr al-Din al-Houthi, who gave his name to the movement. From his mountainous redoubt of Um Issa, where the Imamate had made its last stand in the 1960s, Houthi rallied a public alienated by the regime's corruption, subservience to Saudi and American foreign policies, and support of Wahhabi expansion, and called on Zaydis to rebel. Hundreds were killed in the army offensive that followed, including Houthi himself. His brothers took up the mantle, retreating deeper into the hills. Five years on, government onslaughts had yet to curb the insurgency, but had chased tens of thousands of displaced people into refugee camps.

Sunni Non-state Actors

Sunni Islamist movements also alternated between pursuing civic and violent routes to power. Egypt's Muslim Brotherhood took 20 per cent of the vote in the November 2005 assembly elections, to emerge as the lower house's largest opposition bloc. Two months later Hamas sought to cash in the political capital it had accrued as a resistance force during the Second Intifada by contesting elections for the first time, and won. Prospects for bringing Islamist groups within the constitutional order seemed high.

Their integration coincided with the aimlessness which characterized *jihadi* operations post-9/11. Having seemingly reached the apex in shock value with al-Qaeda's attack on America, global *jihadi* cells appeared to struggle for ideas on where to go next. While tapping local grievances, they continued to strike symbols of

Western cultural or military penetration inside the Muslim world.
These included tourist resorts and hotels (Bali in 2001, Amman and
Sinai each resorts in 2005, and Jakarta in July 2009); foreign residen-
tial compounds (Riyadh in 2003 and Doha in 2005); foreign financial
centres (Istanbul in 2003 and Morocco in 2007); and Jewish sites
(Tunisia in 2002, Morocco in 2003 and Istanbul in 2003). Further
attacks on Western transport networks (Madrid in 2004, London in
2005 and Mumbai in 2006) highlighted the movement's global reach.
But the terrorist campaigns did little to affect the balance of power,
and raised concerns amonst former firebrands about overstretch
and maligning of the faith. In Saudi Arabia, 160 religious scholars
published a manifesto in Riyadh proclaiming Islam to be a religion
of tolerance. One-time firebrands such as Salman al-Awda switched
camp, joining Shia intellectuals to condemn bin Laden and petition
for elections and an end to sectarian discrimination. In Egypt, jailed
leaders of the largest militant group, al-Gamaa al-Islamiya,
renounced violence and former leader Ayman Zawahiri, and sought
entry into civilian politics.

It is an irony of history that the Bush administration did more
to rejuvenate Muslim fundamentalism in the Middle East than
anyone since Ronald Reagan gave the CIA a green light to train
mujahideen in Afghanistan against the Soviet Union. In contrast to
the incoherence and nihilism of the post-9/11 attacks, the invasion
of Iraq refocused *jihadi* efforts on combating their twin foes of
Western expansionism and Shia revivalism, and restored the movement's tarnished appeal amongst the Sunni masses as defenders
against a Western onslaught. Even before the invasion, Arab veterans from Afghanistan began trickling back to Iraq, and by the time
US forces entered Baghdad it had become a magnet for foreign
fighters worldwide, replicating the role Afghanistan played in the
1980s. Led by Musab al-Zarqawi, a Jordanian-born Palestinian whose
thuggery waging the Afghan *jihad* even fellow fighters had found
uncouth, thousands converged on Iraq. They fostered a new generation of trained fighters with active experience in combat. Recalling
the Arab fighters from Afghanistan who had launched local uprisings

after returning home, Arab governments awaited the blowback from their nationals trained in Iraq.

Traditional *jihadi* ideology found new inspiration from another strain of Islam, Salafism, a renewal movement that sought to purify Islam of the sediment of tradition and adhere precisely to the lifestyle of the followers of the Prophet Mohammed. Originating in the Wahhabi schools of Saudi Arabia, it spread rapidly, bank-rolled by Saudi institutions and transmitted by the millions of migrant workers and students passing through the kingdom. It encompassed two broad trends both of which boycotted consti-tutional systems of government (including elections) on the grounds that they were man-made institutions, and preached a virulent anti-Shia creed: political quietists who focused on pros-elytising, and the practitioners of *Salafiya jihadiya*, who used violence to achieve their goals.

Initially fringe, the Salafi *jihadi* movement found growing regional currency, and not only because of Iraq. Unnerved by Islamist success at the ballot box, Arab regimes sharply cracked down on Islamist political action. Thwarted in their efforts to participate in government and with little to show for their pragmatism, Islamist political wings came under mounting pressure from armed *jihadi* militias opposed to collaborating with secular Western-backed regimes.

By the end of the first decade of the twenty-first century, the *jihadis* had evolved from isolated cells into a region-wide presence. After Iraq, their most substantial base was in Yemen, where tribal homelands beyond government control provided similar room for activity to the lawless tribal tracts of Pakistan where al-Qaeda's leaders held sway. Building on an existing base of a first generation of veterans who had fought in Afghanistan and Yugoslavia, incom-ing *jihadis* merged with Saudi counterparts to establish the headquarters of al-Qaeda's Arabian peninsula chapter in January 2009. In August later that year they carried out its first major attack, when a Saudi returning from Yemen attempted to assassinate Prince Muhammad Bin-Nayef, Saudi's deputy interior minister responsible for counterterrorism. Under heavy Saudi and American pressure, in December 2009, President Salih – already fighting on multiple fronts – gave his assent to US bombardment of *jihadi* positions in eastern Yemen.

Salafi *jihadi* groups acquired a further armed presence on the Mediterranean coast. In Gaza Salafi leaders grew increasingly disenchanted with Hamas after the latter sued for ceasefires with Israel, contested elections (within the framework of the Oslo Accords) and, following its takeover of Gaza, backtracked on moves to declare an Islamic state. From pulpits inside and outside Gaza, particularly from Iraq, they repeatedly chided Hamas for selling out and called on its rank-and-file to rebel. In August 2009, a respected preacher in the border town of Rafah, claiming allegiance to al-Qaeda, declared an Islamic emirate. Hopes that followers inside Hamas's armed wing as well as amongst Gaza's clans might join him proved vain. Hamas stormed his mosque and killed him and his followers. But though quickly and brutally suppressed, Salafi discourse continues to erode the monopoly on Islamist activity Hamas craves.

Salafi fighters tried to make similar inroads in Lebanon, particularly around Tripoli and in Palestinian refugee camps. In September 2007, after six months of clashes, Lebanon's armed forces – assisted by covert French forces – succeeded in crushing a *jihadi* group, Fatah al-Islam, in the Nahr al-Bared refugee camp, but only after destroying much of the camp in the process. Having assisted Salafi-oriented insurgents in Iraq and Lebanon in an effort to retain regional leverage, Syria too feared their support might boomerang. Syria's strategic posture – its close ties to Hamas and its promotion of the narrative of resistance against Israel and in Iraq – fuelled the growth of *jihadi* preaching, particularly in mosques. With a majority Sunni population, much of it turning increasingly religious, Syria's social cohesion and stability faced mounting pressure. Turning Syria into a theatre of operations, Lebanon-based *jihadi* groups car-bombed a military intelligence base in Damascus in September 2008, and a year later blew up a busload of Iranian pilgrims visiting Sayyida Zeinab, a Shia shrine.

As significant as the violence was the percolation of Salafi thought into hitherto reformist Islamist groups. Egypt's Muslim Brotherhood, which over the previous two decades had looked to Turkey's ruling Justice and Development Party as a model for operating within a secular system, came under increasing internal pressure from rural hardliners to reduce interaction with the state. In 2009, the movement's 81-year-old Supreme Guide, Mohammed Mehdi Akef, resigned after failing to bring a young advocate of political engagement on to the executive board, and Mohammed Badie, a veterinary professor and ideological sceptic of the political process was elected successor. With Salafi streams and conservatives suspicious of political pluralism and relations with Coptic Christians gaining the upper hand against urban modernizers, a once marginal trend appeared increasingly mainstream.

Defending the Old Order: Reviving the Region's Security States

Buffeted by external and internal challenges, the region's regimes looked ever more vulnerable. Ravaged by civil war, Iraq was falling apart and region-wide, Islamist, clan and ethnic non-state actors garnered strength. After experimenting with co-option through partial and controlled democratic liberalization, the region's regimes retreated into the tried-and-tested formula of repression. Basic civil liberties were routinely infringed, and the communications revolution curbed. Security operatives closed Saudi chat-rooms, interrupted Iranian phone networks, blocked Syrian websites, and fired Jordanian editors. A leading civil rights activist in Cairo, Saad Eddin Ibrahim, was sentenced to seven years' jail for 'tarnishing the image of Egypt'.

Tellingly, Iraq set the pace. Elected in spring 2006, Nuri Kamal al-Maliki entered office as the archetypal weak American puppet: beset by numerous plots to unseat him, a set of powerful cabinet ministers over which he had scant control, a country in the midst of implosion, and above all a US presence which, though bereft of its viceroy, included over 100,000 soldiers and thousands of advisors in ministries and government departments who choreographed his every move. But Maliki's brokerage of a Status of Forces Agreement with Washington marked his first step in boosting his nationalist kudos. Under the agreement, the US committed to withdrawing combat troops by August 2010, and all forces by the end of 2011. Iraq also gained jurisdiction over thousands of advisors and mercenaries Washington planned on leaving behind, tempering fears of continued indirect US rule.

Thanks to the judicious use of US firepower and an injection of oil revenues, Maliki also recovered some of Iraq's central authority. With Shia militias having largely suppressed Sunni armed groups in Baghdad, he sought to rein in their excesses. In April 2008 he defeated the Mahdi Army in Basra and subsequently mastered the Shia slums of Sadr City, and forced Sadr to sue for a ceasefire. Having shored up his credentials as a nationalist willing to face down Shia paramilitary forces, he backed Washington's programme to lure 100,000 Sunni fighters into joining the US-funded Sons of Iraq paramilitary groups. As Iraq recovered a semblance of calm, he dismantled the blast-walls that disfigured and divided Baghdad. Despite sporadic spectacular *jihadi* bombings, by the end of 2009 casualty rates fell to their lowest levels since the invasion. Outside of Baghdad and Mosul, murder rates were lower than most American cities. Iraqis ventured back to restaurants.

The revival of central authority as opposed to the authority of sectarian and often criminalized gangs won him a semblance of popular appeal. His coalition, Dawlat al-Qanun, or 'State of Law', fared well in the January 2009 provincial elections. Touting support for a united Iraq and playing the nationalist card, he outflanked ethnic and confessional rivals including the Kurdish and Shia factions, who favoured federation or partition. While he won nine out of fourteen participating provinces, the support for SCIRI, hitherto the largest Shia faction in Baghdad, collapsed from 39 per cent in 2005 to 5 per cent. In a further sign of a recovery of central authority, Sunni groups returned to the political fold with turnout in Anbar province rising from 2 per cent in 2005 to 40 per cent four years later.

As violence subsided, investors tiptoed back to Iraq. In mid-2009, Iraq began auctioning tenders for its vast untapped reserves. Only partially deterred by a major bomb attack in Baghdad three days before the auction, major oil companies – including BP, China National Petroleum Company, Royal Dutch Shell, Petromas (Malaysia) and Total (France) – bid for the vast oilfields in the more stable south, and left the East Baghdad oilfield, part of which lay beneath Sadr City, for another day. With a touch of hubris, Iraqi officials predicted production, still limping at pre-war levels of around 2 million barrels a day, would double within three years, and rise to 12 million in a decade – close to Saudi capacity, and outstripping Russia and Iran. Thirty years after Saddam Hussein nationalized Iraq's oilfields, the region's sleeping energy giant was slowly awakening from its slumber. In the meantime, corruption became the biggest challenge to rebuilding Iraq. Transparency International placed Iraq third after Somalia and Myanmar in its list of most corrupt countries. Despite the vast billions of dollars spent on paper, virtually nothing had been rebuilt.

Seven hundred miles west, Israel's military also re-established its hegemony. It quelled the *intifada*, in part by removing the Palestinian command. It assassinated Hamas's leaders, including its paraplegic spiritual mentor, Ahmed Yassin, and by natural or other causes disposed of President Arafat. Israeli tanks reoccupied Palestinian towns and pulverized infrastructure funded by earlier European largesse, and with it much of the architecture of the Oslo process. Amid the destruction, the diplomacy limped on. A series of foreign-generated plans – the US-engineered 'Roadmap', King Abdullah's Arab Initiative and the Geneva Initiative – all put the onus on Israel to accept a Palestinian state.

To sidestep them, Sharon crafted his own plan: disengagement from Gaza. There was much debate about his intentions. Some argued he sought to exclude Gaza and its 1.4 million people from the Palestinian equation and shift the demographic balance between the Mediterranean Sea and the Jordan River back in Israel's favour.

Others opined he sought to maintain an aerial occupation, using drones in place of soldiers, while retaining control of Gaza's air, sea and borders. Still others claimed that Gaza was just the first stage in a phased pull-out which would include the West Bank, unilaterally ending Israel's conflict with the Palestinians. In January 2006, Sharon collapsed into a coma, leaving the answer pending.

Most likely he sought to forestall international efforts to achieve a Palestinian state, bifurcating its putative territory into two distinct and geographically separated entities – Gaza and the West Bank. The severe limitations Israel imposed on travel accentuated the distance, as did its subsequent siege of Gaza. The Gaza withdrawal further set the two territories on separate stages of political development. While the Palestinian Authority continued to nominally rule in both, the West Bank remained under Israeli occupation. Gaza was spared the presence of Israeli troops. As Israeli intelligence officers had predicted before the withdrawal, Hamas filled the vacuum. Israel's decision not to facilitate the smooth handover of Gaza to the Palestinian Authority quickened the Islamist rise.

Nevertheless the world, desperate for any sign of progress, applauded. Over the space of three weeks, Sharon, the father of Israel's settlement policy, demolished the Strip's twenty-one settlements, and relocated its 1,700 settler families inside Israel. By September 2005, the last Israeli soldier was out. When his party, Likud, protested, he dumped it and formed a new faction, Kadima.

Sharon's successor, Ehud Olmert – a wheeler-dealing lawyer – promised to continue the work begun in Gaza with a second unilateral pullout from the West Bank. In April 2006, he headed to elections and won convincingly, reducing Likud's representation from a third to a tenth of the Knesset's seats. But despite strong parliamentary backing, outside the Knesset he had to contend with a once pampered but now embittered settler public and the Jewish religious right, opposed to a further pull-out. The demolition of a few houses in Jewish settlements in the West Bank triggered a series of violent clashes and broke his resolve. Rather than confront his internal foes, he embarked on a war against external ones. Intended to rally a divided Jewish public behind him, it did the reverse.

Ostensibly a response to Hizbollah's capture of two Israeli soldiers, the rush to war was initially popular. But poorly planned and lacking in a clear objective, it quickly dragged. Undefeated, Hizbollah's missile salvos sent hundreds of thousands of Israelis fleeing from their homes, and its militia inflicted significant losses on Israeli troops. Popular anger prompted an official commission, which condemned the war's inept prosecution; a series of corruption investigations further sullied Olmert's tenure. Attacked on all fronts, Olmert shied from further action against the assets of the religious right, limiting himself to rhetorical barbs on settlers (whose attacks on Palestinians he called pogroms) while giving free rein to their continued construction. By the end of his tenure there were half a million Jewish settlers in the Palestinian territories of East Jerusalem and the West Bank.

Rather than tackle the reality on the ground, he opted for a politically safer burst of diplomatic activity, negotiating the virtual reality of the final arrangements for an end of conflict. In November 2007 international dignitaries gathered in the American city of Annapolis to celebrate the renewal of Israeli–Palestinian talks and applauded Olmert's promise to deliver a deal within a year. But at home he failed to convince Israelis or Palestinians he was engaged in anything more than a charade.

Pursued by corruption allegations, Olmert bowed out of office, but not before ending his tenure as he had begun it, with another war, this time an attack on Gaza in December 2008. Over the course of a month, Israel killed over a thousand people, as in the 2006 Lebanon war, and destroyed Gaza's government complex, parliament, manufacturing base, and 3,500 homes. The Gaza war and early elections in February 2009 following Olmert's resignation terminated negotiations long before they had reached fruition.

Despairing of a leadership which had promised peace but delivered war, Israel's electorate shifted sharply to the right. Likud led secular right-wing parties into an alliance with Israel's religious right and formed a 'nationalist' bloc led by Binyamin Netanyahu. It was a winning formula that could hold for years: though comprising less than 25 per cent of the population, the Jewish religious public is the country's fastest growing population group – outpacing secular Jewish growth by three to one. Jewish religious factions operate their own education systems, and exert increasing clout inside Israel's judiciary and military. They comprised a near majority of troops in combat units and the officer corps, taking the place of the former secular elite from the kibbutzim, who have opted for more comfortable lives. Army Torah colleges, or *yeshivas*, churn out thousands of soldiers annually, and military rabbis led their troops into Gaza. Backed by a ruling caucus in parliament, they were Israel's ascendant force. The Jewish left wing, meanwhile, has all but collapsed. Labour slipped to fourth place and joined Netanyahu's coalition. Arab parties, excluded from ruling coalitions since the state's birth, remained so.

Nine months into Netanyahu's tenure, the peace process remained grounded. Whatever degree of external pressure the incoming Obama administration and the international community applied failed to match the clout of his right-wing coalition. Netanyahu well remembered how his right-wing allies had ended his previous tenure as prime minister in protest at his withdrawal from part of the West Bank town of Hebron, and he was not going to repeat the mistake. Instead he humoured Washington and uttered the words 'Palestinian state' and 'settlement freeze'. But the small print eroded the meaning of both. Netanyahu's conditions for a Palestinian state rendered it more quisling than sovereign, and his freeze did not preclude the construction of public buildings, thousands of houses on which work had already started, or any construction in East Jerusalem.

Well into its fifth decade, the evolving Israeli occupation was no longer a temporary aberration. Rather its control over Palestinian life, society, space and land remained firmly entrenched, acquiring more sophisticated and enduring forms. To make it more palatable and to consolidate the *status quo*, Netanyahu partially eased the West Bank's checkpoint regime, but Palestinian access and movement remained severely constrained. The West Bank was hemmed in by a matrix of five-metre-high walls, which severed access to Jerusalem, and bypass roads designed for settler not Palestinian use. Palestinians, foreigners and increasingly Israeli Jews were subject to pass laws which increasingly segregated the population along ethnic lines.

Within the multiple cantons, Israel subcontracted responsibility to a pliant Palestinian Authority in the West Bank and a quarantined Hamas in Gaza. It exercised leverage over the latter by controlling movement and trade. Palestinians, except those paying for medical treatment, were denied permission to leave, exports were banned, and imports limited to basics. Adopting the Pavlovian model, Israel rewarded good behaviour. Pasta was allowed in following an appeal from prominent US Congressman and future secretary of state John Kerry, but not honey, canned fruit or construction materials to repair the damage Israel's war had inflicted on Gaza. Israel further punished Gaza's attempts to leverage its way out of its straitjacket by firing rockets with heavy bombing.

Decade by decade, the struggle for Jewish dominance over historic Palestine was growing ever more violent. In the first two decades of occupation after 1967, Israel killed an average of 32 Palestinians each year; in the third decade the average grew to 106, and by the fourth decade Israel was killing over 600 Palestinians per year. The infrastructure of control, too, grew ever more visible. Looming apartheid walls scarred the landscape. The result had been foretold over two decades earlier in the book *Israel's Fateful Decisions* (London, 1988), written at the height of the first *intifada* by a former head of Israeli military intelligence, Yehoshafat Harkabi. He portrays a country at a crossroads, with one path – the destruction of Palestinian national rights – leading to the destruction of Israel's democracy and the loss of international sympathy on which the Zionist state had depended since its foundation. The result, he said, would be national suicide.

At the same time, Israel's own interest in democracy appeared to wane. Given the choice between Arab dictatorships dependent on Western allies, and democratic governments accountable to their people, Israeli strategists publicly stated their preference for the former. Following the January 2006 Palestinian elections, won by Hamas, Israel successfully stymied what had been the high-water mark of Palestinian democracy.

The ascent from *intifada* to democratic elections followed by descent into factional warfare and the takeovers of Gaza and the West Bank by rival security forces mark another sad chapter in Palestine's history of dashed hopes. Broken by Sharon's counter-offensive and bereft of their leadership after five years of *intifada*, Palestinians initially set about rebuilding their shattered political and economic base. In January 2005 a former school teacher and Arafat's sometime negotiator, Mahmoud Abbas, was elected president, and two months later the Palestinian leadership and thirteen Palestinian factions signed a ceasefire, or *tahdia*, in Cairo to which Israel committed (though did not sign). The Cairo Declaration also committed the factions to abandon the use of arms in resolving internal differences, and required President Abbas to bring Hamas into the PLO and launch without delay a process of municipal and legislative elections. It thereby paved the way for Hamas's integration into the political process, something that Arafat had always refused.

The elections for the Palestinian Legislative Council, the Palestinian Authority's parliament, held in January 2006, rank amongst the fairest in Arab history. They were also probably the cruellest. Hamas won 78 of 132 seats, benefitting from a protest vote against the incumbent faction, the nationalist movement Fatah, a sign of their frustration at the endless negotiations with Israel and a political process which had seen their wealth, their freedom of movement and their land all sharply erode to make way for Israeli settlement expansion. But rather than addressing the causes, Israel led the international community in punishing the electorate. Following the inauguration of prime minister Ismail Haniya as head of the Hamas government, Israel moved to torpedo the fledgling democracy. It suspended the transfer of customs duties and donor states withheld aid, together curtailing two-thirds of the Palestinian Authority's revenues. It barred ministers from travelling between the West Bank and Gaza, and following the capture of an Israeli soldier by armed groups in Gaza in June 2006, arrested most of Hamas's ministers and parliamentarians in the West Bank, including the deputy prime minister. Bereft of its quorum, the Palestinian Legislative Council was unable to legislate. The international community watched, and kept quiet.

In addition to undermining the Hamas government, Western powers bolstered Fatah's military capabilities and the forces under President Abbas's command. Hamas responded by raising its own police force, largely manned by fighters from its armed wing, the Ezz al-Din al-Qassam Brigades. Mounting clashes prompted Saudi Arabia to mediate between Fatah and Hamas, resulting in the Mecca Agreement of February 2007, whereby the two factions agreed to form a national unity government. But the failure to agree the command of the security forces was a recipe for further fighting. In June 2007, Hamas's military wing chased Fatah's security commanders from Gaza, and within three days had won control of the Strip. The unity government cleft in two: Prime Minister Haniya continued to govern Gaza. And in the West Bank, President Abbas dismissed Haniya and made finance minister Salam Fayyad, an IMF economist favoured by Washington, prime minister of an 'emergency government'.

Despite their personal and ideological hostility, the two regimes had much in common. Both ruled by decree with questionable respect for the constitution, used their security forces to tamp down dissent inside their respective cantons, and waged a beauty contest, competing over who could deliver most. Despite repeated attempts at national reconciliation, both preferred absolute control of a part of the Palestinian territories to shared rule of all.

Ensconced in Gaza, Hamas raised the democratic drawbridge behind it, relying on force to hold on to power. Its fighters went house to house, armed with Fatah's computer records, searching for senior cadres; dispersed large Fatah-organized demonstrations by shooting into the crowds; broke up wedding parties where guests sang Fatah songs by shooting grooms in the knees; and subdued clans by laying siege to their fiefdoms and lobbing rocket-propelled grenades inside. They thereby created order, if not law, out of the previous security chaos. The population, previously too nervous to venture outdoors for fear of clan and factional violence, flocked to Gaza's beaches and public places. Hamas considered but then backed away from implementing Sharia law, apparently to relieve social dissent.

Seizing the opportunity to cement the rift between Gaza and the West Bank, Israel responded to Hamas's military takeover by Gaza's severing formal trade with the outside world. It declared Gaza 'a hostile entity', interrupting its transactions with Israeli banks. In an attempt to break free of its isolation, Hamas punched through the border fortifications Israel had left behind barring Gaza's access into Egypt in January 2007, but in the process stirred Cairo into joining the blockade. Fearing an Islamist breach of its national security, Egyptian forces pushed back the hundreds of thousands of Gazans who had poured into Sinai on a shopping-spree (hoping to satisfy seven months of pent-up demand), and erected a new wall along Gaza's southern border. Thereafter, Gazans largely relied on underground smuggling from Egypt. By the summer of 2009 Gaza's labyrinth of tunnels under the Egyptian border was so extensive that Gazans could import goods from iPhones to cars at lower prices and faster speeds than when Israel's crossings were open.

At the same time, Hamas's takeover of Gaza dramatically transformed the movement. From a non-state actor operating a social and charitable network and popular armed wing, Hamas morphed into a governing authority with an army and bureaucracy. As it turned from a guerilla movement into the ruling establishment, Hamas's military wing, which had initially begun as a small unit of bodyguards protecting its leaders, dominated the movement. Once unsullied by the exigencies of government, Hamas now had to weigh its ideology against its business and political interests, had to compromise – even to the point of curbing attacks against Israel – to ensure entry of supplies, and in its government offices gave its enemies an address to attack.

For over a year, Hamas lobbed homemade rockets at Israel's border towns in an attempt to pressure Israel to open its crossings.

In July 2008, it agreed a ceasefire on condition Israel ended the siege, and when that proved to no avail, again resorted to rocket fire. In December 2008, Olmert launched his Gaza offensive, sending Hamas scuttling underground. Most of its leaders emerged a month on, celebrating their survival. But Hamas's subsequent ceasefire with Israel without a reciprocal commitment to lift the siege, and the failure of its much-hyped resistance to inflict significant damage on Israel sapped Hamas's credibility. To the movement's loyalists and believers, Hamas's failure either to implement Sharia law or maintain the struggle with Israel smacked of betrayal.

In the West Bank, US military and financial help bolstered Salam Fayyad's hold on the PA. For the first time since the *intifada* the PA resumed formal security coordination with Israel, and by the end of 2009 Fayyad had deployed five of a planned ten US-trained battalions in Palestinian cities. Awash with donor support, the economy briefly notched annual growth rates of 10 per cent. But, as in Gaza, the political price for stability was substantial repression and constitutional contortions. President Abbas's term in office expired and was artificially extended; and Fayyad's government was never elected. Seeking to channel growing resentment into political aspirations, Fayyad outlined a programme to declare a Palestinian state within two years. But he was in danger of doing his donors' rather than his people's bidding. Democratic institutions – particularly the Palestinian Legislative Council – remained moribund, and Hamas's institutional presence in the West Bank was decimated. Fayyad ordered the closure of their charities running schools and hospitals, or appointed intelligence agents to their boards. His security forces detained hundreds of activists, some after their release from Israel's jails. And during the 2008–2009 Gaza war they suppressed anti-Israel demonstrations, clubbing and shooting protestors who sought to rally against Israeli forces in the West Bank.

The trajectory of Palestinian governance matched the times. Across the region, regimes reacted to the internal chaos induced by America's zealous promotion of democracy and the Islamist gains

that resulted by firmly bolting the hatches. Hopes of an era of political reform pregnant during the 1990s dwindled sharply, as did the
distinction between Middle East kingdoms and republics.

Syria was the first Arab state to morph into a *gumlukiyya* (a play
on the Arabic words for republic, *gumhuriya*, and monarchy, *mamla-
kiya*). Despite its more developed civil society, Egypt appeared to
follow in Syria's footsteps. When the elderly president, Hosni
Mubarak, appointed his forty-something son Gamal, a former
investment banker lacking in military experience, general-secretary
of the ruling National Democratic Party in 2002, many feared he
was grooming an heir apparent. The security establishment (who
favoured one of their own and feared that his privatization
programme would threaten the military's copious economic and
land holdings, particularly the tourist enterprises the generals built
along the coasts), liberals and the Muslim Brotherhood all carped
from the sidelines. Other North African rulers followed suit.
Algeria's Abdelaziz Bouteflika favoured his brother, Said; in Tunis,
Ben Ali gave a green light to his son-in-law, Sakhr el-Materi, and
his wife, Leila Trabulsi, a former hairdresser he married five years
after taking power, to amass a business empire apparently as a step-
ping-stone to succession. And in Libya, Muammar Qaddafy, the
leader of Libya's Jamahiriya, or State of the Masses, named his
second son, Saif al-Islam, co-ordinator of the Socialist Popular
Leadership, the second most powerful post in the land, responsible
for internal affairs. Another son, Muatasim, oversaw the oil sector.

Protest at the concentration of the region's substantial energy
and mineral wealth in the hands of the ruler's family while over one
in four people were unemployed was met with repression. After
toying with a brief opening, the Mubarak regime rapidly abandoned
the experiment fearful of the results. In the presidential elections
of 2005 a rival contender stood against Mubarak for the first time,
and the Muslim Brotherhood emerged as the largest opposition in
assembly elections. Determined to limit the fallout, the regime jailed
thousands, including many Brotherhood activists and the presidential candidate, Ayman Nour. Judges who questioned the polls'

integrity became the subject of criminal probes. Municipal elections scheduled for February 2006 were postponed. Elsewhere elections became exercises in *beya*, or traditional allegiance. In October 2009, Tunisian president Ben Ali won a fourth term as president with 90 per cent of the vote. And Algeria's Bouteflika pushed a constitutional amendment through parliament that abolished a limit on the presidential term, granting him life-long rule. With Morocco already a monarchy, North Africa was succumbing to dynastic rule from the Atlantic to the Red Sea.

Perhaps the resentment might have been less had the existing dynasts delivered more. But the brief hope that the region's new generation of leaders who succeeded their fathers might usher in an era of political liberalization flickered and went out. After initially experimenting with a cosmetic glasnost that did little to change the system, Morocco's Mohammed VI, Jordan's King Abdullah and Syria's Bashar al-Assad all tightened their grip. While reining in Islamist opponents, each sought religious legitimacy to compensate for any deficit in a popular mandate. Mohammed VI continued his father's practice of referring to himself as Commander of the Faithful. Abdullah promoted his Hashemite lineage, which had formerly ruled Jerusalem (and Mecca). Even Bashar al-Assad, who was not a Sunni Muslim, tried to fudge his Alawite origins. Distancing himself from his father's narrow Alawite old guard, he sought to broaden his power base beyond minority sects. He promoted Sunnis to positions of power, restored ties to Aleppo – a Sunni stronghold with which relations had been tense since the violent repression of the Muslim Brotherhood in the early 1980s, and adopted a more religious demeanour, leaking videos of one of his sons reciting the Koran. Embittered by Olmert's recourse to war in Lebanon and Gaza (the latter in the midst of Turkish-mediated talks), Assad adopted a 'resistance' discourse that owed more to Syria's potential Islamist challengers than to the pan-Arabism espoused by the Baathist state. The language yielded early dividends, temporarily reducing tensions with the Muslim Brotherhood.

The policy of adopting the *jihadi* discourse on Iraq and Palestine, however, carried inherent risks. By giving vent to Islamist preachers, he enabled previously latent ethnic and sectarian tensions to surface, and Sunni activist groups aspiring to reshape Syria as well as other states to organize. He further unsettled the established non-Sunni elites who had prospered under his father, offering a foretaste of the sectarian strife that was soon to sweep Syria. In 2003, a football clash between Arab and Kurdish teams triggered rioting by their rival supporters; further skirmishes erupted between Christians and Muslims in Hasaka, Druze and Beduin in the south, and Alawites and Ismailis in Damascus. More damaging still were signs of a blowback from Iraq's *jihad*. The attack on a military intelligence base outside Damascus in September 2008 was attributed to *jihadi* groups and prompted a wave of arrests extending well beyond militant circles to individuals reportedly wearing Islamic dress or beards. Fearing an assault on Syria's secular society, security forces placed some neighbourhoods under virtual curfew, and Islamic education and charities under strict regulation.

Amid the crackdown, Assad took significant steps to pave the way for a rapprochement with his Western and Arab foes, particularly following President Obama's election victory. In July 2009, he dismissed his brother-in-law and reputed Assad family strongman, Asef Shawkat, as head of military intelligence, thus ridding the regime of the key suspect in the international investigation into former Lebanese Prime Minister Hariri's assassination. Risking a backlash from both the Islamists and the old guard, he called for a resumption of talks with Israel, exchanged diplomatic relations with Lebanon, attempted to build a new relationship with France and rebalanced his approach toward Iraq.

Jordan maintained the veneer of a constitutional monarchy. King Abdullah, a Western-educated soldier who spoke better English than Arabic, professed commitment to the system his father bequeathed of multi-party elections, trade unions and the co-option of Islamists, including the Islamic Action Front, the Muslim Brotherhood's local parliamentary arm. But to guard against an overspill of tensions from neighbouring Iraq and Palestine, the new king steadily eroded much of the liberalization of the previous decade. He repeatedly dismissed parliament and delayed elections, ruling by temporary decree, sometimes for years on end. When they were finally held, the elections were skewed in favour of indigenous East Bankers, who manned the security forces: constituencies in the mainly Beduin south sometimes comprised a few hundred voters, while those in the predominantly Palestinian cities and refugee camps comprised tens of thousands.

The General Intelligence Department, the *mukhabarat*, maintained a heavy hand over civil institutions from parliament to the press, and only permitted demonstrations if protestors carried the king's portrait. Perhaps its most extensive tool was the department's letter of good behaviour that applicants for jobs ranging from bank clerks to taxi-drivers were required to produce. Any sign of dissent, and the *mukhabarat* would threaten to withhold the letter not just from the applicant, but from his relatives. When such threats proved insufficient, the king resorted to the army, sending in forces to quell the 2003 uprising in Maan, a southern town. Beduin demands for royal intervention were met with insouciance. The day after the suppression of lethal riots in Amman triggered by the death of a Beduin civil servant in custody, the front-page headline on the official press read 'King and Queen head to London'.

To safeguard such a security regime, foreign backing was crucial. The king maintained close ties with the United States and Israel despite public opposition, particularly from the Palestinian majority, many of whom supported Jordan's Islamist opposition, and by extension, Hamas. As Iraq collapsed into chaos, many US companies charged with awarding multi-billion contracts to reconstruct Iraq relocated from Baghdad to Amman, and developed Jordan instead. King Abdullah also proved expert at auctioning his loyalties to the highest bidder. In 2002, he allowed Washington use of his kingdom for covert operations against Iraq only after Washington had outbid Saddam Hussein's delivery of copious quantities of free oil and oil-for-food contracts. In the years following the war, the king received $650 million of US annual aid, making his small kingdom the third largest recipient of US aid.

The largesse was a temporary pacifier. It triggered an explosion of development in the capital. New suburbs sprouted by the season, and the tiny capital mushroomed into a sprawling metropolis. The security agencies joined in the real estate boom, converting their former head-quarters into a vast office development and expanding the limousine 'VIP' business they ran, charging extortionate rates for the short taxi ride over the bridge to Israel. But the boom only deepened social and economic divides. While a few with the right connections grew rich, prices rose beyond levels accessible to the once robust middle class. With government salaries largely static, most Jordanians were penned in a poverty trap, with little disposable income. Absorbed by the strug-gle for daily bread and fed on a diet of consumerism pumped by advertising, few had the energy to pursue political goals.

Denting Lebanon's democratic pretensions, but in keeping with regional trends, the country's factional leaders also groomed their sons for dynastic succession. Saad Hariri replaced his felled father as prime minister and Walid Jumblatt, too, abandoned his progres-sive trappings and, having mended bridges with Syria, nominated his son, Taymur, as his heir.

The oil wealth of the Arab Gulf monarchies largely insulated them from democratic pressures. It spared them from needing to impose taxes, and provided them with the resources to maintain patronage networks. Shrinking capital markets following the 2008 economic crisis further strengthened central government vis-à-vis the private sector. Nevertheless, the belt-tightening provoked broader discussion of issues of management of the public purse, accountability and transparency, amongst subjects who feared insol-vency, particularly in Dubai.

From the first, Dubai had relied on borrowing to develop its coast. In 1954, the ruler of Dubai and father of the current emir, Sheikh Mohammed bin Rashid Al Maktoum, raised £400,000 from Kuwait to clear the creek and create a port that would serve as Dubai's economic base. In the decades that followed a second port, Jebel Ali, the largest man-made harbour in the world, become a trade hub for Asia and the Middle East, particularly Iran. As its fortunes grew, Dubai built ski-slopes in the desert, aquaria with sharks, vast land reclamation schemes and the world's tallest building. It attracted leading companies with tax-free incentives and a cultural life far from the region's conservatism. On the eve of the economic slump, per capita income in an economy without oil was level with that of its neighbouring emirate, Abu Dhabi, which was awash with it.

But to get there, Dubai borrowed at fantastic rates, and in November 2009, in the midst of the global downturn, one of Dubai's state companies, Dubai World, defaulted on its debts. Dubai's inability to bail out the company, coupled with the emir's earlier assurances he would meet its obligations, raised questions about the solvency of the emirate as a whole. Foreign investors carped at the contrast between the transparency of global financial institutions and the secrecy of Gulf economies, noting that in the build-up to the crisis, the UAE had drafted a draconian press law that imposed steep fines for publication of information 'harmful to the economy'. Rents crashed by half, and only after Dubai's public humiliation did Abu Dhabi bail out its brasher neighbour.

Political development in other Gulf states lagged similarly far behind the meteoric modernization of their infrastructure and the evolution of tribal sheikhs into boardroom executives. Across the Gulf, ruling families retained absolute power. For the most part, succession was surprisingly smooth. Only in Kuwait – with its more open legislature – was the process messier. Following the death of Jaber al-Sabah in January 2006, Kuwait's parliament deposed his anointed successor, Crown Prince Saad al-Sabah, apparently because he was too poorly to read his inaugural speech. Presented as a rare display of Arab constitutional monarchy, rivalry between two Sabah branches – the Salims and the Jabirs – fuelled the parliamentary strife. Amid growing dissent at the appointment of numerous Jabirs, some of dubious quality, to senior cabinet positions, parliament grew increasingly feisty. In May 2009, voters elected four women to the legislature, a first in the Gulf, and subsequently forced the prime minister, the emir's nephew, to submit to a vote of confidence.

Further south, the Gulf's new generation of leaders backtracked on earlier promises of sweeping reforms. Qatar's Emir Hamad bin Khalifa al Thani, who had taken power in a palace coup in 1995, repeatedly postponed elections to the country's Consultative Council in contravention of the country's constitution. Hamad Bin Isa al Khalifa of Bahrain won rapturous support by promising to restore the parliament his father had dismissed in 1975, releasing all political prisoners and declaring an amnesty for exiles. In return, in a referendum in 2001, Bahrainis voted to crown him king. But the constitution he presented a year later made criticism of the ruler an offence, guaranteed the continued appointment of his relatives to senior cabinet posts, and by blurring the distinction between his and the public's purse, turned the island from a state into an estate. Shias retained their second-class status: elections were gerrymandered to ensure that parliament kept its Sunni majority; most Shias were barred from the security services; and in a further slight, the government proposed naturalizing foreign Sunnis and paying stipends to poor Shias who converted to Sunnism, in an attempt to rejig the island's confessional composition.

Succeeding to the throne following the death of his half-brother Fahd in 2005, Abdullah bin Abdelaziz continued to inch Saudi Arabia, the region's most conservative state, towards liberalization. Hand-in-hand with a security crackdown on *jihadi* groups, he reined in the Wahhabi establishment, already on the defensive after al-Qaeda's attacks inside and outside the kingdom, and expanded the Ulama Council, the executive body which vetted administrative decrees, to include other Sunni – though not Shia – law schools. He dismissed hardline judges and the head of the Commission of Virtue and Prevention of Vice, or morality police, who barred firemen from rescuing girls from their burning boarding school in Mecca because they were immodestly clad in their nightgowns. Fifteen died, provoking outrage. He unveiled a programme to rehabilitate 4,000 'deviant' clerics, and in a further challenge to Wahhabi tenets, convened an inter-faith conference in Spain in 2008, inviting Jews and Hindus to the podium. Defying clerical backbiting, he appointed the kingdom's first female minister; made a former head of intelligence rather than a cleric his education minister; and launched the kingdom's first co-ed university, the King Abdullah Science and Technology University, or KAUST. Women could drive on campus and take off their veils.

In the wake of the 9/11 attacks and the increasing royal questioning of Wahhabi tenets, some leading preachers began reassessing their creeds. Men and women, some with their faces bared, met in the town of Burayda, the heartland of Arabia's puritanical Islam, to discuss Islamic reform and reversing the Wahhabi *fatwa* that classed Shia as apostates. 'We have to develop a modern, tolerant and inclusive interpretation of faith,' said Muhsen al-Awaji, a participant. Former firebrands, including Salman al-Awda, delivered a withering attack on bin Laden, for perverting Islam's mission of peace. Some called for a government accountable to the people and backed elections. Following a series of petitions, Abdullah announced municipal elections, the kingdom's first, and promised, that within twenty years the kingdom would be a democracy.

And yet the Al Sauds too feared that glasnost could cost them power. Critics dismissed the changes as cosmetic. The kingdom continued to ban non-Muslim places of worship, and bar Shia clerks from serving as judges. Even at their most progressive, the Al Sauds revealed an authoritarian streak: a senior cleric who opposed the mixing of sexes in KAUST University as evil was summarily dismissed. In May 2009 local elections were delayed, and reformers calling for an elected Consultative Council arrested. The two prime contenders for succession when – eventually – the monarchy moves from the generation of the sons of Abdel Aziz to his grandsons were both security personnel.

Central authority looked weakest in Yemen, where old formulae failed to address mounting needs, and transnational movements had made the greatest inroads. Throughout his thirty-year rule, Yemen's President Ali Abdullah Salih had resorted to military and financial means, co-opting one faction or tribe in order to quell another and

bring the long-fragmented state under a semblance of central control.
His task however was complicated by dwindling revenues as Yemen's
oil production fell, coupled with a fast increasing population. Unable
to maintain his patronage networks, by 2009 he was fighting on
multiple fronts against Houthi rebels in the north-west, al-Qaeda
bases in the north-east, and secessionists in the south, killing thousands. The grievances were local – in part related to the battle for
control of local smuggling routes for arms and other commodities
between the Horn of Africa and Saudi Arabia – but all revolved
around Salih's failure to meet the needs of his people. In a bid to
replace oil with aid, he enjoined external allies to lend support. Saudi
Arabia backed his struggle against the Houthis, and the United States
increased military aid and political support in his assault on *jihadi*
groups, particularly after a Nigerian trained in Yemen was caught
trying to blow up his Christmas Day 2009 flight over Detroit. At the
same time Salih's reliance on outsiders carried inherent risks amongst
an intensely proud population. Allegations of US and Saudi logistical support in the bombing of bases where civilians had sought refuge
antagonized the population, boosted the ranks of armed opposition,
and threatened to further fracture Yemen, turning it into a front line
in a simultaneous war on al-Qaeda and Shia revivalism.

From the outset of its Islamic revolution, the Iranian regime accom-
modated popular opposition to its theocratic norms with the safety
valve of elections. Iranians elected a parliament and president, but
only after the Supreme Leader, or *faqih*, and the Council of Guardians
he appointed weeded out candidates deemed unsuitable. In theory
more of an arbiter than a ruler, in practice Ali Khamenei compen-
sated for his embarrassing deficiency of religious qualifications by
assuming even more powers than his predecessor, Khomeini.
Increasingly, he acted as a temporal and infallible pope, vetting legislation, judicial decisions, and presidential decisions. He undermined
President Khatami, rejected reformist candidates for parliamentary
elections in 2004, promoted Iran's nuclear programme, and determined foreign policy.

He derived his legitimacy from Khomeini's political theory of the *velayat al-faqih* – the government of the Supreme Jurist. The doctrine – which roughly parallels the divine right of (religious) kings – held that a cleric should rule as regent for the ninth-century Imam, Mohammad al-Mahdi, who Shias believe remains alive but in occultation pending the Day of Judgement. The theory was the cornerstone of the Islamic Republic's constitution, but it was increasingly contested by a powerful caucus of dissident clerics as well as the newly ascendant Ayatollahs of Iraq, of whom Sistani was the most prominent. The more strident argued instead for a looser relationship, in which the clergy advised not governed the state, akin to the model Sistani promoted in post-Saddam Iraq. A prominent critic, Grand Ayatollah Hossein Ali Montazeri, who had been Khomeini's one-time heir apparent, issued *fatwas* which denounced the regime for betraying the Shia notion of just rule and declared Khamenei unworthy of the status of ayatollah. The authorities responded by placing Montazeri under house arrest and in official statements addressed him as 'Mr', not 'Ayatollah'.

To prop up his rule, Khamenei relied increasingly on the Revolutionary Guard and its vigilante youth organization, the Bassijis, for support. In the June 2005 elections he backed their preferred candidate, Mahmoud Ahmadinejad, a former hardline Tehran mayor, who won on a platform of economic and nationalist populism, becoming the Islamic Republic's first lay president. In power, he oversaw the expansion of the Revolutionary Guard's business interests, particularly in the oil and telecommunications sectors, and appointed defence and oil ministers from its ranks. In the name of social equality, he launched an anti-corruption campaign, clipping the economic clout of former president, business magnate and political rival, Akbar Hashemi Rafsanjani, whose son he arrested for embezzlement.

Presidential elections four years later marked the showdown between the ruling alliance and a mixed bag of Rafsanjani's aggrieved business partners and senior dissident clerics. Khamenei's candidate, Ahmadinejad, had strong rural support, and conceivably could have

won without vote-rigging. But when, before the count was even
near completion, the authorities announced his re-election by a
sweeping margin, the results beggared belief. In cities across Iran an
estimated two million protestors, men and women, took to the
streets to demand a recount.

Echoing the Sistani-backed rallies in Iraq, the rallies were almost
entirely non-violent and at least initially far from anti-clerical.
Activists from the seminary schools, or *madrassas*, featured prominently in the front line of protests. Leading clerics, including
former President Khatami, preached sermons of encouragement,
oftentimes disrupted by Bassijis. State-televised show trials highlighted former regime stalwarts in prison garb, amongst them
Khatami's vice-president, former foreign minister Ibrahim Yazdi,
and the son of the Islamic Republic's first chief justice. In their
struggle for religious legitimacy, loyalists and opposition alike
staged their protests on religious holidays. The funeral of 87-year-
old Montazeri in December 2009 reinvigorated a flagging campaign,
after the opposition declared a day of mourning. And both sides
used Ashura, the symbolic Shia day of mourning for the massacre
of the righteous Imams, Hassan and Hussein, by a dictatorial caliph,
to stage massive rival protests.

As the protests persisted, activists escalated their demands, calling
not only for Ahmadinejad's resignation but for the Supreme Leader's.
Cries of 'Death to the dictator!' punctured the Ashura protests.
Some women danced bareheaded, and activists cried for an Iranian,
not Islamic, revolution. Externally, commentators likened the rallies
to the vast Ashura protests in 1978 that precipitated the Shah's flight
from Iran thirty-six days later, and hailed them as the most vibrant
civil disobedience campaign anywhere in contemporary politics.

On the face of it, that was hyperbole. The Supreme Leader
continued to appoint the heads of all state institutions, including
the judiciary, state media, the Revolutionary Guard, intelligence
agencies, the military and the para-state religious foundations
(*bonyads*) which control large chunks of Iran's non-oil economy. And
the government could still bring large crowds on to the streets. The

opposition failed to muster in the numbers that had unseated the Shah, and unlike in 1979 its leadership was divided. Clerics, concerned that a rebellion might throw out the Islamic baby with the bathwater, cautioned against inter-clerical sparring that would play into secularist hands. In his sermon at Tehran University in September 2009, Rafsanjani pointedly appealed to the opposition to call off its protest.

Yet the authorities appeared confused as to how to respond. Initially, they appeared bent on avoiding the vicious cycle that marked the final five months of the Shah's regime. Riot control techniques included baton charges, impediments to internet and mobile phone use, and rhetoric: Khamenei's Friday prayer sermon at Tehran University denounced dissenters as instruments of foreign 'satanic' powers. But as the protests escalated, the authorities resorted to an increasingly heavy hand. By the end of 2009, 100 people had been killed and over 4,000 detained. Though a tiny fraction of the number of fatalities the Shah took in his attempt to suppress the protests that drove him from power, it nevertheless emphasized the growing gap between the Shia ideals of Islamic rule as defined by Montazeri and Khamenei's bloodied autocracy, and the mounting parallels between the current leadership and the Shah they helped to overthrow.

Preparing for the Showdown

The unfolding drama in Iran had consequences not only domestically, but for the entire region. Throughout the decade, the Islamic Republic had served as the dynamo that galvanized opposition against the region's Western-backed security regimes. The irony was that since al-Qaeda's attacks on America, Iran and the United States had largely shared the same enemies. By overthrowing the Taliban regime in Afghanistan and elevating Shiites in Iraq, Washington helped extend Iran's regional influence east and west. America's remodelling of the region, based on forcible regional regime change and transition from despotism to democracy, further gave voice to the region's (mainly Islamist) dispossessed, whom Iran saw as its natural allies. As late as June 2005, Secretary of State Condoleezza Rice addressed students at the American University in Cairo with the words:

For 60 years my country, the United States, pursued stability at the expense of democracy in this region, here in the Middle East, and we achieved neither. Now we are taking a different course. We are supporting the democratic aspirations of all people . . . [including] freedom from the midnight knock of the secret police.

A series of regional changes prompted a reassessment of this mission of democratization which appeared to dovetail with Iranian interests. In January 2006, following Ahmadinejad's election, Iran relaunched its nuclear enrichment programme, refocusing Western policymakers on the threat Iran posed to their hegemony. By the end of 2009, Iran was operating sufficient centrifuges to produce a nuclear bomb, had tested the solid-fuel Sajjil missile which, it boasted, could deliver a warhead within a 1,300-kilometre radius, and had launched a satellite into orbit. Its capabilities helped project Iran's influence across the region. Secondly, a series of sequential Islamist electoral successes highlighted the fragility of regimes Washington counted amongst its traditional allies, and the possible expansion of an anti-Western camp in an area of strategic and economic primacy. Finally, shaken by their failures in Iraq, America's neo-conservative camp fell from grace. In December 2006, the Bush administration accepted the report of a Congressional panel – the Iraq Study Group, comprised of the leading diplomatic doyens of American realpolitik – which recommended changing tack to 'a US policy that emphasizes political and economic reforms instead of advocating regime change'. Washington abandoned its carping against friendly Arab security regimes, increased its provision of military support, and stoked regional fears of Iran's nuclear and hegemonic ambitions in the Arab heartland.

The volte-face was intended to save the region from metasta-sizing into proxy civil wars and extinguish the sectarian flames. Instead it did the reverse. By reverting to what they knew best — supporting unpopular regimes and deeming tyranny a lesser evil than political Islam, US leaders fuelled a new cycle of confrontation that pitted Sunni Arab security regimes and Israel against trans-national forces egged on by Iran. The mounting tension could be felt across the region. The two rival camps scouted for local pawns to use as leverage, turning the region into a chessboard in which the smallest encounter was a test of the balance of forces.

In Iraq, Iran found leverage in the plethora of armed Shia groups who had surfaced since the invasion, and who in the event of an Israeli or US attack on Iran it hoped to activate in order to bog down US forces. It thus exercised an effective veto over whether American troops made an orderly withdrawal or hurried defeat. It also entered into a formal strategic 'alliance' with Syria in 2006, persuading Damascus to cross a threshold it had hitherto studiously avoided. In Lebanon, Hizbollah gave Iran a bridge to the Mediterranean, leverage against America's 14 March allies, and some deterrence against an Israeli strike in Iran. And in Gaza, Hamas offered Iran a similar base to project its interests against not only Israel, but also Mubarak's Egypt.

The rising levels of acrimony testified to the growing polariza-tion. A senior member of Khamenei's office revived Iranian claims to Bahrain as Iran's fourteenth province, and Khamenei's military advisor warned that Iran had the means to 'burn the region, its military bases, even the oil wells of the Gulf Cooperation Council [the association of Arabian peninsula states] should Iran come under American military attack'. Egypt and Israel tightened their security cooperation, particularly over Gaza. In early 2009, Cairo announced the capture of arms smugglers on its territory allegedly linked to Iran and Hizbollah, and Israel reportedly bombed a convoy trafficking Iranian arms to Gaza as far south as Sudan. Egypt also publicly allowed Israeli submarines to pass through the Suez Canal, suggesting that they were bound for waters off the coast of Iran.

Much of the bile was sectarian. Sunni media outlets fanned alarm-ist reports of a Shia proselytization programme sweeping Arab capitals, particularly Damascus. Iraqi refugees, Iranian funding for schools, Shia religious college stipends, and a surfeit of Persian translation agencies all served as purported covers. Morocco formally accused Iran of spreading Shiism in the Maghreb, and severed ties. The region's fault-lines, hitherto defined by the Arab–Israeli conflict, were increasingly morphing into an Arab–Persian (or Sunni–Shia) divide.

Much as in the Soviet–US Cold War, small fires born of local grievances acquired geo-political strategic import. Flare-ups in Yemen, Lebanon and Gaza became magnets for outside interests, magnifying their intensity.

After four years of relative obscurity, Yemen's offensive against the Houthis in its northern outback showed increasing signs of morphing into a proxy war. Houthi leaders accused Saudi Arabia and US drones of aiding Yemen in its suppression of Zaydi reviv-alists. Yemen and Saudi Arabia both charged Iran with using the Houthis as a cat's paw to establish a foothold on the Arabian Peninsula. In November 2009, Saudi Arabia formally engaged in its first cross-border military intervention since the Gulf War in 1991, using Apache helicopters to repulse what it claimed was Houthi penetration of its border. In a further attempt to prevent a Shia spillover, Riyadh allocated $5 billion to construct a fence the length of its border with Yemen, reportedly imposed a naval blockade around Yemen to prevent Iranian arms shipments, and cleared Shia Ismaili villages on the Saudi side of the border. Presenting the conflict as a showdown between two standard-bearers of the Shia and Sunni branches of Islam, Iranian foreign minister Manouchehr Mottaki denounced Saudi interference as 'deplorable' and a fellow general accused Riyadh of practising 'state terrorism'. Ayatollah Sistani, too, issued a statement condemning 'the repressive persecution of the Zaydi sect' and in Bahrain Shia protestors clashed with Sunni security forces outside the parliament building, as Shia parliamentarians inside opposed a motion support-ing the Saudi offensive.

Lebanon aroused even greater emotions, as both camps poured in political and material capital. Ever since the 1970s, Lebanon had served as the ring within which the region's powerbrokers wrestled to prove their prowess.

Lebanon's 2006 war with Israel elevated Hizbollah's leader, Hassan Nasrallah, from a sectarian Lebanese leader to a regional hero. Remarkably, Yusuf Qaradawi, spiritual mentor of the Sunni Muslim Brotherhood, reversed his earlier anti-Shia rulings and declared it incumbent on all Muslims to support Hizbollah. Even bin Laden's mentor and right-hand man, Ayman al-Zawahiri, called for a pact with 'Lebanon's disinherited', and praised their resistance in the face of official Arab 'treachery'. A newspaper in Cairo hailed Nasrallah a neo-Nasser, the ultimate Egyptian accolade. Harnessing the political capital he had gained, Nasrallah gave a post-war speech addressing the region, not only the Lebanese, in his appeal for people to cast aside their confessional differences and choose between the disenfranchised masses and the perfidious elite; between the followers of *muqawwama* (resistance) and *musawwama* (compromise).

In the aftermath of the war, the 14 March's patrons tried to recoup their losses. Saudi Arabia rushed funds to repair the war damage, in a race with Iran for delivery. The UN sent a European-led force of peacekeepers into South Lebanon, which though more powerful than its UNIFIL predecessor lacked a mandate to disarm Hizbollah. As Iran replenished Hizbollah's depleted arsenal, Washington committed $410 million in post-war military aid for Lebanon's armed forces. The funds, said a visiting senior US commander, would create 'the army that sooner or later will have to stand up to the armed branch of Hizbollah'.

With outside forces bolstering rival security factions, Lebanese politicians feared a descent into civil war. Fearful of the army's rank-and-file Shia, the US diverted funds to such Sunni institutions as the Information Section intelligence agency. But they proved scant match for Hizbollah. When in May 2008, Hizbollah took over West Beirut, Sunni politicians could do little but wail from the

sidelines. 'Are the streets of Beirut the terrain for the resistance? Is
Israel here in Beirut?' asked prime minister Fuad Siniora, as the
country's armed forces stood aside. Hizbollah again proved it was
Lebanon's prevailing power.

Perhaps Iran's most striking success was crossing confessional
boundaries to assume patronage of the ascendant Palestinian force,
the Sunni Islamist movement, Hamas. Although the ties dated back
years, from Hamas's perspective the alignment occurred as much
by default as by design. After Western and neighbouring powers
had rebuffed Hamas's attempts to engage, and stripped it of funding,
it had scant alternative. As Western powers extended political backing and military training and arms to its rival, Fatah, under General
Keith Dayton, the United States Security Coordinator in Jerusalem,
Hamas sought similar support from Iran.

With Palestine's economy almost entirely dependent on outside
sources, the local demand for intra-Palestinian reconciliation was
weaker than the external forces wrenching Hamas and Fatah apart.
Following the bifurcation of Gaza and the West Bank in June 2007,
each camp bolstered their respective proxies with further inflows
of military aid to consolidate their hold in their respective enclaves.
Washington committed $370 million over four years to train West
Bank security forces, which in return it expected to coordinate with
Israel and target Islamists.

As in the Lebanon war, Israel's 2008–2009 war in Gaza was
intended to repulse Iranian influence, and restore the territory from
which Israel had withdrawn to a pro-Western sphere of influence.
Initially it seemed a repeat of the Lebanon fiasco. Hamas fired its
Iranian-supplied arsenal of medium-range rockets, reaching to the
outskirts of Tel Aviv, and accrued political capital by surviving
almost as long as Hizbollah without waving a white flag. At an
emergency Arab League summit in Qatar, attended by the leaders
of its Islamist and regional allies, Hamas successfully portrayed Israel
as a bully state, draining its offensive of international legitimacy.

But as the dust settled, the reality appeared less convincing. With
only a handful of Israelis killed by Hamas fire throughout the

month-long assault, Israel's bombardment revealed the limitations of the deterrence capabilities of Iran's supposed satellites. With much of the Gaza government's infrastructure ravaged, and Iran's supply lines directly targeted, Israel's operation offered a foretaste – or 'pre-introduction' in the words of an Israeli diplomat – of how a future region-wide confrontation might look. Although Hamas survived in Gaza, it henceforth did so as a largely pliant force operating within Egypt's and Israel's orbit. Fearful of an Islamist emirate on its northern border, Egypt intensified its own siege on Gaza. In the midst of the war, pro-Western Arab states boycotted an Arab League gathering attended by Hamas in Doha and mustered a rival summit of their own. More blatantly still, six European leaders travelled together to Jerusalem to dine with Olmert and applaud his victory. Whereas in July 2006, Hizbollah had responded to an Israeli assault on Gaza by launching its own cross-border raid, this time it kept quiet. 'The Iranian camp,' scoffed an Israeli general, 'fights for Palestine to the last Palestinian.'

The Gaza war highlighted how overblown the fear of Iranian hegemony had become. Given its mute response to the assault on Gaza, the idea of a pending attack on or subversion of Gulf Arab states seemed far-fetched. Iran was rather exposed for what it was: a middle-level power ridden with internal woes. To see its hand behind every regional fire was to inflate its capabilities, if not misread its intentions. The balance sheet revealed an Iranian regime in turmoil, its leaders too busy with internal travails to find energy to devote to the tribulations of their external allies. Hizbollah shed support in elections and, confined to its straitjacket in Gaza, Hamas begun to court new allies beyond Iran's orbit. The prospect for Western-backed leaders, by contrast, looked rosier: after six years of chaos, Iraq gained a semblance of stability; the two wars against non-state actors that bookended Olmert's rule delivered Israel's longest period of quiet on its northern border and restored calm to its south. And in a further sign of the shifting balance of power in September 2007, Israel destroyed Syria's nuclear facility, a joint North Korean, Iranian and Syrian venture begun in 2001, with barely a whimper of protest from Damascus.

Most pivotal of all to the regional balance was Iran's nuclear programme. Western-led efforts to clip the country of its aspirations to cast the region under its nuclear umbrella accelerated in 2010, but not fast enough to arrest development. In October 2009, the permanent UN Security Council members plus Germany resumed talks with Iran. They proposed a deal whereby Iran would send the uranium required to power its nuclear reactor for enrichment and conversion into fuel-rods in Russia and France. Had Iran accepted, it would have forfeited the means to produce the highly enriched uranium required for a warhead, since once converted into rods, the uranium could not be further enriched. Beleaguered domestically, Iran initially expressed interest, no doubt noting the precedent of Libya, where Western powers readily acquiesced to Qaddafy's suppression of internal dissent in exchange for jettisoning his nuclear programme. As negotiations continued into 2010, signs of Iranian foot-dragging or defiance were met with US denunciations of Iran's 'military dictatorship'; progress, in talks, by contrast, rendered Western powers surprisingly mute.

With Iran's influence seemingly past its high-water mark, another regional powerbroker made increasing headway. The decision of Turkish prime minister Recep Tayyip Erdogan, leader of the Islamist-leaning Justice and Development Party (AKP), to shift his energies towards the Middle East rekindled the country's Islamist legacy and loosened its moorings to the staunch western secularism of its founder Kemal Ataturk, and his domestic heirs, the generals. Turkey found an alternative field of influence to Europe, which appeared increasingly sceptical of Turkey's accession to the EU despite the submission of its candidacy in October 2005. The policy won Turkey favour with Arab states anxious for allies to stave off Tehran's regional influence – crucially in Iraq. And it offered lucrative commercial benefits.

Turkey's reorientation might have proved less significant had it not been for the dwindling of other traditional regional heavyweights such as Egypt, Iran and Iraq, as well as the waning of US influence following the Iraq imbroglio. As it was, thanks to these factors Turkey recouped an influence not felt since the Ottoman Empire's collapse. By the end of the first decade of the millennium, Ankara had transformed its geopolitical standing in the region. Turkey's exports to the region swelled sevenfold in as many years, reaching $31 billion by 2008, and Turkish companies secured contracts to build airports in Cairo, Libya, Tunisia, Qatar and the UAE, and a crude-oil refinery in Iran. Sidelining his secular-leaning foreign officials, Erdogan projected Turkey's soft power with a vastly expanded Islamic relief network, particularly in Gaza. He further assuaged a series of historic regional grievances, reopening the border with Armenia (closed since 1993), and congratulating 'his friend' Ahmadinejad on his 2009 election victory. In 2005 Syria ended its longstanding territorial claim to Hatay, a province the French mandate granted to Turkey in 1939, and in return Turkey eased Syria's diplomatic isolation, lifting visa restrictions on Syrian nationals, connecting the two countries' gas and electricity networks and laying the foundations for a common market.

More remarkably still, Erdogan made strides to defuse Turkey's 25-year-long domestic war against the Kurdish separatist movement, the PKK, which had cost 40,000 lives. In the summer of 2009, much to his generals' ire, Erdogan offered an estimated 4,000 PKK fighters an amnesty. More broadly, he granted Turkey's own Kurdish population, estimated to number 12 million, limited political and cultural rights in a country which until the late 1980s had called Kurds 'mountain Turks'. He lifted the ban on the use of languages other than Turkish in public and, speaking a few words of Kurdish, in September 2009 he launched a Kurdish-language satellite channel. He sanctioned the teaching of Kurdish in schools, and allowed some towns to again assume their Kurdish names, thereby jettisoning the Turkification plan of the 1940s which had assigned 12,000 localities Turkish names.

The policy was not without setbacks. It stoked Turkish nationalist sentiments inside Turkey, and prompted some to warn of a military backlash. Warnings that Erdogan was opening a Pandora's box proved dangerously plausible after the PKK resumed a bombing campaign against civilians in Istanbul in 2008 and enthusiastic crowds extended a hero's welcome to the beneficiaries of the amnesty, who returned in rebel uniforms. In the 2009 local elections, the main Kurdish party, the Democratic Society Party, fared well, particularly in the predominantly Kurdish south-east, prompting the authorities to ban it for 'damaging the independence of the state and the indivisible integrity of its territory and nation'. At the same time, the reforms eased relations with neighbouring states and the EU, which had long pressed Turkey to improve minority rights, and paved the way for Turkish participation in the exploration of oil in Iraqi Kurdistan.

The flip-side of Turkey's improved stature in the Muslim world was its nose-dive in relations with Israel, souring their military alliance which had followed the Oslo Accords. During the Gaza war, Erdogan – perhaps mindful of imminent elections – publicly rebuked Israel's president, Shimon Peres, during a live debate at the World Economic Forum in Davos and stormed out of the conference hall. Amid mutual recrimination, Turkey barred Israel from a NATO air force exercise and Israel denied Turkish officials access to Gaza, withheld delivery of military drones, substantially reduced its tourist flows, and rebuffed a Turkish offer to renew Israeli–Syrian mediation. Erdogan's stance yielded dividends both at the polls and in the Arab world, where Turkey – not Iran – was hailed as Gaza's standard-bearer during the war. Gazans took to the streets waving Turkish flags.

That said, Erdogan's populism – which occasionally verged on demagoguery – gave some Arab security regimes pause for thought. His promotion of parliamentary sovereignty over military hierarchy, his efforts to clip military influence by putting senior officers on trial, and his powerbase amongst the emerging business-oriented and often Islamist middle class challenged the very pillars on which Arab governance was based. After seven years in power, the Justice and Development Party could reasonably ask whether it offered a model for other regional states to follow. As Turkey consolidated its switch from military to civilian decision-makers, with a resounding national election victory in 2007, the country presented a rare image of a regional power enjoying legitimacy, a popular government, relative economic prosperity and a possible alternative for the region's security regimes to follow.

15. Regime Change from Within not Without

Rarely, if ever, has a street vendor created such turbulence. On 17 December 2010 Mohamed Bouazizi, a young university graduate, set himself on fire after local officials in his scruffy Tunisian town confiscated his unlicensed vegetable cart, and upturned the applecart of the Arab world. Protests at his immolation gathered volume as they swept north. Cries of 'down with prices' morphed into 'down with the regime'. 'Now I understand what you want,' pleaded Tunisia's president for 23 years, Zine al-Abidine Ben Ali. But it was too late. Within days he and his family fled to exile.

It is strange that Tunisia, perhaps the modern Arab world's dullest country, should have cradled its most exciting event. Not since the Fatimids set forth from Mahdiya on Tunis's coast to conquer North Africa over a millennium earlier had the country exercised such regional influence. Within weeks, Tunisia's protests had spread across North Africa and the Middle East, shaking the brittle regimes of Ben Ali's fellow autocrats.

The alarm bells had been ringing for almost a decade. Saddam Hussein's capture in a pit reduced the most brutal of the region's autocrats to a cowering paper tiger, puncturing his invincibility, piercing the fear barrier and launching a new confidence in people power. Backed by their Ayatollahs, Iraqi Shias took to the streets en masse, defying the Arab public's reputation for docility, dubbed by a Tunisian dissident as 'the silence of the Arab lambs'. The protests forced out Bremer, America's appointed CPA chief, and hastened its electoral process. Inspired by Iraq, Lebanon's protestors chased out Syria's forces in 2005, and Palestine's voters turned on their traditional rulers, Fatah, in favour of the Islamist movement Hamas in 2006. In Iran, voters responded to rigged elections with mass protests demanding a fair vote. Egypt, in the years preceding Mubarak's downfall, was mired with strikes; according to Egypt's Land Centre for Human Rights, the number of labour protests rose from 222 in 2006 to over 700 in 2009.

While regime change in Iraq was the catalyst and model for the Arab Awakening, the causes – outlined in preceding chapters – were threefold: the ossification of the existing regimes; the retreat of global powerbrokers – Russia in the late 1980s and America in the late 2000s – and the appeal of transnational identities over outdated national ones.

In response to America's plans for regime change, all the region's autocrats tightened their domestic grip, deploying a mixture of repression, handouts and rise of an external threat, while abandoning anything more than cosmetic reforms. But in so doing they forfeited political consent, becoming ever more estranged from their own increasingly educated, informed and sceptical population. Corruption investigations went nowhere, unless designed to suppress rivals. Governance was top-heavy and sclerotic. The two most important Arab states, Saudi Arabia and Egypt, were both led by octogenarians. Innovation was deemed to threaten the status quo: in Egypt formation of a neighbourhood association to cultivate trees required an interior ministry permit. Discontent was always a security problem, never a sign of social malaise in want of treatment. Economies failed to adapt to a burgeoning middle class. Often the highest unemployment levels were amongst graduates, one of whom was Tunisia's street vendor, Bouazizi.

Although it remained the sole superpower, America's ventures in regime change in Afghanistan and Iraq proved so militarily, financially and strategically draining that it became increasingly wary of intervention – be it to topple autocrats or prop them up. Far from quelling Islamist movements, its efforts to shape the region only emboldened them. Overexposed, the Bush administration began the process of retreat. It agreed a new compact – the 2008 Status of Forces Agreement – with Iraq; and rather than risk opening another front, embarked on tentative talks with Iran aimed at forestalling nuclear proliferation. Barack Obama, who took office in January 2009, hastened the drawdown. Rejecting the neocolonialism inherent in an American-imposed war or peace, he accelerated the US troop withdrawal, pulling troops out of Iraq by the end of 2011 and committing to pull them from Afghanistan by 2014. In his address to Cairo University in June 2009, he quoted Thomas Jefferson, the third US president and principal author of America's Declaration of Independence: 'I hope that our wisdom will grow with our power, and teach us that the less we use our power the greater it will be.'

The retreat was not merely a matter of saving US money, men and prestige. Increasingly the Middle East mattered less. With the growth of alternative energy sources, including ethanol and gas, and the ability to extract gas from shale, offering America vast new untrapped sources of oil, the threat of Armageddon in the event of a conflagration in the Straits of Hormuz, the passageway for oil exports, receded a little. In part, America's diminishing readiness to project its power in the region reflected a diminishing American interest.

Surprisingly, the retreat appeared smoothest in Iraq. The political violence that had racked the country abated as the US prepared to leave Iraq. The great success of the US troop 'surge' in Iraq was to mislead Americans and much of the world into believing the US, not Iraqi's Shias, had won. In fact, the decreasing death-toll owed less to America's military and more to Shia forces which overran Sunni positions. Obama's position on Palestine proved less convincing. In his Cairo declaration he promised to remedy the daily humiliations of Israel's occupation and provide Palestinians with a homeland. But having cavalierly ditched the negotiation framework his predecessor had begun at Annapolis, he failed to coin an alternative, and he frittered away political capital on trying to achieve half-measures, such as a meaningful settlement freeze from Netanyahu.

Sensing waning American clout, the region's leaders grew increasingly defiant. Initially nervous of the new president (so much so that Israel stopped its 2009 Gaza war before he took office), Netanyahu declared a temporary settlement freeze; but it was full of loopholes, and did not include Jerusalem. While Israel defied America by building in occupied territory, small powers, including Mahmoud Abbas's dependency, the Palestinian Authority, rejected Obama's demand to resume negotiations with Israel. The multiple rebuttals damaged US credibility, and prompted some to wonder whether Washington had been relegated from Middle East broker to bit-player. 'Obama would make a good UN Secretary-General,' quipped a UN official in Jerusalem. 'But as the American president, I worry.'

Doomsayers warned that, bereft of a US umpire, Iran or *jihadi* groups would fill the vacuum. But they fared no better. Iran's suppression of popular demonstrations made it look less revolutionary power than another old security regime, particularly after it backed Syria in suppressing a popular revolt, and weakened its capacity to capitalize on the region's popular uprisings when they came. In Lebanon, its closest regional ally, Hizbollah, lost ground at the ballot box. Hamas began the search for alternative, Sunni, patrons. With its regional influence under threat, Iran looked to its future status as a virtual nuclear power to compensate for its waning conventional clout. But here too it faced constraints, precipitating biting sanctions and the threat of military action.

Jihadi groups might also have been expected to thrive in the chaos. Undoubtedly the Arab Awakening presented opportunities, particularly when revolutionaries despaired of mass protests to unseat autocrats and took up arms. But al-Qaeda's central leadership appeared on the defensive. A covert US war continued to debilitate its leadership and demoralize its rank and file. US marines killed Osama Bin Laden in a Pakistani town in May 2011, and drones killed its operatives in Yemen. After the aborted assassination of Saudi Arabia's counter-terrorism chief in December 2009 and the near downing of a Northwest Airlines flight the same month, al-Qaeda in the Arabian Peninsula had little reach beyond its base in Yemen's tribal hinterland. With little to show for its violence, followers increasingly questioned its tactics. High-profile attacks hatched in faraway Afghanistan failed to thwart the Shiite ascendency in Iraq; and in the aftermath of the Arab Awakening most Islamists found ballots more effective than bombs. A civilian Islamist movement unseated the Mubarak regime, where clandestine cells of armed *jihadi* guerrillas had failed. Tellingly, even in Iraq, hitherto the Arab world's leading theatre of *jihad*, Sunnis in northern and central areas staged mass non-violent rallies in late 2012 in protest against their second-class status, seemingly more inspired by Sistani's *modus operandi* than Bin Laden's.

As foreign forces retreated, the region's population was increasingly left to find the solutions for its problems itself. Long-suppressed tribal, ethnic and religious communities rose to the fore, honing coping mechanisms for protection and welfare, which chipped at the glue of the nation-state. The connectivity offered by modern technology proved critical to forming new networks and offering new tools of organization in cities. Facebook pages attracted mass support – one site, 'We are all Khalid Saeed', named after an 18-year-old protestor from Alexandria who died in police hands in June 2010, notched-up two million followers.

Tunisia's ousting of Ben Ali in January 2011 captivated the imagination of the region. Within days, hundreds of thousands had filled the streets of Cairo, the most populous Arab city. As Mubarak fell in February 2011, a huge swathe of Bahrain's population moved into Pearl Monument, a junction in the heart of its capital. Libya's disaffected youth danced in the face of the regime's bullets. And in Syria a month later, youths chanted, '*Ya Doktor, Ijak al-Dour*,' – 'Doctor, now it's your turn.' Social unrest even shook Israel's cities, as Israeli youth occupied Tel Aviv's streets in the summer of 2011, chanting anti-government slogans in Hebrew to the beat of the Arabic anthem that unseated dictators, *Al-Shaab Yurid Isqat al-Nitham*, the people want the regime to fall.

Arguably the autocrats could have deflated the protests had they responded quickly and credibly with reforms, particularly free and

fair presidential elections. Instead hubris and the recourse to violence
unpicked their remaining legitimacy and hastened their end. In Cairo,
Mubarak tried to dislodge the protestors with thugs charging on
camels. In Benghazi in mid-February 2011, Qaddafy's troops sprayed
the protestors with anti-aircraft gunfire. And in Syria, a local intelligence chief and nephew of President Bashar al-Assad dismissed
parental appeals to release the children detained for demonstrating
without a license. 'Forget them,' he is reputed to have told them.
'Our soldiers will help your wives raise more.' The same day Syria's
forces fired on protestors, snipers loyal to Yemen's president, Ali
Abdullah Salih, shot at the crowds from Sanaa's rooftops, killing fifty.
Regimes' excesses quickened the recourse to arms. Libya's opposition
shot back after only a week of street protests. 'I've read about what
Mahatma Gandhi achieved in India and I admire it,' said a Syrian
pharmacist turned fighter. 'But what would have become of him here?
In a week he would have been lying dead in a field.'

Chaos reigned in the territories from which the regime either
collapsed or withdrew, dampening the initial euphoria. In Libya,
children commandeered tanks, and sped them like skateboards
through high streets. Children with machine-guns looted depots.
Bands of thugs, or *beltagiya*, wreaked havoc. Deprived of their
income from bribes, an estimated half a million Egyptians, hitherto
employed as Interior Ministry hands to beat-up opposition candidates in state-rigged elections and such like, preyed on the public,
racketeering and kidnapping. Taxi drivers turned arms-traffickers,
and smuggled sophisticated surface-to-air missiles out of Libya in
the boots of their cabs. In Syria, the price of bread rose sevenfold
and basic supply routes collapsed as the regime resorted to SCUD
missile attacks and what by early 2013 was an average of 40 air strikes
each day on civilian areas in rebel hands. With the proliferation of
rockets, governments worried about the safety of Mediterranean
flight-paths and Suez Canal shipping through which 7.5 percent of
the world's trade chugged, and wondered who would grab Syria's
chemical weapons should the Assad regime collapse.

Compounding the chaos, the seemingly unified forces of the

opposition quickly unravelled into their composite parts as soon as they took control of terrain. Though the social media of the urban educated elite fanned the flames and claimed leadership, the spark of rebellion lay in the anger of the periphery, where the regimes' reach thinned and centrifugal forces prevailed. Bouazizi set himself on fire in Sidi Bouzid a neglected town 260 kilometres south of the capital, Tunis; Jordan's protests were most virulent in the tribal Beduin south and Yemen's in and around Taiz, a city tucked between the traditional powerhouses of the northern highlands and the southern coast. Libya's uprising – which began in the marginalized east – took six months to reach the capital, Tripoli, and Syria's – which first erupted in Dara near the Jordanian border – was a primarily rural struggle, which many urbanites, Sunni as well as other sections, preferred to avoid. It only reached the outskirts of the capital, Damascus, after seven months. Even in Egypt, where Cairo's Tahrir Square was the epicentre, the most brutal confrontations occurred in the provinces.

As the regime retreated, each liberated town, and sometimes neighbourhood, raised its own militia, arming itself from unguarded weapons depots. In Tunisia's hinterland, Salafi groups established their own Islamic courts. In Egypt's peripheral Sinai peninsula, Beduin tribesmen took up arms, chasing out the state security forces, torching their headquarters, ransacking their stations and relishing their first taste of autonomy. They preyed on official trade routes, ambushing tankers and destroying gas regional pipelines while enhancing alternative smuggling routes, particularly with Gaza. Unleashed, these centrifugal forces dogged efforts to stand up a new order. Long after Qaddafy fell and a new government nominally took power, Libya's militiamen – or as they styled themselves the *thuwwar*, or revolutionaries – rejected government demands to disband, hand over their captives and surrender their bases. Security chiefs dispatched by the fledgling government to the provinces were killed.

Fuelling internal rivalries was a broader struggle over the direction and control of the country. Reformers jostled with revolutionaries, peasants with workers, federalists with centralizers, exiles with those who had endured the trauma of totaliterian rule.

Often, the key point of contention was over how much of the regime to replace. Mahmoud Jibril, Libya's first prime minister of the new order, who had acted as chief economic advisor to Qaddafy's son, Saif al-Islam, warned against repeating the mistakes of America's regime-change in Iraq, which had gutted the outgoing administration and disabled Iraq. If the Prophet Mohammed could integrate soldiers from Mecca's army of Unbelievers including its commander, Khalid bin Walid, into its new army of faithful, suggested an advisor, so could the new Libya. But bolstered by arsenals of looted weapons which could outgun anything the central government could muster, Libya's new warlords and militia chiefs were loath to forgo the inheritance they had grabbed and argued for a total overhaul of anything that hinted of old power. Four months after Qaddafy's interior minister, General Abdel Fatah Younes, defected to become the rebel commander in chief, militiamen gunned him down.

In pursuit of a purge of regime remnants, popularly known as *fulul*, or dregs, the militias coined Libya's version of Iraqi de-Baathification. They established tribunals to vet cabinet and parliament for regime loyalists, and vetoed government appointments. 'We want to enter the ministries and cleanse them from the regime,' explained a militiaman from the port city of Misrata, hopeful of a place in Libya's diplomatic corps. The more violent the upheaval, the greater grew the cries for revenge. Despite appeals for an inclusive approach, Syria's rebels drafting a declaration in Cairo for a future Syria in November 2012 insisted on dismantling the Baath party and purging the military.

Transnational identities often exercised as powerful a pull as local allegiances. Once monochrome societies transformed into Lebanese-like patchworks. Following Qaddafy's fall, leaders of the Berber or Tamazight movement waved the flag of their ethnic group which Qaddafy had dismissively called 'mountain Arabs', and set about building alliances from the mountains of Morocco to Saharan oases in Mali and Egypt to promote their separate language and culture. A plethora of Islamist movements filled the newly liberated public space, emerging after decades of persecution and clandestine activ-

ity to give the Arab Awakening a distinctly religious hue. Where
free elections took place, the depth of the support for Islamist politicians was stark. They won 44 percent of Palestine's elections in
2006, 48 percent of Iraq's in 2010, 52 percent of Turkey's in 2011, 41
percent of Tunisia's in 2011, and 69 percent of Egypt's in 2011–12.

Appearing to non-members as irredentist supremacist movements,
new cracks surfaced in the region's old religious melange. Even factions
with reputations for moderation excluded members of other faiths.
Bahrain's parliamentary opposition Wifaq party was headed by a Shia
cleric and its parliamentarians were all Shia. The Muslim Brotherhood,
the oldest and largest of the Islamist movements, was wholly Sunni.
Protests which had begun as revolts against totalitarian regimes rapidly
degenerated into sectarian struggles. Rather than signalling the aspiration for a system of checks and balances against absolute power,
democracy became a euphemism for majority rule. In spite of Syria's
sectarian kaleidoscope the rebel's political arm was top-heavy with
Brotherhood members, and its rebel force, the Syrian Free Army,
almost entirely Sunni. Feeling alienated and fearing a Sunni resurgence, the country's other religious minorities – the Druze, the
plethora of Christian denominations, and the Ismailis – kept to the
sidelines or actively sided with the Alawites, the heterodox Shia sect
of the Assad clan. When fighting erupted it rapidly acquired the overtones of a civil war. Sunnis defected from Assad's forces in increasingly
large numbers, leaving the predominantly Alawite Republican Guard
and special forces to lead the battle. After twenty months, some 60,000
died in the sectarian bloodletting.

   Spread by hundreds of thousands of refugees and partisan media
outlets, the sectarian contagion spilled out of Syria, pulling at the
seams of the region's hybrid states. In Iraq, sectarian tensions which
had begun to subside revived as Sunni tribes and mosques sent medicines and arms to Syria's Sunni rebels, and Shias offered succour to
government forces. Nuri al-Maliki's government made some effort
to inspect cargoes transiting to Iraq, but the border was too long
and too porous to prevent weapons reaching the warring sides. In

July 2012 Iraq's Shia prime minister greeted Assad's foreign minister with a guard of honour, on the same day as Sunni Kurds in their northern autonomous zone feted a Syrian rebel leader as head of state. The spectre of civil war again loomed over Lebanon, as Sunni and Shia activists smuggled aid, arms and men to rival forces over the border. Syria's Sunni rebels threatened to bomb southern Beirut's Shia suburbs after they captured Hizbollah fighters training and arming self-defence squads in Alawite villages. In Lebanon's northern town of Tripoli, fighting erupted between rival Alawite and Sunni suburbs. Fuelling the sectarianism, the region's governments, too, led by Iran and Saudi Arabia, provided political, financial military backing for their respective sects.

Increasingly, the region seemed caught in a tournament between two clashing crescents — a Shia one, identified by Jordan's King Abdullah a decade earlier, running horizontally from Iran via Iraq and Syria to southern Lebanon, and a Sunni rival descending vertically from Turkey through central Syria to Jordan, an increasingly Islamist Palestine and Egypt. Not always by design, global powers sharpened their blades. With overtones of the old Cold War, Russia protected Syria from sanction at the UN, and signed its first arms deal with Iraq since the fall of Saddam Hussein, while the US solidified its ties with the region's Sunni powerhouses, Turkey, Saudi Arabia and Egypt.

The region's other sectarian fires which had subsided flared once more. Yemen's Shia Houthis had agreed to a ceasefire in February 2010, halting a rebellion which had killed some 10,000 in six years of fighting, and left much of northern Yemen and some of the Red Sea coast in their hands. But in October 2011 fighting resumed after the Houthis laid siege to perhaps the Arab world's most prestigious Salafi school, Dammaj, a few kilometres away from their capital, Saada. Of the school's 7,000 students, 100 were killed.

Elsewhere in the peninsula, the Sunni monarchies deflected popular demands to surrender some of their absolute powers by presenting demonstrations as sectarian revolts by their Shia underclass. As the only Sunni-Arab-led country honouring Ashura, the highpoint of the Shia calendar, with two days of national holiday,

Bahrain had prided itself on its tolerance. But when its browbeaten Shia majority converged on the Manama junction of Pearl Monument, its ruling al-Khalifa dynasty, opened its causeway to phalanxes of Saudi tanks, bulldozed the monument and dozens of Shia shrines and smothered its Shia villages with tear gas. Indicative of the sectarian divide, Wifaq, Bahrain's all-Shia party, withdrew its parliamentarians, leaving the legislature bereft of Shia representation. Saudi Arabia's Shias rose up in January 2012, after police shot dead a young Shia protester, Issam Muhammad Abu Abdullah. By the end of 2012, the security forces had killed at least a dozen Shia subjects.

Old and New Autocrats

With identity politics captivating the region, many pundits predicted the break-up of the geopolitical map that colonial powers had carved a century earlier, and its replacement with homogenous atavistic states. "Bouazizi set not just himself on fire, but the order of the Middle East set in place by Mark Sykes and Charles Picot", commented one wag. Libya's vast territory, they posited, would fragment into its three constituent parts: Benghazi in the east, Tripolitania in the West and Fezzan in the south. Syria seemed destined to follow Iraq. As Saddam Hussein in Iraq in the 1990s, the Assad regime appeared to retreat from Syria's northern Kurdish towns, feeding Kurdish aspirations not only for autonomy but a pan-Kurdish state linked to neighbouring Kurdish zones in Turkey and Iraq. Analysts further anticipated Syria's disintegration into a Sunni central spine running north–south linking Syria's most populous cities and Alawite retention of a sausage of territory wiggling from Syria's Mediterranean coast through the anti-Lebanon mountain to Hizbollah-controlled southern Lebanon. Poorer populous states eyed the opportunities afforded by their richer but weaker and dysfunctional desert neighbours. Egyptian security officials toyed with hiving-off Libya's oil-rich eastern province to support Egypt's 90 million people, almost half of whom lived in poverty.

But for all the regional turbulence, as with the previous seismic shocks of September 11 and the Iraq war, the region's borders proved remarkably resilient. In two years of anti-regime protests, only four of the 19 Arab heads of state succumbed. Several deeply polarized states registered little more than murmurings, apparently fatigued from previous bouts of unrest. Having climbed out of its own civil war twenty years earlier, Lebanon's population had no desire to hurl itself headlong into another. Though Syria's feuding pulled at the country's communal seams and there were sporadic attacks, including the assassination of its security chief, a Sunni, Lebanon's army successfully quelled instances of communal fighting. Algeria's Islamists seemed too exhausted to try again; they were still reeling from the generals' success in crushing their rebellion after the army aborted elections in 1992 that they were poised to win. The Palestinian Authority, too, seemed a spent force in the struggle to end Israel's occupation; having ceded Gaza to Hamas, President Abbas hung on shakily in the West Bank, too dependent on Israel for survival to defy it in any court but that of public opinion.

The remaining survivors were all absolute dynastic monarchies. Though many suffered from the same structural problems as the republics, they looked to their oil wealth and a conveniently timed price-hike to buy time. As the world's largest exporter of natural gas and the Arab world's smallest population, Qatar boasted the world's highest per capita annual income of $143,000. Saudi Arabia boosted government spending by 50 percent between 2008 and 2011. The number of universities in Arab Gulf states mushroomed from one in 1950, to 28 in the 1980s, 40 in the 1990s and 120 in 2012. Attracted by booming economies, foreign investment rushed in.

Though it muted the impact, the funding did not render them immune from protest. Despite the repression, Bahrain failed to smother the cries for change. Two years on, its Shia villages remained semi-autonomous zones largely under the control of local activists. On their copious feast and mourning days, Bahrain's Shias processions dominated the streets of their capital, Manama. And the reformist bloc Wifaq which pulled out of parliament lost ground to more radical and clandestine voices, such as al-Haq, which advocated the overthrow of the monarchy. The al-Khalifas imposed emergency law, hauled tortured protestors before military tribunals and allayed more general protest by whipping up Sunnis against Shias with a torrent of propaganda portraying Shias as perfidious blasphemers on state television. Sunni youths toured the streets with swords, boycotted Shia businesses, and erected checkpoints to establish Shia exclusion zones.

Despite the regimes' efforts to paint the stirrings as sectarian, the discontent spanned a cross-section of Gulf society. Tired of a paternalistic system unable to provide jobs and a hereditary system which denied them representation, young people in the Gulf, who are among the best connected and educated in the Arab world increasingly asked when their awakening might come. But their rulers looked on impervious. As per his constitution, the Sultan of Oman retained his titles of head of state and de facto Prime Minister, Supreme Commander of the Armed Forces, Foreign Minister, Defence Minister and governor of the Central Bank. Saudi Arabia dismissed demands for national elections. Kuwait's emir, Sheikh Sabah al-Ahmad al-Sabah, dissolved a newly elected but unruly parliament in June 2012, after it launched an anti-corruption investigation. He issued an emergency decree, amending the electoral law to ensure a more pliant legislature, and had a member of the ruling family, Meshaal al-Malik al-Sabah, detained for tweeting that he would stand in fresh elections on a platform to 'expose corruption among top officials'. Police clashed with protestors after loyalists won all fifty seats in fresh elections in December 2012 that were boycotted by the opposition. Even Qatar, which sold itself as the region's font of cutting-edge critical journalism, replaced Wadah Khanfar, the director of Al Jazeera who was both an Islamist and an ardent supporter of civil rights, with a member of the emir's al-Thani tribe. So quick to report criticism in other Arab states, its editors gagged any mention of the Emir's prison sentence for a Qatari poet who criticized him.

Doubts over the royal successions accentuated concerns over

stability. Oman's ageing sultan is heirless; and Saudi Arabia seems destined for ever-diminishing gaps between its kings as it holds fast to a line of succession which passes from one brother, not one generation, to the next. In 2013 King Abdullah was nearing 90, and by 2015 the youngest of his remaining brothers was set to be over 70 years old. Saudis likened their increasingly hospitalized leadership to that which marred the frequent change of leaders in the dying years of the Soviet Union.

Beset with internal challenges, the monarchs closed ranks. They upgraded the Gulf Cooperation Council into a union; its richer and larger members not only bailed out the smaller ones with less oil, particularly Oman and Bahrain, populations non-Sunni as noted, dispatched their forces to crush unruly Qatar, whose satellite channel goaded other protestors to overthrow their leaders, suspended coverage of Bahrain.

Jordan and Morocco, the Arab world's two monarchies without access to oil wealth, had fewer resources to resist the winds of change. Both applied to join the GCC, but once rebuffed resorted to varying degrees of repression and reform to cushion their rule against protests. Moving quickly to confuse and divide the opposition, Morocco's king Mohammed VI appeared on television promising a new constitution which stripped him of his infallibility. Before the end of the year he had held elections, allowed the country's loyal Islamist movement, Justice and Development, to win, and appointed its leader, Abdullah Benkirane, first minister. A British diplomat likened the country's transition to parliamentary monarchy to England's 17th century Restoration, and compared its monarch's title of Commander of the Faithful to the British monarch's status as head of the Anglican Church. But Morocco remains far from being a constitutional monarchy. Its king presides over the Council of Ministers, the Supreme Security Council, and the Ulama Council, which administers the mosques. He runs the military, the security forces and the intelligence. Tellingly, when US Secretary of State Hillary Clinton travelled to the kingdom in March she met the king's foreign affairs advisor ahead of the government's Islamist foreign minister.

Moving more slowly and less dextrously, King Abdullah of Jordan interpreted any meaningful concession as a sign of weakness and a slippery slope that could lead to his downfall. He tinkered with his powers, touting the tweaks he had made to a third of the constitution. But unlike Morocco, he kept the right to appoint the prime minister, and shied from putting amendments to a referendum. Whereas Morocco's king had courted the Islamists and elevated them to government, Jordan's monarch schemed to exclude them. He endorsed a new electoral law which gerrymandered the seats to favour rural Beduin tribes, so infuriating the Brotherhood whose powerbase was in the cities that it declared a boycott. Exacerbating the unrest in late 2012, the king slashed subsidies to pay for his heavy borrowing used to calm the streets at the start of the Arab Awakening. Protestors, who had initially peppered their protests with cries of 'S-S-S' – hinting at the Arabic for 'dismiss', grew increasingly daring, openly chanting for the toppling of the king.

But though Jordan's Islamist leaders reproved their ruler, few spoke of following Egypt by replacing him. The Brotherhood's politicians still hung portraits of the king in their offices, albeit ones in which he sported a beard, and reluctantly admitted that for all their hunger for power and assets, their monarchs were more tolerant than the republics and slower to kill. Jordanian officials claimed that of some 7,000 protests in the two years of the Arab Awakening, only three people – one of them a policeman – were killed. Bahrain – the most repressive of the monarchies – killed 90 of its citizens in two years of protests, a small fraction of the killing fields in the republics. In an attempt to heal wounds, the al-Khalifas invited an international human rights commission to investigate security force abuses and released some of their political prisoners.

In the four countries which toppled their leaders, new systems of government began to take root. The transition was smoothest in Tunisia and Egypt, where regime change was civil not military. By hiving themselves off from the ruling clan, the old armed forces survived and provided a bridge between new and old. Their criticism of their outgoing presidents for *inter alia* seeking to establish dynasties and their refusal to fire on protestors ensured that the old order was co-opted rather than purged. In Egypt, the generals garnered sufficient legitimacy from their role in deposing Mubarak to form a junta, the Supreme Council of the Armed Forces (SCAF), which provided an interregnum pending transfer to civilian rule. Mubarak's National Democratic Party, which claimed three million members on the eve of the election, was disbanded by court order on 16 April 2011 and its assets nationalized; but its members were allowed to compete for political office, and two of Mubarak's former ministers contested the presidential elections. Similarly, although the Constitutional Democratic Rally (RCD) Party, which had ruled Tunisia since independence in 1956, was dissolved, only a few of its senior members were put on trial. Others, including Ben Ali himself, were allowed to flee into exile. Revenge killings were remarkably rare.

The continuum was even more pronounced in Yemen, where outside parties – primarily Saudi Arabia and the United States – helped negotiate a roadmap for stabilizing the transition. President Salih stepped down in February 2012 after 33 years in power, but he remained in the country, and his cronies and relatives, including his son and three nephews, continued to exercise power as security chiefs. In elections in February 2012, his long-standing deputy was the only candidate. Though the figurehead had changed, the old system survived.

Even Libya, where militias divided up much of the spoils in the post-Qaddafy era, held together. Despite the collapse of the security regimes, the flight of police and surfeit of weaponry, crime levels remained astonishingly low. Close-knit family, religious and tribal ties coupled with the glue of optimism in the dawn of a new era prevented the sort of looting and mugging which might have ravaged western societies faced with a parallel collapse of law and order. Testifying to their desire for central authority despite its absence on the ground, Libyans went to the polls in large numbers in elections which were remarkably unscarred by violence. Federalism remained a dirty word. Militias continued to maintain their own prisons and makeshift judicial systems, but sensing their lack of legitimacy, donned national uniforms and repainted their looted vehicles in the colours of police cars. Along Libya's borders, warlords managed the smuggling routes, reviving the ancient *entrepots* and coastal city-states, but oil revenues remained wholly under central control, ensuring that the government remained the country's primary source of patronage and distributor of wealth.

Indeed, the forces that emerged out of the chaos largely conformed to the historical rule of thumb that authoritarian regimes that break down beget authoritarian successors. From Saddam Hussein onwards, all Arab states which ousted their leaders staged elections to choose their replacements. But as in Russia in 1917 and Iran in 1979, their successors quickly acquired the dictatorial traits of the past. In Iraq, Egypt and Tunisia, the victors were tempted to treat democracy as a system of winner takes all, rather than a mechanism of checks and balances on abuses of absolute power. Establishing democracies proved more complicated than simply erecting polling stations.

After years of bloodshed, Iraq's turnaround was most striking. Far from being overrun after the US withdrawal in December 2011, Prime Minister Nuri al-Maliki's hold strengthened. Unencumbered by US oversight, he tightened his control on the levers of repression. In the run-up to elections, his Shia-led coalition banned 500 candidates deemed to be Baathists, and after winning a second term, Maliki set about eliminating or neutering rivals within his own coalition. He had his Sunni deputy, Tarek al-Hashimi, charged with abetting terrorism, and allowed the Kurds nominally in charge of the Defence Ministry to seek kickbacks from arms contracts, while he filled the ranks of Iraq's special forces, dubbed *Fedayeen al-Maliki* or Maliki's guerrillas, with former Shia militiamen, who exercised control on the ground. When Kurdish leaders went to Washington in 2012, they tried to revive their Saddam-era refrain that Iraq's leader was threatening the autonomy that they had enjoyed since the first Gulf War by stationing his forces along the Green line with Kurdistan, and warned America against supplying Maliki with F16 warplanes. But the US Congress was no longer listening. The economy grew 10 per cent in 2012 and revenues increased as Iraq accelerated oil production, to the point where Maliki suggested that Iraq would challenge Saudi Arabia as the world's swing-producer.

In Egypt, too, the ascendant religious parties seemed prone to the lingering ways of the past. Banned, jailed and downtrodden for 48 years, the Muslim Brotherhood ran election campaigns for parliament and the presidency promising to end the repression of the former security regime. They highlighted their leadership, drawn from the ranks of professionals and technocrats, and trumpeted a new notion of government, in which citizens were equal before the law, civilians exercised oversight over the military and leaders ruled with the consent of the governed. But having won power in both parliamentary and presidential elections, the air of Islamist triumphalism rapidly eroded hopes of a more consensual age. Khairat al-Shatr, a Brotherhood leader, declared his intention to appoint loyalists to 'the 15,000 positions of power'.

As the Brotherhood consolidated its hold on government, its fleeting alliance with secular forces rapidly unravelled. In opposition, both had protested the *mukhabarat*'s pervasive intrusion on personal freedoms, the bureaucracy's repressive and unaccountable ways, the lack of military accountability and the democratic deficit. But in power, the Brotherhood saw advantages in retaining many of Mubarak's powers that they had previously castigated. Five months after winning the June 2012 presidential elections, the triumphant Islamists rushed approval of a constitution through a constituent assembly in a single overnight session, despite the boycott of Copts and liberals. As in the past, it provided for a presidential system and limitations on labour rights and press freedoms. It also gave Al Azhar, the Sunni world's prime theological centre based in Cairo, a degree of oversight over legislation. Rather than bring opposition ministers

into his cabinet, the new president, Mohammed al-Morsi, himself
a former US-trained Brotherhood leader, co-opted conservative
Islamists from the Salafis parties who in the parliamentary elections
of 2011–12 won more than a quarter of the vote. He passed a decree
assuming powers that placed him above the law, and appointed his
own public prosecutor, who set to work investigating opposition
leaders for 'inciting against the president'.

Excluded and targeted by the new power constellation, youth
leaders whose Tahrir protests had ignited the fuse that brought down
Mubarak laid claim to the mantle of popular as opposed to elected
sovereignty and resumed their protests. Judges who had challenged
Mubarak's autocracy laid the same charges at Morsi. 'Mubarak in
beards,' they chided. Former stalwarts of the Muslim Brotherhood
split from the movement in disgust. Kamal al-Helbawi, the
Brotherhood's former spokesman in Europe, returned from exile,
but resigned from the movement in protest at its despotic drift. 'The
Brotherhood left Tahrir Square early. They only went to the square
for their own interests and described the people in the square as
"thugs",' he complained. Protestors broke through the cordon of
the presidential palace threatening a second revolution, only to face
Brotherhood members armed with clubs. Although Morsi managed
to persuade the protestors to disperse after cancelling the decree
that gave him legal immunity, Egypt was increasingly polarized
between rival Islamist and liberal blocs. Sensing the mounting opposition to the Brotherhood's grip on power, the old security forces
flexed their muscles, asserting their authority in Sinai and weighed
their prospects for a comeback.

Sister movements elsewhere in the region appeared similarly bent
on monopolizing power. After its 2006 electoral triumph, the
Palestinian Islamist movement Hamas used its armed wing to oust
Fatah-run security forces from Gaza, and resisted calls to hold elections
long after its term in office had expired. It jailed opponents, banned
protests, and killed armed Salafi *jihadis* that challenged its legitimacy.
Tunisia's new Islamist rulers continued to retain a state media and
censor the press. And they overruled their first prime minister, Hamudi

Jebali, who wanted to hand power to a caretaker government of tech-nocrats, prompting him to resign in February 2012.

As hungry for power as their secular predecessors, the Islamists proved similarly pragmatic. With remarkable ease, they mothballed ideologies which had sustained them in opposition when they cried that Islam is the solution and *Sharia* their constitution. Hizbollah joined Lebanon's ruling coalition and built alliances with non-Shia parties, particularly Christian leader Michel Aoun; it downplayed its earlier aspiration to uphold Islamic law, and in its November 2009 update to its founding manifesto of 1985 the movement abandoned its formal allegiance to Iran's ruling doctrine of *velayat al-faqih*, or theocratic rule. Once in power, Hamas's government in Gaza transformed itself from a guerrilla group into a government, and like Egypt's Brotherhood joined Christians for Christmas celebrations and shelved plans to impose Islamic law. In Cairo, the Brotherhood negotiated backroom deals with Egypt's military. Although he dissolved the SCAF and dismissed its top generals, Morsi left the military's former power largely intact. The Islamists' new constitution left the army in control of its vast assets, spared the defence budget from public scrutiny and pronounced that the defence minister should come from the ranks of the armed forces, an undertaking that Mubarak had shied from.

The Brotherhood was not alone in shedding long-held positions. Pre-revolution, the quietest Salafi preachers had shown a readiness to deal with the Mubarak regime, on the grounds that regime-change was a matter for God not man, and in return secured state licenses for television stations, which broadcast a Muslim version of American TV evangelism. When Brotherhood preachers used their pulpits to summon the faithful to protest, Salafi muezzins kept mum. Yahya Hajouri, a Salafi savant in Yemen, decried the Arab Awakening as a western virus and 'a plague sparked by a Masonic doctrine'. But no sooner had the autocrats fallen, than the Salafis adapted their theology to the new order. Their mentors endorsed participation in politics and sanctioned elections as a manifestation not a sacrilege of the divine will. Devotees hurriedly printed campaign posters and erected coloured billboards promoting candidates, including women – albeit with a rose in place of their faces. Unlike the Brotherhood which was increasingly seen as a middle class and white-collar movement, they fared particularly well in North Africa's urban slums, where their acolytes ran welfare projects reaching the 40 percent of Egyptians who lived on less than a dollar per day.

Salafis with a *jihadi* bent proved equally versatile in jettisoning political violence and entering political systems that they had previously pronounced a sin. Freed from the shackles of Egypt's prisons, which for four decades had served as laboratories for *jihadi* creeds, they swore oaths of allegiance to Egypt's parliament. 'I am taking the political line; I have turned the page on the past, and opened the door to peaceful action,' declared Aboud al-Zumar, a former Egyptian intelligence officer and emir of the *jihad* group which killed Sadat in 1981, released from prison after 30 years in jail. He formed a political party which contested Egypt's first post-Mubarak elections, winning.

Islamists of all hues proved similarly accommodating to external constraints, readily upholding the *status quo* they had challenged in opposition. Continued strategic relations with the US appeared a given not least to ensure the continuation of US aid. 'So long as there is popular will for this, I believe that Egypt will have good relations with the US,' declared al-Zumar. Remarkably, former al-Qaeda fighters appealed for more rather than less western intervention in their struggle to dislodge Qaddafy's regime, adopting a discourse which only a few years earlier would have been condemned as treacherous.

The Brotherhood's U-turn on Israel was as surprising. When the SCAF had run Egypt, its leaders had praised the protestors who had stormed the Israeli embassy in Cairo, demanded Egypt cancel its gas deal with Israel, and sever the remnants of an Israeli–Egyptian relationship. At the rally announcing Morsi as the Brotherhood's candidate for president, a cleric had even hailed Morsi as the liberator of Jerusalem and the harbinger of the Caliphate of the 'United States of the Arabs'. But once in power, Morsi upheld the Camp David accords with Israel. Though he refused to meet with Israelis, he appointed an ambassador to Tel Aviv, and after briefly flirting with the deployment of tanks in Sinai's demilitarized zone, maintained security coordination with Israel. As Mubarak before him, he brokered a ceasefire between Israel and Hamas after their eight-day confrontation in November 2012. Israeli security officials gleefully noted that Morsi did more to constrain the tunnel traffic and arms-trafficking with Gaza than his predecessor.

Egypt's Islamists were not alone in moderating their anti-Israel policies. In its revised manifesto of 2009, Hizbollah advocated the liberation of Jerusalem, whose Eastern half Israel occupied in 1967, but stopped short of calling for Israel's destruction. After its pummelling in the 2006 war, it ensured its southern border was Israel's quietest. Hamas's government in Gaza used its forces to uphold ceasefires with Israel, exposing it to claims, not least from within its own movement, that it had abandoned the founding principles of its full name, the Islamic Resistance Movement, for which hundreds of their comrades had died. It succeeded in rebutting critics who accused it of selling out by launching Palestine's first rockets against Tel Aviv and Jerusalem after Israel killed its military leader, Ahmed Jabbari, in November 2012; it answered Israel's bombardment with hundreds of rockets, winning domestic kudos for building a Palestinian deterrent capability. But immediately afterwards, Hamas headed to Cairo for negotiations with Israel, an act for which it had long berated Abbas. In other signs of growing accommodation, it negotiated a prisoner exchange with Israel and the easing of Israel's siege on Gaza.

The New Old Middle East

Though in many ways the new fledging regimes replicated the old, the hubris of the Islamist revolutionaries set against the conservatism of the monarchies conjured up the geopolitical stand-off of the 1950s, when the Arab world's new republics – with Nasser's Egypt at the helm – waved the revolutionary flag of socialism and anti-colonialism against a bloc of reactionary royals. Like Nasser before him, Morsi sought to restore Egypt's role as the dynamo of the Arab world. And as their fathers before them, the Arab world's kings rallied to resist the regional winds of change.

The two camps jostled for dominance in shaping a post-Assad Syria. The two Abdullah's of Saudi Arabia and Jordan sought to assemble a coalition of southern tribes and Syrian army defectors trained and vetted by western and some Arab governments, who would prevent more fiery Islamists from the north backed by Turkey reaching Damascus first. Fearing that the Brotherhood was plotting to propagate its revolution in the Gulf, the UAE spearheaded a campaign against the Brotherhood, detaining members of the movement, including some of Egyptian origin, eliciting howls of official Egyptian protests. In its bid to amass an anti-Islamist centre of gravity, it hosted Mubarak's last prime minister, Ahmed Shafiq, as well as Mohammed Dahlan, Hamas's bugbear in Gaza and former Fatah strongman, and backed Jordan's efforts to vet and funnel arms finance by Gulf States to cooperative rebel forces.

Much of the sparring occurred on the airwaves. The Islamist republics decried the tired top-heavy systems, which sooner or later would collapse, like their autocrats, under their own weight. For their part, the monarchies peddled the benefits of stability against the bloodshed, chaos and economic recession besetting countries in the grip of transition. Both camps competed for western support. Nervous that the US might abandon them just as it had Mubarak, monarchs toured western capitals warning of the approaching Islamist winter dominated by *jihadis* who were anathema to western notions of human rights. Somewhat disingenuously, for they were no models of western values themselves, they mocked the Islamists for reversing women's rights after their brief appearance on the revolution's barricades. In Morocco, the representation of women fell to one in Benkirane's cabinet from seven under his predecessor. Only 12 of Egypt's 498 elected parliamentarians were women. Jordan's king denounced the Brotherhood as a masonic movement set on establishing another Middle Eastern theocracy, modelled on Iran's in Qom, and waved the standard of a counter-reformation to restore western values.

But oftentimes, the rivalries were more polemical than real – designed to shore up domestic public opinion than stoke a new bout of regional confrontation. Most monarchs were not averse to allying themselves with the Islamists at home or abroad if it furthered their interests. Saudi Arabia and Qatar had long since preceded Morocco in co-opting religious establishments – Wahhabi clerics and the Brotherhood respectively – to cement their hold. And with the new leaderships in desperate need of finance, the Gulf States saw fulsome opportunities to use their budget surpluses to exercise leverage. Gulf investors in post-Mubarak Egypt accounted for 50 percent of the country's stock market, and their governments dangled the promise of aid topping US$20 billion. They were even more proactive in Libya. Ahead of the UN, Saudi Arabia called for international enforcement of a no-fly zone to prevent the Qaddafy regime bombing the rebels, and Qatar and Jordan offered jet fighters. At a time when the rest of the world wrung its hands in Syria, Gulf leaders extended political and military support for the rebels, and dispatched a mission which recommended regime change in Syria and elections – despite their own lack of them.

Qatar perhaps was most agile in finding new territory to promote its influence. Its unelected emir, long seen as the Arabian peninsula's maverick, rushed to patronise the forces of regime change and champion the region's Islamist takeovers. Qatari flags flew from Benghazi's courthouse, the seat of Libya's rebel government, to Gaza's parliament building. After the Assad regime angrily expelled its former ally, Hamas leader Khalid Meshal from Syria in protest at his support for the rebels, Qatar's leader provided him with a haven. He futher became the first Arabic leader to visit Hamas's rulers in Gaza, and provided $400 million for reconstructing the war-ravaged enclave under Hamas rule. In so doing, he de facto recognized the Islamists, not President Abbas, as Palestine's interlocutor. He hosted Yusuf Qaradawi, the ageing Egyptian cleric widely regarded as the Brotherhood's spiritual guide, who in return for his government villa and salary loyally issued *fatwas* endorsing Qatar's foreign policy. From Al Jazeera, Qatar's satellite station, Qaradawi called on Libyans to rise up against Qaddafy, and called on Egypt's security forces not to open fire on civilians, while diplomatically refraining from comment on Bahrain's suppression of Shia demonstrators. Once a respected professional and innovative satellite channel, Al Jazeera degenerated into the Brotherhood's soapbox, inciting rebellion in Egypt, Libya and Syria.

That said, for Gulf monarchs the Arab Awakening carried an inherent risk of backfiring. Local detractors tweeted at the hypocrisy, not to mention audacity, of their support for dissent, violent overthrow and democracy in other autocracies, but repudiation of them in their own. They mocked Bahrain's princes for hosting Syrian rebels on the podia of international conferences while barring their own Shia citizens access to the hall. Saudi Arabia, which remained probably the least democratic country in the world with not even the pretence of legislative elections, looked uneasily at the success of the new democratic strand of Salafism sweeping Egypt, fearing it might yet cast the theologies of their own sheikhs who preached the doctrine that '60 years under an oppressive imam are preferable to one night without one'. Perhaps to give such views a boost, it released a preacher, Suleiman al-Ulwan, in late 2012, who loyally pronounced that 'anyone who calls for democracy does not have any concern for or will to implement Islam.' (For good measure, he also denounced Morsi for not imposing the *jizya*, or non-Muslim tax, on Coptic Christians.)

The other regional players, the non-Arab heavyweights – Israel, Iran and Turkey – used the Arab Spring to jostle for influence. For the most part together with Arab states, they fought their struggle for regional dominance not with armies, most of which had seen little fighting in a generation, but with the supply of guns, money, media coverage, religious polemic and aid. With his defence of the Gaza-bound flotilla, for instance, Prime Minister Recep Tayyib Erdogan asserted his claim to open new maritime sea routes in the eastern Mediterranean, and possibly even to contest Israel's claim to the giant gas fields off the east coast of Cyprus. But while deploying proxies like chess-pieces, rarely did the forces of the region's major powers clash.

Israel feared that the fall of its autocratic allies would give way to revolutionary enemies who would rupture former treaties and trigger its first state-on-state wars since 1973. Prime Minister Netanyahu turned sullenly inwards, telling his public the region was drunk on anti-semitism while fearing that any intervention might only make matters worse. Israel lost its embassy in Cairo after protestors stormed it in September 2011, and Turkey almost severed relations, after Israel refused to apologize for killing nine Turkish nationals when intercepting a Turkish-led flotilla ferrying humanitarian aid to Gaza in the summer of 2010. In the West Bank and the Golan Heights, Netanyahu used Arab preoccupations with their domestic affairs to consolidate his hold with intensified Jewish settlement expansion, effectively annexing swathes of the 60 per cent of the West Bank that the Oslo Accords had designated under full Israeli civil and military control. Further afield, Netanyahu battened down the hatches. He erected a 240-kilometre barrier along Israel's border with Egypt, shutting the region out with walls. Unlike his predecessor, he shied from launching a ground invasion after an escalation of missiles from Gaza in November 2012, and restricted his raids to areas far from the Arab heartland such as a strike on a weapons plant in Sudan. And despite the bluster against Iran's nuclear programme, he refrained from a military strike and left the US and its allies to negotiate.

That said, Israel also saw benefits. The fighting in Syria weakend yet another army fleet that had periodically threatened its border. And over the months, Israel gradually recovered some confidence that its relationship with Egypt would survive the Islamists ascendancy, at least in the medium-term, given their mutual interest in stability. The survival of ties had an impact which rippled beyond their bilateral ties. If the parent organization, the Brotherhood, could maintain relations with Israel, so perhaps one day could other newly ascendant Islamist movements, including its off-spring, Hamas. In the wake of the Arab Awakening, Netanyahu eased Israel's siege on Gaza, agreed a prisoner exchange with Hamas and in the wake of his eight-day bombardment war in November 2012, which killed 160 Palestinians, began negotiations with Hamas without pre-conditions on a longer-term truce (in marked contrast to his position on Abbas, whom he

522   A History of the Middle East

called on to first recognize Israel as a Jewish state). Both parties gathered in Cairo, and negotiated via Egyptian brokers improved access and movement arrangements including the entry of building materials for the first time in five years for the Hamas government to reconstruct Gaza.

Indeed, given the religious composition of Netanyahu's coalition rather than the secular make-up of Israel's Zionist left, some argued that his government belonged to the wave of national-religious sentiment sweeping the Middle East. While the waning Palestinian nationalist movement, Fatah, was the natural partner of Israel's Zionist left, and shared its vision of a two-state settlement, Netanyahu's Likud party mirrored the positions of Hamas. Both flinched from an absolute partition of the holy land, preferring medium-term arrangements which spared either side from ceding their messianic endgame and theological belief in ultimate sovereignty over all of it.

If Israel saw the Arab Awakening as an initial threat to its regional standing which might one day prove advantageous, for Iran the reverse was the case. After almost a decade of growth in regional influence thanks to US policy which had toppled anti-Shia regimes in Iraq and Afghanistan, the Arab Awakening stopped the Shia resurgence in its tracks. At first Iran crowed at the downfall of Mubarak, both Saudi Arabia and the West's closest regional ally, as well as Ben Ali, likening the revolutionary Islamic wave that swept through North Africa to its own Islamic Revolution of 1979. But the Iranian strategic posture changed as soon as the revolution spilled into Syria, their ally and conduit to Hizbollah, their satellite on the Mediterranean coast.

The more Iran invested political, diplomatic and military support to prop up the Assad regime, the faster it haemorrhaged political capital on the Arab street. Iran's Supreme Leader, Ali Khamenei, was lumped with the region's autocrats who repressed the will of the people at home and abroad. He was remembered for rigging the elections in his own country that returned Ahmadinejad to power in 2009 and for crushing the Green movement protests that followed;

four years on, two presidential candidates remained under house arrest. In Bahrain, the initial burst of exuberance was smothered, and the Sunni grip was entrenched. Its other east Mediterranean satellite, Hamas, abandoned its Damascus base and shifted from Syria's orbit to Egypt's and Qatar's. In Gaza, its erstwhile protégés even launched a witch-hunt for Shias. From the sidelines, Israel gleefully watched as western powers imposed sanctions and Arab Gulf states rolled back Iran's influence, not least by promising to meet the shortfall in oil supply when Europe embargoed the purchase of Iran's oil.

Of all the region's powerhouses, Turkey had the most success extending its influence. Unlike Iran and Saudi Arabia, Erdogan viewed the Arab Awakening not only through a sectarian prism, but through his own struggles to replace a security–military establishment with Islamist-leaning civilian rule. In place of his government's 'no problems' foreign policy, he aligned himself against the old order, abandoning former allies in favour of popular Islamist movements. He cut ties with Bashar al-Assad and Qaddafy despite the huge contracts both had awarded to Turkish companies, and recalled his ambassador from Israel following Israel's raid on the Turkish-led aid flotilla. But in return, he garnered fresh support with a new set of allies across the former Ottoman Empire, hosting a summit for its leaders at his party conference in Ankara in September 2012.

Further afield, the US under President Obama gave guaranteed support to the Arab Awakenings, seeking to tweak rather than obstruct the transitions. Rather than risk confrontation with the forces that toppled America's long standing allies, he tried to woo them with praise while moderating their revolutionary zeal. Behind the scenes, he helped engineer the army's takeover in place of Mubarak with Egypt's army chief of staff, Sami Annan, who happened to be in Washington when protests against Mubarak erupted. While critics accused him of turning a revolution into a military coup, he further steered Egypt's US-dependent army – kicking and shoving – to hand over power to elected civilian rule, apparently after helping to broker a deal with the electoral winners, the Brotherhood.

Obama's tactic of leading from behind yielded considerable success. Military intervention continued, but in contrast to its prosecution of high-visibility wars in Afghanistan and Iraq, which one decade on had cost the lives of 6,500 American soldiers, the US ceded successfully much of the action in Libya to other powers, engineering the overthrow of the world's longest-ruling tyrant without the loss of a single US or NATO soldier. Elsewhere, Obama resorted to covert and, where possible, non-human action. On Iran, he and his allies intensified their covert war against Iran's nuclear power programme, using tools ranging from car-bombings to internet viruses. He resorted to drones to pursue al-Qaeda, particularly in Yemen, which in 2012 overtook Pakistan as the CIA's main theatre for drone attacks. US air strikes on Yemen tripled in a year, killing up to 700 people in a little-reported bombardment which forced al-Qaeda to cede ground in Yemen. Despite bloody reprisals and suicide bombings in Yemen's capital, Sanaa, the war continued to enjoy the fulsome support of Yemen's new president, perhaps as the price for US political approval and financial aid underwriting Yemen's transition.

Despite continued US military operations, regional movements found it easier to work with a foreign government which acted less visibly like a superpower. America lost the sureties of its previous satraps, but gained from Iran's retreat – both in Syria and with Hamas's shift into the Sunni camp, and the new-found appeal of Islamic pragmatism over al-Qaeda's unfettered violence. The replacement of autocrats with allies enjoying a more solid popular base put US relations with the Arab world on a more solid footing and, at the level of public opinion, enhanced acceptability of the US. As America appeared to recede, so did the mood of anti-Americanism. Libyans waved rather than burned American flags, and manifested outrage at the killing of the US ambassador, chasing the *jihadi* perpetrators from Benghazi. Conversely, the region's Islamist movements benefited from the welcome they received on the world's stage. In place of the Bush administration which had viewed Islamist groups primarily through a monofocal terrorist lens, Obama dealt with the region as it was, not as America wanted it to be.

That said, America's courting of Islamist movements came at the expense of its traditional relations with the region's surviving old guard. Israel contemplated forging new alliances with the Far East to protect it from the possibility that western criticism of Netanyahu's settlement expansion and European support for UN recognition of Palestine as a state, albeit one with non-member observer status, might grow into broader condemnation of the Jewish state. In Jordan, King Abdullah's men interpreted US criticism of his recalcitrance to reform as proof that Barack Obama was a closet Muslim Brother. And Bahrain's princes angrily rebuffed US pressure to negotiate with their Shia opposition. Four decades earlier, US relations with the region had rested on ties with the region's four powers – Israel, Saudi Arabia, Iran and Turkey. Now each showed signs of strength as the US balanced its old relationships with newer ones.

In compiling a balance sheet, two years into the Arab Awakening there is good cause for hand wringing. Two years after its eruption, the death toll it unleashed topped 100,000. Millions had been displaced, and economies ravaged. But the storm was far from spent, and threatened more carnage to come.

Many caught in its advance feared that as in Afghanistan in the 1980s they had awoken an Islamist Frankenstein that would turn against them. In the West, opponents of regime-change seized on the killing of the US ambassador and four US diplomats in Benghazi on the anniversary of the felling of New York's Twin Towers as a foretaste of attacks to come. After direct intervention in Libya on the grounds of protecting Libyans against a massacre, America shied away from action in Syria where the humanitarian costs were far worse. While there were pressing diplomatic reasons for its hands-off posture – most importantly Russia's resistance to a no-fly zone that could provide cover for military action – the US was unwilling to nurture another *jihadi* theatre, particularly one bordering Israel. It even blacklisted one of Syria's opposition groups, the Nusra Front, an offshoot of al-Qaeda in Iraq, first led by Jordanian Islamist Abu Musab Zarkawi.

As of 2013, an end to the turbulence is not in the offing. Not only does the fighting in Syria continue to rage, but the Brotherhood's autocratic bent in Egypt coupled with continued economic deterioration portends further unrest to come. Continual turmoil has badly tarnished the Islamists image and cost them significant support after the initial election triumphs. Revolutionaries have returned to the street and, based on Gaza's precedent, the hope that the Brotherhood might bow to fresh elections which allow for a smooth handover at the end of their term is far from guaranteed. Even in Palestine, where Hamas's defence against Israel's November 2012 bombardment propelled the movement to its best polling figures since its 2006 victory over Fatah, political rivals staged huge rallies exceeding those of Hamas. Moreover, after their flirtation with electoral politics, the failure of civil means to unseat the autocrats of Libya and Syria helped catapult *jihadi* methods back to centre stage, after their marginalization in the early months of the Arab Awakening. Al-Qaeda increased its chapters from 7 in 2008 to 11 in 2012 retaining its fields of operation in southern Yemen, Algeria and Iraq, and opening new fronts in Libya, Egypt's Sinai and Syria. There was evidence of coordination and some transmission of personnel and arms across the multiple theatres. Abdelkarim Belhaj, a leader of Libya's rebel forces who had trained in Afghanistan, headed via Turkey to Syria after Qaddafy's fall. By March 2013, *jihadi* groups had notched up some 1,400 bomings in Syria. Despite numerous attempts to unseat it, the Taliban evolved from a Luddite organization to a movement with multiple twitter feeds, media outlets and diplomatic relations. And the number of al-Qaeda fighters in Yemen as well as its popular support continued to grow, stoked by anger at US aerial attacks on villages which killed civilians.

If America backed a change of guard only to spawn a new and more antagonistic crop of autocrats, as the Arab revolutions of the

1950s did, history will not likely look kindly on Obama's policy-making. But it is not clear that he had much choice. In the end, abandoning Mubarak and cheerleading Egypt's Revolution proved a more fruitful and subtle path than pinning its colours on a fallen Shah, and stoking a confrontation with Iran's Revolution which still raged forty years on. Moreover, while the Islamist embrace of the principle of a rotation of power remains in doubt, so is Egypt's descent into Islamic dictatorship. Turkey's transition from military to democratic civilian rule – a process greatly enhanced by Erdogan's Islamist Justice and Development Party (AKP) which held power since 2002 and was allied to the Brotherhood – offers a plausible trajectory. Were a number of stable democracies to appear in the Arab world, the blowback effects on and transformative power over the internal dynamics of such oppressive governments as Israel, Iran and Saudi Arabia could be considerable. After decades of suppression, the Arab world might finally experience the independence and self-determination that autocratic regimes denied them when they toppled colonial rule.

Notes on Further Reading

The focus of this history is on the past two centuries since Bonaparte began the second invasion of the world of Islam by the West – the secular crusades. The background of the previous eleven centuries since the coming of Islam which led to the arabization and islamicization of most of the Middle East is covered by the *Cambridge History of Islam* (2 vols, Cambridge, 1971), but a new synthesis of much of this material which can be highly recommended is I. M. Lapidus's *A History of Islamic Societies* (Cambridge, 1988). The collection of essays edited by J. Schacht and C. E. Bosworth, *The Legacy of Islam* (Oxford, 1974), covers all aspects of Islamic society and civilization. For an understanding of Shiite Islam, which plays such an important role in the modern Middle East, M. Moojan's *An Introduction to Shi'i Islam* provides a comprehensive account. A. H. Hourani's *Minorities in the Arab World* (London, 1979) is still the only survey of the religious and national minorities remaining in the Arab countries. The Christians are specifically dealt with in R. B. Betts's *Christians in the Arab East: A Political Study* (London, 1979).

B. Lewis's *The Arabs in History* (4th edn, London, 1968) is brief but still unequalled in its account of the Arabs at the apogee of their power. A more detailed history of the Arab expansion and empire appears in J. B. Glubb's *The Great Arab Conquests* (London, 1963), *The Empire of the Arabs* (London, 1963) and *The Last Centuries, from the Muslim Empires to the Renaissance of Europe 1145–1453* (London, 1967). Hugh Kennedy's *When Baghdad Ruled the World* (New York, 2006) explores the medieval history of Muslim-ruled Iraq and its civilizational glories – people who doubt its importance should try doing maths in Roman numerals with no zero and no algebra. Jonathan Berkley's *The Formation of Islam: Religion and Society in the Near East, 600–1800* (Cambridge, 2002) provides a religious overview of historical developments.

For the first Western invasion of the Middle East, see Steven Runciman's monumental *A History of the Crusades* (3 vols, Harmondsworth, 1978), although in some respects this has been overtaken by more recent research. A. Maalouf's *The Crusades Through Arab Eyes* (London, 1984) is a personal favourite.

My own *The Arabs* (2nd edn, Harmondsworth, 1985) was an attempt to bring the story of the Arab peoples up to the present day but A. H. Hourani's *A History of the Arab Peoples* (London, 1991) is certain to become indispensable. J. Berque's *The Arabs: Their History and Future* (London, 1964) provides the perspective of an outstanding French historian of the Arabs and Islam.

The work of another French scholar, M. Rodinson, *Islam and Capitalism* (London, 1966) helps to enlighten the subject of Chapter 2, 'Islam on the Defensive'. Lord Kinross's *The Ottoman Centuries, the Rise and Fall of the Turkish Empire* (London, 1977) is a highly readable but reliable account of the last Muslim world power and B. Lewis's *The Emergence of Modern Turkey* (2nd edn, London, 1968) remains the best history of the transformation of its heartland into the Turkish Republic. A. Lutfi al-Sayyid Marsot's *Egypt in the Reign of Muhammad Ali* (Cambridge, 1984) is an outstanding study by an Egyptian historian of the Muslim power which came close to repla-cing the Ottoman Empire. Donald Quataert's *The Ottoman Empire, 1700–1922* (Cambridge, 2005) is another social history of the rise and fall of the Middle East's greatest empire.

Modern Egypt by E. Baring, First Earl of Cromer (2 vols, London, 1908) is still essential not only for its account of the British occupation but also as a classic exposition of the British imperial view of the Middle East. It may be balanced by a French view in J. Berque's *Egypt, Imperialism and Revolution* (London, 1972), by an Egyptian one in A. Lutfi al-Sayyid Marsot's *Egypt and Cromer: A Study in Anglo-Egyptian relations* (London, 1968) and possibly by P. Mansfield's *The British in Egypt* (London, 1971).

For the development of Arab nationalism and relations between Arabs and Turks, *Arab Nationalism, an Anthology*, edited by S. Haim, remains invaluable as much for the editor's introduction as for the rare anthology of Arab writing on the subject. E. Dawn's *From Ottomanism to Arabism, Essays on the Origin of Arab Nationalism* (Chicago, 1973) also makes a useful contribution to the subject. *The Arab Awakening: The Story of the Arab*

National Movement (Beirut, 1962) by the Palestinian George Antonius is still unique in the way it shaped the thinking of a generation, but it should be balanced by the differing perspective of Z. Zeine's *Arab–Turkish Relations and the Emergence of Arab Nationalism* (Beirut, 1958). Bassam Tibi's *Arab Nationalism, between Islam and the Nation State* (London, 1997) is a strikingly well-informed account, tracing the European roots of modern Arab identity.

On the subject of modernization and the impact of the West on the Middle East, A. H. Hourani's *Arabic Thought in the Liberal Age 1798–1939* (2nd edn, London, 1983) and his two collections of essays *Europe and the Middle East* (London, 1980) and *The Emergence of the Modern Middle East* (London, 1981) are exceptionally rewarding. *Beginnings of Modernization in the Middle East: The Nineteenth Century* edited by W. R. Polk and R. L. Chambers (Chicago, 1968) also contains useful material. R. Owen's *The Middle East in the World Economy 1800–1914* is a splendidly lucid and comprehensive study of its subject. A unique work of reference is J. C. Hurewitz's *The Middle East and North Africa in World Politics, A Documentary Record: Volume 1 European Expansion 1535–1914* (2nd edn, New Haven, 1975); *Volume 2 British–French Supremacy 1914–1945* (2nd edn, New Haven, 1979). Rashid Khalidi's *Resurrecting Empire: Western Footprints and America's Perilous Path in the Middle East* (Boston, 2004) argues that Western colonialism has continued to the present day.

Sir P. M. Sykes's *History of Persia* (3rd edn, 2 vols, London, 1930) still holds its own for the period before Reza Shah. E. Monroe's *Britain's Moment in the Middle East 1914–71* (new and revised edn, London, 1981) is unlikely to be surpassed as an account of its subject and P. S. Khoury's *Syria and the French Mandate: The Politics of Arab Nationalism 1920–45* is a penetrating study of the French role in the Anglo-French interregnum in the eastern Arab world. J. Wilson's *The Authorized Biography of T. E. Lawrence* (London, 1987) is so exhaustive that it covers most aspects of this period of modern Arab history. International Crisis Group's Middle East programme provides much-respected studies on flashpoints as they unfold across the contemporary Middle East, ranging from North Africa to Iran. The reports offer an invaluable introduction to the region's conflicts based on primary sources and are freely available at www.crisis group.org.

For Turkey since the demise of the Ottoman Empire there is Lord Kinross's *Atatürk: The Rebirth of a Nation* (5th edn, London, 1971) and for the post-Atatürk period of troubled Turkish democracy G. Lewis's *Modern Turkey* (4th edn, London, 1974) and W. R. Hale's *The Political and Economic Development of Turkey* (London, 1981). Erik Zurcher's *Turkey: A Modern History* (London, 1998) is recommended. Ümit Cizre's *Secular and Islamic Politics in Turkey: The Making of the Justice and Development Party* (London, 2008) contains a series of essays on the country's evolution from Kemalism. Iran in the modern period before the Islamic Revolution is well covered in P. Avery's *Modern Iran* (London, 1965) and N. Keddie's *Iran: Religion, Politics and Society* (London, 1980). J. A. Bill and N. R. Louis's *Musaddiq, Iranian Nationalism and Oil* (London, 1988) is a useful account of this crucial episode in modern Middle East history. Nikki Keddie's *Modern Iran: Roots and Results of Revolution* (Yale, 2003) offers a good history of Iran up to and beyond the Islamic Revolution.

There are several books on the Arab states since the end of the Ottoman Empire and their eventual achievement of full independence from the European powers:

1. EGYPT

T. Little's *Modern Egypt* (London, 1967) is to be recommended. P. Vatikiotis's *The History of Modern Egypt, From Muhammad Ali to Mubarak* (London, 1991) is highly recommended. More specifically on the Nasser era, Gamal Abdul Nasser's *Egypt's Liberation: The Philo-sophy of the Revolution* (Buffalo, 1959) still repays study as a seminal manifesto. A. Nutting's *Nasser* is an outstanding biography. P. Mansfield's *Nasser's Egypt* (2nd edn, London, 1969) was an attempt to outline his achievements during his lifetime. A. Sadat's *In Search of Identity: An Autobiography* (London, 1978) reveals the profound difference in outlook of Nasser's successor. W. R. Louis and R. Owen's *Suez 1956: The Crisis and its Consequences* (Oxford, 1989) provides an essential assessment of this watershed in the modern history of the Middle East.

All the books by Mohammed Heikal, Egypt's leading journalist and Nasser's close friend, provide valuable insight but notably *The Road to Ramadan* (London, 1975) on Arab preparations for the 1973 war and *Autumn of Fury* (London, 1983) on the events leading to Sadat's assassination. D. Hopwood's *Egypt: Politics and Society 1945–1981* can be warmly recommended and A. McDermott's *Egypt from Nasser to Mubarak: A Flawed Revolution* (London, 1988) is a useful assessment of the whole post-revolutionary period. Timothy Mitchell's *Colonising Egypt* (University of California Press, 1991) is a staple of university syllabi.

2. SYRIA

N. A. Ziadeh's *Syria and Lebanon* (Troy, 1968) covers the French mandate and the earlier years of independence. Two outstanding books by Patrick Seale are essential reading not only for Syrian affairs but also for the postwar history of the Arab World: *The Struggle for Syria: A Study of Post-war Arab Politics, 1945–1958* (2nd edn, London, 1987) and *Asad: The Struggle for the Middle East* (London, 1988). T. Petran's *Syria* (London, 1972) is still rewarding and D. Hopwood's *Syria, 1948–1956: Politics and Society* is an excellent short survey of its subject. M. Ma'oz's *Asad: The Sphinx of Damascus* (London, 1988) provides a useful Israeli view. Nikolaos Van Dam's *The Struggle for Power in Syria* (London, 1996) is a microscopic breakdown of the sectarian composition of Syrian power by a former Dutch ambassador. Caroline Donati's *L'Exception syrienne: Entre modernisation et résistance* (Paris, 2009) contains much background and detail on the post-Hafez al-Assad era, not available elsewhere.

3. LEBANON

First and foremost are the books by the Lebanese historian Kamal Salibi, notably *The Modern History of Lebanon* (London, 1977), *Crossroads to Civil War: Lebanon, 1958–1976* (Delmar, NY, 1976) and most recently *A House of Many Mansions: The History of Lebanon Reconsidered* (London, 1988). There are various books by close Western observers of the modern Lebanese tragedy, of which H. Cobban's *The Making of Modern Lebanon* (London, 1985) and J. C. Randal's *Going All the Way: Christian Warlords, Israeli Adventures, and the War in Lebanon* (New York, 1983) are perhaps the best. Z. Schiff and E. Ya'ari's *Israel's Lebanon War* (New York, 1984) adds the Israeli dimension, but the impossibility of writing an up-to-date history of modern Lebanon is obvious. For the torment of the civil war following Israel's withdrawal from Beirut read the memoirs of former Lebanese foreign minister Elie Salem in *Violence & Diplomacy in Lebanon* (London, 1995). For two recent studies of the Lebanese Shia movement see Amal Saad-Ghorayeb, *Hizbu'llah: Politics and Religion* (London, 2002) by a Lebanese academic, and Augustus Richard Norton's *Hezbollah: A Short History* (Princeton, 2007) for a concise introduction to the movement. More generally, Fouad Ajami's *The Vanished Imam: Musa Al Sadr and the Shia of Lebanon* (Cornell University Press, 1992) provides an excellent background on Lebanon's Shia revival.

4. JORDAN

M. Wilson's *King Abdullah, Britain and the Making of Jordan* (Cambridge, 1987) deals with the mandate and the early years of independence, as does A. Dearden's *Jordan* (London, 1958). The autobiography by Hussein, King of Jordan, *Uneasy Lies the Head* (London, 1962), may be read in conjunction with an assessment after his thirty-five years on the throne in J. Lunt's *Hussein of Jordan* (London, 1989). P. Gubser's *Jordan: Crossroads of Middle Eastern Events* (London, 1979) places the kingdom in its modern context, although the latest events show that the Jordanian role is subject to continuous change. Kamal Salibi's *History of Jordan* (London, 1998) is a unique contemporary account by an Amman-based academic. Adnan Abu-Odeh, *Jordanians, Palestinians, and the Hashemite Kingdom in the Middle East Peace Process* (2000) is a powerful account of East Bank–West Bank relations by a former senior member of the royal court.

5. IRAQ

For the early modern period S. Longrigg's *Iraq 1900 to 1950* (London, 1953) remains the best account, and for more recent times P. Marr's *The Modern History of Iraq* (Boulder and London, 1985) and P. Sluglett and M. Farouk-Sluglett's *Iraq since 1958: From Revolution to Dictatorship* (London, 1987). H. Batatu's *The Old Social Classes and the Revolutionary Movements of Iraq: A study of Iraq's Old Landed and Commercial Classes, and its Communists, Ba'athists and Free Officers* (Princeton, 1978) is still unequalled as a study of contemporary Iraqi society. D. Hiro's *Neighbours Not Friends, Iraq and Iran after the Gulf Wars* (London, 2001) succinctly summarizes events over the 1990s. *Iraq under Siege: The Deadly Impact of Sanctions and War*, (South End Press, 2000), edited by A. Arnove, details the roots of the 1991 US-Iraq war and the human price of sanctions; A. Cockburn's *Out of the Ashes: The Resurrection of Saddam Hussein* (London, 2002) examines the acme of the Iraqi leader, ahead of any regime change; see also D. McDowall's *A Modern History of the Kurds* (London, 2000). For the case for the weapons inspectors, read former UNSCOM chief R. Butler's personal account in *The Greatest Threat: Iraq, Weapons of Mass Destruction, and the Crisis of Global Security* (New York, 2001). Charles Tripp's *A History of Iraq* (Cambridge, 2002) is the leading political history of modern Iraq. Toby Dodge's well-written *Inventing Iraq: The Failure of Nation-building and a History Denied* (New York, 2003) offers a biting critique of Britain's role in the creation of modern Iraq.

The US invasion and its messy aftermath precipitated a flurry of literature by Western journalists based in Baghdad who mapped the unravelling of US adventurism, of which George Packer's *The Assassins' Gate: America in Iraq* (New York, 2005) and Anthony Shadid's *Night Draws Near: Iraq's People in the Shadow of America's War* (New York, 2005) are the two most insightful. Several studies have also focused on the Arab Shia revivalism it unleashed. Seyyed Vali Reza Nasr's *The Shia Revival: How Conflicts Within Islam Will Shape the Future* (New York, 2006) is a ground-breaking study of global Shia politics by an Iranian-American academic. Yitzhak Nakash's *The Shi'is of Iraq* (Princeton, 2003) is a good historical accompaniment. Nicolas Pelham's *A New Muslim Order: The Shia and the Middle East Sectarian Crisis* (London, 2008) casts a reporter's eye over developments, as do Patrick Cockburn's *Muqtada Al-Sadr and the Battle for the Future of Iraq* (New York, 2008) and Nir Rosen's *In the Belly of the Green Bird: The Triumph of the Martyrs in Iraq* (New York, 2006).

6. ARABIA AND THE GULF

H. St J. B. Philby's *Saudi Arabia* (London, 1968) is a detailed account of the Saudi kingdom before it became wealthy. The two modern studies of the kingdom which appeared almost simultaneously – R. Lacey's *The Kingdom* (London, 1982) and D. Holden and R. Johns's *The House of Saud* (New York, 1981) together provide a highly comprehensive modern history. F. al-Farsy's *Saudi Arabia, a Case Study in Development* (revised 2nd edn, London, 1983) is a useful factual account by a senior Saudi official, and two recent American studies – W. Quandt's *Saudi Arabia in the Nineteen Eighties: Foreign Policy, Security and Oil* (Washington, 1981) and P. N. Woodward's *Oil and Labor in the Middle East: Saudi Arabia and the Oil Boom* (New York, 1988) – are both to be recommended. Mamoun Fandy's *Saudi Arabia and the Politics of Dissent* (New York, 1999) is a scholarly and balanced survey by an Egyptian academic; Said Aburish's *The House of Saud* (London, 1994) is a highly readable diatribe one might expect from a journalist who claims the kingdom tortured his father to death. Jill Crystal's *Oil and Politics in the Gulf* (Cambridge, 1995) remains an incisive account of how the Kuwaiti dynasty survived the Gulf War. M. Klare's *Resource Wars: The New Landscape of Global Conflict* (Metropolitan Books, 2001) is an excellent overview of the struggle for oil in the Middle East and central Asia. A. M. Abu-Hakima's *The Modern History of Kuwait 1750–1965* (London, 1983) is very reliable, as, for the more modern period, is H. V. F. Winstone and Z. Freeth's *Kuwait: Prospect and Reality* (London, 1979). N. Sakr's *The United Arab Emirates to the 1990s* (London, 1986) can be highly recommended, as can R. S. Zahlan's *The Making of the Modern Gulf States* (London, 1989). An entertaining but scholarly study of southern Arabia is provided by R. Bidwell's *The Two Yemens* (London, 1983), and a salutary radical view of the Arabian peninsula is contained in F. Halliday's *Arabia without Sultans* (Harmondsworth, 1974). Mohammad Ayoub and Hasan Kosebalaban (eds), *Religion and Politics in Saudi Arabia: Wahhabism and the State* (London, 2008) contains an important essay on the relationship between the kingdom's royals and religion.

7. ISRAEL/PALESTINE

The literature on the two subjects, whether treated jointly or separately, is large and growing rapidly as contemporary studies soon become out of date. W. Z. Laqueur's *A History of Zionism* (London, 1972) provides the essential background to Israel, and C. Sykes's *Crossroads to Israel* (London, 1965) remains the best account of the moves which led to the creation of the State of Israel, although an Israeli historian, Avi Shlaim, provides some startling new material in *Collusion Across the Jordan: King Abdullah, the Zionist Movement, and the Partition of Palestine* (Oxford, 1988). M. Bar-Zohar's *The Armed Prophet: A Biography of Ben Gurion* (London, 1967) illuminates the creation and early years of the state, and N. Lucas's *The Modern History of Israel* (New York, 1977) is an excellent history of its first three decades. A. Perlmutter's *Military and Politics in Israel: Nation-building and Role Expansion* (London, 1969) remains highly relevant, as does Y. Peri's *Between Battles and Ballots: Israeli Military in Politics* (Cambridge, 1983). S. Flapan's *Zionism and the Palestinians* (London, 1979) is an excellent historical overview by an Israeli peace activist of how the Zionist movement from its inception sought to conquer rather than co-exist with Palestinians. A. Schlaim's *The Iron Wall, Israel and the Arab World* (London, 2000) is a more optimistic account of the relationship. Golda Meir's autobiography *My Life* (London, 1975) illustrates old-style Zionist politics, while that of Ariel Sharon, *Warrior* (New York and London, 1989), may do the same for those of the future. There are several important critiques of official Israeli policies, among which S. Flapan's *Israel: Myths and Realities* (London, 1987) and Y. Harkabi's *Israel's Fateful Decisions* are outstanding. A well-researched account sympathetic to the Palestinian Arabs is D. Hirst's *The Gun and the Olive Branch: The Roots of Violence in the Middle East* (London, 1977), and A. Hart's *Arafat: Terrorist or Peacemaker?* (London, 1984) contains useful material even if it is not always rigorous in its assessment of sources. Andrew Gowers and Tony Walker's *Behind the Myth: Yasser Arafat and the Palestinian Revolution* (London, 1990) is a major new contribution. There are a growing number of works by Palestinian writers, such as H. Cattan's *Palestine and International Law, the Legal Aspects of the Arab–Israeli Conflict* (2nd edn, London, 1976), E. W. Said's *The Question of Palestine* (London, 1980) and M. Tarbush's *Reflections of a Palestinian* (Washington, DC, 1986). Tom Segev's *One Palestine, Complete: Jews and Arabs under the British Mandate* (London, 2000) concludes that Britain during the mandate systematically favoured Jewish claims to Palestine over its Arab counterpart. Charles Smith's *Palestine and the Arab–Israeli Conflict* (Boston, 2004) provides a comprehensive and oft-cited overview. Ilan Pappe's *The Ethnic Cleansing of Palestine* (London, 2006) revives the ghosts of 1948. Yazid Sayigh's masterful *Armed Struggle and the Search for State: The Palestinian National Movement 1949–1993* (Oxford, 1997) highlights the contradictions between the Palestinian movement's statism and its revolutionary rhetoric. Rashid Khalidi's *Palestinian Identity: The Construction of Modern National Consciousness* (New York, 1997) – his most widely cited book – traces the history of Palestinian nationalism back to the early twentieth century. Ahron Bregman, *Elusive Peace: How the Holy Land Defeated America* (London, 2005) offers an illuminating account of the power politics behind the collapse of the Camp David talks in 2000. Several books have studied the rise of Hamas. Halid Harub's *Hamas: Political Thought and Practice* (Washington, 2000) is the perceptive view from within the movement. Azzam Tamimi's *Hamas: Unwritten Chapters* (London, 2007) offers another insider's view; two Israeli academics, Shaul Mishal and Avraham Sela, in their *The Palestinian Hamas: Vision, Violence, and Coexistence* (New York, 2006) offer a remarkably similar portrayal. Jeroen Gunning's *Hamas in Politics: Democracy, Religion, Violence* (New York, 2008) is the best external account.

On relations between the Middle East and the superpowers M. Heikal's *The Sphinx and the Commissar* (London, 1978) is the illuminating and highly readable contribution of an insider, and E. Karsh's *The Soviet Union and Syria, the Asad Years* (London, 1988) is the useful objective work of an Israeli. Said Aburish's *A Brutal Friendship – the West and the Arab Elite* is a journalist's insightful if sensational account of how rulers have juggled the competing interests of their people and their western allies. For the views of leading American and European strategists on shaping the region, *Allies Divided, Transatlanic Policies for the Greater Middle East*, edited by R. Blackwill (Massachusetts, 1997) is highly recommended. The general history of US relations with the Middle East still awaits a new chronicler; meanwhile there are W. R. Polk's *The United States and the Arab World* (Cambridge, Mass., 1965) and personal memoirs such as J. Carter's *The Blood of Abraham, Inside the Middle East* (Boston and London, 1985) and passages in H. Kissinger's *White House Years* (New York and London, 1979) and *Years of Upheaval* (New York and London, 1982). G. Sick's *All Fall Down: America's Fateful Encounter with Iran* (London, 1985) goes far to explain the US débâcle in part of the Middle East.

For the role of oil in Middle East history, S. H. Longrigg's *Oil in the Middle East* (3rd edn, London, 1968) and G. W. Stocking's *Middle East Oil* (London, 1971) are both excellent on the period when the international oil companies were dominant, and A. Sampson's *The Seven Sisters* (London, 1975) sceptically examines the decline in their power and the rise of OPEC.

That a general study of Middle East oil has been lacking since then is not surprising in view of the subject's complexity. OPEC's fortunes and prospects change swiftly and any history soon becomes outdated, but there is A. Skeet's *OPEC: 25 Years of Prices and Politics* (Cambridge, 1988), and M. Arari's *OPEC: The Failing Giant* (Kentucky, 1988) is a pessimistic assessment. W. I. Sharif's *Oil and Development in the Arab Gulf States* (London, 1985) is an annotated bibliography of special value. For a series of essays on the revival of clan identity across the region, F. Jabar and H. Dawod's *Tribes and Power: Nationalism and Ethnicity in the Middle East* (London, 2001) offers an excellent introduction.

Islamic reassertion in the modern world and the Islamic Revolution in Iran are the subjects of numerous books of varied quality. R. Schulze's *A Modern History of the Islamic World* (New York, 2002) is a superb and comprehensive analysis of the Islamist movement. O. Roy's *The Failure of Political Islam* (London, 1994) offers a French antidote to the scaremongers convinced of the inexorable march of the Islamist populism. J. Esposito's *The Islamic Threat: Myth or Reality?* (Oxford University Press, 2002) is a thoughtful history of the cooperation and tensions between Islam and the West. Also recommended: Mahmoud Faksh's *The Future of Islam in the Middle East: Fundamentalism in Egypt, Algeria, and Saudi Arabia* (Praeger, 1997). Two which are likely to stand the test of time are E. Mortimer's *Faith and Power, the Politics of Islam* (London, 1982) and M. Ruthven's *Islam in the World* (Harmondsworth, 1984). On the Khomeini Revolution, S. Bakhash's *The Reign of the Ayatollahs: Iran and the Islamic Revolution* is outstanding, and R. Mottahedeh's *The Mantle of the Prophet: Religion and Politics in Iran* (London, 1986) is a brilliant analysis of the Revolution's antecedents. Baqer Moin's *Khomeini: Life of the Ayatollah* (London, 1999) is a perceptive account by a leading Iranian journalist in Britain. On the Gulf War, S. Chubin and C. Tripp's *Iran and Iraq at War* (London, 1988) is the best study to date.

Political futurology in the Middle East is perhaps best left to astrologers, but some attempts to analyse the present with an eye to the future are worthwhile. Two works by Lebanese writers are F. Ajami's *The Arab Predicament: Arab Political Thought and Practice Since 1967* (Cambridge, 1981) and G. Corm's *Fragmentation of the Middle East* (London, 1988). There are also two excellent collections of essays: H. Sharabi's *The Next Arab Decade:*

Alternative Futures (Boulder and London, 1988) and the series in four volumes edited by Giacomo Lucini of the Istituto Affari Internazionali, Rome, under the general title *Nation, State and Integration in the Arab World* (London and New York, 1988). Y. Sayigh's *The Arab Economy 1930–1980: Past Performance and Future Prospects* (Oxford, 1982) is by one of the Arab world's leading analysts. For a useful collection of essays on the currents of political debate in the region, the reader should consult *Civil Society in the Middle East* (Leiden, 1995). Naomi Sakr's *Satellite Realms: Transnational Television, Globalization and the Middle East* (London, 2002) is an exceptionally sober and sceptical study, which casts doubt on the positive impact of the electronic media age in the Arab world.

For general reference, Europa Publications' *The Middle East and North Africa* (London, 1948–) is published annually. Two more reference works of high standard are *The Cambridge Encyclopaedia of the Middle East and North Africa* (Cambridge, 1988), executive editor Trevor Mostyn and advisory editor Albert Hourani, and the second revised edition of *The Middle East* in the 'Handbooks to the Modern World' series (New York and Oxford, 1987), edited by Michael Adams. D. Hiro's *Dictionary of the Middle East* (London, 1996) is particularly helpful.

TWENTY-FIRST CENTURY ISLAMISM

A vast array of literature of varying quality has emerged in response to 11 September. F. Halliday's essays in *Two Hours That Shook the World* (London, 2002) are among the best. Tariq Ali's *The Clash of Fundamentalisms* (London 2002) is an engaging juxtaposition of the different views of world politics as seen by the White House and al-Qaeda. J. Cooley's *Unholy Wars: Afghanistan, America and International Terrorism* (2002) is a respected journalist's updated account of the collusion between Washington and the Afghan mujahideen. G. Kepel's *Jihad* (London, 2002) charts the development of the Islamist movement from the Iranian Revolution to bin Laden. The 11 September 2001 attacks generated many studies of the neo-*jihadi* movement and its global impact. Among the best are Fawaz Gerges's *The Far Enemy: Why Jihad Went Global* (New York, 2005), Gilles Kepel's *Jihad: The Trail of Political Islam* (Cambridge, Mass., 2003) and François Burgat's *Islamism in the Shadows of al-Qaeda* (Austin, 2008). Reza Aslan's *How to Win a*

Cosmic War: God, Globalization and the End of the War on Terror (New York, 2009) is a religious academic's highly readable account of the appeal of *jihadi* movements. Noah Feldman, *The Fall and Rise of the Islamic State* (Princeton, 2008) provides a sympathetic appraisal of the applicability of *sharia* law both in the past and in the modern world. Omar Ashour's *The De-Radicalization of Jihadists: Transforming Armed Islamist Movements* (London, 2009) traces the experience of the Egyptian and Algerian Islamist movements to explain why some have disarmed.

Index

Index

United States of America (*cont.*)
in Beirut after Iraq revolution 296; Egyptian dependence on 306, 340, 341; and Yom Kippur war 332; supervises Arafat's evacuation 351; marines in Lebanon 352–3, 353; declares prepared for dialogue with PLO 358; and Iraq-Iran war 375; response to invasion of Kuwait 378, 379–80; deployment of troops in the Gulf 382–3; emergence of Pax Americana 382–95; attempt at neutering Iraq 383–93; and Arab-Israeli conflict 395, 397–400, 400; and Palestinian-Israeli conflict 410–11; declaration of war on by Islamic *jihad* 435, 435–6; relations with Saudi Arabia 435–6; war on Afghanistan 438; regime-change policy 439, 440; alliance with Saudi Arabia 439–40; Iraq Liberation Act 440; conquest of Iraq 441–4; reconstruction of Jordan 479; relations with Iran 487–8; influence 498–502; relations with Palestine 499; regimes in power 523–5

UNSCOM, weapons inspections in Iraq 384–5, 391–3
Urban II, Pope 23

Vance, Cyrus 336
Veiled Protectorate 117, 119, 121
velayat-e-faqih 371
Venice Declaration 350
Vichy government 248, 250, 253
Victoria, Queen 84, 84–5, 94
Vienna 27, 38

Wafd party 201, 202, 213–21, 250, 255, 256, 261, 271–2
Wahhab, Ibn Abdel 502
Wahhabis 46, 57, 137–8, 140, 148, 173, 206–10, 235, 365, 460, 481–3, 502
war on terror 438–40
Washington, Treaty of (1979) 340
Weizmann, Chaim 183, 185–6, 262
West Bank 207, 292, 309, 332, 338, 342, 346, 350, 358, 359, 466–7, 472, 474, 492
Western Desert 247–8, 249, 250
Wilhelm II 94–5
Wilson, Woodrow 188, 197, 198, 203–4
Wilson, Harold 318
Wingate, Sir Reginald 179–80
Wolfowitz, Paul 445
Woolf, Sir Drummond 111–12
World Bank 288, 322, 419
World Zionist Organization 183

Yahya, Imam 212
Yemen 17, 29, 58, 129, 148, 207,
    212, 301–2, 416, 432, 441,
    452, 459–60, 462, 483,
    489–90, 505, 511
Yemen, People's Republic of 311,
    338, 382
Yemen Arab Republic 307, 338
Young Arab Society 147
Young Egypt party (Misr al-Fitat)
    219, 273
Young Ottomans 81, 86
Young Turks 141–7, 149, 151, 172,
    183, 190

Zaghloul, Saad 121–2, 126
Zaghloul Pasha 198–9, 200–1, 202,
    214, 218, 220, 260
Al-Zarqawi, Musab 461
al-Zawahari, Ayman 424, 427, 435,
    437, 461, 490
Zayids 17, 154, 459–60
Zenobia, Queen 10
Zionism 182–7, 204, 206, 230–4,
    258, 260, 262, 265–8, 269,
    283, 306, 358, 359, 364